Learn Excel 365 Expert Skills with The Smart Method
Fifth Edition: updated for the Jan 2021 semi-annual version 2008

Make sure that this is the right book for your Excel version

There are two different Windows versions of Excel in common use: Excel 2019 and Excel 365. This book is designed for use with the Excel 365 version (we publish a different book for Excel 2019 users).

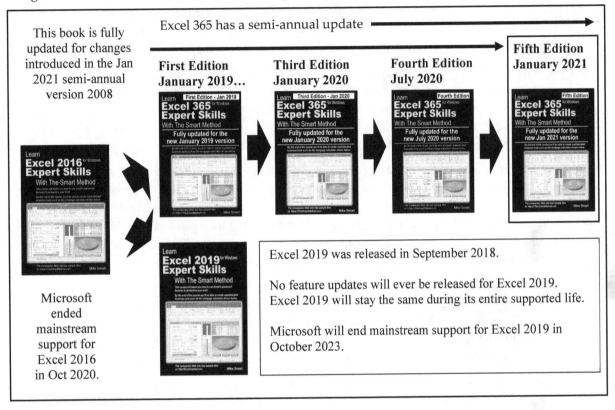

This book is fully updated for changes introduced in the Jan 2021 semi-annual version 2008

Excel 365 has a semi-annual update

First Edition January 2019...

Third Edition January 2020

Fourth Edition July 2020

Fifth Edition January 2021

Microsoft ended mainstream support for Excel 2016 in Oct 2020.

Excel 2019 was released in September 2018.

No feature updates will ever be released for Excel 2019. Excel 2019 will stay the same during its entire supported life.

Microsoft will end mainstream support for Excel 2019 in October 2023.

What is the difference between Excel 2019 (perpetual) and Excel 365 (subscription)?

Excel 2019 (even when first released) had fewer features than Excel 365 and some features worked in a different way. This will always be the case because (unlike Excel 365), Excel 2019 is never updated with new features. For this reason we only need one book to support Excel 2019 learners: *Learn Excel 2019 Expert Skills with The Smart Method*.

Excel 365 is the latest version of Excel. Every six months (in January and July) Microsoft bring out a new major semi-annual update to Excel 365. This update adds new features to Excel and also often changes or retires older features. For this reason we bring out a new edition of our Excel 365 books in January and July each year so that the latest edition of our book always supports the latest version of Excel 365.

How to tell which version you are using

Excel 2019 is a "pay once and use forever" product. Excel 365 is a subscription product (pay monthly or pay annually). When you start Excel, a splash screen showing the words "Office 2019" or "Office 365" is briefly shown on screen.

In: *Lesson 1-2: Check that your Excel version is up to date,* you'll learn more about identifying your version.

Why you should use this book to learn Excel 365

- **It isn't possible to learn Excel 365 with an Excel 2019 book.** The older versions of Excel (Excel 2019 and earlier) are now often referred to as *Legacy Excel* and the modern 365 version as *Excel DA.* This is because Excel 2019 does not support modern analysis using dynamic arrays. Dynamic arrays do not exist (and will never exist) in Excel 2019.

- **It covers all of the new Excel 365 features.** Dynamic Arrays, Comments, Ideas, Fuzzy Matching, Spilled Ranges, and the new dynamic array functions (including XLOOKUP, XMATCH, UNIQUE, SEQUENCE, FILTER, SORT, SORTBY, FILTER) are just a few of the new Excel 365 features. None of these features exist in Excel 2019. Dynamic arrays have been described as a game-changing feature that provide a new way of working that provides a far simpler solution to many common business tasks.

- **It is up-to-date.** This book was written using the *Jan 2021 Semi-Annual version 2008.* A new Excel 365 semi-annual version is released every six months* (in January and July) and automatically updated on your computer. We then publish a new edition of this book to support the latest update. This means that new features are covered and the screen grabs will exactly match what you see on your screen. It can be very frustrating to try to learn Excel 365 using an out-of-date book.

- **It provides a thorough coverage of Power Pivot, Power Query, data modeling and DAX.** Many Excel books regard Excel's sophisticated OLAP tools as being "out of scope". Excel 365 includes Power Pivot, an advanced professional tool for designing OLAP multi-dimensional reporting databases. This book will not only teach you DAX but will also give you all the OLAP data modeling skills you need in order to use Power Pivot, Get & Transform/Power Query and DAX measures effectively. OLAP empowers Excel analysts to work with "Big Data" (data that can potentially have billions of rows).

- **It teaches to true Expert level.** This *Expert Skills* book teaches Excel to an extremely high level of competence that is very rarely found in the workplace (even amongst top professionals). At Expert level your skills will be greater and broader than almost all other Excel users and you will understand (and be able to effectively use) absolutely every Excel and Power Pivot feature (inlcuding dynamic arrays). You'll have a complete mastery of skills that are often even a mystery to Excel power users.

- **It won't waste your time by teaching basic Excel 365 skills that you already know.** This isn't a beginner's book. If you are an absolute beginner, you need our *Excel 365 Essential Skills* book. By assuming that you are already able to use Excel's basic features, far more ground can be covered.

- **It is the book of choice for teachers.** As well as catering for those wishing to learn Excel by self-study, Smart Method® books have long been the preferred choice for Excel teachers as they are designed to teach Excel and not as reference books. Books follow best-practice adult teaching methodology with clearly defined objectives for each learning session and an exercise to confirm skills transfer. With single, self-contained lessons, the books cater for any teaching or self-learning period (from minutes to hours).

- **Smart Method® books are #1 best sellers.** Every paper printed Smart Method® Excel book (and there have been 22 of them starting with Excel 2007) has been an Amazon #1 best seller in its category. This provides you with the confidence that you are using a best-of-breed resource to learn Excel.

Master Excel expert skills by setting aside just a few minutes each day

This book makes it easy to learn at your own pace because of its unique presentational style. The book contains short self-contained lessons and each lesson only takes a few minutes to complete.

You can complete as many, or as few, lessons as you have the time and energy for each day. Many learners have developed expert-level skills by setting aside just a few minutes each day to complete a single lesson.

* Excel 365 Version 2008 was released to the *Semi-Annual* update channel in Jan 2021. An earlier build of the same version was released earlier to the *Current* update channel. You'll learn more about update channels, builds and versions later, in: *Lesson 1-1: Understand Update Channels* and *Lesson 1-2: Check that your Excel version is up to date.*

Who Is This Book for?

This book isn't for absolute beginners

If you're just starting out with Excel, you need to complete the lessons in our *Essential Skills* book to learn all of Excel's basic features.

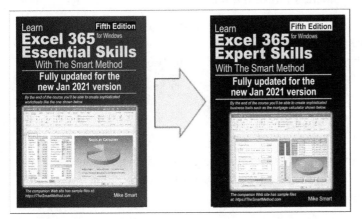

The full course outline for the *Essential Skills* book can be viewed at the end of this book in: *Appendix B: Skills Covered in the Essential Skills Course.*

This *Expert Skills* book teaches Excel to an extremely high level of competence that is very rarely found in the workplace (even amongst top professionals).

At *Expert* level your skills will be greater and broader than almost all other Excel users and you will understand (and be able to use) absolutely every Excel feature.

This book is intended for competent Excel 365 users who:

- Are already comfortable with Excel 365's basic features (ideally by completing all of the lessons in our *Essential Skills* book).
- Want in-depth coverage of all Excel 365's more powerful and complex features rather than a simple overview.
- Want an in-depth knowledge of Excel 365's the new *Dynamic Array Formulas* and associated techniques.
- Want an in-depth knowledge of multidimensional analysis using the OLAP "power" tools now included in all Excel versions: Power Pivot, Get & Transform (previously called: Power Query) and 3D Maps (previously called: Power Maps).
- Schools, colleges and universities who wish to provide advanced Excel 365 training courses.

Use of this book as courseware

While this book is effective for self-instruction, the book is also the official courseware for The Smart Method's *Excel 365 Expert Skills* course.

Smart Method courses have been taken by a varied cross-section of the world's leading companies. We've had fantastic feedback from the vast number of professionals we've empowered with Excel skills.

This book is also suitable for use by other training organizations, teachers, schools, colleges and universities to provide structured, objective-led, and highly effective classroom courses.

Every lesson is presented on two facing pages

> Pray this day, on one side of one sheet of paper, explain how the Royal Navy is prepared to meet the coming conflict.
>
> *Winston Churchill, Letter to the Admiralty, Sep 1, 1939*

Winston Churchill was aware of the power of brevity. The discipline of condensing thoughts into one side of a single sheet of A4 paper resulted in the efficient transfer of information.

A tenet of our teaching system is that every lesson is presented on *two* facing sheets of A4. We've had to double Churchill's rule as they didn't have to contend with screen grabs in 1939! If we can't teach an essential concept in two pages of A4 we know that the subject matter needs to be broken into two smaller lessons.

How this book avoids wasting your time

Over the years I have read many hundreds of computer text books and most of my time was wasted. The big problem with most books is that I must wade through thousands of words just to learn one important technique. If I don't read everything I might miss that one essential insight.

Many presentational methods have been used in this book to help you to avoid reading about things you already know how to do, or things that are of little interest to you.

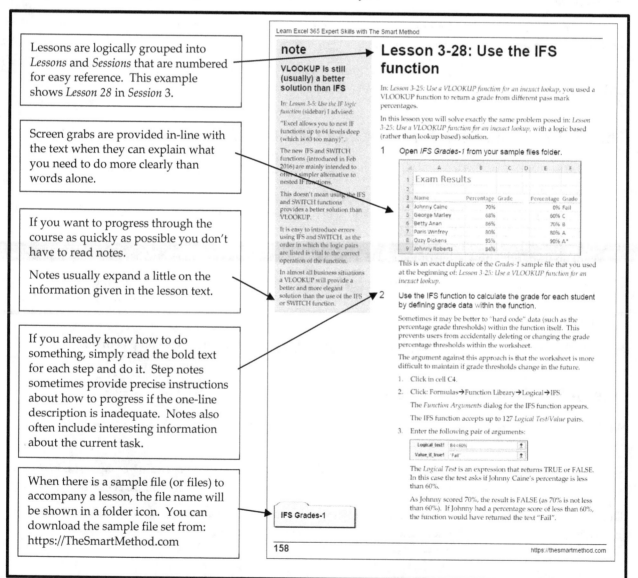

Learning by participation

Tell me, and I will forget. Show me, and I may remember. Involve me, and I will understand.

Confucius, Chinese teacher, editor, politician and philosopher (551-479 BC)

Confucius would probably have agreed that the best way to teach IT skills is hands-on (actively) and not hands-off (passively). This is another of the principal tenets of The Smart Method® teaching method.

Research has backed up the assertion that you will learn more material, learn more quickly, and understand more of what you learn if you learn using active, rather than passive methods.

For this reason, pure theory pages are kept to an absolute minimum with most theory woven into the hands-on lessons, either within the text or in sidebars.

This echoes the teaching method used in Smart Method classroom courses where snippets of pertinent theory are woven into the lessons themselves so that interest and attention is maintained by hands-on involvement, but all necessary theory is still covered.

Learn Excel 365 Expert Skills with The Smart Method

Fifth Edition: updated for the Jan 2021 semi-annual version 2008

Mike Smart

Learn Excel 365 Expert Skills with The Smart Method
Fifth Edition: updated for the Jan 2021 semi-annual version 2008

Published by:

Smart Method Enterprises Ltd
Kemp House
160 City Road
London
EC1V 2NX

The Smart Method® is a trading style of Smart Method Enterprises Ltd.

Tel: +44 (0)845 458 3282

E-mail: Use the contact page at https://thesmartmethod.com/contact
Web: https://thesmartmethod.com

International Standard Book Number (ISBN13): 978-1-909253-48-3

6 8 10 9 7 5

Author's Acknowledgements

> O would some Power, the gift to give us, To see ourselves as others see us!
>
> *Robert Burns, Scottish poet (1759-1796)*

Many people will read this book. Some will be confronting advanced concepts, such as pivot tables and macros, for the very first time. Others will be seasoned professionals with an IT background. Readers will include students, office workers, accountants, administrators, doctors, scientists, engineers, bankers and many other professions.

The book aims to communicate how to use Excel's advanced features in a way that is comprehensible to all.

I couldn't have written the original version of this book without the help of many pairs of eyes. I was extremely lucky to have had this help, throughout the writing process, from a wonderful group of international readers who kindly agreed to test drive the course prior to going to print.

I'm very grateful to Nate Barber (from San Antonio, Texas, USA). Nate was already a seasoned Excel power user and provided some wonderful technical insights. He also highlighted many cases where my British English didn't quite make the journey across the Atlantic. His feedback really helped me to improve the book in so many ways.

Many thanks are also due to Valérie Rousseau (from Quebec, Canada). Valérie spotted an embarrassing number of grammatical errors in my writing and managed to discover errors that had been missed by all other reviewers.

Huge thanks also go out to Mark Casey (from London, England). Mark provided clear and concise feedback that caused me to completely re-write some of the lessons. His excellent command of the written word enabled me to eloquently re-phrase some of my clumsier sentences.

I'd like to show great appreciation to Lorna Henderson (from Auckland, New Zealand). Lorna provided fantastically detailed feedback, resulting in hundreds of improvements to the book. There's hardly a page in the book that has not benefited from her suggestions and comments.

Many thanks also to Heidi Hembree (from Maryville, Tennessee, USA). Heidi highlighted many areas where I hadn't communicated concepts as well as I should have. Her feedback had a significant impact upon every session.

I'm also extremely grateful to Rosalind Johnson (from Pantymwyn, Wales). Rosalind's useful suggestions helped me to improve the readability of many lessons.

Thanks are also due to Jennifer Lashely (from London, England). Jennifer highlighted many potential pitfalls when working through the lessons that I was then able to eliminate from the final copy.

Special thanks are also due to Simon Smart (my son) who took time out of his own busy software development schedule to undertake the original very comprehensive technical proof read.

Huge thanks also to Sue Ferrario (from Douglas, Great Britain) who tirelessly completed the final proofread of the book prior to going to print.

I've also recently received fantastic feedback from Dwayne Roberts (from Arizona, USA). Dwayne provided a huge number of useful ideas as he worked through the entire book between 2018 and 2020. It was wonderful to receive such detailed feedback as the book has changed in so many ways during the last twelve years of updates and regular revisions.

I'd also like to thank the many others that have helped to shape the content of this book that I have not mentioned by name. Your contributions were greatly appreciated.

Contents

Session Three: Advanced Functions   109

Session Four: Working with Dynamic Arrays — 171

Session Ten: 3D Maps   423

Session Eleven: Create Get & Transform queries   457

Introduction to the Data Modeling and Power Pivot sessions   533

Session Twelve: Power Pivot, Data Modeling, OLAP and Business Intelligence   535

Session Thirteen: An introduction to DAX   585

Appendix A: Power Pivot Rules   613

Appendix B: Skills Covered in the Essential Skills Course   621

Index   627

Introduction

Welcome to *Learn Excel 365 Expert Skills with The Smart Method®*. This book has been designed to enable students to master Excel 365 advanced skills by self-study. The book is equally useful as courseware in order to deliver classroom courses.

Smart Method® publications are continually evolving as we discover better ways of explaining or teaching the concepts presented.

Feedback

At The Smart Method® we love feedback – both positive and negative. If you have any suggestions for improvements to future versions of this book, or if you find content or typographical errors, the author would always love to hear from you.

You can make suggestions for improvements to this book using the online form at:

https://thesmartmethod.com/contact

Future editions of this book will always incorporate your feedback so that there are never any known errors at time of publication.

If you have any difficulty understanding or completing a lesson, or if you feel that anything could have been more clearly explained, we'd also love to hear from you. We've made hundreds of detail improvements to our books based upon reader's feedback and continue to chase the impossible goal of 100% perfection.

Downloading the sample files

In order to use this book, it is sometimes necessary to download sample files from the Internet. The process of downloading the free sample files will be explained later, in: *Lesson 1-5: Apply a simple filter to a range.*

Problem resolution

If you encounter any problem using any aspect of the course you can contact us using the online form at:

https://thesmartmethod.com/contact

We'll do everything possible to quickly resolve the problem.

The Excel version and locale that were used to write this book

This edition was written using *Excel 365 semi-annual version 2008*, released on Jan 12, 2021 running under the *Windows 10 operating system version 20H2*. You'll discover which version your computer is running in: *Lesson 1-2: Check that your Excel version is up to date.*

This book was written using English (United States) *Region format* settings. The English - US Region format uses the decimal separator for a period and a comma for the thousands separator, producing formatted numbers such as 12,345.67. Dates are formatted as Month/Day/Year. If you are situated in a different region it is possible to change your region format (in Windows settings) but there is no need to do so. Just be aware that some of the screen grabs in this book will be formatted differently to what you see on your screen.

Typographical Conventions Used in This Book

This guide consistently uses typographical conventions to differentiate parts of the text.

When you see this	Here's what it means
Click *Line Color* on the left-hand bar and then click *No line*.	Italics are used to refer to text that appears in a worksheet cell, an Excel dialog, on the ribbon, or elsewhere within the Excel application. Italics may sometimes also be used for emphasis or distinction.
Click: Home→Font→Underline.	Click on the ribbon's *Home* tab and then look for the *Font* group. Click the *Underline* button within this group (that's the left-hand side of the button, not the drop-down arrow next to it).
Click: Home→Font→ Underline Drop Down→Double Underline.	Click on the ribbon's *Home* tab and then look for the *Font* group. Click the drop-down arrow next to the Underline button (that's the right-hand side of the button) within this group and then choose *Double Underline* from the drop-down list.
Click: File→Options→ Advanced→General→ Edit Custom Lists→Import	This is a more involved example. 1. Click the *File* tab on the ribbon, and then click the *Options* button towards the bottom of the left-hand pane. The *Excel Options* dialog appears. 2. Choose the *Advanced* list item in the left-hand pane and scroll down to the *General* group in the right-hand pane. 3. Click the *Edit Custom Lists…* button. Yet another new dialog pops up. 4. Click the *Import* button.
Type **European Sales** into the cell.	Whenever you are supposed to actually type something on the keyboard it is shown in bold faced text.
Press <Ctrl> + <Z>.	You should hold down the **Ctrl** key and then press the **Z** key.
Σ AutoSum ▾	When a lesson tells you to click a button, an image of the relevant button will often be

shown either in the page margin or within the text itself.

note

Power Pivot tables support up to two thousand million rows. This enables Excel to analyze *Big Data*.

If you want to read through the book as quickly as possible, you don't have to read notes.

Notes usually expand a little on the information given in the lesson text.

important

Do not click the *Delete* button at this point as to do so would erase the entire table.

Whenever something can easily go wrong, or when the subject text is particularly important, you will see the *important* sidebar.

You should always read important sidebars.

tip

Moving between tabs using the keyboard

You can also use the <Ctrl>+<PgUp> and <Ctrl>+<PgDn> keyboard shortcuts to cycle through all of the tabs in your workbook.

Tips add to the lesson text by showing you shortcuts or time-saving techniques relevant to the lesson.

The bold text at the top of the tip box enables you to establish whether the tip is appropriate to your needs without reading all of the text.

In this example if you are not interested in keyboard shortcuts you do not need to read any further.

anecdote

I ran an Excel course for a small company in London a couple of years ago...

Sometimes I add an anecdote gathered over the years from my Excel classes or from other areas of life.

If you simply want to learn Excel as quickly as possible you can ignore my anecdotes.

trivia

The feature that Excel uses to help you out with function calls first made an appearance in Visual Basic 5 back in 1996 ...

Sometimes I indulge myself by adding a little piece of trivia in the context of the skill being taught.

Just like my anecdotes, you can ignore these if you want to. They won't help you to learn Excel any better!

The World's Fastest Cars

When there is a sample file (or files) to accompany a lesson, the file name will be shown in a folder icon. You can download the sample files from: *https://thesmartmethod.com*. Detailed instructions are given in: *Lesson 1-5: Apply a simple filter to a range.*

How to use this course

This course utilizes some of the tried and tested techniques developed after teaching Excel to vast numbers of students during many years of Smart Method classroom courses.

In order to master Excel as quickly and efficiently as possible you should use the recommended learning method described below. If you do this there is absolutely no doubt that you will master the advanced Excel skills taught in this book.

Three important rules

#1 Complete the course from beginning to end

It is always tempting to jump around the course completing lessons in a haphazard way.

We strongly suggest that you start at the beginning and complete lessons sequentially.

That's because each lesson builds upon skills learned in the previous lessons and one of our goals is not to waste your time by teaching the same skill twice. If you miss a skill by skipping a lesson you'll find the later lessons more difficult, or even impossible to follow. This, in turn, may demoralize you and make you abandon the course.

#2 If possible, complete a session in one sitting

The book is arranged into *sessions* and *lessons*.

You can complete as many, or as few, lessons as you have the time and energy for each day. Many learners have developed expert Excel skills by setting aside just a few minutes each day to complete a single lesson.

If it is possible, the most effective way to learn is to lock yourself away, switch off your telephone, and complete a full session, without interruption, except for a 15 minute break each hour. The memory process is associative and we've ensured that the lessons in each session are very closely coupled (contextually) with the others. By learning the whole session in one sitting, you'll store all of that information in the same part of your memory and will find it easier to recall later.

The experience of being able to remember all of the words of a song as soon as somebody has got you "started" with the first line is an example of the memory's associative system of data storage.

#3 Rest at least every hour

In our classroom courses we have often observed a phenomenon that we call "running into a wall". This happens when a student becomes overloaded with new information to the point that they can no longer follow the simplest instruction. If you find this happening to you, you've studied for too long without a rest.

You should take a 15-minute break every hour (or more often if you begin to feel overwhelmed) and spend it relaxing rather than catching up with your e-mails. Ideally you should relax by lying down and closing your eyes. This allows your brain to use all of its processing power to efficiently store and index the skills you've learned. We've found that this hugely improves retention of skills learned.

How to work through the lessons

At the end of each session, complete the session exercise

Keep attempting the exercise at the end of each session until you can complete it without having to refer to lessons in the session. Don't start the next session until you can complete the exercise from memory.

At the end of each session, review the objectives

The session objectives are stated at the beginning of each session.

Read each objective and ask yourself if you have truly mastered each skill. If you are not sure about any of the skills listed, revise the relevant lesson(s) before moving on to the next session.

You will find it very frustrating if you move to a new session before you have truly mastered the skills covered in the previous session. This may demoralize you and make you abandon the course.

How to best use the incremental sample files

Many lessons in this course use a sample file that is incrementally improved during each lesson. At the end of each lesson an interim version is always saved. For example, a sample file called Sales-1 may provide the starting point to a sequence of three lessons. After each lesson, interim versions called Sales-2, Sales-3 and Sales-4 are saved by the student.

A complete set of sample files (including all incremental versions) are provided in the sample file set. This provides three important benefits:

- If you have difficulty with a lesson it is useful to be able to study the completed workbook (at the end of the lesson) by opening the finished version of the lesson's workbook.

- When you have completed the book, you will want to use it as a reference. The sample files allow you to work through any single lesson in isolation, as the workbook's state at the beginning of each lesson is always available.

- When teaching a class one student may corrupt their workbook by a series of errors (or by their computer crashing). It is possible to quickly and easily move the class on to the next lesson by instructing the student to open the next sample file in the set (instead of progressing with their own corrupted file or copying a file from another student).

The time you spend learning Excel will be hugely worthwhile

If you persevere with this course there is no doubt that you will master Excel expert skills. A substantial amount of time and effort is needed but the skills you'll acquire will be hugely valuable for the rest of your life.

Enjoy the course.

Session One: Tables, and Ranges

> As a general rule the most successful man in life is the man who has the best information.
>
> *Benjamin Disraeli, British Politician (1804-1881)*

In this session you'll learn all about tables, how they differ from ranges, and how to use them effectively to manage data.

This session also introduces *structured table references* that provide a completely new way to reference dynamic table data. This has eliminated the need for the complex workarounds previously required when working with dynamic ranges.

Session Objectives

By the end of this session you will be able to:

- Understand update channels
- Check that automatic updates are enabled
- Change the Office Theme
- Apply a simple filter to a range
- Apply a top 10 and custom filter to a range
- Apply an advanced filter with multiple OR criteria
- Apply an advanced filter with complex criteria
- Apply an advanced filter with function-driven criteria
- Extract unique records using an advanced filter
- Add totals using Quick Analysis
- Add percentage and running totals using Quick Analysis
- Convert a range into a table and add a total row
- Format a table using table styles and convert a table into a range
- Create a custom table style
- Sort a range or table by rows
- Sort a range by columns
- Sort a range or table by custom list
- Name a table and create an automatic structured table reference
- Create a manual structured table reference
- Use special items in structured table references
- Understand unqualified structured table references

note

Perpetual license versions have different features

Perpetual license holders still receive monthly updates, but these only include security updates and bug fixes (not new features).

An Excel 2019 user running version 2008 will thus see fewer features than an Excel 365 user running version 2008.

note

Windows also has a semi-annual update channel

The default Windows 10 update is the semi-annual channel.

Starting with version 20H2 windows versions are named as the year of release along with the half of the year they were released in.

The two Windows 10 releases in 2021 will be called Version 21H1 and 21H2 (the year, along with a half-year indicator).

For most users, new Windows 10 versions are supported for 18 months. Some Enterprise and Educational users may have this extended to 30 months.

Microsoft does not force users to accept new Windows 10 versions immediately. Users must initiate updates manually.

If your Windows 10 operating system is approaching the end of its supported life, it is possible that Microsoft will automatically update your computer to keep your computer safe from potential security issues.

Lesson 1-1: Understand Update Channels

In recent years most software vendors have transitioned from the concept of perpetual licenses to Software as a Service (SaaS).

Perpetual license software

There are two current versions of Excel: Excel 2019 and Excel 365. Excel 2019 is a perpetual license product. This means that purchasers "pay once and use forever". Excel 2019 never has new or updated features added during its lifetime. Mainstream support for Excel 2019 ends in October 2023.

There are many disadvantages to the perpetual license model, including:

- Users with different Excel versions can have problems when sharing files with each other. For example, an Excel 365 workbook containing dynamic arrays will often not open correctly in Excel 2019.

- Support and training are difficult as different versions often work in different ways.

Many have speculated that Excel 2019 will be the last perpetual licensed Excel version.

Excel 365 is an SaaS product

The modern method of creating and supporting software is called: *Software as a Service* or *SaaS*. In the SaaS model users pay a low-cost subscription to the software developer (in this case Microsoft) to use the software and receive support and feature updates.

There are many advantages to the SaaS model, including:

- Every user has the latest version. You will see later in this lesson, however, that Excel 365 users that have different update channels may still have different versions.

- The software changes gradually so that users often need no training to adapt to new versions.

The SaaS model does, however, create several development challenges.

How Perpetual Licensed software is developed

The traditional software development cycle involves three stages:

- **Alpha test version:** This is a pre-release version that isn't expected to work very well. Alpha versions are expected to have many bugs and issues and are only used for testing, usually by professional testers working for the development team.

- **Beta test version:** The beta version is feature-complete but many of the features are not thoroughly tested. Beta versions are sometimes given to real-world users who then report bugs to the developer for attention.

- **Release version 1.0:** This version is expected to be solid and reliable and suitable for real-world use.

- **Updated versions 1.01, 1.02 etc** Updates do not add new features but fix bugs and security problems that are found after release.

How SaaS software is developed

SaaS software is constantly updated. To ensure that software is thoroughly tested Microsoft have created update channels. It is possible for users to decide which channel is most suitable for their needs. You'll discover the update channel that your copy of Excel is using later, in: *Lesson 1-2: Check that your Excel version is up to date.*

- **Beta Channel - sometimes called: Insider Fast:** This channel has no support. Features are still in development and may be risky to use. This channel is not suitable for real-world business use.

- **Current Channel (Preview) – sometimes called Insider Slow:** When new features have been tested in the *Insider Fast Channel* they are released to the *Insider Slow Channel*. This channel is more stable and has less risk than the *Insider Fast Channel*. This channel is not suitable for real-world business use.

- **Current Channel:** On June 9, 2020 this became the default channel for all new Excel installations. Current Channel users have an Excel version that can change at any time. Different groups of Current Channel users may be using different versions at any one time as features are not released to all Current Channel users at the same time. Current Channel features can be expected to have more bugs than the *Enterprise* channels.

- **Monthly Enterprise Channel (not available to users of Office Home editions):** This channel is aimed at business rather than home users. Monthly Enterprise Channel users only have access to features that have been thoroughly tested by Current Channel users. Features can appear in the Current Channel months before they are considered ready for the Monthly Enterprise Channel. The Monthly Enterprise Channel in only updated with new features once each month.

- **Semi-Annual Enterprise Channel (not available to users of Office Home editions):** This was the default channel for all business users before June 9, 2020 (when Microsoft changed the default to the Current Channel). Semi-Annual Enterprise Channel users will receive a new, and thoroughly tested, version of Excel in January and July of each year. I would recommend this as the most appropriate channel for serious business use.

If you are a business user of Excel it is most likely that you will be using the *Semi-Annual Enterprise Channel*, but it is also possible that your administrator has decided to use one of the other channels. This book was written using the *Excel 365 Jan 2021 Semi-Annual Enterprise* version.

If your machine is set to use one of the other update channels you may notice some small differences between the version that you are using, and the current semi-annual version described in this book.

Lesson 1-2: Check that your Excel version is up to date

Automatic Updates

Normally Excel will look after updates without you having to do anything. By default, automatic updates are enabled. This means that updates are downloaded from the Internet and installed automatically.

It is possible that automatic updates have been switched off on your computer. In this case there is a danger that you may have an old, buggy, unsupported and out of date version of Excel installed.

This lesson will show you how to make sure that you are using the latest (most complete, and most reliable) version of Excel.

1   Start Excel and open a new blank workbook (if you have not already done this).

2   Make sure that automatic updates are enabled.

   1. Click the *File* button ⬚ File ⬚ at the top-left of the screen.

       This takes you to *Backstage View*. Backstage View allows you to complete an enormous range of common tasks from a single window.

   2. Click: *Account* ⬛ Account ⬛ in the left-hand list.

       Your account details are displayed on screen. Notice the *Office Updates* button displayed in the right-hand pane.

       If all is well, and automatic updates are switched on, you will see a button similar to this:

       If automatic updates have been switched off, you will see a similar button to this.

       In this case you will need to switch automatic updates on (see next step).

3   Switch on automatic updates if necessary.

   Click: Update Options→Enable Updates.

4   If there are updates waiting to install, apply them.

Sometimes Excel will download updates but will not install them automatically.

In this case you will see an update button similar to the following:

You will see this type of button you should apply the update.

Click: Update Options→Apply Updates.

You may be asked to confirm that you want to apply the update, and to close any open programs to apply the update.

5   Notice your version number and update channel.

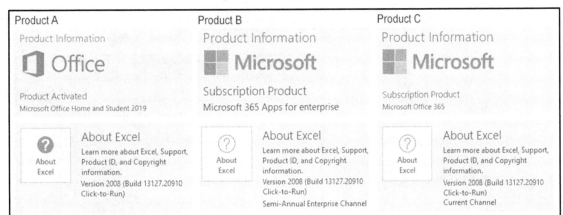

note

Version number and Build

A new Excel version is usually released to the current update channel every month.

Each new version may add new features to Excel 365.

If bugs or security issues are found in a new version, Microsoft will fix them and publish a new *build* of the same version.

You will see product information section displayed. If you see the number *365* or the words *Subscription Product*, you will know that you are using the subscription version (Excel 365) that this book teaches. This is the case for products B and C above. Otherwise you are using the *perpetual license* version (this is the case for product A above). This is not the correct book for learning the perpetual version (we also publish an Excel 2019 book).

Notice also the *Update Channel* (update channels are explained in depth in: *Lesson 1-1: Understand Update Channels*), *Version number* and *Build* (see sidebar).

6   Click the *Back* button to leave *Backstage View* and return to the worksheet.

7   Click the *Close* button ⌧ in the top-right corner of the Excel screen to close Excel.

Lesson 1-3: Change between touch mode and mouse mode

Both Excel and Windows allow you to operate in one of two modes: Touch Mode and Mouse Mode. Excel tries to figure out which mode you want to use and then sets it for you automatically. This lesson will enable you to set the mode you prefer manually.

Touch Mode: In Touch Mode the icons are spaced further apart so that they are easier to tap with your finger.

Mouse Mode: This is the mode preferred by most Excel users. In Mouse Mode the icons are displayed closer together. Unless you have a very large screen you will usually also see more icons on your screen when in Mouse Mode. This means that you can often execute a command with one click rather than two.

For this reason, it is usually more efficient to work with Excel in Mouse Mode (using a mouse to select commands) than to use Touch Mode (using your finger to select commands).

1 Open Excel and open a new blank Excel workbook.

2 Enable the *Touch/Mouse Mode* button on the *Quick Access Toolbar.*

At the top left of the screen you will see several icons. This strip of icons is called the *Quick Access Toolbar.* .

The Quick Access Toolbar

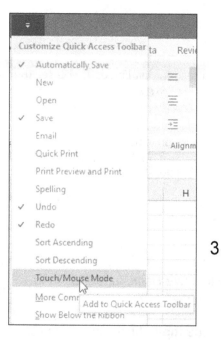

You may already see the *Touch/Mouse Mode* button on the *Quick Access Toolbar.* If you do you can progress to the next step.

If you don't see the *Touch/Mouse Mode* button click the drop-down arrow to the right of the *Quick Access Toolbar* and then click *Touch/Mouse Mode* on the drop-down menu (see sidebar).

The *Touch/Mouse Mode* button is then added to the *Quick Access Toolbar.*

3 Set Excel to use *Touch Mode.*

If you are using a computer that has a touch screen, you may find that Excel is already using touch mode.

1. Click on the *Touch/Mouse Mode* button. Two options appear on the drop-down menu:

note

Windows 10 also has a touch and mouse mode

In Windows 10 *Touch Mode* is called *Tablet Mode*.

Tablet Mode makes all applications run at full screen and shows a different screen when Windows starts.

To enable *Tablet* mode:

1. Click the Windows button:

... on the bottom left of the screen.

2. Click *Settings* on the pop-up menu.

3. Click *System.*

| System |
| Display, sound, notifications, power |

4. Click the *Tablet Mode* button:

Tablet mode

5. Select the option you prefer:

| Use tablet mode |
| Use desktop mode |
| Use the appropriate mode for my hardware |

Optimize spacing between commands

Mouse
Standard ribbon and commands.
Optimized for use with mouse.

Touch
More space between commands.
Optimized for use with touch.

2. Click the *Touch* option.

Notice that fewer icons are now displayed. You are now using Excel in *Touch Mode.*

4 Set Excel to use *Mouse Mode.*

Now do the same thing but this time select *Mouse Mode.*

Notice that the icons are now closer together:

Most of the screen grabs in this book were taken using *Mouse Mode.*

If you decide that you prefer *Touch Mode,* you'll still have no difficulty working through all of the lessons.

note

Themes and Backgrounds affect every Office application on all of your devices

When you set a theme or background in Excel you are actually changing the theme and background for the entire Office suite.

This means that you will have a consistent experience when using other Office applications such as *Word* and *PowerPoint*.

If you are logged in to a *Microsoft Account*, the theme you select will also magically appear on all of your devices (such as a work computer, home computer, laptop, tablet and smartphone). This is part of Microsoft's comprehensive support for cloud computing.

Cloud computing is extensively covered in the *Essential Skills* book in this series, in which a whole session is dedicated to Excel's cloud computing features.

Lesson 1-4: Change the Office Theme

Excel allows you to change the colors of screen elements (such as the title bar and ribbon) by selecting a *theme*. There are four themes available: *Colorful, White, Dark Gray* and *Black*.

Colorful

Excel 365 uses the *Colorful* theme as the default. The colorful theme makes it clear which of the Office applications you are using as Word, Excel, PowerPoint, Outlook and other Office applications each have their own unique color.

White

The *White* theme has very low contrast and shading. Some designers feel that this gives Excel a modern and "minimalist" appearance. This was introduced as the default theme for Excel 2013, but was widely criticized by some users for causing eye strain and being difficult to work with.

In 2016 the default was changed to the (much better) colorful theme.

Dark Gray and Black

note

You can also personalize Excel by changing the background

Background customization can only be done if you are connected to the Internet and logged into a Microsoft Account.

If you are logged into your Microsoft Account, you will see an *Office Background* drop-down list (above the *Office Theme* setting) that enables backgrounds to be set:

When you choose a background a "tattoo" is added to the area above the Ribbon with your chosen design:

note

Audio cues

If you enable *Audio Cues* a different sound will be played whenever you complete common Excel actions (such as cut and paste).

The idea is that you will subconsciously link sounds with actions so that when you make a mistake it will "sound wrong".

To enable Audio cues, click:

File→Options→
Ease of Access→
Feedback options→
Provide feedback with sound.

You are also able to choose between two different *Sound Schemes*.

The *Dark Gray* and *Black* themes provide high contrast between different screen elements. It has been suggested that these themes would be particularly useful for users with impaired vision.

1 Open Excel and open a new blank Excel workbook.

2 Change the *Office Theme*.

　1. Click the *File* button ⬚ File ⬚ at the top-left of the screen.

　2. Click the *Options* button ⬚ Options ⬚ near the bottom of the left-hand menu bar.

　　The *Excel Options* dialog box appears.

　　In the *Personalize your copy of Microsoft Office* section, you'll see an *Office Theme* drop-down list. Click the drop-down arrow to see the different themes available.

> Personalize your copy of Microsoft Office
>
> User name:　　Mike Smart
>
> ☐ Always use these values regardless of sign in to Office.
>
> Office Background:　No Background ▾
>
> Office Theme:　　Colorful ▾
>
> Office intelligent serv　Colorful
> 　　　　　　　　　Dark Gray
> Intelligent services br　Black　　f the cloud to the Office ap
> document content.　　White

　3. Click the *Dark Gray* theme.

　4. Click *OK* to return to the Excel screen.

　　Experiment with each theme until you discover the one you prefer. All of the screen grabs in this book were made using the *Colorful* theme. If you choose a different theme the screen grabs in the book may look slightly different to what you see on your computer screen.

3 Close Excel.

Inventory-1

Lesson 1-5: Apply a simple filter to a range

1 Download the sample files (if you haven't already done so).

   1. Open your web browser and type in the URL:

      https://TheSmartMethod.com

   2. Click the *Sample Files* link on the top menu bar of the home page.

   3. Download the sample files for *Excel 365 Expert Skills Fifth Edition* (also see sidebar: *Organizing your sample files folder*).

      While we provide the sample files in both .EXE and .ZIP file format it is strongly recommended that you download the sample files as a self-extracting .EXE file. This avoids the Protected View issue discussed on the facing page sidebar.

2 Open *Inventory-1* from your sample files folder.

This workbook contains a list showing all goods in stock.

	A	B	C
1	Product Name	Supplier	Category
2	Aniseed Syrup	Exotic Liquids	Condiments
3	Boston Crab Meat	New England Seafood Cannery	Seafood
4	Camembert Pierrot	Gai pâturage	Dairy Products

3 Add a filter to the range.

   1. Click anywhere inside the range.

   2. Click: Data→Sort & Filter→Filter.

Notice that small drop-down arrow buttons have appeared in the range header row:

	A	B	C
1	Product Name ▼	Supplier ▼	Category ▼
2	Aniseed Syrup	Exotic Liquids	Condiments
3	Boston Crab Meat	New England Seafood Cannery	Seafood

4 Use the filter to display products in the *Seafood* category.

   1. Click the drop-down arrow to the right of *Category* in cell C1.

   2. Uncheck the *(Select All)* check box.

   3. Check the *Seafood* checkbox.

   4. Click the *OK* button.

Only Seafood products are now displayed:

	A	B	C
1	Product Name ▼	Supplier ▼	Category ▼
3	Boston Crab Meat	New England Seafood Cannery	Seafood
5	Carnarvon Tigers	Pavlova, Ltd.	Seafood

note

Potential problem when downloading sample files

Protected View is a security feature that was first introduced in Excel 2010. It is designed to protect you from potential viruses by treating all files downloaded from the Internet as being suspicious.

Any workbooks that are downloaded from the Internet, or are sent by e-mail attachment, will open in *Protected View* by default.

PROTECTED VIEW Be careful— to edit, it's s

The user then has to click an *Enable Editing* button to use the file as normal:

Enable Editing

While some users may find it useful to be reminded about the origin of their files, others may find this feature annoying.

To avoid seeing this message whenever you open a sample file, we provide the sample files as a digitally-signed self-extracting download. This means that the sample files will open without warnings.

We also offer an alternative zip file method to download (the link to this page is in the FAQ section at the bottom of the web page).

The alternative zip file has been provided because some companies (or anti-virus products) block the download of executable files.

If you download using the zip file option, you'll have to click the *Enable Editing* button every time you open a sample file.

Notice that the filter button next to *Category* in cell C1 has changed to show that a filter condition is in effect.

Notice also that the row numbers along the left of the worksheet are now shaded blue and are no longer sequential.

5 **Add a second filter condition to show items in the *Seafood* category with an inventory value greater than 1,000.**

1. Click the drop-down arrow to the right of *Value* in cell F1.

2. Click: Number Filters→Greater Than... from the drop-down menu.

3. Type **1000** into the text box.

Custom AutoFilter	?	✕

Show rows where:
Value

is greater than ∨   1000 ∨

⦿ And ◯ Or

∨ ∨

Use ? to represent any single character
Use * to represent any series of characters

OK   Cancel

4. Click the *OK* button.

Only rows that are in the *Seafood* category and exceed a value of 1,000 are now shown.

	A	B	C	D	E	F
				Unit	In	
1	Product Name ⤓	Supplier	Category ⤓	Price ⤓	Stoc ⤓	Value ⤓
3	Boston Crab Meat	New England Seafood Cannery	Seafood	18.40	123	2,263.20
5	Carnarvon Tigers	Pavlova, Ltd.	Seafood	62.50	42	2,625.00
26	Inlagd Sill	Svensk Sjöföda AB	Seafood	19.00	112	2,128.00
51	Röd Kaviar	Svensk Sjöföda AB	Seafood	15.00	101	1,515.00
59	Spegesild	Lyngbysild	Seafood	12.00	95	1,140.00

6 **Remove the filter from the range.**

1. Click anywhere inside the range.

2. Click: Data→Sort & Filter→Filter.

   Notice that the small drop-down handles have disappeared from the range header row and that all rows are now displayed.

7 **Use *Filter by selection* to only show rows in the *Dairy Products* category.**

1. Right-click any cell in the *Category* column containing the text: *Dairy Products*

2. Click: Filter→Filter by Selected Cell's Value from the shortcut menu.

   Notice that only rows that are in the *Dairy Products* category are now displayed.

8 **Remove the filter from the range.**

Lesson 1-6: Apply a top 10 and custom filter to a range

1 Open *Inventory-1* from your sample files folder (if it isn't already open).

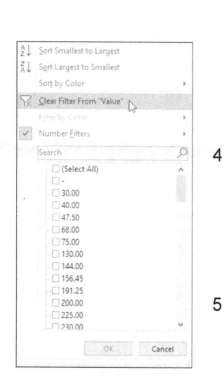

2 Add a filter to the range.

Click anywhere inside the range and then click:

Data→Sort & Filter→Filter

3 Apply a top ten filter to identify the ten items that have the most expensive inventory.

1. Click the drop-down arrow to the right of *Value* in cell F1.

2. Click: *Number Filters.*

3. Click: *Top 10...* from the fly-out menu.

The *Top 10 AutoFilter* dialog is displayed:

Top 10 AutoFilter	?	×
Show		
Top	10	Items
	OK	Cancel

It is possible to use this dialog to filter to a number other than 10 or to filter to the *Bottom* values (if you wanted to show the items with the least expensive inventory).

4. Click the *OK* button.

The ten items with the most expensive inventory are shown. Note that they are still sorted alphabetically, in ascending order, by *Product Name.* You'd probably want to sort the rows by value in descending order. Sorting will be covered later, in: *Lesson 1-16: Sort a range or table by rows.*

4 Clear the filter condition from the *Value* column.

1. Click the button to the right of *Value* in cell F1.

Value

2. Click *Clear Filter From "Value"* from the shortcut menu.

The filter condition is removed and all items in the list are shown.

5 Use a custom filter to show items that have a value between 1,000 and 3,000.

1. Click the drop-down arrow to the right of *Value* in cell F1.

2. Click: Number Filters→Custom Filter on the drop-down menu.

Inventory-1

note

Filtering by color

The *Filter by Color* option is only enabled when at least one cell in the column has a font color or background color.

You can then click the filter arrow at the top of the column and choose *Filter by Color*. This displays a fly-out menu listing every color in the column:

The *Custom AutoFilter* dialog is displayed.

3. Set the filter condition to: *is greater than or equal to 1000* **And** *is less than or equal to 3000*.

4. Click the *OK* button.

Only products with a value between 1,000 and 3,000 are shown.

6 **Remove the filter from the range.**

1. Click anywhere inside the range.

2. Click: Data→Sort & Filter→Filter.

Notice that the small drop-down arrows have disappeared from the range header row and that all rows are now displayed.

Lesson 1-7: Apply an advanced filter with multiple OR criteria

note

The criteria range can appear anywhere on the worksheet and does not have to be complete

It is quick and convenient to place the criteria above the range to be filtered.

You may, however, place the criteria anywhere in the workbook – even on a different worksheet.

In this example, all of the fields in the range are listed by making a complete duplicate of the range headers. The advanced filter will work just as well if the header list is not complete.

Example:

To filter down to the *Seafood* category you could simply type **Category** into cell J1 and **Seafood** into cell J2 and then set the criteria range to J1:J2.

1   Open *Inventory-1* from your sample files folder (if it isn't already open).

2   Create the criteria range.

The criteria range is the area on your worksheet where you define the advanced filter criteria.

1.   Insert five blank rows at the top of the worksheet.

2.   Copy the range headers from row 6 to row 1.

Your worksheet should now look like this:

	A	B	C	D	E	F
				Unit	In	
1	Product Name	Supplier	Category	Price	Stock	Value
2						
3						
4						
5						
				Unit	In	
6	Product Name	Supplier	Category	Price	Stock	Value
7	Aniseed Syrup	Exotic Liquids	Condiments	10.00	13	130.00

Each of the rows 2-4 can now be used to define the criteria needed for each column in the range.

3   Add filter criteria to show all products in the *Condiments*, *Seafood* and *Confections* categories.

This is an example of a filter with three OR criteria. The filter can be defined as:

Condiments OR Seafood OR Confections.

Add the three filter criteria by typing (or copy and pasting) the three category names into cells C2:C4.

	A	B	C	D	E	F
				Unit	In	
1	Product Name	Supplier	Category	Price	Stock	Value
2			Condiments			
3			Seafood			
4			Confections			

note

The criteria range can span any number of rows

In this example a criteria range of four rows is used (A1:F4).

You can use as many rows as you need in your criteria range.

It is crucial that you leave at least one blank row between the criteria range and any other range on the worksheet.

4   Apply the criteria using an advanced filter.

1.   Click anywhere in the range to be filtered (any cell in the range A6:F75).

2.   Click: Data→Sort & Filter→Advanced.

The *Advanced Filter* dialog is displayed with the range already defined. Because you clicked within the range in step one you have saved yourself the trouble of manually selecting the range.

Inventory-1

note

Using wildcards in criteria

Sometimes you will want to filter using a subset of the letters in a text column.

In this case, you can use the wildcard characters – the asterisk (*) and the question mark (?).

The asterisk means that any number of wildcard letters can occur between the letters.

The question mark means that only one wildcard letter can occur between the letters.

Here are some examples:

C*g   Finds **Containing**
           Finds **Citing**
           Doesn't find **Chair**

S?d   Finds **Sid**
           Finds **Sad**
           Doesn't find **Said**
           Doesn't find **Send**

note

Text filters are inexact by default

This lesson's example works just fine but it would have worked just as well if you had entered the filter expression **Cond** instead of **Condiments.**

For the same reason, the filter expression **Dairy** would return the category **Dairy Products.**

Sometimes this isn't what you want and you need an exact match. In this case, you need to enter the filter conditions like this:

=”=Seafood”

=”=Dairy Products”

Unlike **Con**, The filter condition

=”=Con”

... doesn't return the *Condiments* category.

3. Click in the *Criteria range*: text box.

4. Select the range A1:F4 with the mouse.

The criteria range appears as: A1:F4.

5. Click the *OK* button.

The range is now filtered to display only *Condiments, Seafood* and *Confections*.

	Product Name	Supplier	Category	Unit Price	In Stock	Value
6						
7	Aniseed Syrup	Exotic Liquids	Condiments	10.00	13	130.00
8	Boston Crab Meat	New England Seafood Cannery	Seafood	18.40	123	2,263.20
10	Carnarvon Tigers	Pavlova, Ltd.	Seafood	62.50	42	2,625.00
14	Chef Anton's Cajun Seasoning	New Orleans Cajun Delights	Condiments	22.00	53	1,166.00
15	Chocolade	Zaanse Snoepfabriek	Confections	12.75	15	191.25

5   **Remove the advanced filter from the range.**

1. Click anywhere inside the range.

2. Click: Data→Sort & Filter→Clear.

The advanced filter is cleared and all records are displayed.

6   **Save your work as** *Inventory-2.*

Lesson 1-8: Apply an advanced filter with complex criteria

1 Open *Inventory-2* from your sample files folder (if it isn't already open).

2 Create complex advanced filter criteria.

This time you are going to create a filter with both AND and OR criteria. This is an example of a filter that is beyond the scope of a simple filter. Here are the criteria that you are going to apply:

WHERE

Category equals Condiments

OR

(Category equals Seafood AND Value is greater than 2,000)

OR

Value is greater than 3,000

This will list everything in the *Condiments* category.

It will also list products in the *Seafood* category, but only if their value is greater than 2,000.

It will also list all products that have a value greater than 3,000 irrespective of which category they are in.

1. Set the criteria range as follows:

	C	D	E	F
		Unit	In	
1	Category	Price	Stock	Value
2	Condiments			
3	Seafood			>2000
4				>3000

2. Apply the advanced filter using the skills learned in: *Lesson 1-7: Apply an advanced filter with multiple OR criteria.*

3. If you select cells A1:F4 with the mouse (the fastest and easiest way), you may see the following values in the *Advanced Filter* dialog:

List range:	$A$6:$F$75
Criteria range:	Inventory!Criteria

You may wonder why the *Criteria range* displays as *Inventory!Criteria* instead of *Inventory!$A$1:$F$4*.

The reason is that Excel has created something called a *Range Name* behind the scenes. You'll learn all about Range Names

Inventory-2

later, in: *Session Five: Using Names and the Formula Auditing Tools.* Now you can audit the results:

	A	B	C	Unit Price	In Stock	Value
6	Product Name	Supplier	Category			
7	Aniseed Syrup	Exotic Liquids	Condiments	10.00	13	130.00
8	Boston Crab Meat	New England Seafood Cannery	Seafood	18.40	123	2,263.20
10	Carnarvon Tigers	Pavlova, Ltd.	Seafood	62.50	42	2,625.00
14	Chef Anton's Cajun Seasoning	New Orleans Cajun Delights	Condiments	22.00	53	1,166.00
16	Côte de Blaye	Aux joyeux ecclésiastiques	Beverages	263.50	17	4,479.50
21	Genen Shouyu	Mayumi's	Condiments	15.50	39	604.50
24	Grandma's Boysenberry Spread	Grandma Kelly's Homestead	Condiments	25.00	120	3,000.00
27	Gula Malacca	Leka Trading	Condiments	19.45	27	525.15
31	Inlagd Sill	Svensk Sjöföda AB	Seafood	19.00	112	2,128.00
38	Louisiana Fiery Hot Pepper Sauce	New Orleans Cajun Delights	Condiments	21.05	76	1,599.80
39	Louisiana Hot Spiced Okra	New Orleans Cajun Delights	Condiments	17.00	4	68.00
45	Northwoods Cranberry Sauce	Grandma Kelly's Homestead	Condiments	40.00	6	240.00
47	Original Frankfurter grüne Soße	Plutzer Lebensmittelgroßmärkte	Condiments	13.00	32	416.00
52	Queso Manchego La Pastora	Cooperativa de Quesos 'Las Cabr	Dairy Products	38.00	86	3,268.00
53	Raclette Courdavault	Gai pâturage	Dairy Products	55.00	79	4,345.00
61	Sir Rodney's Marmalade	Specialty Biscuits, Ltd.	Confections	81.00	40	3,240.00
63	Sirop d'érable	Forêts d'érables	Condiments	28.50	113	3,220.50
73	Vegie-spread	Pavlova, Ltd.	Condiments	43.90	24	1,053.60

- All eleven *Condiments* products are listed irrespective of their value.

- Only three *Seafood* products are shown – only the items with a value greater than 2,000.

- Items such as *Sir Rodney's Marmalade* are listed even though they do not appear in the *Condiment* or *Seafood* categories. This is because their value is greater than 3,000.

3   Remove the advanced filter from the range.

1.   Click anywhere inside the range.

2.   Click: Data→Sort & Filter→Clear.

The advanced filter is cleared, and all records are displayed.

4   Save your work as *Inventory-3*.

tip

Using the ROW function to remove the need to add a counter column

In the example, you inserted a new column with the row number in it and then used the formula:

=MOD(A7,5)=0

The same problem could have been solved without inserting the new column by using the ROW function.

ROW returns the row number of a reference:

=ROW(A1)

Returns the number 1

=ROW(A2)

Returns the number 2

With this knowledge it is clear that the filter formula would work just as well if it were written:

=MOD(ROW(A7)-6,5)=0

This would work even if column A was deleted.

This works because row 7 originally contained the number 1 in column A.

ROW(A7) brings back a value of 7, so subtracting six from it also results in the value 1 for the first data row in the range.

Remember that you must have a blank space above a formula in order to use it within an advanced filter.

The formula can be placed anywhere on the worksheet.

Lesson 1-9: Apply an advanced filter with function-driven criteria

When a company conducts a physical stock check of its inventory there will always be some errors in the count. Auditors have to verify the accuracy of a stock check. To do this they extract some random samples in order to establish the likely margin of error.

In this lesson, you'll take the *Inventory* workbook and extract an auditing sample by using an advanced filter in conjunction with a MOD (Modulus or Remainder) function.

Excel's MOD function returns the remainder after a number is divided by a divisor. It is often used in conjunction with the INT (integer) function to convert minutes into hours and minutes. For example, to convert 170 minutes into 2 hours 50 minutes you would use the functions like this:

=INT(170/60)   This returns 2, as the whole number part of 2.83 is 2.

=MOD(170,60)   This returns 50, because 60 only divides evenly into 170 twice (120) leaving 50 over.

You're going to use the MOD function in conjunction with an advanced filter to show one transaction in every five, so that you can sample one in five (20%) of the products to check during the audit.

1   Open *Inventory-3* from your sample files folder (if it isn't already open).

2   Add a column to the left of the range, head it with the text: **No,** format the column header to match the style in the other header columns, and fill the column with incremental numbers.

	A	B	C
6	No	Product Name	Supplier
7	1	Aniseed Syrup	Exotic Liquids
8	2	Boston Crab Meat	New England Seafood Cannery
9	3	Camembert Pierrot	Gai pâturage
10	4	Carnarvon Tigers	Pavlova, Ltd.

3   Add a MOD function to cell A2 that will return TRUE when the value in cell A7 is divisible by five.

1.   Type the following function into cell A2:

	A	B
1		Product Name
2	=MOD(A7,5)=0	

2.   Press the **<Enter>** key.

The cell contains the value: *FALSE.*

Inventory-3

note

Using a function-driven criteria to implement a case sensitive filter

Filters are case insensitive by default.

The filters:

Category=Seafood

And

Category=SEAFOOD

… will produce exactly the same result.

You can implement a case sensitive filter by using the EXACT function.

The filter condition:

=EXACT(D7, "Seafood")

… would extract the *Seafood* records in this table.

The filter condition:

=EXACT(D7, "SEAFOOD")

… would not extract any records.

note

Selecting every fifth item is not a truly random sample

In this lesson you select every fifth row to audit.

In a true auditing scenario this would not be a robust approach as a client (who knew your method) could deliberately mislead you by placing false values in other rows.

You could make a truly random selection by using the function:

=RANDBETWEEN(1,5)=1

The formula generates a value between one and five and compares it with one. This returns TRUE in approximately 20% of cases.

	A	B
1		Product Name
2	FALSE	

This is because the number in cell A7 (the value: 1) is not evenly divisible by five.

Here's how the MOD function works:

- The value in cell A7 is divided by five and the remainder is returned. In this case the remainder is 1 because the number 1 is not evenly divisible by 5.

- The expression 1=0 is not true so the cell displays a result of FALSE.

- If cell A7 had contained a value that is evenly divisible by 5 (such as 5 or 10) the MOD function would have returned zero (because the remainder is zero). This would result in the cell displaying a TRUE result because the expression 0=0 is true.

4   **Apply an advanced filter using the *Criteria range* A1:A2.**

Notice that you didn't type the word **No** into cell A1 (a copy of the text header appearing in cell A6).

For a function-driven filter you must leave the cell above the formula blank. This tells the advanced filter to work directly upon the result of the function.

1. Apply an advanced filter in the same way as you did in: *Lesson 1-7: Apply an advanced filter with multiple OR criteria,* using A1:A2 as the *Criteria range.* The *Advanced Filter* dialog should look like this:

Advanced Filter ? ✕

Action
- ⦿ Filter the list, in-place
- ◯ Copy to another location

List range: $SAS6:$GS75
Criteria range: $AS1:$AS2
Copy to:

☐ Unique records only

OK   Cancel

2. Click the *OK* button.

6	No	Product Name	Supplier
11	5	Chai	Exotic Liquids
16	10	Côte de Blaye	Aux joyeux ecclésiastiques
21	15	Genen Shouyu	Mayumi's

Note that the numbers in column A now read 5,10,15,20...

The list now contains the 20% sample needed for the audit.

5   **Save your work as *Inventory-4*.**

important

Other ways to extract unique records

UNIQUE function (not compatible with Excel 2019 and earlier)

The *July 2020 Semi-Annual version 2002* release included a major new feature called *Dynamic Arrays*.

Dynamic Arrays change the way in which many things used to be done in legacy versions of Excel (Excel 2019 and earlier).

If you only need to share your workbooks with other Excel 365 users, there's a new UNIQUE *Dynamic Array Function* that now represents best practice.

You'll learn about this function later, in: *Lesson 4-6: Create a drop-down list using a UNIQUE function.*

Other ways to create unique lists that will also work in older Excel versions

Later, in: *Lesson 2-13: Remove duplicate values from a table,* you'll learn a more powerful way to extract unique records using *Excel's Remove Duplicates* feature.

In *Session Nine: Pivot Tables* you'll also discover an extremely fast way to extract unique records using a pivot table.

Lesson 1-10: Extract unique records using an advanced filter

1   Open *Inventory-4* from your sample files folder (if it isn't already open).

2   Click: Data→Sort & Filter→Clear to show all items in the range.

Notice that one supplier often provides multiple products. For example, *Specialty Biscuits, Ltd.* supplies four different products:

A	B	C
54	Scottish Longbreads	Specialty Biscuits, Ltd.
55	Sir Rodney's Marmalade	Specialty Biscuits, Ltd.
56	Sir Rodney's Scones	Specialty Biscuits, Ltd.
61	Teatime Chocolate Biscuits	Specialty Biscuits, Ltd.

In this lesson you'll extract a list of suppliers from the workbook using an advanced filter. The advanced filter's *Unique records only* feature will be used to ensure that each supplier is only listed once.

You will be amazed at how often you'll find this feature useful in your day-to-day business use of Excel.

3   Delete rows 1-5 (the cells that were previously used to define the advanced filter criteria condition).

After deleting these rows your worksheet should look like this:

	A	B	C
1	No	Product Name	Supplier
2	1	Aniseed Syrup	Exotic Liquids
3	2	Boston Crab Meat	New England Seafood Cannery
4	3	Camembert Pierrot	Gai pâturage
5	4	Carnarvon Tigers	Pavlova, Ltd.

4   Bring up the *Advanced Filter* dialog.

Click: Data→Sort & Filter→Advanced.

5   Set the *List range* to all cells in column C within the range.

   1.   Click in the *List range* text box.

   2.   Click into cell C1.

   3.   Press: **<Ctrl>+<Shift>+<DownArrow>**

   The range C1:C70 appears in the *List range* text box.

   List range: ɔry!$C$1:$C$70   ⬆

6   Leave the *Criteria Range* box blank and check the *Unique records only* check box.

   ☑ Unique records only

7   Click the *Copy to another location* option button.

Inventory-4

8   Click in the *Copy to:* box and then click once in cell I1.

The dialog should now look like this:

F	G	H	I
In			
Stock	Value		
13	130.00		

Advanced Filter   ?   ✕

Action
- ○ Filter the list, in-place
- ◉ Copy to another location

List range: ory!$C$1:$C$70   ⬆

Criteria range: ⬆

Copy to: Inventory!$I$1   ⬆

☑ Unique records only

OK   Cancel

9   Click the *OK* button.

A list of suppliers appears in column I:

F	G	H	I	J	K
In					
Stock	Value		Supplier		
13	130.00		Exotic Liquids		
123	2,263.20		New England Seafood Cannery		
19	646.00		Gai pâturage		
42	2,625.00		Pavlova, Ltd.		
39	702.00		Aux joyeux ecclésiastiques		
17	323.00		New Orleans Cajun Delights		

Notice that there are no duplicate entries in the list. The *Unique records only* feature has ensured that each supplier is only listed once.

10   Delete column I.

11   Save your work as *Inventory-5*.

Lesson 1-11: Add totals using Quick Analysis

Quick Analysis provides a simple way to do simple things. All of the features provided by Quick Analysis are also available (usually with more options and features) by using the Ribbon.

You'll find yourself using Quick Analysis a lot, to save time when adding simple totals to ranges.

1   Open *Hours Worked-1* from your sample files folder (if it isn't already open).

2   Select every cell in the range A3:F8.

    1.   Click anywhere inside the range A3:F8.

    2.   Press the **<Ctrl>+<A>** keys.

        Notice that the *Quick Analysis* button has appeared at the bottom-right corner of the selected range.

3   Understand the Quick Analysis totals options.

    1.   Click the *Quick Analysis* button.

        Five tabs are shown across the top of the Quick Analysis palette:

        Formatting, Charts and *Sparklines* were extensively covered in the *Essential Skills* book in this series.

        The *Tables* quick analysis options will be covered later, in *Lesson 1-13: Convert a range into a table and add a total row (sidebar)* and *Lesson 9-1: Create a one-dimensional pivot table report from a table (sidebar).*

        For this lesson you are only concerned with the *Totals* option.

    2.   Click the *Totals* tab.

        There are ten icons. You need to use the scroll-right arrow to view all of them:

The first five icons will add totals to the bottom of the range. The second five icons will add totals to the right-hand side of the range.

Quick Analysis button

Hours Worked-1

Add totals to bottom of range.

Add totals to the right of the range.

The *Running Total* icon can cause confusion as it has no real purpose when added to the bottom of a range.

4   Click both *Quick Analysis Sum* buttons to show total hours worked for each employee, and total hours worked for each day.

Notice that, as you hover the mouse cursor over each icon, a preview of the result is shown on the worksheet.

	A	B Johnny Caine	C George Marley	D Betty Anan	E Paris Winfrey	F Ozzy Dickens	G Sum
4	Monday	9	10	10	10	7	46
5	Tuesday	8	9	8	6	10	41
6	Wednesday	10	9	8	7	9	43
7	Thursday	6	8	6	10	9	39
8	Friday	10	7	10	7	9	43
9	**Sum**	43	43	42	40	44	

5   Delete the contents of column G and row 9.

6   Use the *Quick Analysis Average* buttons to show average hours worked for each employee, and average hours worked for each day.

	A	B Johnny Caine	C George Marley	D Betty Anan	E Paris Winfrey	F Ozzy Dickens	G Average
4	Monday	9	10	10	10	7	9.2
5	Tuesday	8	9	8	6	10	8.2
6	Wednesday	10	9	8	7	9	8.6
7	Thursday	6	8	6	10	9	7.8
8	Friday	10	7	10	7	9	8.6
9	**Average**	8.6	8.6	8.4	8	8.8	

7   Delete the contents of column G and row 9.

8   Close the workbook without saving.

Lesson 1-12: Add percentage and running totals using Quick Analysis

As you saw in: *Lesson 1-11: Add totals using Quick Analysis,* the Quick Analysis feature provides a simple and easy way to add simple SUM and AVERAGE functions to rows and columns. The COUNT function can be used in the same way to return the number of cells containing values present in a row or column.

Quick Analysis is also able to add some more complex functions to compute *Running Total* and *% Total.*

1   Open *Hours Worked-1* from your sample files folder (if it isn't already open).

2   Select every cell in the range A3:F8.

　　1. Click anywhere inside the range A3:F8.

　　2. Press the **<Ctrl>+<A>** keys.

　　　　Notice that the *Quick Analysis* button has appeared at the bottom-right corner of the selected range.

3   Click the Quick Analysis button.

4   Use both Quick Analysis *% Total* buttons to add percentage totals for each row and column.

　　You learned how to do this in: *Lesson 1-11: Add totals using Quick Analysis.*

	A	B	C	D	E	F	G
4	Monday	9	10	10	10	7	21.70%
5	Tuesday	8	9	8	6	10	19.34%
6	Wednesday	10	9	8	7	9	20.28%
7	Thursday	6	8	6	10	9	18.40%
8	Friday	10	7	10	7	9	20.28%
9	% Total	20.28%	20.28%	19.81%	18.87%	20.75%	

5   Understand how % Totals are calculated.

The *% Total* figures look interesting, but it may not be clear precisely what they relate to.

　　1. Click on cell B9 and examine the formula (shown in the formula bar):

　　　　=SUM(B4:B8)/SUM($B$4:$F$8)

　　This formula represents:

　　Hours worked by Johnny Caine (43)
　　divided by
　　Hours worked by all employees (212)

　　In other words: *of all of the hours worked, by all employees, this week, Johnny Caine worked 20.28% of the total (43/212=0.2028).*

　　2. Click on cell G4 and examine the formula:

f_x =SUM(B4:F4)/SUM($B$4:$F$8)

You can see that the formula is calculating:

Hours worked on Monday (46)
divided by
Hours worked on every day of the week (212)

In other words: *of all of the hours worked, by all employees, this week, 21.70% of them were worked on Monday (46/212=0.2169).*

6   Delete the contents of column G and row 9.

7   Use the Quick Analysis *Column Running Total* button to add a running total to cells G4:G8.

Make sure that you use the *column running total* icon and not the *row running total* (see sidebar).

8   Re-format the running total to show as a number.

Column G was formatted using the percentage style when you added *% Totals* earlier. You may need to return the formatting of these cells to the default *General* format.

1. Select cells G4:G8.

2. Click: Home→Number→
    Number Format Drop-Down→General.

General	˅

    Cell formatting was covered extensively in the *Essential Skills* book in this series.

▲	A	B	C	D	E	F	G
4	Monday	9	10	10	10	7	46
5	Tuesday	8	9	8	6	10	87
6	Wednesday	10	9	8	7	9	130
7	Thursday	6	8	6	10	9	169
8	Friday	10	7	10	7	9	212

You can now see that 46 hours were worked on Monday, and that 87 hours were worked on both Monday and Tuesday.

9   Understand how *Running Totals* are calculated.

Click on cell G4 and examine the formula (shown in the formula bar):

f_x =SUM($B$4:F4)

You can see that Quick Analysis has used an absolute reference for cell $B$4 and used a SUM function to add all of the values in row 4.

Because an absolute reference was used, the formula will correctly adjust when AutoFilled down to G8, maintaining a running total for all hours worked during the week to date.

10   Save your work as *Hours Worked-2.*

Running Total

Running Total

Column Running Total

Row Running Total

note

You can also convert a range into a table by using the Quick Analysis button

When you select an entire range you'll see the *Quick Analysis* button 📊 appear on the bottom right-hand corner of the selected range.

You can also use this button to convert the range into a table by clicking:

Quick Analysis Button→ Tables→Table.

tip

You can also convert a range into a table using the keyboard shortcut:

<Ctrl>+<T>

note

Slicers can be used to visually filter tables

You will learn about slicers later, in: *Lesson 9-7: Filter a pivot table visually using slicers*

Slicers can also be used with normal tables (such as the one used in this lesson) in exactly the same way they are used with pivot tables.

Inventory-5

Lesson 1-13: Convert a range into a table and add a total row

This lesson introduces tables (originally added to Excel in the Excel 2007 version). While tables have now been with us for thirteen years, they remain a mystery to many professional Excel users.

Tables provide a completely new way to work with tabular data and are particularly powerful when dealing with dynamic data. A table is very similar to a range but incorporates several very useful extra features.

You can freely convert a table into a range, or a range into a table. The key difference between ranges and tables is that table references shrink and grow dynamically.

For example, if you create a chart from a table and then add more rows to the table, the chart's source data will automatically adjust to include the new rows. This doesn't happen with a range.

1   Open *Inventory-5* from your sample files folder (if it isn't already open).

2   Convert the range into a table.

 1.   Click anywhere inside the range

 2.   Click: Insert→Tables→Table.

      The *Create Table* dialog is displayed:

Create Table	?	×
Where is the data for your table?		
=$A$1:$G$70		⬆
☑ My table has headers		
OK	Cancel	

 3.   Click the *OK* button.

The range is converted into a table. The appearance of the range changes and filter arrows appear in the header row.

	A	B	C
1	No ▾	Product Name ▾	Supplier ▾
2	1	Aniseed Syrup	Exotic Liquids
3	2	Boston Crab Meat	New England Seafood Cannery
4	3	Camembert Pierrot	Gai pâturage
5	4	Carnarvon Tigers	Pavlova, Ltd.

3   Scroll down the table and notice the "sticky" column headers.

 1.   Click inside the table

 2.   Scroll down the table until the headers disappear from the top row.

      In a range you would have to freeze panes in order to continue to view the range headers (freeze panes was covered in the Essential Skills book in this series). Tables are much easier to work with. The table headers and filter buttons are always visible as they replace the column letters when scrolled off the screen:

	No		Product Name	Supplier	
19	18		Grandma's Boysenberry Spread	Grandma Kelly's Homestead	
20	19		Gravad lax	Svensk Sjöföda AB	
21	20		Gudbrandsdalsost	Norske Meierier	
22	21		Gula Malacca	Leka Trading	

note

Excel's use of the quirky SUBTOTAL function

When Excel adds a total row, the quirky SUBTOTAL function is used. The SUBTOTAL function has a very odd syntax. It is:

SUBTOTAL(function_num, ref1, [ref2], ...)

The *function_num* argument can cause confusion as it has been implemented in a very unusual way.

The *function_num* can be a value from 1 to 11, each corresponding to a different function. For example, function_num 9 is the SUM function and function_num 1 is the AVG function.

The *function_num* argument also supports the same numbers with 100 added to them (ie 101-111) and these correspond to the same functions. For example, function_num 9 is the SUM function and so is function_num 109.

So why does the SUBTOTAL's *function_num* argument accept the values 109 and 9 if they both mean the SUM function?

The reason is that a 109 SUM function ignores any rows that are hidden, while a 9 SUM function will include any hidden rows. (You'll learn about hidden rows later, in: *Lesson 6-7: Hide and unhide worksheets, columns and rows*).

By default, the total row ignores hidden rows meaning that (in this lesson's example) the function used to total (or sum) the column is:

=SUBTOTAL(109,[Value])

Sometimes you might want to include any hidden rows in the total. In this case you would have to change the formula to:

=SUBTOTAL(9,[Value])

4   Add a total row.

Tables have a built-in ability to add total rows.

1.   Click anywhere inside the table.

   The *Table Design* tab appears on the ribbon.

2.   Click: Table Design→Table Style Options→Total Row.

☑ Total Row

   A total row appears at the bottom of the table.

	Category		Unit Price		In Stock		Value	
69	Grains/Cereals		33.25		22		731.50	
70	Confections		9.50		36		342.00	
71							69,598.25	

3.   Re-size the *Value* column if needed to view the total.

   By default, the total row contains the SUM of all values in the right-most column. Excel uses the SUM function indirectly via the rather quirky SUBTOTAL function (see sidebar).

   Note that you can do nearly the same thing by using the *Quick Analysis* feature (used in: *Lesson 1-11: Add totals using Quick Analysis*) to add a SUM total row. The only difference is that a *Quick Analysis* sum is added to every column (rather than only to the right-most column).

5   Change the total from SUM to AVERAGE and add a total for the *In Stock* column.

1.   Click cell G71 (the cell containing the total).

   A drop-down arrow appears next to the total.

2.   Click the drop-down arrow and choose *Average* from the function list.

3.   Click on cell F71 at the bottom of the *In Stock* column (the cell in the dark blue total row).

   A drop-down arrow appears next to the empty cell.

4.   Click the drop-down arrow and then click *Sum* from the function list.

   The sum of units in stock is now also displayed.

6   Change the AVERAGE in cell G71 back to a SUM.

	E	F	G
69	33.25	22	731.50
70	9.50	36	342.00
71		3018	69,598.25

7   Save your work as *Inventory-6*.

note

Formatting mayhem when converting tables into ranges and back

When you convert a table into a range, all of the formatting applied to the table remains.

The biggest problem occurs if you need to convert a formatted range back into a table again.

Because each cell contains formatting information, Excel politely refuses to change any of the colors. This makes it impossible to change the table style using the table styles gallery.

The table's appearance then becomes very strange when you add rows to the table. The added rows will use the table style, while the rows imported from the range will keep their old formatting (because Excel thinks that the formatting has been manually applied).

The simple solution is to always obey the important rule:

Apply the None style before converting a table into a range, except when you are sure that you will never want to convert the range back into a table again.

See facing page sidebar for techniques to clean things up after conversion if you didn't apply this rule.

Inventory-6

Lesson 1-14: Format a table using table styles and convert a table into a range

When you have formatted your data as a table, you can customize the appearance of the table using Excel's powerful *table styles* feature.

You can either apply a table style from the *table styles gallery* or you can create your own custom table styles.

All of the pre-defined styles in the *table styles gallery* follow best practice by restricting color choices to theme colors. Themes are covered in great depth in the *Essential Skills* book in this series.

In this lesson you will explore the simpler of the two options by applying some of the standard pre-defined table styles. Later, in *Lesson 1-15: Create a custom table style,* you'll create your own custom-designed table style.

1 Open *Inventory-6* from your sample files folder (if it isn't already open).

2 Apply the *Berlin* theme to the workbook.

Click: Page Layout→Themes→Themes→Berlin.

The *Berlin* theme is applied and the colors used in the table change.

The reason the colors change is that Microsoft used best practice when creating the built-in table styles and restricted their color and font choices to theme colors and theme fonts.

3 Change the theme back to the default *Office* theme.

4 Choose a new table style from the *Table Styles Gallery*.

1. Click anywhere inside the table.

2. Click: Table Design→Table Styles→More.

The *More* button is located on the right hand side of the *Table Styles* group:

The table styles gallery is displayed.

3. Click any of the table styles that you find attractive.

The chosen table style is applied.

4. Restore the table style to the default *Table Style Medium 9*.

5 Change the table's appearance using *Table Style Options*.

1. Click inside the table.

2. Click the *Table Design* tab and focus upon the *Table Style Options* group.

The easiest way to understand the options is to experiment by switching each option on and off. The function of each option will then be obvious.

6 **Apply the *None* quick table style to remove all table style formatting.**

The *None* style is extremely useful.

In a moment you're going to convert the table back into a range. You'll nearly always want to remove table style formatting prior to conversion (see sidebar for more on this).

1. Click anywhere inside the table.

2. Click: Table Design→Table Styles→ More→None.

   The *None* style is the one in the top left corner of the gallery.

   The table now looks more like a range but it is still a table and still provides all table features.

   (You could also click: Table Design→Table Styles→ More→Clear to achieve a similar result).

7 **Set the *None* style as the default.**

I always like to work with the *None* style as the default. Excel's default table styles are a little too colorful for me. Note that this sets the default style only for this workbook. When you open a different workbook, the default table style will revert to *Table Style Medium 9*.

1. Click inside the table.

2. Click: Table Design→Table Styles→More.

3. Right-click on the *None* style and click *Set As Default* from the shortcut menu.

Every time you create new tables in the *Inventory-6* workbook they will now display with the *None* style.

8 **Convert the table back into a range.**

1. Click anywhere inside the table.

2. Click: Table Design→Tools→Convert to Range.

3. Click the *Yes* button.

The table has now been converted back into a range.

9 **Save your work as *Inventory-7.***

note

Solutions to range and table formatting issues after conversion

The previous page sidebar discusses how to avoid formatting issues when converting tables to ranges (and ranges to tables).

Sometimes you may accidentally convert a richly formatted table or range.

Here are some simple techniques for removing all existing formatting from a range or table:

To remove all formatting information from a range

1. Select all cells in the range (the easiest way is click inside the range and then press the <Ctrl>+<A> keys).

2. Click: Home→Styles→ Cell Styles→Normal.

To remove all formatting information from a table

1. Click inside the table.

2. Click: Table Design→Table Styles→More, to open the *Table Styles Gallery*.

3. Right-click any style and then select: *Apply and Clear Formatting* from the shortcut menu.

4. Apply the *None* style.

tip

How to quickly identify tables and ranges

A quick way to tell tables from ranges is to click inside the table/range.

If you see the *Table Design* tab on the ribbon, you will immediately know that you are looking at a table.

note

Why it is a good idea to restrict custom style colors to theme colors

Themes are covered in great depth in the *Essential Skills* book in this series.

If you restrict your color choice to the 60 *Theme Colors,* your worksheet design will be compatible with documents that use other themes.

If you use non-theme colors, your worksheets will not seamlessly integrate (from a design point of view) with PowerPoint presentations, Word documents, and other Office documents that use a different theme.

Example

John creates a worksheet using the default *Office* theme.

Mary wants to use this in her PowerPoint presentation that uses the *Berlin* theme. John e-mails the worksheet to her and then she simply pastes the required cells into her presentation and changes the theme to *Berlin.*

Joe sees the presentation and wants to use the same worksheet in his Word report that uses the *Circuit* theme. Mary e-mails the presentation to him and then he simply pastes the required slides into his Word document and changes the theme to *Circuit.*

The same worksheet has been used without modification and it blends perfectly into both Joe and Mary's work because John followed best practice and restricted his color choices to theme colors.

Inventory-7

Lesson 1-15: Create a custom table style

Perhaps none of the huge selection of styles in the *table styles gallery* is suitable for your requirements. In this case you can create a custom table style from scratch.

Another great feature of a custom table style is that you can set it as the default for this workbook. This saves you from continually reapplying a style every time you create a table.

1   Open *Inventory-7* from your sample files folder (if it isn't already open).

Notice that this range, (created from a table with a total row in: *Lesson 1-14: Format a table using table styles and convert a table into a range*), has totals in row 71.

2   Convert the range into a table.

You learned how to do this in: *Lesson 1-13: Convert a range into a table and add a total row.*

3   Convert the *range total row* to a *table total row.*

If you click *Table Design* you will see that the *Total Row* check box is unchecked.

View	Help	Power Pivot	Design	🔎
☑ Header Row	☐ First Column		☑ Filter Button	
☑ Total Row	☐ Last Column			
☑ Banded Rows	☐ Banded Columns			
		Table Style Options		

Why then does the table appear to have a total row in row 71?

	D	E	F	G
69	Grains/Cereals	33.25	22	731.50
70	Confections	9.50	36	342.00
71			3018	69,598.25

The reason is that row 71 is the total row defined in the range and has nothing to do with the total row that is available as a table feature.

1.   Check: Table Design→Table Style Options→ Total Row.

A second total row appears beneath the first. This is the *table total row*:

	D	E	F	G
69	Grains/Cereals	33.25	22	731.50
70	Confections	9.50	36	342.00
71			3018	69,598.25
72				69,598.25

2.   Delete row 71 to remove the range total row.

4   Create a custom table style based upon an existing style.

1. Click anywhere inside the table.

2. Click: Table Design→Table Styles→More.

   The *More* button is located on the bottom right hand corner of the Table Styles group:

   The table styles gallery is displayed.

3. Right-click one of the existing styles and then click *Duplicate* from the shortcut menu.

   The *Modify Table Style* dialog is displayed:

4. Name the new table style: **TSM**

Modify Table Style	
Name:	TSM
Table Element:	

   Each of the table's elements are listed on the left of the dialog.

   Each element that has been formatted (in the style you chose to duplicate) is shown in bold face type.

Table Element:	Preview
Whole Table	
First Column Stripe	
Second Column Stripe	
First Row Stripe	
Second Row Stripe	
Last Column	
First Column	
Header Row	
Total Row	

5. Choose a table element and then click the *Format* button to set the *Font, Border* and *Fill* formatting.

   To follow best practice, you should restrict your color and font choices to theme colors and theme fonts (see sidebar on facing page).

6. Customize as many other elements as you wish.

7. Click the *OK* button.

5 Apply your new custom style to the table.

1. Click on any cell inside the table.

2. Click: Table Design→Table Styles→More.

3. Notice the new *Custom* section at the top of the gallery containing your new style.

4. Hover the mouse cursor over your new style. The style name appears in a tip.

5. Click the style to apply it to the worksheet.

6. Change the style back to *None*.

6 Save your work as *Inventory-8*.

Lesson 1-16: Sort a range or table by rows

1   Open *Inventory-8* from your sample files folder (if it isn't already open).

2   Sort the categories from Z-A.

1.   Click anywhere in the *Category* column.

2.   Click: Data→Sort & Filter→Z-A.

The categories are now sorted in reverse alphabetical order:

	Category	Unit Price	In Stock	Value
13	Seafood	12.00	95	1,140.00
14	Produce	10.00	4	40.00
15	Produce	53.00	20	1,060.00
16	Produce	23.25	35	813.75

3   Sort the categories from A-Z.

1.   Click anywhere in the *Category* column.

2.   Click: Data→Sort & Filter→A-Z.

The categories are now sorted in alphabetical order:

	Category	Unit Price	In Stock	Value
11	Beverages	14.00	111	1,554.00
12	Beverages	18.00	20	360.00
13	Condiments	10.00	13	130.00
14	Condiments	22.00	53	1,166.00

4   Sort by both Category and Supplier.

There's a small problem with the existing sort. It can be seen that one category often has many suppliers:

	C	D	E
55	Tokyo Traders	Produce	10.00
56	G'day, Mate	Produce	53.00
57	Mayumi's	Produce	23.25
58	Grandma Kelly's Homestead	Produce	30.00

In the above example it would be nice to also have the suppliers listed in alphabetical order. This can be achieved with a two-column sort.

1.   Click: Data→Sort & Filter→Sort.

The *Sort* dialog appears:

Sort					?	×
Add Level	× Delete Level	Copy Level	^ ∨	Options...	☑ My data has headers	
Column		Sort On		Order		
Sort by	Category	∨	Cell Values	∨	A to Z	∨

2.   Click the *Add Level* button to add a second sort that will sort the *Supplier* column from A-Z.

Inventory-8

note

You can also sort from the Home tab

The *Home* tab also has a *Sort & Filter* menu button in the *Editing* group.

This is one of the unusual cases where a feature is repeated on two different ribbon tabs.

It doesn't matter which you use as the functionality is identical.

tip

Sort with a right-click

The fastest sort method of all is to right-click any cell and select *Sort* from the shortcut menu.

The fly-out menu then provides every sort option available from the ribbon.

note

Sort by font color or cell color

Note that there is also a *Cell Color* and *Font Color* option (in the *Sort On* drop-down list).

These work in exactly the same way as the other options.

3.   Click the *OK* button.

The table is now sorted first by *Category* and then by *Supplier*.

	Supplier	Category
55	G'day, Mate	Produce
56	Grandma Kelly's Homestead	Produce
57	Mayumi's	Produce

5   Select all of the data cells in column G.

1.   Scroll to the top of the table so that row 1 is visible.

2.   Hover the mouse cursor over the top of cell G1 until you see a black down-arrow. Note that the arrow *must* overlap the bottom of the column header button. If you hover inside the button, you'll still see the black arrow but your selection will then include every cell in column G (rather than the value cells within the table).

The arrow must overlap the bottom of this button.

3.   When you see the arrow, click once to select cells G2:G70.

6   Add a *Three Flags* conditional format icon set to column G.

Conditional formatting was covered in depth in the *Essential Skills* book in this series.

1.   Click: Home→Styles→Conditional Formatting→Icon Sets→ 3 Flags.

2.   If necessary, widen column G to make room for the flags.

Values in column G have red, yellow or green flags added depending upon their value.

7   Sort by icon so that the green flagged cells appear first, the yellow flagged second and the red flagged last.

1.   Click any value in column G.

2.   Click: Data→Sort & Filter→Sort.

3.   Click the *Delete Level* button twice to remove existing sort conditions.

4.   Add the following three sort conditions to sort by flag.

Column		Sort On		Order		
Sort by	Value	Conditional Formatting Icon		▶	On Top	
Then by	Value	Conditional Formatting Icon		▶	On Top	
Then by	Value	Conditional Formatting Icon		▶	On Top	

5.   Click the *OK* button.

8   Save your work as *Inventory-9*.

note

Excel 365 now includes new SORT and SORTBY dynamic array functions

The Excel 365 *July 2020 Semi-Annual version 2002* release included a major new feature called *Dynamic Arrays*.

If you only need to share your workbooks with other Excel 365 users, there's are new SORT and SORTBY *Dynamic Array Functions* that provide a powerful way to sort and extract data from a table.

Dynamic arrays are not supported by legacy Excel versions (2019 and earlier).

You'll learn all there is to know about dynamic arrays later, in: *Session Four: Working with Dynamic Arrays*.

You'll also learn about the new SORT and SORTBY dynamic array functions in: *Lesson 4-9: Use a SORT function* and *Lesson 4-10: Use a SORTBY function*.

Lesson 1-17: Sort a range by columns

Students often come to my classes with long "wish lists". Usually by the end of the course they have ticked all of their requirements off and don't have to ask any of the questions they had arrived with.

An item that seems to be on everybody's wish list is a way to sort data by columns. This lesson will teach you a simple technique to achieve this.

Note that this technique will work for ranges but not for tables. If you need to sort a table by columns, you'll have to convert it to a range first. That's exactly what you'll do in this lesson.

1 Open *Inventory-9* from your sample files folder.

2 Convert the table into a range.

You learned how to do this in: *Lesson 1-14: Format a table using table styles and convert a table into a range.*

3 Add a blank row at the top of the range.

4 Add numbers to enable a column sort order of: *No, Category, Supplier, Product Name, Unit Price, In Stock, Value*.

The blank row that you have just added is a dummy row to set the sort order.

Type numbers into row 1 that numerically describe the desired sorted position for each column:

	A	B	C	D	E	F	G
1	1	4	3	2	5.00	6	7
2	No	Product Name	Supplier	Category	Unit Price	In Stock	Value

Note that the value in cell E1 only appears to be different to the others because it has inherited the two decimal place format from the *Price* field in the table.

5 Sort the range by reference to row one.

1. Click anywhere inside the range.

2. Press **<Ctrl>+<A>** to select every cell in the range (including the dummy header row).

3. Click: Data→Sort & Filter→Sort.

Notice that row 1 is no longer included in the selected range. This is because the *My data has headers* box is checked.

☑ My data has <u>h</u>eaders

4. Uncheck the *My data has headers* check box.

☐ My data has <u>h</u>eaders

The entire range (including row 1) is now selected.

5. Remove any existing sort condition(s) by clicking the *Delete Level* button.

Inventory-9

6. Click the *Options...* button.

The *Sort Options* dialog is displayed.

7. Click the *Sort left to right* option button.

Sort Options ? ✕

☐ *C*ase sensitive

Orientation
○ Sort *t*op to bottom
◉ Sort *l*eft to right

OK   Cancel

8. Click the *OK* button.

9. Click the *Add Level* button. + *A*dd Level

10. Set a new sort to sort using *Row 1, Cell Values, Smallest to Largest.*

Sort			? ✕
+ *A*dd Level ✕ *D*elete Level ▢ *C*opy Level ∧ ∨		*O*ptions...	☐ My data has *h*eaders
Row	Sort On	Order	
Sort by Row 1 ∨	Cell Values ∨	Smallest to Largest ∨	

11. Click the *OK* button.

The worksheet is now sorted in the same order as the dummy sort row.

	A	B	C	D	E	F	G
1	1	2	3	4	5.00	6	7
2	No	Category	Supplier	Product Name	Unit Price	In Stock	Value

6   Delete row 1.

7   Convert the range back into a table.

You learned how to do this in: *Lesson 1-13: Convert a range into a table and add a total row.*

8   Save your work as *Inventory-10*.

Lesson 1-18: Sort a range or table by custom list

Sometimes you need a sort order that is not alphabetical.

For example, you might run a support desk and be given support incidents marked as *Low, Medium, High, Urgent* and *Critical*. You would want to sort such a list in order of priority, but these priorities do not lend themselves to an alphabetical sort.

If you create a custom sort list with each incident listed in order of importance, you can then use the list to sort a range or table. This lesson will show you how.

1 Open *Help Desk-1* from your sample files folder.

This worksheet lists several support incidents sent to the help desk and prioritized from *Low* to *Critical*.

	A	B	C	D	E
1	Incident ID	Date Raised	Raised By	Description	Priority
2	10872	27-Jan-16	Barack Obama	Air conditioning not working	Low
3	10873	27-Jan-16	Britney Spears	No hot water in staff kitchen	Medium
4	10874	27-Jan-16	Angelina Jolie	Broken lock on main door	Critical
5	10875	27-Jan-16	Kofi Anan	Freezer has stopped working	Critical

2 Create a custom list.

1. Click: File→Options→Advanced→General→ Edit Custom Lists.

The *Custom Lists* dialog is displayed.

2. Type each of the support incident priority levels followed by the **<Enter>** key into the *List entries* box in the following order:

3. Click the *OK* button twice to close both dialogs.

3 Sort the table using the custom list.

1. Click anywhere in column E.

2. Click: Data→Sort & Filter→Sort.

The *Sort* dialog appears.

3. Select *Priority* from the *Sort by* drop down.

4. Select *Custom List…* for the *Order:*

Help Desk-1

The *Custom Lists* dialog appears showing all defined custom lists.

5. Click on your newly added custom list and then click the *OK* button twice to close both dialogs.

The worksheet is now sorted in order of priority from lowest to highest.

4 Reverse the sort order to show the higher priority incidents first.

1. Click anywhere inside the range.

2. Click: Data→Sort & Filter→Sort.

3. Click the drop-down arrow next to *Order*.

Notice that your custom sort order is shown twice as *Low to Critical* and as *Critical to Low*.

4. Click *Critical to Low*.

5. Click the *OK* button.

The worksheet is now sorted with higher priority incidents listed first.

D	E
Description	Priority
Broken lock on main door	Critical
Freezer has stopped working	Critical
Burst water main is flooding the basement	Critical
Computer not working	Urgent
Broken window on ground floor	Urgent

5 Save your work as *Help Desk-2*.

note

Excel 365 now includes a new SORTBY dynamic array function that can perform a custom sort

The Excel 365 *July 2020 Semi-Annual version 2002* release included a major new feature called *Dynamic Arrays*. This feature will not work in Excel 2019 and earlier.

If you only need to share your workbooks with other Excel 365 users, there are new SORTBY and XMATCH *Dynamic Array Functions* that provide a new, and more powerful way to implement custom sorts.

You'll learn all there is to know about dynamic arrays later, in: *Session Four: Working with Dynamic Arrays*.

You'll also discover an alternative way to perform a custom sort in: *Lesson 4-24: Use a SORTBY function with a custom array*.

important

Because structured table references were only introduced in Excel 2007, this feature will not work if you have saved a workbook in *Excel 97-2003 Workbook* format to maintain compatibility with earlier versions.

note

If this feature doesn't work for you, somebody may have switched it off

Excel allows structured references to be switched off.

You really wouldn't ever want to do this, as structured references are one of the most useful features of tables.

If you simply want to maintain compatibility with Excel 2003 you can save the workbook in *Excel 97/2003 Workbook* format. The structured reference feature will then be automatically disabled.

You can check that this feature is enabled by clicking:

File→Options→
Formulas→
Working with formulas→
Use table names in formulas

When the check box is checked the feature is switched on (the default).

Lesson 1-19: Name a table and create an automatic structured table reference

One of the key differences between a range and a table is that tables shrink and grow dynamically.

The table's ability to shrink and grow wouldn't be useful without a way to enter a cell reference into a formula that points to all of the rows in a table column (no matter how many rows the table contains).

Consider the following range:

	A	B	C	D	E	F	G
1	Sales						
2							
3	Month	Net	Tax	Total		Total Sales	
4	Jan	15,249.00	2,287.35	17,536.35			
5	Feb	18,320.00	2,748.00	21,068.00			
6	Mar	21,260.00	3,189.00	24,449.00			

To calculate the total sales in cell G3 you could use the formula:

=SUM(D4:D6)

A recurring problem with data ranges is that when you add a new row to the range for April's sales, the SUM formula has to be adjusted (to D4:D7).

In order to exploit the power of dynamic tables, the Excel designers had to figure out a whole new way of referencing cell ranges. They needed a cell reference that would mean:

=SUM(All of the cells in column D that are inside this table)

Because there may be several tables on a single worksheet, the cell reference needs to indicate which table the range is in. This has been solved by adding the ability to name tables. If the table in this example was called *Sales* and the column was called *Total*, the formula would be:

=SUM(Sales[Total])

This type of reference is called a *structured reference.*

In this lesson, you'll use structured references to create some formulas that will always give the correct result, no matter how many rows you add or remove from a table.

1   Open *Sales Summary-1* from your sample files folder.

2   Convert the range into a table.

    1.   Click anywhere inside the range (A3:D6).

    2.   Click: Insert→Tables→Table.

        The *Create Table* dialog is displayed.

    3.   Click *OK* to accept the automatically detected range A3:D6.

Sales Summary-1

3   Set the table name to: **Sales**

1.   Click anywhere inside the table.

   Notice that a *Table Design* tab has appeared on the ribbon.

2.   Click: Table Design→Properties→Table Name.

3.   Type **Sales** into the table name text box).

Table Name:
Sales
⊞ Resize Table
Properties

4.   Press the **<Enter>** key.

4   Add a SUM function to cell G3 using a structured reference.

1.   Click in cell G3 and type:

   =SUM(

2.   Hover the mouse cursor over the top of cell D3 until you see a black down-arrow.

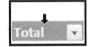

3.   When you see the arrow, click once to select cells D4:D6 (all of the data cells in the column).

4.   Note the structured reference that has been automatically entered:

	F	G	H	I
	Total Sales	=SUM(Sales[Total]		
		SUM(number1, [number2], ...)		

5.   Press the **<Enter>** key.

   There's no need to close the bracket, Excel is clever enough to add this for you automatically.

   The structured reference means:

   The sum of all values in the Total column in the Sales table.

5   Add another row to the Sales table by entering the value: 24,400 in cell B7.

6	Mar	21,260.00	3,189.00	24,449.00
7	Apr	24,400.00	3,660.00	28,060.00

You only have to enter a value in cell B7. Cells C7 and D7 will automatically calculate as Excel automatically adds formulas to new table rows (see *important* sidebar for more on this).

Notice that the total in cell G3 has updated to include April's sales figure. You can now appreciate the power of structured table references.

6   Save your work as *Sales Summary-2*.

Lesson 1-20: Create a manual structured table reference

In the last lesson you created a structured reference automatically by selecting a range inside a table.

In this lesson you'll appreciate the powerful tools that are built into Excel to make the creation of manual structured references very easy and intuitive.

1   Open *Sales Summary-2* from your sample files folder (if it isn't already open).

	A	B	C	D	E	F	G
1	Sales						
2							
3	Month	Net	Tax	Total		Total Sales	91113.35
4	Jan	15,249.00	2,287.35	17,536.35			
5	Feb	18,320.00	2,748.00	21,068.00			
6	Mar	21,260.00	3,189.00	24,449.00			
7	Apr	24,400.00	3,660.00	28,060.00			

2   Add a formula to cell G4 that will calculate average sales using a manual structured reference.

1.   Type the words **Average Sales** into cell F4.

2.   Press the **<Tab>** key to move to cell G4.

3.   Type:

=AVERAGE(Sa

	F	G	H	I
3	Total Sales	91113.35		
4	Average Sales	=AVERAGE(Sa		
5		AVERAGE(number1, [number2], ...)		
6		Sales		

Notice that a small icon of a table has appeared with the name *Sales*. If there was more than one table on any worksheet in this workbook that began with **Sa** you'd see them all listed here. It doesn't matter whether you type **Sa, sa** or **SA**. Table names are not case sensitive.

4.   Press the **<Tab>** key.

The remaining letters in the table name are entered into the formula.

The table name references all of the data in a table excluding the header and totals row.

In this case, and at this time, it will reference cells A4:D7.

As rows are added and removed from the table, the cells referenced by the table name will dynamically adjust to continue to reference all of the data in the table.

5.   Open a square bracket after the word *Sales*.

Sales Summary-2

This time something interesting happens. Excel lists all of the columns in the table:

	F	G	H	I	J
3	Total Sales	91113.35			
4	Average Sales	=AVERAGE(Sales[			
5		AVERAGE(number1, [number2], ...)			
6				@ - This Row ow	
7				Month	
8				Net	
9				Tax	
10				Total	
11				#All	
12				#Data	
13				#Headers	
				#Totals	

There are also some items that begin with a hash (#). These are called *special items*. You'll learn about special items later, in: *Lesson 1-21: Use special items in structured table references.*

6. Use the **<Down Arrow>** key to move the highlight to the *Total* field.

7. Press the **<Tab>** key.

8. Type the closing square bracket.

9. Type the closing curved bracket

The formula should now look like this:

	F	G	H
3	Total Sales	91113.35	
4	Average Sales	=AVERAGE(Sales[Total])	

In a similar way to the table name, the column name will reference all of the data in the *Total* column excluding the header and total rows.

In this case, and at this time, it will reference cells D4:D7.

As rows are added and removed from the table, the cells referenced by the table name and column name will dynamically adjust to continue to reference all of the data in the column.

10. Press the **<Enter>** key to view the result of the formula.

Average sales during the period Jan-Apr were 22,778.34.

	A	B	C	D	E	F	G
1	Sales						
2							
3	Month	Net	Tax	Total		Total Sales	91113.35
4	Jan	15,249.00	2,287.35	17,536.35		Average Sales	22778.34
5	Feb	18,320.00	2,748.00	21,068.00			
6	Mar	21,260.00	3,189.00	24,449.00			
7	Apr	24,400.00	3,660.00	28,060.00			

3   Save your work as *Sales Summary-3*.

Lesson 1-21: Use special items in structured table references

You may have wondered what the items beginning with the hash symbol (#) meant in the last lesson:

These are called *special items*. They can be used to reference different parts of a table.

The #Data special item is rarely used because it is the default and doesn't have to be explicitly stated. In the last lesson you created the structured reference:

Average Sales	=AVERAGE(Sales[Total])

You could have entered the same formula in a different (and needlessly complex) way by adding the #Data special item like this:

=AVERAGE(Sales[[#Data],[Total]])

The #Data special item simply means:

All of the data excluding the header and totals row.

1   Open *Sales Summary-3* from your sample files folder (if it isn't already open).

2   Add a total row to the table.

> You learned how to do this in: *Lesson 1-13: Convert a range into a table and add a total row.*

3   Change the total at the bottom of column D so that it displays the maximum sales in any one month (using the *Max* option).

1.   Click in cell D8.

2.   Click the drop-down arrow next to the cell and select *Max* from the shortcut menu.

4   Type the words: **Max Sales** into cell F5 and then press the **<Tab>** key to move to cell G5.

Sales Summary-3

	A	B	C	D	E	F	G
3	Month ▾	Net ▾	Tax ▾	Total ▾		Total Sales	91113.35
4	Jan	15,249.00	2,287.35	17,536.35		Average Sales	22778.34
5	Feb	18,320.00	2,748.00	21,068.00		Max Sales	
6	Mar	21,260.00	3,189.00	24,449.00			
7	Apr	24,400.00	3,660.00	28,060.00			
8	Total			28,060.00			

This time you're going to reference the value in cell D8 using the special item: *#Totals*.

5   Add an automatic structured reference to cell G5 that will reference the total at the bottom of the *Sales* table.

1.   Press the equals key (=) to start the formula.

2.   Click in cell D8.

An automatic structured reference is created that uses the special item *#Totals* to point to the *Total* row.

Max Sales	=Sales[[#Totals],[Total]]

This means:

Reference the value in the Totals row of the Sales table that is at the bottom of the Total column.

3.   Press the **<Enter>** key to save the formula to the cell.

The *Max Sales* figure is displayed.

6   Apply the comma style to cells G3:G5.

1.   Select cells G3:G5.

2.   Click: Home→Number→Comma Style. ⁹

	A	B	C	D	E	F	G
3	Month ▾	Net ▾	Tax ▾	Total ▾		Total Sales	91,113.35
4	Jan	15,249.00	2,287.35	17,536.35		Average Sales	22,778.34
5	Feb	18,320.00	2,748.00	21,068.00		Max Sales	28,060.00

7   Understand all of the special items.

Here's what the other special items mean:

Special item	What it references
#All	Every cell in the table (this includes the header and total rows).
#Data	The entire contents of the table excluding the header and total rows (this is the default).
#Headers	The header row.
#Totals	The total row.
@ - This Row	Covered in the next lesson.

8   Save your work as *Sales Summary-4*.

Lesson 1-22: Understand unqualified structured table references

A qualified structured reference is a reference that includes the table name such as:

=Sum(Sales[Net])

An unqualified structured reference may be used in formulas within the table itself. In this case you do not have to use the table name as well as the field name because it is obvious.

For example, if you wanted to add *Net sales* and *Tax*, you could use the qualified structured reference:

=Sales[Net]+Sales[Tax]

… but it would be easier and more readable to use the unqualified structured reference:

=[@Net]+[@Tax]

This reference uses the @ (meaning *This Row*) special item.

The @ special item is useful when you want to place a formula *alongside* a table and then want to AutoFill the formula to reference each row in the table.

1   Open *Sales Summary-4* from your sample files folder (if it isn't already open).

2   Convert the A1 style references within the table to unqualified structured references.

   1.   Double-click in cell C4 and note the existing A1 style reference:

      The formula is calculating sales tax as 15% of the net sales value.

   2.   Delete this formula and replace it with the unqualified structured reference:

      =[@Net]*0.15

   3.   Press the **<Enter>** key.

   4.   Double-click in cell D4 and note the existing A1 style reference:

      The formula is adding the sales tax to the net value.

   5.   Delete this formula and replace it with the unqualified structured reference:

      =[@Net]+[@Tax]

tip

You can also convert a table into a range by right-clicking anywhere in the table and then clicking:

Table→Convert to Range

... from the shortcut menu.

The shortcut menu method is much faster than using the Ribbon.

note

When working with tables you don't *have* to convert the old-style A1 references into structured references, but it does make the formulas easier to read if you do.

Sales Summary-4

The *Calculated Columns* feature is switched on by default. You can easily switch off this amazingly useful feature forever by accident.

When you add any formula to an empty table column a calculated column is created and Excel shows a Smart Tag next to the table.

If you click on the Smart Tag you'll see these options:

The dangerous option is: *Stop Automatically Creating Calculated Columns.*

If you click this option, you will switch off the *Calculated Columns* feature.

On all future occasions, when you add a formula to an Excel table, you'll see a Smart Tag with a single option:

10875

Overwrite all cells in this column

The option this time is: *Overwrite all cells in this column with this formula.* It isn't clear from this description that Excel really means that it will create a calculated column.

I strongly recommend that you leave the *Calculated Columns* feature switched on. If you've switched it off by accident, you'll have to do this:

1. Click: File→Options→ Proofing→ AutoCorrect options→ AutoCorrect Options...→ AutoFormat As You Type.

2. Check the checkbox: *Fill formulas in tables to create calculated columns.*

---

6. Press the **<Enter>** key.

7. Click: Formulas→Formula Auditing→Show Formulas to view the formulas in each cell:

	C	D
3	Tax	Total
4	=[@Net]*0.15	=[@Net]+[@Tax]
5	=[@Net]*0.15	=[@Net]+[@Tax]
6	=[@Net]*0.15	=[@Net]+[@Tax]
7	=[@Net]*0.15	=[@Net]+[@Tax]

Notice that, even though you didn't AutoFill the formulas in cells C4 and D4, Excel has automatically converted all of the formulas in columns C and D into structured references.

This has happened because Excel now regards column D as being a *Calculated Column.* This provides a major advantage of tables over ranges.

Unfortunately, there's a huge potential pitfall that you can encounter by accidentally switching off the *Calculated Columns* feature (see important sidebar).

8. Click: Formulas→Formula Auditing→Show Formulas once again to display values.

3 Convert the table back to an unformatted range.

1. Click anywhere inside the table.

2. Click: Table Design→Table Styles→More→None.

The formatting is removed from the table. In: *Lesson 1-14: Format a table using table styles and convert a table into a range,* you learned why this step is essential before converting a table into a range.

3. Click: Table Design→Tools→Convert to Range.

4. Click the *Yes* button.

Notice that the filter buttons have now disappeared.

Notice also that the structured references have now changed into (rather verbose) A1 style references.

4 Convert the range back to a table.

1. Click anywhere inside the range.

2. Click: Insert→Tables→Table.

3. Click the *OK* button to accept the data range A3:D8.

Notice that the filter buttons have now re-appeared. Notice also that the A1 style references remain. They are not converted into structured references when you convert a range into a table.

5 Save your work as *Sales Summary-5.*

Session 1: Exercise

1   Open *Land Speed Records* from your sample files folder.

2   Convert the range A1:F13 into a table.

3   Name the table *SpeedRecord*.

4   Use a simple filter to only show speed records achieved at Bonneville Salt Flats.

5   Remove the filter to show all speed records.

6   Use an advanced filter to show speed records:

- At Bonneville Salt Flats that are greater than 575 mph.

- Together with all records held by Tom Green (irrespective of location and top speed).

    Another way of expressing this is:

    Where Location = Bonneville Salt Flats AND MPH > 575
    OR where Driver = Tom Green.

Here's the result set you should see:

	A	B	C	D	E	F
5	Date	Location	Driver	Vehicle	Power	MPH
7	05-Oct-64	Bonneville Salt Flats	Tom Green	Wingfoot Express	Turbojet	413.199
13	07-Nov-65	Bonneville Salt Flats	Art Arfons	Green Monster	Turbojet	576.553
14	15-Nov-65	Bonneville Salt Flats	Craig Breedlove	Spirit of America - Sonic 1	Turbojet	600.601
15	23-Oct-70	Bonneville Salt Flats	Gary Gabelich	Blue Flame	Rocket	622.407

7   Remove the advanced filter to show all records and remove any rows that you may have added for the advanced filter criteria.

8   Sort the table A-Z, first by *Location* and then by *Driver*.

9   Add a total row to the table and use the MAX function to display the maximum value in column F.

10   Type **Km/h** into cell G1.

11   Use a formula containing a structured reference to show speeds in kilometers per hour in column G.

12   Save your work as *Land Speed Records-1*.

	A	B	C	D	E	F	G
1	Date	Location	Driver	Vehicle	Power	MPH	Km/h
2	15-Oct-97	Black Rock Desert	Andy Green	ThrustSSC	Turbofan	766.000	1232.758
3	04-Oct-83	Black Rock Desert	Richard Noble	Thrust2	Turbojet	633.000	1018.715
4	07-Oct-64	Bonneville Salt Flats	Art Arfons	Green Monster	Turbojet	434.022	698.4907
5	27-Oct-64	Bonneville Salt Flats	Art Arfons	Green Monster	Turbojet	536.710	863.751
6	07-Nov-65	Bonneville Salt Flats	Art Arfons	Green Monster	Turbojet	576.553	927.8721
7	05-Sep-63	Bonneville Salt Flats	Craig Breedlove	Spirit of America	Turbojet	407.447	655.7224
8	13-Oct-64	Bonneville Salt Flats	Craig Breedlove	Spirit of America	Turbojet	468.719	754.3301
9	15-Oct-64	Bonneville Salt Flats	Craig Breedlove	Spirit of America	Turbojet	526.277	846.9607
10	02-Nov-65	Bonneville Salt Flats	Craig Breedlove	Spirit of America - Sonic 1	Turbojet	555.485	893.9665
11	15-Nov-65	Bonneville Salt Flats	Craig Breedlove	Spirit of America - Sonic 1	Turbojet	600.601	966.5736
12	23-Oct-70	Bonneville Salt Flats	Gary Gabelich	Blue Flame	Rocket	622.407	1001.667
13	05-Oct-64	Bonneville Salt Flats	Tom Green	Wingfoot Express	Turbojet	413.199	664.9793
14	Total					766.000	

Land Speed Records

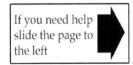

If you need help slide the page to the left

Session 1: Exercise Answers

These are the four questions that students find the most difficult to answer:

Q 11	Q 8	Q 6	Q 2
1. Click in cell G2.	1. Click anywhere inside the table.	1. Insert four blank rows at the top of the worksheet.	1. Click anywhere inside the range.
2. Type:	2. Click: Data→ Sort & Filter→Sort.	2. Copy the table headers from row 5 to row 1.	2. Click:
=			Insert→Tables→Table
3. Click on cell F2.	3. Set the *Sort by* drop-down list to: *Location*	3. In cell F2, type :	You learned how to do this in: *Lesson 1-13: Convert a range into a table and add a total row.*
4. Type:	4. Set the *Sort On* drop-down list to: *Cell Values*	**>575**	
/		4. In cell B2 type:	
5. Click on cell B17.	5. Set the *Order* drop-down list to: *A to Z*	**Bonneville Salt Flats**	
6. Press the **<F4>** key to change the reference to cell B17 into an absolute reference.	6. Click *Add Level.*	5. In cell C3 type:	
	7. Set the *Then by* drop-down list to: *Driver*	**Tom Green**	
Absolute references are covered in depth in the *Essential Skills* book in this series.	8. Set the *Sort On* drop-down list to: *Cell Values*	6. Click anywhere inside the table and then click:	
		Data→Sort & Filter→ Advanced.	
The formula should now read:	9. Set the *Order* drop-down list to: *A to Z*	7. Set the *Criteria Range* to A1:F3.	
=[@MPH]/$B$17	10. Click the *OK* button.	8. Click the *OK* button.	
7. Press the **<Enter>** key.	You learned how to do this in: *Lesson 1-16: Sort a range or table by rows.*	You learned how to do this in: *Lesson 1-8: Apply an advanced filter with complex criteria.*	
You learned how to do this in: *Lesson 1-22: Understand unqualified structured table references.*			

If you have difficulty with the other questions, here are the lessons that cover the relevant skills:

3   Refer to: *Lesson 1-19: Name a table and create an automatic structured table reference.*

4   Refer to: *Lesson 1-5: Apply a simple filter to a range.*

5   Refer to: *Lesson 1-5: Apply a simple filter to a range.*

7   Refer to: *Lesson 1-7: Apply an advanced filter with multiple OR criteria.*

9   Refer to: *Lesson 1-13: Convert a range into a table and add a total row.*

2

Session Two: Data Integrity, Subtotals and Validations

> The longer I live the more I see that I am never wrong about anything, and that all the pains I have so humbly taken to verify my notions have only wasted my time.
>
> *George Bernard Shaw, Irish dramatist & socialist (1856 - 1950)*

In an ideal world all data entry personnel would be just like George Bernard Shaw and never make any mistakes. Unfortunately, the world is not ideal and you will have to give users of your worksheets a little help by validating their input.

In this session you will learn how to validate cells and entire columns in order to restrict the values that users are able to enter. As well as simple validations you'll learn several advanced Excel validation techniques.

Excel's ability to automatically add subtotals never fails to elicit a gasp of amazement during my courses. In this session you'll find out why, when you add sophisticated grouped multi-level subtotals with just a few clicks of the mouse.

Session Objectives

By the end of this session you will be able to:

- Split fixed width data using Text to Columns
- Split delimited data using Text to Columns
- Automatically subtotal a range
- Create nested subtotals
- Consolidate data from multiple data ranges
- Use data consolidation to generate quick subtotals from tables
- Validate numerical data
- Create user-friendly messages for validation errors
- Create data validation input messages
- Add a formula-driven date validation and a text length validation
- Add a table-based dynamic list validation
- Use a formula-driven custom validation to enforce complex business rules
- Remove duplicate values from a table
- Use a custom validation to add a unique constraint to a column

Sales Analysis

Lesson 2-1: Split fixed width data using Text to Columns

Over the years, students have brought some very interesting workbooks to my classes from many diverse areas of business and commerce.

Often the workbook has become extremely complex and unmanageable with convoluted formulas that are difficult to audit.

Many times, all of the problems can be traced to the workbook designer breaking one simple golden rule of data table design:

"Keep data atomic"

This is one of Dr Codd's rules for efficient database design (see sidebar) that is equally relevant to Excel tables and ranges. In the same way that the atom is the smallest basic unit you can divide matter into, a column should contain the smallest possible amount of data.

Here's a simple example to illustrate the concept:

	A	B
1	Name	Age
2	Mr John Smith	42
3	Ms Jane Johnson	28

In the example above it wouldn't be easy to sort or filter column A by first name or last name. If you had observed the *keep data atomic* rule you would have split the data into multiple columns like this:

	A	B	C	D
1	Title	First Name	Last Name	Age
2	Mr	John	Smith	42
3	Ms	Jane	Johnson	28

The benefits provided by this simple example are obvious. It is not as easy to see the problem when a general ledger code or part number contains many different pieces of data. Here's an example:

	A	B	C	D
1	Part Number	Units	Unit Price	Ext Price
2	GB480Z	2	42.70	85.40
3	EU522S	3	22.50	67.50

The error isn't so easy to see here. In this particular example the *Part Number: GB480Z* is actually made up of three pieces of data:

1. GB: Where the product is made (GB=Great Britain, EU=Rest of Europe, US=USA).

2. 480: Product ID.

3. Z: Sales tax rate (Z=Zero rated, S=Standard rated, E=Exempt).

When you see this type of number in your data you should immediately break it up into its constituent parts.

Excel now provides three different ways to split text:

1. **Flash Fill:** This incredibly useful feature is covered comprehensively in Session 2 of the *Essential Skills* book in this series. It is the simplest way to split text.

2. **Using Functions:** You can use the MID, LEFT, RIGHT and FIND functions to split text. (You'll learn about these functions later in: *Lesson 3-20: Extract text from fixed width strings using the LEFT, RIGHT and MID functions*). This is the most complex technique but is the only method that will automatically update when the source text changes.

3. **Using the Get & Transform tool's *Column From Examples* feature:** You'll learn about this feature later in: *Lesson 11-22: Understand Column From Examples.*

4. **Using the *Text to Columns* tool:** This is the method used in this lesson.

1 Open *Sales Analysis* from your sample files folder.

The table contains a list of products sold during March, April and May 2016. But there's a problem with this list. Column B contains part numbers that break the atomic data rule.

	A	B	C	D	E
1	Date	Part Number	Units	Unit Price	Ext Price
2	01-Mar-16	EU812Z	3	72.00	216.00
3	01-Mar-16	EU707Z	4	60.00	240.00
4	01-Mar-16	EU522S	3	22.50	67.50

2 Insert two blank columns to the left of column C.

These columns, along with the original column, will receive the new atomic values.

	B	C	D	E
1	Part Number	Column1	Column2	Units
2	EU812Z			3

3 Split column B into atomic data elements.

1. Select all of the values in column B of the table (B2:B54).

2. Click: Data→Data Tools→Text to Columns.

3. Click *Fixed width* (you'll learn about delimited data in *Lesson 2-2: Split delimited data using Text to Columns*).

> Original data type
>
> Choose the file type that best describes your data:
>
> ○ Delimited   - Characters such as commas or tabs separate each field.
> ● Fixed width   - Fields are aligned in columns with spaces between each field.

4. Click *Next*.

5. Click in the *Data preview* window to break up each data element within the part number (see sidebar).

6. Click the *Finish* button.

The part number is split into atomic data

4 Rename the columns B, C and D as **Region, Part Number** and **Tax**.

	A	B	C	D	E
1	Date	Region	Part Number	Tax	Units
2	01-Mar-14	EU	812	Z	3
3	01-Mar-14	EU	707	Z	4

5 Save your work as *Sales Analysis-2*.

Lesson 2-2: Split delimited data using Text to Columns

Fixed width data

In *Lesson 2-1: Split fixed width data using Text to Columns,* you worked with data that can be split into its constituent parts by reference to the character position of each piece of information.

Several accounting packages export data in a similar fixed width format:

Mr	John	Smith	19-Mar-14	2,220.24	2	4,440.48
Ms	Susan	Phillips	22-Mar-14	125.45	1	125.45
Mrs	Jennifer	Scott	23-Mar-14	1,145.60	2	2,291.20

This type of data is easy to recognize because all of the data elements "line up".

Delimited data

You'll often encounter delimited data. This type of data uses a special character (such as a comma or semicolon) to split each data element. This type of data will be structured like this:

```
Mr;John;Smith;19-Mar-14;2,220.24;2;4,440.48
Ms;Susan;Phillips;22-Mar-14;125.45;1;125.45
Mrs;Jennifer;Scott;23-Mar-14;1,145.60;2;2,291.20
```

In the above example the semicolon (;) is used as the delimiter.

1   Open *US Labor Force-1* from your sample files folder.

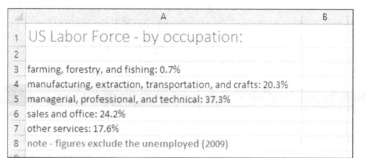

This worksheet contains some data that has been cut and pasted from the *CIA World Fact book* web site.

When you cut and paste information from other documents, (such as web pages), the information often isn't in a format that is "Excel friendly".

In this lesson you'll split this data into a structured table so that you can display the division of labor as a pie chart.

2   Split the data in column A into text and percentages.

1.   Insert a row above row 8.

It is always a good idea to have a blank row separating a range from other data.

US Labor Force-1

2. Select cells A3:A7.

3. Click: Data→Data Tools→Text to Columns.

4. Click *Delimited*.

> Original data type
> Choose the file type that best describes your data:
> ◉ <u>D</u>elimited   - Characters such as commas or tabs separate each field.
> ○ Fixed <u>w</u>idth   - Fields are aligned in columns with spaces between each field.

5. Click the *Next >* button.

6. Set the delimiter to a colon (see sidebar).

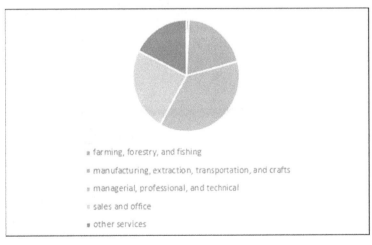

> Delimiters
> ☐ <u>T</u>ab
> ☐ Se<u>m</u>icolon
> ☐ <u>C</u>omma
> ☐ <u>S</u>pace
> ☑ <u>O</u>ther: `:`

You can see that there is a colon before each percentage value in column A. By setting this as a delimiter you can extract the percentages.

7. Click: *Next >*.

8. Click: *Finish*.

The percentages are moved to their own column.

	A	B
1	US Labor Force - by occupation:	
2		
3	farming, forestry, and fishing	0.70%
4	manufacturing, extraction, transportation, and crafts	20.30%
5	managerial, professional, and technical	37.30%
6	sales and office	24.20%
7	other services	17.60%
8		
9	note: figures exclude the unemployed (2009)	

3 Create a pie chart to display the data visually.

1. Select cells A3:B7.

2. Click:

Insert→Charts→Recommended Charts→Pie Chart

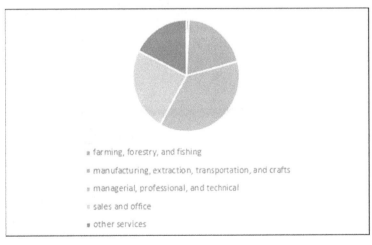

3. Click the *OK* button.

Charting is covered in depth in the *Essential Skills* book in this series.

4 Save your work as *US Labor Force-2*.

Lesson 2-3: Automatically subtotal a range

1   Open *Inventory-10* from your sample files folder.

2   Remove conditional formatting from the table.

Conditional formatting is covered in depth in the *Essential Skills* book in this series.

1. Click anywhere inside the table.

2. Click: Home→Styles→Conditional Formatting→Clear Rules→ Clear Rules from This Table.

3   Sort the table by *Category* in ascending order (A-Z).

You learned how to do this in: *Lesson 1-16: Sort a range or table by rows.*

	A	B	C
11	42	Beverages	Pavlova, Ltd.
12	49	Beverages	Plutzer Lebensmittelgroßmärkte AG
13	57	Condiments	Forêts d'érables
14	18	Condiments	Grandma Kelly's Homestead

4   Convert the table into a range.

You learned how to do this in: *Lesson 1-14: Format a table using table styles and convert a table into a range.*

You must convert the table into a range because you cannot add automatic subtotals to tables.

5   Delete the total row (row 71).

6   Add subtotals to the *In Stock* and *Value* columns for each category.

1. Click anywhere inside the range.

2. Click: Data→Outline→Subtotal.

The *Subtotal* dialog appears:

Inventory-10

note

Other subtotal options

Note the three subtotal options:

- ☑ Replace current subtotals
- ☐ Page break between groups
- ☑ Summary below data

You can use the first option to add different types of subtotal to different columns.

For example, if you wanted to view both the average and the sum at the same time you could add a second subtotal by unchecking this box.

The new subtotal is then shown above the old one:

Beverages Average
Beverages Total

note

Copying subtotals to another location

A very common request in my courses is:

"How can I copy the subtotals only (ie the level two outline) to another worksheet. When I copy the subtotals and paste I get the detail rows as well – but I just want the subtotals".

The secret here is to only select the visible cells on the worksheet before copying.

Here's how it is done:

1. Display level two subtotals by clicking the 2 button.

2. Click: Home→Editing→ Find & Select→Go To Special→ Visible cells only, and then click OK.

OR

Select the range and then press the <Alt>+<;> keys.

4. Copy.

5. Paste to the destination cells.

3. Tell Excel which column of repeating data you wish to add subtotals to by choosing *Category* in the *At each change in:* drop down.

At each change in:
No
No
Category
Supplier

4. Make sure that the *Sum* function is selected.

Use function:
Sum

5. Click the check boxes to add subtotals to the *In Stock* and *Value* columns:

Add subtotal to:
☐ Category
☐ Supplier
☐ Product Name
☐ Unit Price
☑ In Stock
☑ Value

6. Click the *OK* button.

The worksheet is now subtotaled and Excel has added an outline bar to the left hand side:

	A	B	C	D	E	F	G
55	64	Grains/Cereals	PB Knäckebröd AB	Tunnbröd	9.00	61	549.00
56	68	Grains/Cereals	Plutzer Lebensmitte	Wimmers gute Semme	33.25	22	731.50
57		Grains/Cereals Total				282	5,230.50
58	43	Meat/Poultry	Ma Maison	Pâté chinois	24.00	115	2,760.00
59	63	Meat/Poultry	Ma Maison	Tourtière	7.45	21	156.45
60		Meat/Poultry Total				136	2,916.45

7 Collapse and expand the entire outline.

Notice the small 1 2 3 buttons in the top left corner of the worksheet.

- When you click button 1 only the grand total is shown.

- When you click button 2 each category subtotal is shown.

- When you click button 3 all items are shown.

8 Collapse and expand categories within the outline.

Note the ⊞ and ⊟ buttons in the left-hand sidebar.

Experiment by clicking them and notice how you can selectively expand and collapse any group within the outline.

9 Remove the subtotals from the range.

1. Click anywhere within the range.

2. Click: Data→Outline→Subtotal→Remove All.

10 Save your work as *Inventory-11*.

Lesson 2-4: Create nested subtotals

Sometimes you'll find a need for more than one level of subtotal.

Consider this data:

	Category	Supplier	Product Name
4	Beverages	Bigfoot Breweries	Sasquatch Ale
5	Beverages	Bigfoot Breweries	Laughing Lumberjack Lager
6	Beverages	Bigfoot Breweries	Steeleye Stout
7	Beverages	Exotic Liquids	Chai
8	Beverages	Exotic Liquids	Chang

In the example above both *Bigfoot Breweries* and *Exotic Liquids* supply more than one product in the *Beverages* category.

As well as wishing to know subtotals for each *category* you may also wish to know subtotals for each *supplier* within each *category*. In other words:

What is the value of Bigfoot Breweries inventory in each category?

By nesting subtotals, you can quickly cater for this requirement.

1   Open *Inventory-11* from your sample files folder (if it isn't already open).

2   Apply a two-level A-Z sort, first by *Category* and then by *Supplier*.

You learned how to do this in: *Lesson 1-16: Sort a range or table by rows.*

Column		Sort On		Order	
Sort by	Category	Cell Values		A to Z	
Then by	Supplier	Cell Values		A to Z	

3   At each change in *Category* use the *Sum* function to add subtotals to the *In Stock* and *Value* columns.

You learned how to do this in:
Lesson 2-3: Automatically subtotal a range.

At each change in:
Category

Use function:
Sum

Add subtotal to:
- [ ] Category
- [ ] Supplier
- [ ] Product Name
- [ ] Unit Price
- [x] In Stock
- [x] Value

	60		Meat/Poultry Total	
	61	34 Produce	G'day, Mate	Manjimup Dried Apples
	62	65 Produce	Grandma Kelly's Homestead	Uncle Bob's Organic Dried Pears
	63	62 Produce	Mayumi's	Tofu
	64	31 Produce	Tokyo Traders	Longlife Tofu

Inventory-11

4   Add a nested subtotal to show totals by *Supplier* within each category.

1. Click anywhere within the range.

2. Click: Data➔Outline➔Subtotal.

3. Uncheck the *Replace current subtotals* check box.

☐ Replace current subtotals

This is the secret when creating nested subtotals. If you didn't uncheck this box, the new subtotal would simply replace the old one. By keeping the current subtotal you'll add a nested subtotal.

4. At each change in *Supplier* add a *Sum* function to subtotal the *In Stock* and *Value* columns:

Subtotal   ?   ✕

At each change in:

Supplier ⌄

Use function:

Sum ⌄

Add subtotal to:
☐ Category
☐ Supplier
☐ Product Name
☐ Unit Price
☑ In Stock
☑ Value

☐ Replace current subtotals
☐ Page break between groups
☑ Summary below data

Remove All   OK   Cancel

5. Click the *OK* button.

Nested subtotals are now shown by category/by supplier:

1 2 3 4		B	C	D
	52	Confections	Specialty Biscuits, Ltd.	Sir Rodney's Marmalade
	53	Confections	Specialty Biscuits, Ltd.	Scottish Longbreads
	54	Confections	Specialty Biscuits, Ltd.	Sir Rodney's Scones
	55	Confections	Specialty Biscuits, Ltd.	Teatime Chocolate Biscuits
−	56		**Specialty Biscuits, Ltd. Total**	
	57	Confections	Zaanse Snoepfabriek	Chocolade
	58	Confections	Zaanse Snoepfabriek	Zaanse koeken
−	59		**Zaanse Snoepfabriek Total**	

Notice that there's an extra level button too:

The fourth level is the nested subtotal, allowing you to collapse and expand the *Supplier* subtotals.

5   Save your work as *Inventory-12*.

Lesson 2-5: Consolidate data from multiple data ranges

Totaling data from multiple worksheets onto a summary sheet is a very common business requirement. Excel can automatically consolidate data if each worksheet has an identical structure.

If you use this technique, it is a good idea to use templates for each of the worksheets that will be consolidated in order to ensure that they are identical. (Templates are covered in depth in the *Essential Skills* book in this series).

1 Open *Sales and Profit by Employee-1* from your sample files folder.

This worksheet shows each employee's sales, cost and profit data for the first three months in the quarter.

The *January, February, March* and *Summary* worksheets have an identical structure. This makes the consolidation feature very easy to use.

	A	B	C	D	E	F
1	Sales and Profit By Employee					
2						
3	Team	First Name	Last Name	Sales	Cost	Profit
4	Blue	Johnny	Caine	16,756	9,431	7,325
5	Blue	George	Marley	19,437	7,412	12,025
6	Blue	Bill	Spears	14,742	7,960	6,782

2 Consolidate data for the first three months into the summary sheet.

1. Click into the destination cell for the consolidated data. This is cell D4 on the *Summary* sheet.

2. Click: Data→Data Tools→Consolidate.

   The *Consolidate* dialog appears.

3. Make sure that the *Function* drop-down displays the *Sum* function because you want to add together the values in the *January, February* and *March* worksheets:

   Function:
   Sum

4. Click in the *Reference* box.

5. Click the *January* worksheet tab and select cells D4:F17:

   Reference:
   January!$D$4:$F$17

Sales and Profit by Employee-1

6. Click the *Add* button to add the reference to the list of references to be consolidated:

Reference:	
January!$D$4:$F$17|	⬆
All references:	
January!$D$4:$F$17	

7. Click the *February* worksheet tab. This time the same range (on the *February* worksheet) is automatically displayed in the dialog.

8. Click the *Add* button to add the *February* range to the list of references to be consolidated.

9. Repeat the same operation for the *March* range.

    The dialog should now look like this:

Reference:	
March!$D$4:$F$17|	⬆
All references:	
February!$D$4:$F$17	
January!$D$4:$F$17	
March!$D$4:$F$17	

10. Click the *OK* button to display the consolidated totals on the summary sheet:

	A	B	C	D	E	F
1	Sales and Profit By Employee					
2						
3	Team	First Name	Last Name	Sales	Cost	Profit
4	Blue	Johnny	Caine	52,713	22,243	30,470
5	Blue	George	Marley	46,320	20,824	25,496
6	Blue	Bill	Spears	40,847	20,085	20,762

3   **Create a data consolidation that is linked to the source data.**

In the previous operation the consolidated values were not linked to the source worksheets. If a value on a source worksheet changes, the summary worksheet will not update.

1. Delete the range D4:F17 on the *Summary* worksheet.

2. Click in cell D4 on the *Summary* worksheet.

3. Click: Data→Data Tools→Consolidate.

4. Check the *Create links to source data* check box:

    ☑ Create links to source data

5. Click the *OK* button.

This time the data consolidation links to the source data and also displays a grouped outline similar to an automatic subtotal, enabling you to view each of the source data values for the consolidation.

4   **Save your work as *Sales and Profit by Employee-2*.**

1 2		A	B	C
	1	Sales and Profit B		
	2			
	3	Team	First Name	Last Name
+	7	Blue	Johnny	Caine
+	11	Blue	George	Marley
+	15	Blue	Bill	Spears
+	19	Blue	Jamie	Oliver
+	23	Blue	Jack	Nicholson

Lesson 2-6: Use data consolidation to generate quick subtotals from tables

In: *Lesson 2-3: Automatically subtotal a range* you used Excel's fantastic *Automatic Subtotal* feature to quickly add subtotals to a range. Unfortunately, automatic subtotals do not work with tables.

Another problem with automatic subtotals is that you have little control over the formatting of the subtotal data.

Data consolidation can overcome both of these problems by allowing full control of formatting, along with the ability to work with both ranges and tables.

1   Open *Inventory-12* from your sample files folder.

2   Remove subtotals from the range.

     1.   Click anywhere inside the range.

     2.   Click: Data→Outline→Subtotal→Remove All.

3   Convert the range into a table.

     You learned how to do this in: *Lesson 1-13: Convert a range into a table and add a total row.*

4   Add quick subtotals by category using data consolidation.

     1.   Click in cell I1.

     2.   Click: Data→Data Tools→Consolidate.

        The *Consolidate* dialog is displayed:

     3.   Make sure that *Sum* is shown in the *Function* box. This should be the case as *Sum* is the default.

     4.   Click in the *Reference* box and select the range B1:G70.

        A quick way to do this is to click in cell B1, press **<Ctrl>+<Shift>+<DownArrow>**, and then press **<Ctrl>+<Shift>+<RightArrow>**.

Inventory-12

note

Consolidated subtotals cannot be linked to source data on the same worksheet

In: *Lesson 2-5: Consolidate data from multiple data ranges,* you learned how to create consolidated totals that are linked to source data.

You did this by checking the *Create links to source data* checkbox.

☑ Create links to source data

This is really useful as linked consolidated totals will update whenever an existing row in the source data is changed or deleted.

The consolidated totals will not, however, update when new rows are added to the source data.

Unfortunately, the option to link only works when the consolidated data is on a different worksheet to the source data.

If you try to link consolidated totals on the same worksheet as the source data, you will see this dialog:

> Microsoft Excel
>
> ⚠ Cannot create links to consolidation sheet.
>
> OK

If you need to display linked consolidated totals on the same worksheet there's a simple work-around.

1. Create linked consolidated totals on a different worksheet.

2. Create cross-worksheet formulas that reference the values on the worksheet containing the linked consolidated totals.

5. Check the two check boxes: *Use labels in Top row, Left column.*

> Use labels in
> ☑ Top row
> ☑ Left column

6. Click the *OK* button.

Subtotals appear beginning in cell I1 for every column.

			I	J	K	L	M	N
				Supplier	Product N	Unit Price	In Stock	Value
			Beverages			451.25	539	#######
			Condiments			255.40	507	#######
			Confections			327.08	386	#######
			Dairy Products			287.30	393	#######

5 Delete columns J:L.

Subtotals are impossible on the text columns: *Supplier* and *Product Name.* They are also of no interest for the *Unit Price* column.

6 Re-size columns I, J and K.

Useful subtotals are now displayed:

	I	J	K
1		In Stock	Value
2	Beverages	539	12,390.25
3	Condiments	507	12,023.55
4	Confections	386	10,392.20
5	Dairy Products	393	11,271.20
6	Grains/Cereals	282	5,230.50
7	Meat/Poultry	136	2,916.45
8	Produce	74	2,363.75
9	Seafood	701	13,010.35

7 Add averages alongside the totals using the same technique.

1. Click in cell L1.

2. Do exactly the same thing you did for the *Sum* but choose the *Average* function in the consolidate dialog:

> Function:
> Average ▼

3. Click the *OK* button.

4. Delete columns L:O.

5. Change the label in L1 to: **Average In Stock**

6. Change the label in M1 to: **Average Value**

7. Change the number of decimal places shown for the values in column L to zero.

8. Re-size columns L and M.

	I	J	K	L	M
1		In Stock	Value	Average In Stock	Average Value
2	Beverages	539	12,390.25	49	1,126.39
3	Condiments	507	12,023.55	46	1,093.05

8 Save your work as *Inventory-13.*

	I	J
2	The Rules	
3		
4	Age	
5	Minimum age	17
6	Maximum age	100
7		
8	Date	
9	today or later	
10		
11	Names	
12	Min length	2
13	Max length	20
14		
15	Price	
16	Minimum	10.00
17	Maximum	100.00
18		
19	Discounts	
20	Minimum price for discount	20.00
21		

tip

Clearing validation from selected cells

In this lesson you may have noticed that the validation applied to "all of column E" has also been applied to cells E1:E6.

This would prevent you from editing the column header in cell E6.

To quickly clear validation rules from these cells:

1. Right-click on any cell on the worksheet that has no data validation rules.

2. Click: *Copy* from the shortcut menu.

3. Select cells E1:E6.

4. Right-click inside the selected range and select: *Paste Special…* from the shortcut menu.

5. Click the *Validation* option button.

6. Click the *OK* button.

Health Club Bookings-1

Lesson 2-7: Validate numerical data

In the next lessons you'll explore the power of Excel's data validation features. You can prevent a huge number of data entry errors by catching them when they are entered and then politely informing your users that they have made a mistake.

1   Open *Health Club Bookings-1* from your sample files folder.

This worksheet manages all of the treatments sold in a health club.

There are several rules that must not be broken when entering data (see sidebar). These types of rules are often referred to as *business rules* when designing data systems.

At the moment the worksheet doesn't police these rules itself but relies upon all personnel understanding and applying them.

	A	B	C	D	E	F	G
1	Health Club Bookings						
2							
3	Period		From:				
4			To:				
5							
6	Date	Name		Age	Group	Price	Discount	Total
7	05-Apr-16	Depp, Julia		22	Aerobics	22.00	12%	19.36
8	01-Apr-16	Nicholson, Johnny		23	Weight Training	9.00		9.00
9	12-Apr-16	Dickens, Bob		18	Aromatherapy	23.00	10%	20.70
10	15-Apr-16	Oliver, Jamie		38	Weight Training	23.00	15%	19.55

2   Apply the Age rule (see sidebar) to column C.

1. Select all of column C by clicking the column header.

You need to select the entire column when you want to add data validation to every cell in the column.

2. Click: Data→Data Tools→Data Validation.

The data validation dialog appears.

3. Click the *Settings* tab.

At the moment Excel is allowing *Any value*. This is the default, meaning that the user is free to type anything at all into any cell in column C.

4. Choose *Whole number* from the *Allow* drop-down list.

Whole number will not allow the user to enter decimal values such as 22.8. As ages cannot have decimal places this is a good validation rule for a column containing age data.

Criteria now appear that are relevant to whole numbers.

5. Click in the *Data* box and select *between*:

Data:
between

6. Click in the *Minimum* box and then click on cell J5.

7. Make J5 into an absolute reference.

8. Click in the *Maximum* box and then click on cell J6.

9. Make J6 into an absolute reference.

The dialog should now look like this:

Allow:
Whole number ☑ Ignore blank
Data:
between
Minimum:
=$J$5
Maximum:
=$J$6

10. Click the *OK* button.

3 **Test the data validation.**

Data validation will now ensure that any new values entered into column C are valid. It will not change any existing invalid values in the column. (See sidebar for a quick way to find existing invalid values).

Enter an invalid value (such as an age of 101 or 15) into any cell in column C.

A rather unfriendly error message appears advising that an error has occurred:

Microsoft Excel ✕

This value doesn't match the data validation restrictions defined for this cell.

Retry   Cancel   Help

In the next lesson you'll discover how to make this message a little friendlier.

4 **Add another data validation.**

Use the same technique to apply the business rule: *Prices must be between 10.00 and 100.00* (stated in cells I16:J17) to column E.

Allow:
Decimal ☑ Ignore blank
Data:
between
Minimum:
=$J$16
Maximum:
=$J$17

Notice that cell E8 now violates the validation criteria. When you apply a new validation rule to a cell, any values that already exist will remain without any error warnings. It will, however, be impossible to change the value to another that violates the validation criteria.

5 **Save your work as** *Health Club Bookings-2*.

© 2021 The Smart Method® Ltd

---

note

How to quickly find invalid values

The *Data Validation* button on the ribbon is a split button. If you click the small arrow on the:

Data→Data Tools→
Data Validation

… button you'll see some more options:

Data Validation ▾
Consolidate Relati

☑ Data Validation…
◎ Circle Invalid Data
☒ Clear Validation Circles

Click: *Circle Invalid Data* to show red circles around all invalid values on this worksheet:

	D	E	
6	Group	Price	D
7	Aerobics	22.00	
8	Weight Training	9.00	

When you have reviewed the invalid data you can use the *Clear Validation Circles* command to remove the circles.

Lesson 2-8: Create user-friendly messages for validation errors

A very useful design goal when developing computer software is to create a user interface that requires no user training. The interface should be so simple, and the features so obvious, that users can train themselves by experimentation and discovery.

For this reason, a user needs to be provided with an informative error message whenever they do something that is not allowed.

1 Open *Health Club Bookings-2* from your sample files folder (if it isn't already open).

2 Add an error message to column C.

1. Select all of column C.

2. Click: Data→Data Tools→Data Validation.

3. Click the *Error Alert* tab.

4. Type: **Invalid Age** into the *Title* box.

5. Click in the *Error message* box and type:

   Age must be at least 17 and no more than 100.

   Your dialog should now look like this:

6. Click the *OK* button.

3 Test the error message.

When you enter an invalid age into any cell in column C, you will see the error message:

Health Club Bookings-2

4   Change the validation from mandatory to advisory.

This validation is called *mandatory* because there is absolutely no possibility of the user entering an invalid value (other than by copying and pasting a value into the cell).

Sometimes this restriction is too strict. You may want to tell the user that an age of over 100 is unusual, but if the user is really sure that the client is over 100 they can still continue.

1.   Select all of column C.

2.   Click: Data→Data Tools→Data Validation.

3.   Change the error message to read: **Age is usually between 17 and 100. Are you sure this is correct?**

4.   Change the style of the error message from *Stop* to *Warning*.

The dialog should now look like this:

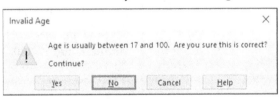

5.   Click the *OK* button.

5   Test the error message.

When you enter an invalid age into any cell in column C you will now see a different style of error message:

You then have the opportunity to click the *Yes* button and override the validation.

6   Add an informative error message to column E.

Use the same technique to add an error message to column E.

7   Save your work as *Health Club Bookings-3*.

© 2021 The Smart Method® Ltd   **91**

---

note

The Stop, Warning and Info error alert styles

Windows users are conditioned to understand the meaning of three different icons.

Stop

    Something terrible has happened!

Warning

    Something quite bad has happened.

Information

We just thought you'd like to know.

Each of these styles produces a slightly different error message dialog.

The *Warning* dialog shows four buttons (see text) and the *Information* dialog shows just three buttons: OK, Cancel and Help.

The only important difference between them is that the *Stop* style is mandatory while the *Information* and *Warning* styles are advisory.

Lesson 2-9: Create data validation input messages

In the last lesson: *Lesson 2-8: Create user-friendly messages for validation errors,* you discovered how to provide an informative error message whenever the user breaks a business rule.

Users can become frustrated if they can only discover business rules by first making mistakes and then being informed of the error. To make applications more efficient and user-friendly, it is sometimes better to inform the user of the business rules before they attempt to enter a value.

In this lesson you'll use data entry input messages to provide a better user experience.

1   Open *Health Club Bookings-3* from your sample files folder (if it isn't already open).

2   Add a data validation input message to column C.

In *Lesson 2-7: Validate numerical data,* you added a validation to column C to ensure that ages are entered as whole numbers between 17 and 100.

You will now use the *Input Message* feature to inform the user of this business rule before an attempt is made to enter an age.

1. Select all of column C by clicking the column header.

You must select the entire column when you want to add an input message to every cell in the column.

2. Click: Data→Data Tools→Data Validation.

The data validation dialog appears.

3. Click the *Input Message* tab.

4. In the *Title* box, type: **Age**

5. In the *Input message* box, type: **Ages must be whole numbers in the range 17-100.**

Data Validation   ?   ×

Settings   Input Message   Error Alert

☑ Show input message when cell is selected

When cell is selected, show this input message:

Title:

Age

Input message:

Ages must be whole numbers in the range 17-100.

Clear All   OK   Cancel

Health Club Bookings-3

6.   Click the *OK* button.

3   Test the data validation input message.

Click any cell in column C. The input message is displayed:

	B	C	D
10	Oliver, Jamie	38	Weight Training
11			
12			
13			Age — Ages must be whole numbers in the range 17-100.
14			
15			
16			

4   Use the same technique to add a data validation input message to column E.

Data Validation   ?   ×

Settings   Input Message   Error Alert

☑ Show input message when cell is selected

When cell is selected, show this input message:

Title:

Price

Input message:

Price must be a minimum of 10.00 and a maximum of 100.00.

Clear All   OK   Cancel

D	E	F	G
Weight Training	23.00	15%	19.55

Price — Price must be a minimum of 10.00 and a maximum of 100.00.

5   Save your work as *Health Club Bookings-4*.

Lesson 2-10: Add a formula-driven date validation and a text length validation

Validation parameters do not have to be simple values. They can also be set to the value returned by a formula.

In this lesson you'll use Excel's TODAY function to add a validation that will not allow a date to be entered that is in the past.

1 Open *Health Club Bookings-4* from your sample files folder (if it isn't already open).

2 Add a validation to column A that will not allow dates that are in the past to be entered.

   1. Select all of column A.

   2. Click: Data→Data Tools→Data Validation.

   3. Click the *Settings* tab.

   4. Set the *Allow:* box to *Date.*

   5. Set the *Data:* box to *greater than or equal to.*

   6. Add a TODAY function to the *Start Date* text box by typing:

      =TODAY()

      The TODAY function returns today's date. The TODAY function will be covered in depth later in: *Lesson 3-8: Understand common date functions.*

      Your dialog should now look like this:

3 Add an appropriate error alert message.

   1. Click the *Error Alert* tab.

   2. Type: **Date Error** into the *Title* box.

   3. Type: **Dates cannot be in the past** into the *Error message* box.

   4. Click the *OK* button.

Health Club Bookings-4

4   Test the validation.

Attempt to enter a date that is in the past.

An error message is displayed:

Date Error	×
⊗ Dates cannot be in the past.	
Retry Cancel Help	

5   Apply a text length validation to column B to enforce the rule: *Minimum name length = 2 characters, Maximum name length = 20 characters*

The validation dialog will look like this:

Data Validation	?	×
Settings Input Message Error Alert		
Validation criteria		
Allow:		
Text length ∨ ☑ Ignore blank		
Data:		
between ∨		
Minimum:		
=$J$12 ↑		
Maximum:		
=$J$13 ↑		
☐ Apply these changes to all other cells with the same settings		
Clear All OK Cancel		

Note that it is important to use the absolute references $J$12 and $J$13 rather than the relative references J12 and J13. Absolute, Relative and Mixed cell references are covered in depth in the *Essential Skills* book in this series.

6   Add an appropriate *Error Alert* for this validation.

7   Test the validation.

Name	×
⊗ Names must have a length of between two and twenty characters.	
Retry Cancel Help	

8   Save your work as *Health Club Bookings-5*.

important

Dynamic ranges have greatly expanded the power of list validations

The technique used in this lesson (and those described on the facing-page sidebar) will also work with legacy Excel versions (Excel 2019 and earlier).

The Excel 365 *July 2020 Semi-Annual version 2002* release included a major new feature called *Dynamic Arrays*. This feature does not work in Excel 2019 and earlier.

If you only need to share your workbooks with other Excel 365 users, there are new techniques that leverage upon dynamic arrays to more simply implement drop down lists.

It is also possible to implement drop-down searchable combo boxes by leveraging upon dynamic array features.

You'll learn all there is to know about dynamic arrays later, in: *Session Four: Working with Dynamic Arrays.*

Lesson 2-11: Add a table-based dynamic list validation

List validations prevent the user from entering any value into a cell that is not contained within a pre-defined list.

1 Open *Health Club Bookings-5* from your sample files folder (if it isn't already open).

2 Create a table (with a header) in cells I24:I30 containing a list of the valid groups: *Yoga, Aerobics, Weight Training, Aromatherapy, Massage* and *Aquarobics.*

   1. Type **Group** into cell I24.

   2. Type the valid group names (shown below) into cells I25:I30.

   3. Convert cells I24:I30 into a table.

      You learned how to do this in: *Lesson 1-13: Convert a range into a table and add a total row.*

	I
24	Group
25	Yoga
26	Aerobics
27	Weight Training
28	Aromatherapy
29	Massage
30	Aquarobics

   4. Name your new table: **ValidGroups**

      You learned how to do this in: *Lesson 1-19: Name a table and create an automatic structured table reference.*

3 Add a validation to column D that will only allow groups defined in the *ValidGroups* table (cells I24:I30) to be entered.

   1. Select all of column D.

   2. Click: Data→Data Tools→Data Validation.

   3. Click the *Settings* tab.

   4. In the *Allow* drop down click *List*.

   5. Click in the *Source* box and then select cells I25:I30 with the mouse.

Allow:
| List | ☑ Ignore blank |

Data:
| between | ☑ In-cell dropdown |

Source:
=$I$25:$I$30

At this point you may wonder why you don't simply type: **=ValidGroups** into the *Source* box. While this makes perfect sense, Excel won't allow it. (See the important sidebar for more on this).

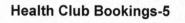
Health Club Bookings-5

important

Some other ways to define validation list source data

1. Type values directly into the source box.

When you do this you need to type a comma in between each value:

Source:

Yoga, Aerobics, Weight Training

2. Define values as a range.

Simply select a regular range to define the values:

Source:

=$I$25:$I$30

3. Define values as a table.

Convert the source values from a range to a table before setting the source data.

Source:

=$I$25:$I$30

This seems to be the same as method 2. It differs because Excel treats source cells that are in a table differently from source cells that are in a range (but only when the table is on the same worksheet as the cells to be validated).

When the source cells originate in a table on the same worksheet, Excel will automatically grow and shrink the range as items are added and removed from the table.

4. Define values as a named range.

You'll learn all about named ranges in: *Session Five: Using Names and the Formula Auditing Tools.*

5. Define values as a named range that references a table.

This is the best method of all as the validation table can then reside on any worksheet. You'll use this technique, in: *Lesson 5-7: Create table-based dynamic range names.*

6. Add an appropriate *Error Alert*.

You learned how to do this in: *Lesson 2-8: Create user-friendly messages for validation errors.*

Title:

Invalid Group

Error message:

The group entered is not a valid group. Click the drop-down arrow to view a list of valid choices.

7. Click the *OK* button.

4 Test the validation.

1. Click anywhere in column D.

Notice that a drop down arrow appears on the right-hand side of the cell.

Weight Training

2. Click the drop-down arrow.

A list of all valid groups is displayed:

Weight Training

Yoga
Aerobics
Weight Training
Aromatherapy
Massage
Aquarobics

3. Click any of the valid groups.

The selected value is displayed in the cell.

5 Add *Circuit Training* as a valid group.

1. Click in cell I31.

2. Type: **Circuit Training**.

3. Press the **<Enter>** key.

The new item is added to the table.

6 Test the validation again.

Click on the drop-down arrow to the right of any cell in column D.

Note that *Circuit Training* is now a valid item in the list.

Aromatherapy
Massage
Aquarobics
Circuit Training

This only happened because you converted the source cells I24:I30 into a table. If you hadn't done this, *Circuit Training* would not have been valid (see the important sidebar for more on this).

7 Save your work as *Health Club Bookings-6*.

Lesson 2-12: Use a formula-driven custom validation to enforce complex business rules

The simple dialog-driven validations have served all of your requirements up to now.

Sometimes you will have to implement a validation that is too complex for any of the dialog-driven validations to handle. In this case you will have to write a formula-driven custom validation.

In the sample file you have been working with, there is a requirement (listed in the business rules) that states:

Discounts	
Minimum price for discount	20.00

This means that the value in column F will depend upon the value in column E.

	E	F	G
6	Price	Discount	Total
7	22.00	12%	19.36
8	9.00		9.00
9	23.00	10%	20.70
10	23.00	15%	19.55

In cell F8 above it is prohibited to enter a discount because the price is less than 20.00. Right now there's nothing to stop a user doing this. You need to enforce this business rule with a formula-driven custom validation.

1 Open *Health Club Bookings-6* from your sample files folder (if it isn't already open).

2 Add a validation to column F that will enforce the business rule: *Minimum price for discount = 20.00*.

   1. Select all of column F.

   2. Click: Data→Data Tools→Data Validation→Data Validation…

   3. Click the *Settings* tab.

   4. Select *Custom* from the *Allow* drop-down list.

Allow:
Custom

     Custom validations require a formula. The validation will only allow a value to be entered if the formula returns a value of TRUE.

   5. Click in the *Formula* text box and type the following text:

     =E1>=$J$20

Health Club Bookings-6

important

Excel's validation mechanism is easily defeated

Excel's validation rules are not very robust.

A user is able to copy and paste any value into any cell to bypass validation rules.

This formula will return FALSE if the value in cell E1 is less than the value in cell J20, and TRUE if the value in cell E1 is greater than or equal to the value in cell J20.

Allow:
| Custom | ☑ Ignore blank |

Data:
between

Formula:
=E1>=$J$20

Note that E1 is a relative cell reference (ie it does not have the dollar prefixes $E$1). This is because you want it to adjust to the current row.

For example, when the user enters a percentage into cell F11 you want to check the value in cell E11 against the value in J20. E1 adjusts to E11 as it is relative but $J$20 is always fixed as it is an absolute reference.

6. Add an appropriate *Error Alert*:

Title:
Invalid Discount

Error message:
You cannot offer a discount on sales values of less than 20.00.

7. Click the *OK* button.

3 Test the validation.

1. Enter a discount into cell F8. Because the value in cell E8 is only 9.00 an error alert is displayed:

Invalid Discount   ✕

❌ You cannot offer a discount on sales values of less than 20.00.

Retry   Cancel   Help

2. Click the *Cancel* button.

3. Change the value in cell E8 to: **21.00**

4. Enter a discount of 10% in cell F8.

This time the value is accepted.

	D	E	F	G
6	Group	Price	Discount	Total
7	Aerobics	22.00	12%	19.36
8	Weight Training	21.00	10%	18.90
9	Aromatherapy	23.00	10%	20.70

4 Save your work as *Health Club Bookings-7*.

Lesson 2-13: Remove duplicate values from a table

Duplicate entries are a common problem in data systems of all types.

When tables contain duplicate entries they are said to be corrupt.

Unfortunately, just about every corporate database I've ever worked with has contained corrupt data. You'll almost certainly have to clean up data sets containing duplicate values at some point in your Excel career.

This lesson will show you how to quickly weed out duplicate entries from tables.

Note that the technique taught in this lesson will only work with tables. If you have a range that needs to have duplicate values removed, you will need to first convert it into a table using the skills learned in: *Lesson 1-13: Convert a range into a table and add a total row.*

1   Open *Employees-1* from your sample files folder.

The table contains a list of employees along with their *EmployeeID* (a unique identification number). Every employee should only be listed once but you suspect that the list contains duplicate entries.

	A	B	C
1	EmployeeID	First Name	Last Name
2	362281	Brad	Cruise
3	324794	Ian	Dean
4	998783	Paris	Smith

2   Sort by *EmployeeID* from smallest to largest.

If the list was very short you could manually identify duplicate *EmployeeID* rows by simply sorting column A. This skill was covered in: *Lesson 1-16: Sort a range or table by rows.*

When the numeric EmployeeID values are sorted, part of the problem is instantly revealed:

	A	B	C
1	EmployeeID	First Name	Last Name
2	117362	Johnny	Caine
3	117362	Johnny	Caine
4	118657	George	Marley
5	118657	George	Marley
6	128947	Bill	Spears

Johnny Caine and George Marley clearly have duplicate entries in the table.

3   Automatically remove employees with duplicate *EmployeeID* values.

1.   Click any cell inside the table.

Employees-1

note

A formula-driven approach to identifying duplicate values

Imagine that the problem posed in this lesson occurred in a real-life business scenario involving a large amount of data.

The primitive "sort and look" or "remove duplicates without review" features discussed in this lesson wouldn't provide a reasonable solution.

Here's one way that you could solve the problem.

1. Close the workbook without saving.

2. Re-open the *Employees-1* sample file (this will still contain duplicate Employee ID numbers).

2. Sort *EmployeeID* (column A) from *Smallest to Largest*.

3. Insert a new column to the left of column B.

4. Type: **Duplicate** into cell B1 (the new column's column header).

5. Enter this formula into cell B2:

= A2=A1

The function only returns TRUE if the value in column A is the same as the value above (ie a duplicate entry).

6. Filter column B so that only TRUE values are shown.

The duplicate entries are now revealed:

	A	B	C	D
1	Emplo	Duplic	First	Last
3	117362	TRUE	Johnny	Caine
5	118657	TRUE	George	Marley
12	186795	TRUE	Gordon	Depp

2. Click: Table Design→Tools→Remove Duplicates.

The *Remove Duplicates* dialog is displayed:

Notice that, by default, Excel has selected every field in the table.

3. Click the *OK* button twice to close both dialogs.

All of the duplicate entries are deleted.

	A	B	C
1	EmployeeID	First Name	Last Name
2	117362	Johnny	Caine
3	118657	George	Marley
4	128947	Bill	Spears
5	170292	Jamie	Oliver
6	171710	Jack	Nicholson

This is a very fast method but not very sophisticated as there's no opportunity to review the values that have been deleted.

In: *Lesson 2-14: Use a custom validation to add a unique constraint to a column*, you'll discover how to catch duplicate entries at the point of entry.

4   Save your work as *Employees-2*.

Lesson 2-14: Use a custom validation to add a unique constraint to a column

You'll often find yourself working with a table or range that contains a column that must have unique values.

For example, consider this list of employees:

	A	B	C
1	EmployeeID	First Name	Last Name
2	117362	Johnny	Caine
3	118657	George	Marley
4	128947	Bill	Spears

The *EmployeeID* column should never contain the same number listed twice. If it does, an error has occurred because no two employees can have the same *EmployeeID*.

In cases such as this, it would be very useful to refuse to let the user add duplicate values to column A. This type of restriction is called a *unique constraint* and is a fundamental feature of database products such as Microsoft Access, SQL Server and Oracle.

Excel doesn't provide an easy way to apply unique constraints directly (hopefully it will in a later version). Fortunately, there's an easy way to leverage upon the custom validation feature to add this functionality to Excel 365 tables.

1 **Open *Employees-2* from your sample files folder (if it isn't already open).**

In this table, each employee should have a unique *EmployeeID*. At the moment the table does not enforce this rule.

2 **Add a duplicate EmployeeID.**

1. Press the **<Ctrl>+<End>** keys to move to the end of the table (cell C120).

2. Press the **<Tab>** key.

If you press the **<Tab>** key in the last cell of a table, a new row is added to the table.

	A	B	C
119	997371	Michal	Marley
120	998783	Paris	Smith
121			

3. Add a duplicate entry for *Paris Smith*.

	A	B	C
119	997371	Michal	Marley
120	998783	Paris	Smith
121	998783	Paris	Smith

Notice that Excel allows the duplicate entry. In a moment you'll add a unique constraint to make this impossible.

Employees-2

3 Delete the duplicate EmployeeID (row 121).

4 Add a unique constraint to column A.

1. Select all of the table cells in column A except the header row.

   A quick way to do this is to click in cell A2 and then press:

   <Ctrl>+<Shift>+<DownArrow>

2. Click: Data→Data Tools→Data Validation.

3. Click the *Settings* tab.

4. In the *Allow* drop-down, select *Custom*.

5. Type the following function into the *Formula* box:

   =COUNTIF(A:A,A2)=1

Formula:
= COUNTIF(A:A,A2) = 1

   See sidebar for a discussion of the COUNTIF function.

6. Add an appropriate error alert.

Title:
Duplicate EmployeeID

   Error message:

   The EmployeeID you have entered already exists in column A.

7. Click the *OK* button.

5 Test the unique constraint.

1. Attempt to change the *EmployeeID* in row 3 so that it is the same as any existing *EmployeeID*.

   Note that you must type the values in. If you copy and paste, the entry is not validated.

	A	B	C	D	E	F	G
1	EmployeeID	First Name	Last Name				
2	117362						
3	117362	Duplicate EmployeeID					×
4	128947						
5	170292	The EmployeeID you have entered already exists in column A.					
6	171710						
7	171841	Retry	Cancel	Help			
8	182991	Ozzy	Roberts				

2. Attempt to add a new row at the end of the table with a duplicate ID:

	EmployeeID	First Name	Last Name	D	E	F	G
118	986334	Marvlyn	Blair				
119	997371	Micl	Duplicate EmployeeID				×
120	998783	Pari					
121	986334		The EmployeeID you have entered already exists in column A.				
122							
123			Retry	Cancel	Help		
124							

6 Save your work as *Employees-3*.

Allow:

Any value
Any value
Whole number
Decimal
List
Date
Time
Text length
Custom

note

The COUNTIF function

The COUNTIF function will be covered in depth later, in: *Lesson 3-6: Use the SUMIF and COUNTIF functions to create conditional totals.*

If you are curious about how it works in this lesson, here's a quick explanation.

COUNTIF(range, criteria)

The COUNTIF function returns the number of cells in a *range* that meet a stated condition (the *criteria* argument).

In this lesson, **A:A** is used for the *range* argument. This means all of the cells in column A.

The relative reference **A2** is used for the *criteria* argument.

The COUNTIF function compares the value in the current row within column A to every other value in column A. It should always result in finding only one value (the value you have entered).

If your entry is unique, the COUNTIF function will return 1. If it is not unique, the function will return a number greater than 1.

As 1=1 is TRUE, the function returns TRUE (passing the validation) when the value is unique and FALSE (failing the validation) when the value is not unique.

Session 2: Exercise

1   Open *Sales Performance Analysis-1* from your sample files folder.

	A	B	C	D
3	Salesman	Country	Salary	Sales
4	Alan Shearer	England	60,000	489,817
5	Bobby Charlton	England	34,000	844,935

2   Using *Text to Columns*, break the data in the *Salesman* column into two columns: *First Name* and *Last Name*.

Make sure that you also type the column labels **First Name** and **Last Name** into cells A3 and B3.

	A	B	C	D	E
3	First Name	Last Name	Country	Salary	Sales
4	Alan	Shearer	England	60,000	489,817
5	Bobby	Charlton	England	34,000	844,935

3   Automatically subtotal by *Country*, showing subtotals for *Salary* and *Sales*.

1 2 3		C	D	E
	3	Country	Salary	Sales
+	11	**England Total**	364,000	3,657,627
+	26	**France Total**	767,000	7,339,298

4   Remove the subtotals.

5   Add a validation to column C so that the country may only be entered as *England, France* or *Germany*.

	A	B	C	D
3	First Name	Last Name	Country	Salary
4	Alan	Shearer	England ▾	60,000
5	Bobby	Charlton	England / France / Germany	34,000
6	David	Beckham		39,000

6   Add a user-friendly Error Alert to column C.

Country Error	✕
✕ Invalid Country. Click the drop-down arrow next to the country to see a list of valid entries.	
Retry Cancel Help	

7   Add an input message to column C to inform users which countries are valid.

	A	B	C	D	E
3	First Name	Last Name	Country	Salary	Sales
4	Alan	Shearer	England ▾	60,000	489,817
5	Bobby	Charlton	England	00	844,935
6	David	Beckham	England	00	766,277
7	Gary	Lineker	England	00	330,707
8	Gordon	Banks	England	00	700,950
9	Kevin	Keegan	England	63,000	334,433

Country
Country must be France, England or Germany.

8   Save your work as *Sales Performance Analysis-2*.

Sales Performance Analysis-1

If you need help slide the page to the left

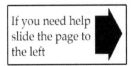

Session 2: Exercise Answers

These are the four questions that students find the most difficult to answer:

Q 6	Q 5	Q 3	Q 2
1. Select all of column C. 2. Click: Data→ Data Tools→ Data Validation. 3. Click the *Error Alert* tab. 4. In the *Title* box, enter the text: **Country Error** 5. In the *Error message* box, enter the text: **Invalid Country. Click the drop-down arrow next to the country to see a list of valid entries.** 6. Click the *OK* button. You learned how to do this in: *Lesson 2-8: Create user-friendly messages for validation errors.*	1. In cell G3 type the text: **Valid Countries** 2. Type the text: **France, England** and **Germany** into cells G4, G5 and G6. 3. Select all of column C. 4. Click: Data→ Data Tools→ Data Validation. 5. Click the *Settings* tab. 6. Set up the dialog as follows: 7. Click the *OK* button. You learned how to do this in: *Lesson 2-11: Add a table-based dynamic list validation.*	1. Click on any of the countries in column C. 2. Click: Data→Sort & Filter→ A-Z …to sort column C in ascending order. 3. Click: Data→Outline→Subtotal 4. Set up the dialog as follows: 5. Click the *OK* button. You learned how to do this in: *Lesson 2-3: Automatically subtotal a range.*	1. Insert a column to the left of column B. 2. Select cells A4:A34. 3. Click: Data→ Data Tools→ Text to Columns. 4. Leave the data type as *Delimited* and click the *Next* button. 5. Select *Space* in the *Delimiters* option group. ☑ Space 6. Click *Finish*. 7. Type: **First Name** and **Last Name** in cells A3 and B3. You learned how to do this in: *Lesson 2-2: Split delimited data using Text to Columns.*

If you have difficulty with the other questions, here are the lessons that cover the relevant skills:

4   Refer to: *Lesson 2-3: Automatically subtotal a range.*

7   Refer to: *Lesson 2-9: Create data validation input messages.*

Session Three: Advanced Functions

3

> All animals are equal, but some animals are more equal than others.
>
> *George Orwell, "Animal Farm"*
> *English essayist, novelist, & satirist (1903 - 1950)*

There are 478 functions in the Excel 365 function library and more are usually added with each new semi-annual version . This would be a very large book if I tried to cover all of them.

In this session, I'll cover the most important Excel functions and put them into context by demonstrating real-world examples of how they can be used.

With the insights that you'll gain from using these functions, you'll be able to confidently explore the vast array of other functions in Excel's huge library should you ever need them.

Session Objectives

- Understand precedence rules and use the Evaluate feature
- Use common functions with Formula AutoComplete
- Use the Insert Function dialog and the PMT function
- Use the PV and FV functions to value investments
- Use the IF logic function
- Use the SUMIF and COUNTIF functions to create conditional totals
- Understand date serial numbers
- Understand common date functions
- Use the DATEDIF function
- Use date offsets to manage projects using the scheduling equation
- Use the DATE function to offset days, months and years
- Enter time values and perform basic time calculations
- Perform time calculations that span midnight

- Understand common time functions and convert date serial numbers to decimal values
- Use the TIME function to offset hours, minutes and seconds
- Use the AND and OR functions to construct complex Boolean criteria
- Understand calculation options (manual and automatic)
- Concatenate strings using the concatenation operator (&)
- Use the TEXT function to format numerical values as strings
- Extract text from fixed width strings using the LEFT, RIGHT and MID functions
- Extract text from delimited strings using the FIND and LEN functions
- Use a VLOOKUP function for an exact or inexact lookup
- Use an IFERROR function to suppress error messages
- Use the SWITCH, MATCH, INDEX and IFS functions

Payroll-1

Lesson 3-1: Understand precedence rules and use the Evaluate feature

Here are Excel's precedence rules:

Operator	Description
Parentheses (brackets)	Any expression in brackets is always evaluated first. **(6+2)*3=24**
Exponent	Exponents are always evaluated next. Exponents tend to be used in engineering/scientific scenarios and are rarely seen in accounting scenarios. **(1+1)*6^2=72**
Multiply and Divide	Multiplication and Division operators have the same precedence and are evaluated from left to right.
Add and Subtract	Addition and Subtraction operators have the same precedence and are evaluated from left to right.

If you only ever work with accounting scenarios, all you really need to remember is:

- Brackets are evaluated first.

- Multiplication and Division are evaluated next.

- Addition and Subtraction are evaluated last.

1   Open *Payroll-1* from your sample files folder.

This worksheet contains some simple formulas required to compute *Net Pay* from *Hours Worked* (see *Payroll Rules* grab on facing page).

Most tax regimes have more complicated rules than those defined in this simple example. Employees are paid the same hourly rate for all hours worked. A different percentage of gross pay is then deducted for Tax, Social Security and Pension contributions.

2   Evaluate the formula in cell B17.

Cell B17 contains the simple formula:

f_x =B15*B4

There's really not much that can go wrong with such a simple formula, but you can see how it works using Excel's evaluation feature.

1. Click on cell B17.

2. Click: Formulas→Formula Auditing→Evaluate Formula.

	A	B
1	Payroll	
2		
3	Payroll Rules	
4	Hourly rate	12.00
5	Tax	32%
6	Social Security	8%
7	Pension	5%
8		
9	Day	Hours Worked
10	Monday	10
11	Tuesday	8
12	Wednesday	12
13	Thursday	7
14	Friday	9
15	Total	46
16		
17	Gross	552.00
18	Tax	176.64
19	Social Security	44.16
20	Pension	27.60
21	Net Pay	303.60
22		
23	Net Pay	303.60

The *Evaluate Formula* dialog appears. You can see that the first part of the formula that will be evaluated is **B15**. This is indicated by an underline:

3. Click the *Step In* button. This will show the formula behind cell B15.

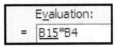

4. Click the *Step Out* button.

    The value in cell B15 now replaces the cell reference:

> Evaluation:
> = 46*B4

5. Click the *Evaluate* button. The value in cell B4 now replaces the cell reference:

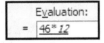

6. Click the *Evaluate* button again. You can now see the result of the evaluation:

> Evaluation:
> = 552.00

    The *Evaluate* button has now changed its caption to *Restart*. If you wanted to, you could click this button to start the evaluation process all over again.

7. Click the *Close* button.

3 Evaluate the formula in cell B23.

To better illustrate precedence rules, a formula that uses a rather long winded way of calculating *Net Pay* has been inserted into cell B23:

> f_x =B15*B4-B15*B4*B5-B4*B15*B6-B4*B15*B7

Because of the rules of precedence, the formula works correctly. It could also have been written with parentheses like this:

> f_x =(B15*B4)-(B15*B4*B5)-(B4*B15*B6)-(B4*B15*B7)

The parentheses are not needed because the precedence rules state that multiplication happens before subtraction. I still prefer the formula with redundant parentheses (see sidebar).

4 Save your work as *Payroll-2*.

trivia

The feature that Excel uses to help you out with function calls first made an appearance in Visual Basic 5 back in 1996 and had the wonderful name: *IntelliSense.* The Excel implementation is called *Formula AutoComplete.*

In 1996, I was working in Switzerland developing a ski-school management application. I was extremely impressed by *IntelliSense* as I didn't have to remember hundreds of function names any more. I was even slightly worried that just about anybody could now program (but, of course, I was wrong).

Recently, I was in London being driven by a Hackney cab driver. (Hackney cab drivers know every shortcut and back street in London). He was worried that satellite navigation would now mean that anybody could become a London cabbie.

Of course, he really had nothing to worry about either.

note

If AutoComplete doesn't work

As with so many other features, Microsoft allows you to turn this very useful feature off.

You'd never want to do this, but you may work on a machine that has had *Formula AutoComplete* switched off and need to turn it on again. To do this, click:

File→Options→Formulas→ Working with formulas

...and make sure that the *Formula AutoComplete* box is checked.

The World's Tallest Buildings-1

Lesson 3-2: Use common functions with Formula AutoComplete

The functions most often seen in workbooks are: SUM, AVERAGE, COUNT, MAX and MIN. In this lesson, you'll use Excel's *Formula AutoComplete* feature to add these formulas to a workbook.

1 Open *The World's Tallest Buildings-1* from your sample files folder.

This worksheet contains information about the world's 20 tallest buildings. You'll use the SUM, MAX, MIN, AVERAGE and COUNT functions to populate cells B25:B29.

2 Click into cell B25 and type **=S** into the cell.

	A	B
25	Total number of floors:	=S
26	Height of tallest building (meters):	ƒx SEARCH
27	Height of shortest building (meters):	ƒx SEC

A list appears showing every function in the Excel function library beginning with S. This feature (introduced in Excel 2007) is called *Formula AutoComplete.* (If this didn't work for you, see the sidebar).

3 Continue typing: **=SU**

Notice that the list now only shows functions beginning with SU. You can see the SUM function, three down in the list.

4 Select the SUM function.

There are two methods for selecting the SUM function:

Press the **<Down Arrow>** key twice.

OR

Click on the function name with the mouse.

The SUM function now displays a tip telling you what the function does:

	A	B
25	Total number of floors:	=SU
26	Height of tallest building (meters):	ƒx SUBSTITUTE
27	Height of shortest building (meters):	ƒx SUBTOTAL
28	Ave. Adds all the numbers in a range of cells	ƒx SUM
20	Number of buildings in the list:	ƒx SUMIF

5 Display detailed help for the SUM function.

The tip tells you a little about the SUM function but to get the full story press the **<F1>** key while *SUM* is still highlighted in the dropdown list.

The Excel help system opens, showing detailed help for the SUM function (this will only work if your are connected to the Internet).

This will not work if you are not connected to the Internet as the help system in Excel 365 is only available online.

note

The Syntax box

The Syntax box tells you which arguments (sometimes called parameters) the function needs.

Arguments in square brackets are optional.

In the case of the SUM function, the first argument does not have square brackets, meaning that you can't leave it out.

For such a simple function as SUM, the syntax box is hardly needed, but later you'll discover functions that require several arguments and then the syntax box will be invaluable.

trivia

How the foot got shorter in 1959

This workbook uses the foot-to-meter conversion factor of 0.3048. Before 1959, a foot was slightly longer at 0.3048006096012 meters.

In 1893, the US Office of Weights and Measures (now the National Bureau of Standards) fixed the value of the US foot at 0.3048006096012 Meters. Unfortunately, the rest of the world used a slightly different factor.

Because this caused problems, an international agreement was reached in 1959 to re-define the standard conversion factor at exactly 0.3048 meters, making a post-1959 foot slightly shorter than a pre-1959 foot!

Because the new standard upset existing survey data, it was further agreed that, for geodetic purposes only, the old conversion factor would remain valid. To avoid confusion, survey data is now defined in a new unit called the *US Survey Foot*.

Read the help text if you are interested and then close the help window.

Complete the formula so that you see: **=SUM(**

```
=SUM(
SUM(number1, [number2], ...)
```

Notice that a little box has appeared beneath the function call. This is the *Syntax box* (see sidebar for more information).

6 **Select the cells that you need to sum (cells F4:F23) with the mouse or keyboard.**

You can select the cells with the keyboard using the following technique:

1. Erase the current contents of cell B25 (to start again).

2. Type: **=SUM(**

3. Press the **<Up Arrow>** and **<Right Arrow>** keys until you reach cell F4.

4. Press **<Ctrl>+<Shift>+<Down Arrow>** to select cells F4:F23.

7 **Press the <Enter> key to finish the formula.**

There's no need to type the closing bracket as Excel is clever enough to enter it for you. The total number of floors in all 20 buildings is now displayed in cell B25.

8 **Use the same technique to add a MAX function to cell B26.**

1. Click in cell B26.

2. Type **=MA**

3. Press the **<Down Arrow>** key once to move the cursor over the MAX function.

4. Press the **<Tab>** key to automatically enter the MAX function into cell B26.

5. Select the range D4:D23 using either the mouse or the keyboard.

   The formula should now be: **=MAX(D4:D23**

6. Press the **<Enter>** key.

   There's no need to type the closing bracket as, once again, Excel helps you out by entering it automatically.

9 **Use the same technique to add MIN, AVERAGE and COUNT functions to cells B27:B29.**

	A	B
25	Total number of floors:	=SUM(F4:F23)
26	Height of tallest building (meters):	=MAX(D4:D23)
27	Height of shortest building (meters):	=MIN(D4:D23)
28	Average number of floors:	=AVERAGE(F4:F23)
29	Number of buildings in the list:	=COUNT(D4:D23)

10 **Save your work as *The World's Tallest Buildings-2*.**

Lesson 3-3: Use the Insert Function dialog and the PMT function

In this lesson, you'll use a complex function with five parameters that will calculate the monthly repayments on a mortgage loan.

1   Open *Mortgage Repayments-1* from your sample files folder.

This worksheet contains details of mortgages for loans from 50,000 to 300,000 with a 25-year term and an interest rate of 6.7%. You will use the PMT function to calculate the monthly repayments.

	A	B	C	D
			Interest	Monthly
3	Price		Term (Years) (APR)	Repayment
4	50,000	25	6.70%	
5	100,000	25	6.70%	

2   Calculate the monthly repayments using the PMT function and the *Insert Function* dialog.

1.   Click in cell D4.

2.   Click the *Insert Function* button at the left of the formula bar:

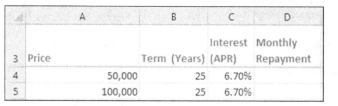

The *Insert Function* dialog appears.

3.   Type **Loan** into the *Search for a function* text box and then click the *Go* button:

> Search for a function:
>
> Loan   Go

A list of functions is shown in the *Select a function* list. Excel's second best guess is the PMT function. Click once on the PMT function and look at the help text below the list. You can see what the PMT function is used for:

> PMT(rate,nper,pv,fv,type)
> Calculates the payment for a loan based on constant payments and a constant interest rate.

While the help lets you know what the function does, it is unclear (at this stage) what the arguments mean. Note also that there is a hyperlink pointing to the help page for this function.

> Help on this function

The help page provides detailed information about each argument. It is, however, more convenient to obtain interactive help as each argument is entered.

Mortgage Repayments-1

note

What are the Fv and Type arguments used for?

Fv

Fv is the Future Value. It is an amount that will still be owed, or a cash bonus that will be paid to the borrower at the end of the loan. This is sometimes called a balloon payment.

If a positive amount is entered into the Fv box, this amount will be paid to the borrower at the end of the loan.

If a negative amount is entered, it will represent an amount still owed at the end of the loan.

This type of loan is common in vehicle loan agreements and can also be used to model *interest only* mortgages.

Example:

A car is sold for 10,000 across three years. At the end of the three years, the borrower is able to buy the car for 3,000 or to hand it back to the dealer.

To model this loan, the Pv would be 10,000 and the Fv would be -3,000.

Type

Most loans require the repayment to be made at the end of the period (in this example, at the end of each month). Some insurance-backed loans require the repayment to be made at the beginning of the period.

Payments for this type of loan can be calculated by setting the *Type* argument to 1.

	C	D
3	Interest (APR)	Monthly Repayment
4	6.70%	$343.88
5	6.70%	$687.76
6	6.70%	$1,031.64
7	6.70%	$1,375.51
8	6.70%	$1,719.39
9	6.70%	$2,063.27

4. Click the *OK* button.

The *Function Arguments* dialog is displayed.

Rate		↑	= number
Nper		↑	= number
Pv		↑	= number
Fv		↑	= number
Type		↑	= number

The arguments shown in bold face are required (**Rate, Nper** and **Pv**). The last two arguments are optional (Fv and Type). You won't be using the Fv and Type arguments, but if you are interested in their purpose see the sidebar for more information.

5. Click in the first box (*Rate*). Notice that help is provided at the bottom of the dialog:

> **Rate** is the interest rate per period for the loan. For example, use 6%/4 for quarterly payments at 6% APR.

6. Click in cell C4 and then type **/12**. You need to divide the annual interest rate by twelve to calculate the monthly interest rate.

7. Complete the next two arguments by studying the help text for each. Your dialog should now look like this:

Rate	C4/12	↑	= 0.005583333
Nper	B4*12	↑	= 300
Pv	A4	↑	= 50000

8. Click the *OK* button.

The monthly repayment is now shown in cell D4 but the amount shown is negative. The number is shown as negative because it represents money going out of your account (a negative cash flow).

The PMT function automatically formats the repayment with a currency prefix matching the currency locale on your computer.

9. Click in cell D4 and add a minus operator to the front of the formula:

f_x	=-PMT(C4/12,B4*12,A4)

10. Press the **<Enter>** key.

The value is now displayed as a positive number, which is more visually pleasing:

	A	B	C	D
3	Price	Term (Years)	Interest (APR)	Monthly Repayment
4	50,000	25	6.70%	$343.88

11. AutoFill the formula to the end of the list to show monthly repayments for all six loan amounts.

3   Save your work as *Mortgage Repayments-2*.

Lesson 3-4: Use the PV and FV functions to value investments

> Compound interest is the eighth wonder of the world. He who understands it, earns it … he who doesn't … pays it
>
> *Albert Einstein, theoretical physicist (1879-1955)*

Present Value

Present Value is the total amount that a series of future payments is worth now.

Present Value can be used to value an existing loan. This would be useful if you wanted to sell the loan to another party.

In this lesson, you will explore the following scenario:

I have loaned my friend John $20,000 to buy a car. John has agreed to repay $1,000 per month for two years (making me $4,000 in interest on the deal). I want to sell the loan on to my other friend Bill. Bill says he is happy to buy it from me, but he needs a return of 12% on his investment. I can use the PV function to work out what the loan is worth today based upon Bill's requirement for a 12% return.

Future Value

Future value is used to work out how much capital will accumulate if a fixed amount is saved each month at a specified compound interest rate.

In this lesson, you will also explore the following scenario:

I save $100 each month towards my retirement fund. If I save for 30 years and the interest rate during this time will be 10%, how much money will I have in my fund upon retirement?

	A	B
1	Retirement Fund	
2		
3	Monthly Savings	100.00
4	Number of years	30
5	Interest Rate	10%
6		
7	**Value upon retirement**	
8		
9	Car Loan	
10		
11	Monthly repayment	1,000.00
12	Number of years	2
13	Interest rate	12%
14		
15	**Value of investment**	

Investments-1

1 Open *Investments-1* from your sample files folder.

This worksheet contains details of the retirement fund and car loan scenarios described above.

2 Use the FV function to calculate the retirement fund value.

In the last lesson, you discovered how to use the *Insert Function* button f_x to access functions in Excel's vast function library.

You can also access the library by using the *Function Library* buttons on the ribbon.

1. Click in cell B7.

2. Click: Formulas→Function Library→Financial→FV.

Notice that when you hover the mouse cursor over the FV option a tip appears showing a short description of the function:

FV(rate,nper,pmt,pv,type)

Returns the future value of an investment based on periodic, constant payments and a constant interest rate.

(?) Tell me more

3. Add the correct values to the *Function Arguments* dialog:

Rate	B5/12	↑	= 0.008333333
Nper	B4*12	↑	= 360
Pmt	B3	↑	= 100
Pv		↑	= number
Type		↑	= number

4. Click the *OK* button. The retirement fund is shown as a negative because it represents money leaving your account.

5. Add a minus sign in front of *FV* in the formula bar to convert it to a more visually pleasing positive value:

fx   =-FV(B5/12,B4*12,B3)

Although only 36,000 was paid into the retirement fund, compound interest has boosted the amount saved to 226,048.79.

You can now appreciate why Einstein described compound interest as the eighth wonder of the world.

3 **Use the PV function to calculate the value of the car loan.**

1. Click in cell B15.

2. Click: Formulas→Function Library→Financial→PV.

3. Add the correct values to the *Function Arguments* dialog:

Rate	B13/12	↑	= 0.01
Nper	B12*12	↑	= 24
Pmt	B11	↑	= 1000
Fv		↑	= number
Type		↑	= number

4. Click the *OK* button.

5. Add a minus sign in front of *PV* in the formula bar to convert it to a positive value:

fx   =-PV(B13/12,B12*12,B11)

6. Press the **<Enter>** key. The result is 21,243.39 so you turned a profit on the deal.

(The *Fv* and *Type* arguments are discussed in: *Lesson 3-3: Use the Insert Function dialog and the PMT function*).

4 **Save your work as *Investments-2*.**

	A	B
1	Retirement Fund	
2		
3	Monthly Savings	100.00
4	Number of years	30
5	Interest Rate	10%
6		
7	Value upon retirement	226,048.79
8		
9	Car Loan	
10		
11	Monthly repayment	1,000.00
12	Number of years	2
13	Interest rate	12%
14		
15	Value of investment	21,243.39

Lesson 3-5: Use the IF logic function

The IF function is one of Excel's most widely used and useful functions. It is also a function that often confuses my students, so I'll begin this lesson by explaining the concept of the logical test. Later, you'll construct a worksheet containing three examples of the IF function at work.

The IF function requires a *logical test* and then performs one action if the test returns TRUE and a different action if the test returns FALSE.

Here are some examples of logical tests:

Expression	Returns	Why?
6=2	FALSE	Because six does not equal two.
100<90	FALSE	Because 100 is not less than 90.
6+2 = 4+4	TRUE	Because eight does equal eight.

In this lesson, you'll use three different logical tests in order to calculate several employees' earnings during a week.

1   Open *Earnings Summary-1* from your sample files folder.

Notice the *Payroll Rules* section:

	A	B	C	D	E	F
3	Payroll Rules:					
4	All hours up to 35 hours per week paid at hourly rate					
5	All hours over 35 hours per week paid at time and a half (150% of hourly rate)					
6	Bonus of 5% paid on all sales above target					

Logical tests will be constructed to calculate *Standard Pay, Overtime Pay* and *Bonus*:

	A	B	C	D	E	F	G	H	I
				Hourly	Hours	Standard	Overtime		
8	Name	Sales	Target	Rate	Worked	Pay	Pay	Bonus	Total
9	Brad Cruise	22,000	10,000	15.00	40				

2   Use an IF function to calculate standard pay.

In the case of *Standard Pay*, the logical test will be:

"Did this employee work more than 35 hours this week?"

The formula for the logical test is: **E9<=35** (cell E9 is less than or equal to 35).

If this returns *TRUE*, then standard pay will be:

*Hours Worked * Hourly Rate*, (E9*D9)

…because the employee worked for 35 hours or less.

If this returns **FALSE**, then standard pay will be:

*35*Hourly Rate* (35*D9)

… because the employee worked more than 35 hours (and the first 35 hours of this time will be paid at standard rate).

tip

Avoid nesting IF functions

Here's an example of a two-level nested IF function:

=IF(A31="Apples",10%,IF(A31="Lemons",20%,0))

This would return 10% if the value in A31 was *Apples,* 20% if the value was *Lemons* and zero if the value was anything else. Note that the words *Apples* and *Lemons* are enclosed in quotation marks. You must refer to text in this way within Excel formulas.

Whenever you see nested IF functions be aware that there is almost surely a better, less complex, less error-prone and more elegant solution.

Excel allows you to nest IF functions up to 64 levels deep (which is 63 too many).

Most problems that you will find solved with a nested IF function could be better solved using a SWITCH, IFS, VLOOKUP or XLOOKUP function. These function will be covered later, in:

Lesson 3-22: Use a VLOOKUP function for an exact lookup.

Lesson 3-23: Use the SWITCH function

Lesson 3-28: Use the IFS function.

…and

Lesson 4-18: Understand XLOOKUP (part one)

1. Click in cell F9.

2. Click: Formulas→Logical→IF.

    The *Function Arguments* dialog appears.

3. Complete the dialog as follows:

Logical_test	E9<=35	⬆	=	FALSE
Value_if_true	E9*D9	⬆	=	600
Value_if_false	35*D9	⬆	=	525

    If you do not completely understand why the above formulas are used, read the introduction to this lesson again.

4. Click the *OK* button.

    Standard Pay is correctly displayed in cell F9 (525.00).

3   Use an IF function to calculate overtime pay in cell G9.

    It should now be clear to you why the correct arguments for the IF function, this time, are:

Logical_test	E9<=35	⬆	=	FALSE
Value_if_true	0	⬆	=	0
Value_if_false	(E9-35)*D9*1.5	⬆	=	112.5

    (The *Value_if_false* argument would have worked in exactly the same way if you had used a value of 150% instead of 1.5 as Excel recognizes both as having the same value but different formats).

4   Use the IF function to calculate the bonus in cell H9.

    Once again, it should be clear to you why the correct arguments for the IF function this time are:

Logical_test	B9>C9	⬆	=	TRUE
Value_if_true	(B9-C9)*5%	⬆	=	600
Value_if_false	0	⬆	=	0

5   Add a formula to cell I9 to calculate total pay.

    The correct formula could be either of the following:

    =F9+G9+H9
    =SUM(F9:H9)

6   AutoFill the formulas in cells F9:I9 to cells F10:I17.

    The payroll worksheet is now complete.

	A	B	C	D	E	F	G	H	I
				Hourly	Hours	Standard	Overtime		
8	Name	Sales	Target	Rate	Worked	Pay	Pay	Bonus	Total
9	Brad Cruise	22,000	10,000	15.00	40	525.00	112.50	600.00	1,237.50
10	Ian Dean	9,000	8,000	13.00	35	455.00	-	50.00	505.00
11	Paris Smith	10,000	12,000	15.00	42	525.00	157.50	-	682.50

7   Save your work as *Earnings Summary-2*.

note

The SUMIFS and COUNTIFS functions

The SUMIFS and COUNTIFS functions work in exactly the same way as the SUMIF and COUNTIF functions used in this lesson but they accept multiple criteria.

For example, if you needed to know the combined total salary for Male employees in the *Sales* department, you'd set the SUMIFS arguments as follows:

SUMIFS	
Sum_range	C4:C17
Criteria_range1	D4:D17
Criteria1	'Sales'
Criteria_range2	B4:B17
Criteria2	'M'

tip

Quickly make a range reference absolute

Many users type in those little dollar signs by hand, which is very time consuming.

Here's a great time saver:

1. Select the entire range reference (for example **D4:D17**).

2. Press the **<F4>** key once. The range is then converted to absolute (for example **$D$4:$D$17**).

If you press the **<F4>** key more than once, you'll cycle through all possible mixed cell references for the range.

Headcount & Salaries-1

Lesson 3-6: Use the SUMIF and COUNTIF functions to create conditional totals

In the previous lesson, you used the IF logical function to return different values based upon a logical test that returned TRUE or FALSE.

SUMIF and COUNTIF are similar functions but are used to sum or count values within a range based upon a similar logical test.

This lesson's sample workbook lists all of an organization's employees along with their gender and department:

	A	B	C	D
3	Name	Sex	Salary	Department
4	Johnny Caine	M	37,864	Sales
5	George Marley	M	26,148	Purchasing
6	Betty Anan	F	26,345	Logistics
7	Paris Winfrey	F	23,562	Sales

You'll use the SUMIF and COUNTIF functions to list the total salary and headcount for each department, along with the total salary and headcount for each gender.

1   Open *Headcount & Salaries-1* from your sample files folder.

2   Use the SUMIF function to calculate the total salary for each department.

    1.   Click in cell B21.

    2.   Click: Formulas→Function Library→Math & Trig→SUMIF.

        The *Function Arguments* dialog appears.

        There are three arguments for the SUMIF function:

        The *Range* argument defines the range in which to look for the department name. In this case, it is the range D4:D17 (the cells containing the *Departments*).

        The *Criteria* argument is the thing to look for within the stated range. In this case, it is the word "Sales" contained in cell A21.

        The *Sum_range* argument is the range containing numerical data that needs to be added up when the criteria is true. In this case, it is the range C4:C17 (the cells containing *Salary* values).

    3.   Complete the dialog with the following arguments:

Range	$D$4:$D$17	↑
Criteria	A21	↑
Sum_range	$C$4:$C$17	↑

Note the use of absolute references for each range. This will allow you to AutoFill the function for the *Purchasing* and *Logistics* totals.

4. Click the *OK* button.

5. AutoFill cell B21 to cells B22:B23 to display the total salaries for the *Purchasing* and *Logistics* departments.

3   Use the COUNTIF function to calculate the headcount for each department.

COUNTIF works in exactly the same way as SUMIF but returns a count of all cells that match the criteria.

1. Click in cell C21.

2. Click: Formulas→Function Library→ More Functions→Statistical→COUNTIF.

3. Complete the dialog with the following arguments:

Range	$D$4:$D$17
Criteria	A21

4. Click the *OK* button.

5. AutoFill cell C21 to cells C22:C23 to display the headcount for the *Purchasing* and *Logistics* departments.

4   Use SUMIF and COUNTIF functions to calculate the salary and headcount for male and female employees in cells B27:C28.

Use exactly the same technique as you did for *Salary* and *Headcount by Department*. The correct arguments for cells B27 and C27 are:

Range	$B$4:$B$17
Criteria	A27
Sum_range	$C$4:$C$17

And:

Range	$B$4:$B$17
Criteria	A27

	A	B	C
20	Department	Salary	Headcount
21	Sales	179,898	6
22	Purchasing	137,557	5
23	Logistics	73,601	3
24	**Total:**	**391,056**	**14**
25			
26	Gender	Salary	Headcount
27	M	253,587	9
28	F	137,469	5
29	**Total:**	**391,056**	**14**

5   Save your work as *Headcount & Salaries-2*.

Lesson 3-7: Understand date serial numbers

This lesson was included in the *Essential Skills* book in this series and has also been included in this book as a recap. A full understanding of the date serial number concept is essential in order to understand the date and time functions that will be introduced in later lessons.

Excel stores dates in a very clever way. Understanding Excel's date storage system empowers you to use date arithmetic. You can use date arithmetic to compute the difference between two dates (in days) or to shift date ranges by a given time interval.

How Excel stores dates

Dates are stored as simple numbers called *date serial numbers*. The serial number contains the number of days that have elapsed since 1st January 1900 (where 1st January 1900 is 1).

The world began in 1900

An interesting shortcoming of Excel is its inability to easily work with dates before 1900. Excel simply doesn't acknowledge that there were any dates before this time. If you work with older dates, you will have to work-around this limitation.

In Excel, every time is a date, and every date is a time

You've already realized that 5th January 1900 is stored as the number 5. What would the number 5.5 mean? It would mean midday on 5th January 1900.

It is possible to format a date to show only the date, only the time, or both a time and a date.

When you enter a time into a cell without a date, the time is stored as a number less than one. Excel regards this as having the non-existent date of 00 January 1900!

When you enter a date into a cell without a time, the time is stored as midnight at the beginning of that day.

1 Create a new blank workbook and put the numbers 1 to 5 in cells A1:A5.

2 Type the formula **=A1** into cell B1 followed by the **<Enter>** key, and then AutoFill the formula to the end of the list.

	A	B
1	1	1
2	2	2
3	3	3
4	4	4
5	5	5

3   Apply a date format to column A that will show a four-digit year.

	A	B
1	Sunday, January 1, 1900	1
2	Monday, January 2, 1900	2

This reveals that the numbers 1 to 5 represent the dates 1-Jan-1900 to 05-Jan-1900.

4   Set a custom format of **dd mmm yyyy hh:mm** for the dates in column A (to show both dates and times).

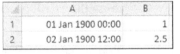

Notice that when you enter a date without a time, the time is set to midnight at the beginning of that day.

	A	B
1	01 Jan 1900 00:00	1
2	02 Jan 1900 00:00	2

5   Change the time in cell A2 to: **12:00:00 PM**

Notice that the number in cell B2 has changed to 2.5, showing that times are stored by Excel as the decimal part of a number.

	A	B
1	01 Jan 1900 00:00	1
2	02 Jan 1900 12:00	2.5

6   Compute the number of days that occurred between 01 Jan 1900 and 01 Jan 2000.

Now that you have a good grasp of Excel's serial numbers, this task is easy.

1.   Enter the two dates in cells A7 and A8, one beneath the other.

2.   Subtract one date from the other by entering the formula: **=A8-A7** into cell A9.

3.   Format cell A9 to display numeric (rather than date) values.

7	Sunday, January 1, 1900
8	Saturday, January 1, 2000
9	36,525.00

You now know that 36,525 days occurred during the last century (actually 36,524 due to the Lotus 1-2-3 bug – see sidebar).

7   Close the workbook without saving.

Lesson 3-8: Understand common date functions

Excel's primary date functions are TODAY, DAY, MONTH and YEAR. In the previous lesson, you gained an understanding of how Excel stores dates as serial numbers. You can now use this knowledge in conjunction with the above date functions to create some very useful date related formulas.

1 Open *Resources-1* from your sample files folder.

This worksheet contains a list of employees along with their dates of birth.

	A	B	C
3	First Name	Last Name	Date of Birth
4	Brad	Cruise	15-Apr-65
5	Ian	Dean	22-May-67
6	Paris	Smith	16-Jul-72

2 Use the YEAR function to calculate the year in which each employee was born.

1. Click in cell D4.

2. Click: Formulas→Function Library→Date & Time→Year.

   The *Function Arguments* dialog is displayed.

3. Click in cell C4.

   Because you know that all dates are represented by a serial number, and because cell C4 contains a date, this reference will cause the YEAR function to return 1965 (the year Brad Cruise was born).

   Notice that the dialog previews the result as = *1965* and also lets you know that the date serial number for 15th April 1965 is *23,847*.

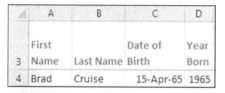

4. Click the *OK* button.

   The year in which Brad Cruise was born is now displayed in cell D4.

	A	B	C	D
3	First Name	Last Name	Date of Birth	Year Born
4	Brad	Cruise	15-Apr-65	1965

3 Use the DAY function to place the day when Brad Cruise was born into cell E4.

Resources-1

4   Use the MONTH function to calculate the month when Brad Cruise was born into cell F4.

	D	E	F
3	Year Born	Day Born	Month Born
4	=YEAR(C4)	=DAY(C4)	=MONTH(C4)

	A	B	C	D	E	F
3	First Name	Last Name	Date of Birth	Year Born	Day Born	Month Born
4	Brad	Cruise	15-Apr-65	1965	15	4

5   Use the TODAY function to place a volatile current date into cell G4.

	G
3	Today
4	=TODAY()

	G
	Today
	26-Jun-19

The TODAY function returns the current date. The date is volatile. This means that if you were to open this worksheet again tomorrow, you would see tomorrow's date in cell G4.

6   Use the YEAR function to place the current year into cell H4.

By using the value in cell G4 as the argument for the YEAR function, it is possible to insert the current year into cell H4.

Because the value in cell G4 is volatile, the value in H4 is also volatile. This means that if this worksheet was opened again in the year 2021, you would see the value 2021 in cell H4.

	H
3	Current Year
4	=YEAR(G4)

	H
3	Current Year
4	2019

7   Add a formula to cell I4 to calculate the employee's maximum age this year.

Calculating the employee's current age from their date of birth using the YEAR, MONTH and DAY functions is quite a feat (although it can be done). You'll discover an easy way to do this in the next lesson using a different technique.

In this lesson, you'll simply calculate what the employee's maximum age will be this year with a simple subtraction of the year born from the current year.

	A	B	C	D	E	F	G	H	I
3	First Name	Last Name	Date of Birth	Year Born	Day Born	Month Born	Today	Current Year	Max Age This Year
4	Brad	Cruise	15-Apr-65	1965	15	4	26-Jun-19	2019	=H4-D4

8   AutoFill cells D4:I4 down to row 12.

9   Save your work as *Resources-2*.

note

Why calculating age from date of birth is so difficult

I've seen some weird and wonderful attempts to calculate age from date of birth in my student's worksheets.

At first, it doesn't seem such a big deal. The first solution that occurs is to simply convert each date to days and then divide by 365. Like this:

(TODAY() – BirthDate)/365

If it wasn't for leap years, this would work. To overcome the leap year issue, I've seen solutions based upon the assumption that a year is, on average, 365.25 days long. So why won't this work?

(TODAY() – BirthDate)/365.25

There are two reasons why.

The first reason is that the date may belong to a child who has not yet lived through a leap year.

The second reason is caused by the Gregorian leap year rule that skips a leap year in centurial years (see: *Lesson 3-7: Understand date serial numbers,* sidebar).

Lesson 3-9: Use the DATEDIF function

Three may keep a secret, if two of them are dead.

Benjamin Franklin (1706 - 1790)

One of the most useful date-related functions available in Excel is the DATEDIF function. For some reason this is a secret, and you'll find nothing about this wonderful function anywhere in the Excel 365 documentation. Some have speculated that this may be for legal reasons as the function was originally included for compatibility with Lotus 1-2-3.

Microsoft documented the function in Excel 2000 so, in their spirit of backward compatibility, they continue to support it in Excel 365 and can be expected to also support it in all future Excel versions.

DATEDIF is able to calculate the difference between two dates for several intervals. In this lesson, you'll use it to calculate an age from a date of birth. This is hugely complex using the YEAR, MONTH and DAY functions (see sidebar).

Because you probably don't have a copy of the Excel 2000 manual, here is the syntax for the function:

=DATEDIF(StartDate, EndDate, Interval)

StartDate: The first date.

EndDate: The second date.

Interval: The interval to return, such as the number of months or years between the two dates.

The interval arguments are:

"m"   Months between two dates.

"d"   Days between two dates.

"y"   Years between two dates.

"ym"   Months between two dates, ignoring the year (ie as if both dates were the same year).

"yd"   Days between two dates, ignoring the year.

"md"   Days between two dates, ignoring the months and years.

1   Open *Resources-2* from your sample files folder (if it isn't already open).

2   Change the text in cell I3 to: **Age (Years)**

Resources-2

note

Calculating age from date of birth using the YEARFRAC and INT functions

Excel is also able to calculate an age from a date of birth using the INT and YEARFRAC functions.

YEARFRAC returns the number of years between two dates expressed as a fraction.

The syntax is:

YEARFRAC(start_date,end_date,basis)

In this lesson's sample file, you would use the function (in cell I4) like this:

=YEARFRAC(C4, G4, 1)

The last argument (basis) tells Excel to take leap years into account when calculating the fractional part of the year.

In this lesson's sample file YEARFRAC produced these results (on 26th June 2019):

	A	B	I
3	First Name	Last Name	Age (Years)
4	Brad	Cruise	54.198
5	Ian	Dean	52.096

This means that Brad Cruise was 53.198 years old.

In: *Lesson 1-9: Apply an advanced filter with function-driven criteria*, you learned about the INT function. This returns the whole number portion of a number. For example, **=INT(25.99)** would return the whole number **25.**

In the example above, the formula:

=INT(I4)

… would return **54** (Brad Cruise's age).

You could also combine the two functions like this:

=INT(YEARFRAC(C4, G4, 1))

3 Delete cells I4:I12.

	C	D	E	F	G	H	I
3	Date of Birth	Year Born	Day Born	Month Born	Today	Current Year	Age (Years)
4	15-Apr-65	1965	15	4	26-Jun-19	2019	
5	22-May-67	1967	22	5	26-Jun-19	2019	
6	16-Jul-72	1972	16	7	26-Jun-19	2019	

4 Add the following formula to cell I4:

=DATEDIF(C4,TODAY(),"y")

Notice that *Formula AutoComplete* doesn't even want to admit that this function exists.

The function works by comparing the date of birth (in cell C4) with today's date (returned by the TODAY function) and returns the interval between the date of birth, and today's date, in years.

5 Calculate each resource's precise age in years, months and days.

This requirement illustrates the use of the "ym" and "md" arguments.

1. Type the text: **Age (Months)** into cell J3.

2. Type the text: **Age (Days)** into cell K3.

3. Match the formatting of cells J3 and K3 to that in cell I3.

    (Formatting is an elementary skill covered in the *Essential Skills* book in this series).

	E	F	G	H	I	J	K
3	Day Born	Month Born	Today	Current Year	Age (Years)	Age (Months)	Age (Days)
4	15	4	26-Jun-19	2019	54		

(You will probably see a different age depending upon whatever today's date is at the time you read this book).

4. Add the following formula to cell J4:

    =DATEDIF(C4,TODAY(),"ym")

5. Add the following formula to cell K4:

    =DATEDIF(C4,TODAY(),"md")

6. AutoFill cells I4:K4 to the end of the range.

	A	B	C	D	I	J	K
3	First Name	Last Name	Date of Birth	Year Born	Age (Years)	Age (Months)	Age (Days)
4	Brad	Cruise	15-Apr-65	1965	54	2	11
5	Ian	Dean	22-May-67	1967	52	1	4

The above was calculated on 26th June 2019. They'll all be a little older by the time you complete this exercise.

6 Save your work as *Resources-3*.

note

Project Management and Excel

Excel is often misused to manage projects.

Project Management involves scheduling tasks and assigning resources to complete each task. For example, to build a house you would have tasks such as *lay bricks* and *fit windows*.

Each task has a *start* and *end* date, along with one or more *dependencies* (for example you cannot fit the windows until you have laid the bricks).

Each task also has one or more *resources* assigned to it (for example you may assign Bill and Bob to lay the bricks and Colin to fit the windows).

The best way to illustrate a project plan is the Gantt chart, named after Henry Gantt (1861–1919). It is quite easy to produce a primitive Gantt chart using Excel (but not a true Gantt chart showing inter-task dependencies).

Now that you understand Excel's date functions, you might think that Excel is a great tool for managing projects – but there's a far, far better way.

Microsoft Project is a tool designed specifically to manage projects and produce excellent Gantt charts.

If you have complex workbooks that seek to manage the type of scenario described above, you really should check out Microsoft Project – it is a superb tool.

Many students that attend my Project Management courses have first tried hard and failed using Excel.

Project-1

Lesson 3-10: Use date offsets to manage projects using the scheduling equation

In this lesson, you'll use date offsets in conjunction with the scheduling equation to create a worksheet that will manage a small project.

In order to understand project management, you need to first understand the scheduling equation:

Time = Work/Units

Let's pose the age-old primary school math problem:

"If it takes one man ten days to dig a hole, how long will it take two men to dig the same hole"?

The answer is, of course, five days (in mathematics, if not in reality).

To use the scheduling equation, each unit can be described (in this example) as being a man and the work can be defined in days.

In the first example:

10 days = 10 days/1 Man

In the second example:

5 days = 10 days/2 Men

If you increase your estimate of 10 days work, then the time will increase. If you add more men to the task, then the time will decrease, as the equation will always balance.

In this lesson, you'll learn how to create formulas that will enable task lengths to dynamically re-scale as you either add more resources to each task, or revise your estimate for the amount of work needed to complete each task.

1 Open *Project-1* from your sample files folder.

The worksheet contains a simple project plan consisting of four linked tasks:

	A	B	C	D
			Work	
3	Task Name	Start date	(Man-Days)	Units
4	Dig Foundations	15-Jun-16	3	3
5	Pour Footings		2	1
6	Lay Bricks to DPC		8	4
7	Pour floor slab		2	1

Each task has a *start to finish dependency*. This means that each task must complete before the following task can begin.

2 Calculate the *End Date* for the first task.

Enter the formula: **=B4+C4/D4-1** into cell E4.

Note that, because of the rules of precedence, this is the equivalent of **=B4+(C4/D4)-1**

important

Refining the example worksheet

The example presented in this lesson is very simple as its aim is to teach the use of date offsets (rather than to create a useful project management system).

Here are some of the worksheet's shortcomings:

1. If you assign more units to a task than there is work, the task will finish in the past.

This could be overcome by adding a MAX function to column E as follows:

=MAX(B4+C4/D4-1,B4)

This would ensure that the *End Date* of a task could never be earlier than the *Start Date*.

2. The worksheet can only deal with whole days.

With the refinement suggested above:

(a) When a task ends early in the day all workers are assumed to stop work for the day (rather than move to the next task).

(b) Where *Work/Units* does not result in a whole number the *End Date* will not be accurately calculated.

For example, if 8 men were allocated to a 7 man-day task, the worksheet would assume that the task would be completed in one day (as 0.875 is not a whole number).

This could be overcome by adding a formula-driven custom validation to column D that would only allow *Units* to be entered when *Work/Units* produced a whole number result.

Formula-driven validations were covered in: *Lesson 2-10: Add a formula-driven date validation and a text length validation.*

(Precedence was covered in: *Lesson 3-1: Understand precedence rules and use the Evaluate feature*).

One day is subtracted because a job of one day's duration will begin and end on the same day. The formula calculates the *End Date* using the scheduling equation discussed at the beginning of this lesson (see sidebar for a more in-depth discussion).

	A	B	C	D	E
			Work		
3	Task Name	Start date	(Man-Days)	Units	End Date
4	Dig Foundations	15-Jun-16	3	3	15-Jun-16
5	Pour Footings		2	1	
6	Lay Bricks to DPC		8	4	
7	Pour floor slab		2	1	

The *End Date* is 15-Jun-16 because three men have been assigned to a task that has three man-days' work. The task thus takes one day to complete and so begins and ends on the same day.

3 Test the scheduling equation.

If you were to take two men off the job, the single remaining man would take three days to complete the task.

1. Change the value in cell D4 to 1.

   Notice that the task now takes three days to complete.

	A	B	C	D	E
			Work		
3	Task Name	Start date	(Man-Days)	Units	End Date
4	Dig Foundations	15-Jun-16	3	1	17-Jun-16

2. Revise your estimate of the work to 8 Man-Days and assign two men to the task.

   This time, the task takes four days to complete.

	A	B	C	D	E
			Work		
3	Task Name	Start date	(Man-Days)	Units	End Date
4	Dig Foundations	15-Jun-16	8	2	18-Jun-16

4 Add a formula to show the start date for the *Pour Footings* task.

The start date of the *Pour Footings* task will be the day after the end date of the *Dig Foundations* task.

Enter the formula: **=E4+1** into cell B5.

5 AutoFill cells B5 and E4 to the end of the range.

You now have a dynamic project plan that will adjust the end date of the project based upon your work estimates and the number of resources that you assign to each task.

	A	B	C	D	E
			Work		
3	Task Name	Start date	(Man-Days)	Units	End Date
4	Dig Foundations	15-Jun-16	8	2	18-Jun-16
5	Pour Footings	19-Jun-16	2	1	20-Jun-16
6	Lay Bricks to DPC	21-Jun-16	8	4	22-Jun-16
7	Pour floor slab	23-Jun-16	2	1	24-Jun-16

6 Save your work as *Project-2*.

Lesson 3-11: Use the DATE function to offset days, months and years

Now that you understand the TODAY, DAY, MONTH and YEAR functions, you will be able to use the DATE function to dynamically manage more sophisticated date offsets.

1   Open *Service Schedule-1* from your sample files folder.

In this example, the service schedule requires that vehicles are inspected 20 days after first supply, 3 months after the 20-day inspection, and then every year thereafter.

	A	B	C	D	E	F
1	Service Schedule					
2						
3	Vehicle Supplied On	20 Day Inspection	3 month Inspection	12 Month Services Thereafter...		
4	16-Jan-15					
5	18-Feb-16					
6	16-Mar-16					

2   Put a formula in cell B4 that will calculate the date for the 20-day inspection based upon the date in cell A4.

1.   Type **=D** into cell B4.

The DATE function is the first in the drop-down list:

	A	B	C
3	Vehicle Supplied On	20 Day Inspection	3 mon Inspe
4	16-Jan-15	=D	
5	18-Feb-16	*fx* DATE	
6	16-Mar-16	*fx* DATEVALUE	
7		*fx* DAVERAGE	

2.   Press the **<Tab>** key to enter the formula into the cell.

3.   Click the *Insert Function* button on the left of the formula bar:

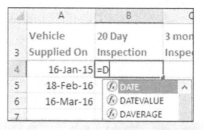

The *Function Arguments* dialog is displayed.

The DATE function demands three numerical arguments: *Year, Month* and *Day.* For example:

=DATE(2020,07,29)

… would return 29th July 2020.

Because the DATE function requires numerical arguments, you need to use the YEAR, MONTH and DAY functions to convert each part of the date into numbers.

tip

You can also use the keyboard shortcut:

<Ctrl>+<A>

…to bring up the *Function Arguments* dialog when you are entering a function.

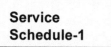

Service
Schedule-1

4. Complete the dialog as follows:

Year	YEAR(A4)	↟	= 2015
Month	MONTH(A4)	↟	= 1
Day	DAY(A4)+20	↟	= 36

Notice that in the *Day* argument, the number 20 has been added to 16 create 36 for the day argument. You can see from the argument result values on the right of the above grab that you are requesting the date: *36th January 2015*. This is not, of course, a valid date.

Fortunately, Excel is intelligent enough to understand that you really require the date: *5th February 2015*.

5. Click the *OK* button.

A date is shown that is 20 days after 16th January 2015:

	A	B
	Vehicle	20 Day
3	Supplied On	Inspection
4	16-Jan-15	5-Feb-15

3   Put a DATE formula in cell C4 that will calculate a date that is three months later than the 20-day inspection date.

This time your dialog should look like this:

Year	YEAR(B4)	↟	= 2015
Month	MONTH(B4)+3	↟	= 5
Day	DAY(B4)	↟	= 5

4   Put a DATE formula in cell D4 that will calculate a date that is one year later than the 3-month inspection date.

This time your dialog should look like this:

Year	YEAR(C4)+1	↟	= 2016
Month	MONTH(C4)	↟	= 5
Day	DAY(C4)	↟	= 5

5   AutoFill the formula in cell D4 to cells E4:G4.

6   AutoFill the formulas in cells B4:G4 to the end of the range.

	A	B	C	D	E	F	G
	Vehicle	20 Day	3 month				
3	Supplied On	Inspection	Inspection	12 Month Services Thereafter...			
4	16-Jan-15	5-Feb-15	5-May-15	5-May-16	5-May-17	5-May-18	5-May-19
5	18-Feb-16	9-Mar-16	9-Jun-16	9-Jun-17	9-Jun-18	9-Jun-19	9-Jun-20
6	16-Mar-16	5-Apr-16	5-Jul-16	5-Jul-17	5-Jul-18	5-Jul-19	5-Jul-20

7   Save your work as *Service Schedule-2*.

important

Why do my times and dates look different from the ones in the screen grabs?

The default formats for times and dates are based upon the *Region Settings* set up in Windows. To view your regional settings:

Type: *Region settings* into the Windows 10 search box and then click *Region settings*.

Windows then displays your current Regional format data:

Short date:	6/26/2019
Long date:	Wednesday, June 26, 2019
Short time:	5:26 PM
Long time:	5:26:30 PM
Change data formats	

The above settings are the default regional formats for the *United States* region. These are the settings used for all of the screen grabs in this book.

Short date:	26/06/2019
Long date:	26 June 2019
Short time:	17:24
Long time:	17:24:45
Change data formats	

The above settings are the default regional formats for the *United Kingdom* region.

There's also a *Change Data Formats* hyperlink that allows you to change the formats if you wish.

These are, of course, only the defaults and you will normally apply a specific format to times as you do at the end of this lesson.

If your region format is set to another country there is no need to change it. Just be aware that some of the screen grabs in this book will be formatted differently to those on your screen.

Lesson 3-12: Enter time values and perform basic time calculations

Serial number recap

In: *Lesson 3-7: Understand date serial numbers,* you learned how Excel combines time and date information in a single date serial number.

Excel represents dates by counting from 1st January 1900 to the present day. For example, the date serial number 2.0 represents midnight (00:00) on 2nd January 1900.

Excel represents time using the decimal part of the serial number. For example, the date serial number 3.5 represents midday on 3rd January 1900.

Excel also allows you to work with pure time values (times that do not have an associated date). In this case, the non-existent date of 0 Jan 1900 is used. For example, the date serial number 0.3333 represents the time 08:00 but does not represent any date.

In this lesson, you'll focus on entering time values into a worksheet without any associated date and learn how to avoid the mistakes commonly made when working with time values.

1 Open *Time Sheet-1* from your sample files folder.

This worksheet contains details of the hours worked by an employee during a single week.

2 Add a start time of 08:00 and finish time 17:00 for Monday.

24-hour notation is the best way to enter times as it is the least error prone and easiest to read.

Type **08:00** into cell B8 and **17:00** into cell C8.

	A	B	C
7	Day	Start	Finish
8	Monday	8:00	17:00

3 Add a start time of 10:00 AM and finish time 6:00 PM for Tuesday.

AM/PM notation is preferred by some users, but is more error prone than the recommended 24-hour notation.

Type **10:00 AM** into cell B9 and **6:00 PM** into cell C9. Make sure that you leave a space between the time and the AM/PM indicator, otherwise Excel will interpret the value as text rather than time.

	A	B	C
7	Day	Start	Finish
8	Monday	8:00	17:00
9	Tuesday	10:00 AM	6:00 PM

Time Sheet-1

4 Complete the rest of the time sheet as follows:

	A	B	C
7	Day	Start	Finish
8	Monday	8:00	17:00
9	Tuesday	10:00 AM	6:00 PM
10	Wednesday	21:00	3:00
11	Thursday	10:00 PM	4:00 AM
12	Friday	8:00	17:00

Depending upon your *Windows Region settings*, your dates and times may display differently to those shown above. See the sidebar on the facing page for more information about how your regional settings affect the default format of dates and times.

5 Examine the date serial numbers in cells B8:C12.

1. Select cells B8:C12.

2. Right-click the selected cells and click *Format Cells…* from the shortcut menu.

3. Click *General* in the *Category* list.

4. Click the *OK* button.

   Notice that all of the time values begin with zero. This is because no date is associated with them. Understanding this is very important when creating time formulas.

   Notice that the time in cell B8 is 0.333333. This is because at 08:00 approximately 33.333333% of the day has elapsed, as eight hours is approximately 33.333333% of 24.

6 Add a formula to cell D8 that will calculate the number of hours worked.

Add the formula **=C8-B8** to cell D8.

	A	B	C	D
7	Day	Start	Finish	Hours Worked
8	Monday	0.333333	0.708333	0.375

The result shows that Frank worked for 37.5% of the day on Monday.

7 Format cells B8:D12 to show times in the 24-hour format.

1. Select cells B8:D12.

2. Right-click the selected cells and click *Format Cells…* from the shortcut menu.

3. From the *Custom* category, set the format to: **hh:mm**

4. Click the *OK* button.

   The number of hours and minutes worked is now shown in cell D8.

	A	B	C	D
7	Day	Start	Finish	Hours Worked
8	Monday	08:00	17:00	09:00
9	Tuesday	10:00	18:00	

8 Save your work as *Time Sheet-2*.

Lesson 3-13: Perform time calculations that span midnight

1 Open *Time Sheet-2* from your sample files folder (if it isn't already open).

2 AutoFill the formula in cell D8 to cells D9:D12.

	A	B	C	D
7	Day	Start	Finish	Hours Worked
8	Monday	8:00	17:00	9:00
9	Tuesday	10:00	18:00	8:00
10	Wednesday	21:00	3:00	##############
11	Thursday	22:00	4:00	#############
12	Friday	8:00	17:00	9:00
13	Total:			

A problem is now revealed. On Wednesday and Thursday, Frank's working times spanned midnight. A row of hashes is shown to signify an error as Excel cannot display a time value that is negative (Frank's Wednesday hours would result in minus 18 hours worked).

3 Correct the formulas in cells D8:D12 so that time is correctly calculated, even when the times span midnight.

Fortunately, it is very easy to correct the formula using the IF logic function covered in: *Lesson 3-5: Use the IF logic function.*

1. Change the formula in cell D8 to the following:

   =IF(C8>B8, C8-B8, C8+1-B8)

   The formula works by adding the number one (representing one day) to the finish time when the finish time is earlier than the start time.

IF	
Logical_test	C8>B8
Value_if_true	C8-B8
Value_if_false	C8+1-B8

2. AutoFill the formula from cell D8 to cells D9:D12.

   The times are now correctly calculated:

	A	B	C	D
7	Day	Start	Finish	Hours Worked
8	Monday	8:00	17:00	9:00
9	Tuesday	10:00	18:00	8:00
10	Wednesday	21:00	3:00	6:00
11	Thursday	22:00	4:00	6:00
12	Friday	8:00	17:00	9:00

4 Add a formula to show the total hours worked this week in cell D13.

Add a SUM function to cell D13 to sum the values in cells D8:D12.

	D
13	=SUM(D8:D12)

Time Sheet-2

The formula doesn't return an error but it seems to produce the wrong answer:

	A	B	C	D
7	Day	Start	Finish	Hours Worked
8	Monday	8:00	17:00	9:00
9	Tuesday	10:00	18:00	8:00
10	Wednesday	21:00	3:00	6:00
11	Thursday	22:00	4:00	6:00
12	Friday	8:00	17:00	9:00
13	Total:			14:00

tip

Another way to sum time serial numbers that exceed 24 hours

In this lesson, you use the **[h]:mm** custom format to display the time data correctly.

The value of **1.5833** then correctly displayed as **38:00**.

The value 1.5833 actually means 158.33% of a 24-hour day, so another method of correcting the result would be to multiply it by 24:

=SUM(D8:D12)*24

...and then to format cell D13 as a number.

The advantage of this method is that it is often easier to work with numerical values than with date serial numbers if you need to perform further mathematical calculations.

You'll see this technique in action in: *Lesson 3-14: Understand common time functions and convert date serial numbers to decimal values.*

tip

You can also open the Format Cells dialog using the shortcut key:

<Ctrl>+<1>

The value in cell D13 is actually correct. The problem lies in the way in which cell D13 is formatted.

Remember that the date serial numbers in cells D8:D12 contain the percentage of each 24-hour day that was worked. When they are added together they will add up to more than one. Because cell D13 is formatted to show times, it will ignore the whole number part of the date/time serial number, believing that this represents a date.

The actual value in cell D13 is 1.583333 and that represents 14:00 on 1st January 1900.

5   Display the value in cell D13 correctly by adjusting the format.

There are two ways to solve this problem. In this lesson a custom format is used. The other potential method is discussed in the sidebar.

Because adding time values is a common requirement, Excel provides a special custom format to display times that exceed 24 hours.

1. Click on cell D13.

2. Click: Home→Number→Dialog Launcher.

    The *Format Cells* dialog appears.

3. Click the *Custom* category.

    Notice that the current format is: **hh:mm**

4. Manually type in the new custom format: **[h]:mm**

    The square brackets around the [h] means that where there is a whole number in the date serial number it should be regarded as time data.

    For example, the date serial number 2.0 will be interpreted as meaning 48 hours and not midnight on 2nd January 1900. The serial number 1.5 will be interpreted as 36 hours and not midday on 1st January 1900.

5. Click the *OK* button.

    The *total hours worked* in cell D13 now displays correctly:

	A	B	C	D
11	Thursday	22:00	4:00	6:00
12	Friday	8:00	17:00	9:00
13	Total:			38:00

6   Save your work as *Time Sheet-3*.

Lesson 3-14: Understand common time functions and convert date serial numbers to decimal values

Excel's primary time functions are NOW, HOUR, MINUTE and SECOND. In this lesson, you'll learn how to use all of them along with some important techniques that are useful when performing calculations with time values.

1   Open *Time Sheet-3* from your sample files folder (if it isn't already open).

2   Add formulas to cells E8:E12 to calculate earnings.

This isn't as straightforward as it first seems.

The actual values in cells D8:D12 represent the percentage of each day that was worked. For example, cell D9 actually contains the value 0.333333, as eight hours are approximately 33.3333% of one 24-hour day.

In order to calculate the correct earnings figure, it is necessary to multiply the date serial number in column D by 24 to convert the date serial number into hours.

1. Type the formula: **=D8*24*$B$5** into cell E8.

    Note the absolute reference for cell B5. This will enable the formula to be AutoFilled to the cells below without adjusting the reference to cell B5.

2. AutoFill the formula in cell E8 down to cells E9:E12.

3. Select cells E8:E13.

4. Click: Home→Number→Comma Style $\boxed{\text{,}}$ to show two decimal places.

    The correct earnings figure is now shown in every case.

5. Use a SUM function to show total earnings for the week in cell E13.

	A	B	C	D	E
5	Hourly Rate:	15.00			
6					
7	Day	Start	Finish	Hours Worked	Earnings
8	Monday	8:00	17:00	9:00	135.00
9	Tuesday	10:00	18:00	8:00	120.00
10	Wednesday	21:00	3:00	6:00	90.00
11	Thursday	22:00	4:00	6:00	90.00
12	Friday	8:00	17:00	9:00	135.00
13	Total:			38:00	570.00

3   Add a NOW function to cell B15 to display the current date and time.

1. Type **Current Date and Time** into cell A15.

Time Sheet-3

tip

Entering a non-volatile current time

The NOW function is very useful but it inserts a volatile date and time. This means that the date and time will change to reflect the current date and time whenever the worksheet opens or is recalculated.

You'll often want to place the current date and time into a worksheet in a non-volatile way. For example, where you want to include a *Date and Time Created* cell at the top of the worksheet, but you never want this date and time to change.

To enter the current time into a cell, press the keys:

<Ctrl>+<Shift>+<;>

(Control plus Shift plus semicolon)

To place the current date into a cell press the keys:

<Ctrl>+<;>

(Control plus semicolon)

tip

Recalculate the workbook or a single sheet using a shortcut key

To recalculate the entire workbook, press:

<F9>

If you have a very large workbook with multiple pages and hundreds of formulas, it can take a significant time to recalculate. In this case, you can recalculate only the currently selected worksheet by pressing:

<Shift>+<F9>

2. Click on cell B15.

3. Type **=NOW**

The tip advises that this function returns the current date and time. This is a little like the TODAY function encountered in *Lesson 3-8: Understand common date functions* except that it returns the current date *and* time rather than midnight on the current date.

The current date and time is the time that the worksheet was last recalculated (you'll learn how to recalculate the worksheet later in this lesson).

4. Press the **<Tab>** key twice. Notice that Excel has added brackets for you to create the formula: **=NOW()**

5. If necessary, widen columns A and B so that they are wide enough to see all of their contents.

4 Add a TIME function to cell B16 to display the current time.

The TIME function works in a similar way to the DATE function encountered in: *Lesson 3-10: Use date offsets to manage projects using the scheduling equation.*

1. Type **Current Time** into cell A16.

2. Click in cell B16.

3. Click: Formulas→Function Library→Date & Time→TIME.

The *Function Arguments* dialog is displayed.

4. Enter the following values for each argument:

5. Click the *OK* button.

The current time appears in cell B16.

5 Re-calculate the worksheet to update the current time.

Click: Formulas→Calculation→Calculate Sheet.

Provided that at least a minute has passed since you created the NOW and TIME functions, you will see the time update to the current time.

6 Save your work as *Time Sheet-4.*

Lesson 3-15: Use the TIME function to offset hours, minutes and seconds

In this lesson, you will use the TIME function in conjunction with the HOUR, MINUTE and SECOND functions to offset time data.

You'll construct a train timetable that will run a service every 10 minutes before 09:00 and every hour thereafter.

1   Open *Train Timetable-1* from your sample files folder.

The formulas in this worksheet will be constructed so that the entire timetable can be automatically updated by simply changing the *First Train* times in column B.

This will work because all of the subsequent journeys will be defined as offsets from the first train's arrival time using the TIME function.

	A	B	C	D	E	F	G
3	Trains run every 10 minutes before 09:00 and every hour at other times.						
4							
5	Route	First Train	Further trains at...				
6	Northern	8:30					
7	Jubilee	8:20					

2   Put formulas into cells C6:K6 that will calculate the arrival times of subsequent trains on the Northern line.

You know that trains arrive every 10 minutes before 09:00 so would expect trains at 08:40, 08:50 and 09:00. After that, you would expect trains each hour at 10:00, 11:00, 12:00...

1.   Click in cell C6.

2.   Click: Formulas→Function Library→Date & Time→TIME.

The *Function Arguments* dialog appears.

3.   Enter the following values for each argument:

TIME			
Hour	HOUR(B6)	↑	= 8
Minute	MINUTE(B6)+10	↑	= 40
Second	SECOND(B6)	↑	= 0

4.   Click the *OK* button.

The correct time of the next train appears in cell C6.

	A	B	C	D
5	Route	First Train	Further trains at...	
6	Northern	8:30	8:40	

5.   AutoFill the formula in cell C6 to cells D6:K6.

Unsurprisingly, the formula applies an offset of 10 minutes to each cell:

Train Timetable-1

	A	B	C	D	E	F
5	Route	First Train	Further trains at...			
6	Northern	8:30	8:40	8:50	9:00	9:10

Unfortunately, that isn't what is needed. After the 09:00 train there shouldn't be another until 10:00.

To fix the formula, you need to add an IF function that will check the time of the previous train. If the time is later than or equal to 09:00, the increment should be one hour and not 10 minutes (the IF function was covered in: *Lesson 3-5: Use the IF logic function*).

6. Copy the function from cell C6 *excluding the = sign* by clicking in cell C6, selecting the function in the formula bar (but not the = sign) and then copying (by pressing **<Ctrl>+<C>** or by right-clicking and then selecting *Copy* from the shortcut menu).

> *fx* =TIME(HOUR(B6),MINUTE(B6)+10,SECOND(B6))

7. Press the **<ESCAPE>** key to exit cell edit mode

8. Click cell C6 again and then press the **<Delete>** key to remove the existing formula from the cell.

9. Click: Formulas→Function Library→Logical→IF.

The *Function Arguments* dialog is displayed.

10. Paste the function (previously copied) into the **Value_if_true** and **Value_if_false** text boxes.

The dialog should now look like this:

Logical_test	
Value_if_true	TIME(HOUR(B6),MINUTE(B6)+10,
Value_if_false	TIME(HOUR(B6),MINUTE(B6)+10,

11. Set the Logical_test argument to:

HOUR(B6)>=9

12. Edit the *Value_if_true* argument so that it offsets the previous train time by one hour rather than ten minutes:

TIME(HOUR(B6)+1,MINUTE(B6),SECOND(B6))

13. Click the *OK* button.

14. AutoFill cell C6 to cells D6:K6.

3   AutoFill cells C6:K6 down to cells C7:K10 to complete the timetable.

The timetable is now complete and correct:

	A	B	C	D	E	F	G
5	Route	First Train	Further trains at...				
6	Northern	8:30	8:40	8:50	9:00	10:00	11:00
7	Jubilee	8:20	8:30	8:40	8:50	9:00	10:00
8	Circle	8:27	8:37	8:47	8:57	9:07	10:07

4   Save your work as *Train Timetable-2*.

note

The NOT logical function

This session introduces the two Excel logical functions:

AND
OR

There's another logical function that can sometimes make your formulas easier to read (though it is never actually necessary).

This is the NOT function that will invert a logical result.

In other words, it will change TRUE to FALSE and FALSE to TRUE.

The rule:

If Sales > Target AND Years Service > 2

OR

Years Service > 5

Could also be written as:

If Sales > Target AND NOT Years Service < 2

OR

Years Service NOT < 5

Lesson 3-16: Use the AND and OR functions to construct complex Boolean criteria

When using logical functions such as IF, COUNTIF and SUMIF, you need to construct a logical test (sometimes also called Boolean criteria) that will return TRUE or FALSE.

You've already used simple Boolean criteria such as:

E9<=35

This Boolean expression returns TRUE if the value in cell E9 is less than or equal to 35, otherwise it returns FALSE.

In this lesson, you'll use the logical functions AND and OR to create more complex Boolean criteria.

The sample file for this lesson computes bonuses for employees, based upon the following rules:

Bonus rules
A bonus of 2% of sales will be paid to employees who meet the following criteria:
1/ Sales are above target.
2/ Have worked for the company for more than two years.
Note: *Employees with more than five years service will receive the bonus even if sales are below target.*

Here are the bonus figures for the first three employees:

	A	B	C	D	E
9	Name	Years service	Sales	Target	Bonus
10	Johnny Caine	2	11,000	9,000	-
11	George Marley	7	7,000	9,000	140
12	Betty Anan	3	13,000	5,000	260

- You can see that Johnny Caine exceeded his target but received no bonus because he only has two years' service.

- George Marley has over five years' service and thus receives a bonus even though he didn't reach his sales target.

- Betty Annan has three years' service and she has also exceeded her sales target, so she receives a bonus.

Another way of expressing the logical test that governs when bonus will be paid is:

If Sales > Target AND Years Service > 2
OR
Years Service > 5

A logical expression can be created to implement the rules using Excel's AND and OR functions.

Here's how you can use the AND function to test that Johnny Caine's sales are above his target AND that he has more than two years' service:

Bonus Calculator-1

=AND(C10>D10, B10>2)

The AND function will return TRUE only if both expressions evaluate TRUE. In Johnny's case, it will return FALSE because Johnny only has two years' service.

You also need to check whether the employee has over five years' service. Here's how you can use the OR function to do this:

=OR(B10>5, AND(C10>D10, B10>2)**)**

The OR function will return TRUE if either of the arguments return TRUE. In Johnny's case, this will still return FALSE as he also has less than five years' service, but in George's case it would return TRUE since George has seven years' service.

Now that you understand how to construct the logical test for the bonus calculation, you can create the IF function for the sample file.

1   Open *Bonus Calculator-1* from your sample files folder.

    1.   Click in cell E10.

    2.   Click: Formulas→Function Library→Logical→IF.

    3.   Enter the following values into the dialog (see text above for explanation):

Logical_test	OR(B10>5,AND(C10>D10,B10>2))
Value_if_true	C10*0.02
Value_if_false	0

    4.   Click the *OK* button.

    5.   AutoFill the formula from cell E10 to the end of the range.

	A	B	C	D	E
9	Name	Years service	Sales	Target	Bonus
10	Johnny Caine	2	11,000	9,000	-
11	George Marley	7	7,000	9,000	140
12	Betty Anan	3	13,000	5,000	260
13	Paris Winfrey	1	11,000	10,000	-
14	Ozzy Dickens	5	9,000	9,000	-
15	Johnny Roberts	2	6,000	7,000	-
16	Charles Monroe	8	10,000	5,000	200

2   Save your work as *Bonus Calculator-2*.

note

Gross profit and mark up

Newcomers to the retail business often confuse mark up with gross profit.

In general business, gross profit is the more widely accepted metric when discussing profits.

Here's an example of mark up:

Bob buys a watch for $500 and marks it up by 50%. This means that he adds 50% to the cost price and sells it for $750. In this case, the formula is:

Selling Price = Cost Price * (1+MarkUp)

$750 = $500 * 1.5

Here's an example of gross profit:

Bill buys a hard disk for $100. His company needs to make 50% gross profit on all goods sold. This means that they need to sell the hard drive for $200, making 50% of the selling price ($100) in profit. In this case, the formula is:

Selling Price = Cost Price/ (1-Gross Profit%)

$200 = $100/(1-0.5)

You can see from the above example that a gross profit of 50% is the same as a mark up of 100%.

Terminology

I use the terms *Gross Profit* when discussing both cash amounts and percentages.

There's a lot of controversy about correct terminology. Some purists would argue that the correct terms are *Gross Margin* (or simply *Margin*) for *% Gross Profit*, and *Gross Profit* for a Gross Profit cash value.

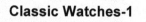

Classic Watches-1

Lesson 3-17: Understand calculation options (manual and automatic)

It is possible to change the calculation mode used by Excel. The three modes available are:

1. *Automatic:* Whenever you change the value in a cell, all values that reference that cell are automatically recalculated. This is the default.

2. *Automatic except for data tables:* This is similar to *Automatic*, but data tables will only be recalculated when the **<F9>** key is pressed. (you will learn about data tables later, in: *Lesson 6-1: Create a single-input data table*).

3. *Manual:* Calculation will only take place when the **<F9>** key is pressed.

Most users are unaware that the calculation options exist and leave Excel set to the default *Automatic* at all times.

So why would you ever need the other two options? The answer is that Excel worksheets can be very large indeed (over a million rows and over 16,500 columns). A workbook could contain many millions (or even many billions) of formulas. Such a workbook is very unusual, but could take a substantial amount of time to recalculate. You wouldn't want to have to pause for recalculation every time you edited any cell in such a workbook, so you would switch to one of the other two calculation modes under those circumstances.

1 Open *Classic Watches-1* from your sample files folder.

This worksheet calculates the selling prices for a classic watch dealer.

	A	B	C	D	E
5			Gross Profit	33%	
7	Description	Date	Cost price	Selling Price	Profit
8	Breitling Duograph 18K	1948	11,500.00	17,164.18	5,664.18
9	Cartier Tank 18K	1974	3,200.00	4,776.12	1,576.12
10	Rolex Tudor Oyster	1966	300.00	447.76	147.76

The dealer makes 33% Gross Profit (sometimes also called *Margin, Gross Margin* or *Gross Profit Margin*) on all watch sales (see sidebar for a discussion of the difference between gross profit and mark up).

The formula in column D:

=C8/(1-$D$5)

... calculates the selling price based upon the gross profit stated in cell D5.

2 Change the gross profit to 25%.

When the value in cell D5 is changed to 25%, the worksheet recalculates to show the new selling prices.

important

Calculation mode is set at application level

It would be quite reasonable to assume that the calculation mode could be set for a specific worksheet or workbook. Unfortunately, Excel doesn't work in this way, causing great confusion amongst users who begin to believe that Excel is randomly changing the calculation mode.

You can't set the calculation mode for a single worksheet or workbook. When you change the calculation mode, it also changes for all other worksheets and all other open workbooks.

Consider the following scenario:

1/ You create a workbook and set the calculation mode to *Manual*.

2/ You then open another workbook without closing the first one. The second workbook is also in manual calculation mode because only one calculation mode can exist for all open workbooks.

Things become even more confusing because the calculation mode is saved with the workbook.

Suppose that you had two workbooks called *Manual* and *Automatic*. The first was saved in manual calculation mode and the second saved in automatic calculation mode.

If you open the *Manual* workbook followed by the *Automatic* workbook, then both workbooks will be set to *Manual* calculation mode, as this was the mode of the first workbook opened.

If you open the *Automatic* workbook followed by the *Manual* workbook, then both workbooks will be set to *Automatic* calculation mode.

	A	B	C	D	E
5			Gross Profit	25%	
7	Description	Date	Cost price	Selling Price	Profit
8	Breitling Duograph 18K	1948	11,500.00	15,333.33	3,833.33
9	Cartier Tank 18K	1974	3,200.00	4,266.67	1,066.67
10	Rolex Tudor Oyster	1966	300.00	400.00	100.00

This is exactly what you would expect because this workbook is using the default *automatic* calculation mode.

3   Change the calculation mode to manual.

Click: Formulas→Calculation→Calculation Options→Manual.

4   Change the gross profit to 30%.

This time nothing happens to the other values, because the worksheet will only recalculate when you explicitly request a recalculation.

	A	B	C	D	E
5			Gross Profit	30%	
7	Description	Date	Cost price	Selling Price	Profit
8	Breitling Duograph 18K	1948	11,500.00	15,333.33	3,833.33
9	Cartier Tank 18K	1974	3,200.00	4,266.67	1,066.67
10	Rolex Tudor Oyster	1966	300.00	400.00	100.00

5   Manually recalculate the workbook.

EITHER

Press the **<F9>** key.

OR

Click: Formulas→Calculation→Calculate Now.

The workbook recalculates to show the new selling prices at 30% gross profit.

	A	B	C	D	E
5			Gross Profit	30%	
7	Description	Date	Cost price	Selling Price	Profit
8	Breitling Duograph 18K	1948	11,500.00	16,428.57	4,928.57
9	Cartier Tank 18K	1974	3,200.00	4,571.43	1,371.43
10	Rolex Tudor Oyster	1966	300.00	428.57	128.57

Note that you can also click:

Formulas→Calculation→Calculate Sheet

You would use this option to save calculation time when other worksheets in the workbook contained large numbers of formulas. In the case of this simple workbook (that contains only one worksheet), there is no calculation time difference between using *Calculate Now* and *Calculate Sheet*.

6   Change the calculation mode back to automatic.

Click: Formulas→Calculation→Calculation Options→Automatic.

7   Save your work as *Classic Watches-2*.

note

ASCII

ASCII (pronounced Askey) is an acronym for: *American Standard Code for Information Interchange.*

In 1968, the US President (Lyndon B. Johnson) ordered that all computers purchased by the United States Federal Government must support ASCII.

ASCII defines a number (between 0 and 127) for the numbers **0-9**, lowercase letters **a** to **z**, uppercase letters **A** to **Z**, basic punctuation symbols, the space character, and 33 non-printable control characters (many of which are now obsolete).

For example, the ASCII code for an upper-case **A** character is 65.

Excel has two ASCII related functions:

CHAR(number)

This function returns an ASCII character from the corresponding ASCII code. For example:

=CHAR(65)

… would result in an upper-case **A** character appearing in the cell.

CODE(text)

This function returns an ASCII code number from a character. For example:

=CODE("A")

… would return the number 65 (the ASCII code number for an upper-case A).

Lesson 3-18: Concatenate strings using the concatenation operator (&)

About strings

In the world of computers, letters, numbers, spaces, punctuation marks and other symbols are referred to as *characters*.

When several characters are grouped together (perhaps to spell out words), they are referred to as a *string.*

Here are some examples of strings:

Abc123

John Smith

Strings may be of any length, from a single character to thousands of words.

The concatenation operator (&)

When numbers are added together, the addition operator (+) is used to return the sum of the numbers. For example, the formula:

 … returns:

The concatenation operator joins two strings together. For example, the formula:

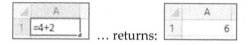 … returns:

Concatenation is rarely used with numbers. It is more likely that you may wish to concatenate *Title*, *First Name* and *Last Name* cells to produce a full name. For example:

 … returns:

Note the use of double quotation marks to indicate that each value is a string.

In this example, it would be nice to have spaces between each of the words. To do this, you would concatenate a string containing only a space between each word. Here's how it's done:

 … returns:

1   Open *Classic Watches-2* from your sample files folder (if it isn't already open).

Classic Watches-2

note

Using a control code to add a line break

In the (previous page) sidebar, it was stated that there are 33 non-printable control characters defined by ASCII, many of which are now obsolete.

Two of these control codes can sometimes be very useful when you need to create a formula that outputs multiple-line text. These are:

Line Feed (ASCII 10) and
Carriage Return (ASCII 13)

The term *Carriage Return* comes from the age of mechanical typewriters. In computer terms it is a control code that is used to move the cursor to the first position on the same line. A *Carriage Return* control code is often used with a *Line Feed* control code in order to begin a new line. This sequence is often referred to as CRLF (or, in Excel terms, =CHR(10) & CHR(13).

To force a line break in a cell Excel only requires a line feed.

Here's an example of concatenating an ASCII 10 control code (in a cell with word-wrap enabled) in order to force a line break:

⊿	A
1	="One, Two"

Results in:

⊿	A
1	One, Two

... While

⊿	A
1	="One,"& CHR(10) & "Two"

Results in:

⊿	A
1	One, Two

2 Type **Classified Ad** into cell F7 and apply the *Heading 3* style.

To apply the *Heading 3* style, select cell F7 and then click:

Home→Styles→Style Gallery→Titles and Headings→Heading 3

Cell styles were covered in depth in Session 4 of the *Essential Skills* book in this series.

Cells F8:F17 will contain text to be included in a classified ad listing in the local newspaper. You want to show the description of the watch, the year of manufacture and the selling price.

⊿	A	B	C	D	E
7	Description	Date	Cost price	Selling Price	Profit
8	Breitling Duograph 18K	1948	11,500.00	16,428.57	4,928.57

3 Round the values in cells D8:D17 to the nearest five dollars.

The Breitling Duograph is priced at $16,428.57. It would be cleaner to round all of the prices up (or down) to the nearest five dollars. This can easily be achieved using the MROUND (multiple round) function.

1. Change the formula in cell D8 from:

   =C8/(1-$D$5)

   TO

   =MROUND(C8/(1-$D$5),5)

2. AutoFill the formula to the end of the range.

4 Use the concatenation operator to place the classified ad into cell F8 in the format:
Breitling Duograph 18K (1948) -$16,430

As described in the introduction to this lesson, this can easily be achieved using the concatenation operator. The correct formula is:

f_x	=A8 & " (" & B8 & ") -$" & D8

This very nearly provides the required result:

⊿	E	F	G	H	I
7	Profit	Classified Ad			
8	4,930.00	Breitling Duograph 18K (1948) -$16430			

The only thing that isn't correct is the comma thousand separator in the cash price of the watch ($16430 should be $16,430). In the next lesson, you'll discover how to solve this problem using the TEXT function.

5 AutoFill the formula in cell F8 to cells F9:F17.

⊿	E	F	G	H	I
7	Profit	Classified Ad			
8	4,930.00	Breitling Duograph 18K (1948) -$16430			
9	1,370.00	Cartier Tank 18K (1974) -$4570			
10	130.00	Rolex Tudor Oyster (1966) -$430			

6 Save your work as *Classic Watches-3*.

Lesson 3-19: Use the TEXT function to format numerical values as strings

Custom format strings recap

The TEXT function allows numbers to be explicitly formatted as strings. The *Essential Skills* book in this series extensively covers the (rather cryptic) formatting codes available in Excel.

Zeroes are used in formatting codes to define the number of decimal places that are required, along with leading and trailing zeroes. Here are some examples (reproduced from the *Essential Skills* book).

Custom Format String	Value	Display
0	1234.56	1235
0.0	1234.56	1234.6
	1234.5	1234.5
	.5	0.5
0.00	1234.56	1234.56
	1234.5	1234.50
	.5	0.50
00.000	4.56	04.560
0.000	1234.56	1234.560

The hash symbol (#) is mainly used to add comma separators to thousands and millions. Here are some examples (once again, reproduced from the *Essential Skills* book).

Custom Format String	Value	Display
#	123.4500	123
#.##	123.45	123.45
	123.50	123.5
#,#	1234.56	1,235
#,#.##	1234.56	1,234.56
	1234.50	1,234.5
	12341234.56	12,341,234.56

Because the hash symbol can be used in conjunction with zeroes, it is also possible to indicate that you want both thousand separators *and* a specific number of leading or trailing zeroes.

Custom Format String	Value	Display
#,#0.00	12341234.5	12,341,234.50

Classic Watches-3

https://thesmartmethod.com

note

The TEXTJOIN function

The (hugely useful) TEXTJOIN function is unfamiliar to most Excel 365 users as it was only added in February 2016.

The TEXTJOIN function syntax is:

TEXTJOIN(delimiter, ignore_empty, text1, [text2], …)

This new function makes it very easy to add spaces or commas between text strings. Here is an example:

	A	B	C	D
1	First	Middle	Last	Full Name
2	John	Paul	Smith	John, Paul, Smith
3	Henry		Jones	Henry, Jones

In the above example a TEXTJOIN function has been placed in cell D2 and then AutoFilled down to cell D3.

The argument values used were:

Delimiter	", "
Ignore_empty	TRUE
Text1	A2:C2

The *Delimiter* argument has been specified as a comma followed by a space.

The *Ignore_empty* argument prevents two commas from being added between *Henry* and *Jones*.

The TEXTJOIN function's ability to simply concatenate a range will solve many concatenation problems that would previously have been very tedious using the CONCAT (or older CONCATENATE) functions.

1 Open *Classic Watches-3* from your sample files folder (if it isn't already open).

2 Delete the contents of cells F8:F17.

3 Use the CONCAT function to place the classified ad into cell F8 in the format:
Breitling Duograph 18K (1948) - $16,430

The concatenation operator (&) used in the last lesson provides a quick and easy way to concatenate text:

f_x	=A8 & " (" & B8 & ") -$" &D8

It would be possible to use the TEXT function in conjunction with the concatenation operator (&) to construct the formula, but this approach would result in the formula:

f_x	=A8 & " (" & B8 & ") -" &TEXT(D8, "$#,#0")

… which is difficult to read and prone to error. Instead, you'll use the CONCAT function.

1. Click in cell F8.

2. Click: Formulas→Function Library→Text→CONCAT.

3. Populate the dialog as follows:

CONCATENATE

Text1	A8	↑	= "Breitling Duograph 18K"
Text2	" ("	↑	= " ("
Text3	B8	↑	= "1948"
Text4	") -"	↑	= ") -"
Text5	TEXT(D8, "$#,#0")	↑	= "$16,430"

Note that each string is enclosed in double quotation marks to denote text.

Note also the use of the TEXT function with a reference to cell D8 followed by the custom format string:

"$#,#0"

This format string means "show a leading dollar sign, show a comma after thousands and show only whole numbers (no decimal places)".

4. Click the *OK* button.

The text is displayed as specified:

	F	G	H	I
7	Classified Ad			
8	Breitling Duograph 18K (1948) - $16,430			

4 AutoFill cell F8 to the end of the range (cells F9:F17).

5 Save your work as *Classic Watches-4*.

important

Allow for formatting characters when using the LEFT RIGHT and MID functions

Consider a cell that contains the value 28 in cell A1 and has been formatted as *currency* using the dollar currency prefix. The cell would display the value:

$28.00

But the actual value in the cell (and displayed on the formula bar) would be:

28

If you were to extract the first character using the LEFT function

=LEFT(A1, 1)

...you would extract 2 and not $ because the $ character is simply displayed as a result of the cell's formatting and is not part of the value in the cell.

Lesson 3-20: Extract text from fixed width strings using the LEFT, RIGHT and MID functions

In *Lesson 2-1: Split fixed width data using Text to Columns*, you learned how to extract fixed width data using Excel's *Text to Columns* feature.

It is also possible to split data using Excel's Flash Fill feature (covered extensively in the *Essential Skills* book in this series).

While these methods work well, you'll often need to extract data dynamically using a formula. In this lesson, you'll use the LEFT, RIGHT and MID functions to do just that.

1 Open *Best Selling Books-1* from your sample files folder.

This worksheet lists some of the bestselling fiction books of all time:

	A	B	C	D	E
3	Title	Author	Year	Copies (millions)	ISBN-13
4	A Tale of Two Cities	Charles Dickens	1859	200	978-0141439600
5	The Lord of the Rings	J.R.R. Tolkein	1954	150	978-0618640157

For this lesson, the interesting data is in column E: the *International Standard Book Number* (ISBN-13).

ISBN numbers are a good example of fixed-width strings. At first they simply seem to be a jumble of numbers but they actually contain four discrete pieces of data:

	A	B	C	D
17	Anatomy of an ISBN Number			
18	Digits 1-3	EAN (European Article Number)		
19	Digit 4	Group Identifier (country or language code)		
20	Digits 5-12	publisher prefix and title identifier		
21	Digit 13	Check digit (proves accuracy)		

2 Use a LEFT function to extract the EAN from the ISBN code.

You know that the leftmost three digits represent the EAN. The LEFT function extracts a given number of characters from the left part of a string.

1. Click in cell F4.

2. Click: Formulas→Function Library→Text→LEFT.

3. Complete the dialog as follows:

Text	E4	↑	= "978-0141439600"
Num_chars	3	↑	= 3
		=	"978"

4. Click the *OK* button.

Best Selling Books-1

Converting a textual result to a numerical result

In this lesson, you extract several numeric codes from an ISBN number.

Notice that the results are left aligned in each cell. This tells you that they are textual, rather than numeric values.

Often you will wish the results to be numeric values. There are many ways to do this in Excel.

Multiply by a numeric value

To convert the textual return value of a formula to a true number, simply multiply the result of the formula by 1.

For example, to return the EAN as a numeric value you would use the following formula:

=LEFT(E4,3)*1

Use a mathematical operator upon the textual value

It is interesting to note that there are many other mathematical operations that will achieve the same result, such as adding 0 (+0), dividing by 1 (/1) adding two negative signs in front of the number (--) and even raising to the power of 1 (^1).

Use the VALUE function

There's also a function-based method using the VALUE function. You could wrap the LEFT function with a VALUE function like this:

=VALUE(LEFT(E4,3))

The EAN is extracted into cell F4.

3 Use a RIGHT function to extract the Check Digit from the ISBN code.

You know that the rightmost single digit represents the *Check Digit*. The RIGHT function extracts a given number of digits from the right part of a string.

1. Click in cell I4.

2. Click: Formulas→Function Library→Text→RIGHT.

3. Complete the dialog as follows:

Text	E4	⬆	=	'978-0141439600'
Num_chars	1	⬆	=	1
			=	'0'

4. Click the *OK* button.

The *Check Digit* is extracted into cell I4.

4 Use a MID function to extract the Group from the ISBN code.

The MID function extracts text from within a string. You know that digit 4 is the *Group Identifier* that indicates the language that the book is written in. Because the ISBN has a hyphen between the third and fourth digits, you'll have to extract a single character from position five in the string.

1. Click in cell G4.

2. Click: Formulas→Function Library→Text→MID.

3. Complete the dialog as follows:

Text	E4	⬆	=	'978-0141439600'
Start_num	5	⬆	=	5
Num_chars	1	⬆	=	1
			=	'0'

4. Click the *OK* button.

The *Group* is extracted into cell G4.

5 Use a MID function to extract the *Publisher and Title* code from the ISBN code.

This time, the correct arguments for the dialog will be:

Text	E4	⬆	=	'978-0141439600'
Start_num	6	⬆	=	6
Num_chars	8	⬆	=	8
			=	'14143960'

6 AutoFill the formulas in cells F4:I4 to cells F15:I15.

You can now see from the Group (country or language code) that *Le Petit Prince* was published in French.

7 Save your work as *Best Selling Books-2*.

Lesson 3-21: Extract text from delimited strings using the FIND and LEN functions

Here are two examples of international telephone numbers.

+44 (0)113-4960227 (a UK telephone number)
+356 (0)2138-3393 (a Maltese telephone number)

The *country code* (or international dialing code) is shown as a + symbol followed by one or more numbers. The *NDD* (National Direct Dialing prefix) is shown in brackets. This is the access code used to make a call within the relevant country but it is omitted when calling from outside the country. The *Area Code* consists of the numbers after the closing bracket but before the hyphen.

In this lesson, you'll use the FIND and LEN functions, in combination with the LEFT and MID functions, to extract the country code, area code and phone number from an international telephone number.

1   Open *Phone Book-1* from your sample files folder.

2   Insert a FIND function into cell C4 to find the first occurrence of an opening bracket within the telephone number.

   1.   Click in cell C4.

   2.   Click: Formulas→Function Library→Text→FIND.

      The FIND function demands three arguments. The first is the character to find (in this case the opening bracket), the second is the text to search within (in this case the telephone number in cell B4). There's also an optional argument that allows you to begin the search at a specified position within the string.

   3.   Complete the dialog as follows:

Find_text	"(	↑	=	"("
Within_text	B4	↑	=	"+44 (0)113-4960227"
Start_num		↑	=	number

      Note that you don't have to manually type the quotation marks around the text in the *Find_text* argument. Excel will helpfully add them for you automatically.

   4.   Click the *OK* button.

      The number 5 is shown in cell C4. This is because the opening bracket is positioned five characters from the left of the string **+44 (**. Note that the space before the opening bracket is counted as a character.

3   Insert a FIND function into cell D4 to find the first occurrence of a closing bracket within the telephone number.

    Repeat *Step 2,* but use a closing bracket for the *Find_text* argument.

4   Insert a FIND function into cell E4 to find the first occurrence of a hyphen within the telephone number.

Phone Book-1

note

Avoid leading and trailing spaces with the TRIM function

In *Step 6* you extracted the country code using the LEFT function. This could result in strings with a trailing space such as:

"+44 "
"+356 "

Because you can't see the trailing space, this doesn't seem to matter.

Trailing spaces cause many problems when comparing data because strings that appear to be the same visually are, in fact, different:

="+44 " = "+44"
(returns FALSE)

="+44" = "+44"
(returns TRUE)

For this reason, it is good practice to always remove leading and trailing spaces using the TRIM function.

You could have used the TRIM function in *Step 6* like this:

=TRIM(LEFT(B4,C4-1))

If this seems a little too complex, you could also have placed the trimmed country code in a different column and then used the untrimmed result as an argument like this:

=TRIM(G4)

Repeat *Step 2,* but use a hyphen ("-") for the *Find_text* argument.

5 Insert a LEN function into cell F4 to find the total number of characters in the telephone number.

1. Click in cell F4.

2. Click: Formulas→Text→LEN.

3. Click cell B4 for the single argument for this function.

4. Click the *OK* button.

    The length of the telephone number string (18 characters) is displayed in cell F4.

6 Insert a LEFT function into cell G4 to extract the country code.

The correct arguments are:

Text	B4	↑	= "+44 (0)113-4960227"
Num_chars	C4-1	↑	= 4

Note that C4-1 is used for the number of characters to avoid returning the opening bracket. This could result in a trailing space (see sidebar for a way to remove trailing spaces).

7 Insert a MID function into cell H4 to extract the area code.

The MID function was covered in: *Lesson 3-20: Extract text from fixed width strings using the LEFT, RIGHT and MID functions.*

The correct arguments are:

Text	B4	↑	= "+44 (0)113-4960227"
Start_num	D4+1	↑	= 8
Num_chars	E4-D4-1	↑	= 3

8 Insert a MID function into cell I4 to extract the phone number.

The correct arguments are:

Text	B4	↑	= "+44 (0)113-4960227"
Start_num	E4+1	↑	= 12
Num_chars	F4-E4	↑	= 7

9 AutoFill cells C4:I4 into cells C5:I18.

	A	B	C	D	E	F	G	H	I
			Position of opening bracket (	Position of closing bracket)	Position of Hyphen	Length of entire string	Country Code	Area Code	Phone Number
3	Company	Telephone							
4	Books A Million	+44 (0)113-4960227	5	7	11	18	+44	113	4960227
5	Maltese Books	+356 (0)2138-3393	6	8	13	17	+356	2138	3393

10 Hide columns C:F.

Select columns C:F, right click the mouse and then click *Hide* from the shortcut menu.

11 Save your work as *Phone Book-2.*

important

The XLOOKUP dynamic array function has now replaced VLOOKUP in Excel 365

The Excel 365 *July 2020 semi-annual version (2002)* added support for dynamic arrays to Excel.

Dynamic arrays are a huge step forward and change best-practice for many business tasks in Excel 365.

Unfortunately dynamic arrays are incompatible with Excel 2019 and earlier versions.

If your workbooks need to be used by non-Excel 365 users you will not be able to use functions that rely upon dynamic arrays.

XLOOKUP is the new dynamic array function that completely replaces VLOOKUP. It is easier to use and far more powerful. If you do not need to share your workbooks with users of older Excel versions you should no longer use VLOOKUP in new work.

Because VLOOKUP was one of the most used Excel functions in the past, you will need a good understanding of it in order to understand legacy workbooks that were created using older version of Excel.

You'll learn about dynamic arrays later, in: *Session Four: Working with Dynamic Arrays.*

You'll learn about the modern XLOOKUP replacement for VLOOKUP later, in:

Lesson 4-18: Understand XLOOKUP (part one) and *Lesson 4-19: Understand XLOOKUP (part two)*

Invoice-1

Lesson 3-22: Use a VLOOKUP function for an exact lookup

Consider the following worksheet:

	A	B	C	D	E
5	Code	Description	Date	Cost price	Selling Price
6	BR48	Breitling Duograph 18K	1948	11,500.00	16,430.00
7	CA74	Cartier Tank 18K	1974	3,200.00	4,570.00
8	RO66	Rolex Tudor Oyster	1966	300.00	430.00

The retailer has created a stock code to save time when creating invoices. The code is made up of the first two letters of the watch description, along with the last two numbers of the date of manufacture.

When provided with a stock code, the VLOOKUP function can scan all of the codes in column A until a match is found and then return a value from the same row for any of the other columns.

1 **Open *Invoice-1* from your sample files folder.**

	A	B	C
5	Code	Description	Price
6	CA74		
7			
8			
9		Total:	-

In this lesson, you will create a VLOOKUP formula that will automatically return the *Description* of any watch into column B when the user enters a stock code into column A.

2 **Convert the range A5:G15 on the *Stock* worksheet into a table named: Stock**

This was covered in: *Lesson 1-13: Convert a range into a table and add a total row* and *Lesson 1-19: Name a table and create an automatic structured table reference.*

When working with the VLOOKUP function it is best practice to use a table for the *Table_array* argument (see sidebar on facing page).

Using a table will make the data dynamic. In other words, the VLOOKUP function will still work correctly if you add and remove rows from the *Stock* table.

3 **Insert a VLOOKUP function into cell B6 on the *Invoice* worksheet to find the description that matches the *Code* in cell A6 on the *Stock* worksheet.**

1. Click in cell B6 on the *Invoice* worksheet.

2. Click: Formulas→Function Library→ Lookup & Reference→VLOOKUP.

The VLOOKUP *Function Arguments* dialog appears. It can be seen that the VLOOKUP function has three required arguments (shown in bold face) and one optional argument:

important

It is best practice to use tables with your VLOOKUP functions

In this lesson I've shown you how to construct a VLOOKUP function that uses a table for the *Table_array* argument.

This has been best practice since the release of Excel 2007, but it wasn't possible in Excel 2003 as the (fantastically useful) table feature wasn't available.

In worksheets constructed using pre-2007 versions of Excel (or those created by novice users) it is common to see absolute range references for *Table_array* arguments like this:

Table_array	$A$5:$G$15

More sophisticated users of pre-2007 Excel versions learned how to use *Range Names*. (You'll learn all about Range Names in: *Session Five: Using Names and the Formula Auditing Tools*).

When you see a *Range Name* reference, it looks the same as a table reference. This example shows the use of a *Range Name* also called *Stock*:

Table_array	Stock

While *Range Names* were best practice in pre-2007 Excel versions, they have a fatal flaw as they are not truly dynamic.

Users of earlier versions had to resort to a complex work-around to make their Range Names dynamic. You'll learn about this workaround in: *Lesson 5-6: Create dynamic formula-based range names using the OFFSET function.*

This information is provided so that you will understand any older Excel worksheets you may inherit, (or worksheets that were created by users that haven't yet learned how to use tables).

Lookup_value		⬆	=	any
Table_array		⬆	=	number
Col_index_num		⬆	=	number
Range_lookup		⬆	=	logical

4 Set the *Lookup_value* argument to: **A6**

This is the cell on the *Invoice* worksheet that provides the value to be searched for in column A of the *Stock* worksheet. You want to look up the description for the watch that has the code *CA74*. This is contained in cell **A6**.

Lookup_value	A6	⬆	=	`CA74`

5 Set the *Table_array* argument to: **Stock**

The table array is the *range, table* or *name* (see sidebar) you will search for a match to the value in cell A6. VLOOKUP always searches the left-most column of the *range, table* or *name*.

Type: **Stock** into the *Table_array* text box.

Table_array	Stock	⬆

It is best practice to use a table for the *Table_array* argument (see sidebar).

6 Set the *Col_index_num* argument to: **2**

	A	B	C	D	E
5	Code ▾	Description ▾	Date ▾	Cost price ▾	Selling Price ▾
6	BR48	Breitling Duograph 18K	1948	11,500.00	16,430.00
7	CA74	Cartier Tank 18K	1974	3,200.00	4,570.00

Counting from left to right, the *Col_index_num* argument is the column that contains the value you want to return. In this case, it is the *Description* column, so you want to return column **2**.

Col_index_num	2	⬆	=	2

7 Set the *Range_lookup* argument to: **FALSE**

Beginners often overlook this vital argument because it is optional.

If it is left blank, VLOOKUP will return an inexact match. Later, in *Lesson 3-25: Use a VLOOKUP function for an inexact lookup*, you'll find out why that might be useful, but in this case you want an error to be returned if the stock code is not found, so it is vital to set this argument to **FALSE**.

Range_lookup	FALSE	⬆	=	FALSE

8 Click the *OK* button.

The description of the *Cartier Tank 18K* is returned to cell B6.

	A	B
6	CA74	Cartier Tank 18K

9 Save your work as *Invoice-2*.

note

VLOOKUP is usually a better solution than SWITCH

The SWITCH function is mainly intended to offer a simpler and more elegant alternative to many common uses of nested IF functions.

This doesn't mean that using the SWITCH function provides a better solution than VLOOKUP.

You could have completed this lesson by using a VLOOKUP function like this:

1. Make the range A27:B32 into a table and name it: **Category**

2. Add this VLOOKUP function into cell E4:

=VLOOKUP(
D4, Category, 2,FALSE)

3. AutoFill to the end of the range.

This solution would allow users to add or edit rows in the Category table.

Lesson 3-23: Use the SWITCH function

In: *Lesson 3-22: Use a VLOOKUP function for an exact lookup,* you used a VLOOKUP function to return price information from a watch retailer's constantly changing stock list.

When you need to lookup values from this type of dynamically changing table VLOOKUP is always the best approach.

A very useful SWITCH function was added to Excel in February 2016. This may be a better solution when you have lookup data that is not expected to change (or at least rarely changes). This type of data is often called *static data* by IT professionals.

In this lesson you will use the maximum wind speeds defined by the *Saffir-Simpson Hurricane Wind Scale* for category 1 to 5 hurricanes. The defined SSHS maximum wind speeds are extremely unlikely to change in the future, so it is reasonable to describe this as static data.

1   Open *Biggest Atlantic Hurricanes-1* from your sample files folder.

The sample file for this lesson lists some of the biggest Atlantic hurricanes from 1870 to present. Each hurricane is categorized (from 1-5).

	A	B	C	D	E
			Damage (USD		Max Wind
3	Name	Start Date	Millions)	Category*	Speed
4	San Marcos	October 5, 1870	12	3	
5	Sea Islands	August 15, 1893	1	3	
6	Chenier Caminanda	September 27, 1893	5	4	
7	San Ciriaco	August 3, 1899	20	4	

2   Use the SWITCH function to calculate the maximum wind speed for each hurricane.

The maximum wind speed for each hurricane category is shown at the bottom of the list:

	A	B
27	Hurricane Category	Max Wind Speed (mph)
28	5	157 and over
29	4	156
30	3	129
31	2	110
32	1	95

With the skills you learned in: *Lesson 3-22: Use a VLOOKUP function for an exact lookup,* you could easily have calculated the maximum wind speed by looking up the *Hurricane Category* in cells A28:B32 (see sidebar).

By using a SWITCH function instead, there will be no danger of a user editing the contents of cells A28:B32 causing the worksheet to become inaccurate.

1.   Click in cell E4.

Biggest Atlantic Hurricanes-1

2. Click: Formulas→Function Library→Logical→SWITCH.

   The *Function Arguments* dialog appears.

3. Click in the *Expression* box.

4. Click once on cell D4.

5. In the *Value1* box enter the value: **1**

6. In the *Result1* box enter the value: **95**

   You have now defined a *Value/Result* pair for a *Category 1* hurricane.

Expression	D4	⬆	=	3
Value1	1	⬆	=	1
Result1	95	⬆	=	95
Default_or_value2		⬆	=	any

7. Continue to define pairs of values for category 2 to 5 hurricanes (see sidebar).

   The SWITCH function allows you to add up to 127 *Value/Result* pairs.

8. In the final *Default_or_value6 box,* type: **"Error"**

   This text will be displayed in the event that a category cell is out of range or empty.

   See sidebar for all of the values that you should have entered.

9. Click the OK button.

3 AutoFill the formula in cell E4 down to the end of the range.

The maximum wind speed is now shown for each hurricane.

Expression	D4	⬆		
Value1	1	⬆		
Result1	95	⬆		
Default_or_value2	2	⬆		
Result2	110	⬆		
Default_or_value3	3	⬆		
Result3	129	⬆		
Default_or_value4	4	⬆		
Result4	156	⬆		
Default_or_value5	5	⬆		
Result5	"over 156"	⬆		
Default_or_value6	"Error"	⬆		

▲	A	B	C	D	E
1	Strongest Atlantic Hurricanes				
2					
3	Name	Start Date	Damage (USD Millions)	Category*	Max Wind Speed
4	San Marcos	October 5, 1870	12	3	129
5	Sea Islands	August 15, 1893	1	3	129
6	Chenier Caminanda	September 27, 1893	5	4	156

4 Save your work as *Biggest Atlantic Hurricanes-2.*

note

The IFS function is more sophisticated than SWITCH

Many common uses of nested IF functions can be solved using a SWITCH function.

In February 2016 a more sophisticated function called IFS was added to Excel 365.

The IFS function is able to replace **all** uses of nested IF functions.

You'll learn to use the IFS function later, in: *Lesson 3-28: Use the IFS function.*

Lesson 3-24: Use an IFERROR function to suppress error messages

1   Open *Invoice-2* from your sample files folder (if it isn't already open).

2   Select the *Invoice* worksheet.

3   Add a VLOOKUP formula to cell C6 to return the price that corresponds to the *Code* in cell A6.

You learned how to add a VLOOKUP function in *Lesson 3-22: Use a VLOOKUP function for an exact lookup*. This time, the correct arguments are:

Lookup_value	A6
Table_array	Stock
Col_index_num	5
Range_lookup	False

4   AutoFill cells B6:C6 to cells B7:C8.

	A	B	C
5	Code	Description	Price
6	CA74	Cartier Tank 18K	4,570.00
7		#N/A	#N/A
8		#N/A	#N/A
9		Total:	#N/A

This is nearly what is needed. The invoice will work just fine when all three lines are populated:

	A	B	C
5	Code	Description	Price
6	CA74	Cartier Tank 18K	4,570.00
7	RO66	Rolex Tudor Oyster	430.00
8	BR43	Breitling Chronomat 18K	3,070.00
9		Total:	8,070.00

But you need to cater for customers that only wish to purchase one watch. To make this work, you need to suppress the error messages when some invoice lines have no stock code.

Fortunately, the IFERROR function is designed precisely for this purpose.

5   Wrap each VLOOKUP function with an IFERROR function to return a blank space when an error is encountered.

The IFERROR function can return the value of your choice whenever a formula returns an error.

1.   Click in cell B6.

Look at the formula in the formula bar:

Invoice-2

This is the VLOOKUP function that returns the description. You're going to use this formula as the *value* argument for the IFERROR function. When one function is used inside another function in this way, the outside function is sometimes referred to as a *wrapper*.

2. Click just to the right of the equals sign in the formula bar.

   `𝑓ₓ  =VLOOKUP`

3. Type **IFERROR(**

   `𝑓ₓ  =IFERROR(VLOOKUP(A6,Stock,2,FALSE)`
   `      IFERROR(value, value_if_error)          E`

   Notice the tip that has appeared. The entire VLOOKUP function is now being used as the *value* argument for the IFERROR function.

4. Click to the extreme right of the formula in the formula bar and add a comma:

   `𝑓ₓ  =IFERROR(VLOOKUP(A6,Stock,2,FALSE),`

   You are now ready to add the second argument for the IFERROR function. This argument defines what will be displayed if the VLOOKUP function returns an error.

5. Add an empty string to the IFERROR function.

   Type **""**. This is an empty string and tells Excel to keep the cell blank when an error is returned.

   `𝑓ₓ  =IFERROR(VLOOKUP(A6,Stock,2,FALSE), ""`

6. Close the bracket to complete the formula.

   `𝑓ₓ  =IFERROR(VLOOKUP(A6,Stock,2,FALSE), "")`

7. Press the **<Enter>** key.

8. Do the same thing for the *Price* formula in cell C6.

   `𝑓ₓ  =IFERROR(VLOOKUP(A6,Stock,5,FALSE), "" )`

6 AutoFill the formulas in cells B6:C6 to cells B7:C8.

The invoice now works correctly, even when some stock codes are left blank.

⊿	A	B	C
5	Code	Description	Price
6	CA74	Cartier Tank 18K	4,570.00
7			
8	PA83	Patek Phillipe Jumbo Nautilus	20,355.00
9		Total:	24,925.00

7 Save your work as *Invoice-3*.

---

note

The HLOOKUP function works in the same way as the VLOOKUP function

In the VLOOKUP function, V is an abbreviation of *Vertical*. This means that you search for a matching value in a (vertical) column and return a value from any column in that row.

In the HLOOKUP function, H is an abbreviation of Horizontal. This means that you can search for a matching value in a (horizontal) row and return a value from any row in that column.

You'll see the VLOOKUP function used far more often than HLOOKUP but you may find a scenario where it is useful.

In: *Lesson 3-22: Use a VLOOKUP function for an exact lookup (sidebar),* you learned that the new XLOOKUP dynamic array function has now completely replaced VLOOKUP.

XLOOKUP also replaces HLOOKUP as it is able to lookup both horizontally and vertically.

Unless you need to share your workbooks with users of Excel 2019 and earlier, you should use XLOOKUP for all new work.

You'll learn about dynamic arrays later, in: *Session Four: Working with Dynamic Arrays.*

You'll learn about the modern XLOOKUP replacement for VLOOKUP and HLOOKUP later, in:

Lesson 4-18: Understand XLOOKUP (part one) and *Lesson 4-19: Understand XLOOKUP (part two)*

Grades-1

Lesson 3-25: Use a VLOOKUP function for an inexact lookup

In: *Lesson 3-22: Use a VLOOKUP function for an exact lookup,* you set the fourth argument of the VLOOKUP to FALSE in order to achieve an *exact* lookup. Most of the time, that's exactly what you want to do.

Sometimes you don't want to search for an exact match but are interested in a close match. This is called an *inexact* lookup. Consider the following exam grades:

	E	F
3	Percentage	Grade
4	0%	Fail
5	60%	C
6	70%	B
7	80%	A
8	90%	A*

An *exact* VLOOKUP for a student with a mark of 80% would correctly return a grade of A.

An *exact* VLOOKUP for a student with a mark of 77% would result in an error because there is no exact value of 77% in column E.

If you ask VLOOKUP to perform an *inexact* lookup, it will return an exact match if one is found. If an exact match is not found, it will return the largest value *that is less than* the lookup value.

For VLOOKUP to work with inexact matches, it is vital that the lookup column is sorted in ascending order (from the lowest to the highest value).

In the above example, an inexact search for 68% would find row 5 (a C grade) because 60% is the largest value that is less than 68%.

1 Open *Grades-1* from your sample files folder.

	A	B	C	D	E	F
1	Exam Results					
2						
3	Name	Percentage	Grade		Percentage	Grade
4	Johnny Caine	70%			0%	Fail
5	George Marley	68%			60%	C
6	Betty Anan	86%			70%	B
7	Paris Winfrey	80%			80%	A
8	Ozzy Dickens	95%			90%	A*
9	Johnny Roberts	84%				

2 Convert cells E3:F8 into a table named: **Grade**

This was covered in: *Lesson 1-13: Convert a range into a table and add a total row* and *Lesson 1-19: Name a table and create an automatic structured table reference.*

When working with the VLOOKUP function it is best practice to use a table for the *Table_array* argument.

XLOOKUP is more sophisticated than VLOOKUP

In: *Lesson 3-22: Use a VLOOKUP function for an exact lookup (sidebar)*, you learned that the new XLOOKUP dynamic array function has now completely replaced VLOOKUP.

You should only use VLOOKUP in new work when you need to maintain compatibility with Excel 2019 and earlier versions.

XLOOKUP can perform more advanced inexact lookups than VLOOKUP:

* VLOOKUP always returns an *exact match or next smaller item*. XLOOKUP can return either the *next smaller* or *next larger* item when an exact match is not found.

0 - Exact match
-1 - Exact match or next smaller item
1 - Exact match or next larger item
2 - Wildcard character match

* XLOOKUP does not require a range to be sorted in ascending order.

* XLOOKUP supports wildcard character matches.

You'll learn about dynamic arrays later, in: *Session Four: Working with Dynamic Arrays.*

Lesson 4-18: Understand XLOOKUP (part one)
and
Lesson 4-19: Understand XLOOKUP (part two)

This will make the data dynamic. In other words, the VLOOKUP function will still work correctly if you add and remove grades from the *Grade* table.

3 Add an inexact VLOOKUP to cell C4 to return the grade that corresponds to the percentage mark in cell B4.

You learned how to add an exact VLOOKUP in *Lesson 3-22: Use a VLOOKUP function for an exact lookup*. An inexact lookup is done in exactly the same way, except that the *Range_lookup* argument is set to TRUE (or omitted, as the default is TRUE).

This time, the correct arguments are therefore:

Lookup_value	B4
Table_array	Grade
Col_index_num	2
Range_lookup	TRUE

4 AutoFill cell C4 to cells C5:C17.

The correct grades are now shown for each student.

	A	B	C
3	Name	Percentage	Grade
4	Johnny Caine	70%	B
5	George Marley	68%	C
6	Betty Anan	86%	A
7	Paris Winfrey	80%	A
8	Ozzy Dickens	95%	A*
9	Johnny Roberts	84%	A
10	Charles Monroe	55%	Fail
11	Ronnie Bush	58%	Fail
12	Michal Jolie	69%	C
13	JK Spears	77%	B
14	Ozzy Rowling	84%	A
15	Oprah Hilton	60%	C
16	Bill Biggs	58%	Fail
17	Angelina Osbourne	30%	Fail

5 Save your work as *Grades-2*.

important

The XMATCH function has replaced MATCH

Excel 365 *July 2020 version 2002* added dynamic arrays to Excel.

There is now a new XMATCH dynamic array function that replaces MATCH.

You should use XMATCH for new work unless you need to maintain combability with Excel 2019 and earlier versions.

You'll learn about XMATCH later, in: *Lesson 4 21: Use an XMATCH function.*

⬦	A	B	C
3	Distance		
5	City	Anchorage	Atlanta
6	Anchorage	-	3,400
7	Atlanta	3,400	-
8	Austin	3,164	817

⬦	A	B
37	Fare	
39	Min Passengers	Per Mile
40	1	$ 1.25
41	2	$ 0.65
42	3	$ 0.50
43	4	$ 0.40
44	5	$ 0.30
45	10	$ 0.15

51	Fare Calculator	
53	From	Atlanta
54	To	
55	From Row	Anchorage / Atlanta / Austin
56	To Col	Baltimore / Boston
57	Distance (Miles)	Chicago
58	Min Passengers	Dallas / Denver
59	Per Mile	
60	Fare	

Bus Fare Calculator-1

Lesson 3-26: Use a MATCH function for an exact lookup

1 Open *Bus Fare Calculator-1* from your sample files folder.

In the next two lessons you will create a fare calculator for a long-distance bus company.

There are two tables in the sample file. The *Distance* table (see sidebar) shows the distance between major US cities. You can see at a glance that the distance between Austin and Atlanta is 817 miles. The second table shows the *Fare*. As more passengers share the vehicle it is possible to charge a lower fare per passenger.

When the worksheet is completed, the operator will select a *From* and *To* destination and enter the *Min Passengers* (minimum number of passengers who will travel). The worksheet will then automatically calculate the *Distance* and *Fare*.

In this lesson you will use the MATCH function to identify the cell in the *Distance* table that contains the correct distance value for the selected *From* and *To* cities.

2 Unhide all rows between row 53 and 60.

1. Select rows 53 to 60

2. Right click on one of the selected column headers.

3. Click: *Unhide* from the shortcut menu.

    Several new rows are now revealed. These are often called helper cells. They will make the formulas more readable. Later, when the worksheet is complete, you will hide these cells again.

3 Add a list validation to cells B53 and B54 to show a drop-down list of all cities.

You learned how to do this in: *Lesson 2-11: Add a table-based dynamic list validation.*

You can use cells A6:A35 as the source of both lists as the row and column City names in the *Distance* table are (and always will be) identical.

4 Select **Atlanta** as the *From* city and **Chicago** as the *To* city.

5 Add a MATCH function to cell B55 to find which row in the *City* column of the *Distance* table contains the text: *Atlanta*

1. Click in cell B55.

2. Click: Formulas→Function Library→ Lookup & Reference→MATCH.

    The *Function Arguments* dialog for the MATCH function appears.

3. Click in the *Lookup_value* box.

4. Click on cell B53.

note

The MATCH function offers three different match types

MATCH(lookup_value, lookup_array, [match_type])

MATCH offers a choice of three values for the *match_type* argument:

1 - Less than
0 - Exact match
-1 - Greater than

For a **Less than** match the list must be sorted in ascending order.

For a **Greater than** match the list must be sorted in descending order.

For an **Exact match** the list does not have to be sorted in any particular order.

Here is a table named *Price*:

	A	B
1	Qty	Price
2	5	$ 10.00
3	10	$ 9.00
4	15	$ 8.00

MATCH(13, Price[Qty], 1)

In this case **10** is the largest value that is less than, or equal to **13**. For this reason, the function returns 2 (the second data row in the table).

MATCH(13, Price[Qty], 0)

This would return an error as there is no *Qty* value that is exactly equal to 13.

MATCH(13, Price[Qty], -1)

Remember that, to use this match type, the *Qty* column would have to be sorted in descending order.

In this case **15** is the largest value that is greater than, or equal to **13**. For this reason, the function returns 1 (the first data row in the table after the table has been sorted in descending order).

5. Click in the *Lookup_array* box

6. Select the range A6:A35 in the distance table.

   Note that this results in the structured reference: *Distance[City]*.

7. Click in the *Match_type* box.

   The *Match_type* is very similar to the *Exact Match* and *Inexact Match* arguments of the VLOOKUP function. See sidebar for a discussion of the three possible arguments. Enter a value of **0** (meaning an *Exact Match*).

   The dialog should now look like this.

Lookup_value	B53
Lookup_array	Distance[City]
Match_type	0

8. Click the *OK* button.

   A value of 2 is returned to cell B55. Notice that *Atlanta* is the second city listed in the *Distance* table.

6 Insert a MATCH function into cell B56 to define the column in the *Distance* table that contains the header text: **Chicago**

   This time the function arguments should be:

Lookup_value	B54
Lookup_array	Distance[#Headers]
Match_type	0

	A	B
51	Fare Calculator	
52		
53	From	Atlanta
54	To	Chicago
55	From Row	2
56	To Col	7
57	Distance (Miles)	
58	Min Passengers	
59	Per Mile	
60	Fare	

   A value of 7 is returned to cell B56. Notice that the text **Chicago** appears in the seventh row of the *Distance* table.

	A	B	C	D	E	F	G
5	City	Anchorage	Atlanta	Austin	Baltimore	Boston	Chicago
6	Anchorage	-	3,400	3,164	3,351	3,366	2,849
7	Atlanta	3,400	-	817	576	935	587
8	Austin	3,164	817	-	1,346	1,693	977

   In the next lesson you will use these row and column references within an INDEX function to return the correct *Distance (Miles)* value from the *Distance* table.

7 Save your work as *Bus Fare Calculator-2*.

note

A combined INDEX and MATCH formula can be used to emulate a VLOOKUP

In this lesson you use this simple VLOOKUP function to calculate the *Fare Per Mile*:

=VLOOKUP(B58, Fare, 2,TRUE)

You could emulate this single function using a combined INDEX and MATCH formula like this:

=INDEX(Fare[PerMile],MATCH(B58,Fare[Min Passengers],1))

With your understanding of the INDEX and MATCH functions you should understand how this formula works.

I'm sure that you will agree that this approach seems pointless but if you search the web you might find arguments that this is a "better" approach.

In almost every case it isn't (though in older versions of Excel it used to execute a little faster).

One argument for the INDEX/MATCH approach is that the function cannot be broken by a user inserting or deleting a column in the lookup table. If this robustness is required it is better achieved by using a MATCH function in combination with a VLOOKUP function. See: *Lesson 3-22: Use a VLOOKUP function for an exact lookup,* (sidebar) for an example of this technique.

It is still useful to understand how the above INDEX/MATCH approach works as you may have to maintain an older workbook that has used this function combination.

Bus Fare Calculator-2

Lesson 3-27: Use the INDEX function

In: *Lesson 3-26: Use a MATCH function for an exact lookup* you determined row and column co-ordinates to identify a value within a range.

Specifically, you identified that the driving distance from Atlanta to Chicago was contained in row 2 and column 7 of the *Distance* table.

	A	B	C	D	E	F	G
5	City	Anchorage	Atlanta	Austin	Baltimore	Boston	Chicago
6	Anchorage	-	3,400	3,164	3,351	3,366	2,849
7	Atlanta	3,400	-	817	576	935	587
8	Austin	3,164	817	-	1,346	1,693	977

The INDEX function can be used to retrieve a value from a range or table when the numerical co-ordinates are known.

1   Open *Bus Fare Calculator-2* from your sample files folder.

2   Place an INDEX function in cell B57 that will return the value in the *Distance* table that is identified by the row and column references in cells B55 and B56.

1. Click in cell B57.

2. Click: Formulas→Function Library→ Lookup & Reference→INDEX.

   A *Select Arguments* dialog appears

   The INDEX function is quite unusual because it is said to be *overloaded*. An overloaded function can accept different sets of arguments.

   The function decides the form it will take by examining the arguments provided. See sidebar (facing page) for examples of the different sets of arguments that can be used.

3. Click the first set of arguments (the set beginning with *array*) and click the *OK* button. This is the more commonly used form of the INDEX function.

4. Click in the *Array* box.

5. Type: **Distance** to reference the *Distance* table.

6. Click in the *Row_num* box.

7. Click on cell B55 (this identifies the row in the table that has *Atlanta* in the *City* column).

8. Click in the *Column_num* box.

9. Click on cell B56 (this identifies the column in the table that has *Chicago* in the header row).

   The *Function Arguments* dialog should now look like this:

Array	Distance
Row_num	B55
Column_num	B56

note

There are many ways to use the INDEX function

Using this lesson's sample file:

INDEX(Distance, 2, 7)

This was used in this lesson (by referencing the values in cells B55 and B56) to return the single value of 587 miles (the distance from Atlanta to Chicago).

INDEX(Distance, 2)

This example returns an array of all of the values in the Atlanta row.

INDEX(Distance,,7)

This example returns an array of all of the values in the Chicago column.

INDEX(A7:AE7,,7)

This example references the seventh column in the *Atlanta row* (cells A7:AE7). 587 miles is returned (the distance from Atlanta to Chicago).

=INDEX(Distance[Chicago],2)

This example references the second row in the Chicago column. 587 miles is returned (the distance from Atlanta to Chicago).

=INDEX((Distance,Fare),2,7,1)

This example uses the lesser-used *reference* form of the INDEX function. You won't often see this form in real-world workbooks.

In this example both the *Distance* and *Fare* tables have been referenced, followed by the usual row and column references (2 and 7).

The last argument is the *Area_num*. It identifies which table to use for the lookup (in this case the first table: *Distance*).

587 miles is returned (the distance from Atlanta to Chicago).

10. Click the *OK* button

    Notice that the distance from Atlanta to Chicago is now shown in cell B57 (587 miles).

3 Type: **14** into cell B58 (to define a test value for *Min Passengers*).

4 Add a VLOOKUP formula to cell B59 to retrieve the *Fare per mile* from the *Fare* table.

As more passengers share the vehicle it is possible to charge a lower fare per passenger. The *Fare* table defines the cost per mile based upon a minimum number of passengers.

In: *Lesson 3-25: Use a VLOOKUP function for an inexact lookup* you learned how to find the correct value in the *Fare* table. Here are the correct arguments for the VLOOKUP:

Lookup_value	B58
Table_array	Fare
Col_index_num	2
Range_lookup	TRUE

5 Add a function to cell B60 to calculate the fare for this journey.

This is simply the distance multiplied by the fare per mile:

=B57*B59

6 Hide rows 55, 56 and 59.

It is always a good idea to hide helper cells when a worksheet is completed. This keeps the worksheet simple and clear.

1. Select rows 55, 56 and 59.

2. Right click on one of the selected row headers and click *Hide* from the shortcut menu.

7 Test the bus fare calculator

	A	B
51	Fare Calculator	
52		
53	From	Atlanta
54	To	Chicago
57	Distance (Miles)	587
58	Min Passengers	14
60	Fare	$ 88.02

Later, in: *Lesson 6-11: Restrict the cells users are allowed to change,* you will learn how to lock cells B57 and B60 to prevent users from over-writing the formulas by mistake.

8 Save your work as *Bus Fare Calculator-3.*

note

VLOOKUP is still (usually) a better solution than IFS

In: *Lesson 3-5: Use the IF logic function* (sidebar) I advised:

"Excel allows you to nest IF functions up to 64 levels deep (which is 63 too many)".

The new IFS and SWITCH functions (added to Excel 365 in Feb 2016) are mainly intended to offer a simpler alternative to nested IF functions.

This doesn't mean using the IFS and SWITCH functions provides a better solution than VLOOKUP.

It is easy to introduce errors using IFS and SWITCH, as the order in which the logic pairs are listed is vital to the correct operation of the function.

In this lesson the arguments are ordered correctly (as shown on the facing page sidebar).

If you were to state the grades in reverse order like this:

Logical_test1	B4<90%
Value_if_true1	"A"
Logical_test2	B4<80%
Value_if_true2	"B"

… most students would have a Grade A pass:

3	Name	Percentage	Grade
4	Johnny Caine	70%	A
5	George Marley	68%	A
6	Betty Anan	86%	A

This happens because the first logical test is applied and, because most students have a grade of less than 90%, a grade A pass is returned.

In almost all business situations a VLOOKUP will provide a better and more elegant solution than the use of the IFS or SWITCH function.

IFS Grades-1

Lesson 3-28: Use the IFS function

In: *Lesson 3-25: Use a VLOOKUP function for an inexact lookup*, you used a VLOOKUP function to return a grade from different pass mark percentages.

In this lesson you will solve exactly the same problem posed in: *Lesson 3-25: Use a VLOOKUP function for an inexact lookup,* with a logic based (rather than lookup based) solution.

1   Open *IFS Grades-1* from your sample files folder.

	A	B	C	D	E	F
1	Exam Results					
2						
3	Name	Percentage	Grade		Percentage	Grade
4	Johnny Caine	70%			0%	Fail
5	George Marley	68%			60%	C
6	Betty Anan	86%			70%	B
7	Paris Winfrey	80%			80%	A
8	Ozzy Dickens	95%			90%	A*
9	Johnny Roberts	84%				

This is an exact duplicate of the *Grades-1* sample file that you used at the beginning of: *Lesson 3-25: Use a VLOOKUP function for an inexact lookup.*

2   Use the IFS function to calculate the grade for each student by defining grade data within the function.

Sometimes it may be better to "hard code" data (such as the percentage grade thresholds) within the function itself. This prevents users from accidentally deleting or changing the grade percentage thresholds within the worksheet.

The argument against this approach is that the worksheet is more difficult to maintain if grade thresholds change in the future.

1.   Click in cell C4.

2.   Click: Formulas→Function Library→Logical→IFS.

The *Function Arguments* dialog for the IFS function appears.

The IFS function accepts up to 127 *Logical Test/Value* pairs.

3.   Enter the following pair of arguments:

Logical_test1	B4<60%
Value_if_true1	"Fail"

The *Logical Test* is an expression that returns TRUE or FALSE. In this case the test asks if Johnny Caine's percentage is less than 60%.

As Johnny scored 70%, the result is FALSE (as 70% is not less than 60%). If Johnny had a percentage score of less than 60%, the function would have returned the text "Fail".

Logical_test1	B4<60%
Value_if_true1	"Fail"
Logical_test2	B4<70%
Value_if_true2	"C"
Logical_test3	B4<80%
Value_if_true3	"B"
Logical_test4	B4<90%
Value_if_true4	"A"
Logical_test5	B4>=90%
Value_if_true5	"A*"

important

Excel recognizes text as having a value in logical expressions

If you try entering text into the *Percentage* column you might be surprised to find this result:

	A	B	C
3	Name	Percentage	Grade
4	Johnny Caine	teacup	A*
5	George Marley	68%	C

Excel has evaluated this logic expression:

="teacup">90%

… and has surprisingly returned TRUE.

This seems puzzling at first until you realize that (behind the scenes) Excel assigns numeric values to text in order to implement alphabetical sorting.

These numeric values are always higher than any number so that (in an A-Z sort) numbers will always come before text.

To work around this peculiarity, you could add a new first *Logical Test/Value* pair to ensure that the value in column B was numeric like this:

Logical_test1	ISNUMBER(B4)=FALSE
Value_if_true1	"Error"

Note that textual values must be placed in double quotation marks. If you omit to do this Excel will add them for you.

4.   Add *Logical Test/Value* pairs for the other grades (see sidebar).

It is vital that these arguments are added in the correct order (see facing page sidebar for the reason for this).

5.   Click the OK button.

Johnny Caine's B grade is shown in cell C4.

6.   AutoFill cell C4 to the end of the range.

All grades are now correctly shown.

	A	B	C	D	E	F
3	Name	Percentage	Grade		Percentage	Grade
4	Johnny Caine	70%	B		0%	Fail
5	George Marley	68%	C		60%	C
6	Betty Anan	86%	A		70%	B
7	Paris Winfrey	80%	A		80%	A
8	Ozzy Dickens	95%	A*		90%	A*

3   Use the IFS function to calculate the grade for each student using the grade data defined in cells E3:F8.

1.   Delete the functions in column C.

2.   Add a new IFS function to cell C4.

3.   Enter the following pair of *Logical Test/Value* arguments:

Logical_test1	B4<$E$5	↑	= FALSE
Value_if_true1	"Fail"	↑	= "Fail"

Notice the use of an absolute reference for cell E5. This is needed to make sure that the formula AutoFills correctly.

You could also have used $F$4 to reference the text: "Fail" in cell F4 like this:

Logical_test1	B4<$E$5	↑	= FALSE
Value_if_true1	$F$4	↑	= "Fail"

Personally I prefer the literal text approach in this case as it makes the formula easier to read and thus less prone to error.

4.   Add appropriate *Logical Test/Value* pairs for the other grades.

5.   Click the *OK* button.

6.   AutoFill cell C4 down to the end of the range.

Exactly the same grade values are now shown. The difference from the first approach is that the grades will change if the Percentage thresholds shown in cells E4:E8 change in the future.

4   Save your work as *IFS Grades-2*.

Session 3: Exercise

1 Open *Employee Summary-1* from your sample files folder.

	A	B	C	D	E	F	G
					Date	Year	
3	Full Name	Last Name	First Name	Department	Started	Started	Bonus
4	Johnny Caine				16-Jan-04		
5	George Marley				18-Feb-08		

2 Using the RIGHT, LEFT, LEN and FIND functions, split the *Full Name* in column A into *Last Name* and *First Name* in columns B and C.

	A	B	C
3	Full Name	Last Name	First Name
4	Johnny Caine	Caine	Johnny

3 Use an exact VLOOKUP to return the *Department* for each employee (departments are listed on the *Departments* worksheet).

	A	B	C	D
3	Full Name	Last Name	First Name	Department
4	Johnny Caine	Caine	Johnny	Sales

4 Use a COUNTIF function to return the headcount for each department in cells B20:B22.

	A	B
19	Department	Headcount
20	Sales	6
21	Purchasing	5
22	Logistics	3

5 Use the YEAR function to populate column F with the year each employee started.

	A	B	C	D	E	F
					Date	Year
3	Full Name	Last Name	First Name	Department	Started	Started
4	Johnny Caine	Caine	Johnny	Sales	16-Jan-04	2004
5	George Marley	Marley	George	Purchasing	18-Feb-08	2008

6 Each employee in the *Sales* department receives a 10% bonus, while all other employees receive a 5% bonus. Use an IF function to populate column G with the correct bonus percentage.

	A	B	C	D	E	F	G
					Date	Year	
3	Full Name	Last Name	First Name	Department	Started	Started	Bonus
4	Johnny Caine	Caine	Johnny	Sales	16-Jan-04	2004	10%
5	George Marley	Marley	George	Purchasing	18-Feb-08	2008	5%

7 Save your work as *Employee Summary-2*.

Employee Summary-1

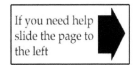

If you need help slide the page to the left

Session 3: Exercise Answers

These are the four questions that students find the most difficult to answer:

Q 6	Q 4	Q 3	Q 2
1. Click in cell G4. 2. Click: Formulas→ Function Library→ Logical→IF. 3. Add the following arguments: Logical_test D4="Sales" Value_if_true 10% Value_if_false 5% 4. Click the *OK* button. 5. AutoFill the formula in cell G4 to cells G5:G17. This was covered in: *Lesson 3-5: Use the IF logic function.*	1. Click in cell B20. 2. Click: Formulas→ Function Library→ More Functions→ Statistical→ COUNTIF. 3. Add the following arguments: Range $D$4:$D$17 Criteria A20 4. Click the *OK* button. 5. AutoFill the formula in cell B20 to cells B21:B22. This was covered in: *Lesson 3-6: Use the SUMIF and COUNTIF functions to create conditional totals.*	1. Select the *Departments* worksheet. 2. Convert the range A3:B17 into a table named: **Department** 3. Select the *Employees* worksheet. 4. Click in cell D4. 5. Click: Formulas→ Function Library→ Lookup & Reference→ VLOOKUP. 6. Add the following arguments: Lookup_value A4 Table_array Department Col_index_num 2 Range_lookup False 7. Click the *OK* button. 8. AutoFill the formula in cell D4 to cells D5:D17. This was covered in: *Lesson 3-22: Use a VLOOKUP function for an exact lookup.*	The easiest way to do this is to use the LEFT and RIGHT functions to return a specified number of characters from the left and right hand side of the *Full Name* string. The formula for the *First Name* (in cell C4) is quite easy. You can simply use the FIND function to find the first space and return that number of characters from the left hand side of the string: **=LEFT(A4, FIND(" ",A4)-1)** The *Last Name* is a little more involved. You also need to use the LEN function to return the total number of characters in the string: **=RIGHT(A4,LEN(A4)-FIND(" ",A4))** This was covered in: *Lesson 3-21: Extract text from delimited strings using the FIND and LEN functions.*

If you have difficulty with the other questions, here are the lessons that cover the relevant skills:

5   Refer to: *Lesson 3-8: Understand common date functions.*

4

Session Four: Working with Dynamic Arrays

> The measure of intelligence is the ability to change.
>
> *Albert Einstein, theoretical physicist (1879 – 1955)*

Dynamic arrays were introduced in the *Jan 2021 semi-annual version 2008* release. Dynamic arrays make many previously complex business tasks simple to implement.

Dynamic arrays are such a major change that the terms: *DA Excel* (Excel with dynamic arrays) and *Legacy Excel* (Excel 2019 and older versions) are often used to distinguish Excel 365 from older versions.

Session Objectives

By the end of this session you will be able to:

- Understand one-dimensional arrays
- Understand two-dimensional arrays
- Create a legacy CSE array formula
- Understand dynamic arrays
- Understand dynamic array compatibility
- Create a drop-down list using a UNIQUE function
- Use a FILTER function
- Create a searchable drop-down list
- Use the SORT and SORTBY functions
- Create two linked drop-down lists using dynamic arrays
- Use a FILTER function with a custom logic array
- Construct Boolean AND/OR arrays
- Use a FILTER function with AND/OR custom logic arrays
- Use a SEQUENCE function
- Create a perpetual calendar using the SEQUENCE function
- Use a RANDARRAY function
- Understand XLOOKUP (part one)
- Understand XLOOKUP (part two)
- Use XLOOKUP to perform a two-dimensional lookup
- Use XLOOKUP with boolean criteria
- Use an XMATCH function
- Use the SUMPRODUCT function with a logic array
- Use a SORTBY function with a custom array

note

You can view the contents of an array using the F9 key

The F9 key provides a useful way to audit formulas.

If a formula (or part of a formula) is selected and then F9 is pressed you will see the result of the formula.

You can use the F9 key to view an array.

	A
1	London
2	Paris
3	New York

If I type this formula:

=A1:A3

… and then press the **[F9]** key, the array that will be returned is shown:

	A	B	C
1	London		
2	Paris		
3	New York		
4	={"London";"Paris";"New York"}		

Lesson 4-1: Understand one-dimensional arrays

What is an array?

Whenever you include a range argument in an Excel function you are providing the function with an array.

Here is a very simple worksheet:

	A	B	C	D	E
1	City	Jan	Feb	Mar	Total
2	London	3	4	6	13
3	Paris	5	7	8	20
4	New York	6	7	9	22
5	**Total**	**14**	**18**	**23**	

… and here are the formulas that are used to calculate the totals:

	A	B	C	D	E
1	City	Jan	Feb	Mar	Total
2	London	3	4	6	=SUM(B2:D2)
3	Paris	5	7	8	=SUM(B3:D3)
4	New York	6	7	9	=SUM(B4:D4)
5	Total	=SUM(B2:B4)	=SUM(C2:C4)	=SUM(D2:D4)	

Consider the **=SUM(B2:B4)** function in cell B5.

Here is the *Function Arguments* dialog for this function:

You may not have noticed the numbers in the curly brackets before. This is an *array*.

When you entered the formula =SUM(B2:B4) you were instructing Excel to do this:

1. Take the values from cells B2:B4 and store them in an array (that resides in the computer's memory).

2. Add each number in the array together.

3. Return the sum of all values in the array to cell B5.

One-dimensional vertical arrays

In the above example the array is:

{3;5;6}

Each of the values within the array is called an *element*.

This array could be more accurately described as a *one-dimensional vertical array*.

- It is a *vertical* array because the data originated in a column.

- It is *one-dimensional* because the data is in only one column. Arrays that are made from a single row or column are one-dimensional. Later, in: *Lesson 4-2: Understand two-dimensional arrays*, you'll learn about the more complex two-dimensional type of array.

One-dimensional horizontal arrays

Now consider the =SUM(B2:D2) function in cell E2. The array shown in the *Function Arguments* dialog for the range B2:D2 is slightly different:

SUM			
Number1	B2:D2	↑	= {3,4,6}
Number2		↑	= number

You can tell at a glance that this is a horizontal array because it uses a comma to delimit the values rather than a semicolon.

- One-dimensional vertical array: **{3;5;6}**

- One-dimensional horizontal array: **{3,4,6}**

Now that you understand one-dimensional arrays you are able to substitute an array for a range in any Excel function.

1   Open a new blank worksheet.

2   Create a SUM function that adds together four numbers using a single array argument.

1.   Enter this function into any cell:

   f_x =SUM({1,3,4,6})

2.   Press the **[Enter]** key.

   The correct value 14 is returned to the cell.

   14

You may wish to experiment with different functions that accept ranges (arrays) as arguments.

When an array contains values that are not present in worksheet cells the array is sometimes called a *constant array*.

3   Close the workbook without saving.

note

Arrays can contain different data types

You cannot use formulas in an array. Arrays can only contain values.

The following data types can be used in an array:

- **Numbers:** Numbers cannot contain parentheses, currency prefixes or percent symbols.

- **Text:** Text must be enclosed in double quotation marks.

- **Logical values:** (TRUE or FALSE).

Different data types can be used in the same array.

Lesson 4-2: Understand two-dimensional arrays

In: *Lesson 4-1: Understand one-dimensional arrays,* you learned about arrays that can contain values found in a single column or row. You learned that there are two types of one dimensional array:

- One-dimensional vertical array, for example: {3;5;6}

- One-dimensional horizontal array, for example: {3,4,6}

Consider this very simple worksheet:

	A	B	C	D
1	City	Jan	Feb	Mar
2	London	3	4	6
3	Paris	5	7	8
4	New York	6	7	9
5				
6	Quarterly Total for all cities:			55

… and here is the formula used to calculate the total of all values:

	A	B	C	D
1	City	Jan	Feb	Mar
2	London	3	4	6
3	Paris	5	7	8
4	New York	6	7	9
5				
6	Quarterly Total			=SUM(B2:D4)

Consider the **=SUM(B2:D4)** function in cell B5.

Here is the *Function Arguments* dialog for this function:

Function Arguments			
SUM			
Number1	B2:D4	⬆	= {3,4,6;5,7,8;6,7,9}
Number2		⬆	= number

Notice that this time the array contains both commas and semicolons:

{3,4,6; 5,7,8; 6,7,9}

You can see that the semicolons delimit the rows and the commas delimit the values in each row. It may be clearer if I show this array on three lines:

{   3,4,6;
    5,7,8;
    6,7,9   }

This type of array is called a *two-dimensional array.*

As an Excel range is always rectangular you can see that each row in an Excel two-dimensional array must contain the same number of values (in this case three per row).

1   Open *Product List* from your sample files folder.

note

Arrays can be defined as named constants

Later, in: *Lesson 5-2: Manually create single cell range names and named constants,* you will learn how to create a named constant.

A named constant is a symbolic name that can be used in the place of a constant value (or an array containing several constant values).

It is also possible to create a named array using the technique you will learn in this lesson.

note

A two-dimensional array is an array of one-dimensional arrays

In this lesson you considered the array:

three lines:

{
3,4,6;
5,7,8;
6,7,9
}

You can see that a two dimensional array is really a one-dimensional array where each element is, itself, a one-dimensional array.

For example, the second element of this array contains the array element:

{5,7,8}

This worksheet uses a VLOOKUP function in column D to return the *Tax Rate* from the defined rates in cells A10:B12.

You learned how to create a VLOOKUP function in: *Lesson 3-22: Use a VLOOKUP function for an exact lookup.*

	A	B	C	D
1	Product	Price	Tax Code	Tax Rate
2	Fruit of the Loom children's T Shirt	$ 2.95	L	5%
3	Second class stamps (12-pack)	$ 7.80	Z	0%
4	Kids sports socks (3 pack)	$ 8.95	L	5%
5	Seagate 5Tb external hard drive	$ 109.99	S	20%
6	Microsoft Wireless Keyboard	$ 22.99	S	20%
7	First Class Stamps (12-pack)	$ 9.12	Z	0%
8				
9	Tax Code	Tax Rate		
10	Z	0%		
11	L	5%		
12	S	20%		

2 Replace two-dimension range referenced by the VLOOKUP function in cells D2:D7 with an in-memory array.

When an array contains values that are not present in worksheet cells the array is sometimes called a *constant array* or an *in-memory array*.

1. Double-click in cell D2 and then click the *Insert Function* button next to the formula bar to display the *Function Arguments* dialog.

   =VLOOKUP(C2,$A$10:$B$12,2,FALSE)

   Note the two-dimensional array shown next to the *Table_array* argument:

   | Table_array | $A$10:$B$12 | ↑ | = {"Z",0;"L",0.05;"S",0.2} |

2. Replace the range shown in the *Table_array* argument with the two-dimensional array.

   | Table_array | {"Z",0;"L",0.05;"S",0.2} | ↑ | = {"Z",0;"L",0.05;"S",0.2} |

3. Click the *OK* button.

4. Autofill the formula down to cells D3:D7.

5. Delete rows 9:12 as they are no longer needed.

	Product	Price	Tax Code	Tax Rate
1	Product	Price	Tax Code	Tax Rate
2	Fruit of the Loom children's T Shirt	$ 2.95	L	5%
3	Second class stamps (12-pack)	$ 7.80	Z	0%
4	Kids sports socks (3 pack)	$ 8.95	L	5%
5	Seagate 5Tb external hard drive	$ 109.99	S	20%
6	Microsoft Wireless Keyboard	$ 22.99	S	20%
7	First Class Stamps (12-pack)	$ 9.12	Z	0%

3 Save your work as *Product List-1*

Product List

note

CSE array formulas were never very useful

In the past most Excel users did not understand or use CSE array formulas.

Even Expert-level Excel users that completely understood CSE array formulas often avoided using them. In recent Excel versions there was nearly always a better way of achieving your goal.

This is not the case for Excel's new *Dynamic Array Formulas.* As you will discover later in this session, they are easy to understand and are now best practice when solving many real-world business problems.

Lesson 4-3: Create a legacy CSE array formula

You should not use legacy CSE array formulas in new work

Legacy CSE (Ctrl+Shift+Enter) array formulas are an outdated feature that should not be used in new work. *Dynamic array formulas* have now completely replaced them.

Legacy versions of Excel (Excel 2019 and earlier) included the ability to create what were called *CSE array formulas* though most Excel users never found this feature very useful.

Later, in: *Lesson 4-4: Understand dynamic array formulas,* you will encounter the modern replacement for CSE array formulas.

As you'll discover later, in: *Lesson 4 6: Understand dynamic array compatibility,* you will need an understanding of these outdated functions only to understand compatibility issues if an Excel 365 workbook is opened in a legacy version of Excel (Excel 2019 or earlier).

1   Open *Distance Converter* from your sample files folder.

This worksheet contains a simple Excel utility that uses simple formulas to convert miles into four other units of distance. Because the conversion ratios will never change they are referred to as constants:

	A	B	C
3	Enter Distance in Miles Here:	3	
4			
5		Conversion Ratio	Distance
6	Nautical Miles	0.8689	=$B$3*B6
7	Kilometers	1.6093	=$B$3*B7
8	Furlongs	8	=$B$3*B8
9	Chains	80	=$B$3*B9

It is possible to use a single multicell CSE array formula that has these constants embedded within the formula. The array formula will return five different results.

2   Delete cells B5:C9.

3   Delete column C.

4   Type: **Distance** into cell B5.

Your worksheet should now look like this:

	A	B
3	Enter Distance in Miles Here:	3
4		
5		Distance
6	Nautical Miles	
7	Kilometers	
8	Furlongs	
9	Chains	

Distance Converter

note

Editing CSE array formulas

When you click on any cell within an CSE formula array range you will see the formula (contained within curly brackets) in the formula bar:

| f_x | {=$B$3*{0.8689;1.6093;8;80}} |

When you click in the formula bar the outside pair of curly brackets disappear:

| f_x | =$B$3*{0.8689;1.6093;8;80} |

When you have finished editing you must remember to press:

[Ctrl]+[Shift]+[Enter]

… in order to save your changes.

note

In a CSE array formula the result cells must match the number of values in the array arguments

In this lesson you created the CSE array formula:

=$B$3*{0.8689;1.6093;8;80}

This array formula includes an array containing four values.

Before you saved the array formula you selected cells B6:B9 – a range that contained four cells.

Before creating a CSE array formula you must always select a range that contains the same number of cells as the number of values in the array.

5 Add a single CSE array formula to cells B6:B9 that will correctly calculate distances using array constants for the conversion ratios.

1. Select cells B6:B9.

2. Type the following CSE array formula:

   =$B$3*{0.8689;1.6093;8;80}

   Make sure that you use a semicolon to delimit each value in the constant array.

   Semicolons are used because the array represents values in four rows (a one-dimensional vertical array).

   If you needed to enter values in a constant array that represented a single row that spanned four columns (a one-dimensional horizontal array), you would use commas instead of semi colons.

3. Press: **[Ctrl]+[Shift]+[Enter]**

   The same CSE array formula is added to each cell in the range B6:B9 and the correct results are displayed.

   Click in cell B6 and examine the function shown in the formula bar:

   | f_x | {=$B$3*{0.8689;1.6093;8;80}} |

   Notice the curly brackets on the outside of the CSE array formula.

   Click: Formulas→Formula Auditing→Show Formulas to examine the array functions in cells B6:B9.

	A	B
3	Enter Distance in Miles Here:	3
4		
5		Distance
6	Nautical Miles	2.6067
7	Kilometers	4.8279
8	Furlongs	24
9	Chains	240

	A	B
3	Enter Distance in Miles Here:	3
4		
5		Distance
6	Nautical Miles	=$B$3*{0.8689;1.6093;8;80}
7	Kilometers	=$B$3*{0.8689;1.6093;8;80}
8	Furlongs	=$B$3*{0.8689;1.6093;8;80}
9	Chains	=$B$3*{0.8689;1.6093;8;80}

   Notice that the same CSE array formula has returned four different results.

4. Click: Formulas→Formula Auditing→Show Formulas once more to show values upon the worksheet instead of formulas.

6 Save your work as *Distance Converter-1*.

Lesson 4-4: Understand dynamic array formulas

The *Jul 2020 semi-annual version 2002* introduced a brand new concept to Excel. The *Dynamic Array Formula*.

This concept of dynamic arrays also enabled the addition of six new dynamic array functions that you'll learn about later in this session.

The Excel calculation engine has been fundamentally changed. The concept of Dynamic Array Formulas is a major advancement that has changed the way that many existing Excel functions can now be used.

Spilling

Dynamic Array Formulas introduce the concept of *Spilling*.

Before dynamic arrays were introduced, Excel functions could only return a single value to a single cell. Dynamic array formulas are formulas that can return arrays of variable size that can *Spill* into the cells to the right and below the cell containing the function.

For example, the new RANDARRAY dynamic array function returns a two-dimensional array of random numbers and uses Excel's new ability to *Spill* the array to adjacent cells:

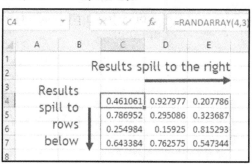

The example above uses the formula: **=RANDARRAY(4,3)** to return a two-dimensional array of random numbers and spills them into four rows and three columns. It is important to understand that (in the above example) there is only one dynamic array function that resides in cell D4. The other cells only contain spilled values.

Spilling is now enabled for many other Excel functions

Consider an IF function. Here's a solution from a legacy Excel version (Excel 2019 and earlier):

	A	B	C
3	Employee	Sales	Bonus?
4	John Smith	12200	=IF(B4<10000, "Yes", "No")
5	Fred Jones	9500	=IF(B5<10000, "Yes", "No")
6	Bill Bragg	14400	=IF(B6<10000, "Yes", "No")

	A	B	C
3	Employee	Sales	Bonus?
4	John Smith	$12,200.00	Yes
5	Fred Jones	$ 9,500.00	No
6	Bill Bragg	$14,400.00	Yes

The example shown supposes that employees receive a bonus if their sales exceed $10,000. An IF function is used to compare sales to 10,000 and return the text *Yes* or *No*. You learned about the IF function in: *Lesson 3-5: Use the IF logic function.*

Here is a modern way to do the same thing now that Excel supports dynamic arrays:

	A	B	C
3	Employee	Sales	Bonus?
4	John Smith	12200	=IF(B4:B6>10000, "Yes", "No")
5	Fred Jones	9500	
6	Bill Bragg	14400	

	A	B	C
3	Employee	Sales	Bonus?
4	John Smith	$12,200.00	Yes
5	Fred Jones	$ 9,500.00	No
6	Bill Bragg	$14,400.00	Yes

You can see that the single IF function has returned a dynamic array that has *spilled* into cells C5 and C6 (even though these cells do not contain a formula).

It is also possible to use formulas like LEN and VLOOKUP in this new way.

The new #SPILL and #CALC! errors

	B	C
3	Sales	Bonus?
4	$12,200.00	Yes
5	$ 9,500.00	No
6	$14,400.00	Yes

Excel now has two new errors that support dynamic ranges.

If any of the cells that results should spill into are not empty, a #SPILL error will occur.

	B	C
3	Sales	Bonus?
4	$12,200.00	#SPILL!
5	$ 9,500.00	
6	$14,400.00	test

If Excel detects a calculation error within an array a #CALC error will occur.

The # spilled range operator

Excel now has a new operator to reference dynamic spilled ranges. In the example shown earlier you might want to use a COUNTIF function to count how many employees earned bonus. You learned how to use the COUNTIF function in: *Lesson 3-6: Use the SUMIF and COUNTIF functions to create conditional totals.*

Here's the formulas you might use.

	A	B	C
3	Employee	Sales	Bonus?
4	John Smith	12200	=IF(B4:B6>10000, "Yes", "No")
5	Fred Jones	9500	
6	Bill Bragg	14400	
7			
8	Total Bonus Earners:		=COUNTIF(C4#,"Yes")

	A	B	C
3	Employee	Sales	Bonus?
4	John Smith	$12,200.00	Yes
5	Fred Jones	$ 9,500.00	No
6	Bill Bragg	$14,400.00	Yes
7			
8	Total Bonus Earners:		2

Dynamic arrays make CSE array formulas redundant

Dynamic array functions are intended to entirely replace the older *CSE Array Formulas* that you learned about in: *Lesson 4-3: Create a legacy CSE array formula.*

For new work you should always use *Dynamic Array Functions*. Support for the older *CSE Array Formulas* is only retained for compatibility reasons.

note

You can use the compatibility checker to determine whether a DA Excel workbook will open in Legacy Excel.

To check an Excel 365 workbook for compatibility with earlier versions click:

File→Info→Check for Issues→ Check compatibility

… you will then be able to choose a legacy version of Excel in order to identify potential problems when your workbook is viewed in the legacy version.

Lesson 4-5: Understand dynamic array compatibility

Dynamic arrays are a brand new concept for the *Jan 2021 semi-annual version 2008*.

Dynamic arrays are such an important new feature that many commentators are now using the terms:

- **DA Excel:**   Excel that supports dynamic arrays.
- **Legacy Excel:**   Excel 2019 and earlier versions.

There are, of course, many millions of users with older (pre Excel 365) versions of Excel. If backward compatibility with these older versions is important you may have to consider limiting your use of dynamic arrays and dynamic array functions.

Microsoft have worked hard to make DA Excel workbooks still function where possible in Legacy Excel versions. Some changes have also been needed to ensure that Legacy Excel workbooks continue to work without issues in DA Excel.

How Legacy Excel will attempt to maintain compatibility with DA Excel

When you write a formula in DA Excel the calculation engine determines if the function can potentially return multiple values (even if it is only returning one value). If the formula does have the potential to do this then it is saved as a dynamic array formula.

When a workbook is opened in Legacy Excel the workbook will attempt to convert any dynamic array formulas found into legacy CSE array formulas but this will not always be possible.

The main differences between Dynamic Array formulas and legacy CSE Array Formulas

In many cases it will be possible to convert a dynamic array formula to a legacy CSE array formula. This will not be successful in every case due to some fundamental differences.

- Legacy CSE array formulas are unable to automatically re-size.
- Legacy CSE array formulas have no spill border
- Columns and rows cannot be inserted and deleted within a CSE array formula range.
- The # spilled range operator cannot be used by Legacy Excel as there is no spill range to reference.

DA Excel may add @ implicit intersection operators to some Legacy Excel formulas

Implicit intersection occurs when a Legacy Excel formula attempts to return more than one value. In this case Legacy Excel will return a single value to the cell.

Legacy Excel Example

Cell B2 above contains the formula:

=A1:A4*2

Legacy Excel can only return one value so it uses the correct value for row 2.

DA Excel Example

Because DA Excel supports dynamic arrays the formula is processed in a different way. A four-row spilled range is created.

This inconsistency had the potential to cause an error when a Legacy Excel workbook is opened in DA Excel.

For this reason DA Excel adds an *implicit intersection* operator to the formula:

=@A1:A4*2

This makes DA Excel process the formula in the same way that Legacy Excel used to.

It is recommended that you do not use the @ implicit intersection operator yourself in your own Excel 365 formulas as this may create problems when opening the workbook in Legacy Excel.

The # spilled range operator is not supported by Legacy Excel

If you use the # spilled range operator in an DA Excel workbook the formula will result in an error when opened using Legacy Excel.

Lesson 4-6: Create a drop-down list using a UNIQUE function

Later, in: *Lesson 4-7: Use a FILTER function*, you'll create this simple filtered product list:

	A	B	C	D	E	F	G
1	Products				Single Category (Filtered)		
3					Category	Condiments	
4						Beverages	
5	Supplier	Product Name	Category		Supplier	Condiments / Confections	tegory
6	Exotic Liquids	Aniseed Syrup	Condiments		Exotic Liquids	Dairy Products / Grains/Cereals	ndiments
7	New England Seafood Cannery	Boston Crab Meat	Seafood		New Orleans Cajun Delights	Meat/Poultry	ndiments
8	Gai pâturage	Camembert Pierrot	Dairy Products		Mayumi's	Produce / Seafood	ndiments
9	Pavlova, Ltd.	Carnarvon Tigers	Seafood		Grandma Kelly's Homestead	Grandma's Boysenberry Spread	Condiments

This worksheet allows a user to select a *Category* from a drop-down list. When a category has been chosen, a filtered extract of values from the *Product* table is displayed (beginning in cell E6).

Notice that:

- The user has been provided with a drop-down list (in cell F3) that makes it easy to select a single category.

- The category names appear multiple times in the *Product* table (the table appearing in columns A:C), but only appear once in the drop-down list.

- The drop-down list has been sorted to show the categories in A-Z order.

It used to be quite challenging to create this type of drop-down list in legacy Excel but dynamic arrays have made this task very simple.

1 Open *Filtered Product List* from your sample files folder.

2 Add a new worksheet called: **Dynamic Data**

Whenever a new category is added to the *Product* table, the new category should also appear in the drop-down list. The data that will be needed for the drop-down list is often referred to as *Dynamic Data*.

It is useful to place this data on a second worksheet that can be later hidden from users.

3 Add a spilled range to the *Dynamic Data* worksheet that contains a list of unique values found in the *Category* column of the *Products* table.

1. Select the *Dynamic Data* worksheet.

2. Type: **Dynamic Data** into cell A1.

3. Type: **Category** into cell A3.

4. Apply the *Title* cell style to cell A1.

5. Apply the *Heading 4* style to cell A3.

6. Click in cell A4.

Filtered Product List

7. Click: Formulas→Function Library→
Lookup & Reference→UNIQUE.

The *Function Arguments* dialog for the UNIQUE function appears.

The UNIQUE function is one of the six new dynamic array functions added in *Jul 2020 version 2002.*

8. **Click in the *Array* box and type: Product[Category]**

This structured reference returns a dynamic array containing every value shown in the *Category* column of the *Product* table. This array will contain many duplicate values.

The UNIQUE function will remove any duplicates to return an array containing no duplicates.

Function Arguments			?	×
UNIQUE				
Array	Product[Category]	⬆	=	{"Condiments";"Seafood";"Dairy Produ
By_col		⬆	=	logical
Exactly_once		⬆	=	logical

9. Click the OK button.

A spilled range containing each unique *Category* found in the *Product* table is now shown in cells A3:A11 (see sidebar).

4 **Apply an A-Z sort to the values returned by the UNIQUE function.**

When the return value of one function is used as an argument for another function, the outside function is sometimes referred to as a *wrapper*. It is easy to sort the dynamic array returned by the UNIQUE function by wrapping it inside a SORT function.

The SORT function is one of the new dynamic array functions and will be covered in depth later, in: *Lesson 4-9: Use a SORT function.*

Edit the dynamic array formula to the following:

fx	=SORT(UNIQUE(Product[Category]))

The spilled range is now sorted in alphabetical order.

5 **Apply a list validation to cell F3 on the Filtered Products worksheet.**

You learned how to do this in: *Lesson 2-11: Add a table-based dynamic list validation.* You can reference the entire spilled range on the *Dynamic Data* worksheet using the spilled range operator (#) (see sidebar).

6 **Test the new list validation.**

When you click in cell F3 a down arrow should appear. When you click the down arrow a drop-down list should appear containing every unique *Category* value found in the *Product* table (see sidebar).

7 **Save your work as *Filtered Product List-1.***

Lesson 4-7: Use a FILTER function

The FILTER function provides the ability to extract a filtered range of values from a table or range.

1   Open *Filtered Product List-1* from your sample files folder (if it isn't already open).

This worksheet contains the *Category* drop-down list that you created in: *Lesson 4-6: Create a drop-down list* using a UNIQUE function.

2   Add a FILTER dynamic array function to cell E6 on the *Filtered Products* worksheet that will display a filtered list using the value shown in cell F3.

1.   Select the *Filtered Products* worksheet.

2.   Click in Cell E6.

3.   Click: Formulas→Function Library→ Lookup & Reference→FILTER.

The *Function Arguments* dialog for the FILTER dynamic array function appears.

3   Add an *Array* argument to the FILTER dynamic array function.

The first argument for the FILTER function is an array containing the range to filter.

In this case you want to return all of the columns from the *Product* table. This is easily done by adding a reference to all of the data within the *Product* table with the structured reference:

Product

If you wanted to return selected columns from the table you could use a structured reference such as:

Product[[Supplier]:[Product Name]]

The above reference would return a filtered dynamic range that only contained the *Supplier* and *Product Name* columns. Even though you will filter using the *Category* column there is no requirement to include this column in the returned results.

1.   Click in the *Array* argument box.

2.   Hover the mouse cursor over the top-left corner of the *Product* table until you see the angled arrow cursor shape.

4		
5	Supplier	Product Name
6	Exotic Liquids	Aniseed Syrup

3.   Click when you see the angled arrow cursor shape.

This is a quick way to return a structured reference that returns all of the data in a table.

Filtered Product List-1

note

Removing blank spaces from a dropdown list

In the sample file for this lesson there are no blank categories in the *Category* column of the *Product* table.

Not all data is as clean as this and it is a common requirement to create a drop-down list that filters out any blank entries.

To appreciate the problem try deleting one of the *Category* cells in the *Product* table. You'll see the following appear in the drop-down list:

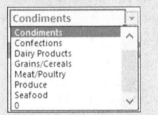

Notice the zero at the end of this list. This has happened because Excel has interpreted the empty call as having a value of zero.

Now that you understand the FILTER function it is easy to correct the problem.

1. Select the *Dynamic Data* tab.

2. Click in cell A4.

The current formula is:

=SORT(UNIQUE(Product[Category]))

3. Change the formula to:

=FILTER(SORT(UNIQUE(Product[Category])), SORT(UNIQUE(Product[Category]))<>0)

This removes any zero values found from the list.

The structured reference is returned to the *Function Arguments* dialog.

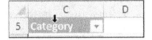

4 Add an *Include* argument to the FILTER dynamic array function that will only return rows that match the category defined in cell F3.

The *Include* argument defines the filter condition to be used.

The *Include* argument must be an array that contains the same number of rows as the array defined in the *Array* argument.

In this case the filter condition is very simple.

1. Click in the *Include* argument box.

2. Hover the mouse cursor over the top of the *Category* column header until you see the down-arrow cursor shape:

	C	D
5	Category ▼	

3. Click when you see the down-arrow cursor shape.

This is a quick way to return a structured reference that returns all of the data in a single table column.

4. Type: = and then click in cell F3.

The correct filter condition is returned.

Array	Product	↑	=	{"Exotic Liquids","Anis
Include	Product[Category]=F3	↑	=	{FALSE;TRUE;FALSE;TR

5. Notice that the array returned contains a series of TRUE or FALSE values, one for each data row in the table. Only the rows that contain a TRUE value will be returned.

5 Add an *If_empty argument* that will return the text: **No Rows Found** if the filter does not return any rows

1. Click in the *If_empty* argument box.

2. Type: **"No Rows Found"** (make sure that you include the double quotation marks).

Array	Product	↑	=	{"Exotic Liquids
Include	Product[Category]=F3	↑	=	{FALSE;TRUE;FA
If_empty	"No Rows Found"	↑	=	"No Rows Four

3. Click the OK button.

A filtered list is returned:

	E	F	G
1	Single Category (Filtered)		
3	Category	Seafood	
4			
5	Supplier	Product Name	Category
6	New England Seafood Cannery	Boston Crab Meat	Seafood
7	Pavlova, Ltd.	Carnarvon Tigers	Seafood
8	Escargots Nouveaux	Escargots de Bourgogne	Seafood

6 Save your work as *Filtered Product List-2*.

Searchable Drop Down List

Lesson 4-8: Create a searchable drop-down list

1 Open *Searchable Drop Down List* from your sample files folder.

This worksheet is very similar to the one you worked with in: *Lesson 4-7: Use a FILTER function.*

2 Select a supplier from the drop-down list in cell F3.

It can take some time to scroll down the list and identify the supplier. In this lesson you will make this task easier by making the drop-down list searchable.

3 Select the *Dynamic Data* worksheet.

There is a formula in cell A7 that displays a sorted list of all unique values found in the *Supplier* column in the *Product Table*. This list is being used as the source data of the list validation in cell F3 on the *Products* worksheet.

4 Add a test search expression to cell A4

Type: **aux** into cell A4 on the *Dynamic Data* worksheet. This is only for testing purposes and is to simulate a search expression that a user might enter later into the search box on the *Products* worksheet.

5 Add a SEARCH function to cell C7 to identify suppliers that contain the search expression in cell A4

The SEARCH function returns a number showing the position within a string where a character or string is first found.

- **=SEARCH("b","abcde")**   returns 2.
- **=SEARCH("cd", "abcde"**   returns 3
- **=SEARCH("z", "abcde")**   returns an error

1. Type this function into cell C7:

    =SEARCH(A4, A7#)

2. Press the **[Enter]** key

	A	B	C
6	Supplier		Found?
7	Aux joyeux ecclésiastiques		1
8	Bigfoot Breweries		#VALUE!
9	Cooperativa de Quesos 'Las Cabras'		#VALUE!
10	Escargots Nouveaux		16

You can see that a number is only returned when the search text exists in the *Supplier Name* shown in column A.

6 Add an ISNUMBER function to cell D7 that will return TRUE for any cell in column C that contains a number.

Type this function into cell D7:

=ISNUMBER(C7#)

	A	B	C	D
6	Supplier		Found?	Logic Array
7	Aux joyeux ecclésiastiques		1	TRUE
8	Bigfoot Breweries		#VALUE!	FALSE
9	Cooperativa de Quesos 'Las Cabras'		#VALUE!	FALSE
10	Escargots Nouveaux		16	TRUE

7 Add a FILTER function to cell E7 that will return supplier names that have a TRUE value in column D.

Type this function into cell E7:

=FILTER(A7#,D7#,"Type some letters to find a match")

You learned to use the FILTER function in: *Lesson 4-7: Use a FILTER function.*

	E
6	Filtered List
7	Aux joyeux ecclésiastiques
8	Escargots Nouveaux

8 Convert the list validation in cell F3 on the *Products* worksheet so that it results in a searchable combo box.

1. Select the *Products* worksheet.

2. Click in cell F3

3. Click Data→Data Tools→Data Validation.

4. Click the *Error Alert* tab and clear the *Show error alert after invalid data is entered* check box.

   This is needed to prevent the list validation from rejecting a search expression if it does not exactly match a supplier name.

5. Click the *Settings* tab and change the *Source* to:

Source:
='Dynamic Data'!$E$7#

6. Select the *Dynamic Data* worksheet.

7. Type this formula into cell A4:

f_x	=Products!F3

   The *Search Expression* will now match the search expression that the user types into the searchable list box on the *Products* worksheet.

9 Test the searchable drop-down list.

1. Type: **new** into cell F3 on the *Products* worksheet

2. Click the drop-down arrow on the right-hand side of the cell.

new
New England Seafood Cannery
New Orleans Cajun Delights

   Both suppliers with the text: **new** in their names appear on the drop-down list.

3. Click on one of the suppliers.

   A filtered list appears showing all products sold by the selected supplier.

10 Save your work as *Searchable Drop Down List-1.*

---

note

It is easy to change the search logic from *within* to *begins with*

In this lesson you implemented a search that found the text: **aux** anywhere *within* the name of each supplier.

This resulted in these rows being matched:

	E
6	Filtered List
7	Aux joyeux ecclésiastiques
8	Escargots Nouveaux

It is easy to change the search logic so that rows are found that *begin with* a search term.

In this case the formula in column D would be:

=IFERROR(C7#,0)=1

The IFERROR function returns 0 only when there is an error in column C. Provided there is no error the value in column C is compared with 1, a match on the first letter(s) of the search expression.

A search for the letter: **s** would then result in:

	E
6	Filtered List
7	Specialty Biscuits, Ltd.
8	Svensk Sjöföda AB

Lesson 4-9: Use a SORT function

1   Open *2019 Film Sales* from your sample files folder.

Notice some features of this sample file.

- This worksheet contains an Excel table named *FilmSales.*

- There is an area in columns G:K that will later contain a sorted extract of the data in columns A:E.

	A	B	C	D	E	F	G	H	I	J	K
1	2019 Film Sales						2019 Film Sales (Sorted)				
2											
3							Sort By:	Order Date			
4							Sort Order:	Ascending			
5											
6	Order No	Order Date	Title		Qty	Total	Order No	Order Date	Title	Qty	Total
7	136584	2-Jan-19	The Lord of the Rings: The Two Towers		14	129.84					
8	136585	3-Jan-19	The Fly		10	71.94					

In this lesson you will create two drop-down lists in cells H3 and H4 and populate the filtered extract using a SORT dynamic array function.

2   Create a spilled range to provide the data for the *Sort By:* drop-down lists.

1.   Click on the *Dynamic Data* worksheet tab.

2.   Type this formula in cell A4:

   =TRANSPOSE(FilmSales[#Headers])

   FilmSales[#Headers] is a structured table reference that references the *#Headers* special item.

   Because there is more than one header this function returns a spilled range of all headers and displays them in cells A4:A8.

   The TRANSPOSE function has been used to show the returned headers vertically (in cells A4:A8) rather than horizontally (in cells A4:E4).

3   Add a list validation to cell H3 on the *Data* worksheet that will show a drop-down list containing all of the *FilmSales* table's row headers.

You learned how to do this in: *Lesson 2-11: Add a table-based dynamic list validation.* The correct validation criteria is shown in the sidebar.

4   Add a list validation to cell H4 that will show a drop-down list containing the words "Ascending" and "Descending".

You can type these values directly into the List Validation's *Source* box (see sidebar).

5   Test your new drop-down lists.

Sidebar 1:

Allow:
| List | ∨ |

Data:
| between | ∨ |

Source:
= 'Dynamic Data'!$A$4#

Sidebar 2:

Validation criteria

Allow:
| List | ∨ |

Data:
| between | ∨ |

Source:
Ascending, Descending

2019 Film Sales

Note

For the problem posed in this lesson SORT is not the best option

The SORT function is very useful for doing simple things.

For example, if you simply wanted an A-Z sorted array containing all of the values in the *Title* column you could use this simple formula:

=SORT(FilmSales[Title])

In this lesson you have stretched the powers of the SORT function by using the optional *Sort_index* and *Sort_order* arguments.

In: *Lesson 4-10: Use a SORTBY function* you'll use the more powerful SORTBY function to perform a two-column sort.

Even though SORTBY can sort by multiple columns, to my mind it is also a simpler function to use when performing a more complex single column sort.

Compare the function used in this lesson:

=SORT(FilmSales, XMATCH(H3, FilmSales[#Headers]), IF(H4="Ascending",1,-1))

… with the SORTBY equivalent:

=SORTBY(FilmSales, INDIRECT("FilmSales["& H3 & "]"), IF(H4="Ascending",1,-1))

They both do exactly the same thing but I think that the latter solution is more readable.

6   Understand the SORT function's arguments.

- *Array:* The array to sort.

  In this case you want to sort all of the data in the *FilmSales* table so the correct argument is the structured reference: **FilmSales**

- *Sort_index:* This argument requires a number to indicate the position of the column to be sorted (for example, *Order No* is column 1 and *Total* is column 5).

  In Legacy Excel (Excel 2019 and earlier) you would use the MATCH function that you learned about in: *Lesson 3-26: Use a MATCH function for an exact lookup* like this:

  =MATCH(H3,FilmSales[#Headers],0)

  The above function would return 3 if the selected column was *Title* because *Title* is the third column from the left of the table.

  To use the modern replacement for MATCH you can use this formula instead:

  =XMATCH(H3,FilmSales[#Headers])

  The XMATCH function will be covered in depth later, in*: Lesson 4-21: Use an XMATCH function.* This will return exactly the same value as the MATCH example above.

- *Sort_order:* This argument requires the number 1 for an ascending order sort and the number -1 for a descending order sort. You can use an IF function to convert the text in cell H4 into the required argument. You learned to use the IF function in: *Lesson 3-5: Use the IF logic function.* The correct formula is:

  IF(H4="Ascending",1,-1))

7   Add a SORT dynamic array function to cell G7.

The correct dynamic array formula is:

=SORT(FilmSales, XMATCH(H3,FilmSales[#Headers]), IF(H4="Ascending",1,-1))

When viewed in the *Insert Function* dialog the arguments appear like this:

Array	FilmSales	↑	=	{136584,43467,'The Lord
Sort_index	XMATCH(H3,FilmSales[#Headers	↑	=	{3}
Sort_order	IF(H4='Ascending',1,-1)	↑	=	{1}

8   Test the worksheet.

Sort By:	Total	▼		
Sort Order:	Descending			

Order No	Order Date	Title	Qty	Total
136645	2-Mar-19	Nayagan	24	302.25
137040	22-Dec-19	Chungking Express	24	297.45
136804	6-Jul-19	Chungking Express	25	289.86

9   Save your work as *2019 Film Sales-1.*

Lesson 4-10: Use a SORTBY function

The SORTBY dynamic array function allows multiple-level sorts to be defined.

1 **Open *Two Field Sorted Product List* from your sample files folder.**

This sample file is very similar to the one you worked with in: *Lesson 4-8: Create a searchable drop-down list.*

Instead of one sort order this worksheet provides two.

This time all of the functionality of the drop-down lists (in cells E4:F5) has already been enabled for you. If you do not understand how the drop-down lists have been implemented refer back to: *Lesson 4-9: Use a SORT function.*

	A	B	C	D	E	F	G
1	Stock List				Stock List (Sorted)		
2							
3					Column	Order	
4				Sort By	Supplier	Ascending	
5				Then By	Product Name	Ascending	
6							
7	Supplier	Product Name	Category		Supplier	Product Name	Category
8	Exotic Liquids	Aniseed Syrup	Condiments				
9	New England Seafood Cannery	Boston Crab Meat	Seafood				
10	Gai pâturage	Camembert Pierrot	Dairy Products				

You can make this worksheet fully functional simply by adding a SORTBY dynamic array function to cell E8.

2 **Add a SORTBY dynamic array function to cell E8 that will perform a two-level sort based upon the criteria chosen by the user.**

1. Click in cell E8.

2. Type: **=SORTBY(**

3. Click on the *Insert Function* button to the left of the formula bar to open the *Function Arguments* dialog.

The *Function Arguments* dialog appears.

SORTBY			
Array		↑	= array
By_array1		↑	= array

The *Array* argument of the SORTBY function requires a reference to the range to sort.

4. Type: **Product** into the *Array* argument box.

You can then see the beginning of the array that Excel has retrieved from the table:

Array	Product	↑	= {"Exotic Liquids","Aniseed Syrup","Con
By_array1		↑	= array

The second argument requires another range to use for the sort. This array will contain all values in the column that the user wishes to sort.

If you were typing in the array reference directly things would be very simple. You'd just type a structured reference such as:

Array	Product	↑	=	{"Exotic Liquids","Aniseed Syrup","Con
By_array1	Product[Supplier]	↑	=	{"Exotic Liquids";"New England Seafo(

… and that would sort the results by Supplier.

Because you want the user to be able to select the sort column from the drop-down list in cell E4, the structured reference will need to reference the *Product* table column name shown in cell E4.

5. Type: **INDIRECT("Product["& E4 & "]")** for the second argument.

Array	Product	↑
By_array1	INDIRECT("Product["& E4 & "]")	↑

This function wraps a structured reference such as:

Product[Supplier]

… inside an INDIRECT function. The INDIRECT function is needed as otherwise Excel would regard the concatenated structured reference as being a text string.

Placing the reference inside an INDIRECT function will cause an array to be returned.

6. For the *Sort_order1* argument you need to reference cell F4 in the same way you did in: *Lesson 4-9: Use a SORT function.*

Array	Product	↑	=	{"Exotic Liquids","Aniseed Syrup","C...
By_array1	INDIRECT("Product["& E4 & "]")	↑	=	Volatile
Sort_order1	IF(F4="Ascending",1,-1)	↑	=	1

Array	Product
By_array1	INDIRECT("Product["& E4 & "]")
Sort_order1	IF(F4="Ascending",1,-1)
By_array2	INDIRECT("Product["& E5 & "]")
Sort_order2	IF(F5="Ascending",1,-1)

Now that you have defined the first sort condition it is easy to complete the second (see sidebar for argument values).

3 Test the worksheet.

When you specify two *Sort By* and *Sort Order* arguments the relevant records are extracted and shown in a range that begins in cell G6.

	D	E	F	G
1		Products (Sorted)		
3		Column	Order	
4	Sort By	Supplier	Ascending	
5	Then By	Product Name	Ascending	
6				
7		Supplier	Product Name	Category
8		Aux joyeux ecclésiastiques	Chartreuse verte	Beverages
9		Aux joyeux ecclésiastiques	Côte de Blaye	Beverages

4 Save your work as *Two Field Sorted Product List-1.*

note

The linked drop-down lists created in this lesson will not work in legacy Excel versions

Dependent drop-down lists are a lot more difficult to create using legacy Excel (Excel 2019 and earlier).

If you need to create linked drop-down lists that will work with legacy versions you'll find a more limited way of doing this later, in: *Lesson 5-8: Create two linked drop-down lists using range names.*

Lesson 4-11: Create two linked drop-down lists using dynamic arrays

In this lesson you'll allow a user to select any column and any filter condition (unique value) from the selected column. You'll achieve this by linking two drop-down lists together.

1 Open *Filtered Product List-2* from your sample files folder.

This worksheet contains the *Category* drop-down list that you created in: *Lesson 4-6: Create a drop-down list* using a UNIQUE function.

2 Edit the *Dynamic Data* worksheet so that it looks like this:

	A	B
1	Dynamic Data	
2		
3	Selected Column:	
4	Selected Filter:	
5		
6	Columns:	Unique Filter By List:
7		

3 Add a formula to cell A7 that will display a spilled range of column names, sorted A-Z, starting in cell A7.

You learned how to do this in: *Lesson 4-9: Use a SORT function.* The correct formula is:

=SORT(TRANSPOSE(UNIQUE(Product[#Headers])))

See sidebar for how the list should look.

	A
6	Columns:
7	Category
8	Product Name
9	Supplier
10	

4 Select the *Filtered Products* worksheet.

5 Remove the list validation from cell F3.

    1. Click in cell F3.

    2. Click: Data→Data Tools→Data Validation→Clear All.

6 Edit the *Filtered Products* worksheet so that it looks like this:

	E	F	G
1	Filter By Column		
2			
3	Column:	Filter By:	
4			
5			
6	Supplier	Product Name	Category
7			

Paste Special

Paste
- ○ All
- ○ Formulas
- ○ Values
- ○ Formats
- ○ Comments and Notes
- ◉ Validation

Allow:
List

Data:
between

Source:
= 'Dynamic Data'!$A$7#

7 Add a validation to cell E4 that allows the user to select any of the columns listed in cell A7 of the *Dynamic Data* worksheet.

You learned how to do this in: *Lesson 4-6: Create a drop-down list using a UNIQUE function.* See sidebar for validation *Source* formula.

Filtered Product List-2

8   Add a formula to cell B3 on the *Dynamic Data* worksheet that will reference the value in cell E4 on the *Filtered Products* worksheet.

The correct formula is: **='Filtered Products'!E4**

Your worksheet should now look like the one shown in the sidebar.

	A	B
1	Dynamic Data	
2		
3	Selected Column:	Category
4	Selected Filter:	
5		
6	Columns:	Unique Fi
7	Category	
8	Product Name	
9	Supplier	
10		

9   Create a dynamic list in cell B7 that will show unique values for the column selected by the user.

You know that if the user had selected the *Category* column you would create the correct dynamic array using the formula:

=UNIQUE(Product[Category])

But in this case you want to create the string: **Product[Category]** so that it will change if a different column is selected. This can be done with the concatenated formula:

= "Product["&B3 & "]"

This formula returns the string:

Product[Category]

You might think that this formula would work:

=UNIQUE(Product["&B3 & "]")

Unfortunately this will not work as Excel will see the concatenated expression as a string. In order to make it work you'll need to wrap the concatenated string in an INDIRECT function like this:

=UNIQUE(INDIRECT("Product["&B3 & "]"))

And to sort the resulting list from A-Z you'll need to wrap the formula in a SORT function like this:

=SORT(UNIQUE(INDIRECT("Product["&B3 & "]")))

Type the above function into cell B7. A unique sorted dynamic list of all unique values in the selected column is now displayed beginning in cell B7 (see sidebar).

	A	B
3	Selected Column	Category
4	Selected Filter:	
5		
6	Columns:	Unique Filter By
7	Category	Beverages
8	Product Name	Condiments
9	Supplier	Confections
10		Dairy Products
11		Grains/Cereals
12		Meat/Poultry
13		Produce
14		Seafood

10 Add a list validation to cell F4 on the *Filtered Products* worksheet that will display the spilled range in cell B7 on the *Dynamic Data* worksheet.

You learned how to do this in: *Lesson 4-6: Create a drop-down list using a UNIQUE function.*

11 Test the linked drop-down lists.

When you select a column from the *Column* drop-down list on the *Filtered Products* worksheet, you should see that the corresponding unique column values are available in the *Filter By* drop down list. You will make the filter conditions return the correct results later, in: *Lesson 4-12: Use a FILTER function with a custom logic array*

	E	F
3	Column:	Filter By:
4	Category	Confections
5		Beverages
6	Supplier	Condiments / Confections
7	No Rows Four	Dairy Products / Grains/Cereals
8		Meat/Poultry
9		Produce / Seafood

12 Save your work as *Filtered Product List-3*.

Lesson 4-12: Use a FILTER function with a custom logic array

In: *Lesson 4-11: Create two linked drop-down lists using dynamic arrays,* you created an intuitive user interface that allows a user to select any column and any filter condition that could be applied to the selected column. In this lesson you'll create a filtered list that will only display table rows that match the user's selections.

In order to do this you'll use a custom logic array (an array that contains a TRUE or FALSE value for each element in the array that will be filtered). This custom logic array will be used as the second argument for the FILTER function.

1   Open *Filtered Product List-3* from your sample files folder.

This worksheet has the user interface you implemented in: *Lesson 4-11: Create two linked drop-down lists using dynamic arrays.*

	E	F	G
3	Column:	Filter By:	
4	Category	Dairy Products	▾
5			
6	Supplier	Product Name	Category

In: *Lesson 4-11: Create two linked drop-down lists using dynamic arrays,* you created two drop-down lists in cells E4 allowing the user to select a column and filter condition. In this lesson you'll add a FILTER function to cell E7 on the *Filtered Products* worksheet that will return all rows that match the values chosen in the drop-down lists.

2   Use the drop-down lists to set the *Column* to *Category* and *Filter By* to *Seafood.*

This will make it easier for you to follow the examples.

3   Add a formula to cell B4 on the *Dynamic Data* worksheet that will contain the value chosen by the user in cell F4 on the *Filtered Products* worksheet.

The correct formula is:

='Filtered Products'!F4

You could reference these values directly from the *Filtered Products* list but by echoing them to the *Dynamic Data* worksheet it is easier to understand how the worksheet works.

4   Type: **Filter By List:** into cell D6 and **Filter Match:** into cell E6.

5   Apply the *Header 4* cell style to cells D6:E6.

	A	B	C	D	E
3	Selected Column:	Category			
4	Selected Filter:	Seafood			
5					
6	Columns:	Unique Filter By List:		Filter By List:	Filter Match:
7	Supplier	Beverages			

Filtered Product List-3

6 Add a function to cell D7 that will add a spilled range containing all of the values in the column that corresponds to the column selected in cell B3

In: *Lesson 4-11: Create two linked drop-down lists using dynamic arrays,* you learned how the INDIRECT function could be used to convert a string into an expression.

You can use the same technique to return the selected column.

Type this formula into cell D7:

=INDIRECT("Product["&B3 & "]")

	D
6	Filter By List:
7	Condiments
8	Seafood
9	Dairy Products
10	Seafood
11	Beverages
12	Beverages

A spilled range is returned containing every value in the selected column (in this example the *Category* column).

Notice that this range contains one row to match each row in the *Product* table.

7 Add a formula to cell E7 that will add a spilled range containing TRUE if the filter condition in cell B4 is met, and FALSE if it is not met.

This is the logic array you will later use with the FILTER function.

The formula is very simple:

=D7#=B4

	D	E
6	Filte By List:	Filter Match:
7	Condiments	FALSE
8	Seafood	TRUE
9	Dairy Products	FALSE
10	Seafood	TRUE
11	Beverages	FALSE

Observe the values that are returned. Every row containing the text: *Seafood* has a TRUE value and every other row has a FALSE value (see sidebar).

This logic array will work perfectly with the FILTER function.

8 Add a FILTER function to cell E7 on the *Filtered Products* worksheet that will return the rows requested by the user.

1. Select the *Filtered Products* worksheet.

2. Click in cell E7.

3. Delete the current contents of the cell.

4. Click: Formulas→Function Library→ Lookup & Reference→Filter

   The *Function Arguments* dialog appears.

5. Add these arguments to the *Function Arguments* dialog:

Array	Product	↑	= {"Exotic Liquids","Aniseed Syrup"
Include	'Dynamic Data'!E7#	↑	= {TRUE;FALSE;FALSE;FALSE;FALSE;
If_empty	"None Found"	↑	= "None Found"

You can see that the logic array (defined on the *Dynamic Data* worksheet) is used for the *Include* argument. Every row that has a TRUE value defined will be returned.

9 Test the worksheet.

Add some different *Column* and *Filter By* values using the drop-down lists in cells E4 and F4. Notice that the filtered results are correct no matter which row or filter you choose.

10 Save your work as *Filtered Product List-4.*

Lesson 4-13: Construct Boolean AND/OR logic arrays

The FILTER function accepts two arrays as its main arguments. The first array (the *Array* argument) contains a number of data elements, and the second array (the *Include* argument) contains TRUE or FALSE values.

For example:

Array	{"Apples", "Pears", "Oranges"}	↑	= {"Apples","Pears","Oranges"}
Include	{TRUE, FALSE, TRUE}	↑	= {TRUE,FALSE,TRUE}
If_empty		↑	= any
			= {"Apples","Oranges"}

This example defines a simple one-dimensional array as the *Array* argument – the equivalent of a single three-cell row of cells.

You can see that only the *Array* elements that have a matching TRUE value in the *Include* elements will be returned by the FILTER function (in this example, *Apples* and *Oranges*).

When you want to model more complex Boolean expressions it is necessary to use Boolean arithmetic to construct the *Include* array.

AND and OR arrays

Here's an example of some AND and OR arrays:

◢	A	B	C	D
1	First Array	Second Array	AND Array	OR Array
2	TRUE	TRUE	TRUE	TRUE
3	TRUE	FALSE	FALSE	TRUE
4	FALSE	TRUE	FALSE	TRUE
5	FALSE	FALSE	FALSE	FALSE

The AND array value is TRUE when the *First Array* **AND** *Second Array* values are both TRUE.

The OR array value is TRUE when either or both the *First Array* **OR** *Second Array* values are TRUE.

TRUE and FALSE have values of 1 and 0

Behind the scenes Excel uses the value 1 for TRUE and 0 for false. You can see this by adding the following formulas to a worksheet:

This can also be done with the *double unary operator* (see sidebar).

If the values in the above example are converted to their numeric values you can see the values that are required in the AND and OR arrays:

	A	B	C	D
1	First Array	Second Array	AND Array	OR Array
2	1	1	1	1
3	1	0	0	1
4	0	1	0	1
5	0	0	0	0

AND arrays are constructed by multiplication

Multiplying the values in the *First Array* and *Second Array* will result in the correct values for the AND array.

Here is the result of multiplying the two values:

	A	B	C
1	First Array	Second Array	AND Array
2	TRUE	TRUE	=A2*B2
3	TRUE	FALSE	=A3*B3
4	FALSE	TRUE	=A4*B4
5	FALSE	FALSE	=A5*B5

	A	B	C
1	First Array	Second Array	AND Array
2	TRUE	TRUE	1
3	TRUE	FALSE	0
4	FALSE	TRUE	0
5	FALSE	FALSE	0

You can then convert the AND array numbers back to logic values using simple logic expression:

	A	B	C
1	First Array	Second Array	AND Array
2	TRUE	TRUE	=A2*B2=1
3	TRUE	FALSE	=A3*B3=1
4	FALSE	TRUE	=A4*B4=1
5	FALSE	FALSE	=A5*B5=1

	A	B	C
1	First Array	Second Array	AND Array
2	TRUE	TRUE	TRUE
3	TRUE	FALSE	FALSE
4	FALSE	TRUE	FALSE
5	FALSE	FALSE	FALSE

OR arrays are constructed by addition

To create an OR array the first step is to add the first and second array values together:

	A	B	C
1	First Array	Second Array	OR Array
2	TRUE	TRUE	=A2+B2
3	TRUE	FALSE	=A3+B3
4	FALSE	TRUE	=A4+B4
5	FALSE	FALSE	=A5+B5

	A	B	C
1	First Array	Second Array	OR Array
2	TRUE	TRUE	2
3	TRUE	FALSE	1
4	FALSE	TRUE	1
5	FALSE	FALSE	0

You can see that when the first array value OR second array value is TRUE, the addition of the values is always greater than zero.

You can thus convert the values with this formula:

	A	B	C
1	First Array	Second Array	OR Array
2	TRUE	TRUE	=A2+B2>0
3	TRUE	FALSE	=A3+B3>0
4	FALSE	TRUE	=A4+B4>0
5	FALSE	FALSE	=A5+B5>0

	A	B	C
1	First Array	Second Array	OR Array
2	TRUE	TRUE	TRUE
3	TRUE	FALSE	TRUE
4	FALSE	TRUE	TRUE
5	FALSE	FALSE	FALSE

trivia

George Boole (1815-1864)

The concept of Boolean algebra was first defined in George Boole's book: *The Laws of Thought (1854).*

I'm sure that George would have been pleased to have known that his work established the foundation of modern computing over 100 years later.

According to GeorgeBoole.com (a website dedicated to him):

"His legacy surrounds us everywhere, in the computers, information storage and retrieval, electronic circuits and controls that support life, learning and communications in the 21st century".

Boole was largely self-taught and had little formal education.

As well as Boolean Algebra George has a lunar crater named after him. His legacy also lives on in most modern computer languages and database systems where logical values are usually referred to as having a *Boolean data type.*

Google marked the 200th anniversary of George's birth (2 November 2015) with a special commemorative *Google Doodle.*

Lesson 4-14: Use a FILTER function with AND/OR custom logic arrays

In: *Lesson 4-13: Construct Boolean AND/OR logic* arrays, you learned how to combine arrays to satisfy AND and OR logical conditions.

In this lesson you will put this understanding to practical use by creating a two-column filter that allows the user to select AND and OR filter conditions.

1 Open *Boolean Filtered Product List* from your sample files folder.

This worksheet is very similar to the one you created in: *Lesson 4-12: Use a FILTER function with a custom logic array.*

A second filter has been added using the same technique you used to create the first:

	E	F	G
3	Column:	Filter By:	
4	Supplier	Exotic Liquids	
5		AND	
6	Category	Beverages	
7			
8	Supplier	Product Name	Category

There is also a drop-down list enabling the user to select between three conditions:

	E	F
5		OR
6	No second condition	
7	AND	
	OR	

2 Create an AND custom logic array for use with the FILTER function.

Examine the *Dynamic Data* worksheet.

Everything is as you would expect except that columns J and K have a column header indicating that they will contain AND and OR custom logic arrays:

	H	I	J	K
3	Category			
4	Beverages			
5				
6	Filter By List:	Logic Array:	AND Logic Array	OR Logic Array
7	Beverages	TRUE		
8	Beverages	TRUE		

As you learned in: *Lesson 4-13: Construct Boolean AND/OR logic arrays,* you can construct an AND array by multiplying together two arrays.

1. Click in cell J7.

2. Type this formula into the cell: **=E7#*I7#=1**

The AND array appears in column J as TRUE/FALSE values.

Boolean Filtered Product List

note

The value of helper columns

It always annoys me when some people use many words in conversation when one is sufficient.

In the world of programming the opposite is true.

When I have led programming teams I've always encouraged programmers to write more code rather than less, documenting each step in a process.

Unfortunately many programmers prefer to write huge unfathomable expressions in a single line of code. I've never understood why they do this – though I suspect that they rather enjoy nobody else being able to understand their code.

I feel exactly the same way when tackling a problem in Excel. The use of intermediate results in the *Dynamic Data* worksheet allow you to see exactly how the FILTER function works. These intermediate results are often referred to as *helper columns*.

For example, you could use this less understandable formula for the FILTER function in this lesson:

=FILTER(Product,SWITCH(E5, "AND",'Dynamic Data'!E7#*'Dynamic Data'!I7#=1,"OR",'Dynamic Data'!E7#+'Dynamic Data'!I7#>0,+'Dynamic Data'!E7#), "None Found")

You would then have no need for the AND and OR columns on the *Dynamic Data* worksheet.

However, you'd make the formula more error prone and difficult for others to understand.

My advice is to use as many helper columns as you can. You can always hide the *Dynamic Data* worksheet before giving the workbook to users.

If you had used the formula: **=E7#*I7#,** you would have seen 1 and 0 values in column J. This would have also worked (see facing page sidebar).

3 Create an OR custom logic array for use with the FILTER function.

As you learned in: *Lesson 4-13: Construct Boolean AND/OR logic* arrays, you can construct an OR array by adding together two arrays and comparing the resulting value with zero.

1. Click in cell K7.

2. Type this formula into the cell:

   =E7#+I7#>0

   The OR array appears in column K.

4 Add a FILTER function to cell E9 in the *Filtered Products* worksheet to display the rows chosen by the user.

The user interface enables the user to select between three options.

You've already created three custom logic arrays that will satisfy each option.

1. Select the *Filtered Product* worksheet.

2. Click in cell E9.

3. Click: Formulas→Function Library→ Lookup & Reference→FILTER.

   The *Function Arguments* dialog appears.

4. Type: **Product** into the *Array* argument box as you want to return all columns in the *Product* table.

5. Type the following into the *Include* argument box:

   **SWITCH(E5,
   "AND",'Dynamic Data'!J7#,
   "OR",'Dynamic Data'!K7#,
   +'Dynamic Data'!E7#)**

   (shown above broken into four lines for clarity)

   You learned about the SWITCH function in: *Lesson 3-23: Use the SWITCH function*. You can see that the correct array will be used depending upon the Boolean operator chosen by the user.

6. Type the following into the *if_empty* argument box:

   "None Found"

5 Test the worksheet.

If you find that the filter is not showing the correct results it should be easy to examine the values in the *Dynamic Data* worksheet to discover the source of the error.

6 Save your work as *Boolean Filtered Product List-1.*

Lesson 4-15: Use a SEQUENCE function

SEQUENCE is another of the six new dynamic array functions that were added in *Jul 2020 semi-annual version 2002.* The syntax is:

=SEQUENCE(rows,[columns],[start],[step])

The SEQUENCE function generates a one or two dimensional array that contains sequential numbers. The function also optionally allows you to specify *start* and *step* values.

The SEQUENCE function is useful for generating date and time sequences (when used in conjunction with Excel's date and time functions).

1   Open *Calendar* from your sample files folder.

This sample file contains a non-functioning calendar. In this lesson you'll use SEQUENCE functions to add drop-down list validations that will allow users to easily select a year and month.

The *Year* drop-down data will dynamically adjust to display years that are ten years in the past and future from the current year.

2   Add *Month* data to the *Data* worksheet.

1.   Select the *Data* worksheet.

2.   Type this function into cell A6:

=TEXT(DATE(2020,SEQUENCE(12),1), "mmm")

You learned about the DATE function in: *Lesson 3-11: Use the DATE function to offset days, months and years.* Note the use of the SEQUENCE function to produce twelve consecutive numbers.

This will cause the DATE function to return the first day of each month in 2020. Any year could be used, the aim is simply to return one date for each month.

The date function is wrapped in a TEXT function. You learned about the TEXT function in: *Lesson 3-19: Use the TEXT function to format numerical values as strings.*

The TEXT function uses the format **"mmm"** to convert each date value into a three letter month (see sidebar).

	A
5	Month
6	Jan
7	Feb
8	Mar
9	Apr
10	May
11	Jun
12	Jul
13	Aug
14	Sep
15	Oct
16	Nov
17	Dec

Calendar

3   Add Year data to the *Data* worksheet.

A SEQUENCE function will be used to return a dynamic array containing 21 sequential year values beginning ten years before the current year.

Type this function into cell C6:

=SEQUENCE(21,1,YEAR(TODAY())-10)

This function returns 21 rows and 1 column beginning with a year that is ten years earlier than the current year (see sidebar).

	C
5	Year
6	2010
7	2011
8	2012
9	2013
10	2014
11	2015
12	2016
13	2017
14	2018
15	2019
16	2020
17	2021
18	2022
19	2023
20	2024
21	2025
22	2026
23	2027
24	2028
25	2029
26	2030

4 Add list validations to cells C4 and C5 on the *Calendar* worksheet that use the *Month* and *Year* dynamic arrays defined on the *Data* worksheet.

You learned how to do this in: *Lesson 4-6: Create a drop-down list using a UNIQUE function.* The correct source formulas are:

5 Add an XMATCH function to cell B5 on the Data worksheet that will return the Month number selected on the Calendar worksheet.

Excel's DATE function needs to work with month numbers rather than text. You need to convert the chosen textual month into a month number.

1. Select the *Data* worksheet.

2. Type this function into cell B3:

    =XMATCH(Calendar!C5,Data!A6#)

    The selected month number now appears in cell B3.

    In this case this gives exactly the same result as:

    =MATCH(Calendar!C5,Data!A6#)

    You *learned about the MATCH function in: Lesson 3-26: Use a MATCH function for an exact lookup.* XMATCH is the modern replacement for MATCH and can do many more things. You'll learn about the XMATCH function later, in: *Lesson 4-21: Use an XMATCH function.*

6 Test the drop-down lists

1. Select the *Calendar* Worksheet.

2. Select *July 2020.*

3. Select the *Data* worksheet.

4. Make sure that the *Selected Month* (in cell B3) contains the number: 7

The calendar does not yet work but you have created a functioning user interface.

You will complete the calendar in: *Lesson 4-16: Create a perpetual calendar using the SEQUENCE function*

7 Save your work as *Calendar-1.*

Lesson 4-16: Create a perpetual calendar using the SEQUENCE function

1   Open *Calendar-1* from your sample files folder.

The user interface allows a user to select a year and month. You created year and month data for the drop-down lists using the SEQUENCE function in: *Lesson 4-15: Use a SEQUENCE function.*

2   Add a SEQUENCE function to cell B8 to populate the calendar with date serial numbers that relate to the chosen *Year* and *Month*.

You'll now use another SEQUENCE function to populate the calendar area in cells B8:H12 with the correct dates for the selected *Month* and *Year*.

1. Click in cell B8.

2. Click: Formulas→Function Library→Math & Trig→Sequence. The *Function Arguments* dialog appears:

SEQUENCE			
Rows		↑	= number
Columns		↑	= number
Start		↑	= number

Clearly you need to populate five rows and seven columns with dates to complete the calendar.

3. Type: **5** into the *Rows* box.

4. Type: **7** into the *Columns* box.

You now need to consider the starting value.

In: *Lesson 3-7: Understand date serial numbers,* you learned that every date in Excel is represented by a number.

The *Start* argument (the number that needs to be returned to cell B8) needs to be the serial number for the first day in the month defined in the *Year* and *Month* drop-down lists (in cells C4 and C5).

In: *Lesson 3-11: Use the DATE function to offset days, months and years,* you learned about the DATE function. The DATE function accepts a *Year, Month* and *Day* argument (all of which must be numbers) and returns a date serial number

It should be clear that the function:

DATE(C4, Data!B3, 1)

… will return the correct date serial number for cell B8 (the number that starts the sequence).

5. Type :

DATE(C4, Data!B3, 1)

Calendar-1

… into the *Start* box. The *Insert Function* dialog should now look like this:

Rows	5	↑	= 5
Columns	7	↑	= 7
Start	DATE(C4,Data!B3,1)	↑	= 44013
Step		↑	= number
			= {44013,44014,44015,

You can see that the first date serial number returned (in this example) is 44013. That's because I had selected *Jul* for the month and *2020* for the year.

44013 is the date serial number for 1st July 2020.

6. Click the OK button.

The calendar is filled with date serial numbers:

A	B	C	D	E
6				
7				
8	44713	44714	44715	44716
9	44720	44721	44722	44723

3 Format the date serial numbers to display as days.

Because the calendar only needs to show day numbers it is necessary to format the date serial numbers to display as days.

1. Select cells B8:H12.

2. Right-click on any selected cell.

3. Click *Format Cells…* from the shortcut menu.

4. Click *Custom* in the left-hand *Category* list.

5. Type the format character: **d** into the *Type* box (see sidebar).

This custom format code formats a date as a single number (with no leading zeroes) representing the day.

6. Click the OK button.

Day numbers are now shown in the body of the calendar.

A	B	C	D	E	F
7					
8	1	2	3	4	5
9	8	9	10	11	12

Number	Alignment	Font
Category:		
General		Sample
Number		1
Currency		
Accounting		Type:
Date		d
Time		
Percentage		h:mm
Fraction		h:mm:ss
Scientific		m/d/yyyy
Text		mm:ss
Special		mm:ss.0
Custom		@
		[h]:mm:ss

4 Add the correct days of the week to cells B7:H7.

1. Type this function into Cell B7:

=TEXT(B8:H8,"ddd")

This function takes the date serial numbers found in cells B8:H8 and formats them as three-letter day names.

A	B	C	D	E	F	G	H
7	Wed	Thu	Fri	Sat	Sun	Mon	Tue
8	1	2	3	4	5	6	7

5 Save your work as *Calendar-2*.

Lesson 4-17: Use a RANDARRAY function

The RANDARRAY syntax is:

=RANDARRAY([rows],[columns],[min],[max],[whole_number])

This function generates a one or two dimensional array of random numbers between a maximum and minimum value.

RANDARRAY can be configured to return both whole and decimal numbers using the whole number argument.

RANDARRAY is very useful when you need to create some random test data.

1   Open *Dummy Data* from your sample files folder.

Imagine that you need a sample file that contains monthly sales data for ten employees. In this lesson you'll create ten fictitious names along with their sales data using a RANDARRAY function.

	C	D	E	F	G	H
3	First Name	Last Name	Jan	Feb	Mar	Total
4	Coco	Lewis	$ 20,764.27	$ 20,424.15	$ 21,557.85	$ 62,746.28
5	Joseph	Sellers	$ 18,372.07	$ 21,484.91	$ 19,626.71	$ 59,483.69
6	Greta	Parks	$ 18,715.59	$ 5,157.69	$ 4,519.21	$ 28,392.49
7	Paul	Antoinette	$ 16,040.09	$ 8,316.39	$ 12,605.14	$ 36,961.62

2   Add a RANDARRAY function to cells A4:B13 on the *Dummy* worksheet that returns a random row number from the *FamousNames* table.

1. Select the *Dummy* worksheet.

2. Click in cell A4.

3. Click: Formulas→Function Library→ Math & Trig→RANDARRAY.

The *Function Arguments* dialog appears:

You need to populate a matrix of ten rows and two columns with random whole numbers that reference a row in the *FamousNames* table.

The *Rows, Columns* and *Min* arguments will thus be:

Rows	10
Columns	2
Min	1

For the *Max* argument you will need to determine the total number of data rows in the *FamousNames* table. This can easily be done using the ROWS function. The ROWS function returns the number of data rows in a table (excluding the header row).

4. Type this function into the *Max* argument box:

ROWS(FamousNames)

You now need to consider the last argument: *Integer.*

Dummy Data

The Integer argument allows you to specify whether you require a whole number (called an integer) or decimal value.

Because you want to return a whole number this argument needs to be set to TRUE.

5. Type: **TRUE** in the *Integer* argument box.

The dialog should now be the same as shown in the sidebar.

6. Click the *OK* button.

Random numbers are shown in cells A4:B13.

3   Use the random numbers in cells A4:B13 to return random *First* and *Last* Names to cells C4:D13.

1. Add this function into cell C4:

   =INDEX(FamousNames[First Name],A4)

   This INDEX function returns the *First Name* found in the data row of the *FamousNames* table defined in cell A4.

2. Add this function into cell D4:

   =INDEX(FamousNames[Last Name],B4)

   Autofill cells C4:D4 down to row 13.

   Random names are now shown in each cell (see sidebar).

	A	B	C	D
3	Ran	Ranc	First Name	Last Name
4	34	77	George	Ali
5	58	98	Lech	Freud
6	48	63	John	Johnson
7	29	23	Eva	Tutu
8	53	13	Joseph	Geldof
9	74	79	Michael	Mandela
10	97	32	Shakira	Roosevelt
11	104	52	Thomas	Stewart
12	72	16	Mata	Darwin
13	64	16	Madonna	Darwin

4   Use a RANDARRAY function to add random monthly sales figures between $4,000 and $22,000 into cells E4:G13 showing sales to two decimal places.

Type this function into cell E4:

=RANDARRAY(10,3,4000,22000,FALSE)

You can see that this will return a two-dimensional array of 10 rows by 3 columns containing random numbers between 4000 and 22000. The FALSE last argument causes the function to return decimal numbers.

Random sales figures now appear in each cell and the data refreshes if you press the **[F9]** (recalculate) key:

	A	B	C	D	E	F	G	H
3	Ran	Ranc	First Name	Last Name	Jan	Feb	Mar	Total
4	65	4	Mahatma	Hitchcock	$ 19,871.20	$ 4,448.16	$ 4,994.95	$ 29,314.31
5	65	78	Mahatma	Armstrong	$ 21,203.63	$ 12,323.16	$ 10,032.07	$ 43,558.85
6	24	64	Donald	American	$ 13,119.03	$ 11,656.53	$ 4,265.37	$ 29,040.92
7	41	30	Ingrid	Castro	$ 8,597.08	$ 16,717.36	$ 20,254.77	$ 45,569.21
8	108	65	Usain	Gandhi	$ 21,651.80	$ 18,788.20	$ 19,247.95	$ 59,687.94
9	20	35	Coco	Clooney	$ 21,131.83	$ 14,554.18	$ 9,102.92	$ 44,788.93
10	66	15	Malala	Lewis	$ 20,255.06	$ 6,160.48	$ 9,778.20	$ 36,193.74
11	36	75	Grace	Gorbachev	$ 9,296.73	$ 18,680.38	$ 4,761.91	$ 32,739.02
12	112	102	Wilbur	Jobs	$ 9,131.23	$ 21,853.74	$ 13,485.05	$ 44,470.02
13	3	99	Albert	Bolivar	$ 14,324.86	$ 13,114.65	$ 15,046.63	$ 42,486.14
14					$158,582.43	$138,296.84	$110,969.81	

5   Hide columns A and B on the Dummy worksheet.

1. Select columns A and B.

2. Right-click on one of the selected cells.

3. Click *Hide* from the shortcut menu.

6   Save your work as *Dummy Data-1.*

note

XLOOKUP will not work in legacy Excel versions (Excel 2019 and earlier)

The XLOOKUP function was added in the *Jul 2020 semi-annual version 2002.*

If you must share your workbooks with users of legacy versions of Excel (Excel 2019 and earlier) you will not be able to make use of this feature.

You can expect the deprecated VLOOKUP and HLOOKUP functions to continue to be supported in future Excel versions.

Microsoft have stated:

"VLOOKUP and HLOOKUP will both continue to be supported by Excel. That said, we strongly recommend using XLOOKUP in favor of VLOOKUP and HLOOKUP".

Lesson 4-18: Understand XLOOKUP (part one)

You should use XLOOKUP and not VLOOKUP, HLOOKUP or INDEX/MATCH in new work

XLOOKUP was introduced in the *Jul 2020 semi-annual version 2002.* This was a landmark release as it added support for dynamic arrays.

You learned to use VLOOKUP and HLOOKUP in*: Lesson 3-25: Use a VLOOKUP function for an inexact lookup.*

You learned to use INDEX and MATCH together to emulate a VLOOKUP in: *Lesson 3-27: Use the INDEX function.*

Unless backward compatibility with legacy Excel versions (Excel 2019 and earlier) is required, you should use XLOOKUP for new work. As XLOOKUP is far more versatile and is easier to use.

Later, in: *Lesson 4-21: Use an XMATCH function,* you'll learn about the new XMATCH function, the modern replacement for the old MATCH function.

XLOOKUP simple example

Here is the XLOOKUP syntax:

=XLOOKUP (lookup, lookup_array, return_array, [not_found], [match_mode], [search_mode])

The first three arguments (those without square brackets) are required and the last three (those inside square brackets) are optional.

XLOOKUP can return a single value or an array of values. Here's how it works:

You can see that XLOOKUP requires a lookup value and two arrays. In this example the Lookup value is "Apples".

 The *lookup_array* contains:

{ "Pears"; "Apples"; "Bananas"}

and the *return_array* contains:

{22;33;50}.

XLOOKUP searches for the *lookup* value *Apples* in the *lookup_array*. When the value is found XLOOKUP remembers that *Apples* is the second element in the *lookup_array*.

XLOOKUP then fetches the value contained in the second element in the *return_array* (33) and returns it to the cell containing the function (cell F4).

Of course, you could have done almost the same thing with the old VLOOKUP function but, as you'll see in a moment, re-designing VLOOKUP as an array function provides many advantages.

XLOOKUP can return a custom error message

When a VLOOKUP function cannot find any matching values it returns a *#N/A* error.

When an XLOOKUP function cannot find any matching values it is able to return a custom *Not Found* message

F4				f_x	=XLOOKUP(B4,C4:C6,D4:D6,"No fruit found")		
	A	B	C	D	E	F	G	H
2								
3		Lookup	Lookup Array	Return Array		Returns		
4		Grapes	Pears	22		No fruit found		
5			Apples	33				
6			Bananas	50				

Notice that the fourth *not_found* argument has been used to return the custom text: *No Fruit Found* when the *lookup* value does not appear in the *lookup_array*.

XLOOKUP can use any column for the lookup and return arrays

C11				f_x	=XLOOKUP(C10,E4:E6,C4:C6)		
	A	B	C	D	E	F	G
2							
3		Date	Category	Supplier	Code	Qty	Price
4		1-Jan-20	Pears	Best Buys	P03	5	$0.78
5		15-Jan-20	Apples	Top Discounts	A22	12	$0.85
6		18-Jan-20	Bananas	Exotic Fruit	B30	14	$0.92
7			⬆		⬆		
8			Return Array		Lookup Array		
9							
10		Lookup:	B30				
11		Returns:	Bananas				

In this example you can see that XLOOKUP has achieved something that isn't possible with VLOOKUP. You'd have had to use an INDEX/MATCH combination in legacy excel to achieve this.

Lesson 4-19: Understand XLOOKUP (part two)

XLOOKUP can return more than one value

VLOOKUP is only able to return a single value.

In this example the XLOOKUP function in cell B13 is returning an array of six values because the return array has been defined as the entire range B4:G6.

XLOOKUP can search both horizontally and vertically

Legacy Excel provided both VLOOKUP (vertical lookup) and HLOOKUP (horizontal lookup) functions.

The XLOOKUP function can replace both the VLOOKUP and HLOOKUP functions as arrays can model both horizontal and vertical ranges.

In this example the lookup and return arrays are horizontal. The products shown in cells B6:B8 are searched for in cells C2:E2. When a match is found, a value is returned from cells C3:E3.

An interesting feature in this example is the use of an array (B6:B8) for the first (lookup) argument. This makes the XLOOKUP function return a spilled range into cells D6:D8.

XLOOKUP has more powerful inexact lookup features than VLOOKUP

In: *Lesson 3-25: Use a VLOOKUP function for an inexact lookup*, you learned about the concept of exact and inexact lookups.

Just like VLOOKUP, XLOOKUP can perform an inexact lookup but XLOOKUP has some additional features that are not available in VLOOKUP:

- There is no need to sort a table or range before using XLOOKUP.

- XLOOKUP is able to search a lookup array from last-to-first as well as first-to-last. This is useful when there are multiple matches present in the lookup array. The search direction is defined using the *search_mode* argument:

> 1 - Search first-to-last
> -1 - Search last-to-first
> 2 - Binary search (sorted ascending order)
> -2 - Binary search (sorted descending order)

The *Binary Search* options are not very useful but if you are curious about their purpose see sidebar.

- VLOOKUP is only able to return the *next smallest* item when performing an inexact lookup. XLOOKUP is able to return the *next smallest* or *next largest* item. The type of inexact match is defined using the *match_mode* argument:

> 0 - Exact match
> -1 - Exact match or next smaller item
> 1 - Exact match or next larger item
> 2 - Wildcard character match

XLOOKUP can match using wildcards

You learned about wildcards in: *Lesson 3-6: Use the SUMIF and COUNTIF functions to create conditional totals (sidebar)*.

Wildcards are search strings that can include the * and ? wildcard symbols.

The XLOOKUP function's *match_mode* argument enables you to define a wildcard search.

> 0 - Exact match
> -1 - Exact match or next smaller item
> 1 - Exact match or next larger item
> 2 - Wildcard character match   Return the index of a wildcard match where *, ? and ~ have special meaning

important

A two-dimensional array is an "array of arrays"

Consider this simple two-dimensional array:

{
3,4,6;
5,7,8;
6,7,9
}

You could think of this as a single array with three elements. Each element contains an array rather than a single value.

For example, the second element of the array contains the one-dimensional array:

{5,7,8}

It is important to realize that XLOOKUP cannot easily return a column array from a two-dimensional array.

In the above example XLOOKUP alone cannot return the second column:

{4;7;7}

You could not have completed the problem that you solved in this lesson by first extracting the *Birmingham* column array as XLOOKUP cannot return a column array.

Later, in *Lesson 4-21: Use an XMATCH function* you'll find a simpler solution to the problem posed in this lesson using the INDEX and XMATCH functions.

Lesson 4-20: Use XLOOKUP to perform a two-dimensional lookup

1 Open *Distance Chart* from your sample files folder.

The sample file contains a matrix showing the distance between several British towns and cities:

	A	B York	C Southampton	D Sheffield	E Portsmouth	F Oxford	G Nottingham	H Norwich
3								
4	Aberdeen	307	538	347	552	473	379	480
5	Aberystwyth	195	198	156	218	157	156	271
6	Birmingham	129	128	76	141	63	49	161
7	Bristol	217	74	164	94	70	137	209
8	Cardiff	231	118	178	138	104	151	235

Simple list validations have been placed in cells B30 and B31 to enable the user to select a *From* and *To* destination. You learned how to create list validations in: *Lesson 2-11: Add a table-based dynamic list validation.*

	A	B	C	D	E	F	G	H	I
28	The above are the shortest business routes in miles								
29									
30	From:	Birmingham							
31	To:	Sheffield							
32									
33	Miles:								
34									

A formula is needed in cell B33 that will return the correct number of miles from the matrix above.

This type of lookup is often called an *X/Y lookup* or a *Two Dimensional Lookup.*

2 Select *Birmingham* as the *From:* location and *Sheffield* as the *To:* location.

This will make the screen grabs below match your own work.

	A	B York	C Southampton	D Sheffield	E Portsmouth
3					
4	Aberdeen	307	538	347	552
5	Aberystwyth	195	198	156	218
6	Birmingham	129	128	76	141

You can see that the correct answer will be 76 miles.

3 Extract all of the values in the *From:* row into a spilled range in cell B35.

1. Type **From Array:** into cell A35.

Distance Chart

note

It is often useful to break complex formulas up into several simpler formulas

In: *Lesson 4-14: Use a FILTER function with AND/OR custom logic arrays (sidebar),* I discussed the value of breaking a complex formula into several simpler formulas.

In this lesson you use a helper spilled range in row 35 and later hide the row to maintain a clean user interface.

You could also use this less understandable formula (in cell B33) to return the distance between locations:

**=XLOOKUP(B31,
B3:X3,
XLOOKUP(B30,
A4:A26,
B4:X26))**

You would then have no need for the spilled range you created in cell B35.

If you did this you'd make the formula more error prone and difficult for others to understand.

My advice is to always break complex functions into as many simple steps as possible.

2. Add an XLOOKUP function to cell B35 using the following arguments:

Lookup_value	B30	↑	=	`Birmingham`
Lookup_array	A4:A26	↑	=	{"Aberdeen";"A
Return_array	B4:X26	↑	=	{307,538,347,55

The *Lookup_value* argument is the cell containing the selected *From:* location (*Birmingham*). In this example: **B30**

The *Lookup_array* is the range in which to search for the text: *Birmingham*. Because you want to return the location of a row you need to search the range **A4:A26**.

The *Return_array* is the entire data matrix **B4:X26**.

XLOOKUP will find the correct row element in this array (element 3) and return an array containing all of the values in the third row. An array of all data corresponding to the *Birmingham* row is returned:

	A	B	C	D	E	F
35	From Array:	129	128	76	141	63

4 **Extract the value in the *From Array:* (located in cell B35) that corresponds to the chosen *To:* location.**

You can see that the *To:* location (*Sheffield*) is the third element in the *From Array:* and contains the correct distance between Birmingham and Sheffield (76 miles).

Add an XLOOKUP function to cell B33 using the following arguments:

Lookup_value	B31	↑	=	`Sheffield`
Lookup_array	B3:X3	↑	=	{"York","Sou
Return_array	B35#	↑	=	{129,128,76

The *Lookup_value* argument is the cell containing the selected *To:* location: *Sheffield*. In this example: **B31**

The *Lookup_array* is the range in which to search for the text: *Sheffield*. Because you want to find the correct column, you need to search the range **B3:X3**.

The *Return_array* is the array containing all of the data in the *Birmingham* row. This is the spilled range you extracted into cell B35.

The correct value is returned to cell B33.

	A	B	C	D	E	F
30	From:	Birmingham				
31	To:	Sheffield				
32						
33	Miles:	76				

5 **Hide row 35.**

Right-click on the row 35 row header and select *Hide* from the shortcut menu.

6 **Save your work as *Distance Chart-1*.**

note

Using XMATCH to return a single column from a two-dimensional array

Consider this simple two-dimensional array:

{
3,4,6;
5,7,8;
6,7,9
}

You could think of this as a single array with three elements. Each element contains a row array rather than a single value.

For example, the second element of the array contains the one-dimensional array:

{5,7,8}

In some scenarios you may wish to return a column rather than a row. For example the second column:

{4;7;7}

The INDEX function can do this by specifying 0 as the *Row_num* argument:

Array	{3,4,6;5,7,8;6,7,9}
Row_num	0
Column_num	2

When you use the above arguments for the INDEX function it will return the array:

{4;7;7}

This is because if you set the *row_num* or *col_num* argument to 0, INDEX will return an array containing all of the values in the corresponding column or row.

Row number 0 and column number 2 will thus return an array containing all of the values in the second column of the array.

Lesson 4-21: Use an XMATCH function

You should use XMATCH and not MATCH in new work

XMATCH was introduced in the *Jul 2020 semi-annual version 2002* release as a modern replacement for the old MATCH function that you learned about in: *Lesson 3-26: Use a MATCH function for an exact lookup.*

Unless backward compatibility with legacy Excel versions (Excel 2019 and earlier) is required, you should use XMATCH for new work. XMATCH is more versatile and easier to use than the older MATCH function that it replaces.

How XMATCH works

The syntax for the XMATCH function is:

XMATCH (lookup_value, lookup_array, [match_mode], [search_mode])

You can think of the XMATCH functions as being XLOOKUP but without the return array. XMATCH has identical *match_mode* and *search_mode* options.

Instead of a value from an element of a return array, XMATCH returns the element number of a specific value found in a one-dimensional array. For example:

=XMATCH("Apples", {"Apples", "Pears", "Oranges"})

… returns the number 1, as the value *Apples* is found in the first element in the array.

In this lesson you'll create an alternative solution to the problem posed in: *Lesson 4-20: Use XLOOKUP to perform a two-dimensional lookup.* Instead of XLOOKUP you'll use a combination of XMATCH and INDEX functions.

1   Open USA *Distance Chart* from your sample files folder.

This is similar to the workbook you created in: *Lesson 4-20: Use XLOOKUP to perform a two-dimensional lookup* except that this workbook shows USA cities rather than UK cities.

⊿	A	B	C	D	E
22	From:	Chicago			
23	To:	Dallas			
24					
25	Miles:				
26					

2   Select *Chicago* as the *From* city and *Dallas* as the *To city*.

3   Type: **From Row:** into cell A27.

4   Type: **To Column:** into cell A28.

Your worksheet should now look like this:

note

How does XMATCH differ from MATCH

XMATCH defaults to an exact match.

The old VLOOKUP and MATCH functions defaulted to an inexact match. In almost every business scenario an exact match is needed.

XLOOKUP and XMATCH sensibly correct this anomaly and the new default is now an exact match.

MATCH(B22, A5:A20)
... results in an inexact match

XMATCH(B22, A5:A20)
... results in an exact match

XMATCH has an optional search_mode argument

The *search_mode* argument can be used to set the direction in which XMATCH searches.

	1 - Search first-to-last
	-1 - Search last-to-first
	2 - Binary search (sorted ascending order)
	-2 - Binary search (sorted descending order)

The last two options (*Binary search*) are not very useful. *See: Lesson 4-19: Understand XLOOKUP (part two) sidebar*, for more information.

The first two options are very useful as they allow the direction of the search to be set. For example:

Apples
Pears
Apples

In the above range a first-to-last search will return 1 but a last-to-first search will return 3.

XMATCH supports wildcards

You learned about wildcard searches in: *Lesson 4-19: Understand XLOOKUP (part two).*

The XMATCH function has the same wildcard search option as XLOOOKUP that can be specified in the optional *match_mode* argument.

	A	B	C	D
22	From:	Chicago		
23	To:	Dallas		
24				
25	Miles:			
26				
27	From Row:			
28	To Column:			

5 Add an XMATCH function to cell B27 that will find the *Chicago* row.

Type this function into cell B27:

=XMATCH(B22,A5:A20)

The function returns 2 because Chicago is the second row in the list of locations in column A (see sidebar).

6 Add an XMATCH function to cell B28 that will find the *Dallas* column.

Type this function into cell B28:

=XMATCH(B23,B4:Q4)

The function returns 3 because *Dallas* is the third column in the list of locations in row 4 (see sidebar).

	A	B	C	D
4		Austin	Chicago	Dallas
5	Austin	-	1,572	294
6	Chicago	1,572	-	1,290
7	Dallas	294	1,290	-
8	Denver	1,241	1,474	1,064

7 Add an INDEX function to cell B25 that will return the number of miles from Chicago to Dallas.

Type this function into cell B25:

=INDEX(B5:Q20,B27,B28)

The correct mileage appears in cell B25.

	A	B	C	D
22	From:	Chicago		
23	To:	Dallas		
24				
25	Miles:		1,290	
26				
27	From Row:	2		
28	To Column:	3		

Each of the three formulas used for this solution are very simple to understand.

You could, of course, hide rows 27 and 28 to maintain a clean user interface.

You could also eliminate the need for the Row and Column cells by combining the three functions like this:

=INDEX(B5:Q20,XMATCH(B22,A5:A20),XMATCH(B23,B4:Q4))

8 Save your work as *USA Distance Chart-1*.

Lesson 4-22: Use the SUMPRODUCT function

How SUMPRODUCT works

The SUMPRODUCT function syntax is:

=SUMPRODUCT (array1, [array2], ...)

It is easiest to explain what SUMPRODUCT does using an example.

SUMPRODUCT is usually used with two or more arrays. Each array must have the same number of elements.

Consider these two arrays:

Array 1:   {1, 2, 3}

Array 2:   {6, 5, 4}

The result of =SUMPRODUCT(Array 1, Array 2) would be 28.

This is calculated as (1*6) + (2*5) + (3*4).

This calculation can be referred to as: "The sum of the products of corresponding arrays".

1   Open *New Car Sales* from your sample files folder.

This worksheet contains a car dealer's new car sales figures.

	A	B	C
1	New Model 3 Car Sales		
2			
3	Model	Cost per unit	Quantity
4	Model 3 Standard Range Plus	$ 39,900.00	22
5	Model 3 Long Range	$ 48,990.00	18
6	Model 3 Performance	$ 56,990.00	9
7			
8		Total Sales:	

2   Add a SUMPRODUCT function to cell C8 that will return the total sales value.

1.   Click in cell C8.

2.   Click: Formulas→Function Library→ Math & Trig→SUMPRODUCT.

The *Function Arguments* dialog appears.

Function Arguments			
SUMPRODUCT			
Array1		↑	= array
Array2		↑	= array
Array3		↑	= array

You can see that the SUMPRODUCT function accepts one or more arrays as arguments.

New Car Sales

3. Add the following ranges to the *Function Arguments* dialog:

Function Arguments

SUMPRODUCT

Array1	B4:B6	↑	=	{39900;48990;56990}
Array2	C4:C6	↑	=	{22;18;9}
Array3		↑	=	array

= 2272530

4. Click the OK button.

The correct value is returned to cell C8.

⊿	A	B	C
1	New Model 3 Car Sales		
2			
3	Model	Cost per unit	Quantity
4	Model 3 Standard Range Plus	$ 39,900	22
5	Model 3 Long Range	$ 48,990	18
6	Model 3 Performance	$ 56,990	9
7			
8		Total Sales:	$ 2,272,530

SUMPRODUCT has performed several calculations using the two arrays provided:

(39,900*22) + (48,990*18) + (56,990*9)

This is quite a trivial way to use a SUMPRODUCT function. You could have achieved the same result in many other ways.

The real power of SUMPRODUCT comes from its use with numeric and logic arrays.

Later, in: *Lesson 4-23: Use the SUMPRODUCT function with a logic array,* you'll address a business problem that would be difficult to solve without SUMPRODUCT.

3   Save your work as *New Car Sales-1*

note

Helper columns keep worksheets understandable

In this lesson you use helper columns to move the work of calculating the *Price Array* and *Logic Array* into two separate columns on the worksheet.

This results in a very simple SUMPRODUCT function to calculate the total price:

=SUMPRODUCT(J5#,K5#)

You could have avoided the need to create helper columns by moving all of the logic inside the SUMPRODUCT function like this:

**=SUMPRODUCT(
INDEX(HirePrices,0,
XMATCH(
H7,HirePrices[#Headers])),
(HirePrices[Date]>=H5)*
(HirePrices[Date]<=H6))**

This formula is far more difficult to understand. It is also more prone to error and more difficult to audit.

I recommend that you keep your workbooks as simple as possible. You can always hide the helper columns if you want to.

Lesson 4-23: Use the SUMPRODUCT function with a logic array

1   Open *Car Hire* from your sample files folder.

This worksheet contains a utility that will quote the total cost of car hire for a selected model and date period.

	G	H
5	Collection Date:	10-Jul-20
6	Return Date:	12-Jul-20
7	Model:	Ford Focus
8	Days on hire:	3
9	Total Price:	$ 345.00

This could be quite a difficult problem to solve without the SUMPRODUCT function.

2   Extract an array from the *HirePrices* table that contains all prices for the chosen car model.

In: *Lesson 4-21: Use an XMATCH function,* you learned that XMATCH returns the numerical position (element number) of a string found in an array of values.

In this lesson's example (and with *Ford Focus* chosen as the model) the function:

=XMATCH(H7,HirePrices[#Headers])

… will return 3. This is because *Ford Focus* is the third column in the *HirePrices* table:

	A	B	C	D	E
4	Date	Fiesta	Ford Focus	Ford Fusion	Mustang
5	1-Jul-20	$ 100	$ 110	$ 155	$ 165
6	2-Jul-20	$ 110	$ 105	$ 120	$ 140

To extract all of the prices in the third (*Ford Focus*) column you will use an INDEX function. The function:

=INDEX(HirePrices,0,3)

…would extract an array containing all of the values in the third (*Ford Focus)* column. That's because when either of the INDEX function's *row_num* or *column_num* arguments is zero, an array containing the entire row or column is returned

Type this formula into cell J5:

=INDEX(HirePrices,0,XMATCH(H7,HirePrices[#Headers]))

This formula combines the XMATCH and INDEX functions together.

All of the *Ford Focus* prices are now shown in a dynamic spilled range beginning in cell J5 (see sidebar).

	J
4	Price Array
5	$ 110
6	$ 105
7	$ 105
8	$ 135
9	$ 125
10	$ 135
11	$ 135
12	$ 135

Car Hire

3   Create a logic array that will indicate which rows in the *HirePrices* table fall between the selected dates.

Notice that this car hire company charges for the day of collection and the day of return. For this reason the Boolean logic test that needs to be applied is:

For each row:

Row *Date* is greater than or equal to *Collection Date*

AND

Row *Date* is less than or equal to *Return Date.*

This is a Boolean AND expression that you learned about in: *Lesson 4-13: Construct Boolean AND/OR logic arrays.* You also learned that multiplying two arrays together will result in an AND logic array.

Type this formula into cell K5:

=(HirePrices[Date]>=H5)*(HirePrices[Date]<=H6)

A dynamic spilled range containing logic values (expressed as numbers where one=true and zero=false) appears, beginning in cell K5 (see sidebar).

In this example the dates *10-Jul-2020* to *12-Jul-2020* were chosen. Notice how the number 1 appears next to the correct rows (rows 14-16) that correspond with the chosen dates in the *HirePrices* table.

4   Use a SUMPRODUCT function to calculate the total hire cost for the chosen date range and model.

Type this formula into cell H9:

=SUMPRODUCT(J5#,K5#)

SUMPRODUCT begins by multiplying the values found in the *Price Array* (J5#) and *Logic Array* (K5#). When the logic array's value is zero this will result in a zero result, but when the logic array's value is 1 it will multiply (sum) the daily price by one (returning the daily price).

When SUMPRODUCT has completed this task it adds together (calculates the product of) the resulting values.

The total hire cost for the period is thus returned:

	J	K
4	Price Array	Logic Array
5	$ 110	0
6	$ 105	0
7	$ 105	0
8	$ 135	0
9	$ 125	0

	A	B	C	D	E	F	G	H	I	J	K
4	Date	Fiesta	Ford Focus	Ford Fusion	Mustang					Price Array	Logic Array
5	1-Jul-20	$ 100	$ 110	$ 155	$ 165		Collection Date:	10-Jul-20		$ 110	0
6	2-Jul-20	$ 110	$ 105	$ 120	$ 140		Return Date:	12-Jul-20		$ 105	0
7	3-Jul-20	$ 120	$ 105	$ 140	$ 165		Model:	Ford Focus		$ 105	0
8	4-Jul-20	$ 115	$ 135	$ 120	$ 145		Days on hire:	3		$ 135	0
9	5-Jul-20	$ 115	$ 125	$ 135	$ 165		Total Price:	$ 345.00		$ 125	0
10	6-Jul-20	$ 80	$ 135	$ 140	$ 145					$ 135	0

5   Save your work as *Car Hire-1*

Lesson 4-24: Use a SORTBY function with a custom array

1　Open *DA Help Desk from your sample files folder*.

	A	B	C	D	E	F	G	H
3	Incident ID	Date Raised	Raised By	Description	Priority		Sort By	
4	10872	27-Jan-16	Barack Obama	Air conditioning not working	Low		Critical	
5	10873	27-Jan-16	Britney Spears	No hot water in staff kitchen	Medium		Urgent	
6	10874	27-Jan-16	Angelina Jolie	Broken lock on main door	Critical		High	
7	10875	27-Jan-16	Kofi Anan	Freezer has stopped working	Critical		Medium	
8	10876	27-Jan-16	Oprah Winfrey	Internet down	High		Low	
9	10877	27-Jan-16	Bill Clinton	TV in canteen doesn't pick up sky sports	Low			

This is very similar to the sample file used previously in: *Lesson 1-18: Sort a range or table by custom list*.

The worksheet has an *Incident* table that lists several support incidents sent to a help desk that are prioritized from *Low* to *Critical*. There is a requirement to sort the table into the order defined in the *SortBy* table in column G.

In this lesson you will create a solution using the SORTBY function along with a custom sort array created by the XMATCH function.

2　Add a SORTBY dynamic array function to cell I4 that will return the entire Incident table sorted in the order defined in the *SortBy* table.

You only need to consider the first three arguments of the SORTBY function, as this will be a single level sort:

=SORTBY(array, by_array, sort_order)

The first argument (array) contains the array that should be returned. Because you want to return the entire table you need a structured reference that returns all of the data in the table ie:

Incident

The second argument (*by_array*) will contain a custom array that will be returned by the XMATCH function.

You only need to consider the first two arguments of the XMATCH function, as the *Match_mode* default is an exact match and the *Search_mode* default is first to last. The syntax is thus:

=XMATCH (lookup_value, lookup_array)

Up until now you've used a single *lookup_value* with XMATCH to return the element of an array that contains the value. For example:

=XMATCH("apples", {"pears", "apples", "oranges", "apples"})

… returns a value of 2 because *apples* is the second value in the *lookup_array* (and is also the first match found in the array).

If an array is used for the first argument XMATCH will return an array. For example:

=XMATCH({"apples", "oranges"}, {"apples", "apples", "oranges"})

DA Help Desk

… returns the array {1,3}

- **1** is returned because the first incidence of "apples" appears in the first element of the lookup array.

- **3** is returned because the first incidence of "oranges" appears in the third element of the lookup array.

It should thus be clear that this function:

=XMATCH(Incident[Priority],CustomSort[Sort By])

… will return an array of numbers between 1 and 5 (depending upon the position of the text in the *Priority* column within the *SortBy* table).

1. Click in cell I4.

2. Click: Formulas→Function Library→ Lookup & Reference→SORTBY

   The *Function Arguments* dialog appears.

3. Add the following arguments to the *Function Arguments* dialog. The *By_array1* argument is:

   XMATCH(Incident[Priority],CustomSort[Sort By])

Array	Incident	⬆	=	{10872,42396,"Barack Obama"
By_array1	XMATCH(Incident[Priority], Custc	⬆	=	{5;4;1;1;3;5;2;5;5;2;4;4;5;3;1;4;5
Sort_order1	1	⬆	=	1

   Notice the values shown next to the *By_array1* argument.

   You can see how sorting this array will return the table sorted in the priority order required.

4. Click the OK button.

   The table is returned in the correct sorted order.

	F	G	H	I	J	K	L	M
1				Prioritized List				
2								
3		Sort By ▼		Incident ID	Date Raised	Raised By	Description	Priority
4		Critical		10874	42396	Angelina Jolie	Broken lock on main door	Critical
5		Urgent		10875	42396	Kofi Anan	Freezer has stopped working	Critical
6		High		10886	42397	Bob Marley	Burst water main is flooding the basement	Critical
7		Medium		10878	42396	Marylyn Monroe	Computer not working	Urgent
8		Low		10881	42396	Warren E Buffett	Broken window on ground floor	Urgent
9				10891	42397	Johnny Depp	Our web site is down	Urgent
10				10896	42398	Roald Dahl	Staff minibus has flat battery	Urgent
11				10897	42398	Ian Fleming	Heating oil is low in the warehouse	Urgent
12				10901	42398	George Osborne	I can't connect to the database	Urgent
13				10876	42396	Oprah Winfrey	Internet down	High

3   Save your work as *DA Help Desk-1*

Session 4: Exercise

1 Open *Highest Grossing Movies of 2019* from your sample files folder.

This workbook contains a table listing the highest grossing movies of 2019 along with a non-functioning user interface that will later allow you to filter the table by any column:

	H	I	J	K
3	Column:		Total Gross: $	-
4	Filter:		Total Tickets Sold	

2 Add a dynamic spilled range to cell A7 on the *Data* tab that will list all of the column headers in the *Movie* table.

3 Add a list validation to cell I3 on the *Movie* worksheet that will provide a drop-down list listing all of the columns defined in the dynamic spilled range you have just created.

4 Select a column using the drop-down list you have just created.

5 Add a dynamic spilled range to cell B7 on the *Data* worksheet that will show a unique list of all values in the column shown in the selected column (shown in cell B3). Sort the list in A-Z order.

6 Add a list validation to cell I4 on the *Movie* worksheet that will provide a drop-down list listing all of the columns defined in the *Unique Filter By:* dynamic spilled range you have just created.

7 Select a filter value from the drop-down list you have just created.

8 Add a dynamic spilled range to cell D7 on the *Data* tab that will list all of the values in the column the user has chosen (shown in cell B3). Note that this is not a unique list but will contain all of the rows (from the selected column) in the *Movies* table. Do not sort the list.

9 Add a dynamic spilled range to cell E7 on the *Data* tab that will have a value of TRUE if the value shown in column D is equal to the selected filter shown in cell B4. If the value is not equal show a value of FALSE.

10 Add a FILTER function to cell H7 on the *Movie* worksheet that will create a dynamic spilled range listing all of the columns in the *Movie* table that match the column and filter condition defined in cells I3 and I4.

11 Add SUMPRODUCT functions to cells K3 and K4 to report total values for filtered results. (Tip: you will need to use the double unary operator (--) to convert the TRUE/FALSE values in the logic array into 1 and 0 values.

12 Save your work as: *Highest Grossing Movies of 2019-1*.

	H	I	J	K	L	M
3	Column:	Genre	Total Gross: $	633,893,893		
4	Filter:	Comedy	Total Tickets Sold	69,582,200		
5						
6	Movie	Released	Distributor	Genre	2019 Gross	Tickets Sold
7	The Upside	11-Jan-19	STX Entertainment	Comedy	$ 108,235,497	11,880,954
8	Good Boys	16-Aug-19	Universal	Comedy	$ 83,140,306	9,126,268
9	Tyler Perry's A Madea Famil...	1-Mar-19	Lionsgate	Comedy	$ 73,257,045	8,041,388

Highest Grossing Movies of 2019

If you need help, answers are shown on the next page

Session 4: Exercise Answers

If you have difficulty completing the exercise, here are the lessons that cover the relevant skills:

2   You learned how to do this in: *Lesson 4-9: Use a SORT function.*

The correct formula is: **=TRANSPOSE(Movie[#Headers])**

3   You learned how to do this in: *Lesson 4-6: Create a drop-down list using a UNIQUE function.*

1. Click in cell I3 on the *Movie* worksheet.

2. Click: Data→Data Tools→Data Validation→Data Validation…

3. Click: Settings→Allow→List

4. Type: **=Data!$A$7#** into the *Source* box.

5   You learned how to do this in: *Lesson 4-11: Create two linked drop-down lists using dynamic arrays.*

The correct formula is: **=SORT(UNIQUE(INDIRECT("Movie["&B3 & "]")))**

6   You learned how to do this in: *Lesson 4-6: Create a drop-down list using a UNIQUE function.*

1. Click in cell I4 on the *Movie* worksheet.

2. Click: Data→Data Tools→Data Validation.

3. Click: Settings→Allow→List

4. Type: **=Data!$B$7#** into the *Source* box.

8   You learned how to do this in: *Lesson 4-11: Create two linked drop-down lists using dynamic arrays.*

The correct formula is: **=INDIRECT("Movie["&B3 & "]")**

9   You learned how to do this in: *Lesson 4-12: Use a FILTER function with a custom logic array.*

The correct formula is: **=D7#=B4**

10   You learned how to do this in: *Lesson 4-12: Use a FILTER function with a custom logic array.*

The correct formula is: **=FILTER(Movie,Data!E7#,"None Found")**

11   You learned how to do this in: *Lesson 4-23: Use the SUMPRODUCT function with a logic array.*

The correct formulas are:

=SUMPRODUCT(Movie[2019 Gross],--Data!E7#)

=SUMPRODUCT(Movie[Tickets Sold],--Data!E7#)

5

Session Five: Using Names and the Formula Auditing Tools

> To make no mistakes is not in the power of man; but from their errors and mistakes, the wise and good learn wisdom for the future.
>
> *Plutarch (46 AD - 120 AD)*

This session introduces Excel's ability to apply a name to a range of cells, a single cell, a formula, a constant or a table. Some problems are almost impossible to solve without names. In this session, you'll use name-based techniques to address several common business scenarios.

This session also introduces Excel's superb formula auditing tools. These will allow you to check your work for mistakes or track down errors when you know that something is wrong. As Plutarch asserts, you *will* make errors when working with Excel (assuming that you are human of course).

By the end of this session, you'll be able to use all of the auditing tools to track down and repair workbook errors.

Session Objectives

By the end of this session you will be able to:

- Automatically create single-cell range names
- Manually create single cell range names and named constants
- Use range names to make formulas more readable
- Automatically create range names in two dimensions
- Use intersection range names and the INDIRECT function
- Create dynamic formula-based range names using the OFFSET function
- Create table based dynamic range names
- Create two linked drop-down lists using range names
- Understand the #NUM!, #DIV/0! and #NAME? error values
- Understand the #VALUE!, #REF! and #NULL! error values
- Understand background error checking and error checking rules
- Manually check a worksheet for errors
- Audit a formula by tracing precedents
- Audit a formula by tracing dependents
- Use the Watch Window to monitor cell values
- Use Speak Cells to eliminate data entry errors

Lesson 5-1: Automatically create single-cell range names

The sample worksheet for this lesson contains prices that need to be expressed in different currencies. When you have this type of data, a separate exchange rate worksheet makes the exchange rates easy to maintain.

Here's how the exchange rates will be defined:

	A	B
3	GBP/USD	1.45427
4	EUR/USD	1.0923
5	JPY/USD	0.00852

A range name will then be automatically created for each of the values in column B. Excel will choose range names for column B based upon the values in column A. For the exchange rate in cell B3, it will automatically create the range name:

GBP_USD

You can then use the range name to make your formulas more readable.

	A	B	C	D
3	Description	Year	US Dollars	British Pounds
4	Chateau Lafite	1787	160000	=C4/USD_GBP

note

About names

A name can be applied to a range of cells, a single cell, a formula, a constant or a table.

When a name has been applied, it can be referred to within a formula in place of the item that it represents. For example, if the range A5:A45 was given the name *Sales*, the formulas:

=SUM(A5:A45)

and

=SUM(Sales)

…would produce exactly the same result.

1 Open *Vintage Wines-1* from your sample files folder.

2 Automatically create a range name for each of the exchange rates.

   1. Click the *ExchangeRates* worksheet tab.

   2. Select the range A3:B5.

   3. Click: Formulas→Defined Names→Create from Selection.

   The *Create Names from Selection* dialog appears:

   Create Names from Selection ? ✕

   Create names from values in the:
   ☐ Top row
   ☑ Left column
   ☐ Bottom row
   ☐ Right column

   OK   Cancel

   Notice that Excel has correctly guessed that the labels for each exchange rate are in the left column.

tip

You can also bring up the *Create Names from Selection* dialog using the keyboard shortcut:

<Ctrl>+<Shift>+<F3>

   4. Click the *OK* button.

Vintage Wines-1

note

Syntax rules for Range Names

Range names cannot contain spaces and may only begin with a letter, an underscore character (_), or a backslash (\).

Only letters, numbers, periods, question marks and underscores can be included within a name.

Range names are not case sensitive, so the name **SALES** or **Sales** can be used to reference a range name defined as **sales**.

Range names cannot be the same as any valid cell reference.

Good:
Boeing737
Boeing_737
_Boeing737
\Boeing.737

Bad:
737Boeing (number at start)
Boeing 737 (contains space)
BOE737 (same as a cell reference)

Excel uses range names for some of its own features. For this reason, you should never use any of the following range names:

Print_Area
Sheet_Title
Consolidate_Area
Print_Titles
Criteria

My preferred naming convention is to always spell out names in full, using mixed case with no underscores:

Good:
SalesTarget

Bad:
Sales_Target (underscore)
SlsTgt (abbreviation)

Nothing seems to have happened, but Excel has actually created a range name for each of the values in cells B3:B5.

3   Click the drop-down arrow on the right of the *Name* box to view the range names.

Notice that Excel hasn't used the exact names shown in column A, but has changed each forward slash to an underscore. This is because a forward slash isn't valid syntax for a range name (see sidebar for more on range name syntax).

4   Use formulas containing a range name to calculate prices in Great Britain Pounds, Euros and Japanese Yen.

1.   Click the *Prices* worksheet tab.

2.   Click in cell D4.

3.   Type **=C4/** to begin the formula.

4.   Click: Formulas→Defined Names→Use in Formula.

A drop-down list appears containing all defined range names.

Name Manager	Define Name
	Use in Formula
	EUR_USD
	GBP_USD
	JPY_USD

5.   Click: *GBP_USD* to insert the range name.

	C	D	E
3	US Dollars	British Pounds	Euros
4	$160,000.00	=C4/GBP_USD	

6.   Press the **<Enter>** Key.

7.   Use the same technique to enter a formula to calculate the *Euro* and *Japanese Yen* prices in cells E4 and F4.

5   AutoFill the formulas in cells D4:F4 to cells D5:F11.

	C	D	E	F
3	US Dollars	British Pounds	Euros	Japanese Yen
4	$160,000.00	£ 110,020.84	€ 146,479.90	¥18,779,342.72
5	$ 43,500.00	£ 29,911.91	€ 39,824.22	¥5,105,633.80

6   Save your work as *Vintage Wines-2*.

note

Qualified and Unqualified range name references

An unqualified reference means that the range name is used on its own. For example:

=C4*KilometerToMile

Qualified references state the worksheet name, then an exclamation mark, and then the *range name*. For example:

ConversionFactors! KilometerToMile

Range Name scope

Scope means the places in your workbook where an *unqualified* range name may be used. There are two possible scopes:

Workbook Scope – The name may be used within any of the worksheets in the workbook.

Worksheet Scope – The name may only be used within a specified worksheet.

Scope mayhem

Excel confusingly allows a *workbook scope* and a *worksheet scope* range name to share the same name. If this is done, the *worksheet scope* name takes precedence within the specified worksheet and the *workbook scope* name has precedence everywhere else.

Lesson 5-2: Manually create single cell range names and named constants

1 Open *Distances-1* from your sample files folder.

2 Manually create a range name for the *Kilometer to Mile* conversion factor using the *Name* box.

1. Click the *ConversionFactors* worksheet.

	A	B	C
3	From	To	Multiply By
4	Kilometer	Mile	0.621371192
5	Meter	Foot	3.28083

This time you are unable to automatically create range names because the values in column B are not descriptive enough to easily identify each conversion factor.

2. Click in cell C4.

3. Type **KilometerToMile** into the *Name* box.

KilometerToMile	▾	:	✕	✓	*fx*	0.621371192

	A	B	C	D	E
3	From	To	Multiply By		
4	Kilometer	Mile	0.621371192		

4. Press the **<Enter>** key.

3 Manually create a range name for the Meter to Foot conversion factor using the *Define Name* dialog.

This is an alternative method of defining range names.

1. Click in cell C5.

2. Click: Formulas→Defined Names→Define Name.

The *New Name* dialog appears.

3. Type the name **MeterToFoot** into the *Name* box.

Leave the scope as *Workbook* (see sidebar for an explanation of scope).

4. Click the *OK* button.

4 Use formulas containing range names to calculate distances in miles on the *Distances* worksheet.

	A	B	C	D
3	From	To	Km	Miles
4	London	Paris		343

1. Click in cell D4 on the *Distances* worksheet.

2. Type: **=C4***

Distances-1

note

When to use constants rather than range names

You should use single-cell range names when a value may possibly change in the future.

This was the case in: *Lesson 5-1: Automatically create single-cell range names* because you were dealing with currency exchange rates that fluctuate.

Constants are more appropriate when a value is never expected to change. For this reason, constants would be more appropriate for the conversion factors used in this lesson.

You now need to insert the conversion factor to convert Kilometers to Miles.

3. Click: Formulas→Defined Names→Use in Formula.

    A drop-down list appears showing all currently defined range names.

4. Click *KilometerToMile*.

    f_x =C4*KilometerToMile

5. Press the **<Enter>** key.

5   AutoFill cell D4 to cells D5:D11.

	A	B	C	D
3	From	To	Km	Miles
4	London	Paris	343	213.13
5	New York	Sydney	15,989	9,935.10

6   Given that one Kilometer = 0.539956803 Nautical Miles, create a named constant that will convert Kilometers into Nautical Miles.

Constants are used for values that will rarely change. Named constants are useful because they are difficult to change and are thus less likely to be changed accidentally.

When you create a named constant, there is no cell on the worksheet that contains the constant value.

1. Click: Formulas→Defined Names→Define Name.

2. Type **KilometerToNauticalMile** into the *Name* box:

    Name: KilometerToNauticalMile

3. Type: **=0.539956803** into the *Refers to* box.

    Refers to: =0.539956803

4. Click the *OK* button.

7   Use the *KilometerToNauticalMile* named constant to add a formula to cell E4 that will calculate the distance from London to Paris in nautical miles.

1. Click in cell E4.

2. Type **=C4*** to start the formula.

3. Click: Formulas→Defined Names→Use in Formula to see the list of defined names.

4. Click *KilometerToNauticalMile* from the drop-down list.

    f_x =C4*KilometerToNauticalMile

5. Press the **<Enter>** Key.

8   AutoFill cell E4 to cells E5:E11.

9   Save your work as *Distances-2.*

Lesson 5-3: Use range names to make formulas more readable

1   Open *Sales and Profit-1* from your sample files folder.

	A	B
3	Sales	10,000.00
4	Cost	8,000.00
5	Gross Profit	2,000.00
6	Commission	100.00
7	Tax	200.00
8	Net Profit	1,700.00

2   Show formulas instead of values within the worksheet.

Click: Formulas→Formula Auditing→Show Formulas.

	A	B
3	Sales	10000
4	Cost	8000
5	Gross Profit	=B3-B4
6	Commission	=B5*5%
7	Tax	=B5*10%
8	Net Profit	=B5-B6-B7

It is reasonably clear from the formulas that:

Gross Profit = Sales - Cost

... and that five percent commission and ten percent tax are being deducted.

You can make the formulas a lot easier to read using range names.

3   Create automatic range names for all of the values in cells B3:B8.

This was covered in depth in: *Lesson 5-1: Automatically create single-cell range name.*

1.   Select cells A3:B8.

2.   Click: Formulas→Defined Names→Create from Selection.

3.   Click *OK*.

4   View the range names created by Excel.

The easiest way to view the range names is to click the drop-down arrow to the right of the *Name* box:

D14		× ✓ fx
Commission		B
Cost		
Gross_Profit		10000
Net_Profit		8000
Sales		=B3-B4
Tax		=B5*5%
		=B5*10%

Sales and Profit-1

5 **Apply the new range names to the existing formulas.**

1. Make sure that cells A3:B8 are still selected.

2. Click: Formulas→Defined Names→
   Define Name (Drop-down arrow)→Apply Names…

   The *Apply Names* dialog appears.

3. Click the *OK* button.

   The formulas should now show range names instead of cell references, making them a lot easier to read:

	A	B
3	Sales	10000
4	Cost	8000
5	Gross Profit	=Sales-Cost
6	Commission	=Gross_Profit*5%
7	Tax	=Gross_Profit*10%
8	Net Profit	=Gross_Profit - Commission -Tax

6 **Show values instead of formulas within the worksheet.**

Click: Formulas→Formula Auditing→Show Formulas.

Values are now displayed rather than formulas:

	A	B
3	Sales	10,000.00
4	Cost	8,000.00
5	Gross Profit	2,000.00
6	Commission	100.00
7	Tax	200.00
8	Net Profit	1,700.00

7 **Save your work as** *Sales and Profit-2.*

Lesson 5-4: Automatically create range names in two dimensions

1   Open *Earnings Summary-2* from your sample files folder.

	A	B	C	D	E	F	G	H	I
8	Name	Sales	Target	Hourly Rate	Hours Worked	Standard Pay	Overtime Pay	Bonus	Total
9	Brad Cruise	22,000	10,000	15.00	40	525.00	112.50	600.00	1,237.50
10	Ian Dean	9,000	8,000	13.00	35	455.00	-	50.00	505.00
11	Paris Smith	10,000	12,000	15.00	42	525.00	157.50	-	682.50
12	Gordon Ramsay	12,000	14,000	17.00	45	595.00	255.00	-	850.00
13	Barack Brown	15,000	9,000	13.00	35	455.00	-	300.00	755.00
14	Johnny Nicholson	18,000	14,000	17.00	40	595.00	127.50	200.00	922.50
15	Tony Blair	9,000	10,000	15.00	42	525.00	157.50	-	682.50
16	Jack Nicholson	10,000	9,000	13.00	30	390.00	-	50.00	440.00
17	Bob Clinton	9,000	11,000	15.00	35	525.00	-	-	525.00
18	Totals:	114,000	97,000		344	4,590.00	810.00	1,200.00	6,600.00

This worksheet was previously created in Session 3.

2   Create automatic range names based upon the labels in column A and row 8.

1.   Select the range A8:I17.

2.   Click: Formulas→Defined Names→Create from Selection.

Excel correctly guesses that the labels are in the *Top row* and *Left column*.

3.   Click the *OK* button.

3   View the range names created using the *Name Manager*.

1.   Click: Formulas→Defined Names→Name Manager.

The *Name Manager* dialog appears.

tip

You can also bring up the Name Manager using the keyboard shortcut:

<Ctrl>+<F3>

Name Manager	? ✕
New... *Edit...* *Delete*	*Filter ▾*

Name	Value	Refers To	Scope
Barack_Brown	{" 15,000 "," 9,000 ",...	=Sheet1!$B$13:$I$13	Workbo...
Bob_Clinton	{" 9,000 "," 11,000 ",...	=Sheet1!$B$17:$I$17	Workbo...
Bonus	{" 600.00 ";" 50.00 ";...	=Sheet1!$H$9:$H$17	Workbo...

The *Name Manager* is fantastically useful when working with names. It lists all currently defined names and allows you to edit them. Note the *Filter* drop-down that allows you to show a subset of names. This is useful when working with workbooks that contain large numbers of names.

You can see that you have created a range name for each employee (named in column A) and for each of the columns (named in row 8).

Earnings Summary-2

2.   Click the *Close* button.

4   Type **Average Sales** into cell A20.

5   Type **Average Bonus** into cell A21.

6   Add a formula to cell B20 that uses a range name to calculate the average sales.

This time, you'll use Excel's *formula AutoComplete* feature to insert the range name into an AVERAGE formula.

1.   Click in cell B20 and type:

=AVERAGE(S

Notice that *Formula AutoComplete* shows both functions and defined names beginning with S:

Average Sales	=AVERAGE(S
Average Bonus	AVERAGE(**number1**, [number2], ...)
	Sales
	fx SEARCH
	fx SEC

2.   Press the **<Tab>** key to insert the *Sales* range name.

20	Average Sales	=AVERAGE(Sales

3.   Press the **<Enter>** key (the closing bracket is automatically added).

7   Add a formula to cell B21 that uses a range name to calculate the average bonus.

The correct formula is:

20	Average Sales	12666.67
21	Average Bonus	=AVERAGE(Bonus)

8   Apply the *Comma Style* to cells B20:B21.

1.   Select cells B20:B21.

2.   Click: Home→Number→Comma Style.

9   Widen column B slightly so that both values are visible.

10   Add a new worksheet (you can leave it at the default name of *Sheet2*).

11   Copy cells A20:B21 from the Sheet1 worksheet and then paste into cells A1:B2 on the *Sheet2* worksheet.

	A	B
1	Average Sales	12,666.67
2	Average Bonus	133.33

You can now appreciate one of the great advantages of range names. The formula on *Sheet2* is exactly the same as that on *Sheet1* and still works correctly.

Without the use of range names, it wouldn't have been possible to copy and paste the formulas between worksheets. You would have had to re-write the formula as:

=AVERAGE(Sheet1!B9:B17)

12   Save your work as *Earnings Summary-3*.

Lesson 5-5: Use intersection range names and the INDIRECT function

1   Open *Distance Chart-1* from your sample files folder.

	A	B	C	D	E	F	G	H	I
3		York	Southampton	Sheffield	Portsmouth	Oxford	Nottingham	Norwich	Newcastle
4	Aberdeen_	307	538	347	552	473	379	480	228
5	Aberystwyth_	195	198	156	218	157	156	271	259
6	Birmingham_	129	128	76	141	63	49	161	204

The chart allows you to quickly find the distance between two UK locations. For example, it is clear that the distance from Birmingham to Oxford is 63 miles.

2   Create automatic range names based upon the labels in column A and row 3.

1. Select the range A3:X26.

2. Click: Formulas→Defined Names→Create from Selection.

Excel correctly guesses that the labels are in the *Top row* and *Left column*.

3. Click the *OK* button.

3   View the range names created using the *Name Manager*.

1. Click: Formulas→Defined Names→Name Manager.

The *Name Manager* dialog appears.

It is now clear why trailing underscores were used for the labels in column A. Without them, there would have been a naming conflict as each place name appears for both a row and a column.

2. Click the *Close* button.

4   Type **From** into cell A30.

5   Type **To** into cell A31.

6   Type **Miles** into cell A32.

7   Merge cells B30:E30, B31:E31 and B32:E32 (see sidebar if you are unable to do this).

Note

Merging cells

Merging cells is a basic skill covered in depth in *Lesson 4-6* of the *Essential Skills* book in this series.

To merge the cells:

1. Select cells B30:E30.

2. Click:

Home→Alignment→ Merge & Center→ Merge Across

Distance Chart-1

Note

The indirect function converts text to references

Consider this worksheet:

	A	B
1	Item	Cell Reference
2	Sales Total	A19
3	Cost Total	A35
4	**Profit**	

In this example the *Sales Total* value is present in cell A19 and the *Cost Total* value is present in cell A35.

If you placed this formula into cell B4:

=B2-B3

... the formula would fail:

	A	B
1	Item	Cell Reference
2	Sales Total	A19
3	Cost Total	A35
4	**Profit**	#VALUE!

The formula fails because Excel sees the values in cells B2 and B3 as simple text.

The correct formula would be:

=INDIRECT(B2)-INDIRECT(B3)

This formula succeeds:

	A	B
1	Item	Cell Reference
2	Sales Total	A19
3	Cost Total	A35
4	**Profit**	6,895.00

... because you have instructed Excel to regard the values in cells B2 and B3 as cell references rather than values.

	A	B	C	D
30	From	Derby_		
31	To	Manchester		
32	Miles		59	

8 Add a list validation to cell B30 that will restrict the cell to the items appearing in cells A4:A26.

This was covered in: *Lesson 2-11: Add a table-based dynamic list validation.*

9 Add a list validation to cell B31 that will restrict the cell to the items appearing in cells B3:X3.

10 Click in cell B30 and choose *Birmingham_* from the drop down list.

11 Click in cell B31 and choose *Oxford* from the drop down list.

Your worksheet should now look like this:

	A	B	C	D
30	From		Birmingham_	
31	To		Oxford	
32	Miles			

12 Use the intersection operator to create a formula in cell B32 that will show the distance from Birmingham to Oxford.

1. Click in cell B32.

2. Type the formula:

    =Birmingham_ Oxford

    Note that there is a space between the words *Birmingham_* and *Oxford*.

3. Press the **<Enter>** key.

The space is the intersection operator. The correct mileage is displayed in cell B32 (63 miles).

13 Use the INDIRECT function and the intersection operator (space) to show the correct distance in cell B32 based upon the values in cells B30 and B31.

This is more difficult than it first seems.

You could be forgiven for thinking that the formula:

=B30 B31

...would work.

Unfortunately, you can't refer to range names in this way. Excel provides the INDIRECT function to solve this problem (see sidebar).

1. Type the following formula into cell B32:

f_x	=INDIRECT(B30) INDIRECT(B31)

    Note that there is a space between *=INDIRECT(B30)* and *INDIRECT(B31)*.

2. Press the **<Enter>** key.

    The correct mileage is now shown in cell B32 for any journey that you select in cells B30 and B31.

14 Save your work as *Distance Chart-2*.

Lesson 5-6: Create dynamic formula-based range names using the OFFSET function

The technique shown in this lesson is a work-around that, in most cases, hasn't been needed since 2007 when the *table* feature was introduced. (You learned about tables in: *Session One: Tables, and Ranges*).

Feel free to skip this lesson if it is not relevant to you (see sidebar).

The range referred to by a range name is already dynamic to a point. If the range has rows or columns added or removed *inside the range,* the range name will automatically adjust. Problems occur when a new value is added to a blank row immediately below a range. In this case, the range name does not automatically adjust.

1   Open *Human Resources-1* from your sample files folder.

This is a simple workbook containing two worksheets. One worksheet lists employees and the other lists all of the company's current offices and departments.

2   Create automatic range names for cells A4:A6 and C4:C7 on the *Validations* worksheet.

1.   Select the *Validations* worksheet.

2.   Select cells A3:A6 (to include the range header).

3.   Click: Formulas→Defined Names→Create from Selection.

Note that the actual range name will be A4:A6. Cell A3 was only included in order to define the automatic name: *Offices*.

4.   Click the *OK* button.

5.   Repeat for the range C3:C7.

3   Create list validations for columns B and C on the *Employees* worksheet.

1.   Select all of the cells in column B on the *Employees* worksheet.

2.   Click: Data→Data Tools→Data Validation.

3.   Select *List* in the *Allow* drop-down list.

4.   Type **=Offices** into the *Source* box.

5.   Click the *OK* button.

6.   Use the same technique to add a list validation for *Departments* to column C.

4   Use the drop-down lists to add some random *Offices* and *Departments* for Brad Cruise, Ian Dean and Paris Smith.

5   Type **Rome** into cell A7 on the *Validations* worksheet.

6   Select the *Employees* worksheet.

7   Add an office for Gordon Ramsay.

Allow:	
List	⌄

Data:	
between	⌄

Source:	
=Offices	

▲	A	B	C
3	Name	Office	Department
4	Brad Cruise	London	Purchasing
5	Ian Dean	Paris	Credit Control
6	Paris Smith	New York	Sales

Human Resources-1

Notice that the new *Rome* office can't be added. That's because the range name does not adjust itself when a new value is added to a blank row immediately below a range.

8   **Convert the *Offices* range name into a formula-based name that is able to automatically re-size.**

To do this you need to use the OFFSET function. This returns a range reference that is a given number of rows or columns from a specified cell, or from an offset from a specified cell.

In this case, the specified cell will be A4 (on the *Validations* worksheet) as this contains the first *Office,* but how can you automatically detect how many offices there are?

The answer is to use the COUNTA function to return the number of cells in column A that are not empty. COUNTA needs a range to examine for non-blank cells. You'll use the range A4:A200 on the basis that you're unlikely to ever have more than 197 offices.

=COUNTA(Validations!\$A\$4:\$A\$200) will thus return 4: the current number of offices in the range.

To convert the *Offices* range name into a formula-based range name, you will need to use the *Name Manager.*

1.   Click: Formulas→Defined Names→Name Manager.

2.   Click the *Offices* range name.

3.   Click the *Edit* button.

Note that this name currently refers to the range:

> Refers to: =Validations!\$A\$4:\$A\$6

4.   Type the following formula into the *Refers to* box:

> =OFFSET(Validations!\$A\$4,0,0,COUNTA(Validations!\$A\$4:\$A\$200))

The four arguments specify where the range will begin, the number of rows to offset the start of the range by, the number of columns to offset the start of the range by, and the number of rows in the range.

5.   Click the *OK* button.

9   **Convert the *Departments* range name into a formula-based range name that is able to automatically re-size.**

Do this in exactly the same way as for the *Offices* range. This time, the formula in the *Refers to* box will be:

> =OFFSET(Validations!\$C\$4,0,0,COUNTA(Validations!\$C\$4:\$C\$200))

10   **Test the validation by adding *Offices* and *Departments.***

When you add a new *Office* or *Department,* the range names now dynamically expand to include the new item. Note that there should never be any blank entries within the list.

11   **Save your work as *Human Resources-2.***

Lesson 5-7: Create table-based dynamic range names

In the last lesson: *Lesson 5-6: Create dynamic formula-based range names using the OFFSET function*, you used a complex method based on the OFFSET and COUNTA functions to implement a dynamic formula-based range name.

You'll be pleased to know that (since 2007) there has been a much simpler way to achieve the same thing using a table-based range name. The technique described in this lesson is also more elegant and less prone to error.

1   Open *Human Resources-2* from your sample files folder (if it isn't already open).

This is a simple workbook containing two worksheets. One worksheet lists employees and the other lists all of the company's current offices and departments.

2   Delete the existing range names for *Departments* and *Offices*.

1. Click: Formulas→Defined Names→Name Manager.

2. Select *Departments* and *Offices* and then click the *Delete* button.

3. Click *OK* to confirm that you want to delete.

4. Click the *Close* button to close the *Name Manager*.

3   Convert the ranges A3:A7 and C3:C7 on the *Validations* worksheet into tables.

This was covered in depth in: *Lesson 1-13: Convert a range into a table and add a total row.*

1. Click anywhere in the range A3:A7 on the *Validation* worksheet.

2. Click: Insert→Tables→Table.

3. Click the *OK* button.

4. Do exactly the same thing for the *Departments* range.

4   Name the two new tables *Office* and *Department*.

1. Click anywhere inside the range A3:A7.

2. Click Table Design→Properties→Table Name.

3. Type **Office** into the text box.

4. Do exactly the same thing to name the *Department* table.

Human Resources-2

5 Create range names called *OfficeTable* and *DepartmentTable* based upon the two new tables.

Unfortunately, Excel doesn't accept a table name for a list validation. Fortunately, it is happy to accept a range name associated with a table.

1. Select all of the values in the *Office* table (cells A4:A7), being careful not to include the header row.

2. Click: Formulas→Defined Names→Define Name.

    The *New Name* dialog appears.

3. Type **OfficeTable** in the *Name* text box.

Name:	OfficeTable

    Note that the *Refers to* box now contains the structured reference:

Refers to:	=Office[Offices]

    This means that the structured reference refers to all of the data in the *Office* table. In other words, it is a dynamic named range that will shrink and grow with the *Office* table.

4. Click the *OK* button.

5. Create a *DepartmentTable* range name in exactly the same way.

6 Edit the list validation on columns B and C in the *Employees* worksheet to reference the *OfficeTable* and *DepartmentTable* range names.

1. Select column B on the *Employees* worksheet.

2. Click: Data→Data Tools→Data Validation.

3. Delete *=Offices* from the *Source* text box.

4. Press the **<F3>** key to bring up a list of range names.

    This is the fastest way to bring up the *Paste Name* dialog. The slower ribbon method is to click:

    Formulas→Defined Names→Use In Formula→Paste Names

5. Click: *OfficeTable*.

6. Click the *OK* button.

7. Click the OK button on the *Data Validation* dialog.

8. Use the same method to edit the list validation for column C.

Paste Name

Paste name

DepartmentTable
OfficeTable

OK

7 Test the validations.

As items are added and deleted from the tables in the *Validations* worksheet, the changes are reflected in the contents of the drop-down validation lists on the *Employees* worksheet.

8 Save your work as *Human Resources-3*.

Lesson 5-8: Create two linked drop-down lists using range names

In this lesson, you're going to push Excel's validation feature into bold new territory by addressing a common business requirement.

Here's the sample worksheet for this session:

	A	B	C
3	Make	Model	
4	Jaguar	X-Type	
5			

Cars — Model Range

You want to add a validation to columns A and B (to allow users to select a *Make* and *Model*) for each row.

The *Make* validation is easy to implement as a simple list validation.

The *Model* validation is not so simple. The values that are valid need to change depending upon the selected *Make*.

Here's what you want to see:

- When the Make is *Ford,* valid models are *Fusion, Mustang* and *C-Max*.

- When the Make is *Fiat*, valid models are *500, 124 Spider* and *Abarth*.

This lesson provides a solution to the problem by dynamically selecting the correct *Model* range name that matches the selected *Make*.

1. Open *New Car Model Range-1* from your sample files folder.

2. Create an automatic range name for the *Make* table on the *Model Range* worksheet.

   1. Select the *Model Range* worksheet.

   2. Select cells A5:A8.

   3. Click: Formulas→Defined Names→Create From Selection.

   4. Click the *OK* button.

3. Create automatic range names for each *Model* on the *Model Range* worksheet.

   1. Select cells A12:C15.

   2. Click Formulas→Defined Names→Create from Selection.

   3. De-select the *Left column* check box because you only want the range names to use the labels from the *Top row*.

   4. Click the *OK* button.

Create Names from Selection dialog:

Create Names from Selection ? ✕

Create names from values in the:
☑ Top row
☐ Left column
☐ Bottom row
☐ Right column

OK   Cancel

New Car Model Range-1

4 **Apply a list validation to column A of the *Cars* worksheet that uses the *Make* range name as its source.**

1. Select column A on the *Cars* worksheet.

2. Click: Data→Data Tools→Data Validation.

3. Enter the following values into the dialog:

> Allow:
> List
> Data:
> between
> Source:
> =Make

4. Click the *OK* button.

5 **Use the drop-down list to select a car make in cell A4.**

6 **Apply a list validation to cell B4 that will display a list of models based upon the make displayed in cell A4.**

1. Click in cell B4.

2. Click: Data→Data Tools→Data Validation.

3. Enter the following values into the dialog:

> Allow:
> List
> Data:
> between
> Source:
> =INDIRECT(A4)

It is very important that the reference to cell A4 is relative (A4) and not absolute ($A$4) because you are going to copy the validation to the other cells in column B in a moment.

4. Click the *OK* button.

7 **Copy and paste the validation to all of the cells in column B.**

1. Copy the contents of cell B4.

2. Select all of column B.

3. Right-click inside the selected range and click *Paste Special...* from the shortcut menu.

4. Select *Validation* from the *Paste Special* dialog.

5. Click the *OK* button.

8 **Test the validation.**

The valid choices for *Model* now change based upon the *Make* selected in column A.

	A	B
3	Make	Model
4	Ford	Mustang
5		Fusion
6		Mustang / C-Max

	A	B
3	Make	Model
4	Fiat	124 Spider
5		500
6		124 Spider / Abarth

9 **Save your work as *New Car Model Range-2*.**

---

tip

Removing validation from the label row

It is quick and convenient to add validation to an entire column because you are never sure how many entries will ultimately be added to the range.

An unfortunate side-effect of this is that the validation drop-down arrows also appear when you click in the header and label rows (in this example rows 1 to 3).

To solve this problem:

1. Click on any empty cell in the worksheet *that contains no validation constraint.*

2. Press **<Ctrl> + <C>** to copy.

3. Select the cells that you want to remove validation from, and then click:

Home→Clipboard→Paste→ Paste Special→Validation

...to clear the validation.

> Paste Special
>
> Paste
> ○ All   ○ All
> ○ Formulas   ○ All
> ○ Values   ○ Col
> ○ Formats   ○ For
> ○ Comments   ○ Val
> ◉ Validation   All
> Operation

Lesson 5-9: Understand the #NUM!, #DIV/0! and #NAME? error values

Excel has eight specific error values that it is able to display in cells containing formulas. It's important that you understand the type of problem that causes Excel to display each of these errors.

The error values are:

#DIV/0!, #NAME?, #NULL!, #NUM!, #REF!, #VALUE!, #SPILL and **#CALC**

There's also a nonspecific error value called **#N/A** (see sidebar).

The sample worksheet for this lesson has faulty formulas that produce all eight errors.

1   Open *Errors-1* from your sample files folder.

This worksheet has a lot of problems. You can see each of the eight error messages appearing in different cells.

2   Diagnose and solve the problem causing the #NUM! error in cell D4.

	A	B	C	D
				Above/Below
3	Month	Sales	Target	Target
4	Jan	$ 5,210.00	$ 3,500.00	#NUM!
5	Feb	$ 5,650.00	$ -	$ 5,650.00

The #NUM! error is usually caused by a formula that returns a number that is too large, or too small for Excel to handle.

Another possible cause is a non-numeric value entered as an argument for a function that expects a numeric value.

1.   Examine the formula in cell D4:

Here lies the problem. Excel is trying to calculate B4 *exponent* C4, which results in a huge number that Excel isn't capable of handling.

2.   Correct the formula.

As you need to calculate how far sales are above or below target you will need to correct the formula to:

The problem then vanishes. Notice that the formula in cell D10 now also displays correctly as it was simply inheriting the #NUM! error from cell D4.

Errors-1

3   Diagnose and solve the problem causing the #DIV/0! error in cell E5.

	A	B	C	D	E
				Above/Below	% of
3	Month	Sales	Target	Target	Target
4	Jan	$ 5,210.00	$ 3,500.00	$ 1,710.00	149%
5	Feb	$ 5,650.00	$ -	$ 5,650.00	#DIV/0!
6	Mar	$ 6,092.00	$ 4,000.00	$ 2,092.00	152%

Dividing by zero causes Excel's "Divide by Zero" error to be displayed.

1. Examine the formula in cell E5.

	E
5	=B5/C5

You know that the zero value must be in cell C5. Sure enough, no sales target was entered for February.

2. Enter a sales target of **3,250** for February.

The problem is solved.

If you didn't know the target for February and wanted to suppress the error message, you could use the IFERROR function as described in: *Lesson 3-24: Use an IFERROR function to suppress error messages.*

4   Diagnose and solve the problem causing the #NAME? error in cell C10.

	A	B	C	D
9	Jun	$ 7,130.00	$ 4,750.00	$ 2,380.00
10	Totals:	$ 34,292.00	#NAME?	$ 10,042.00

The #NAME? error means that Excel has encountered a name it doesn't understand. The most likely cause is that you've used a range name that doesn't exist.

1. Examine the formula in cell C10.

	C
10	=SUM(Target)

Because there was a #NAME? error you know that there is no range name called *Target.*

2. Select cells C3:C9.

3. Click: Formulas→Defined Names→Create from Selection.

4. Click the *OK* button.

The problem is now solved.

5   Save your work as *Errors-2.*

Lesson 5-10: Understand the #VALUE!, #REF! and #NULL! error values

1   Open *Errors-2* from your sample files folder (if it isn't already open).

2   Diagnose and solve the problem causing the #VALUE! error in cell F8.

	A	B	C	D	E	F
				Above/Below	% of	Exceeded
3	Month	Sales	Target	Target	Target	Target?
4	Jan	$ 5,210.00	$ 3,500.00	$ 1,710.00	149%	Yes
5	Feb	$ 5,650.00	$ 3,250.00	$ 2,400.00	174%	Yes
6	Mar	$ 6,092.00	$ 4,000.00	$ 2,092.00	152%	Yes
7	Apr	$ 3,955.00	$ 4,250.00	$ -295.00	93%	No
8	May	$ 6,255.00	$ 4,500.00	$ 1,755.00	139%	#VALUE!

The #VALUE! error means that a function contains an invalid argument.

1. Examine the formula in cell F8.

f_x	=IF("B8>C8", "Yes", "No")

    The IF function was covered in: *Lesson 3-5: Use the IF logic function.*

    The first argument of an IF function demands a logical expression that evaluates TRUE or FALSE.

    There's nothing wrong with the logical expression: **B8>C8**. The problem is caused by the quotation marks that cause Excel to interpret it as text.

2. Correct the formula in cell F8 by removing the quotation marks from the expression **B8>C8** (the IF function's first argument).

f_x	=IF(B8>C8, "Yes", "No")

    The problem is solved.

3   Diagnose and solve the problem causing the #REF! error in cell B11.

	A	B	C
10	Totals:	$ 34,292.00	$ 24,250.00
11	GBP Totals:	#REF!	

The #REF! error means that a formula refers to a cell that isn't valid. This happens when you reference a cell from a formula and then delete the row or column that used to contain the referenced cell.

Errors-2

1. Examine the formula in cell B11

| f_x | =B10/#REF! |

Because this cell needs to convert the dollar sales figure in cell B10 to Great Britain Pounds (GBP), the missing reference is the USD/GBP exchange rate.

2. Replace the #REF! part of the formula with **1.30** (the USD/GBP exchange rate when this lesson was first written).

| f_x | =B10/1.62 |

3. Press the **<Enter>** key.

The problem is solved.

4   Diagnose and solve the problem causing the #NULL! error in cell B16.

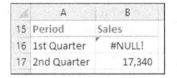

◢	A	B
15	Period	Sales
16	1st Quarter	#NULL!
17	2nd Quarter	17,340

The #NULL! error occurred because Excel is confused by the use of the intersection (space) operator. It usually simply means that you've incorrectly typed one of a function's arguments.

1. Examine the formula in cell B16.

| f_x | =B4+B5 B6 |

It is clear that there is a missing addition (+) operator between B5 and B6.

Excel has interpreted the missing operator as an attempt to reference the intersection of cells B5 and B6. It is, of course, impossible to have an intersection between two single cell references.

The intersection operator was covered in: *Lesson 5-5: Use intersection range names and the INDIRECT function.*

2. Correct the formula in cell B16 by adding the missing addition operator.

| f_x | =B4+B5+B6 |

3. Press the **<Enter>** key.

The problem is solved.

5   Save your work as *Errors-3*.

Lesson 5-11: Understand the #SPILL and #CALC error values

The #SPILL and #CALC error values were introduced in the *July 2020 semi-annual version 2002* release to support Excel 365's new *Dynamic Array* capability. You learned about dynamic arrays in: *Session Four: Working with Dynamic Arrays*.

1 Open *Errors-3* from your sample files folder (if it isn't already open).

2 Diagnose and solve the problem causing the #SPILL error in cell H4.

The #SPILL error occurs when a spilled range is unable to occupy cells because the cells are not presently empty.

1. Click in cell H4

Look at the formula (shown in the formula bar):

f_x	=UNIQUE(A4:A9)

=UNIQUE(A4:A9)

UNIQUE is one of Excel's new dynamic range functions and returns a spilled array.

Notice that there is a dotted outline showing the cells that the spilled range needs to occupy:

⊿	G	H	I	J
		Months for		
3		drop-down		
4		A9)		
5				
6				
7		April closed for two weeks.		
8				
9				
10				

You can see that the spilled range needs to occupy cells H4:H9 but is unable to do so due to the presence of text in cell H7.

2. Delete the text in cell H7.

The problem vanishes and the spilled range occupies cells H4:H9:

Errors-3

	G	H
3		Months for drop-down
4		Jan
5		Feb
6		Mar
7		Apr
8		May
9		Jun

3   Diagnose and solve the problem causing the #CALC error in cell A23.

The #CALC error occurs when Excel's calculation engine encounters a calculation error when performing an array operation.

1. Click in cell A23.

    Look at the formula (shown in the formula bar):

    =FILTER(A4:F9,A4:A9=A20)

    =FILTER(A4:F9,A4:A9=A20)

    You can see that the FILTER function is trying to find a value that matches the month selected in cell A20. Unfortunately no month has yet been selected causing an error.

	A	B	C	D
19	Select a Month:			
20				
21				
22	Month	Sales	Target	Above/Below Target
23	#CALC!			

2. Click in cell A20 and select a month from the drop-down list.

    The problem is now solved:

	A	B	C	D
19	Select a Month:			
20	Mar			
21				
22	Month	Sales	Target	Above/Below Target
23	Mar	6092	4000	2092
24				

4   Save your work as *Errors-4.*

Lesson 5-12: Understand background error checking and error checking rules

Excel is constantly working in the background, automatically checking for errors. Whenever Excel thinks you've made a mistake, it will politely let you know. Of course, Excel isn't always correct. It can only guess that you've made a mistake and it is often wrong.

1   Open *Daily Profit Report-1* from your sample files folder.

This workbook contains two errors. Excel has automatically detected them and indicates each by a small green triangle in the top left hand corner of each cell containing a suspected error.

If you don't see the green triangles on your computer, somebody has switched automatic error checking off. See the sidebar for instructions on how to switch it back on.

	A	B	C	D
3	Date	Sales	Costs	Profit
4	18-Sep-16	20,000	12,000	8,000
5	19-Sep-16	21,000	12,500	8,500
6	20-Sep-16	22,800	12,600	35,400
7	21-Sep-16	23,500	13,000	10,500
8	Total:	87,300	50,100	62,400

> ## note
>
> ### Why can't I see any green triangles?
>
> If you don't see the green triangles, somebody has switched off automatic error checking.
>
> To switch it back on, check the check box:
>
> File→Options→
> Formulas→Error Checking→
> Enable background error checking

2   Understand error checking rules.

1. Click: File→Options→Formulas.

Note that Excel monitors for nine different error conditions by default. There's a tenth that is switched off by default but can be enabled if required:

☑ Cells containing formulas that result in an error ⓘ
☑ Inconsistent calculated column formula in tables ⓘ
☑ Cells containing years represented as 2 digits ⓘ
☑ Numbers formatted as text or preceded by an apostrophe ⓘ
☑ Formulas inconsistent with other formulas in the region ⓘ

☑ Formulas which omit cells in a region ⓘ
☑ Unlocked cells containing formulas ⓘ
☐ Formulas referring to empty cells ⓘ
☑ Data entered in a table is invalid ⓘ
☑ Misleading number formats ⓘ

2. Click the *Cancel* button.

3   Remove the error warning from cell A5.

1. Click on cell A5. Notice that an *Error Smart Tag* has appeared to the right of the cell.

2. Hover the mouse cursor over the *Smart Tag*.

> Daily Profit Report-1

A tip appears showing the rule that Excel believes has been violated:

3. Click the down arrow on the Smart Tag.

Excel is worried because the date (unlike the other dates in the column) has been entered as a text value with two digits for the year. This is a throw-back to the problems caused in the year 2000 when such dates were predicted to bring about the end of the world (see sidebar).

A date can be entered in this way by preceding the date by an apostrophe to indicate that the entry is a textual value:

'19-Sep-16

Notice that two of the options in the *Smart Tag list* offer to convert the date to 2016 or to 1916.

4. Click *Ignore Error.*

The green triangle vanishes.

4 Correct the error in cell D6.

1. Click on cell D6 and hover the mouse cursor over the *Smart Tag.*

This time Excel has found a real error. It has noticed that the formula in cell D6 is inconsistent with the other formulas in column D. The formula is adding costs to sales when it should be subtracting them.

2. Click the down arrow on the *Smart Tag* and click *Copy Formula From Above* from the shortcut menu.

The error is corrected.

5 Save your work as *Daily Profit Report-2.*

Lesson 5-13: Manually check a worksheet for errors

Sometimes those little green triangles can be annoying. Excel often picks up "errors" that are not really errors at all.

Some Excel users would prefer to switch off background error checking and instead run a manual error check when the worksheet is complete.

In this lesson, you'll switch off Excel's background error checking and then manually scan a worksheet for errors.

1   Open *Operating Expenses-1* from your sample files folder.

This workbook contains three errors. Excel has automatically detected them and indicates each by a small green triangle in the top left-hand corner of each cell containing a suspected error.

	A	B	C	D
3	Month	Budget	Actual	Variance
4	Jan-13	42,000	45000	3,000
5	Feb-13	45,000	42000	-3,000
6	Mar-13	47,500	46000	-2,500
7	Apr-13	48,000	53000	5,000
8	May-13	47,000	47000	0
9	Jun-13	46,000	45000	-1,000
10	Total	275,500	186000	1,500

2   Switch off background error checking.

1.   Click: File→Options→Formulas.

2.   Clear the *Enable background error checking* check box:

> Error Checking
>
> ☐ Enable background error checking

3.   Click the *OK* button.

Notice that the green triangles have now vanished, even though the error conditions remain.

3   Manually check the worksheet for errors.

1.   Click: Formulas→Formula Auditing→Error Checking.

Cell D6 is selected (the first cell in the worksheet containing a suspected error) and the *Error Checking* dialog appears:

> Error Checking   ?   ×
>
> Error in cell D6
>
> =C6-B6-1000   Copy Formula from Above
>
> Inconsistent Formula   Help on this error
>
> The formula in this cell differs from the
> formulas in this area of the spreadsheet.   Ignore Error
>
>   Edit in Formula Bar
>
> Options...   Previous   Next

The dialog indicates that Excel has detected an inconsistent formula. This means that the formula in cell D6 is not consistent with the other formulas in column D.

2. Click: Formulas→Formula Auditing→Show Formulas.

    The formulas behind the cells are now displayed:

	D
3	Variance
4	=C4-B4
5	=C5-B5
6	=C6-B6-1000
7	=C7-B7

    The error is now apparent. For some reason an extra 1,000 has been deducted from the variance for March 2016.

3. Click: Formulas→Formula Auditing→Show Formulas.

    Values are once again shown in all cells.

4. Click the *Resume* button on the *Error Checking* dialog.

5. Click *Copy Formula from Above* to correct the error.

    The error is corrected, and the active cell moves to cell C8. Cell C8 is the next cell in the worksheet that contains a suspected error.

    This time, the error is caused by a number being stored as text. This can happen when a numeric cell is formatted as text or when a value is typed into a cell preceded with an apostrophe like this:

    '47000

Error in cell C8

47000

Number Stored as Text

The number in this cell is formatted as text or preceded by an apostrophe.

6. Click *Convert to Number*.

    The error is corrected, and the active cell moves to cell C10. Cell C10 is the next cell in the worksheet that contains a suspected error.

    This time the error is another inconsistent formula. The formula in cell C10 is incorrectly adding the values in cells C4:C8 instead of C4:C9. Excel has noticed that this is inconsistent with the formulas in cells B10 and D10.

Error in cell C10

=SUM(C4:C8)

Inconsistent Formula

The formula in this cell differs from the formulas in this area of the spreadsheet.

7. Click *Copy Formula from Left* to correct the error.

8. Click the *OK* button to end the error check.

Re-enable background error checking.

Microsoft Excel   ✕

⚠   The error check is complete for the entire sheet.

OK

1. Click: File→Options→Formulas.

2. Check the *Enable background error checking* check box.

3. Click the *OK* button.

    Notice that there are no longer any green triangles as you've corrected all of the errors.

5   Save your work as *Operating Expenses-2*.

Lesson 5-14: Audit a formula by tracing precedents

When you have a worksheet with cross-worksheet formulas and range names, there is a lot of scope for error. Ranges and formulas can often reference the wrong cells.

Excel's *trace precedents* tool provides an easy way to quickly audit cell references in order to confirm the integrity of your workbook.

1   Open *Profit Analysis-1* from your sample files folder.

This workbook summarizes data from the *January, February* and *March* worksheets into a *First Quarter Summary*. The workbook also makes extensive use of range names.

	A	B	C	D	E	F	G	H
1	First Quarter Summary							
2								
3		Sales	Cost	Profit				
4	Jan	89,199	45,318	43,881				
5	Feb	99,197	42,510	56,687				
6	Mar	87,194	45,025	42,169				
7	Totals:	275,590	132,853	142,737				
8								

First Quarter Summary | January | February | March

2   Audit the formula in cell D7 of the *First Quarter Summary* worksheet using *Trace Precedents*.

1.   Click into cell D7.

Notice that it isn't possible to immediately see which cells are referenced by the *Profit* range name.

f_x =SUM(Profit)

2.   Click: Formulas→Formula Auditing→Trace Precedents.

The cells referenced by the *Profit* range name are now apparent.

	A	B	C	D
3		Sales	Cost	Profit
4	Jan	89,199	45,318	43,881
5	Feb	99,197	42,510	56,687
6	Mar	87,194	45,025	42,169
7	Totals:	275,590	132,853	142,737

You might think that this isn't very impressive. You could have done the same thing by pressing the **<F2>** key, or by clicking the word *Profit* in the formula bar. But there's more to come!

3.   Click: Formulas→Formula Auditing→Trace Precedents again.

This time the next level of precedents is shown:

Profit Analysis-1

	A	B	C	D
3		Sales	Cost	Profit
4	Jan	89,199	45,318	43,881
5	Feb	99,197	42,510	56,687
6	Mar	87,194	45,025	42,169
7	Totals:	275,590	132,853	142,737

You can see that the value in cell D4 is calculated from the values in cells B4 and C4. You can also see that the value in cell D7 is calculated from the range D4:D6.

But where are the values in cells B4:C6 coming from?

4. Click: Formulas→Formula Auditing→Trace Precedents again.

	A	B	C	D
2				
3		Sales	Cost	ofit
4	Jan	89,199	45,318	43,881
5	Feb	99,197	42,510	56,687
6	Mar	87,194	45,025	42,169
7	Totals:	275,590	132,853	142,737

The icons pointing to cells B4:C6 indicate that their values come from different worksheets in this (or even another) workbook.

5. Double-click the dotted line joining cell B4 and the icon.

The *Go To* dialog appears, showing the source of the value in cell B4.

6. Select the item shown in the *Go To* window and then click the *OK* button.

Reference:
'[Profit Analysis-1.xlsx]January'!$D$10

Special...   OK   Cancel

You are taken to the cell in the *January* worksheet that provides the value shown in cell B4 on the *First Quarter Summary* worksheet.

7. Click: Formulas→Formula Auditing→Trace Precedents again.

Now you can see the precedents of cell D10 in the *January* worksheet (see sidebar).

8. Click: Formulas→Formula Auditing→Remove Arrows.

The precedent arrows are removed from the *January* worksheet.

9. Select the *First Quarter Summary* worksheet.

10. Click: Formulas→Formula Auditing→Remove Arrows.

The precedent arrows are removed from the *First Quarter Summary* worksheet.

note

Use Trace Error to quickly find the first error in a chain

When a cell shows an error condition (such as **#DIV/0!**), it is often caused by an error in a precedent cell.

It is possible to click:

Formulas→
Formula Auditing→
Trace Precedents

... several times in order to trace the cell causing the error.

Excel also provides a way of tracing all precedents in a single click when a cell shows an error condition, allowing you to save a few mouse clicks.

When the active cell contains an error condition, you can click:

Formulas→
Formula Auditing→
Error Checking→
Trace Error

This shows all precedents, at all levels, with a single click.

	D	E	
3	Sales	Cost	
4	16,756	9,431	
5	19,437	7,412	
6	14,742	7,960	
7	15,881	6,214	
8	11,835	8,714	
9	10,548	5,587	
10	89,199	45,318	

Lesson 5-15: Audit a formula by tracing dependents

1   Open *Profit Analysis-1* from your sample files folder (if it isn't already open).

2   Select the *January* worksheet.

3   Audit the formula in cell D6 using *Trace Dependents*.

     1.   Click cell D6 to make it the active cell.

     2.   Click: Formulas→Formula Auditing→Trace Dependents.

        The direct dependents are shown for cell D6. These cells have formulas that directly reference cell D6.

	A	B	C	D	E	F
3	Team	First Name	Last Name	Sales	Cost	Profit
4	Blue	Johnny	Caine	16,756	9,431	7,325
5	Blue	George	Marley	19,437	7,412	12,025
6	Blue	Bill	Spears	14,742	7,960	6,782
7	Red	Gordon	Depp	15,881	6,214	9,667
8	Red	Tom	Marley	11,835	8,714	3,121
9	Red	Charles	Blair	10,548	5,587	4,961
10	Totals:			89,199	45,318	43,881
11						
12	Team			Average Sales	Average Cost	Average Profit
13	Blue			16,978	8,268	8,711
14	Red			12,755	6,838	5,916

        You can see that:

- The *Profit* in cell F6 depends upon *Sales* in D6 (because Profit = Sales-Cost).

- The *Total Sales* in cell D10 depends upon the *Sales* in D6.

- The *Average Sales* for the *Blue* team also depends upon the value in D6 because Bill Spears is in the *Blue* team.

     3.   Click: Formulas→Formula Auditing→Trace Dependents again.

	A	B	C	D	E	F
3	Team	First Name	Last Name	Sales	Cost	Profit
4	Blue	Johnny	Caine	16,756	9,431	7,325
5	Blue	George	Marley	19,437	7,412	12,025
6	Blue	Bill	Spears	14,742	7,960	6,782
7	Red	Gordon	Depp	15,881	6,214	9,667
8	Red	Tom	Marley	11,835	8,714	3,121
9	Red	Charles	Blair	10,548	5,587	4,961
10	Totals:			89,199	45,318	43,881
11						
12	Team			Average Sales	Average Cost	Average Profit
13	Blue			16,978	8,268	8,711
14	Red			12,755	6,838	5,916

The next level of dependents is shown. You can now see that:

Profit Analysis-1

- The *Total* in cell F10 depends upon the *Profit* value in cell F6.

- The Blue Team's *Average Profit* in cell F13 depends upon the *Average Sales* in cell D13.

There is also an icon pointing to cell D10 indicating that there is a dependent value in a different worksheet in this (or even another) workbook.

4. Double-click the dotted line joining cell D10 and the icon.

The *Go To* dialog appears showing the source of the value in cell D10.

5. Select the item shown in the *Go To* window and then click the *OK* button.

Reference:

'[Profit Analysis-1.xlsx]First Quarter Summary'!$B$4

Special...   OK   Cancel

You are taken to cell B4 in the *First Quarter Summary* worksheet as this cell depends upon the value in cell D10 on the *January* worksheet.

6. Click: Formulas→Formula Auditing→Trace Dependents again.

You can now see the cells whose formulas directly depend upon the value in cell B4.

	A	B	C	D
3		Sales	Cost	Profit
4	Jan	89,199	45,318	43,881
5	Feb	99,197	42,510	56,687
6	Mar	87,194	45,025	42,169
7	Totals:	275,590	132,853	142,737

7. Click: Formulas→Formula Auditing→Trace Dependents again.

The final level of dependents is shown:

	A	B	C	D
3		Sales	Cost	Profit
4	Jan	89,199	45,318	43,881
5	Feb	99,197	42,510	56,687
6	Mar	87,194	45,025	42,169
7	Totals:	275,590	132,853	142,737

8. Click: Formulas→Formula Auditing→Remove Arrows.

The dependent arrows are removed from the *First Quarter Summary* worksheet.

9. Select the *January* worksheet.

10. Click: Formulas→Formula Auditing→Remove Arrows.

The dependent arrows are removed from the *January* worksheet.

Lesson 5-16: Use the Watch Window to monitor cell values

The *Watch Window* is useful when developing workbooks that contain cross-worksheet formulas. You'll often want to monitor one or more result cells on a summary worksheet as you edit values in source worksheets.

1   Open *Profit Analysis-1* from your sample files folder (if it isn't already open).

2   Select the *First Quarter Summary* worksheet.

◢	A	B	C	D
3		Sales	Cost	Profit
4	Jan	89,199	45,318	43,881
5	Feb	99,197	42,510	56,687
6	Mar	87,194	45,025	42,169
7	Totals:	275,590	132,853	142,737

3   Set up a *Watch Window* to monitor the values in cells B7, C7 and D7.

1.   Click cell B7 to make it the active cell.

2.   Click: Formulas→Formula Auditing→Watch Window.

     The *Watch Window* appears.

3.   Click the *Add Watch…* button.

     The *Add Watch* dialog appears:

4.   Click the *Add* button.

     The watched cell's details appear in the *Watch Window*.

5.   Click the *Add Watch...* button again.

6.   Click on cell C7.

7.   Click the *Add* button.

     A second watch appears in the *Watch Window*.

8.   Add a watch for cell D7 in the same way.

     The *Watch Window* now contains three watched cells.

Profit Analysis-1

4   Dock the *Watch Window* to the top of the screen.

Drag the *Watch Window* to the top of the screen. It then snaps into place above the formula bar:

Book	Sheet	Name	Cell	Value	Formula
Profit ...	First Q...		B7	275,590	=SUM(Sales)
Profit ...	First Q...		C7	132,853	=SUM(Cost)
Profit ...	First Q...		D7	142,737	=SUM(Profit)

	A	B	C	D	E	F
3		Sales	Cost	Profit		
4	Jan	89,199	45,318	43,881		
5	Feb	99,197	42,510	56,687		
6	Mar	87,194	45,025	42,169		
7	Totals:	275,590	132,853	142,737		

5   Convert the watch window into a floating dialog box.

1. Click the drop down menu at the top right corner of the *Watch Window* and then click *Move* from the shortcut menu.

Book	Sheet	Name	Cell	Value	Fo	Move
						Size
Profit ...	First Q...		B7	275,590	=S	Close
Profit ...	First Q...		C7	132,853	=SUM(Cost)	
Profit ...	First Q...		D7	142,737	=SUM(Profit)	

2. Move the cursor into the worksheet grid.

The window is converted back into a floating dialog box.

(You can also do this simply by dragging the top window downward).

6   Change some values on the *February* worksheet while monitoring the values defined in the Watch Window.

1. Click on the *February* worksheet tab.

2. Change Johnny Caine's sales (in cell D4) to 20,000 and press the **<Enter>** key.

Note that the values in the *Watch Window* have changed to reflect the new value.

Book	Sheet	Name	Cell	Value
Profit ...	First Quarter Summary		B7	276,841
Profit ...	First Quarter Summary		C7	132,853
Profit ...	First Quarter Summary		D7	143,988

3. Close the *Watch Window*.

7   Save your work as *Profit Analysis-2*.

note

Access Excel's hidden features using Tell Me help.

Tell Me help is covered in depth in *Lesson 1-19* of the *Essential Skills* book in this series.

Tell Me help is different from all previous versions of Excel help, as it allows you to both access help topics and execute Excel commands directly from the help system. This feature enables you to execute all of the *Commands Not in the Ribbon* that you saw listed in this lesson.

There are over 250 of these "secret" Excel commands and now, for the first time, you can execute any of them instantly using *Tell Me help*.

Here's how you could access the (very useful) *Speak Cells* hidden feature using *Tell Me help*:

1. Select some cells that have numbers, text or dates in them.

2. Click on the *Search* box in the menu bar:

3. Type: **Speak Cells** into the *Search* box.

A menu appears showing the *Speak Cells* command:

4. Click on the *Speak Cells* menu item.

Excel will then read the selected cells to you.

Profit Analysis-2

Lesson 5-17: Use Speak Cells to eliminate data entry errors

One of my favorite Excel features is its ability to read the workbook to me via the *Speak Cells* facility. When I need to input lots of numbers from a sheet of paper and want to check them, I get Excel to read them to me as I tick each off my list. This is much faster and nicer than continuously looking first at the screen, and then at the paper, for each entry.

This is one of those "secret" features that most Excel users will never discover because you won't find it anywhere on the ribbon or standard Excel dialogs.

In pre-2016 versions of Excel, you had to add some custom buttons to the Quick Access Toolbar or ribbon in order to use this feature (you'll learn how to create a custom ribbon tab later in: *Lesson 8-20: Create a custom ribbon tab*). The *Tell Me help* system (accessed via the *Search* box at the top right of the menu bar) now provides a new way of accessing Excel's hidden features (discussed in the sidebar).

1   Open *Profit Analysis-2* from your sample files folder (if it isn't already open).

2   Add custom buttons to the Quick Access Toolbar for all of the *Speak Cells* commands.

   1. Click: File→Options→Quick Access Toolbar.

      The *Customize the Quick Access Toolbar* pane appears.

   2. Select *Commands Not in the Ribbon* from the *Choose commands from* drop-down list:

   3. Click the *Speak Cells* command in the list of commands:

   4. Click the *Add* button.

   5. Click the *Add* button four more times to add all *Speak Cells* commands to the Quick Access Toolbar.

6.   Click the *OK* button.

3   Type **Bonus** into cell G3 on the *January* worksheet.

4   If necessary, apply the *Heading 3* cell style to cell G3.

5   Click in cell G4.

6   Click the *Speak Cells on Enter* button that you added to the Quick Access Toolbar.

You should hear the words "Cells will now be spoken on enter". If you don't hear this, your speakers are either muted or not working.

7   Add the following values to column G without looking at the Excel screen.

	E	F	G
3	Cost	Profit	Bonus
4	9,431	7,325	700
5	7,412	12,025	1200
6	7,960	6,782	600
7	6,214	9,667	900
8	8,714	3,121	300
9	5,587	4,961	400
10	45,318	43,881	

Notice that Excel speaks the number back to you every time that you press the **<Enter>** key. This means that you can be sure that you added the correct value without having to continually look from paper to screen.

8   Select cells G4:G9.

9   Click the *Speak Cells* button that you added to the Quick Access Toolbar.

This time Excel speaks each value in the column in sequence. This is an alternative way to double-check that figures have been entered correctly.

10   Click the *Speak Cells on Enter* button that you added to the Quick Access Toolbar.

You should hear the words "Turned off speak on enter". If you don't do this, Excel will continue to speak to you when you remove the toolbar buttons!

11   Remove the *Speak Cells* buttons from the Quick Access Toolbar.

Right-click on each *Speak Cells* button in turn and then click *Remove from Quick Access Toolbar*.

12   Save your work as *Profit Analysis-3*.

note

Excel won't stop talking!

You may delete your *Quick Access Toolbar* buttons and then find that Excel continues to talk to you.

It's easy to run into this problem, as you would reasonably expect the *Stop Speaking Cells* button to switch off the voice.

However, Excel will continue speaking as long as the *Speak Cells on Enter* button is pressed.

Session 5: Exercise

1   Open *Excel Quiz-1* from your sample files folder.

2   Select cells A5:E9 on the *Choices* worksheet.

	A	B	C	D	E
4					
5	1	64,000	128,000	512,000	1,048,576
6	2	1985	1992	1995	1997
7	3	Excel 7	Excel 12	Excel 9	Excel 16
8	4	Lotus 1-2-3	SuperCalc	VisiCalc	Multiplan
9	5	256	512	16,384	22,256

3   Create range names from the selected cells, using the value in the left column to name each range.

4   Apply a list validation to cell C4 on the *Quiz* worksheet that will show a list of all valid answers to the first question by referencing the range name matching the value in cell A4 on the *Quiz* worksheet using the INDIRECT function.

	A	B	C	D
3	No	Question	Answer	Correct A
4	1	How many rows does Excel have?	64000 ▾	1,0
5	2	When was the first Excel version released?	64,000	
6	3	What is another name for Excel 2016?	128,000 512,000	cel 16
7	4	What was the most popular spreadsheet product before Excel?	1,048,576	tus 1-2-
8	5	How many columns does Excel support		

5   Copy and paste the validation from cell C4 to cells C5:C8.

6   Put an IF function into cell E4 that will show the text "CORRECT" if the answer in cell C4 equals the correct answer in cell D4, and a blank space if the answer is not correct.

	C	D	E
3	Answer	Correct Answer	Correct?
4	1048576	1,048,576	CORRECT

7   AutoFill cell E4 down to cells E5:E8.

8   Hide columns A and D.

9   Save your work as *Excel Quiz-2.*

	B	C	E
3	Question	Answer	Correct?
4	How many rows does Excel have?	1048576	CORRECT
5	When was the first Excel version released?	1985	CORRECT
6	What is another name for Excel 2016?	▾	
7	What was the most popular worksheet before Excel?	Excel 7	
8	How many columns does Excel support	Excel 12	
9		Excel 9 Excel 16	

Excel Quiz-1

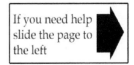

If you need help slide the page to the left

Session 5: Exercise Answers

These are the four questions that students find the most difficult to answer:

Q 6	Q 5	Q 4	Q 3
The correct function is: **=IF(D4=C4, "CORRECT", "")** This was covered in: *Lesson 3-5: Use the IF logic function.*	1. Click in cell C4. 2. Click: Home→ Clipboard→Copy. 3. Select the range C5:C8. 4. Click: Home→ Clipboard→ Paste→ Paste Special… 5. Select *Validation* in the *Paste Special* dialog. Paste ○ All ○ Formulas ○ Values ○ Formats ○ Comments ⦿ Validation 6. Click the *OK* button. This was covered in: *Lesson 5-8: Create two linked drop-down lists using range names.*	1. Click in cell C4 on the *Quiz* worksheet. 2. Click: Data→ Data Tools→ Data Validation. 3. Complete the Data Validation dialog like this: Allow: List Data: between Source: =INDIRECT(A4) The INDIRECT function allows you to use the value in column A to reference the range name (with the same name) that contains the correct multiple-choice answers. This was covered in: *Lesson 5-8: Create two linked drop-down lists using range names.*	1. Click: Formulas→ Defined Names→ Create from Selection. 2. Make sure that only the *Left column* is checked in the *Create Names from Selection* dialog. Create names from ☐ Top row ☑ Left column ☐ Bottom row ☐ Right column 3. Click the *OK* button. This was covered in: *Lesson 5-1: Automatically create single-cell range names.*

If you have difficulty with the other questions, here are the lessons that cover the relevant skills:

8 In order to hide a column, right-click the column header and select *Hide* from the shortcut menu.

This skill is covered in: *Lesson 3-27: Use the INDEX function.*

6

Session Six: What If Analysis and Security

> The superior man, when resting in safety, does not forget that danger may come. When in a state of security, he does not forget the possibility of ruin. When all is orderly, he does not forget that disorder may come. Thus his person is not endangered, and his States and all their clans are preserved.
>
> *Confucius (551 BC - 479 BC)*

The concept of "What If" is very simple. A business may wish to know what will happen in a given set of circumstances (called a scenario). For example, a simple scenario might be: "What if I reduced my profit margins by 5% and this caused my sales to increase by 20%?" Excel provides several tools that are geared to more complex scenarios. In this session you'll learn how to use these tools effectively.

Sometimes you'll want to keep the contents of a workbook secure. This session will show you how to prevent unauthorized users from opening or changing your workbooks. You'll also learn how to restrict the cells that a user is able to edit within a workbook. This session will also show you how to hide rows and columns and then create multiple custom views of the worksheet – each view hiding and showing different information.

Session Objectives

By the end of this session you will be able to:

- Create a single-input data table
- Create a two-input data table
- Define scenarios
- Create a scenario summary report
- Use Goal Seek
- Use Solver
- Hide and unhide worksheets, columns and rows
- Create custom views
- Prevent unauthorized users from opening or modifying workbooks
- Control the changes users can make to workbooks
- Restrict the cells users are allowed to change
- Allow different levels of access to a worksheet with multiple passwords
- Create a digital certificate
- Add an invisible digital signature to a workbook
- Add a visible digital signature to a workbook

Lesson 6-1: Create a single-input data table

Don't be fooled by the name. A *data table* has nothing to do with a regular Excel table. Data tables are another of those wonderful Excel features that are a complete mystery to virtually all Excel users.

In this lesson you'll use a data table to list the monthly repayments for a loan at different interest rates.

1   Open *Mortgage-1* from your sample files folder.

	A	B
3	Input Cells	
4	Loan Amount	250,000
5	Deposit (%)	10%
6	Term (Years)	25
7	Interest Rate (APR%)	6.6%
8		
9	Result Cells	
10	Loan Financed	225,000
11	Monthly Repayment	1,533.31
12	Total amount to be repaid	459,992
13	Total interest to be repaid	234,992

This is a simple worksheet that calculates four result values from four input values. When performing what-if analysis, it is a good idea to separate the input values from the result values on your worksheet.

The worksheet uses the PMT function that was covered in: *Lesson 3-3: Use the Insert Function dialog and the PMT function.*

During the last 25 years, mortgage interest rates have never dropped below 2.5% or increased to more than 15.5%.

Based upon the assumption that future rates will stay in this range, you will create a data table to show how potential changes in interest rates will affect monthly payments.

2   Create a single input data table to display all result cells for interest rates between 2.5% and 15.5% in half percent increments.

1. Type **Interest %** into cell D3.

2. Type **Monthly Payment** into cell E3.

3. Type **Total Payments** into cell F3.

4. Type **Total Interest** into cell G3.

5. AutoSize columns D, E, F and G so that all of the headers are readable.

6. Select cells D3:G3.

7. Click: Home→Styles→Cell Styles→Heading 3.

8. Type **2.5%** into cell B7.

   When you create a data table, you should always put the lowest input value into the relevant input cell. You'll see why in a moment.

9. Add formulas to cells D4:G4 that refer to the relevant input and result cells. The correct formulas are shown below:

	D	E	F	G
3	Interest %	Monthly Payment	Total Payments	Total Interest
4	=B7	=B11	=B12	=B13

10. Type **=D4+0.005** into cell D5 (the formula **=D4+0.5%** would produce an identical result).

11. AutoFill cell D5 down to cell D30 (15.5%).

Mortgage-1

12. Select cells D4:D30.

13. Use the Home→Number→Decrease Decimal and Home→Number→Increase Decimal buttons, to show interest rates to only one decimal place.

Your worksheet should now look like this:

	D	E	F	G
3	Interest %	Monthly Payment	Total Payments	Total Interest
4	2.5%	1,009.39	302,816	77,816
5	3.0%			

14. Convert cells D4:D30 from formulas to values.

Excel data tables have a problem with certain formulas in the left-hand column. For this reason, you need to *Copy* the values in cells D4:D30 and then *Paste Special* them back to the same location as *Values.*

Another work-around for this limitation is discussed in: *Lesson 8-8: Add a single input data table to a form.*

You are now ready to create your data table.

15. Select cells D4:G30.

16. Click: Data→Forecast→What-If Analysis→Data Table...

The *Data Table* dialog appears.

17. Click once in the *Column input cell* text box.

18. Click on cell B7.

This sets the *Column input cell* to the absolute cell reference: $B$7.

Because the interest rates are shown in column D, Excel must change the input value in cell B7 (to each value in column D) in order to calculate result values for columns E, F and G.

19. Click the *OK* button.

The data table is populated to show all result cells for all interest rates.

20. Select cells E4:G30.

21. Click: Home→Styles→Cell Styles→Comma[0].

	D	E	F	G
3	Interest %	Monthly Payment	Total Payments	Total Interest
4	2.5%	1,009	302,816	77,816
5	3.0%	1,067	320,093	95,093

You are now able to change the *Loan Amount, Deposit* or *Term* input values to update the data table.

3 Save your work as *Mortgage-2.*

Lesson 6-2: Create a two-input data table

A two-input data table is similar to a one-input data table.

However, in a two-input data table, input cells are arranged along both the top and the left-hand side of the table.

In this lesson you'll use a two-input data table to show monthly repayments for different loan amounts and different interest rates.

1   Open *Mortgage-2* from your sample files folder (if it isn't already open).

2   Create a new worksheet and name it: **Variable Interest and Capital**

	Variable Interest	Variable Interest and Capital	⊕

3   Copy cells A1:B13 from the *Variable Interest* worksheet and paste them into the same cells in the *Variable Interest and Capital* worksheet.

4   AutoSize columns A and B so that they are wide enough to display all values.

5   Create rows for your data table in cells E3:L3, showing capital amounts from 125,000 to 300,000 in increments of 25,000.

   1.   Type **125,000** into cell E3.

   2.   Type **150,000** into cell F3.

	E	F	G	H
3	125,000	150,000	175,000	200,000

   3.   Select cells E3:F3 and AutoFill across to cell L3.

6   Create row labels for your data table in cells D4:D30, showing interest rates from 2.5% to 15.5% in increments of 0.5%.

   1.   Type **2.5%** into cell D4.

   2.   Type **3%** into cell D5.

   3.   Select cells D4:D5 and AutoFill down to cell D30 (15.5%).

7   Format cells D4:D30 to show one decimal place.

   1.   Select cells D4:D30.

   2.   Click: Home→Number→Decrease Decimal. [.00→.0]

8   Add a formula to cell D3 that will reference the *Monthly Repayment* result cell.

	D	E	F	G
3	=B11	125000	150000	175000

9   If necessary, AutoSize column D so that it is wide enough to display all values.

10   Apply the *Note* cell style to cells D3:D30 and cells E3:L3.

   1.   Select cells D3:D30 and cells E3:L3.

Mortgage-2

tip

Hiding values with the three-semicolon custom format

You will often want to hide numbers or text in specific cells.

A common way of doing this is to format the cell as white text upon a white background.

A better solution is to create a custom format consisting of three semicolons. This is better because the cell contents will remain hidden no matter which background and foreground colors are set for the cell.

Here's how you would hide the value in cell D3:

1. Right-click cell D3.

2. Click *Format Cells...* from the shortcut menu.

3. Click the *Custom* category.

4. Type three semicolons into the *Type* box.

Type:
;;;

5. Click the *OK* button.

The value in cell D3 has now become invisible:

	D	E
3		125000
4	2.5%	504.69
5	3.0%	533.49

Custom formats are covered in depth in the *Essential Skills* book in this series.

2. Click: Home→Styles→Cell Styles→Note.

Your worksheet should now look like this:

	C	D	E	F	G
2					
3		1,009.39	125000	150000	175000
4		2.5%			
5		3.0%			
6		3.5%			
7		4.0%			

You are now ready to create your two-input data table.

11 Create a two-input data table to show monthly payments for each capital amount and interest rate.

1. Select cells D3:L30.

2. Click: Data→Forecast→What-If Analysis→Data Table...

   The *Data Table* dialog appears.

   The *Row input cell* is the *Loan Amount* in cell B4.

   The *Column input cell* is the *Interest Rate* in cell B7.

   Note that you could take the view that the amount financed in cell B10 is the correct row input cell. You're using cell B4 as it represents how much capital you would have available if your lender demands a 10% deposit.

3. Enter these values into the dialog and then click the *OK* button.

Data Table	?	×
Row input cell:	$B$4	↑
Column input cell:	$B$7	↑
	OK	Cancel

4. Select cells E4:L30.

5. Click: Home→Number→Comma Style.

   The numbers are formatted with a thousand comma separator and two decimal places.

   The two-input data table is complete.

	C	D	E	F	G
2					
3		1,009.39	125000	150000	175000
4		2.5%	504.69	605.63	706.57
5		3.0%	533.49	640.19	746.88
6		3.5%	563.20	675.84	788.48
7		4.0%	593.82	712.58	831.34

The value in cell D3 looks a little untidy. See the sidebar tip if you'd like it to become invisible.

12 Save your work as *Mortgage-3*.

Lesson 6-3: Define scenarios

When you create a set of input values, it is referred to as a scenario.

For example, here's a scenario:

Forecasted sales for next month are: 1,500 Grommets, 4,300 Sprockets, 3,100 Widgets and 2,800 Flugel Valves.

You enter the scenario's values into the input cells:

	A	B
3	Input Cells	Units
4	Grommets	1,500
5	Sprockets	4,300
6	Widgets	3,100
7	Flugel valves	2,800

… and the result cells display the result:

	A	B
15	Result Cells	
16	Sales	842,280.00
17	Cost	643,230.00
18	Profit	199,050.00
19	Gross Profit Pct	23.6%

Sometimes, you will have several different scenarios that you want to compare side-by-side. For example, you may ask your salesmen for *"worst case, expected case* and *best case"* scenarios.

	A	B	C	D
21	Scenarios			
22	Product	Worst Case	Expected Case	Best Case
23	Grommets	750	1,500	2,200
24	Sprockets	4,100	4,300	4,350
25	Widgets	2,000	3,100	3,750
26	Flugel valves	2,400	2,800	2,950

Excel's *Scenario Manager* is designed to enable you to easily compare these scenarios side-by-side.

1 Open *Profit Forecast-1* from your sample files folder.

Notice that this worksheet has been grouped to show four sets of values:

- Input Cells (referred to as *changing cells* in Excel scenarios).

- Constants (cells that do not, or rarely, change their values).

- Result Cells (cells that change when input cells change).

- Scenarios (values for best, worst and expected case).

2 Create single-cell range names for the input and result cells.

This was covered in depth in: *Lesson 5-1: Automatically create single-cell range names.*

As you'll see later, in: *Lesson 6-4: Create a scenario summary report,* the *Scenario Manager* expects you to define range names for input

note

The scenario manager can only handle 32 changing cells

If you try to define more than 32 changing cells, Excel will display an error message.

Profit Forecast-1

and result cells in order to correctly display scenario summary reports.

1. Select cells A4:B7.

2. Click: Formulas→Defined Names→Create from Selection.

3. Click the *OK* button.

4. Repeat for cells A16:B19.

3 **Define the scenarios listed in cells A22:D26.**

1. Click: Data→Forecast→What-If Analysis→ Scenario Manager...

   The *Scenario Manager* dialog appears.

2. Click the *Add* button to add a new scenario.

3. Type **Worst Case** into the *Scenario name* box.

4. Click in the *Changing cells* box and select cells B4:B7 with the mouse.

   > Scenario name:
   >
   > Worst Case
   >
   > Changing cells:
   >
   > $B$4:$B$7

   The *Scenario Manager* uses the term *Changing cells* to refer to *Input Cells*.

5. Click the *OK* button.

6. Enter the following values for the *Worst Case* scenario:

Scenario Values	?	×
Enter values for each of the changing cells.		
1: Grommets	750	
2: Sprockets	4100	
3: Widgets	2000	
4: Flugel_valves	2400	
Add	OK	Cancel

7. Click the *Add* button and then use the same technique to add the *Expected Case* and *Best Case* scenarios.

8. Click OK when finished.

4 **Use the Scenario Manager to view result cells for each scenario.**

1. Select one of the cases in the *Scenarios* list.

2. Click the *Show* button to display the scenario on the worksheet.

3. Select a different case and click the *Show* button.

4. Click the *Close* button to close the Scenario Manager.

5 **Save your work as *Profit Forecast-2*.**

note

Merging scenarios

Excel allows you to merge scenarios from one or more other workbooks.

Imagine that you send a worksheet out to three salesmen: Tom, Dick and Harry. Your salesmen are well trained in Excel and know how to define a scenario.

You instruct each of them to forecast their sales by completing the input cells on their worksheet. They then name a scenario with their own name which references the input cells.

When you receive their workbooks, you merge them with your summary workbook like this:

1. Make sure that the *Tom, Dick, Harry,* and *Summary* workbooks are open (they are in the sample files if you want to follow through).

2. Make sure that you are viewing the *Summary* workbook.

3. Click: Data→Forecast→ What-If Analysis→ Scenario Manager.

You should see the *Tom, Dick* and *Harry* scenarios listed.

4. Click the *Merge...* button.

5. Select *Sheet1* of the *Tom* workbook.

6. Click the *OK* button.

7. Do the same for *Dick* and *Harry.*

8. Close the *Tom, Dick* and *Harry* workbooks.

The three merged scenarios *Tom, Dick* and *Harry* are now available in the *Summary* workbook. (You may also see duplicate scenarios listed and can delete them if you wish)

Profit Forecast-2

Lesson 6-4: Create a scenario summary report

When scenarios have been defined, it is possible to display a neatly formatted report or pivot table, showing each scenario side-by-side.

1 Open *Profit Forecast-2* from your sample files folder (if it isn't already open).

2 Open the Scenario Manager.

Click: Data→Forecast→What-If Analysis→Scenario Manager…

The *Scenario Manager* dialog is displayed:

3 Create a *Scenario Summary* Report.

1. Click the *Summary…* button.

The *Scenario Summary* dialog is displayed.

This dialog asks which result cells should be displayed on the report.

2. Delete the current contents of the *Result cells* box.

3. Select cells B16:B19 with the mouse:

Note that it is possible to show the report as either a *Scenario summary* or as a *Scenario PivotTable report.* You'll learn about PivotTable reports later, in: *Session Nine: Pivot Tables.*

4. Click the *OK* button.

The *Scenario Summary* report is displayed on its own worksheet.

Scenario Summary		Current Values:	Worst Case	Expected Case	Best Case
Changing Cells:					
	Grommets	1,500	750	1,500	2,200
	Sprockets	4,300	4,100	4,300	4,350
	Widgets	3,100	2,000	3,100	3,750
	Flugel_valves	2,800	2,400	2,800	2,950
Result Cells:					
	Sales	842,280.00	661,725.00	842,280.00	950,415.00
	Cost	643,230.00	519,680.00	643,230.00	715,235.00
	Profit	199,050.00	142,045.00	199,050.00	235,180.00
	Gross_Profit_Pct	23.6%	21.5%	23.6%	24.7%

Notes: Current Values column represents values of changing cells at time Scenario Summary Report was created. Changing cells for each scenario are highlighted in gray.

Notice that the report is shown as an outline and that it is possible to collapse and expand the outline by clicking on the plus and minus buttons or on the number buttons in the top left corner.

You can now see how important it was to define named ranges for the input and result cells. Without these, the report would show cell references rather than descriptive names such as *Flugel_valves*.

4   Save your work as *Profit Forecast-3*.

Lesson 6-5: Use Goal Seek

It is very easy to view result values by changing input values. You simply type the new values into the input cells.

	A	B
1	Mortgage	
2		
3	Input Cells	
4	Loan Amount	300,000
5	Deposit (%)	20%
6	Term (Years)	20
7	Interest Rate (APR%)	6.6%
8		
9	Result Cells	
10	Loan Financed	240,000
11	Monthly Repayment	1,803.53
12	Total amount to be repaid	432,848
13	Total interest to be repaid	192,848

In the above worksheet, I wanted to know the monthly repayment for a 300,000 loan with a 20% deposit over 20 years at 6.6% interest. I simply typed the values into the input cells and viewed the results in the result cells.

Consider the case where you want to know the maximum *Loan Amount* if you can only afford a monthly payment of 1,000. This is more difficult because the result cells contain formulas rather than values.

By using Goal Seek, Excel will change one (and only one) input cell so that the desired value is shown in one result cell.

There's a much more complex tool called Solver. You'll learn about this later in: *Lesson 6-6: Use Solver*. Solver is a more advanced goal seek tool, able to automatically set multiple input cells.

For now, you'll examine the simple and extremely useful Goal Seek tool.

1   Open *Mortgage-3* from your sample files folder.

2   Create a new worksheet called: **Goal Seek**

3   Copy cells A1:B13 from the *Variable Interest and Capital* worksheet into the same cells on the *Goal Seek* worksheet.

4   AutoSize columns A and B so that all text and values are visible.

5   Use *Goal Seek* to find the maximum *Loan Amount* available if you can afford only 1,000 per month.

1.   Click in cell B11 (the *Monthly Repayment* cell).

Mortgage-3

2. Click: Data→Forecast→What-If Analysis→Goal Seek...

The *Goal Seek* dialog appears:

Goal Seek	?	✕
Se̲t cell:	B11	⬆
To v̲alue:		
By c̲hanging cell:		⬆
	OK	Cancel

You want to set the *Monthly Repayment* (B11) to the value 1,000 by changing the *Loan Amount* (B4).

3. Complete the dialog as follows:

Goal Seek	?	✕
Se̲t cell:	B11	⬆
To v̲alue:	1000	
By c̲hanging cell:	$B$4	⬆
	OK	Cancel

4. Click the *OK* button.

Goal Seek advises you that it has found a solution:

Goal Seek Status	?	✕
Goal Seeking with Cell B11 found a solution.	Step	
Target value: 1000	Pause	
Current value: 1,000.00		
	OK	Cancel

5. Click the *OK* button.

The solution to the problem is shown on the worksheet:

	A	B
3	Input Cells	
4	Loan Amount	247,675
5	Deposit (%)	10%
6	Term (Years)	25
7	Interest Rate (APR%)	2.5%
8		
9	Result Cells	
10	Loan Financed	222,907
11	Monthly Repayment	1,000.00
12	Total amount to be repaid	300,000
13	Total interest to be repaid	77,093

The maximum *Loan Amount* I could raise will be 247,675 if I can only afford 1,000 per month. I could, of course, have also used Goal Seek to change any of the other input cells. The key limitation of Goal Seek is that it can only change one input cell.

6 Save your work as *Mortgage-4.*

Lesson 6-6: Use Solver

What is Solver?

Conceptually, Solver is similar to Goal Seek. While Goal Seek can only change one input cell to set a value in one result cell, Solver can change any number of input cells. This makes the tool a lot more complex.

You can also define a set of rules (called constraints) that Solver needs to observe when finding a solution.

1   Open *Bicycle Manufacturing Schedule-1* from your sample files folder.

This worksheet models a bicycle manufacturing company. The company manufactures four different types of bicycle but has a limited number of parts available.

- Cells B4:E4 are the input cells (or changing cells) for the worksheet. They define how many bicycles of each model will be manufactured.

- The parts needed to manufacture each type of bicycle are shown in cells B7:E11. For example, a *Street Bike* needs 2 wheels, 1 steel chassis and 1 set of derailleur gears.

- Column I shows how many parts are available.

- Cells B14:F14 show the profit for each bicycle type, along with the total profit for all bicycle types.

	A	B	C	D	E	F	G	H	I
3		Mountain Bike	Street Bike	Racing Bike	Commuter Bike		Input (Changing) Cells		
4	Qty To Manufacture	20	20	20	20				
5								Constraints	
6	Parts List						Parts needed	Operator	Parts Available
7	Wheels	2	2	2	2		160	<=	180
8	Alloy Chassis	1		1			40	<=	40
9	Steel Chassis		1		1		40	<=	60
10	Hub Gears	1			1		40	<=	50
11	Derailleur Gears		1	1			40	<=	40
12									
13	Profit Analysis		Profit Per Unit			Total Profit			
14		$ 45	$ 60	$ 55	$ 50	$ 4,200			

Your challenge is to maximize profit by manufacturing the optimum number of each type of bicycle.

2   Install the Solver add-in (if it is not already installed).

1.   Click: File→Options→Add-ins.

2.   Click the *Go…* button.

3.   Check the *Solver Add-in* check box and click the *OK* button.

Bicycle Manufacturing Schedule-1

Solver now appears on the ribbon's *Data* tab in a new *Analyze* group.

3   **Open Solver.**

Click: Data→Analyze→Solver.

Solver appears.

4   **Let Solver know which are the *Changing* (Input) cells and which is the *Objective* (Result) cell.**

Complete the dialog as follows:

Set Objective:	$F$14
To: ● Max ○ Min ○ Value Of:	
By Changing Variable Cells:	
$B$4:$E$4	

You are telling Solver to maximize the profit (shown in cell F14) by changing the *Input Cells* (or *Changing Cells*) B4:E4.

5   **Define the constraints for the problem.**

1.   Click the *Add* button next to the *Subject to the Constraints* list box.

2.   Complete the dialog as follows:

Cell Reference:				Constraint:	
$B$4:$E$4	↥	>=	∨	0	↥

This tells Solver that it cannot manufacture a negative number of bicycles.

3.   Click the *Add* button.

4.   Set up a second constraint as follows:

Cell Reference:				Constraint:	
$G$7:$G$11	↥	<=	∨	$I$7:$I$11	↥

This tells Solver that it cannot use more parts than are available.

5.   Click the *OK* button.

6   **Solve the problem.**

1.   Click the *Solve* button.

2.   Click the *OK* button.

Solver has solved the problem.

	A	B	C	D	E
3		Mountain Bike	Street Bike	Racing Bike	Commuter Bike
4	Qty To Manufacture	25	35	5	25

This mix of bicycles maximizes profits to $4,750.

7   **Save your work as *Bicycle Manufacturing Schedule-2*.**

---

note

This workbook uses an array function

This worksheet uses the SUMPRODUCT array function to calculate the *Parts Needed* in column G and the *Total Profit* in cell F14.

You learned about the SUMPRODUCT function in: *Lesson 4-22: Use the SUMPRODUCT function*.

Unlike the new dynamic array functions, SUMPRODUCT is compatible with legacy Excel versions (Excel 2019 and earlier).

trivia

Solver wasn't developed by Microsoft

Solver is a product developed by Frontline Systems who have now distributed over a billion copies of their product to users.

As well as Excel's Solver, Frontline also developed the solvers included in Lotus 1-2-3 and Quattro Pro.

Every copy of Excel sold since 1990 has included Frontline's Solver.

Frontline also produce a more advanced version of Solver (available at extra cost) called *Premium Solver*. There's also a *Risk Solver* product that enables Excel to model Monte Carlo simulations (an advanced mathematical technique that relies upon random sampling to obtain numerical results).

Lesson 6-7: Hide and unhide worksheets, columns and rows

note

Hiding and unhiding a worksheet using the ribbon

The right-click method is much faster than using the ribbon but here's how it can be done:

To hide a worksheet:

Click: Home→Cells→ Format→Hide & Unhide→ Hide Sheet.

To Unhide a worksheet:

Click: Home→Cells→ Format→Hide & Unhide→ Unhide Sheet.

Then select the sheet that you want to hide/unhide from the dialog and click the *OK* button.

important

Don't rely on hidden worksheets for security

There is no password associated with hiding and unhiding a worksheet, row or column. A knowledgeable user can easily unhide any hidden item.

If you need to hide items more securely, it is possible to protect the structure before distributing a workbook.

When this is done, it isn't possible to unhide and view the hidden items unless you know the password.

Protecting the structure of a workbook will be covered in: *Lesson 6-10: Control the changes users can make to workbooks*.

1   Open *Human Resources-1* from your sample files folder.

2   Hide the *Headcount & Salaries* worksheet.

The *Payroll* worksheet depends upon the *Headcount & Salaries* worksheet in order to calculate each employee's hourly rate.

Because this data is sensitive, you may decide to hide the entire *Headcount & Salaries* worksheet.

1. Select the *Headcount & Salaries* worksheet.

2. Right-click the worksheet tab.

3. Click *Hide* from the shortcut menu.

The worksheet disappears.

3   Unhide the *Headcount & Salaries* worksheet.

1. Right-click on any worksheet tab (at the moment the only visible worksheet tab is *Payroll*).

2. Click *Unhide* from the shortcut menu.

    The *Unhide* dialog is displayed, listing all currently hidden worksheets.

3. Click the *OK* button.

    The *Headcount & Salaries* worksheet reappears.

    You can see that this is not a good way to hide confidential information, as any knowledgeable user can simply unhide the worksheet (see sidebar).

4   Hide rows 3:6, rows 19:23 and row 9 on the *Payroll* worksheet.

Perhaps you would like to print out the *Payroll* worksheet for the floor manager so that each employee's hours can be reviewed.

This might be a problem if the salaries had to be kept confidential.

For this reason, you are going to hide the confidential rows on the *Payroll* worksheet before printing.

1. Select the *Payroll* worksheet.

2. Select rows 3 to 6.

3. Right-click anywhere within the selected cells.

4. Click *Hide* from the shortcut menu.

Human Resources-1

note

Sharing information using screenshots

A screenshot is a little like a photograph of all, or part of a worksheet.

You will often want to paste a read-only depiction of part of a worksheet into an e-mail, Word document, PowerPoint presentation or other Office document.

To take a screenshot:

1. Select the cells that you want to take a screenshot of.

2. Click:
Home→Clipboard→Copy→ Copy as Picture…

You'll then see the *Copy Picture* dialog with two sets of option buttons:

Appearance
- ● As shown on screen
- ○ As shown when printed

Format
- ● Picture
- ○ Bitmap

If you choose: *As shown on the screen,* you are able to choose a *Picture* or *Bitmap.*

The main difference between these options is that a *Picture* will have a transparent background and a *Bitmap* will have a white background (unless you have set a background color for the cells that you are copying).

tip

A faster way to hide a single row or column

A hidden column is simply a column that has its width set to zero.

You can quickly hide a row or column by dragging its border to make it so narrow that it is no longer visible.

The rows disappear.

5. Do the same to hide rows 19:23.

6. Do the same to hide row 9.

   The payroll no longer shows any financial values. It would now be possible to print the worksheet (or take a screenshot of the worksheet – see sidebar) without showing the hidden rows.

5 Hide columns E:O on the *Payroll* worksheet.

This is very similar to hiding rows.

1. Select columns E:O.

2. Right-click anywhere in the selected area.

3. Click *Hide* from the shortcut menu.

   The columns disappear.

6 Unhide columns E:O on the *Payroll* worksheet.

1. Select columns D:P (the columns that are on either side of the hidden columns).

2. Right-click anywhere in the selected area.

3. Click *Unhide* from the shortcut menu.

   The columns re-appear.

7 Unhide all hidden rows on the *Payroll* worksheet.

1. Click the *Select All* button (in the top left corner of the worksheet) to select every cell.

2. Right-click any of the row headers (the numbered buttons on the left of the worksheet).

3. Click *Unhide* from the shortcut menu.

4. All hidden rows re-appear.

There is no need to save this workbook as it has not been changed in any way.

important

Custom views don't work if there is a table anywhere in the workbook

In *Excel 365 version 2008 Jan 2021*, custom views could not be used in any workbook that contains a table (though I expect that this will be fixed in a future version).

If there's a table anywhere in the workbook, the *Custom Views* button will be grayed out for all worksheets.

You can work-around this limitation by using range names in place of tables when you really need the *Custom Views* feature.

In: *Lesson 5-6: Create dynamic formula-based range names using the OFFSET function*, there's a description of a technique that allows you to create range names that have the same dynamic features as tables.

Lesson 6-8: Create custom views

In: *Lesson 6-7: Hide and unhide worksheets, columns and rows*, you learned how useful it can be to hide columns and rows when printing (or taking a screenshot from) a worksheet.

Sometimes you may find that you are continuously hiding and unhiding the same rows and columns in order to print selected parts of a worksheet. When you notice that this is happening, you have an ideal candidate for a custom view.

Custom views allow you to save and recall worksheet layouts that have hidden columns and rows.

1   Open *Human Resources-1* from your sample files folder (if it isn't already open).

2   Select the *Payroll* worksheet.

3   Save the current view as *HR*.

    1.   Click: View→Workbook Views→Custom Views.

        The *Custom Views* dialog appears:

    2.   Click the *Add…* button.

        The *Add View* dialog appears.

    3.   Type **HR** into the *Name* box.

Human Resources-1

Notice that custom views don't only save hidden rows and columns.

Custom views also save all of the following:

- *Print settings*, including any *Page Layout* settings.

- Any filters that are currently applied to the worksheet.

- The zoom factor.

- Window sizes and positions.

- The currently active cell.

- The current worksheet view (*Normal, Page Layout* or *Page Break Preview*).

4. Click the *OK* button.

Nothing seems to have happened, but you have, in fact, stored a view with all rows and columns visible.

4 Hide rows 3:6, rows 19:23 and row 9 on the *Payroll* worksheet.

This was covered in: *Lesson 6-7: Hide and unhide worksheets, columns and rows.*

5 Save the current view as: **Hours Worked**

Do this in the same way that you saved the HR custom view earlier.

6 Hide columns B,C,F,G,H,I,J,K,L and N.

7 Save the current view as: **Hours Worked (Female)**

8 Show the *Hours Worked* view.

1. Click: View→Workbook Views→Custom Views.

The *Custom Views* dialog is displayed, showing the three saved views:

2. Click the *Hours Worked* view in the *Views* list.

3. Click the *Show* button.

The worksheet changes to show the *Hours Worked* view.

9 Show the *Hours Worked (Female)* view.

10 Show the *HR* view.

11 Save your work as *Human Resources-2*.

important

Secure passwords

Hacking tools (freely available on the Internet) commonly use five methods to discover passwords:

1. Dictionary attack

In a matter of seconds, the tool tries every word in the dictionary. For this reason, your password should never be a real word such as *London*.

2. Dictionary + numbers

The tool makes several passes through the dictionary, appending a sequential number to the front or back of the password. For this reason, your password should never be a real word with leading or trailing numbers, such as *London99* or *99London*.

3. Reverse words

The tool tries every word in the dictionary spelled backwards.

4. Words with the letter O replaced with a zero

5. *Brute force* **attack**

The tool tries every possible combination of the letters of the alphabet. A 2017 test showed that it takes less than 10 minutes for an Intel core i5-6600K dual-core Pentium to crack a seven letter single-case password such as: *xcoekfh*

For ultimate security against brute force attacks, include upper and lower case letters, numbers, and symbols in your passwords. The best approach is to create a password from a phrase such as: "I like to ride my Honda motorcycle at 100 MPH". This gives the extremely secure password: *IltrmHm@100MPH*

This password would take up to 5 million years to crack using an Intel i5.

Human Resources-2

Lesson 6-9: Prevent unauthorized users from opening or modifying workbooks

There are two levels of password protection available when you save a workbook. You can:

- Prevent users from opening the workbook.

- Prevent users from changing a workbook once they have opened it.

In this lesson you'll implement both types of protection.

1 Open *Human Resources-2* from your sample files folder (if it isn't already open).

2 Protect the workbook with a password that will prevent other users from opening it.

1. Click: File→Save As→Browse.

   The *Save As* dialog is displayed.

2. Click: Tools→General Options at the bottom-right of the dialog.

3. Type a password in the *Password to open* box.

   See the *secure passwords* sidebar for important information about choosing an appropriate password.

   See the facing page sidebar for a discussion of the *Always create backup* and *Read-only recommended* check box options.

4. Click the *OK* button.

   Excel reminds you not to forget the password and prompts for it again to protect against accidental typing errors.

5. Type the password again.

6. Click the *OK* button.

note

Excel passwords do not provide 100% security

Even if you choose a secure password that is nine or more characters long, there are tools freely available on the Internet that can crack most Excel 365 worksheet protection passwords in minutes. Currently, only the *password to open* is not easily cracked.

The *password to open* is encrypted using the AES 128 standard.

This encryption standard is approved by the US government to encrypt classified documents up to SECRET level. This suggests that it is extremely secure.

note

General Options check boxes

The *Always create backup* check box provides you with an escape route if you need to return to the previous version of the workbook. A copy of the old workbook is saved every time you save, so that you always have two copies of each workbook. One copy is a *Microsoft Excel Backup* file with the file extension .xlk.

If you check the *Read-only recommended* check box, the user is presented with a dialog when opening a protected workbook. The dialog suggests that the workbook be opened read-only.

If the user ignores this suggestion, a read/write copy will be opened. As you discovered in this lesson, this copy cannot be used to over-write the protected file but can be used to create a new file with a different name.

7. Click the *Save* button.

8. If necessary, click *Yes* to overwrite the existing file.

3 Close the *Human Resources-2* workbook and then try to re-open it.

You are unable to open the workbook without the password.

4 Enter the password and click OK to open the workbook.

5 Remove the password from the workbook.

1. Click: File→Save As→Browse.

2. Click: Tools→General Options at the bottom-right of the dialog.

3. Remove the password from the *Passsword to open* box.

4. Click the *OK* button.

5. Click the *Save* button.

6. Click *Yes* to overwrite the existing file.

6 Protect the workbook with a password that will prevent other users from changing it.

Follow the same procedure as you did when adding a *Password to open*, but this time specify a *Password to modify*.

7 Save and Close the workbook.

8 Open *Human Resources-2* read only.

1. Click: File→Open→Human Resources-2.

2. The *Password* dialog appears.

3. Click the *Read Only* button without entering a password.

This doesn't have the effect you might expect. You've opened the workbook without a password and are able to change it.

9 Attempt to save the workbook.

Surprisingly, Excel will only prevent you from saving the workbook with the same name as the password-protected workbook. Excel is quite happy for you to make a copy and even prompts you to do so when you attempt to save the file.

10 Save the workbook as *Human Resources-3*.

This workbook no longer has password protection.

Lesson 6-10: Control the changes users can make to workbooks

Sometimes you are quite happy for any user to open your workbook, but you need to prevent them from inserting, deleting, renaming, moving, hiding or unhiding any of the worksheets.

This is called protecting the *Structure* of a workbook.

1 Open *Human Resources-3* from your sample files folder (if it isn't already open).

2 Display the *Hours Worked (Female)* custom view.

This was covered in: *Lesson 6-8: Create custom views.*

3 Hide the Headcount & Salaries worksheet

This was covered in: *Lesson 6-7: Hide and unhide worksheets, columns and rows.*

4 Protect the structure of the workbook.

1. Click: Review→Protect→Protect Workbook.

The *Protect Structure and Windows* dialog is displayed.

In Excel 365, it is no longer possible to protect windows, making the *Windows* option redundant (see sidebar).

2. Check the *Structure* check box (if necessary) and add a password.

Protect Structure and Windows   ?   ✕

Password (optional):

Protect workbook for
☑ Structure
☐ Windows

OK   Cancel

3. Click the *OK* button.

4. Enter the password again when prompted and click *OK*.

Because you checked the *Structure* check box you are now unable to add, delete, rename, move, hide or unhide any of the worksheets in this workbook.

5 Attempt to unhide the Headcount & Salaries worksheet.

Right-click on the *Payroll* worksheet tab.

Human Resources-3

important

Do not rely upon Protect Structure to hide confidential data

Protect Structure is not a secure method to hide confidential data.

Protect Structure does its job well only if the Excel file is opened (in Excel) in the normal and intended way.

I managed to hack this protected worksheet in less than a minute using only common tools found on every desktop computer. Most users with basic IT skills could figure out how to do the same thing.

note

Protection options are also available from File→info→Protect Workbook

The features demonstrated in: *Lesson 6-9: Prevent unauthorized users from opening or modifying workbooks, Lesson 6-10: Control the changes users can make to workbooks* and *Lesson 6-11: Restrict the cells users are allowed to change* can also be accessed from File→Info→Protect Workbook.

Notice that the *Unhide* option is grayed out and unavailable. This has happened because you have protected the structure of the workbook.

Notice also that the *Insert, Delete, Rename, Move or Copy, Tab Color* and *Hide* options are now unavailable.

6 **Remove password protection from the structure.**

1. Click: Review→Protect→Protect Workbook.

   You are prompted for the password to remove protection:

2. Enter the password and click the *OK* button.

   Protection is removed.

7 **Unhide the *Headcount & Salaries* worksheet.**

This time you are permitted to unhide the worksheet as the structure is no longer protected.

8 **Display the *HR* custom view.**

There's no need to save the workbook as it has not changed.

tip

Use cell locking to make forms more user-friendly

Excel is often used to create forms (such as booking forms). The form is sent to the user by e-mail and the user completes and returns it.

This type of form becomes much easier to use if you do the following:

1. Unlock the cells that the user should type data into.

2. Protect the worksheet making sure that only the *Select unlocked cells* option is checked.

When this is done, the user can use the **<Tab>** key to navigate through all of the cells in the form that need to be completed.

note

Cells can also be locked and unlocked using the Ribbon

To do this you need to first select the cell(s) to be locked or unlocked and then click:

Home→Cells→Format→ Lock Cell

You might have thought that the menu option would show the text: *Lock Cell* or *Unlock Cell* depending upon whether the range selected was already locked.

Confusingly, the icon always displays *Lock Cell* but is highlighted in gray if the selected range is locked.

Lesson 6-11: Restrict the cells users are allowed to change

1   Open *Human Resources-3* from your sample files folder (if it isn't already open).

2   Display the *Hours Worked* custom view.

This was covered in: *Lesson 6-8: Create custom views*.

3   Hide the *Headcount and Salaries* worksheet.

This was covered in: *Lesson 6-7: Hide and unhide worksheets, columns and rows*.

4   Re-size columns B:O so that they are just wide enough to display their contents:

	A	B	C	D	E	F	G	H	I	J	K	L	M	N	O
1	Payroll														
8		Johnny Caine	George Marley	Betty Anan	Paris Winfrey	Ozzy Dickens	Johnny Roberts	Charles Monroe	Ronnie Bush	Michal Jolie	JK Spears	Ozzy Rowling	Oprah Hilton	Bill Biggs	Angelina Osbourne
11	Hours Worked														
12	Monday	9	10	10	10	7	7	7	7	7	7	7	10	8	6
13	Tuesday	8	9	8	6	10	10	10	7	6	10	7	8	7	9
14	Wednesday	10	9	8	7	9	8	6	8	7	8	8	6	6	8
15	Thursday	6	8	6	10	9	7	6	6	7	8	8	6	6	9
16	Friday	10	7	10	7	9	10	9	8	8	10	8	9	10	6
17	Total	43	43	42	40	44	42	38	36	35	43	38	39	37	38

The challenge this time will be to prevent the user from changing any value other than those in the yellow shaded cells (cells B12:O16).

You will solve this problem by *unlocking* these cells and then *protecting* the worksheet. This will only allow the user to enter values into the *unlocked* cells.

5   Unlock cells B12:O16.

All cells on a worksheet are (by default) *locked*. You are able to type values into them because the worksheet is not yet *protected*.

In order to prevent the user from changing any cell except cells B12:O16 you need to do two things:

•   Unlock the cells that you want the user to be able to change.

•   Protect the worksheet.

Here's how to unlock the cells:

1.   Select cells B12:O16.

2.   Right click anywhere in the selected area.

Human Resources-3

note

You can keep your formulas secret with the Hidden attribute

If you set the *Hidden* attribute on the *Format Cells* dialog's *Protection* tab, users cannot see any of your formulas.

Even if a cell is unlocked, the formula does not display in the formula bar when the cell is selected. This could be used if the formula used to calculate a value was a "trade secret".

This will only take effect when the worksheet is protected.

tip

Leave all cells locked to distribute a read-only workbook

If you protect a workbook without unlocking any cells, you have effectively created a read-only workbook.

To prevent the user from copying and pasting the contents, you should also un-check the *Select locked cells* check box. Note that the user will still be able to click:

Insert➔Illustrations➔ Screenshot

… from any another Office application to copy an image of the worksheet.

3. Click *Format Cells…* from the shortcut menu.

4. Click the *Protection* tab.

5. Uncheck the *Locked* check box.

See sidebar for more about the *Hidden* attribute.

6. Click the *OK* button.

6 **Protect the *Payroll* worksheet so that the user is unable to change or select any of the locked cells.**

When you protect a worksheet, it is no longer possible to change the contents of a *locked* cell.

1. Click: Review➔Protect➔Protect Sheet.

   The *Protect Sheet* dialog appears

   The default settings allow the user to select (but not change) the contents of locked cells. This normally makes sense as you want the user to be able to copy and paste any part of the worksheet.

   In this case, however, it creates a huge security problem as the user can easily copy the entire worksheet, paste it into a new worksheet, and then unhide the hidden rows.

   For this reason, you want to prevent the user from selecting locked cells.

2. Uncheck the *Select locked cells* check box.

   Notice that, by default, the user is prevented from doing many more things to the worksheet (such as formatting cells). You can selectively allow these actions by checking the appropriate check boxes.

3. Enter a password.

4. Click the *OK* button, confirm the password and then click the *OK* button once more.

7 **Test the protected worksheet.**

You are unable to change (or even select) any of the locked cells but you can select and change any of the unlocked cells.

8 **Unprotect the worksheet.**

1. Click: Review➔Protect➔Unprotect Sheet.

2. Enter the password, and then click the *OK* button.

9 **Lock cells B12:O16.**

Do this in the same way that you unlocked the cells, but this time check the *Locked* check box (instead of un-checking it).

10 **Save your work as *Human Resources-4*.**

note

You can allow access based upon the Windows log-in password or user group

You can also use your existing Windows passwords and user groups to allow access to specific ranges of cells.

To use Windows permissions, click:

Review→Protect→ Allow Edit Ranges→ New...→Permissions...

Lesson 6-12: Allow different levels of access to a worksheet with multiple passwords

Sometimes you will want different users to be able to change different ranges in your worksheet. In this lesson, you'll set the following levels of access to the *Hours Worked* worksheet.

	A	B	C	D	E
3	Payroll Rules				
4	Tax	32%			
5	Social Security	8%			
6	Pension	5%			
7					
8		Johnny Caine	George Marley	Betty Anam	Paris Winfrey
9	Hourly Rate	18.20	12.57	12.66	11.32
10					
11	Hours Worked				
12	Monday	9	10	10	10
13	Tuesday	8	9	8	6
14	Wednesday	10	9	8	7
15	Thursday	6	8	6	10
16	Friday	10	7	10	7
17	Total	43	43	42	40

Group	Permission	Password
Human Resources	Access to cells B4:B6, B9:O9 and B12:O16. This allows the HR department to change *Tax, Social Security, Pension, Hours Worked* and *Hourly Rate* values.	cat
Floor Manager	Access to cells B12:O16 only. Floor managers can only change the *Hours Worked* values.	dog
Administrator	All rights (this is the unprotect password).	cow

I have deliberately used very insecure passwords in order to save you the effort of typing longer (and more secure) ones. If security was important, you would use secure passwords (see sidebar in: *Lesson 6-9: Prevent unauthorized users from opening or modifying workbooks,* for details of how to construct a secure password).

1 Open *Hours Worked-1* from your sample files folder.

2 Set up the *Human Resources* password and permissions.

   1. Select cells B4:B6.

Hours Worked-1

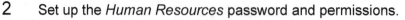

2. Hold down the **<Ctrl>** key and select cells B9:O9 and cells B12:O16.

3. Click: Review→Protect→Allow Edit Ranges.

The *Allow Users to Edit Ranges* dialog appears.

4. Click the *New…* button

5. Type **Human Resources** as the *Title.*

6. Type **cat** as the *Range password.*

7. Click the *OK* button.

8. Type the password again when prompted and click the *OK* button.

3 Set up the *Floor Manager* password and permissions.

1. Click the *New…* button.

Ranges unlocked by a password when sheet is protected:		
Title	Refers to cells	New...
Human Resources	$B$4:$B$6,$B$9:O...	Modify...

2. Type **Floor Manager** as the *Title.*

3. Click in the *Refers to cells* box and delete the current contents.

4. Select cells B12:O16.

5. Type **dog** as the *Range password.*

6. Click the *OK* button.

7. Type the password again when prompted and click the *OK* button.

8. Click the *OK* button to close the dialog.

Allow Users to Edit Ranges

Ranges unlocked by a password when sheet is prot

Title	Refers to cells
Floor Manager	$B$12:$O$16
Human Resources	$B$4:$B$6,$B$9:O...

4 Protect the worksheet.

1. Click: Review→Protect→Protect Sheet.

2. Type the administrator password: **cow** into the *Password to unprotect sheet* box.

3. Click *OK*, re-enter the password when prompted and click *OK.*

5 Test the worksheet.

1. Try to change any of the numbers in cells B12:O16.

A dialog appears asking for a password.

2. Type **dog** as the password.

You are now able to freely change any value in cells B12:O16 for as long as the workbook stays open.

3. Try to change any of the values in cells B4:B6 or cells B9:O9.

In each case, a dialog appears asking for a password.

4. Type **cat** as the password.

You are now able to freely change any value in cells B4:B6, B9:O9 or B12:O16 for as long as the workbook stays open.

Unlock Range

A cell you are trying to change is password protected.

Enter the password to change this cell:

OK   Cancel

6 Save your work as *Hours Worked-2.*

Lesson 6-13: Create a digital certificate

Why digital certificates are needed

If you receive a workbook via e-mail, you cannot be sure where it has really come from. It is remarkably easy to send an e-mail that appears to have been sent by a different person.

You may also worry that the workbook may have been altered by somebody since the author sent it to you.

The solution to both of these problems is to digitally sign your workbooks.

If a workbook is digitally signed, it confirms the identity of the author. Excel will also warn the recipient if the workbook has been changed since the author signed it.

Digital certificates are of great use when you need to distribute workbooks that contain macros within an organization. (You'll learn all about macros in: *Session Eight: Forms and Macros*). Macros can contain destructive macro viruses and you wouldn't ever want to open a workbook containing macros without being absolutely sure of its origin.

Self-certification and third-party certification

There are two ways to create a digital certificate in Excel 365:

1. Create your own digital certificate. This isn't very secure, as it is easy to forge a self-certified digital certificate. When another user opens a workbook with a self-certified signature it will display the message:

    > ℹ SIGNATURES   This document contains recoverable signatures.   View Signatures...

    This isn't likely to inspire a great deal of confidence in the recipient. In fact, I'd go so far as to say that a self-certified digital certificate has no value as it doesn't really increase security at all.

    The terminology *recoverable signature* isn't very descriptive (see sidebar). In this case it means that the certificate issuer isn't trusted. You'll learn more about trusted issuers later, in: *Lesson 8-13: Implement macro security.*

2. Buy a certificate from a trusted third party such as VersiSign. Third-party certificates provide a high level of security as they are certified to be genuine by an outside agency. When a user opens a workbook, Excel will confirm that the certificate is genuine by contacting the third-party's server. Most third-party subscriptions cost between US$100 and US$500 per year.

In this lesson, you'll create your own digital certificate. Although this doesn't really improve security, it will give you all of the skills you need to effectively use digital certificates should you eventually purchase a third-party subscription.

1   Open the Windows digital certificate dialog.

As mentioned in the introduction, the ability to create a self-certified digital certificate is a contradiction in terms.

Microsoft also must have thought it a pointless feature as they still allow you (but have recently made it rather difficult) to create a self-certified digital certificate.

If you do want to work through the remainder of this lesson here's how it can be done (at least how it could be done at time of writing in Jan 2021).

1. Navigate to:

   C:\Program Files\Microsoft Office\root\Office16

   Or for some users:

   C:\Program Files (x86)\Microsoft Office\root\Office16

   In this folder you should find an application called:

   SELFCERT.exe

2. Double-click *SELFCERT.exe* to open it.

2 Create a self-certified digital certificate.

The *Create Digital Certificate* dialog should now be shown:

The dialog refers to macros because workbooks containing macros present the most serious security threat. You'll learn more about macros in: *Session Eight: Forms and Macros.*

Notice that there is a hyperlink on this dialog that will direct you to several commercial certificate authorities should you wish to purchase a third-party certificate.

1. Type a name for your certificate into the *Your certificate's name* box.

2. Click the *OK* button.

   A dialog appears confirming that the certificate has been created.

Lesson 6-14: Add an invisible digital signature to a workbook

As discussed in: *Lesson 6-13: Create a digital certificate*, a self-certified digital certificate has little value as it doesn't increase security at all. As you'll see in this lesson, Microsoft go out of their way to warn the user of this.

Should your organization purchase a "real" digital certificate this lesson will give you all of the skills you need to effectively attach certificates to workbooks.

1   Open *Salary Increase-1* from your sample files folder.

This worksheet details salary increases for the coming year:

You want your HR department to be confident that this workbook was really created by you and that nobody has changed any of the salary increases since it was sent out.

This can be achieved by adding a digital certificate.

2   Add an invisible digital signature.

1.   Click: File→Info→Protect Workbook→Add a digital signature.

The *Sign* dialog appears.

2.   Use the *Commitment Type* drop-down to add a *Commitment Type* of: *Created and approved this document.*

3.   Enter a *Purpose for signing this document* into the text box:

4.   Click the *Sign* button.

5.   You are warned that a self-certified certificate cannot be verified. Click *Yes* to confirm that you really do want to use the self-certified certificate.

The document is now digitally signed.

Notice that Excel warns you (in a rather cryptic way) that a self-certified signature cannot be relied upon as it cannot be

Salary Increase-1

verified. Recoverable signatures are discussed in: *Lesson 6-13: Create a digital certificate (sidebar)*.

> ### Recoverable Signatures
> One or more of the digital signatures in this workbook is recoverable or could not be verified. A recoverable signature may indicate that an error occurred when the workbook was signed.
>
> View Signatures

6. Click the *Back Button* to return to the worksheet.

Notice that two things have changed on the worksheet.

There is a warning at the top of the worksheet that it has been marked as final (by adding the certificate):

> (i) MARKED AS FINAL   An author has marked this workbook as final to discourage editing.   Edit Anyway

There is also an icon at the bottom left corner showing that the workbook contains a digital signature:

> Ready
>
> This document contains signatures.

3   Close the workbook.

You don't have to save the workbook. It is automatically saved when you add a signature.

4   Close Excel.

5   Re-open Excel.

6   Re-open the *Salary Increase-1* workbook.

Note the two status bars at the top of the screen:

> (i) MARKED AS FINAL   An author has marked this workbook as final to discourage editing.   Edit Anyway
> (i) SIGNATURES   This document contains recoverable signatures.   View Signatures...

You can see that a self-certified digital signature is presented to the user as *recoverable* by Microsoft. This is Microsoft's way of saying "the signature is not verified by a third-party agency and cannot be relied upon".

Note also that the top status bar indicates that the workbook has been opened as read-only.

Lesson 6-15: Add a visible digital signature to a workbook

1 Open *Salary Increase-1* from your sample files folder (if it isn't already open).

2 Remove the invisible digital signature.

    1. Click the signature icon at the bottom-left of the screen.

    The *Signatures* pane appears.

    2. Click the certificate issuer name in the task pane.

    A drop-down arrow appears to the right of the certificate issuer.

    3. Click the drop-down arrow and then click *Remove Signature* from the menu.

    The *Remove Signature* dialog appears.

> **Remove Signature** ✕
>
> **?** Are you sure you want to permanently remove this signature? This action cannot be undone.
>
>   Yes   No

    4. Click *Yes*.

    This *Signature Removed* dialog may appear.

> **Signature Removed** ✕
>
> **i** The signature has been removed and the document has been saved.
>
> ☐ Don't show this message again
>
>   OK

    5. Check the *Don't show this message again* check box to prevent this dialog from displaying in future.

    6. Click the *OK* button.

3 Add a visible signature.

    1. Click: Insert→Text→Signature Line→ Microsoft Office Signature Line.

    The *Signature Setup* dialog appears.

    2. Enter a *Name, Title* and *E-mail Address* into the relevant boxes:

Salary Increase-1

3. Click the *OK* button.

A graphic appears on the worksheet with a blank space for the signature. This graphic may be freely dragged to any location on the screen.

4. Double-click the signature graphic.

The *Sign* dialog appears.

The *Sign* dialog allows you to either select a signature image (created from a scan of your handwritten signature) or to type a name into the box.

5. Type a name into the box.

6. Click the *Sign* button.

A signature confirmation dialog appears, warning you that your self-certified digital signature cannot be verified.

7. Click the *Yes* button.

8. If a confirmation dialog appears, click the *OK* button.

Microsoft flags the signature as *recoverable* because it is self-certified, easily forged, and thus not of any real use as a security measure.

4 Close the *Salary Increase-1* workbook without saving.

Session 6: Exercise

1 Open *Selling Price Calculator-1* from your sample files folder.

	A	B
3	Input Cells	
4	Cost	$ 4.50
5	Retail Price	$ 17.95
6	Wholesale Discount	60%
7	Annual Units	2,000.00
8		
9	Result Cells	
10	Sales (at wholesale price)	$14,360.00
11	Total Cost	$ 9,000.00
12	Gross Profit	$ 5,360.00
13	Gross Profit Percent	37%

2 Create an attractively formatted single input data table in cells D3:F18 to display the *Gross Profit* and *Gross Profit Percent* that would result from a *Retail Price* of $17.95 to $24.95 in increments of $0.50.

	D	E	F
3	Retail Price	Gross Profit	Gross Profit Percent
4	$ 17.95	$ 5,360.00	37%
5	$ 18.45	$ 5,760.00	39%
6	$ 18.95	$ 6,160.00	41%

3 Hide columns D:F.

4 Use *Goal Seek* to calculate the *Retail Price* that would be needed to produce a *Gross Profit Percent* of exactly *50%*.

5 Create range names for cells B4:B7 and cells B10:B13 using the names in cells A4:A7 and A10:A13.

6 Use the scenario manager to create three scenarios:

Worst Case: 2,000 Annual Units
Expected Case: 3,500 Annual Units
Best Case: 5,000 Annual Units

7 Create a *Scenario Summary* report to show *Sales (at wholesale price), Total Cost, Gross Profit* and *Gross Profit Percent* values for each scenario.

Scenario Summary		Current Values:	Worst Case	Expected Case	Best Case
Changing Cells:					
Annual_Units		2,000.00	2,000.00	3,500.00	5,000.00
Result Cells:					
Sales__at_wholesale_price		$ 17,998.98	$ 17,998.98	$ 31,498.22	$ 44,997.45
Total_Cost		$ 9,000.00	$ 9,000.00	$ 15,750.00	$ 22,500.00
Gross_Profit		$ 8,998.98	$ 8,998.98	$ 15,748.22	$ 22,497.45
Gross_Profit_Percent		50%	50%	50%	50%

8 Protect the *Selling Price Calculator* worksheet so that only cells B4:B7 (the cells shaded yellow) can be changed.

9 Save your work as *Selling Price Calculator-2*.

Selling Price Calculator-1

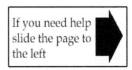
If you need help slide the page to the left

Session 6: Exercise Answers

These are the four questions that students find the most difficult to answer:

Q 6	Q 5	Q 4	Q 2
1. Click: Data→Forecast→ What-If Analysis→ Scenario Manager… 2. Click the *Add…* button. 3. Type **Worst Case** into the *Scenario name* box. Scenario name: Worst Case 4. Click in the *Changing cells* box and then click on cell B7. Changing cells: $B$7 5. Click the *OK* button. 6. Type **2000** into the value box. $B$7 2000 7. Click the *OK* button. 8. Click the *Add…* button. 9. Complete the same steps for the *Expected Case* and *Best Case* scenarios. This was covered in: *Lesson 6-3: Define scenarios.*	1. Select cells A4:B7. 2. Click: Formulas→ Defined Names→ Create from Selection. 3. Click the *OK* button. 4. Repeat for cells A10:B13. This was covered in: *Lesson 5-1: Automatically create single-cell range names.*	1. Click: Data→ Forecast→ What-If Analysis→ Goal Seek… 2. Complete the dialog as follows: Set cell: $B$13 To value: 50% By changing cell: $B$5 3. Click *OK* and *OK* again. This was covered in: *Lesson 6-5: Use Goal Seek.*	1. Type **Retail Price, Gross Profit** and **Gross Profit Percent** into cells D3, E3 and F3. 2. AutoSize columns D:F so that all text is visible. 3. Enter the formula: **=B5** into cell D4, **=B12** into cell E4 and **=B13** into cell F4. 4. Enter the formula: **=D4+0.5** into cell D5. 5. AutoFill cell D5 to cells D6:D18. 6. Copy cells D5:D18 and then paste them back into the same location using *Paste Values*. 7. Select cells D4:F18. 8. Click: Data→Forecast→ What-If Analysis→ Data Table… 9. Set the *Column input cell* to: $B$5 and click the *OK* button. 10. Use the *Format Painter* to attractively format each column and the column headers. This was covered in: *Lesson 6-1: Create a single-input data table.*

If you have difficulty with the other questions, here are the lessons that cover the relevant skills:

3   Refer to: *Lesson 6-7: Hide and unhide worksheets, columns and rows.*

7   Refer to: *Lesson 6-4: Create a scenario summary report.*

8   Refer to: *Lesson 6-11: Restrict the cells users are allowed to change.*

7

Session Seven: Working with Hyperlinks and Other Applications

> Every generation brings something new to the workplace, and millennials are no exception. As a group, they tend to be highly educated, love to learn, and grew up with the Internet and digital tools in a way that can be highly useful when leveraged properly.
>
> *Kathryn Minshew (1985-)*
> *CEO and co-founder of The Muse*

Anybody who opens an Excel workbook these days will have also spent many hours navigating the Internet using a web browser. Navigating web sites by clicking on hyperlinks will feel natural and intuitive to them.

In this session you'll discover how you can also implement a hyperlink-based navigation system in large workbooks so that even users with no Excel skills will immediately feel at home when viewing your work.

This session will also show you how to embed Excel objects into other Office applications such as Word, PowerPoint and Outlook.

Session Objectives

By the end of this session you will be able to:

- Hyperlink to worksheets and ranges

- Hyperlink to other workbooks and the Internet

- Hyperlink to an e-mail address and enhance the browsing experience

- Embed an Excel worksheet object into a Word document

- Embed an Excel chart object into a Word document

- Link an Excel worksheet to a Word document

Lesson 7-1: Hyperlink to worksheets and ranges

Because just about everybody uses a web browser, the "point and click" method of doing things comes naturally to most users.

It is possible to give users the same browser-like experience by adding hyperlinks to your workbooks in order to mimic web browser navigation. This isn't just a presentational gimmick. Hyperlink browsing is the most efficient way to quickly navigate to specific parts of long multi-page documents.

1 **Open *Monaco-1* from your sample files folder.**

This worksheet has a lot of information about Monaco (the second smallest independent state in the world at only 2 sq km).

2 **Create a worksheet hyperlink from cell A5 in the *Main Menu* worksheet to the *Background* worksheet.**

1. Select cell A5 on the *Main Menu* worksheet.

2. Click: Insert→Links→Link.

    The *Insert Hyperlink* dialog appears.

3. Select *Place in this Document* from the left-hand navigation bar.

4. Select *Background* from the *Or select a place in this document* tree view.

Insert Hyperlink	
Link to:	Text to display: Background
Existing File or Web Page	Type the cell reference: A1 Or select a place in this document:

Place in This Document	⊟ Cell Reference
	  'Main Menu'
	  Background
	  Geography
	  People
	  Defined Names

Create New Document	
E-mail Address	

5. Click the *OK* button.

The text in cell A5 has been changed into a hyperlink:

	A
3	Main Sections
5	Background
6	Geography
7	People

It is also possible to define a screen tip for the hyperlink (see sidebar).

Monaco-1

3   Create worksheet hyperlinks from cells A6 and A7 to the *Geography* and *People* worksheets.

Do this in the same way that you created the *Background* hyperlink.

4   Create a range name called *Climate* for cells A32:A33 on the *Geography* worksheet.

1.   Select cells A32:A33 on the *Geography* worksheet.

2.   Click: Formulas→Defined Names→Create from Selection.

3.   Click the *OK* button.

5   Create range names called *Population* and *Life expectancy at birth* for cells A3:A5 and A50:A54 on the *People* worksheet.

Note that the range name: *Life_expectancy_at_birth* will be created with underscores, as range names cannot contain spaces.

6   Make cells A12, A13 and A14 on the *Main Menu* worksheet into hyperlinks pointing to the range names that you created.

1.   Select cell A12 on the *Main Menu* worksheet.

2.   Click: Insert→Links→Link.

The *Insert Hyperlink* dialog appears.

3.   Select *Place in this Document* from the left-hand navigation bar.

4.   Select *Climate* from the *Or select a place in this document* tree view (*Defined Names* section).

5.   Click the *OK* button.

6.   Do the same for *Population* and *Life Expectancy*.

7   Test your hyperlinks.

When you click upon any of the six defined hyperlinks, you are taken to the relevant defined worksheet or range.

8   Save your work as *Monaco-2*.

Lesson 7-2: Hyperlink to other workbooks and the Internet

1   Open *Monaco-2* from your sample files folder (if it isn't already open).

2   Create a hyperlink from cell A8 in the *Main Menu* worksheet to the *Monaco Economy-1* workbook.

1.   Select cell A8.

2.   Click: Insert→Links→Link.

3.   Click: *Existing File or Web Page* in the left-hand navigation bar.

4.   Select *Current Folder* and then the *Monaco Economy-1* file in the central window.

Existing File or Web Page	Look in:	Session 6
	Current Folder	International Customers-1
		Monaco Economy-1
		Monaco-1

5.   Click the *OK* button.

6.   Click the *Imports* hyperlink in cell A8.

The *Monaco Economy-1* workbook opens. Note that the hyperlink took you to cell A1 but the *Imports* data is actually in cells A74:A77.

	A
74	Imports:
75	$916.1 million (2005)
76	country comparison to the world: 171
	note: full customs integration with France, which collects and rebates M
77	participates in EU market system through customs union with France
78	

3   Expand the hyperlink to include cells A74:A77.

Once Excel has done the hard work of constructing a hyperlink to a different workbook it is easy to expand it to point to a range if required.

1.   Click: View→Window→Switch Windows→Monaco-2.

You are returned to the *Monaco-2* workbook.

2.   If not already selected, move the cursor to cell A8 using the keyboard arrow keys (if you simply click the cell you will execute the hyperlink).

3.   Click: Insert→Links→Link.

The hyperlink address is visible in the *Address* box.

Address:	Monaco%20Economy-1.xlsx

Notice that a hyperlink must have a *%20* code in place of any spaces.

Monaco-2

note

You can also hyperlink to non-Excel files such as Word documents

When you set the *Link to* type to *Existing File or Web Page,* you are able to link to any file on your computer.

Windows knows which application is used to open most file types, so if you link to a Word document, the document will open in Word when you click the hyperlink.

This opens up a huge range of possibilities. You could create a hyperlink on a worksheet that will:

- Play an MP3 sound file.
- View an MP4 video.
- Open a Word document.

... and do anything else that any application installed on your computer is capable of.

4. Edit the hyperlink to reference the range A74:A77 on the *Economy* worksheet by changing the *Address* to the following:

Address:	Monaco%20Economy-1.xlsx#Economy!A74:A77

5. Click the *OK* button.

4 Test the hyperlink.

When you click the *Imports* hyperlink, you are taken to the *Economy* worksheet in the *Monaco Economy-1* workbook with cells A74:A77 selected.

	A
73	
74	Imports:
75	$916.1 million (2005)
76	country comparison to the world: 171
77	note: full customs integration with France, which collects and rebates Monegasque trade duties; also participates in EU market system through customs union with France

5 Return to the *Monaco-2* workbook.

Click: View→Window→Switch Windows→Monaco-2.

6 Make cell A17 on the *Main Menu* worksheet into a *Web Page* hyperlink pointing to the *Monaco Tourist Office* website at: www.visitmonaco.com

1. Select cell A17 on the *Main Menu* worksheet.

2. Click: Insert→Links→Link.

3. Click *Existing File or Web Page* in the *Link to* navigation bar.

4. Type **http://www.visitmonaco.com** into the *Address* box.

Address:	https://www.visitmonaco.com/

5. Click the *OK* button.

Cell A17 is converted into a hyperlink pointing to the *Monaco Government Tourist Office* website.

	A
16	Useful Web resources
17	Monaco Government Tourist Office

7 Save your work as *Monaco-3*.

Lesson 7-3: Hyperlink to an e-mail address and enhance the browsing experience

By now you've probably noticed a big problem when creating Excel hyperlinks. The links take you to the desired destination without problems, but how do you get back to the main menu? Excel has sold you a one-way ticket!

In a regular web browser, you have a *Back Button, Forward Button* and *Document Location Box:*

This lesson will show you how to add the same controls to Excel.

You may also want to allow your users to quickly send you e-mail feedback. The easiest way to do this is to add a clickable e-mail link to the worksheet.

1   Open *Monaco-3* from your sample files folder (if it isn't already open).

2   Add a *Back* button to the *Quick Access Toolbar*.

This is another of those really useful Excel features that can only be accessed by customizing the *Quick Access Toolbar* or the ribbon. You'll learn how to create a custom ribbon tab later in: *Lesson 8-20: Create a custom ribbon tab.*

1.   Click the drop-down arrow on the right of the *Quick Access Toolbar*.

2.   Click *More Commands...* from the drop-down menu.

The *Customize the Quick Access Toolbar* dialog appears.

3.   Click *Commands Not in the Ribbon* from the *Choose commands from* drop-down list.

A list appears showing all of the commands that are not normally available in Excel.

4.   Select the *Back* command from the commands list.

5.   Click the *Add>>* button to add the *Back* command to the *Quick Access Toolbar*.

Monaco-3

6.   Click the *OK* button.

A back button is now displayed on the *Quick Access Toolbar*.

3   Add a *Forward* button to the *Quick Access Toolbar*.

Do this in the same way that you added the back button.

→ Forward

4   Add a *Document Location* box to the *Quick Access Toolbar*.

Document Location

5   Click the *OK* button to close the dialog.

6   Test the new navigation controls.

Your Quick Access Toolbar now has familiar browser-like controls.

← → C:\Practice\Excel 365 Expert Skil ▾ ⇄

Click on an Excel hyperlink and then use the *Back* button to return to the *Main Menu* worksheet.

7   Add an e-mail hyperlink to cell A20 on the *Main Menu* worksheet.

1.   Type your e-mail address into cell A20 on the *Main Menu* worksheet.

2.   Press the **<Enter>** key.

When you press the **<Enter>** key, the e-mail address changes into a hyperlink.

	A
19	Any questions e-mail me...
20	notta.realname@notreal.com

8   Edit the hyperlink to show a subject line for any generated e-mails.

1.   If not already selected, move the cursor to cell A20 using the keyboard arrow keys (if you simply click the cell you will execute the hyperlink).

2.   Click: Insert→Links→Link.

3.   Type **Feedback from Monaco Excel workbook** into the *Subject* box.

Subject:
Feedback from Monaco Excel workbook

4.   Click the *OK* button.

9   Test the hyperlink.

When you click the hyperlink, you are taken to your default e-mail application with the destination e-mail address and subject lines already completed.

10   Save your work as *Monaco-4.*

Lesson 7-4: Embed an Excel worksheet object into a Word document

Microsoft Office is an object-orientated application. Simply put, this means that everything you work with in Office is an object.

An Excel cell, an Excel range of cells, an Excel table, an Excel chart, a Word document and a PowerPoint slide are all objects.

The wonderful thing about this object-orientated architecture is that you can freely embed objects inside other objects. For example, you can embed an Excel range into a Word document, or an Excel chart into a PowerPoint presentation.

In this lesson you'll embed an Excel worksheet into a Word document.

1　Open Microsoft Word.

2　Use Word to open *The World's Best Selling Cars-1* (Word document) from your sample files folder.

This file contains the beginning of a Word document:

> The World's Best Selling Cars
>
> Some cars sell well, others hardly sell at all. Once every few years a car comes along that is demonstrably better than its competition. The car may beat the competition on price, performance, reliability, style or a combination of these factors.
>
> Here is a list of the world's most successful cars to date:

3　Embed an Excel worksheet at the end of the word document.

1. Click just to the right of the sentence *"Here is a list of the world's most successful cars to date:"*.

2. Press the **<Enter>** key to move to the next line.

3. Click: Insert→Text→Object→Object…

   The *Object* dialog appears.

4. Select *Microsoft Excel Worksheet* from the *Object type* list.

   Object type:
Microsoft Excel Chart
Microsoft Excel Macro-Enabled Worksheet
Microsoft Excel Worksheet
Microsoft Graph Chart

5. Click the *OK* button.

   An empty Excel worksheet is embedded into the Word document.

   Here is a list of the world's most successful cars to date:

	A	B	C	D	E
1					

   Notice that something has happened to the ribbon. The Word ribbon has been replaced by the Excel ribbon.

The World's Best Selling Cars-1

4　Enter the following data into the worksheet:

◢	A	B	C
1	Make	Model	Sales (Million)
2	Ford	Escort	18
3	Volkswagen	Beetle	23.5
4	Volkswagen	Golf	27.5
5	Ford	F Series	35
6	Toyota	Corolla	40

(When you have entered the data, AutoSize each column so that each is wide enough to display the contents).

5 Return to Word.

Click anywhere in the Word document's text (outside the Excel object).

Notice that the appearance of the worksheet has changed and that the Excel ribbon has changed back to the Word ribbon.

6 *Print Preview* the document.

Click: File→Print.

Notice that the worksheet looks just as it would in Excel. The worksheet is too big, however, as there are many empty cells.

7 Return to Excel.

1. Click the *Back Button*.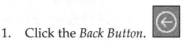

2. Double click anywhere in the Excel object.

   Notice that the Excel ribbon has returned.

8 Size the worksheet window so that it is the same size as the data entered.

1. Hover the mouse cursor over the sizing handle in the bottom right corner of the worksheet until you see the double-headed arrow cursor shape.

2. Click and drag upwards and to the left to re-size the worksheet object so that it is the same size as its contents.

9 Return to Word.

Click anywhere in the Word document's text (outside the Excel object).

Here is a list of the world's most successful cars to date:		
Make	Model	Sales (Million)
Ford	Escort	18
Volkswagen	Beetle	23.5
Volkswagen	Golf	27.5
Ford	F Series	35
Toyota	Corolla	40

10 Save your work as *The World's Best Selling Cars-2*.

Lesson 7-5: Embed an Excel chart object into a Word document

1   Open Microsoft Word.

2   Use Word to open *The World's Best Selling Cars-2* (a Word document) from your sample files folder (if it isn't already open).

3   Convert the range into a table.

1.   Double-click the Excel object to return to Excel.

The Excel ribbon replaces the Word ribbon.

2.   Click inside the range.

3.   Click: Insert→Tables→Table.

4.   Click *OK* to accept the automatically detected range.

The range is converted into a table.

4   Remove the AutoFilter from the table.

The AutoFilter buttons don't look good in a Word document.

Click: Data→Sort & Filter→Filter.

The filter buttons vanish.

5   Sort the table from bestselling to least selling.

1.   Click anywhere in column C.

2.   Click: Data→Sort & Filter→Sort Largest to Smallest.

6   Format the values in column C so that they display one decimal place.

1.   Select the values in column C.

2.   Click Home→Number→Increase Decimal.

7   Add the text **... and here is the same data as a chart** to the end of the document.

1.   Click anywhere in the document's text to return to Word.

2.   Click slightly to the right of the table.

3.   Press the **<Enter>** key to move to the next line.

4.   Type the text: **... and here is the same data as a chart.**

5.   Press the **<Enter>** key to move to the next line.

Make	Model	Sales (Million)
Toyota	Corolla	40.0
Ford	F Series	35.0
Volkswagen	Golf	27.5
Volkswagen	Beetle	23.5
Ford	Escort	18.0

... and here is the same data as a chart.

Create Table

Where is the data for your table?

=$A$1:$C$6

☑ My table has headers

OK   Cancel

The World's Best Selling Cars-2

note

Use the same technique to embed objects into (and from) PowerPoint and other applications

The mechanism that allows you to embed and link documents is called OLE (Object Linking and Embedding).

Any application that supports OLE is happy to work with any other OLE compatible application.

Applications supporting OLE include (of course) the entire Office suite along with many Adobe and other third-party applications.

You'll find OLE fantastically useful to add Excel ranges and charts to Word documents and PowerPoint presentations, but there's no need to stop there.

8   Copy the Excel object to the end of the document.

1. Click the Excel object once to select it. Be careful to only click once. If you double-click you will go back into Excel.

2. Copy the Excel object.

3. Click on the line after the text: **... and here is the same data as a chart**.

4. Paste.

   An identical Excel object now appears in both places.

9   Convert the duplicated Excel object into a chart.

1. Double-click the lower Excel object to go back into Excel.

2. Select cells A1:C6.

3. Click: Insert→Charts→Insert Pie or Doughnut Chart→ 2-D Pie→Pie.

   The worksheet now contains a pie chart.

4. Right-click just inside the top-left corner of the pie chart.

5. Click *Move Chart...* from the shortcut menu.

6. Click the *New Sheet* option button.

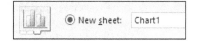

7. Click the *OK* button.

   A portion of the pie chart is now visible in the Excel object.

10   Re-size the Excel chart object to an attractive size.

This was covered in: *Lesson 7-4: Embed an Excel worksheet object into a Word document.*

11   Return to Word.

Click anywhere in the document's text.

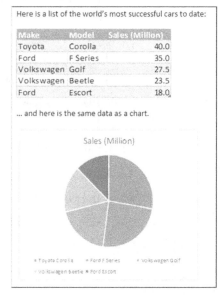

12   Save your work as *The World's Best Selling Cars-3*.

Lesson 7-6: Link an Excel worksheet to a Word document

1   Open Microsoft Word.

2   Open *International Customers-1* from your sample files folder.

This file contains the beginning of a document:

> **Information for International Customers**
> We are happy to supply our products to any world location and to bill you in your own currency.
>
> We convert our prices using the following exchange rates:

3   Insert the *International Customer Rates-1* Excel Workbook at the end of the document as a linked object.

The *International Customer Rates-1* workbook contains exchange rates for eleven currencies. They will all have changed by the time you read this book.

1.   Click just to the right of the sentence: *We convert our prices using the following exchange rates:*

2.   Press the **<Enter>** key to move down to the next line.

3.   Click: Insert→Text→Object→Object.

The *Object* dialog is displayed.

4.   Click the *Create from File* tab.

5.   Check the *Link to file* check box.

☑ Link to file

6.   Notice the help text that has appeared:

This means that any changes to the Excel worksheet will immediately appear in the linked Excel object.

7.   Click the *Browse...* button.

8.   Navigate to the *International Customer Rates-1* workbook.

9.   Click the *Insert* button.

10.   Click the *OK* button.

The exchange rates are now displayed inside the Word document.

International Customers-1

note

Link and embed objects using drag and drop

You can simply drag and drop a range of cells from Excel to Word. Make sure that you <Ctrl>-click-drag if you want to copy the range. If you simply click and drag, you'll remove the range from the workbook.

To drag and drop, you'll need to arrange your screen so that you can see both the Excel and Word document windows at the same time.

When you drag and drop, Word has to guess whether you want to link or embed.

If you drag and drop a chart, Word will link. If you drag and drop a range of cells, Word will embed.

Because of this limitation, the other methods are preferable when you need to control linking and embedding.

We convert our prices using the following exchange rates:

Exchange Rates

Country	Multiply GBP Price by:	To get price in:
USA	1.44662	US Dollar
Australia	2.04065	Australian Dollar
Canada	2.01132	Canadian Dollar
Euro	1.29759	Euro
Hong Kong	11.267	Hong Kong Dollar
Indonesia	19,681.80	Indonesian Rupiah
Japan	168.69	Japanese Yen
Singapore	2.0333	Singapore Dollar
Sweden	12.2389	Swedish Krona
Switzerland	1.43485	Swiss Franc
Thailand	51.3285	Thai Baht

4 **Test the link by changing values in the Excel workbook.**

Linked objects work in a different way to embedded objects.

When you double-click an embedded object, you are able to edit it inside the Word document.

When you double-click a linked object, Excel will open and display the linked file.

1. Double-click the Excel object.

   Excel opens with the *International Customer Rates-1* workbook.

2. Re-size the Excel and Word windows so that you can see both documents.

3. Change one of the exchange rates in the *International Customer Rates-1* workbook.

4. Click once in the Word document window to make it the active window.

5. Right-click the Excel linked object in the *International Customers-1* Word document.

6. Click *Update Link* from the shortcut menu.

   Notice that the values update to match those in the workbook.

   Values are normally only updated when you open the Word document. The *Update Link* command tells Word to refresh the data it is displaying.

5 **Close the Excel window without saving.**

6 **Save the Word document as *International Customers-2*.**

Session 7: Exercise

1   Open the *Spectrum Car Sales-1* Excel workbook from your sample files folder.

2   Hyperlink the *What is your budget?* cells (F7, F8, F9 and F10) to the relevant worksheets.

3   Hyperlink the *Car of the week BMW 3 Series* text (cell D11) to the *£1,000 - £3,000* worksheet.

4   Hyperlink the *Just arrived Lamborghini Gallardo* text (cell H11) to the *Over £5,000* worksheet.

5   Make the *e-mail sales@spectrum.test* text in cell D13 into an e-mail hyperlink that will send an e-mail to the e-mail address: *sales@spectrum.test* with the subject: *Car sales enquiry.*

6   Save the workbook as *Spectrum Car Sales-2* and close Excel.

7   Open the *Stock List-1* sample file in Microsoft Word.

8   Place a linked object after the text in the *Stock List-1* Word document that will show the contents of the *Over £5,000* worksheet in the *Spectrum Car Sales-2* workbook.

Here is our current stock list of cars in the over £5,000 category:

Cars over £5,000

All of these cars have a six month warranty

Make	Model	Year	Miles	Price
Ferrari	348 TB 2dr	1992	15,246	£44,995
Rolls Royce	Silver Spur 6.8 III 4dr	1994	21,900	£23,950
Aston Martin	Vantage 4.7 V8 Sportshift 2dr	2010	33,345	£49,995
Lamborghini	Gallardo 5.0 V10 2dr	2005	18,861	£54,999

9   Save the Word document as *Stock List-2.*

Spectrum Car Sales-1   Stock List-1

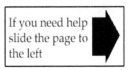

If you need help slide the page to the left

Session 7: Exercise Answers

These are the five questions that students find the most difficult to answer:

Q 8	Q 5	Q 2, 3, 4
1. Open the *Spectrum Car Sales-2 workbook* in Excel.	1. Select cell D13 on the *Home* worksheet.	1. Click in cell F7.
2. Select the *Over £5,000* worksheet.	2. Click: Insert→Links→ Link.	2. Click: Insert→Links→ Link.
3. Save and close the *Spectrum Car Sales-2* workbook.	3. Click *E-mail Address* on the left-hand selection bar.	3. Click: *Place in This Document* in the left-hand menu bar.
4. Open the *Stock List-1* document in Microsoft Word.	4. Complete the dialog as follows:	4. Click on *'Under £1,000'* in the central pane.
5. Click just to the right of the ... *£5,000 category:* text.	E-mail address: mailto:sales@spectrum.test Subject: Car sales enquiry	
6. Press the **<Enter>** key to move to the next line.	5. Click the *OK* button.	5. Repeat the same steps to add hyperlinks to cells F8, F9, F10, D11 and H11.
7. Click: Insert→Text→Object→ Object.	This was covered in: *Lesson 7-3: Hyperlink to an e-mail address and enhance the browsing experience.*	This was covered in: *Lesson 7-1: Hyperlink to worksheets and ranges.*
8. Select the *Create from File* tab.		
9. Click the *Browse* button and select the *Spectrum Car Sales-2* workbook.		
10. Click the *Insert* button.		
11. Check the *Link to File* check box.		
12. Click the *OK* button.		
This was covered in: *Lesson 7-6: Link an Excel worksheet to a Word document.*		

8

Session Eight: Forms and Macros

You don't need to know how an engine works to drive a car.

Proverb, unknown authors

You can design Excel applications for users who have no Excel skills.

When you create this type of application, you need to provide a simple and intuitive form-based user interface. The user interface should be so simple that the application can be used without any training or assumed Excel skills.

In this session you'll create a powerful, form-based, Excel application with a simple and intuitive user interface.

You'll also learn how to record and run macros. Macros allow you to provide users with simple form controls that execute a complex sequence of Excel actions.

Session Objectives

By the end of this session you will be able to:

- Add group box and option button controls to a worksheet form
- Add a combo box control to a worksheet form
- Set form control cell links
- Connect result cells to a form
- Add a check box control to a worksheet form
- Use check box data in result cells
- Add a temperature gauge chart to a form
- Add a single input data table to a form
- Improve form appearance and usability
- Understand macros and VBA
- Record a macro with absolute references
- Understand macro security
- Implement macro security
- Understand trusted documents
- Record a macro with relative references
- Use shapes to run macros
- Run a macro from a button control
- Show and hide ribbon tabs
- Add custom groups to standard ribbon tabs
- Create a custom ribbon tab

Lesson 8-1: Add group box and option button controls to a worksheet form

1 Open *Mortgage Calculator-1* from your sample files folder.

2 Add the *Developer* tab to the ribbon.

Because form controls are an advanced feature of Excel, Microsoft hides them from normal users. You must add the *Developer* tab to the ribbon in order to reveal them.

1. Click: File→Options→Customize Ribbon.

2. Check the *Developer* check box in the right-hand pane.

3. Click the *OK* button.

The *Developer* tab is now visible on the ribbon.

3 Delete row 5 and then insert two new blank rows so that there are four blank rows between *Property Price* and *Arrangement Fee*.

4 Add a *Group Box* control so that it completely fills cells B5:D6.

1. Click: Developer→Controls→Insert→Form Controls→ Group Box (Form Control).

2. Hold down the **<Alt>** key. This will make the group box snap to the corners of the selected cells.

3. Carefully position the black cross cursor near the top left corner of cell B5.

4. Click and drag to the bottom right corner of cell D6 and release the mouse button.

A group box appears.

5 Change the caption of the group box to: **Deposit:**

1. Click on a blank area of the worksheet to de-select the group box.

2. Double click the *Group Box 1* caption on the border of the group box.

3. Delete the existing *Group Box 1* text and then type: **Deposit:**

6 Add six option button controls to the group box.

1. Click: Developer→Controls→Insert→Form Controls→ Option Button (Form Control).

2. Click and drag inside the group box to add an option button. Keep the button small, as you need space for six buttons and they should not overlap. Be careful to keep the border of each option button inside the group box.

3. Repeat for the other five buttons. It is important that you add them in sequence from left to right.

Mortgage Calculator-1

note

Why are there two sets of form controls?

When you click:

Developer→Controls→Insert

...you are confronted with two sets of similar controls:

The Form Controls are designed to be used without any understanding of the Visual Basic for Applications (VBA) programming language.

The ActiveX controls are intended to be used as part of the Visual Basic programming environment.

Unless you have Visual Basic programming skills, you will probably not find a use for ActiveX controls.

You'll learn a little more about VBA's relationship with Excel in: *Lesson 8-10: Understand macros and VBA.*

7 Change the option button captions to **5%** to **30%** (reading left to right).

1. Right-click the first option button to select it.

   A box appears around the option button, along with a shortcut menu.

2. Press the **<Esc>** key or click once again inside the control to close the shortcut menu (an even faster way to do steps one and two in a single operation is to double right-click the control).

3. Double-click the text next to the option button.

4. Delete the existing text and type: **5%**

5. Do the same for the **10%** to **30%** option buttons.

8 Move and re-size the option buttons so that they are evenly spaced inside the group box.

1. Select an option button and close the shortcut menu.

2. Use the arrow keys on the keyboard to move the option button to its new position.

3. Click and drag one of the white circles (sizing handles) on the border of the option button to re-size if necessary.

4. Hover over the border of the selected option button control (but not on one of the white circles until you see the four-headed arrow cursor shape).

5. Click and drag to move the option button control.

6. Your option group should now look like this:

9 Add another set of option buttons to show terms from 5 to 30 years.

1. Delete row 12 and then insert three new rows.

2. Add a group box form control so that it completely fills cells B12:D14.

3. Add the caption and option buttons. It is important that you add them in sequence (in ascending order).

10 Save your work as *Mortgage Calculator-2*.

Lesson 8-2: Add a combo box control to a worksheet form

1   Open *Mortgage Calculator-2* from your sample files folder (if it isn't already open).

2   Delete the contents of cell D16.

3   Remove the black border from cell D16.

   1.   Select cell D16.

   2.   Click: Home→Font→Borders→No Border.

4   Place a combo box control in cell D16.

   1.   Select cell D16.

   2.   Click: Developer→Controls→Insert→Form Controls→ Combo Box (Form Control).

   3.   Hold down the **<Alt>** Key. This will make the control fit perfectly in the cell.

   4.   Click just inside the top left border of cell D16 and drag to just inside the bottom right border.

   5.   Release the mouse button.

        The control is inserted into the cell (and fits perfectly).

	A	B	C	D
15				
16		Interest:		▼

5   Create a new worksheet called *Data* to provide interest rate data from 2% to 15% in increments of 0.5%.

   1.   Create a new worksheet called *Data*.

   2.   Select the *Data* worksheet.

   3.   Type: **Interest Rates** into cell A1.

   4.   Type: **2.0%** into cell A2.

   5.   Type the formula: **=A2+0.5%** into cell A3.

   6.   AutoFill cell A3 into cells A4:A28.

6   Format cells A2:A28 so that only one decimal place is shown.

   1.   Select cells A2:A28.

   2.   Click: Home→Number→Decrease Decimal.

	A	B
1	Interest Rates	
2	2.0%	
3	2.5%	
4	3.0%	

Mortgage Calculator-2

7 Create a range name for the interest rate values in cells A2:A28.

1. Select cells A1:A28.

2. Click: Formulas→Defined Names→Create from Selection.

3. Click the *OK* button.

8 Set the combo box's *Input Range* to reference the interest rate data.

1. Select the *Mortgage Calculator* worksheet.

2. Right-click inside the combo box control.

3. Click *Format Control…* from the shortcut menu.

4. Select the *Control* tab.

5. Click in the *Input Range* box.

6. Type **Interest_Rates** into the *Input range* box.

Input range:	Interest_Rates	⬆

7. Click the *OK* button.

9 Test the combo box control.

1. Click away from the control to de-select it.

2. Click the drop-down arrow on the combo box.

Notice that the combo box displays all of the interest rates defined by the *Interest_Rates* range name.

10 Save your work as *Mortgage Calculator-3.*

Lesson 8-3: Set form control cell links

When working with forms, it is useful to separate the user interface from the input and result cells. The user interface is the part of the worksheet where the user enters values and views results. In this lesson's worksheet the user interface comprises of cells B3:D20.

Calculations are done in a different section of the worksheet where you will define *Input Cells* and *Result Cells*. You'll recognize this method of working from the lessons in: *Session Six: What If Analysis and Security.*

In this lesson's worksheet the *Input Cells* and *Result Cells* are shown in cells B23:D36. Later you will hide these rows from the user.

In this lesson you'll connect the *User Interface* with the *Input Cells*.

1   Open *Mortgage Calculator-3* from your sample files folder (if it isn't already open).

2   Link the user interface's *Property Price, Arrangement Fee,* and *Annual Income (after tax)* cells to the relevant *Input Cells.*

This is extremely easy, as it can be done using simple cell references:

	B	C	D
23	Input Cells	Value	Actual
24	Property Price		=D3
25	Deposit		
26	Arrangement Fee		=D8
27	Term		
28	Interest		
29	Annual Income (after tax)		=D18
30			

3   Connect the data from the *Deposit* group box to cell C25.

1.   Right-click the *5% Deposit* option button.

2.   Select *Format Control...* from the shortcut menu.

3.   Click the *Control* tab.

4.   Click in the *Cell link* box.

5.   Click in cell C25.

Cell link:	$C$25

6.   Click the *OK* button.

4   Test the cell link.

1.   Click away from the option buttons to de-select.

2.   Left-click each option button in turn.

3.   Notice that numbers from 1 to 6 appear in cell C25 as each option button is clicked. Option 5% results in 1, option 10% results in 2... and so on.

Mortgage Calculator-3

If you find that the wrong numbers are appearing, it is because you added the option buttons in the wrong order. In this case you'll have to move the buttons around and change their captions, until you have the correct number associated with each button.

5   Add a formula to cell D25 so that it displays the correct percentage for each option.

1.   Type **=C25*0.05** into cell D25.

2.   Test again. This time the actual percentage of the selected option button should display in cell D25.

6   Connect the data from the *Term* group box to cell C27.

Do this in exactly the same way that you connected the *Deposit* group box to cell C25.

7   Add a formula to cell D27 to show the actual term.

1.   Type **=C27*5** into cell D27.

2.   Test the *Term* option buttons.

8   Connect the data from the *Interest* combo box to cell C28.

1.   Right-click the combo box control.

2.   Click *Format Control…* from the shortcut menu.

3.   Click the *Control* Tab.

4.   Click in the *Cell link* box.

5.   Click in cell C28.

6.   Click the *OK* button.

9   Test the *Interest* combo box cell link.

Just like the option button controls, the value returned from the combo box is a number representing which option was selected. 2% returns the number 1, 2.5% returns the number 2… and so on.

10   Add a formula to cell D28 so that it displays the correct interest rate.

Type the formula **=(C28*0.5+1.5)/100** into cell D28.

11   Test the combo box.

12   Save your work as *Mortgage Calculator-4.*

Lesson 8-4: Connect result cells to a form

In the previous lessons you created a user interface using Excel's form controls.

The form now collects data from the user, and uses this data to update the input cells.

In this lesson you'll use the input cells to calculate the result cells, and then use the result cells to update the form.

1   Open *Mortgage Calculator-4* from your sample files folder (if it isn't already open).

2   Add a formula to cell D32 that will calculate the *Amount Financed*.

Amount Financed = Property Price – Deposit + Arrangement Fee

To perform this calculation, you need to type the following formula into cell D32:

=D24-(D24*D25)+D26

3   Add a formula to cell D33 to calculate the *Monthly Repayment*.

For this calculation you will use the PMT function that was covered in: *Lesson 3-3: Use the Insert Function dialog and the PMT function.*

The function arguments will be:

Rate	D28/12
Nper	D27*12
Pv	D32
Fv	
Type	

4   Convert the negative *Monthly Repayment* into a positive value.

The easiest way to do this is to place a minus operator in front of the function:

f_x =-PMT(D28/12,D27*12,D32)

5   Add a formula to cell D34 to calculate the *Total Repaid* amount.

Total Repaid = Monthly Repayment * 12 * Term

To perform this calculation, you need to type the following formula into cell D34:

=D33*12*D27

6   Add a formula to cell D35 to calculate the *Total Interest*.

Total Interest = Total Repaid – Amount Financed

Mortgage Calculator-4

To perform this calculation, you need to use the following formula into cell D35:

=D34-D32

7 Add a formula to cell D36 to calculate the *Repayment as % of Income*.

Repayment as % of Income =
Monthly Repayment * 12/Annual Income (after tax)

To perform this calculation, you need to type the following formula into cell D36:

=D33*12/D29

8 Connect the *Amount Financed* result cell (D32) to the *Amount Financed* form cell (D10).

Enter the following formula into cell D10:

=D32

9 Connect the *Monthly Repayment* result cell (D33) to the *Monthly Repayment* form cell (D20).

Enter the following formula into cell D20:

=D33

10 Test the form.

Enter the values shown below into the form. The result cells should match those shown:

	B	C	D
3	Property Price:		350,000
4			
5	Deposit: ○ 5% ○ 10% ○ 15% ◉ 20% ○ 25% ○ 30%		
6			
7			
8	Arrangement Fee:		5,000
9			
10	Amount Financed:		285,000
11			
12	Term: ○ 5 Years ○ 10 Years ○ 15 Years		
13	○ 20 Years ◉ 25 Years ○ 30 Years		
14			
15			
16	Interest:		5.0% ▼
17			
18	Annual Income (after tax):		38,000

	B	C	D
31	Result Cells		
32	Amount Financed		285,000
33	Monthly Repayment		£1,666.08
34	Total Repaid		499,824
35	Total Interest		214,824
36	Repayment as % of Income		53%

11 Save your work as *Mortgage Calculator-5*.

Lesson 8-5: Add a check box control to a worksheet form

In this lesson you will improve the form to model interest-only mortgages.

1 Open *Mortgage Calculator-5* from your sample files folder (if it isn't already open).

2 Left-align the text in cell B16.

 1. Select cell B16.

 2. Click: Home→Alignment→Align Left.

3 Move the combo box so that it appears directly after the *Interest:* text in cell B16.

 1. Right-click the combo box.

 If a shortcut menu appears either press the **<Esc>** key or click once again inside the control to close it.

 2. Use the arrow keys on the keyboard to move the combo box to its new position.

 Your combo box should now look like this:

4 Add a check box control so that it completely fills cells C16:D16.

 1. Click: Developer→Controls→Insert→ Check Box (Form Control).

 2. Hold down the **<Alt>** key. This will make the control fit perfectly in the cells.

 3. Click just inside the top left border of cell C16 and drag to just inside the bottom right border of cell D16.

 4. Release the mouse button.

 The control is inserted into the cells (and aligns perfectly).

 Your check box may have a different caption, such as *Check Box 20* as the control number is not consistently applied.

5 Change the check box caption to: **Interest Only Loan**

 Change this in the same way that you changed the option button captions in: *Lesson 8-1: Add group box and option button controls to a worksheet form.*

Mortgage Calculator-5

	A	B	C	D
15				
16		Interest: 5.0% ▼	☐ Interest Only Loan	

6 Add an input cell to link to the new check box.

1. Insert a row above row 29.

2. Type the text **Interest Only?** into cell B29.

	B	C	D
28	Interest	7	5.0%
29	Interest Only?		
30	Annual Income (after tax)		38,000

7 Connect the data from the *Interest Only Loan* check box to cell D29.

1. Right-click the *Interest Only Loan* check box.

2. Select *Format Control...* from the shortcut menu.

3. Click the *Control* tab.

4. Click in the *Cell link* box.

5. Click in cell D29.

Cell link: $D$29

6. Click the *OK* button.

8 Test the cell link.

1. Click away from the check box to de-select it.

2. Click the *Interest Only Loan* check box a few times.

   When the box is checked, TRUE appears in cell D29. When the box is unchecked, FALSE appears in cell D29.

	C	D
16	☑ Interest Only Loan	

	B	C	D
29	Interest Only?		TRUE

	C	D
16	☐ Interest Only Loan	

	B	C	D
29	Interest Only?		FALSE

9 Save your work as *Mortgage Calculator-6*.

Lesson 8-6: Use check box data in result cells

1 Open *Mortgage Calculator-6* from your sample files folder (if it isn't already open).

2 Correct the formula in the *Monthly Repayment* result cell (D34) to allow for interest only loans.

    1. Click in cell D34.

    2. Click the *Insert Function* button to the left of the formula bar.

D34	▼	:	×	✓	*fx*	=-PMT(D28/12,D27*12,D33)

    3. The *Function Arguments* dialog appears.

    The capital owed at the end of an interest only loan (Excel's terminology for this is: *Future Value*) will be a negative number that is the same as the *Amount Financed*. The *Future Value* will thus be:

    Amount Financed * -1

    A normal capital and repayment loan will have been fully repaid by the end of the term, so there will be no future value.

    In order to make the PMT function return the correct value for both types of loan, you will have to use an IF logic function to set the future value. The IF function was covered in: *Lesson 3-5: Use the IF logic function.*

    4. Type the following formula into the *Fv* argument box:

Fv	IF(D29=TRUE,D33*-1,0)	⬆

    This will set the *Future Value* to be the same as the **Amount Financed*-1** for an interest only loan, and to **zero** for a capital and repayment loan.

    5. Click the *OK* button.

3 Correct the *Total Interest* result cell (D36) to allow for interest only loans.

    A capital and repayment loan will incur interest of:

    Total Repaid – Amount Financed.

    Every payment in an *interest only* loan consists only of interest. This means that the *Total Interest* will be the same as the *Total Repaid.*

    In order to correct the *Total Interest* result cell, you will, once again, have to use an IF logic function.

    1. Click in cell D36.

    2. Delete the previous formula.

    3. Add an IF function. The function arguments are:

Mortgage Calculator-6

Logical_test	D29	↑
Value_if_true	D35	↑
Value_if_false	D35-D33	↑

4   Test the check box.

I tested with the following form values:

	B	C	D
1	Mortgage Calculator		
2			
3	Property Price:		350,000
4			
5	Deposit: ○ 5% ○ 10% ○ 15% ◉ 20% ○ 25% ○ 30%		
6			
7			
8	Arrangement Fee:		5,000
9			
10	Amount Financed:		285,000
11			
12	Term: ○ 5 Years ○ 10 Years ○ 15 Years		
13	◉ 20 Years ○ 25 Years ○ 30 Years		
14			
15			
16	Interest: 5.0% ▼ ☐ Interest Only Loan		
17			
18	Annual Income (after tax):		38,000
19			
20	Monthly Repayment:		£1,880.87

When the *Interest Only Loan* box was unchecked, the *Result Cells* were:

	B	C	D
32	Result Cells		
33	Amount Financed		285,000
34	Monthly Repayment		£1,880.87
35	Total Repaid		451,410
36	Total Interest		166,410
37	Repayment as % of Income		59%

When the *Interest Only Loan* box was checked, the *Result Cells* were:

	B	C	D
32	Result Cells		
33	Amount Financed		285,000
34	Monthly Repayment		£1,187.50
35	Total Repaid		285,000
36	Total Interest		285,000
37	Repayment as % of Income		38%

5   Save your work as *Mortgage Calculator-7*.

Lesson 8-7: Add a temperature gauge chart to a form

Charting is covered in depth in session 5 of the *Essential Skills* book in this series. Excel doesn't have a temperature gauge chart in its pre-defined range of charts. It is possible, however, to create this type of chart by formatting a regular bar chart in a special way.

1   Open *Mortgage Calculator-7* from your sample files folder.

2   Add a column chart to the worksheet with the single data value of *Repayment as % of Income.*

1. Select cell D37.

2. Click: Insert→Charts→Column or Bar Chart→2-D Column→ Clustered Column.

3. Right-click the center of the chart and then click *Select Data...* from the shortcut menu.

4. Click the *Edit* button above the *Legend Entries (Series)* list box.

5. Remove all of the text from the *Series values* box.

6. Click in the *Series values* box and then click cell D37.

7. Click *OK* and then *OK* again.

    You now have a chart with a single bar showing the loan affordability as a percentage of income.

3   Change the vertical axis so that it begins at 0% and ends at 100%.

1. Click the chart to activate it.

2. Right click on the *Vertical (Value Axis)* (one of the percentages).

3. Click *Format Axis:* from the shortcut menu.

4. Set the *Minimum* and *Maximum* values to **0** and **1**.

4   Remove the gap from the left hand side of the column.

1. Right-click on the chart column and then click *Format Data Series...* from the shortcut menu.

    The *Format Data Series* task pane appears.

2. Change the *Gap Width* to *0%*.

5   Remove the *Horizontal Axis* and *Chart Title* elements from the chart.

1. Click on the chart to activate it.

2. Click the *Chart Elements* button just outside the top right of the chart.

3. Clear the *Chart Title* check box.

4. Click the *Axes* flyout menu

5. Clear the *Primary Horizontal* check box.

6   Apply a thin black line around the Plot Area.

1. Right-click in the center of the chart (but not on the bar or a gridline).

2. Click *Format Plot Area…* from the shortcut menu.

   The *Format Plot Area* task pane appears.

3. Click on the *Border* fly-out menu.

4. Click the *Solid Line* option button.

5. Click the *Color* button and select *Black.*

7   Re-size the chart so that it resembles a temperature gauge that is the same height as the form.

1. Click on the chart to select it.

2. Click and drag the bottom right-hand corner sizing handle to size as required.

3. Click and drag anywhere on the border of the chart that is not a sizing handle to move it to the required position (see the cover of this book for an idea of roughly where that should be).

8   Remove the border around the chart.

1. Click on the chart to select it.

2. Right-click on the border of the chart.

3. Click *Format Chart Area…* from the shortcut menu.

   The *Format Chart Area* task pane appears.

4. Click: Border→No Line.

9   Add an oval shape to mimic the bulb at the bottom of a thermometer.

1. Click away from the chart to de-select it.

2. Click: Insert→Illustrations→Shapes→Basic Shapes→Oval.

3. Click and drag to draw an oval at the bottom of the chart.

4. Right-click the oval shape and select *Format Shape…* from the shortcut menu.

5. Click Line→No Line in the *Format Shape* task pane.

6. Click the *Close* button ☒ at the top right of the *Format Shape* task pane.

   Your chart should now look similar to the sidebar.

10 Save your work as *Mortgage Calculator-8.*

Lesson 8-8: Add a single input data table to a form

You covered single-input data tables in: *Lesson 6-1: Create a single-input data table.* In this lesson you'll recap this skill by adding a single-input data table to the form to show how repayments could increase if interest rates were to rise by up to 4% more than the current rate.

1 Open *Mortgage Calculator-8* from your sample files folder (if it isn't already open).

2 Add titles for each of the data table's columns.

Type labels into cells H2:L2 so that they are the same as the following:

H	I	J	K	L
2 Interest	Monthly Repayment	Repayment as % of Income	Total Repaid	Total Interest

3 Merge cells H1:H2, I1:I2, J1:J2, K1:K2 and L1:L2.

 1. Select cells H1:H2.

 2. Click: Home→Alignment→Merge & Center→Merge Cells.

 3. Repeat for the other cell pairs.

4 Switch text wrapping on for cells H1:L1.

 1. Select cells H1:L1.

 2. Click: Home→Alignment→Wrap Text.

5 Arrange the labels so that they appear on two lines where necessary.

 1. Double-click just before the word *Repayment* in cell I1 (*Monthly Repayment*).

 2. Hold down the **<Alt>** key.

 3. Press the **<Enter>** key.

 4. Repeat for the other column labels.

 5. Re-size each column.

   Your column headers should now look like this:

H	I	J	K	L
1	Monthly	Repayment	Total	Total
2 Interest	Repayment	as % of Income	Repaid	Interest

6 Add a formula to cell H3 that will show the interest rate selected on the form.

 1. Click in cell H3.

 2. Add the formula: **=(C28*0.5+1.5)/100**

   You need to refer to cell C28 rather than D28 to work-around an odd quirk in Excel data tables (see sidebar).

7 Add a formula to cell H4 that will show an interest rate 1% higher than the rate in cell H3.

Mortgage Calculator-8

1. Click in cell H4.

2. Add the formula: **=H3+0.01**

8 AutoFill the formula in cell H4 to cells H5:H7.

9 Format the formulas in cells H3:H7 so that they are formatted as percentages and display one decimal place.

1. Select cells H3:H7 and click: Home→Number→Percent Style.

2. Click: Home→Number→Increase Decimal.

10 Add formulas to cells I3:L3 that will reference the relative result cells.

The correct formulas are:

▲	I	J	K	L
1	Monthly	Repayment	Total	Total
2	Repayment	as % of Income	Repaid	Interest
3	=D34	=D37	=D35	=D36

11 Add a single input data table to cells H3:L7.

1. Select cells H3:L7.

2. Click: Data→Forecast→What-If Analysis→Data Table…

The *Data Table* dialog appears.

3. Click in the *Column input cell* box.

4. Click in cell D28.

5. Click the *OK* button.

Data Table dialog:

Data Table ? ✕

Row input cell: [   ] ↑

Column input cell: SD$28 ↑

[OK] [Cancel]

12 Copy the formats in cells I3:L3 to cells I4:L7.

1. Select cells I3:L3.

2. Click: Home→Clipboard→Copy.

3. Select cells I4:L7.

4. Click: Home→Clipboard→Paste→Paste Special…

5. Select the *Formats* option button.

6. Click the *OK* button.

Paste Special dialog:

Paste Special

Paste
○ All
○ Formulas
○ Values
◉ Formats
○ Comments
○ Validation

13 Resize the columns if necessary.

Your data table should now look like this:

▲	H	I	J	K	L
1		Monthly	Repayment	Total	Total
2	Interest	Repayment	as % of Income	Repaid	Interest
3	5.0%	£1,187.50	38%	285,000	285,000
4	6.0%	£1,425.00	45%	342,000	342,000
5	7.0%	£1,662.50	53%	399,000	399,000
6	8.0%	£1,900.00	60%	456,000	456,000
7	9.0%	£2,137.50	68%	513,000	513,000

The actual values shown on your worksheet may differ depending upon the values selected in your form.

14 Save your work as *Mortgage Calculator-9.*

Lesson 8-9: Improve form appearance and usability

An elegant form-based user interface enables you to create utilities for users with no Excel skills. The form should be so intuitive that staff training is not needed. In its present form the Mortgage Calculator might intimidate non-technical users. You need to do a few more things to make this into a really professional form. They are:

- Improve the appearance of the form.

- Hide irrelevant worksheets and cells. In this case you need to hide the *Input Cells, Result Cells* and the *Data* worksheet.

- Protect the form so that users cannot alter the functionality or layout.

1 Open *Mortgage Calculator-9* from your sample files folder.

2 Add a pie chart to show the *Amount Financed* and *Total Interest*.

1. Click in cell D33, hold down the **<Ctrl>** key and click cell D36.

2. Click: Insert→Charts→Insert Pie or Doughnut Chart→ 3-D Pie→3-D Pie.

3. Move and re-size the chart so that it fills cells H9:L20.

4. Right-click on the center of the pie chart.

5. Click *Select Data...* from the shortcut menu.

6. Click the *Edit* button at the top of the *Horizontal (Category) Axis Labels* list box.

7. Click on cell B33, hold down the **<Ctrl>** key and click on cell B36.

8. Click *OK,* and then click *OK* again.

3 Surround the form area with two narrow padding columns.

It is useful for a form to be clearly delineated from the worksheet. This is best achieved by adding two narrow padding columns to each border of the form (see the screen grab on the front cover of this book).

The borders can then be shaded to clearly mark the form edges.

1. Add two narrow columns (about 9 pixels wide) to the left of column A.

2. Add two narrow rows (about 9 pixels deep) above row 1.

3. Add two narrow rows (about 9 pixels deep) above row 24.

4. Resize columns P and Q so that they are about 9 pixels wide.

4 Shade the form area (excluding controls and cells that the user will enter data into) light yellow.

1. Click in cell D22.

2. Set the background color to very light yellow.

Mortgage Calculator-9

3. Double-click: Home→Clipboard→Format Painter.

4. Click once in each cell in the range: C4:G23 that should be yellow (see cover of this book for guidance).

   You may have to move the checkbox control in order to shade the cells behind it, and then move it back again.

5. Click: Home→Clipboard→Format Painter to switch the format painter off.

5 **Use a similar technique to format the worksheet to match the design shown (in color) on the cover of this book.**

You will have to add a padding column to the left of the temperature gauge chart. Sample file *Mortgage Calculator-10* has the end result as shown on the book cover. You can use different formatting and colors if you think that they look better.

6 **Switch off the gridlines.**

The gridlines are spoiling the appearance of the group boxes.

Click: View→Show→Gridlines.

7 **Unlock cells F5, F10, F20, E29, E31, E32 and F33.**

In a moment you will protect the workbook. At this point it will only be possible to change unlocked cells. Notice that you have to unlock cells E29, E31, E32 and F33 because a control cannot change a value in a locked cell.

1. Select all of the cells to be unlocked.

2. Right-click one of the selected cells.

3. Click *Format Cells...* from the shortcut menu.

4. Click the *Protection* tab and clear the *Locked* check box.

   Cell locking and protection were covered in: *Lesson 6-11: Restrict the cells users are allowed to change.*

8 **Configure the charts to use data in hidden rows and columns.**

See sidebar if you are unsure how to do this.

9 **Hide the *Data* worksheet, *Input Cells* and *Result Cells* (rows 27:41).**

1. Right-click the Data tab and click *Hide* from the shortcut menu.

2. Select rows 27:41, right-click in the selected area and click *Hide* from the shortcut menu.

10 **Protect the worksheet.**

1. Click: Review→Protect→Protect Sheet.

2. Add a password if you want greater security.

3. Check the *Select unlocked cells* check box.

4. Uncheck the *Select locked cells* check box.

5. Click the *OK* button.

11 **Save your work as *Mortgage Calculator-10*.**

© 2021 The Smart Method® Ltd

---

note

Charting data in hidden rows and columns

By default, a chart cannot use source data that is in a hidden row or column.

To chart data in hidden rows and columns:

1. Right-click in the center of the chart.

2. Click *Select Data...* from the shortcut menu.

3. Click the *Hidden and Empty Cells* button.

4. Check the *Show data in hidden rows and columns* check box.

☑ Show data in hidden rows and columns

5. Click *OK* and *OK* again.

Charting was covered in depth in the *Essential Skills* book in this series.

Allow all users of this worksheet to:
☐ Select locked cells
☑ Select unlocked cells

note

VBA is a programming language that can be used to write custom extensions to Excel

Microsoft Office is written in a very special way. It consists of several hundred objects all "glued" together with programming code. In: *Lesson 7-5: Embed an Excel chart object into a Word document,* you saw how easy it was to place one object inside another object.

Microsoft has documented all of the objects that make up Office, so that programmers can use Office objects in their own applications.

VBA also makes it possible to add new functions and features to Excel that Microsoft didn't anticipate you would want.

Excel is now such a well-featured application that very few reasonable business requirements now need custom VBA programming to implement.

Custom functions are, perhaps, the most likely candidates for the use of VBA programming skills. I have taught VBA classes to oil industry engineers who needed some very specialized functions that were not available within the Excel function library. Of course, only one of the engineers really needed to learn VBA while everybody could use the functions he had created.

VBA isn't an Excel-specific skill. The Visual Basic language can be used to add functionality to Excel, Word, PowerPoint, Visio, Project… and many other Microsoft and third party applications.

Lesson 8-10: Understand macros and VBA

Macros are a very misunderstood concept. Most books cause terrible confusion by mixing up the twin subjects of macros and the VBA (Visual Basic for Applications) programming language.

You don't need to know anything about the VBA programming language to use macros.

Macros record keystrokes and mouse-clicks

The macro recorder is able to record (and play back) every mouse click or key stroke that you make. Here's how I would record a simple macro:

1. Start the recorder to record a macro called *TypeMikeIntoCellA5.*

2. Click into cell A5 to make it the active cell.

3. Type: **Mike** into cell A5.

4. Press the **<Enter>** key.

5. Stop the recorder.

This would record a macro that I would be able to play back in future. The macro recorded the following key presses:

Move to cell A5, Press the **<M>** key, press the **<i>** key, press the **<k>** key, press the **<e>** key, press the **<Enter>** key.

If I wanted to play back the *Mike* macro in the future I would simply run the *TypeMikeIntoCellA5* macro.

The word *Mike* would then magically appear in cell A5 and the cursor would move down to cell A6. The macro would have effectively pressed all of the keys for me automatically.

The actual method that Excel uses, to save and play back your key presses and mouse clicks, is to automatically write VBA code. But you don't need to know anything about those technicalities in order to record and play macros.

1   Open a new blank workbook.

2   Begin recording a macro called *MyName* with a shortcut key of **<Ctrl>+<m>**.

   1. Click: View→Macros→Macros→Record Macro.

   2. Type **MyName** into the *Macro name* box.

      Note that macro names cannot contain spaces.

   3. Type a lower case **m** into the *Ctrl+* box.

   4. Select *This Workbook* from the *Store macro in* drop-down list.

   Store macro in:
   | This Workbook | ∨ |

   The other options for this setting will be explained later.

note

A little knowledge is a dangerous thing

Alexander Pope, poet (1688-1744)

While I can teach you all you need to know about macros in less than an hour, I'd need several days to teach you to be a competent and professional Visual Basic programmer.

I run my Excel VBA programming courses across two to five days and still don't have enough time to cover really advanced topics (such as user defined classes). VBA is one of those subjects that it isn't useful to know a tiny bit about, so I am not going to attempt to teach you even a tiny bit in this book.

Of the hundreds of students that I've taught in my Excel VBA programming courses, a large number found that the skills were not useful. Many of them would have benefited far more from this *Expert Skills* course.

Most of the problems that they had imagined needed custom VBA coding could be better (and more easily) solved by the correct use of the Excel features you've learned about in this book.

5. Describe your macro in the *Description* box.

Description:
Puts my name into the active cell

6. Click the *OK* button – but do nothing else!

   You are now recording your macro. There's no time element to a macro recording, so you can be relaxed. The macro will record every key press and every mouse click, so it is important that you do not press any keys or click anywhere with the mouse.

3 **Record a macro that will put your name into the active cell.**

Remember that every click and keystroke are recorded, so be careful not to move to any other cell. If you did, your name would always appear in the cell you had moved to when the macro was played.

1. Type your name into the currently active cell.

   Mike

2. Press **<Ctrl>+<Enter>**.

   When you press **<Ctrl>+<Enter>** you save the value into the cell without moving to the next line. This keystroke combination is very useful when recording macros.

4 **Stop the macro recording.**

You can do this in two ways:

Click: View→Macros→Macros→Stop Recording.

OR

Click the *Stop* button at the bottom left of the screen.

Sheet1
Ready

It is a common error to forget to stop a macro recording. I've seen Excel crash in my classes when a student had forgotten and then accidentally continued to record for a long period.

5 **Test the macro.**

1. Click in any blank cell.

2. Click: View→Macros→Macros→View Macros.

   The *Macro* dialog appears, listing only the *MyName* macro (as you have only recorded one macro so far).

3. Click the *Run* button.

   Your name appears in the currently active cell.

4. Click in another blank cell and press: **<Ctrl>+<m>**

   Once again your name appears in the currently active cell.

6 **Close the workbook without saving.**

note

Choosing where to store your macros

There are three possible places to store a macro:

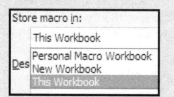

Macros stored in *This Workbook* are also available to other workbooks – but only if the workbook containing the macro is open!

The *Personal Macro Workbook* is a special workbook called *Personal.xlsb*. This is stored in a folder called XLSTART buried deep in the file system where nobody is likely to find and change it.

Whenever you open Excel, the Personal Macro Workbook opens in the background (but it is hidden so you never see it). Because it is always open, every workbook has access to its macros at all times. The only purpose of the Personal Macro Workbook is to act as a container to store macros that you want to be available to every workbook.

Remember that if you store macros in the Personal Macro Workbook, they will only work on your machine. If you e-mail a workbook that depends upon one of these macros, it will not work on the recipient's machine. In this type of scenario, you'd want to store the macro in *This Workbook*.

You'll rarely want to use the *New Workbook* option. If you record a macro in a new workbook, you would have to always make sure that it was open before you could access its macros.

Expenses Claim-1

Lesson 8-11: Record a macro with absolute references

1　Open *Expenses Claim-1* from your sample files folder.

Imagine this is a form that you need to fill in every week. Every time you make an expenses claim, you have to add your *Employee Number* and other details. This isn't very efficient, so you decide to record a macro that will automatically complete part of the form.

2　Begin recording a macro.

Click: View→Macros→Macros→Record Macro.

The *Record Macro* dialog appears.

3　Name the macro *FillInExpenseForm*.

Type **FillInExpenseForm** into the *Macro name* box.

Note that macro names cannot contain spaces. Always use mixed case for macro names and do not abbreviate. (For example, don't use names such as **FillExpFrm** – they will only confuse).

4　Assign a shortcut key of **<Ctrl>+<e>** to the macro.

Type a lower case **e** into the *Ctrl+* box.

See the sidebar on facing page for more about choosing macro shortcut keys.

5　Store the macro in *This Workbook*.

Note that there are three possible places to store a macro

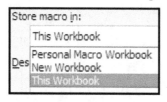

Normally you'll simply want to choose between *This Workbook* (when the macro is only useful in one workbook) and the *Personal Macro Workbook* (when the macro may be used by all workbooks). See the sidebar for more details.

This macro will only ever be used in the *Expenses Claim-1* workbook, so the most appropriate location is in *This Workbook*.

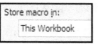

If there were many expense claim forms that all had the same data in cells B3, B5, B7, B9 and B11, you'd want to store the macro in the *Personal Macro Workbook* to make it available to all workbooks on your computer.

6　Add a *Description* to the macro.

It is good practice to describe your macros so that other users will understand what they are used for. The description is displayed in the *Macro* dialog when the user runs the macro.

Describe your macro in the *Description* box.

> Description:
> Fill in the Name, Department, Employee Number, Bank Account No and Sort Code in the Expenses Claim form

7 Record the macro.

1. Click the *OK* button.

2. Make cell B3 the active cell.

   This is a potential pitfall. If B3 is already the active cell (when you begin recording the macro) and you simply type your name, the recorder will place your name into whichever cell is the active cell when the macro is run. This may not be B3.

   For this reason, if B3 was active when you began recording you would have to click into a different cell, and then back again into cell B3 to explicitly record your intention to move the cursor to cell B3.

3. Fill in each box (with fictitious details). Here's the ones I used:

	A	B
3	Name:	Elvis Presley
5	Department:	Rock and Roll
7	Employee Number:	EP999
9	Bank Account No:	398724789A
11	Sort Code:	32-77-63

3. Click in cell A16, as this is the most likely cell that the user would want to enter text into after the macro has run.

4. Click: View→Macros→Macros→Stop Recording.

8 Test the macro.

1. Delete the contents of cells B3:B11.

2. Click: View→Macros→Macros→View Macros.

   The macro dialog appears, listing only the *FillInExpenseForm* macro (as you have only recorded one macro so far).

3. Click the *Run* button.

   All of the details that you previously recorded appear in the relevant cells.

4. Delete the contents of cells B3:B11.

5. Press **<Ctrl>+<e>**.

   Once again the form is completed with the recorded details.

9 Don't save your work yet but keep the workbook open.

   You need to understand more about security and workbook formats before you can save. You'll save this workbook in the next lesson: *Lesson 8-12: Understand macro security.*

You must begin this sequence of two lessons at: Lesson 7-11

Lesson 8-12: Understand macro security

Why is security needed?

Macros are a wonderful Excel feature but they can also be dangerous. It is possible to record a macro that will damage your computer in many ways.

Macro security provides several methods to identify which macros you can trust and which you can't.

You shouldn't trust any macro enabled workbook that is sent to you across the Internet (unless it is digitally signed). You learned about digital signatures in: *Lesson 6-14: Add an invisible digital signature to a workbook*. Without a digital signature it is impossible to be sure of an e-mail sender's identity. It is extremely easy to send an e-mail with a forged name and e-mail address.

The Excel Workbook and Excel Macro Enabled Workbook formats

There are two commonly used Excel formats:

- Excel Workbook (.xlsx file extension).

  This type of workbook can always be trusted, because it is incapable of storing a macro.

- Excel Macro Enabled Workbook (.xlsm file extension).

  You must ensure that you can trust the origin of this type of workbook as it is capable of carrying destructive macro viruses.

Four ways to trust a macro enabled workbook

Excel 365 provides four mechanisms for recognizing a trusted workbook.

- Make the workbook a *trusted document.* When a workbook becomes a trusted document you will no longer receive a warning when opening it. In: *Lesson 8-14: Understand trusted documents,* you'll learn about trusted documents in depth.

  This is probably the easiest and best way to manage macro security.

- Place the workbook in a trusted folder.

  Excel allows you to designate a folder as a trusted location. You are then able to open macro enabled workbooks that are saved to this location without warnings or restrictions.

  You'll learn about trusted folders in: *Lesson 8-13: Implement macro security.*

- Digitally sign the macro.

You learned about digital signatures in: *Lesson 6-14: Add an invisible digital signature to a workbook.*

Excel can be configured to run digitally signed macros from trusted publishers without warnings or restrictions. You'll discover how to do this in: *Lesson 8-13: Implement macro security.*

- Warn the user before enabling macros.

Excel warns you that a workbook contains macros and asks whether you wish to enable them. You'll see this working in: *Lesson 8-13: Implement macro security.*

1 *Expenses Claim-1* should still be open from the previous lesson.

In the previous lesson you recorded a macro within this workbook.

The workbook is currently an anomaly – a regular Excel Workbook that contains a macro. Excel cannot allow such a workbook to be saved.

2 Attempt to save the workbook.

Excel warns you (in a rather cryptic way) that you cannot save this workbook as a regular (macro free) workbook.

3 Click the *No* button to close the dialog.

The *Save As* dialog opens.

4 Save the workbook as an *Excel Macro Enabled* Workbook named *Expenses Claim-2.*

1. Navigate to the folder that you wish to save the file to.

2. Change the *Save as type* to: *Excel Macro-Enabled Workbook.*

3. Change the file name to: *Expenses Claim-2.*

4. Click the *Save* button.

You have now saved your first macro enabled workbook.

5 Close *Expenses Claim-2.*

Lesson 8-13: Implement macro security

1   Open *Expenses Claim-2* from your sample files folder.

Remember that this is a macro-enabled workbook. When you open it, one of three things will happen:

- The workbook opens without warnings and macros are enabled.

- Excel displays a security warning (this is the default setting). The warning is sometimes not shown if the user is the same user who last saved the workbook (as it is illogical to distrust yourself).

> ⚠ SECURITY WARNING   Macros have been disabled.   Enable Content

- The workbook opens without warnings, but the macros are disabled.

It doesn't matter which is the case on your computer at the moment. This lesson will show you how to set up the macro security options to any one of the above.

2   Set the Trust Center's Macro Settings to: *Disable all macros with notification.*

1. Click: File→Options→Trust Center.

2. Click the *Trust Center Settings…* button.

3. Click *Macro Settings* in the left-hand selection bar.

   Macro settings are displayed.

4. Click the option: *Disable all macros with notification.*

   This is the default setting for Excel, so it will probably already be selected. This option displays a warning when a workbook containing macros is opened (unless it is digitally signed by a trusted publisher or opened by its own author – see facing page sidebar). It is the best setting for an informed user.

> **Macro Settings**
>
> ○ Disable all macros without notification
> ⦿ Disable all macros with notification
> ○ Disable all macros except digitally signed macros
> ○ Enable all macros (not recommended; potentially dangerous code can run)

5. Click *OK* and *OK* again.

3   Test macro security.

As you are the user who last saved the *Expenses Claim-2* workbook you will often not see a warning when you open it.

To test security, you will open a workbook that I created containing a simple macro. This will always cause Excel to display a warning.

> **Created by Mike Smart**

> **Expenses Claim-2**

note

Controlling macro security using digital certificates

In: *Lesson 6-14: Add an invisible digital signature to a workbook,* you learned that it is possible to obtain a digital certificate by paying a third-party authority for an annual subscription.

By signing a workbook with a digital signature, it is possible to confirm that you are the *publisher* of the workbook.

In order for Excel to suppress the normal security warning, five conditions must be met:

1. The workbook must be signed with a digital signature.

2. The macro must not have been changed since the digital certificate was issued.

3. The digital certificate must not have expired.

4. The digital certificate must have been issued by a certificate authority recognized as reputable by Microsoft.

5. The publisher must appear in your trusted publishers list.

When you open a workbook with a valid digital certificate, you are prompted with the name of the publisher and asked whether you want to add the publisher to your trusted publishers list.

To view publishers currently appearing on your trusted publisher list:

1. Click: File→ Options→Trust Center→ Trust Center Settings...

2. Click *Trusted Publishers* on the left-hand selection bar.

You will then see a list of all trusted publishers and are able to view details of their digital certificates or remove them from the list.

1. Open the *Created by Mike Smart* workbook from your sample files folder.

2. Notice the warning that is displayed:

> ⚠ SECURITY WARNING   Macros have been disabled.   [Enable Content]

3. Do not click the *Enable Content...* button (if you did this you would create a trusted document). Trusted documents will be covered later, in: *Lesson 8-14: Understand trusted documents.*

4. Close the *Created by Mike Smart* workbook.

4 Set a trusted folder for your macro-enabled workbooks.

If you designate a folder for your trusted macro-enabled workbooks, Excel will know that they are trusted and not bother you with any warnings in future.

For extra security, the trusted folder should always be a non-shared folder on your local hard drive (not a network drive).

1. Create a folder for your trusted macro-enabled workbooks.

   I created a folder called: **C:\Trusted Files** on my own computer just to illustrate how this works.

2. Open a new blank workbook in Excel.

3. Click: File→Options→Trust Center.

4. Click the *Trust Center Settings...* button.

5. Click *Trusted Locations* on the left-hand selection bar.

6. Click the *Add new location...* button.

7. Click the *Browse...* button.

8. Navigate to the folder that your trusted files will be placed in.

9. Click the *OK* button.

10. Click *OK* and *OK* again to close the dialogs.

5 Test the trusted folder.

1. Copy the *Created by Mike Smart* workbook into the trusted folder.

2. Open the *Created by Mike Smart* workbook from the trusted folder.

   This time the workbook opens without warnings.

3. Click in a blank cell.

4. Run the *Test* macro contained within this workbook.

   The word: *Test* appears in the cell, proving that macros are enabled.

6 Close the *Expenses Claim-2* workbook.

7 Close the *Created by Mike Smart* workbook (without saving).

Lesson 8-14: Understand trusted documents

In Excel 2007 (and earlier versions) it was only possible to open a macro-enabled workbook without a security prompt if it was either placed in a trusted document folder or digitally signed.

Most users had to deal with this prompt every time they opened a macro-enabled workbook:

> ⚠ SECURITY WARNING Macros have been disabled. | Enable Content

The Excel designers realized that showing the prompt every time didn't really add any security. If you had decided to trust the workbook the first time you opened it, you were hardly likely to change your mind the next time. For this reason, it was decided that Excel would remember which documents you have already trusted and open them without prompts forever more.

Despite the name, Excel does not make the workbook itself "trusted". Excel stores the *location* (also called *path*), *file name* and *file creation time* in a table that is linked to your user name. This means that the macro-enabled workbook will no longer be trusted in any of the following cases:

- A different user logs onto your machine and tries to open the workbook (in this case the user name will be different).

- You change the file name or move the file to a different directory.

- A malicious user deletes the old file and replaces it with another of the same name (in this case the file creation time will not be correct).

1   Open *Created by Mike Smart* from your sample files folder.

Note that this file must be opened from your sample files folder and not from the trusted folder that you created in: *Lesson 8-13: Implement macro security.*

Because you have never clicked the *Enable Content* button for this file, the security message bar appears:

> ⚠ SECURITY WARNING Macros have been disabled. | Enable Content

2   Click the *Enable Content* button to allow macros to run.

3   Run the *Test* macro to prove that macros are enabled.

(You learned how to do this in: *Lesson 8-11: Record a macro with absolute references*).

The macro runs as intended because you have previously clicked the *Enable Content* button.

4   Close the *Created by Mike Smart* file and re-open it.

This time the file opens without showing the security message bar because Excel knows that you have previously trusted the file.

In other words, *Created by Mike Smart* has become a *trusted document.*

5   Run a macro to prove that they are enabled.

Created by Mike Smart

Expenses Claim-2

Run the *Test* macro.

The macro runs as intended because this is now a trusted document.

6   Close *Created by Mike Smart*.

7   Clear your trusted documents list.

As mentioned in the introduction to this lesson, no information is saved in the workbook file when you approve it. Instead a trusted files list is maintained by Excel.

Sometimes you may want to clear the trusted files list. When you do this, all macro-enabled files will once again display the security message bar the first time they are opened (unless, of course, they are in a trusted folder or have a digital certificate).

1. Open Excel and create a new blank workbook.

2. Click: File→Options→Trust Center→
   Trust Center Settings…→Trusted Documents.

   The *Trusted Documents* pane appears.

Trusted Documents

Warning: Trusted Documents open without any security prompts for macros, ActiveX controls and other types of active content in the document. For a Trusted Document, you will not be prompted the next time you open the document, even if new active content was added to the document or changes were made to existing active content. Therefore, you should only trust documents if you trust the source.

☑ Allow documents on a network to be trusted

☐ Disable Trusted Documents

Clear all Trusted Documents so that they are no longer trusted   [Clear]

You can see that this pane can also be used to permanently disable the *Trusted Documents* feature for network drives only or for all file locations.

3. Click the *Clear* button.

4. Click *Yes, OK* and *OK* again to clear the dialogs.

   All trusted documents in the trusted documents list are now cleared. This means that all macro-enabled workbooks (including ones you created yourself) will now display the security message bar the first time they are opened.

8   Open *Expenses Claim-2* from your sample files folder.

Notice that the security message bar is shown because *Expenses Claim-2* is no longer a trusted document.

⚠ SECURITY WARNING   Macros have been disabled.   [Enable Content]

---

9   Click the *Enable Content* button.

Expenses Claim-2 has once again become a trusted document. This means that the security message bar will not display the next time that you open it.

Lesson 8-15: Record a macro with relative references

1   Open *Company List-1* from your sample files folder.

This workbook contains a list of 88 companies. The list will be used to perform a mail merge (using Microsoft Word).

In order to perform a mail merge, the data needs to be converted into a format that Word can understand. Instead of:

	A
3	Contact Name
4	Alejandra Camino
5	Romero y tomillo
6	Gran Vía, 1
7	Madrid
8	28001
9	Spain
10	
11	
12	
13	Alexander Feuer
14	Morgenstern Gesundkost
15	Heerstr. 22
16	Leipzig
17	4179
18	Germany
19	

The data needs to be re-formatted like this:

	A	B	C	D	E	F
3	Contact Name	Company Name	Address	City	Post Code	Country
4	Alejandra Camino	Romero y tomillo	Gran Vía, 1	Madrid	28001	Spain
5	Alexander Feuer	Morgenstern Gesundkost	Heerstr. 22	Leipzig	4179	Germany

To do this manually would take a long time, but you can convert all 88 records in less than five seconds by creating a macro recorded with relative references.

Relative reference macros record an offset from the active cell. Imagine that the active cell is A4 (Alejandra Camino). The relative macro that you are about to record will record the actions:

• Move one cell down.

• Cut.

• Move one cell up and one cell to the right.

• Paste.

... and so on until all of Alejandra's details are moved to row 4. The macro will then delete the blank rows and be ready to start again with Alexander Feuer.

2   Set up the macro recorder to use relative references.

Click: View→Macros→Macros→Use Relative References.

Company List-1

3   Make cell A4 the active cell.

When recording a relative reference macro, it is vital that you select the active cell <u>before</u> beginning the recording.

4 **Record a macro with the name *MoveAddress* and save it in *This Workbook* with the shortcut key <Ctrl>+<m>.**

1. Click: View→Macros→Macros→Record Macro.

2. Type **MoveAddress** into the *Macro name* box.

3. Type a lower case **m** into the *Shortcut key* box.

4. Select *This Workbook* from the *Store macro in* drop-down list.

5. Click *OK* to begin recording the macro.

6. Click in cell A5 and cut.

7. Click in cell B4 and paste.

8. Continue until the complete address is pasted into row 4.

	A	B	C	D	E	F
3	Contact Name	Company Name	Address	City	Post Code	Country
4	Alejandra Camino	Romero y tomillo	Gran Vía, 1	Madrid	28001	Spain
5						

9. Select rows 5:12.

10. Right-click inside the selected cells.

11. Click *Delete* from the shortcut menu.

12. Click in cell A5 to make it the active cell.

	A	B	C
3	Contact Name	Company Name	Address
4	Alejandra Camino	Romero y tomillo	Gran Vía, 1
5	Alexander Feuer		
6	Morgenstern Gesundkost		

The macro will be run multiple times to convert all of the addresses. By placing the cursor in cell A5 before you stop recording, it will be in the right position to convert the next address.

13. Click: View→Macros→Macros→Stop Recording.

5 **Convert the other 87 addresses by running the macro multiple times.**

1. Make sure that A5 is the active cell.

2. Press: **<Ctrl>+<m>**

3. The next address is converted.

4. Hold down the **<Ctrl>+<m>** keys and let the keyboard automatically repeat.

   If this macro runs very slowly see sidebar for more details.

	A	B	C	D	E	F
3	Contact Name	Company Name	Address	City	Post Code	Country
4	Alejandra Camino	Romero y tomillo	Gran Vía, 1	Madrid	28001	Spain
5	Alexander Feuer	Morgenstern Gesundkost	Heerstr. 22	Leipzig	4179	Germany

6 **Save your work as a macro enabled workbook called: *Company List-2*.**

Lesson 8-16: Use shapes to run macros

1 Open *Mortgage Calculator-10* from your sample files folder.

2 Record a macro in *This Workbook* called *PrintWorkbook*.

1. Click: View→Macros→Macros→Record Macro.

2. Type **PrintWorkbook** in the *Macro name* box.

3. Describe what the macro does in the *Description* box (see sidebar).

4. Click the *OK* button.

5. Click: File→Print→Print.

   The worksheet will print out on your default printer.

6. Click: View→Macros→Macros→Stop Recording.

3 Save the workbook as a macro enabled workbook called *Mortgage Calculator-11*.

1. Click: File→Save As→This PC→Browse.

2. Navigate to the folder that you wish to save the file in.

3. Select *Excel Macro-Enabled Workbook* from the *Save as type* dropdown list.

4. Type: **Mortgage Calculator-11** in the *File Name* box.

5. Click the *Save* button.

4 Record a macro in *This Workbook* called *SaveWorkbook*.

1. Click: View→Macros→Macros→Record Macro.

2. Type **SaveWorkbook** in the *Macro name* box.

3. Describe what the macro does in the *Description* box (see sidebar).

4. Click the *OK* button.

5. Click: File→Save.

6. Click: View→Macros→Macros→Stop Recording.

5 Add three shape controls to the worksheet.

1. If the worksheet is protected:

   Click: Review→Protect→Unprotect Sheet.

2. Re-size the pie chart to make space for a row of buttons underneath.

3. Click: Insert→Illustrations→Shapes→Rectangles→ Rectangle: Rounded Corners.

4. Click and drag on the worksheet to draw the button.

5. Click: Shape Format→Shape Styles→ More→Intense Effect – Blue, Accent 1.

Mortgage Calculator-10

6. Click: Shape Format→Shape Styles→Shape Effects→Bevel→Round.

7. Right-click on the button and click *Edit Text* from the shortcut menu.

8. Type: **Save Quote** to add a caption to the shape.

9. Click: Home→Alignment→Middle Align.

10. Click: Home→Alignment→Center.

11. Copy and paste the shape twice.

12. Change the captions on the other two shapes to read **Print Quote** and **Go To Website**.

6 Connect the *Save Quote* and *Print Quote* shapes to the *SaveWorkbook* and *PrintWorkbook* macros.

1. Right-click the *Save Quote* shape.

2. Click *Assign Macro…* from the shortcut menu.

3. Select the *SaveWorkbook* macro.

4. Click the *OK* button.

5. Follow the same procedure to assign the *PrintWorkbook* macro to the *Print Quote* shape.

7 Connect the *Go To Website* shape to the website at https://TheSmartMethod.com.

1. Right-click the *Go To Website* shape.

2. Click: *Link* from the shortcut menu.

3. Click: *Existing File or Web Page* on the left hand selection bar.

4. Type **https://TheSmartMethod.com** into the *Address* box.

5. Click the *OK* button.

8 Protect the worksheet.

1. Click: Review→Protect→Protect Sheet.

2. Click the *OK* button.

9 Save your work as *Mortgage Calculator-11.*

10 Test the shapes.

1. Close and re-open the workbook.

Note that you may need to enable macros after re-opening (see: *Lesson 8-14: Understand trusted documents*).

2. Click upon each shape.

The relevant macro or hyperlink executes.

Lesson 8-17: Run a macro from a button control

note

You can also run macros from the Quick Access Toolbar

If you have general-purpose macros (saved in the Personal Macro Workbook) that you would like to run with a single click, you can add them to the Quick Access Toolbar.

1. Click: File→Options→ Quick Access Toolbar.

2. Select *Macros* in the *Choose commands from* drop-down list.

3. Select the macro that you want to add to the Quick Access Toolbar.

4. Click the *Add>>* button.

5. Select the macro in the right-hand pane.

6. Click the *Modify...* button to change the icon and tip text for the macro.

🖬	Save
⤺	Undo ▸
⤻	Redo ▸
⊚	Compare and Merge Workbooks...
⟲	HR
👤	Hours Worked (Female)
🕵	Total Hours Worked

7. Click the *OK* button.

The macros can then be run from the *Quick Access Toolbar* with a single click.

You can also add macro buttons to the ribbon in a similar way. You'll learn how to do this in: *Lesson 8-20: Create a custom ribbon tab.*

Human Resources-2

1 Open *Human Resources-2* from your sample files folder.

This is the workbook created in: *Lesson 6-8: Create custom views.* The workbook contains three custom views:

- Hours Worked
- Hours Worked (Female)
- HR

It is not obvious that the workbook contains custom views. You can make users more aware of the feature, and make the feature easier to use, by adding button controls to move between the custom views.

2 Record macros in *This Workbook* that will show each custom view.

1. Click: View→Macros→Macros→Record Macro.

2. Type **ShowHoursWorkedView** in the *Macro name* box.

Macro name:

ShowHoursWorkedView

3. Describe what the macro does in the *Description* box.

Description:

Display the hours worked custom view.

4. Click the *OK* button to begin recording the macro.

5. Click: View→Workbook Views→Custom Views.

6. Select the *Hours Worked* view.

7. Click the *Show* button.

8. Click: View→Macros→Macros→Stop Recording.

9. Create a **ShowHoursWorkedFemaleView** macro that will display the *Hours Worked (Female)* custom view.

10. Create a **ShowHRView** macro that will display the *HR* custom view.

3 Add a button control to cell A8 with the caption *Hours Worked* that will run the *ShowHoursWorkedView* macro.

1. If the *Developer* tab is not shown in the ribbon, click: File→Options→Customize Ribbon and check the *Developer* check box in the right-hand pane.

2. Click: Developer→Controls→Insert→ Form Controls→Button (Form Control).

3. Click and drag in the top of cell A8 to add a button.

4. The *Assign Macro* dialog appears.

5. Select the *ShowHoursWorkedView* macro.

6. Click the *OK* button.

7. Click on the face of the button, delete the existing text and type: **Hours Worked**.

	A	B	C	D
6	Pension	5%		
	Hours Worked			
		Johnny Caine	George Marley	Betty Anan
8				
9	Hourly Rate	18.20	12.57	12.67

4   Add another button control to cell A8 with the caption *Hours Worked (Female)* that will run the *ShowHoursWorkedFemaleView* macro.

5   Add another button control to cell A8 with the caption *HR* that will run the *ShowHRView* macro.

	A	B	C	D	E	F	G
1	Payroll						
2							
	Hours Worked						
	Hours Worked (Female)	Johnny Caine	George Marley	Betty Anan	Paris Winfrey	Ozzy Dickens	Johnny Roberts
8	HR						
11	Hours Worked						
12	Monday	9	10	10	10	7	7
13	Tuesday	8	9	8	6	10	10

6   Test the workbook.

Click on each of the command buttons. The workbook should display each custom view as the command buttons are clicked.

7   Save your work as a macro-enabled workbook with the name *Human Resources-3*.

Lesson 8-18: Show and hide ribbon tabs

Excel 365 allows you to customize both the Quick Access Toolbar and ribbon.

You can:

* Show and hide ribbon tabs.

* Add your own custom command groups to standard ribbon tabs.

* Add your own custom tab(s) to the ribbon and add custom command groups to them.

1 Open *Mortgage Calculator-11* from your sample files folder.

The Mortgage Calculator has a very simple user interface that non-Excel users will find easy and intuitive to use.

The screen still looks intimidating to a non-Excel user (even though most of the ribbon buttons are grayed out).

If you hide all of the standard ribbon tabs, the screen will seem a lot simpler.

2 Hide all of the standard ribbon tabs.

1. Right-click anywhere in a blank area of the ribbon and select *Customize the Ribbon…* from the shortcut menu.

The *Excel Options* dialog appears with the *Customize Ribbon* pane selected.

2. Select *Main Tabs* in the *Customize the Ribbon* drop-down list on the right-hand pane of the dialog:

Customize the Ribbon: ⓘ

Main Tabs ▼

3. Clear the check boxes next to each of the main tabs:

Main Tabs
⊞ ☐ Background Removal
⊞ ☐ Home
⊞ ☐ Insert
⊞ ☐ Draw
⊞ ☐ Page Layout
⊞ ☐ Formulas
⊞ ☐ Data
⊞ ☐ Review
⊞ ☐ View
⊞ ☐ Developer
    ☐ Add-ins
⊞ ☐ Help
⊞ ☐ Power Pivot

4. Click the *OK* button.

The user interface is now a lot cleaner with only the *File* tab displayed:

Mortgage Calculator-11

---

note

Ribbon customizations are set at application level

When you customize the ribbon, you are customizing Excel itself and not the current workbook.

For applications such as the Mortgage Calculator it would be great if you could save customizations that only applied to the current workbook.

Unfortunately, you cannot easily do this but perhaps we'll see this feature in a future Excel release.

3 **Bring the tabs back again.**

1. Right-click on the *File* tab and click: *Customize the Ribbon...* from the shortcut menu.

2. The *Excel Options* dialog appears with the *Customize Ribbon* pane selected.

3. Check each of the check boxes that you unchecked earlier.

4. Click the *OK* button.

5. The standard ribbon tabs are restored.

note

Why it is a bad idea to customize standard ribbon tabs

A common attraction at fairgrounds is the "reverse steering bicycle".

The showman has a bicycle that has special steering. When the handlebars are steered left the bicycle turns right, and when steered right the bicycle turns left.

The showman competently rides the bicycle, demonstrating how easy it is, and challenges the public to ride just five meters to win a prize. Of course, nobody that takes the challenge is able to ride the bicycle.

This works because the showman has learned to ride the bicycle with reverse steering.

Because riding a bicycle is a subconscious process, nobody that has learned to ride a regular bicycle can ride a reverse steering bicycle. In computer terminology, the bicycle has a non-standard user interface.

As a side-effect, the showman will also be unable to ride a normal bicycle.

If you extensively customize standard ribbon tabs, you may find it difficult to work with the unfamiliar standard ribbon on other computers. You may effectively turn yourself into a reverse cyclist!

For this reason, I suggest that you refrain from customizing the standard ribbon tabs but, instead, add any extra functionality you need to a custom ribbon tab.

Lesson 8-19: Add custom groups to standard ribbon tabs

While I was very pleased when Excel 2010 introduced the ability to add new custom tabs to the ribbon, I was less pleased to find that users can also add and remove command groups on the standard ribbon tabs.

In my opinion it would be best to refrain from doing this (see sidebar). Despite my opinion, this lesson demonstrates this feature.

1   Open *Passwords-1* from your sample files folder.

This workbook has been created so that the user does not forget passwords. Unfortunately, the passwords used are very insecure, in fact they are among the world's top 20 most commonly used passwords. It would be very easy to hack into this user's sites!

	A	B
3	Web Site	Password
4	YouTube.com	qwerty
5	Facebook.com	123456
6	PayPal.com	letmein

The user has wisely decided to change the passwords to secure ones (secure passwords were discussed in: *Lesson 6-9: Prevent unauthorized users from opening or modifying workbooks*). In order to do this the user has created a secure password generator (see facing page sidebar if you are interested in how this works).

2   Generate a new password and copy it to cell C4.

1.   Press the <F9> key to generate a new password.

2.   Copy the password from cell C21.

3.   Right-click in cell C4.

4.   Click: Paste Options→Values from the shortcut menu.

3   Apply the strikethrough style to the old password.

The strikethrough style is very useful when you have replaced text but still wish to retain it. Unfortunately, this style is not included on the ribbon and it is necessary to use a dialog launcher to access it.

1.   Click in cell B4.

2.   Click: Home→Font→Dialog Launcher.

3.   Check the *Strikethrough* check box.

	A	B	C
3	Web Site	Password	New Password
4	YouTube.com	~~qwerty~~	Zbx1JhQlQpf%

note

How the secure password generator works

The secure password generator is constructed using skills covered in earlier lessons in this book.

Look at the *Password Characters* worksheet. This contains a table named *Password*. The first column contains sequential numbers and the second contains all of the letters, numbers and special symbols that may be used in the generated password. You learned about tables in: *Session One: Tables, and Ranges*.

Return to the *Passwords* worksheet and unhide rows 23 to 34. You learned how to do this in: *Lesson 6-7: Hide and unhide worksheets, columns and rows*.

Look at the formula in cell A23. This uses the RANDBETWEEN function in conjunction with a VLOOKUP function to return a random letter from the *Password* table. You learned about VLOOKUP in: *Lesson 3-22: Use a VLOOKUP function for an exact lookup*.

Look at the formula in cell C21. This uses the CONCAT function to construct the password from the random characters in cells A23:A34. You learned about the CONCAT function in: *Lesson 3-19: Use the TEXT function to format numerical values as strings*.

It is standard behaviour for a worksheet to recalculate when the **<F9>** key is pressed. Each time this is done, the RANDBETWEEN function generates new random numbers which, in turn, look up new random letters. This is discussed in depth in: *Lesson 3-17: Understand calculation options (manual and automatic)*.

4   Add a custom group called *Special Formatting* to the right of the *Font* command group in the *Home* ribbon.

1. Right-click in a blank area of the ribbon and select *Customize the Ribbon…* from the shortcut menu.

    The *Customize the Ribbon* dialog appears.

2. Click the *Home* tab in the right-hand pane of the dialog.

3. Click the *New Group* button.

    A new group appears within the *Home* tab.

4. Click the *Rename…* button and type **Special Formatting** into the *Display name* text box.

5. Click the *OK* button.

6. Use the up and down arrow buttons to move the group so that it appears after the *Alignment* group.

Main Tabs
⊞ ☑ Background Removal
⊟ ☑ Home
   ⊞ Clipboard
   ⊞ Font
   ⊞ Alignment
   Special Formatting (Custom)
   ⊞ Number

5   Add the *Strikethrough* command to the *Special Formatting* custom group.

1. Select *Commands Not in the Ribbon* from the *Choose commands from* drop-down list at the top of the dialog.

2. Select the *Strikethrough* command from the left-hand list.

3. Click the *Add>>* button.

    The *Strikethrough* command now appears within the *Special Formatting* custom group.

4. Click the *OK* button.

    The *Home* ribbon now contains a *Special Formatting* custom group with a single *Strikethrough* command.

6   Add a new secure password for *Facebook.com* and strikethrough the old password using the new ribbon command.

	A	B	C
3	Web Site	Password	
4	YouTube.com	~~qwerty~~	2UE5vl@y77e7
5	Facebook.com	~~123456~~	S#yQk1rH#!pS

7   Save your work as *Passwords-2.*

Lesson 8-20: Create a custom ribbon tab

Excel has many really useful features that hardly any user will ever discover. A good example is the Speak Cells feature covered in: *Lesson 5-17: Use Speak Cells to eliminate data entry errors.* The only way to access these features is by adding commands to the Quick Access Toolbar or ribbon or by using *Tell Me help.*

In this lesson you'll create a special ribbon tab containing my own favorite selection of hidden Excel features. You may find that you want to keep this ribbon permanently.

The ribbon tab that you will create is shown in the sidebar.

1 Open a new blank workbook.

2 Create a custom ribbon tab called *Extras.*

1. Right-click the ribbon and click: *Customize the Ribbon…* from the shortcut menu.

   The *Customize the Ribbon* dialog appears.

2. Click the *New Tab* button at the bottom of the right-hand pane.

   A new custom tab and single new custom group appear in the *Main Tabs* window.

   ```
   ☐ ☑ New Tab (Custom)
          New Group (Custom)
   ```

3. Select the new tab and click the *Rename…* button.

   Be careful to click the *New Tab* and not the *New Group* item.

   The *Rename* dialog appears.

4. Type **Extras** into the *Display Name* text box.

Rename	? ✕
Display name:	Extras
	OK Cancel

5. Click the *OK* button.

   ```
   Main Tabs
   ☐ ☑ Background Removal
   ☐ ☑ Home
   ☐ ☑ Extras (Custom)
            New Group (Custom)
   ☐ ☑ Insert
   ```

3 Add six more custom groups to the *Extras* tab.

Click the *New Group* button six times.

4 Name the custom groups: *Hyperlinks, Speak, Collaboration, Format, Widgets, Quick Paste* and *File/Print.*

1. Select the first *New Group*.

2. Click the *Rename…* button.

Sidebar (ribbon tab illustration):

Tabs: File | Home | Extras | Insert | Draw | Page Layout | Formulas | Data | Review | View | Developer | Help | Power Pivot | Search | Share | Quick Print | Close All

Groups and buttons:

Hyperlinks: Forward, Back
Speak: Speak Cells, Stop Speaking Cells, By Columns, By Rows, On Enter
Collaboration: Compare and Merge Workbooks, Mail Recipient
Format: Strikethrough
Widgets: Freeform: Scribble
Quick Paste: Left Brace {, Right Brace }, Equal Sign =, Left Parenthesis (, Right Parenthesis), Multiplication Sign *, Plus Sign +, Minus Sign −, Division Sign /
File/Print: Quick Print, Close All

The *Rename* dialog appears.

Notice that you are able to select a symbol as well as define a name. The symbols will display when the application window is made so narrow that the commands have no room to display... like this:

Note that the new *Format* and *Widgets* command groups have only one command, meaning that no symbol is ever shown.

3. Select the cloud symbol ▢ and type **Hyperlinks** into the *Display Name* text box.

4. Click the *OK* button.

5. Repeat for the other command groups.

5   Add *Forward* and *Back* commands to the *Hyperlinks* command group.

In: *Lesson 7-3: Hyperlink to an e-mail address and enhance the browsing experience,* you discovered how useful a forward and backward button were when constructing workbooks that had hyperlink-based navigation systems.

1. Select the *Hyperlinks* custom group in the right-hand pane of the *Customize the Ribbon* dialog.

2. Select *Commands Not In the Ribbon* from the drop-down list above the left-hand pane.

3. Click the *Forward* command in the left-hand pane.

4. Click the *Add>>* button.

5. Repeat for the *Back* command.

6   Add all of the other commands to the relevant ribbon groups.

Use the screen grab on the facing page as a guide. If you don't find a command in the *Commands Not in the Ribbon* group, look in the *All Commands* group.

7   Save your ribbon customizations to a file.

You may wish to share your custom ribbon with other users or to load it onto a different computer.

1. Right-click the ribbon and select *Customize the Ribbon...* from the shortcut menu.

    The *Customize the Ribbon* dialog appears.

2. Click the *Import/Export* button at the bottom of the right-hand pane.

3. Click *Export all customizations* from the drop down list.

4. Name the customizations *Extras Bar* and click *Save.*

Session 8: Exercise

1 Open *Gala Dinner-1* from your sample files folder.

2 Add combo box, group box, option button and check box form controls, so that the user interface looks like this:

3 Add a new worksheet called *Data*.

4 Add a named range to the *Data* worksheet called *Tickets*, containing the numbers 1-10.

5 Set the *Input range* of the combo box control to the *Tickets* range name.

6 Link the combo box and check box controls to the input cells (B19, B20 and B21).

7 Add formulas to the result cells (B24, B25, B26 and B27) to calculate the total cost of the order.

8 Add a formula to cell B13 so that it displays the same value as cell B27 and hide rows 18 to 27.

9 Record a macro named *PrintOrder* in *This Worksheet* that will print the worksheet.

10 Add a button control to the form that will run the *PrintOrder* macro.

11 Save your work as a *Macro-Enabled Workbook* named *Gala Dinner-2*.

Gala Dinner-1

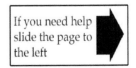
If you need help slide the page to the left

Session 8: Exercise Answers

These are the four questions that students find the most difficult to answer:

Q 9	Q 7	Q 6	Q 3 & 4
1. Click: View→Macros→Macros→Record Macro…	The correct formulas are:	1. Right-click the combo box.	1. Click the *New Sheet* button at the bottom left of the screen to insert a new worksheet.
2. Type **PrintOrder** into the *Macro name* box.	*Ticket Cost* (B24): **=B19*22.5**	2. Click *Format Control…* from the shortcut menu.	2. Double-click on the new tab and change the worksheet name to: **Data**
3. Select *This Workbook* from the *Store macro in* drop-down list.	*Water Cost* (B25): **=IF(B20=TRUE, B19*2.5,0)**	3. Click the *Control* tab.	3. Select the *Data* worksheet and type **Tickets** into cell A1.
4. Click the *OK* button.	*Wine Cost* (B26): **=IF(B21=TRUE, B19*5.5,0)**	4. Click in the *Cell Link* box.	4. Type the numbers 1 to 10 in cells A2:A11.
5. Click: File→Print.	*Total Cost* (B27): **=SUM(B24:B26)**	5. Click in cell B19.	5. Select cells A1:A11.
6. Click the *Print* button.	This was covered in: *Lesson 8-6: Use check box data in result cells.*	6. Click the *OK* button.	6. Click: Formula→Defined Names→Create from Selection.
7. Click: View→Macros→Macros→Stop Recording.		7. Follow the same steps for the check boxes, linking the *Water* check box to cell B20 and the *Wine* check box to cell B21.	7. Click the *OK* button.
This was covered in: *Lesson 8-16: Use shapes to run macros.*		This was covered in: *Lesson 8-3: Set form control cell links.*	You have now created a named range called *Tickets* that references cells A2:A11.
			This was covered in: *Lesson 5-1: Automatically create single-cell range names.*

If you have difficulty with the other questions, here are the lessons that cover the relevant skills:

2   Refer to: *Lesson 8-1: Add group box and option button controls to a worksheet form, Lesson 8-2: Add a combo box control to a worksheet form* and *Lesson 8-5: Add a check box control to a worksheet form.*

5   Refer to: *Lesson 8-2: Add a combo box control to a worksheet form.*

8   The correct formula is: **=B27**. To hide the rows, select them, right-click inside the selected range and click *Hide* from the shortcut menu.

10   Refer to: *Lesson 8-17: Run a macro from a button control.*

Session Nine: Pivot Tables

I'm constantly amazed at how many highly experienced Excel users are unable to understand pivot tables.

I've seen many cases where a user has spent hours creating a worksheet-based solution that could have been addressed in a few seconds using a pivot table. This session will empower you with a complete mastery of this powerful Excel feature.

Session Objectives

By the end of this session you will be able to:

- Create a one dimensional pivot table report from a table
- Create a grouped pivot table report
- Understand pivot table rows and columns
- Understand the pivot table data cache
- Apply a simple filter and sort to a pivot table
- Use report filter fields
- Filter a pivot table visually using slicers
- Add a timeline control to a pivot table
- Use slicers to create a custom timeline
- Use report filter fields to automatically create multiple pages
- Format a pivot table using PivotTable styles
- Create a custom pivot table style
- Understand pivot table report layouts
- Add/remove subtotals and apply cell styles to pivot table fields
- Display multiple summations within a single pivot table
- Add a calculated field to a pivot table
- Add a calculated item to a pivot table
- Group by text, date and numeric value ranges
- Show row data by percentage of total rather than value
- Use pivot table values in simple formulas
- Use the GETPIVOTDATA function
- Create a pivot chart from a pivot table
- Embed multiple pivot tables onto a worksheet
- Use slicers to filter multiple pivot tables

Lesson 9-1: Create a one-dimensional pivot table report from a table

In this lesson, you'll create a simple one-dimensional pivot table. There's a huge amount to learn about pivot tables but it will be fun to do some useful work with one straight away.

Here's the sample file that you'll use in this lesson:

	A	B	C	D	E	F	G	H
1	Order No	Order Date	Customer	Employee	Title	Genre	Qty	Total
2	136438	02-Oct-14	Silver Screen Video	Lee,Frank	Lawrence of Arabia	Biography	15	122.76
3	136438	02-Oct-14	Silver Screen Video	Lee,Frank	The Discreet Charm of the Bourgeoisie	Comedy	9	67.46
4	136438	02-Oct-14	Silver Screen Video	Lee,Frank	Berlin Alexanderplatz	Drama	25	250.60
5	136438	02-Oct-14	Silver Screen Video	Lee,Frank	Gone With The Wind	Drama	14	107.72
6	136439	03-Oct-14	Cinefocus DVD	Diamond,Elizabeth	Mouchette	Drama	5	31.77

This is the type of worksheet that pivot tables can work well with because the columns contain repeating data.

The sample file contains over 2,000 rows of transactional data listing sales during the 18-month period from October 2014 to March 2016 inclusive.

You can see from the data that the worksheet contains details of orders sold by a DVD wholesaler, along with the titles supplied on each order. Order *136438* was placed on *2nd-Oct-14* and was ordered by *Silver Screen Video*. The order was sold by *Frank Lee* and there were four items on the order. Two of the films ordered were in the *Drama* genre and the other two were in the *Biography* and *Comedy* genres.

A business may wish to ask several questions about sales during this period such as:

- What were my sales by *Genre*?

- How many units did each *Employee* sell?

In this lesson, you'll use a simple pivot table to answer both questions in less than 10 seconds!

1   Open *Transactions-1* from your sample files folder.

This worksheet contains a large table named *Data* (see sidebar for more on using tables with pivot tables).

The table looks like a regular range because the *Filter* buttons have been switched off and the *Table Style* has been set to *None*.

2   Click anywhere inside the table.

3   Click Insert→Tables→PivotTable.

The *Create PivotTable* dialog appears.

Notice that, because you clicked inside the table, the dialog has automatically detected the table's name of *Data*.

Transactions-1

4   Click the *OK* button.

An empty pivot table is shown on screen and the *PivotTable Fields* task pane appears on the right of the screen.

5   Check the *Genre*, *Qty* and *Total* check boxes (in that order) in the *PivotTable Fields* task pane.

Simply by clicking on three fields you have answered the first question:

- What were my sales by *Genre*?

6   Format the values shown in column C of the pivot table so that they show two decimal places with a comma separator.

1. Right-click on any value in column C.

2. Click *Number Format...* from the shortcut menu.

3. Click *Number* in the *Category* list.

4. Click the *Use 1000 Separator* check box.

5. Click the *OK* button.

7   Clear all check boxes and then select the *Employee* and *Qty* check boxes.

Once again, with very little effort, you have answered the second question:

- How many units did each *Employee* sell?

8   Name the pivot table: **Transactions**

1. Click inside the pivot table.

2. Click: PivotTable Analyze→PivotTable→PivotTable Name.

3. Type **Transactions** into the *PivotTable Name* box.

9   Name the pivot table worksheet tab: **Pivot Table**

10   Save your work as *Transactions-2*.

Lesson 9-2: Create a grouped pivot table report

1   Open *Transactions-2* from your sample files folder (if it isn't already open).

2   Select the *Pivot Table* worksheet (if it isn't already selected).

3   Click inside the pivot table to show the *PivotTable Fields* task pane.

4   Check *Genre* in the *PivotTable Fields* list.

Each Employee's sales for each genre are now shown in the report.

5   Add *Title* information to the pivot table.

Check *Title* in the *PivotTable Field List*.

The report now breaks sales down by *Employee*, *Genre* and *Title*.

Transactions-2

6 Collapse the outline to show only sales by *Employee.*

1. Right-click in cell A4.

   A shortcut menu appears.

2. Click: Expand/Collapse→Collapse Entire Field.

   The pivot table collapses to the level of *Employee.*

	A	B
3	Row Labels	Sum of Qty
4	⊞ Anderson,Jane	1109
5	⊞ Armstrong,Dan	1000
6	⊞ Ashe,Lucille	1116
7	⊞ Bell,Stephen	1409

7 Expand Dan Armstrong's sales to show full details.

Click the small + sign to the left of cell A5.

	A	B
5	Armstrong,Dan	1000
6	Ashe,Lucille	1116

Sales are expanded to show full details of Dan's sales.

	A	B
5	⊟ Armstrong,Dan	1000
6	⊟ Action	136
7	A Touch of Zen	24
8	Drunken Master II	22

8 Collapse the outline so that Dan's sales by *Genre* are shown without *Title* details.

1. Right-click in cell A6.

   A shortcut menu appears.

2. Click: Expand/Collapse→Collapse Entire Field.

   The *Title* level of the Pivot Table collapses to show Dan's sales by *Genre* but not by *Title.*

	A	B
5	⊟ Armstrong,Dan	1000
6	⊞ Action	136
7	⊞ Adventure	26
8	⊞ Animation	22

9 Collapse the outline to only show sales by *Employee.*

Click the small minus sign to the left of cell A5.

The outline collapses to show only the *Employee* level.

	A	B
5	⊞ Armstrong,Dan	1000
6	⊞ Ashe,Lucille	1116
7	⊞ Bell,Stephen	1409

10 Save your work as *Transactions-3.*

---

trivia

PivotTable or Pivot Table?

The term *Pivot Table* has been used for a long time to describe the general concept of summarizing data.

One of the earliest implementations of pivot tables was introduced in *Lotus Improv* (released in 1991).

Pivot tables also featured in the 1992 release of *Quattro Pro.* Quattro called this feature *DataPivot.*

Pivot tables first appeared in Excel in the 1994 *Excel 5* release. The Excel pivot table feature was called *PivotTable* (without a space). This name was registered as a trademark by Microsoft in December 1994.

In the ribbon and in most Microsoft documentation you'll see the pivot table spelled as *PivotTable* rather than *pivot table.*

It would be correct to refer to an Excel pivot table both in the more general way (*pivot table*) and also using the Microsoft trademark (*PivotTable*).

In this book I try to consistently use the *PivotTable* terminology only when referring to a feature within the user interface where this spelling is used. At all other times I find *pivot table* (with a space) to be more elegant.

Lesson 9-3: Understand pivot table rows and columns

1 Open *Transactions-3* from your sample files folder (if it isn't already open).

2 Select the *Pivot Table* worksheet (if it isn't already selected).

3 Click inside the pivot table to display the *PivotTable Fields* task pane.

At the lower right of the screen, you can see four panes:

At the moment, you have three columns in the *Rows* list and one in the *Values* list. This creates a pivot table that shows sales grouped first by *Employee,* then grouped by *Genre* and then grouped by *Title.*

4 Remove the *Genre* and *Title* rows from the Rows list.

1. Click *Genre* in the *Rows* pane of the *PivotTable Fields* task pane and then click *Remove Field* from the shortcut menu.

2. Click *Title* and then click *Remove Field* from the shortcut menu.

5 Add the *Genre* to the pivot table as a *Column Label.*

Instead of checking the *Genre* box in the *PivotTable Fields* task pane, you need to drag it from the *PivotTable Fields* task pane to the *Columns* list below.

Transactions-3

note

The Defer Layout Update check box

You may have noticed a check box at the bottom left of the *PivotTable Fields* task pane that is labelled: *Defer Layout Update* and a button to the right (that is normally grayed out) labelled *Update*.

Rows	Σ Values
Employee ▾	Sum of Qty ▾
☐ Defer Layout Update	Update

This option is useful if you work with very large data sets.

Pivot tables normally update as soon as you add a field to them. On small data sets (such as the 2,155 row data set used in the sample data for this lesson) there is no problem. The pivot table updates in a fraction of a second.

If you find that you have to wait a significant amount of time after adding a field before you can add another, you've found a use for *Defer Layout Update*.

Here's what you need to do:

1. Click the *Defer Layout Update* check box.

The *Update* button will then become enabled.

2. Add all of the fields you need.

3. Click the *Update* button. With a very large data set it could take some time for the pivot table to update.

4. Uncheck the check box.

This is usually a lot faster than adding fields one by one.

It is really important that you remember to uncheck the box. You won't be able to use any of the interactive features of the pivot table (such as filtering, sorting and grouping) until you do.

The pivot table now shows sales for each employee by genre with the genres listed along the top row as column labels:

	A	B	C	D	E
4	Row Labels ▾	Action	Adventure	Animation	Biography
5	Anderson,Jane	199	30		134
6	Armstrong,Dan	136	26	22	79
7	Ashe,Lucille	176	42	23	54

6 Add the *Title* field to the *Columns* list.

Drag the *Title* field from the *PivotTable Fields* task pane to the *Columns* list.

Make sure that you place *Title* below *Genre*.

▼ Filters	▦ Columns
	Genre ▾
	Title ▾
▦ Rows	Σ Values
Employee ▾	Sum of Qty ▾

A small + sign is now displayed next to each genre:

	A	B	C	D	E
4		⊞ Action	⊞ Adventure	⊞ Animation	⊞ Biography
5	Row Labels ▾				
6	Anderson,Jane	199	30		134
7	Armstrong,Dan	136	26	22	79
8	Ashe,Lucille	176	42	23	54

7 Expand and collapse the *Action* genre.

1. Click the small + sign to the left of *Action* in cell *B4*.

The field expands to show each title within the *Action* genre:

	A	B	C	D
4		⊟ Action		
5	Row Labels ▾	A Touch of Zen	Drunken Master II	Get Carter
6	Anderson,Jane	41	3	31

2. Click the small – sign that has now appeared to the left of *Action* in cell B4.

The outline collapses back to the genre level:

	A	B	C	D
4		⊞ Action	⊞ Adventure	⊞ Animation
5	Row Labels ▾			
6	Anderson,Jane	199	30	
7	Armstrong,Dan	136	26	22

8 Save your work as *Transactions-4.*

note

Can a Pivot Table be set up to auto-refresh?

While a Pivot Table cannot automatically update (without resorting to custom VBA programming), it is possible to emulate a pivot table design using three simple dynamic array formulas.

You learned about dynamic array formulas in in: *Session Four: Working with Dynamic Arrays.*

The resulting dynamic arrays will then update whenever the source data changes.

I've included a sample file: *Transactions-4 Dynamic Array Emulation* in the sample files set. This workbook contains the pivot table used in this lesson along with an identical emulation of the same pivot table created using three simple dynamic array formulas.

The emulation uses the UNIQUE dynamic array function to create the row and column headers. You learned about the UNIQUE function in: *Lesson 4-6: Create a drop-down list using a UNIQUE function.*

To fill the data area, the emulation uses a SUMIFS function that points to the spilled ranges using the spilled range operator (#). You learned about the SUMIFS function in: *Lesson 3-6: Use the SUMIF and COUNTIF functions to create conditional totals.*

Lesson 9-4: Understand the pivot table data cache

Data sources

Your data source will typically be one of the following:

1. **A single table on a single worksheet.**

   This the most common data source for a pivot table and is the type of data source you've been using up until now.

2. **Several tables (on the same, or different worksheets) joined by primary key/foreign key relationships.**

   You'll learn more about primary and foreign keys later in: *Lesson 11-26: Understand primary and foreign keys.*

3. **A table or view residing in an external relational database such as Access, Oracle or SQL Server.**

   You'll learn more about this type of data source later, in: *Lesson 11-30: Load a query directly into the PivotTable cache.*

Pivot tables do not directly use the data source

When you first create a pivot table, a hidden copy of the data source (called the *pivot table data cache*), is created and held in the computer's memory. This is a specially structured version of the data source that includes many pre-computed subtotals as well as all of the source data.

If you change the source data (for example by adding a new row to a table) the change does not appear in the pivot table until you refresh (create a new copy of) the *pivot table data cache.* You'll see how to refresh the cache later in this lesson.

If you need data to automatically update whenever the source data changes, consider creating an emulation of the pivot table using dynamic array formulas. This will automatically update whenever source data changes because only regular Excel functions are used.

Pivot tables can work without the data source

When you save a workbook containing a pivot table, the *pivot table data cache* is saved along with the workbook, providing several advantages:

1. If your data source is an external database, your pivot table will still work perfectly when the database is not connected. This means that you could (for example) e-mail the workbook to another user that has no access to the database.

2. If your data source was a worksheet, the pivot table will still work perfectly even if the worksheet is deleted.

The downside is that workbooks containing both the source data and the *pivot table data cache* can have huge file sizes as all data is effectively

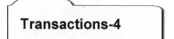

Transactions-4

https://thesmartmethod.com

tip

You can refresh a pivot table more quickly using the right-click method

In this lesson you refreshed the pivot table using the ribbon.

If you right-click inside a pivot table, you'll also see a *Refresh* option on the shortcut menu.

	A	E
4		⊞ Biography
5	Row Labels ▾	
18	Lee,Frank	157

stored twice. For this reason, it is possible to ask Excel not to save the *pivot table data cache* with the workbook in the *PivotTable Options* (as you will see later in this lesson).

Workbooks that use external data (such as the one you will create in: *Lesson 11-30: Load a query directly into the PivotTable cache*), are more efficient (in terms of both file size and use of computer memory) as they save only one copy of the data (the *pivot table data cache*) and do not have to hold both the workbook source data and the *pivot table data cache* in memory at the same time.

1 Open *Transactions-4* from your sample files folder.

This pivot table uses the *Data* table on the *Data* worksheet as its data source. Notice that Frank Lee has sold a total of 157 videos in the *Biography* genre.

2 Change the source data to add ten more sales for Frank Lee in the Biography genre.

1. Click the *Data* worksheet tab.

2. Increase Frank Lee's sale (in cell G2) from 15 units to 25 units.

	D	E	F	G	H
1	Employee	Title	Genre	Qty	Total
2	Lee,Frank	Lawrence of Arabia	Biography	25	122.76

3 Notice that the pivot table does not show any change.

Click the *Pivot Table* worksheet tab. Notice that Frank Lee's *Biography* genre sales remain the same at 157.

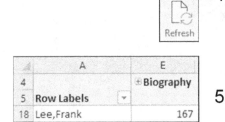

Refresh

4 Refresh the PivotTable data cache and observe the change.

1. Click inside the pivot table to activate it.

2. Click: PivotTable Analyze→Data→Refresh.

Notice that Frank Lee's sales have now updated.

	A	E
4		⊞ Biography
5	Row Labels ▾	
18	Lee,Frank	167

5 Restore Frank Lee's sales (on row 2 of the *Data* table) to the original value (of 15 units) and refresh the pivot table data cache.

6 Examine options relating to the pivot table data cache.

1. Click inside the pivot table to activate it.

2. Click: PivotTable Analyze→ PivotTable→Options→Options.

3. Click the *Data* tab.

Save source data with file: Unchecking this option prevents Excel from saving the *pivot table data cache*. Doing this can result in greatly reduced file sizes.

Enable show details: This option controls whether you can drill-down to see the transactions that were used to calculate any total. For more on this, see: *Lesson 9-2: Create a grouped pivot table report (sidebar)*.

Refresh data when opening the file: Selecting this option refreshes the pivot table data cache when the workbook is opened.

PivotTable Data
- ☑ Save source data with file
- ☑ Enable show details
- ☐ Refresh data when opening the file

Lesson 9-5: Apply a simple filter and sort to a pivot table

1   Open *Transactions-4* from your sample files folder (if it isn't already open).

2   Select the *Pivot Table* worksheet (if it isn't already selected).

3   Click inside the pivot table to display the *PivotTable Fields* task pane.

4   Remove the *Genre* and *Title* column fields.

This was covered in: *Lesson 9-3: Understand pivot table rows and columns.*

5   Click the drop-down arrow next to *Row Labels* in cell A3.

Filter options appear.

These are very similar to the options that you learned how to use in: *Lesson 1-5: Apply a simple filter to a range* and *Lesson 1-6: Apply a top 10 and custom filter to a range.*

6   Filter the pivot table so that only female employees are shown.

1.   Uncheck the check boxes next to each male employee (see sidebar).

2.   Click the *OK* button.

	A	B
3	**Row Labels** .T	**Sum of Qty**
4	Anderson,Jane	1109
5	Ashe,Lucille	1116
6	Carrey,Julia	770
7	Diamond,Elizabeth	1153

Notice the filter icon in cell A3 has changed to indicate that the pivot table has been filtered.

This is a very long winded way to filter out the male employees.

In a real-world workbook you'd probably create a *Gender* column in the source data containing the values **M** or **F**.

You could then filter by gender with a single check box.

7   Sort *Employee* names in Z-A order.

At the moment, the names are sorted in A-Z order.

1.   Right-click on any of the employee names in column A.

2.   Click: Sort→Sort Z to A from the shortcut menu.

**Sidebar checklist:**

- ☐ (Select All)
- ☑ Anderson,Jane
- ☐ Armstrong,Dan
- ☑ Ashe,Lucille
- ☐ Bell,Stephen
- ☐ Bradshaw,John
- ☑ Carrey,Julia
- ☐ Davis,Charles
- ☑ Diamond,Elizabeth
- ☐ Goodman,Paul
- ☐ Hawking,Alfred
- ☐ Hicks,Michael
- ☐ Jennings,John
- ☐ Lee,Frank
- ☑ Manning,Marilyn
- ☑ Newhart,Anna
- ☑ Putin,Julia
- ☐ Richards,Andy
- ☑ Sagan,Jessica
- ☑ Silverstone,Gloria
- ☐ Simpson,Howard
- ☑ Simpson,Meryl
- ☑ Spears,Julie
- ☑ Streep,Margaret
- ☐ West,Chuck

Shortcut menu:

Sort	▶	A↓	Sort A to Z
Filter	▶	Z↓	Sort Z to A
✓ Subtotal "Genre"			More Sort Options...

Transactions-4

note

Filters are not inherited from source data

If the data associated with a pivot table (whether a table, range or named range) has a filter applied to it (or contains subtotals) this will not be carried forward into the pivot table.

If you need the same filter in your pivot table, you must first create the pivot table and then apply the same filter.

Another way to achieve this is to copy the (filtered) data to a new worksheet and then create the pivot table from this subset of the actual data.

A useful technique for copying and pasting filtered data (visible cells) is described in: *Lesson 2-3: Automatically subtotal a range (sidebar).*

	A	B
3	Row Labels	Sum of Qty
4	Newhart,Anna	1081
5	Diamond,Elizabeth	1153
6	Silverstone,Gloria	1040
7	Anderson,Jane	1109
8	Sagan,Jessica	1407
9	Carrey,Julia	770
10	Putin,Julia	1054
11	Spears,Julie	1314
12	Ashe,Lucille	1116
13	Streep,Margaret	1772
14	Manning,Marilyn	1161
15	Simpson,Meryl	822
16	**Grand Total**	**13799**

The pivot table is sorted in Z-A order.

	A	B
3	Row Labels	Sum of Qty
4	Streep,Margaret	1772
5	Spears,Julie	1314
6	Simpson,Meryl	822
7	Silverstone,Gloria	1040
8	Sagan,Jessica	1407
9	Putin,Julia	1054
10	Newhart,Anna	1081

8 Sort *Employee* names by first name.

It isn't possible to automatically sort by first name. To do this, you would need *First Name* to be a different field to *Last Name*.

If there were a lot of names, you could attend to this in the source data by splitting the *Employee* column into two. (You learned how to do this in: *Lesson 2-1: Split fixed width data using Text to Columns* and in *Lesson 3-21: Extract text from delimited strings using the FIND and LEN functions*).

Because there are only twelve names, it will be quicker to manually sort the list.

1. Right-click on any of the employee names in column A.

2. Click: Sort→More Sort Options... from the shortcut menu.

   The *Sort* dialog appears.

3. Click the *Manual* option button.

Sort (Employee)	?	×
Sort options		
⦿ Manual (you can drag items to rearrange them)		

4. Click the *OK* button.

5. Click and drag the border of each *Employee* name to move them to the desired position. Look for the four headed arrow cursor shape before clicking the mouse (sidebar shows sorted order).

11	Manning,Marilyn	1161
12	Diamond,Elizabeth	1153
13	Carrey,Julia	770

9 Remove the filter.

1. Click the filter button at the top right of cell A3.

2. Check the *Select All* check box at the top of the list of names.

3. Click the *OK* button.

10 Save your work as *Transactions-5*.

Lesson 9-6: Use report filter fields

In pre-2007 versions of Excel, report filters were called *Page Fields*.

1   Open *Transactions-5* from your sample files folder (if it isn't already open).

2   Select the *Pivot Table* worksheet (if it isn't already selected).

3   Click inside the pivot table to display the *PivotTable Fields* task pane.

4   Drag the *Genre* field from the field list at the top of the task pane to the *Filters* list below.

	A	B
1	Genre	(All)
2		
3	**Row Labels**	**Sum of Qty**
4	West,Chuck	886
5	Newhart,Anna	1081
6	Diamond,Elizabeth	1153
7	Silverstone,Gloria	1040
8	Anderson,Jane	1109
9	Sagan,Jessica	1407
10	Carrey,Julia	770
11	Putin,Julia	1054
12	Spears,Julie	1314
13	Ashe,Lucille	1116
14	Streep,Margaret	1772
15	Manning,Marilyn	1161
16	Simpson,Meryl	822
17	Simpson,Howard	1190
18	Richards,Andy	998
19	Lee Frank	1645

PivotTable Fields

Choose fields to add to report:

Search

- ☐ Customer
- ☑ Employee
- ☐ Title
- ☑ Genre
- ☑ Qty

Drag fields between areas below:

▼ Filters   ⬛ Columns
Genre ▼

⬛ Rows   Σ Values
Employee ▼   Sum of Qty ▼

☐ Defer Layout Update   Update

Notice that a filter has appeared at the top left of the pivot table (in cells A1 and B1):

	A	B
1	Genre	(All)

The filter currently shows all sales for all genres.

5   Use the report filter field to display sales for the *Comedy* genre.

1.   Click the drop-down list arrow in cell B1.

2.   Click *Comedy* in the drop-down list.

3.   Click the *OK* button.

   Notice that the *Sum of Qty* values now change to only show quantities sold in the *Comedy* genre.

6   Use a report filter field to show sales in the *Comedy* genre for June 2015.

1.   Drag the *Order Date* field from the *PivotTable Fields* task pane down to the *Filters* List.

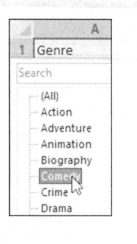

	Filters		Columns
	Genre ▼		
	Order Date ▼		

2. Click the drop-down arrow in cell B2.

	A	B
1	Genre	Comedy ▾Ⓣ
2	Order Date	(All) ▾
3		

3. Type **jun-15** into the *Search* box.

(The search text is not case sensitive so exactly the same results would be displayed if you had typed JUN-15).

jun-15	✕
02-Jun-15	⌃
03-Jun-15	

The *Search* box filters the entries in the list to dates containing the text *jun-15.*

4. Check the *Select Multiple Items* check box.

☑ Select Multiple Items

Every June 2015 date is now checked.

jun-15	✕
☑ (Select All Search Results)	⌃
☐ Add current selection to filter	
☑ 02-Jun-15	
☑ 03-Jun-15	

5. Click the *OK* button.

The total quantities of goods sold in the *Comedy* genre during *June 2015* are now displayed.

	A	B
1	Genre	Comedy ▾Ⓣ
2	Order Date	(Multiple Items) ▾Ⓣ
3		
4	**Row Labels** ▾	**Sum of Qty**
5	West,Chuck	22
6	Silverstone,Gloria	22
7	Anderson,Jane	17
8	Sagan,Jessica	22
9	Putin,Julia	40
10	Spears,Julie	19
11	Ashe,Lucille	15
12	Simpson,Meryl	9
13	Richards,Andy	24
14	Lee,Frank	6
15	Bradshaw,John	43
16	Bell,Stephen	37
17	**Grand Total**	276

Notice that the filter information in cell B2 *(Multiple Items)* gives no information to the user about the filter currently in place. In *Lesson 9-7: Filter a pivot table visually using slicers* you'll discover a much better way of showing the user which multiple item filters are currently active.

7   Save your work as *Transactions-6.*

Lesson 9-7: Filter a pivot table visually using slicers

Unlike report filter fields, slicers show which filters are in place when a multiple-item filter is applied.

Slicers are also very useful for designing touch-screen user interfaces for tablet personal computers.

1 Open *Transactions-6* from your sample files folder (if it isn't already open).

2 Remove all existing fields and filters from the pivot table.

Sometimes you will want to completely clear all filters and fields from a pivot table.

1. Click inside the pivot table to activate it.

2. Click PivotTable Analyze→Actions→Clear→Clear All.

3 Display the *Total* and *Qty* values for each genre.

Click the check-boxes for *Genre, Qty* and *Total* (in that order) in the field list on the *PivotTable Fields* task pane.

4 Change the number format for the values shown in column C to show two decimal places with a comma thousand separator.

You learned how to do this in: *Lesson 9-1: Create a one-dimensional pivot table report from a table.*

5 Change the number format for the values shown in column B to show no decimal places and a comma thousand separator.

You learned how to do this in: *Lesson 9-1: Create a one-dimensional pivot table report from a table.*

6 Change the text in cell A4 to: **Genre**, in cell B4 to: **Sales Qty** and in cell C4 to: **Total Sales**

Click in each cell and type the new text.

Your pivot table should now look like this:

	A	B	C
4	Genre	Sales Qty	Total Sales
5	Action	4,699	37,411.40
6	Adventure	1,149	8,588.03

7 Add slicers to filter by Genre and Customer.

In *Lesson 9-6: Use report filter fields*, you saw how filtering could be done using report filter fields. This time you'll implement the filters using slicers.

1. Click anywhere in the pivot table to activate it.

2. Click: PivotTable Analyze→Filter→Insert Slicer.

The *Insert Slicers* dialog appears.

PivotTable Fields

Choose fields to add to report:

Search

☐ Order No
☐ Order Date
☐ Customer
☐ Employee
☐ Title
☑ Genre
☑ Qty
☑ Total

More Tables...

---

note

Slicers can also be used to visually filter tables

Slicers can be used with tables in exactly the same way that they are used with pivot tables.

Transactions-6

3. Check the *Genre* and *Customer* check boxes.

4. Click the *OK* button.

Two slicers appear on the worksheet.

8 Move and format the slicers so that they have an attractive appearance.

1. Click on the *Genre* slicer to select it and then click and drag the border to move it next to the pivot table.

2. Click: Slicer Tools→Options→Buttons→Columns and type **6** into the text box.

	Columns:	6

3. Re-size the slicer so that all genre names are visible.

4. Click: Slicer→Slicer Styles and select an attractive style.

5. Do the same for the *Customer* slicer, setting the *Columns* to 3.

	A	B	C	D	E	F	G	H	I
3									
4	Genre	Sales Qty	Total Sales	Genre					
5	Action	4,699	37,411.40	Action	Adventure	Animation	Biography	Comedy	Crime
6	Adventure	1,149	8,588.03	Drama	Fantasy	Sci Fi	Thriller		
7	Animation	574	5,098.87						
8	Biography	2,229	17,174.78						
9	Comedy	4,747	37,614.16						
10	Crime	2,960	25,212.68	Customer					
11	Drama	8,439	67,097.47	Addison-Freelander Screen...	AV Supplies		Box Office Supplies		
12	Fantasy	1,252	11,785.28	Cheapo Cheap DVD's Ltd	Cinefocus DVD		Classic Films		
13	Sci Fi	989	7,289.18	Creative Films	Lights-Camera-Action Ltd		Magic Lantern Classic Film ...		
14	Thriller	765	5,514.95	Silver Screen Video	Soft Focus Video Rental		Video Flicks International		
15	Grand Total	27,803	222,786.80						
16									
17									

note

Slicers have a multi-select button ⌄☰

When you want to select more than one item in a slicer you normally hold down the **<Ctrl>** key as you click each item.

This is the preferred technique on a desktop computer but isn't possible on a touchscreen. For this reason, a multi-select button is provided on the top-right corner of slicers.

Click (or touch) the multi-select icon once to enter multi-select mode, select two or more slicer buttons and then click (or touch) the multi-select icon once more to exit multi-select mode.

9 Test the slicers.

1. Click the *Action* button on the *Genre* slicer.

Notice that the pivot table is filtered to only show sales values for the *Action* genre.

2. Click the *Cinefocus DVD* button on the *Customer* slicer and then hold down the **<Ctrl>** key and click the *Classic Films* button.

Notice that only sales to the selected customers for the *Action* genre are now shown.

3. Clear the slicer filters by clicking the *Clear Filter* buttons 🔲 in each slicer's top right corner.

10 Save your work as *Transactions-7*.

Lesson 9-8: Add a timeline control to a pivot table

1   Open *Transactions-7* from your sample files folder (if it isn't already open).

2   Add a timeline control to the pivot table.

1. Click anywhere inside the pivot table to activate it.

2. Click: PivotTable Analyze→Filter→Insert Timeline.

    The *Insert Timelines* dialog appears.

3. Check the *Order Date* check box.

4. Click the *OK* button.

    A *Timeline* control appears on the worksheet.

3   Move the timeline control so that it is neatly placed beneath the two slicers added in the previous lesson.

4   Use the timeline control to show a summary of transactions taking place only in 2014.

1. Click the drop-down arrow in the top right corner of the timeline control.

note

You cannot add a timeline control to all pivot tables

Before inserting a timeline control, Excel will make sure that there is at least one column in the source data that contains valid date values that are formatted as dates.

Excel will not allow a timeline control to be added if this is not the case.

Order...							🏮
All Periods						MONTHS	
	2016					YEARS	
JN	JUL	AUG	SEP	OCT	NOV	QUARTERS	
						✓ MONTHS	
◀						DAYS	

You are now able to select *YEARS, QUARTERS, MONTHS or DAYS.*

2. Select *YEARS*.

    The three years 2014, 2015 and 2016 are shown in the timeline control.

3. Click on the 2014 button to select sales in the year 2014.

Order...			🏮
All Periods			YEARS ˅
2014	2015	2016	
◀			▶

Only sales that occurred in 2014 are now shown in the pivot table.

Transactions-7

5   Use the timeline to show a summary of transactions occurring in 2014 and 2015.

Hover the mouse cursor over the 2014 button.

Notice that a sizing handle has appeared on the right-hand side of the button.

Click and drag the right-hand border of the button so that both the 2014 and 2015 buttons are selected.

2014	2015	2016

Only sales that occurred in 2014 or 2015 are now shown in the pivot table.

6   Use the timeline to show a summary of transactions occurring in the period January 2014 to June 2015.

1. Click the drop-down arrow in the top right corner of the timeline control and select *MONTHS* from the drop-down menu.

2. Widen the timeline control so that you can see the months JAN 2014 to JUN 2015.

3. Click on JAN and then drag the right-hand border of the button so that months JAN 2014 to JUN 2015 are selected.

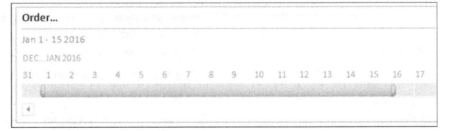

Only sales that occurred between January 2014 and June 2015 are now shown in the pivot table.

7   Use the timeline control to show a summary of all transactions occurring between 1ˢᵗ Jan 2016 and 15ᵗʰ Jan 2016.

Select *DAYS* from the drop-down menu in the top right-hand corner of the timeline and select the days: 1st JAN 2016 to 15th JAN 2016

The pivot table will now only summarize transactions occurring within this date range.

8   Save your work as *Transactions-8.*

note

Creating Years, Months, Days and Quarters from a date value

Year

The YEAR function is covered in: *Lesson 3-8: Understand common date functions.*

Month as a string

The TEXT function is covered in *Lesson 3-19: Use the TEXT function to format numerical values as strings.*

The custom format code: "mmm" formats a date as a three character text value (such as *Jan*). The *Essential Skills* book in this series extensively covers the (rather cryptic) formatting codes available in Excel.

Day

The DAY function is covered in: *Lesson 3-8: Understand common date functions.*

Quarter

1. The month is first returned as a number (1-12) using the MONTH function (covered in: *Lesson 3-8: Understand common date functions*).

2. The number of the month returned is then divided by three. For example, May would return 5/3 = 2.666.

3. The ROUNDUP function is used to round the number up to the nearest whole number. This returns the correct quarter (1-4).

The completed formula can be seen in the *Data* worksheet:

=ROUNDUP(MONTH([@Date])/3,0)

Lesson 9-9: Use slicers to create a custom timeline

In *Lesson 9-8: Add a timeline control to a pivot table,* you learned how to use a timeline control. While the timeline control offers a quick and convenient way to add a timeline, you are unable to significantly customize its appearance. In this lesson you'll create the same timeline functionality using slicers to provide a more elegant user interface.

Before you can add a date-driven interface to a pivot table you will need to create fields in the underlying data table for *Year, Month, Day* and *Quarter*. This has already been done in the sample file for this session:

Before beginning this lesson, you may find it useful to study the formulas used to create these fields from the *Date* field. If you do not understand how these formulas work, refer to the sidebar for more information.

1   Open *Executive Summary-1* from your sample files folder (if it isn't already open).

2   Add slicers to the pivot table for *Year, Quarter, Month* and *Day*.

You learned how to do this in: *Lesson 9-7: Filter a pivot table visually using slicers.*

3   Format the slicers so that they look the same as the screen grab at the bottom of the facing page.

You learned how to do this in: *Lesson 9-7: Filter a pivot table visually using slicers.*

Notice that a *Year* slicer has been included even though the underlying data only has a single year (2015).

When you use slicers to create a timeline, it is good practice to always include a *Year* slicer because you can never be sure that more data will not be added to the underlying data table.

For example, if 2016 sales data were added to the table, selecting *Jan* would show sales for both Jan 2015 and Jan 2016 if the *Year* slicer was not included.

4   Use the slicers to show sales for the first two quarters of 2015 in the *Action, Animation and Comedy* genres.

1.   Click the *1* button in the *Quarter* slicer and then hold down the **<Ctrl>** key and click the *2* button.

Executive Summary-1

Notice that the months Jan-Jun are now selected in the *Month* slicer.

OR

Click the *Jan* button in the *Month* slicer and then hold down the **<Shift>** key and click the *Jun* button.

Month				🗓 🏷
Jan	Feb	Mar	Apr	May
Jun	Jul	Aug	Sep	Oct
Nov	Dec			

Notice that the 1 and 2 buttons are now selected in the *Quarter* slicer

2. Click the *Action* button in the *Genre* slicer and then hold down the **<Ctrl>** key and click the *Animation* and *Comedy* buttons.

Sales are now shown for the first two quarters of 2015 in the *Action, Comedy* and *Animation* genres.

	A	B	C	D	E	F	G	H	I	J	K	L	M
2													
3	Genre	Sales Qty	Total Sales		Year			Quarter					
4	Action	890	6,916.98		2015			1	2	3	4		
5	Animation	143	1,297.74										
6	Comedy	1,255	10,103.79										
7	Grand Total	2,288	18,318.51		Month								
8					Jan	Feb	Mar	Apr	May				
9													
10					Jun	Jul	Aug	Sep	Oct				
11													
12					Nov	Dec							
13													
14					Day								
15													
16					1	2	3	4	5	6	7		
17					8	9	10	11	12	13	14		
18					15	16	17	18	19	20	21		
19													
20					22	23	24	25	26	27	28		
21					29	30	31						
22													
23					Genre								
24					Action	Adventure		Animation		Biography		Comedy	
25													
26					Crime	Drama		Fantasy		Sci Fi		Thriller	
27													
28													
29					Customer								
30					Addison-Freelander Scr...		AV Supplies		Box Office Supplies				
31													
32					Cheapo Cheap DVD's Ltd		Cinefocus DVD		Classic Films				
33					Creative Films		Lights-Camera-Action Ltd		Magic Lantern Classic Fi...				
34					Silver Screen Video		Soft Focus Video Rental		Video Flicks International				
35													

5 Save your work as *Executive Summary-2*.

note

Report filter fields are not supported by OLAP pivot tables

Later, in: *Lesson 12-7: Understand OLAP pivot tables,* you'll learn about a new type of pivot table called an *OLAP pivot table.*

OLAP pivot tables are created in a different way to the regular pivot tables you work with in this session.

Regular pivot tables can do some things that OLAP pivot tables are not capable of. Conversely, OLAP pivot tables have some extra features that regular pivot tables do not have.

Report filter fields are one of those features that are not supported by OLAP pivot tables.

Lesson 9-10: Use report filter fields to automatically create multiple pages

In this lesson, you will cater for the following scenario:

You have been asked to print out a sales listing for each employee. This involves printing a total of 23 separate reports.

It is easy, but time consuming, to print each sheet manually. You would need to perform 23 filter and print operations. Surely there's a better way?

Of course there is. You can use a report filter to automate the whole task and print all 23 reports in one operation.

1   Open *Transactions-8* from your sample files folder.

2   Select the *Pivot Table* worksheet (if it isn't already selected).

3   Remove all filters and fields from the pivot table.

There's a quick way to remove all filters and fields from a pivot table. This is very useful when you want to start again with an empty pivot table.

1.   Click inside the pivot table to activate it.

2.   Click: PivotTable Analyze→Actions→Clear→ Clear All.

4   Change the fields displayed by the pivot table so that they match the following:

▼ Filters		▮▮ Columns	
Employee	▼	Σ Values	▼
▤ Rows		Σ Values	
Genre	▼	Sum of Qty	▼
		Sum of Total	▼

You learned how to do this in: *Lesson 9-3: Understand pivot table rows and columns.* Note that the ⌞ Σ Values ▼ ⌟ field automatically appears in the *Columns* list when you add more than one field to the *Values* list.

Your pivot table now looks like this:

⏴	A	B	C
2	Employee	(All) ▾	
3			
4	Row Labels ▾	Sum of Qty	Sum of Total
5	Action	4699	37411.4
6	Adventure	1149	8588.03

5   Create separate worksheets detailing each employee's sales.

1.   Click anywhere within the pivot table.

Transactions-8

2. Click: PivotTable Analyze→PivotTable→Options→
    Show Report Filter Pages…

The *Show Report Filter Pages* dialog appears.

Show Report Filter Pages	?	X
Show all report filter pages of:		
Employee		
	OK	Cancel

Because there is only one report filter, there's only one choice.

If you had multiple filters, you could choose which filter you wanted to use.

3. Click the *OK* button.

Something amazing happens.

24 worksheets are instantly created, one for each employee.

◄ ►	Anderson, Jane	Armstrong, Dan	Ashe, Lucille

Here's Jane Anderson's sheet:

	A	B	C
1	Employee	Anderson, Jane ⊤	
2			
3	Row Labels ▾	Sum of Qty	Sum of Total
4	Action	199	1556.48
5	Adventure	30	257.29
6	Biography	134	1046

You can see that it contains a copy of the original pivot table with a filter set for *Anderson, Jane.*

6   Print preview all worksheets.

1. Click on the first employee's tab (Anderson, Jane).

2. Use the worksheet scroll bar buttons so that the last employee's tab (West, Chuck) is visible.

3. Hold down the **<Shift>** key.

4. Click on the last employee's tab (West, Chuck).

    You have now selected all of the employee worksheets (you don't want to print the *Pivot Table* or *Data* worksheets).

5. Click: File→Print.

    Notice that *Print Active Sheets* is selected by default.

    Notice the preview pane. All employee sheets will be printed.

Settings	
▦ Print Active Sheets	▾
Only print the active sheets	

6. Click the *Back Button* ⊖ to return to the worksheet.

7   Save your work as *Multiple Sheets-1.*

Lesson 9-11: Format a pivot table using PivotTable styles

In: *Lesson 1-14: Format a table using table styles and convert a table into a range,* you learned how to use a built-in style to format an Excel table. PivotTable styles are used in a similar way.

1   Open *Transactions-8* from your sample files folder.

2   Remove all existing fields and filters from the pivot table.

   1.   Select the *Pivot Table* worksheet.

   2.   Click inside the pivot table to activate it.

   3.   Click: PivotTable Analyze→Actions→Clear→ Clear All.

3   Delete the three slicers from the pivot table.

Click on each slicer and then press the **<Delete>** key.

4   Select the fields shown below.

▼ Filters		⦀ Columns	
		Genre	▼
⦀ Rows		Σ Values	
Employee	▼	Sum of Total	▼

5   Filter to only show the genres: *Action, Adventure* and *Animation* for employees: *Dan Armstrong, Julie Spears* and *Chuck West.*

You learned how to do this in: *Lesson 9-5: Apply a simple filter and sort to a pivot table.*

	A	B	C	D	E
4	Sum of Total	Column Labels .T			
5	Row Labels .T	Action	Adventure	Animation	Grand Total
6	Armstrong,Dan	1199.7	195.56	218.1	1613.36
7	Spears,Julie	1032.11	284.58	109.37	1426.06
8	West,Chuck	861.84	44.77	677.02	1583.63
9	Grand Total	3093.65	524.91	1004.49	4623.05

6   Apply the PivotTable style: *Light 17.*

Click: Design→PivotTable Styles→ Light→Light Orange, Pivot Style Light 17.

Light Orange, Pivot Style Light 17

	A	B	C	D	E
4	Sum of Total	Column Labels ⊤			
5	Row Labels ⊤	Action	Adventure	Animation	Grand Total
6	Armstrong,Dan	1199.7	195.56	218.1	1613.36
7	Spears,Julie	1032.11	284.58	109.37	1426.06
8	West,Chuck	861.84	44.77	677.02	1583.63
9	Grand Total	3093.65	524.91	1004.49	4623.05

7 Enable *Banded Rows.*

Check: Design→PivotTable Style Options→
Banded Rows.

☑ Row Headers   ☑ Banded Rows

☑ Column Headers   ☐ Banded Columns

PivotTable Style Options

The pivot table changes to show colored shading on alternate rows.

	A	B	C	D	E
4	Sum of Total	Column Labels ⊤			
5	Row Labels ⊤	Action	Adventure	Animation	Grand Total
6	Armstrong,Dan	1199.7	195.56	218.1	1613.36
7	Spears,Julie	1032.11	284.58	109.37	1426.06
8	West,Chuck	861.84	44.77	677.02	1583.63
9	Grand Total	3093.65	524.91	1004.49	4623.05

The colored bands can help the eye to track across rows, especially when a pivot table is printed.

8 Disable *Banded Rows* and enable *Banded Columns.*

Check: Design→PivotTable Style Options→
Banded Columns.

	A	B	C	D	E
4	Sum of Total	Column Labels ⊤			
5	Row Labels ⊤	Action	Adventure	Animation	Grand Total
6	Armstrong,Dan	1199.7	195.56	218.1	1613.36
7	Spears,Julie	1032.11	284.58	109.37	1426.06
8	West,Chuck	861.84	44.77	677.02	1583.63
9	Grand Total	3093.65	524.91	1004.49	4623.05

9 Disable *Banded Columns.*

Clear the *Banded Columns* check box.

10 Understand the two other *PivotTable Style Options.*

The other two options in the *PivotTable Style Options* group are: *Row Headers* and *Column Headers*.

In the *Light 17* style, the column headers are shown in a contrasting color. The *Column Headers* check box allows you to switch this color off.

Some of the other styles also show row headers (cells A6:A8) in a contrasting color. If you were using this type of style, you could switch this color off with the *Row Headers* check box.

11 Save your work as *Transactions-9.*

Lesson 9-12: Create a custom pivot table style

In: *Lesson 1-15: Create a custom table style,* you learned how to create a custom style for an Excel table. Pivot table custom styles are applied in a similar way.

1   Open *Transactions-9* from your sample files folder (if it isn't already open).

2   Remove the existing style.

    1.   Click the pivot table to activate it.

    2.   Click: Design→PivotTable Styles→ Light→None.

3   Create a custom pivot table style called *Corporate* by duplicating the *Medium8* built in style.

You'll usually find that modifying a duplicate of an existing style is easier than creating a style from scratch.

    1.   Right-click on:

       Design→PivotTable Styles→
       Medium→White, Pivot Style Medium 8

    2.   Click *Duplicate...* from the shortcut menu.

The *Modify PivotTable Style* dialog appears.

Transactions-9

Notice that some of the *Table Elements* are shown in bold face. These are the elements that have had formatting applied to them:

Table Element:

Whole Table
Report Filter Labels
Report Filter Values
First Column Stripe
Second Column Stripe
First Row Stripe
Second Row Stripe
First Column
Header Row

3. Type the name **Corporate** into the *Name* text box.

Modify PivotTable Style

Name: Corporate

4. Click the *OK* button to dismiss the dialog.

4 Apply the new *Corporate* style to the pivot table.

Click: Design→PivotTable Styles→
Custom→Corporate.

You'll see the new *Corporate* style at the top of the *PivotTable Styles* gallery in a new group called *Custom*.

5 Modify the *Corporate* style so that it shows the *Grand Total* column in bold face.

1. Right-click on:

Design→PivotTable Styles→
Custom→Corporate.

2. Click *Modify…* from the shortcut menu.

3. Select *Grand Total Column* from the *Table Element* list.

4. Click the *Format* button.

5. Select the *Font* tab.

6. Select the *Font style:* Bold.

7. Click the *OK* button.

8. Click the *OK* button again.

The *Grand Total* column is now shown in bold face.

	A	B	C	D	E
4	Sum of Total	Column Labels			
5	Row Labels	Action	Adventure	Animation	Grand Total
6	Armstrong,Dan	1199.7	195.56	218.1	**1613.36**
7	Spears,Julie	1032.11	284.58	109.37	**1426.06**
8	West,Chuck	861.84	44.77	677.02	**1583.63**
9	**Grand Total**	3093.65	524.91	1004.49	**4623.05**

6 Save your work as *Transactions-10*.

note

You can change the default Pivot Table report layout

If you would like the default pivot table report layout to be different to the *compact form layout,* you can set a new default like this:

1. Setup the pivot table with the layout options you would like to be the new default and click anywhere inside it.

2. Click: File→Options→ Data→Data options.

3. Click the *Edit Default Layout...* button .

4. Click the *Import* button.

The settings from the existing pivot table will now become the default for any future pivot tables.

Lesson 9-13: Understand pivot table report layouts

1 Open *Transactions-10* from your sample files folder (if it isn't already open).

2 Remove all existing fields from the pivot table by dragging them up into the *PivotTable Fields* list.

This is another way to remove selected fields. You can also drag and drop them onto the worksheet grid area if you wish.

It's important to realize that when you drag a field back to the *PivotTable Fields* list, you do not clear any filter conditions associated with the field. You can still see a filter icon next to each filtered field (see sidebar).

3 Select the fields shown below.

You learned how to do this in: *Lesson 9-3: Understand pivot table rows and columns.*

The pivot table is shown in *compact form layout.* This is the default layout.

	A	B
4	Row Labels	Sum of Total
5	Armstrong,Dan	1613.36
6	Action	1199.7
7	Adventure	195.56
8	Animation	218.1
9	Spears,Julie	1426.06
10	Action	1032.11

This layout is useful when you need the report to take up the minimum amount of space on screen or paper.

Subsidiary fields are only slightly indented from their parent field.

Transactions-10

note

The Repeat All Item Labels option

Sometimes you may want to copy and paste values from a pivot table into a regular range. This can be of particular use when you want to create a regular chart from data summarized by a pivot table.

The best way to do this is to use *Tabular Form* layout in conjunction with the *Repeat All Item Labels* option.

Here's how you could achieve this with this lesson's sample file:

1. Click inside the pivot table to activate it.

2. Click: Design→Layout→ Report Layout→ Show in Tabular Form

3. Click: Design→Layout→ Report Layout→ Repeat All Item Labels.

4. Click: Design→Layout→ Subtotals→ Do Not Show Subtotals.

5. Click: Design→Layout→ Grand Totals→ Off for Rows and Columns.

Instead of only showing the *Employee Name* once (in column A) it is now shown on every row in the column.

Subtotals and *Grand Totals* have also been removed.

You now have a format that is easy to copy and paste into a normal range. The best *Paste Special* option would be: *Paste Values and Number Formats:*

◉ Values and number formats

4   Change the report layout to *Outline Form*.

Click:

Design→Layout→
Report Layout→Show in Outline Form

	A	B	C
4	Employee ⏷	Genre ⏷	Sum of Total
5	⊟ Armstrong,Dan		1613.36
6		Action	1199.7
7		Adventure	195.56
8		Animation	218.1
9	⊟ Spears,Julie		1426.06
10		Action	1032.11

Outline Form is the classic pivot table layout that was the default in pre-2007 versions of Excel.

Outline Form takes up more space but is more readable as each field has its own column label.

5   Change the report layout to *Tabular Form*.

Click:

Design→Layout→
Report Layout→Show in Tabular Form

	A	B	C
4	Employee ⏷	Genre ⏷	Sum of Total
5	⊟ Armstrong,Dan	Action	1199.7
6		Adventure	195.56
7		Animation	218.1
8	Armstrong,Dan Total		1613.36
9	⊟ Spears,Julie	Action	1032.11
10		Adventure	284.58
11		Animation	109.37
12	Spears,Julie Total		1426.06
13	⊟ West,Chuck	Action	861.84
14		Adventure	44.77
15		Animation	677.02
16	West,Chuck Total		1583.63
17	Grand Total		4623.05

This layout is very easy to read because it is similar to a regular Excel table with totals shown at the bottom of each column.

This layout is also very useful when you want to copy the values in a Pivot Table into a regular range (especially when combined with the *Repeat All Item Labels option* – see sidebar).

6   Save your work as *Transactions-11*.

Lesson 9-14: Add/remove subtotals and apply cell styles to pivot table fields

1 Open *Transactions-11* from your sample files folder (if it isn't already open).

2 Apply a Filter to show only the *Biography* and *Thriller* genres.

You learned how to do this in: *Lesson 9-5: Apply a simple filter and sort to a pivot table.*

3 Add the *Title* field to the pivot table as a third-level row label.

Drag the *Title* field from the *PivotTable Fields* task pane to the *Rows* list.

▼ Filters	▦ Columns
▦ Rows	Σ Values
Employee ▼	Sum of Total ▼
Genre ▼	
Title ▼	

4 If necessary, expand all of the *Genre* fields to show all *Titles*.

You learned how to do this in: *Lesson 9-2: Create a grouped pivot table report.*

Because the pivot table layout is set to *Tabular Form,* subtotals are displayed for all subsidiary groups. Both *Employee* and *Genre* are showing subtotals.

	A	B	C	D
4	Employee ⬇	Genre ⬇	Title ▼	Sum of Total
5	⊟Armstrong,Dan	⊟Biography	Bonnie and Clyde	96.53
6			Lawrence of Arabia	230.31
7			Raging Bull	329.88
8			Schindler's List	9.14
9		Biography Total		665.86
10		⊟Thriller	Psycho	51.44
11		Thriller Total		51.44
12	Armstrong,Dan Total			717.3

5 Format the *Genre* subtotal fields using the *Total* cell style.

1. Hover the mouse cursor over the left edge of the *Biography Total* label in cell B9.

2. Make sure you see the black arrow cursor shape and then click to select.

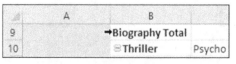

	A	B	
9		➡Biography Total	
10		⊟Thriller	Psycho

Transactions-11

Notice that when you select the field all *Genre subtotal* cells are selected.

3. Click: Home→Styles→Cell Styles→Total.

The *Total* style is applied to all *Genre subtotal* fields.

	A	B	C	D
4	Employee	Genre	Title	Sum of Total
5	Armstrong,Dan	Biography	Bonnie and Clyde	96.53
6			Lawrence of Arabia	230.31
7			Raging Bull	329.88
8			Schindler's List	9.14
9		Biography Total		665.86
10		Thriller	Psycho	51.44
11		Thriller Total		51.44
12	Armstrong,Dan Total			717.3
13	Spears,Julie	Biography	Bonnie and Clyde	58.2

6 **Remove the *Genre* subtotals.**

1. Right-click on any of the genres in column B.

2. Click Subtotal "Genre" from the shortcut menu.

The *Genre* subtotal fields are removed.

7 **Remove the *Grand Total.***

Click: Design→Layout→
Grand Totals→Off for Rows and Columns.

8 **Save your work as *Transactions-12.***

Lesson 9-15: Display multiple summations within a single pivot table

It is possible to show the same *Value* field many times in the same pivot table.

This is useful when you need to display different summations (such as Average, Sum and Max) on a single pivot table.

1   Open *Transactions-12* from your sample files folder (if it isn't already open).

2   Remove the *Genre* and *Title* fields from the *Rows* list.

3   Add two more *Total* fields to the *Values* list.

Drag the *Total* field from the *PivotTable Fields* pane to the *Values* pane twice.

▼ Filters	▥ Columns
	Σ Values ▾

▤ Rows	Σ Values
Employee ▾	Sum of Total ▾
	Sum of Total2 ▾
	Sum of Total3 ▾

4   Change the new totals to show *Average* sales and *Maximum* sales for each employee.

1.   Right-click anywhere in column C within the pivot table.

2.   Click *Value Field Settings…* from the shortcut menu.

3.   Select *Average* in the *Summarize value field by* list.

Value Field Settings ? ✕

Source Name: Total

Custom Name: Average of Total2

Summarize Values By   Show Values As

Summarize value field by

Choose the type of calculation that you want to use to summarize data from the selected field

Sum
Count
Average
Max
Min
Product

Number Format   OK   Cancel

4.   Click the *OK* button.

Transactions-12

5. Use the same technique to make the *Sum of Total3* field display the maximum (*Max*) value.

	A	B	C	D
4	Employee	Sum of Total	Average of Total2	Max of Total3
5	Armstrong,Dan	7880.51	96.10378049	248.73
6	Spears,Julie	10683.14	99.84242991	243.85
7	West,Chuck	6847.74	96.44704225	239.05

5 Format the *Average of Total2* field so that it displays two decimal places.

1. Right-click on any value in column C within the pivot table.

2. Click *Number Format…* from the shortcut menu.

3. Select the *Number* category and set two decimal places.

> Number
>
> Category:
> General
> Number
> Currency
> Accounting
> Date
>
> Sample
>
> Decimal places: 2

4. Click the *OK* button.

	A	B	C	D
4	Employee	Sum of Total	Average of Total2	Max of Total3
5	Armstrong,Dan	7880.51	96.10	248.73
6	Spears,Julie	10683.14	99.84	243.85
7	West,Chuck	6847.74	96.45	239.05

6 Add a *Grand Total*.

Click anywhere inside the pivot table to activate it.

Click: Design→Layout→
Grand Totals→On for Columns Only.

	A	B	C	D
4	Employee	Sum of Total	Average of Total2	Max of Total3
5	Armstrong,Dan	7880.51	96.10	248.73
6	Spears,Julie	10683.14	99.84	243.85
7	West,Chuck	6847.74	96.45	239.05
8	Grand Total	25411.39	97.74	248.73

7 Save your work as *Transactions-13*.

tip

It is often easier to add calculated fields to the source data

When the data source is a worksheet (as is the case in this lesson) it is usually faster and more efficient to add the calculated field to the source data on the worksheet.

You will then see the new field appear in the *PivotTable Fields* list when you refresh the pivot table.

You learned how to refresh a pivot table in: *Lesson 9-4: Understand the pivot table data cache.*

Later, in: *Lesson 11-30: Load a query directly into the PivotTable cache,* you will learn how to connect a pivot table to an Access database.

When working with external data sources, the calculated fields you need may not exist in the data source.

The calculated fields you have learned about in this lesson provide a useful solution to this problem.

Lesson 9-16: Add a calculated field to a pivot table

1 Open *Transactions-13* from your sample files folder (if it isn't already open).

2 Remove the *Average of Total2* and *Max of Total3* fields.

   You learned how to do this in: *Lesson 9-3: Understand pivot table rows and columns.*

	A	B
3		
4	**Employee**	**Sum of Total**
5	Armstrong,Dan	7880.51
6	Spears,Julie	10683.14
7	West,Chuck	6847.74
8	**Grand Total**	25411.39

3 Format the *Sum of Total* field to show a comma thousand separator.

   1. Right-click any of the values in column B within the pivot table.

   2. Click *Number Format…* from the shortcut menu.

   3. Click the *Number* category.

   4. Check the *Use 1000 Separator (,)* check box.

   5. Click *OK.*

4 Add a calculated field called *Bonus* that will calculate 3% of total sales.

   1. Click: PivotTable Analyze→Calculations→ Fields, Items & Sets→Calculated Field…

      The *Insert Calculated Field* dialog appears.

   2. Type **Bonus** into the *Name* text box.

Insert Calculated Field	
Name:	Bonus

   3. Click in the *Formula* text box and remove the zero, leaving only an = sign.

Formula:	=

   4. Select *Total* in the *Fields* list and then click the *Insert Field* button.

      The word **Total** is added to the formula.

Formula:	= Total

   5. Type ***3%** to complete the formula.

Formula:	= Total*3%

Transactions-11

tip

Creating a custom header row

In this lesson, you switched off the field headers in order to remove the filter button from cell A4. This had the side-effect of also removing the word *Employee* from cell A4. It isn't then possible to type any text into cell A4.

If you wanted to keep the *Employee* label but suppress the filter button, you would need to hide row 4 and then re-create the headers in row 3. Here's how you could do this:

1. Copy cells A4:C4 into cells A3:C3.

2. To hide row 4, right-click the row header (the number 4 on the left of the row) and then click *Hide* from the shortcut menu.

3. Type: **Employee** into cell A3.

	A	B
2		
3	**Employee**	**Sales**
5	Armstrong,Dan	7,880.51
6	Spears,Julie	10,683.14
7	West,Chuck	6,847.74
8	**Grand Total**	**25,411.39**

6. Click the *OK* button.

A new field called *Bonus* has now appeared in the *PivotTable Fields* task pane and a *Sum of Bonus* field has appeared in column C.

	A	B	C
4	Employee ▾	Sum of Total	Sum of Bonus
5	Armstrong,Dan	7,880.51	236.42
6	Spears,Julie	10,683.14	320.49
7	West,Chuck	6,847.74	205.43
8	**Grand Total**	**25,411.39**	**762.34**

5   Change the names at the top of columns B and C to *Sales* and *Bonus Due*.

1. Click cell B4.

2. Type the new name: **Sales**

3. Press the **<Tab>** key to save the value and move to cell C4.

4. Type: **Bonus Due** into cell C4.

6   Remove the *Field Header* (this is currently shown in row 4).

The pivot table looks untidy because cell A4 includes a filter button. If you wanted to print the pivot table, you would also want to remove the filter button.

	A	B	C
3			
4	Employee ▾	Sales	Bonus Due
5	Armstrong,Dan	7,880.51	236.42

Click: PivotTable Analyze→Show→Field Headers.

The three items in the *Show* group are toggle buttons which allow you to show and hide different pivot table artefacts.

The pivot table is now well formatted.

	A	B	C
3			
4		Sales	Bonus Due
5	Armstrong,Dan	7,880.51	236.42
6	Spears,Julie	10,683.14	320.49
7	West,Chuck	6,847.74	205.43
8	**Grand Total**	**25,411.39**	**762.34**

The filter button has disappeared, but so has the *Employee* label.

It is possible to show the *Employee* label without the filter icon. See sidebar for a special technique you can use to make this possible.

7   Save your work as *Transactions-14*.

note

Calculated items are not supported by OLAP pivot tables

Later, in: *Lesson 12-7: Understand OLAP pivot tables,* you'll learn about a new type of pivot table called an *OLAP pivot table.*

Calculated items are not supported by OLAP pivot tables. They provide an alternative (and more powerful) replacement called *calculated measures.*

You'll learn about these later, in: *Lesson 13-3: Create a DAX calculated measure.*

Lesson 9-17: Add a calculated item to a pivot table

One *field* will usually consist of several *items*. For example, the *Genre* field consists of items such as *Drama, Comedy, Action, Biography* etc.

If you wanted to show a sales target of **Sales + 10%**, you'd simply create a calculated field (as described in: *Lesson 9-16: Add a calculated field to a pivot table*).

Sometimes you will want to perform a calculation upon an arbitrary group of items. In this lesson's example, you are interested in combined sales for the *Drama, Comedy* and *Action* genres, as they are your top sellers.

Calculated items provide a solution to this problem. In this lesson, you'll add a calculated item to find the total sales in these genres.

1 Open *Transactions-14* from your sample files folder (if it isn't already open).

2 Clear all filters and fields from the pivot table.

Click: PivotTable Analyze→Actions→Clear→Clear All.

3 Add the following fields to the pivot table:

▼ Filters		▥ Columns	
☰ Rows		Σ Values	
Genre	▼	Sum of Total	▼

4 Format the *Sum of Total* field to show two decimal places with a thousand comma separator.

1. Right-click on any of the values in column B within the pivot table.

2. Click *Number Format* from the shortcut menu.

3. Click the *Number* category.

4. Check the *Use 1000 Separator (,)* check box.

5. Click the *OK* button.

Your pivot table now looks like the one shown in the sidebar.

	A	B
4		**Sum of Total**
5	Action	37,411.40
6	Adventure	8,588.03
7	Animation	5,098.87
8	Biography	17,174.78
9	Comedy	37,614.16
10	Crime	25,212.68
11	Drama	67,097.47
12	Fantasy	11,785.28
13	Sci Fi	7,289.18
14	Thriller	5,514.95
15	**Grand Total**	**222,786.80**

5 Add a calculated item to show total sales for the genres: *Drama, Comedy and Action.*

1. Click any pivot table cell in column A.

2. Click: PivotTable Analyze→Calculations→ Fields, Items & Sets→Calculated Item...

The *Insert Calculated Item* dialog appears.

This is very similar to the *Insert Calculated Field* dialog. The dialog can be confusing because it shows many fields and items that would not be valid for the *Genre* field. They are not grayed out as you would expect.

Transactions-14

3. Name the calculated item: **Drama, Comedy & Action**

4. Select the *Genre* field and the *Drama* item and then click the *Insert Item* button.

   The formula changes to include the *Drama* item.

   Formula: =Drama

5. Type a **+** operator into the formula.

   Formula: =Drama+

6. Add the *Comedy* and *Action* items in the same way so that your formula is the same as the following:

   Formula: =Drama+Comedy+Action

7. Click the *OK* button.

   A total for *Drama, Comedy & Action* appears at the bottom of the pivot table.

	A	B
14	Thriller	5,514.95
15	Drama, Comedy & Action	142,123.03
16	**Grand Total**	**364,909.83**

   Notice that this addition has corrupted the *Grand Total* as *Drama, Comedy & Action* are now included in the *Grand Total* twice.

6 **Filter the individual *Drama*, *Comedy* and *Action* fields so that they are no longer shown or included in the *Grand Total*.**

   Because the *Field Headers* are currently switched off, you cannot apply a filter.

   1. Click: PivotTable Analyze→Show→Field Headers.

   2. The *Genre* field header appears in cell A4.

	A	B
4	Genre ▼	**Sum of Total**
5	Action	**37,411.40**

   3. Click the drop-down arrow to the right of cell A4.

   4. Remove the individual *Drama*, *Comedy* and *Action* items by unchecking their check boxes.

   5. Click: *OK*.

   The *Grand Total* is now correct.

	A	B
11	Thriller	5,514.95
12	Drama, Comedy & Action	142,123.03
13	**Grand Total**	**222,786.80**

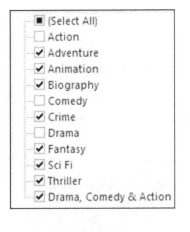

7 **Save your work as *Transactions-15*.**

Lesson 9-18: Group by text

In *Lesson 9-17: Add a calculated item to a pivot table*, you used a calculated item to show a group total for the *Action, Comedy & Drama* genres.

Another solution to this requirement would be to create a *group* for these three genres. The pivot table could then show group totals.

You'll push things a little further in this lesson by placing each of the genres into three groups:

- Action, Comedy & Drama
- Crime, Biography & Fantasy
- Adventure, Sci Fi, Thriller & Animation

1 Open *Transactions-15* from your sample files folder (if it isn't already open).

2 Remove all of the existing fields and filters from the pivot table (including the calculated item added in the last lesson).

You'll often want to remove all items from your pivot table to start again. To do this, click:

PivotTable Analyze→Actions→Clear→Clear All

3 Add the following fields to the pivot table.

4 Format the *Sum of Qty* field so that it shows 0 decimal places and a comma separator for thousands.

1. Right-click anywhere in column B within the pivot table.

2. Click *Number Format…* from the shortcut menu.

3. Click the *Number* category.

4. Set 0 decimal places with a thousand separator.

Decimal places: 0

☑ Use 1000 Separator (,)

5. Click the *OK* button.

5 Add a group for the *Action, Comedy* and *Drama* genres.

1. Click on the *Drama* field in column A (cell A11).

2. Hold down the **<Ctrl>** key and then click on the *Comedy* (A9) and *Action* (A5) fields in column A.

Cells A11, A9 and A5 are now selected.

3. Right-click on any of the selected cells and click *Group* from the shortcut menu.

The fields are grouped:

Transactions-15

	A	B	C
4	Genre2 ▼	Genre ▼	Sum of Qty
5	⊟ Group1	Action	4,699
6		Comedy	4,747
7		Drama	8,439

note

You can also group selected fields using the Ribbon

The right-click method is usually the fastest way to group but you can also use the Ribbon command:

PivotTable Analyze→ Group→Group Selection

6 Change the *Genre2* label to: **Category** and the *Group1* label to: **Action, Comedy & Drama**

The default names are not very descriptive. Single-click (be careful not to double-click) on each field (cells A4 and A5) and then type in the new labels.

	A	B	C
4	**Category** ▼	**Genre** ▼	**Sum of Qty**
5	⊟ **Action, Comedy & Drama**	Action	**4,699**
6		Comedy	**4,747**

7 Create the *Crime, Biography & Fantasy* group and the *Adventure, Sci Fi, Thriller & Animation* group.

Do this in exactly the same way (this time you will select the *Genres* in column B).

8 AutoSize column A.

Your pivot table should now look like this:

	A	B	C
4	**Category**	▼ **Genre** ▼	**Sum of Qty**
5	⊟ **Action, Comedy & Drama**	Action	4,699
6		Comedy	4,747
7		Drama	8,439
8	**Action, Comedy & Drama Total**		**17,885**
9	⊟ **Adventure, Sci-Fi, Thriller & Animation**	Adventure	1,149
10		Animation	574
11		Sci Fi	989
12		Thriller	765
13	**Adventure, Sci-Fi, Thriller & Animation Total**		**3,477**
14	⊟ **Crime, Biography & Fantasy**	Biography	2,229
15		Crime	2,960
16		Fantasy	1,252
17	**Crime, Biography & Fantasy Total**		**6,441**
18	**Grand Total**		**27,803**

Notice how Excel has automatically added subtotals for each group.

9 Collapse all categories.

This was covered in: *Lesson 9-2: Create a grouped pivot table report.*

Your pivot table should now look like this:

	A	B	C
4	**Category**	▼ **Genre** ▼	**Sum of Qty**
5	⊞ **Action, Comedy & Drama**		17,885
6	⊞ **Adventure, Sci-Fi, Thriller & Animation**		3,477
7	⊞ **Crime, Biography & Fantasy**		6,441
8	**Grand Total**		**27,803**

10 Save your work as *Transactions-16*.

note

Excel automatically adds a collection of date related fields

In: *Lesson 9-4: Understand the pivot table data cache,* you learned that a pivot table accesses values stored in its data cache.

In this lesson the data cache is created from the Excel table called *Data* in the *Data* worksheet. This data only has an *Order Date* (in column B).

In: *Lesson 3-7: Understand date serial numbers,* you learned that date serial numbers can contain only a time or both a time and a date.

When the data cache is created Excel doesn't only store the *Order Date* field. It also pre-computes subtotals for seven different values:

Seconds, Minutes, Hours, Days, Months, Quarters and *Years.*

This set of date/time fields are added according to a set of rules.

1. If the source data spans less than one year, Excel will automatically add the *Year* and *Month* fields.

2. If the source data spans more than one year, Excel will automatically add the *Year, Month* and *Quarter* fields (as it did in this lesson).

3. If the data only contains time values, Excel will automatically add the *Seconds, Minutes* and *Hours* fields.

Lesson 9-19: Group by date

Out of all of the skills covered in my classroom *Expert Skills* course, this is surely the star of the show.

Excel's ability to summarize transactional data by daily, monthly, quarterly and yearly totals is extremely difficult to achieve without a pivot table.

1 Open *Transactions-16* from your sample files folder (if it isn't already open).

2 Remove all of the existing fields from the pivot table.

Click:

PivotTable Analyze→Actions→Clear→Clear All

3 Add the following fields to the pivot table.

Total sales are now shown for each employee.

	A	B	C
4	Employee	Sum of Total	
5	Anderson,Jane	8833.4	
6	Armstrong,Dan	7880.51	

4 Add the *Order Date* field to the *Columns* pane.

When you do this something unusual happens:

Notice that Excel has created two extra fields: *Quarters* and *Years* (see sidebar for more information about this feature). You can see that the fields are collapsed to show the total sales figure for each year:

	A	B	C	D
5		2014	2015	2016
6				
7	Employee			
8	Anderson,Jane	1551.33	5855.67	1426.4
9	Armstrong,Dan	2526.81	4511.81	841.89

Transactions-16

In: *Lesson 9-4: Understand the pivot table data cache,* you learned that pivot tables obtain their values from a *pivot table data cache* and not from the original data source.

If you create two pivot tables (in the same workbook) that use the same data source (in this lesson the data source is the *Data* table on the *Data* worksheet), Excel will only create one *pivot table data cache* and share it between the two pivot tables.

Normally this is exactly what you want, as it will result in a lower file size. Unfortunately, this leads to a problem with grouping.

Suppose that you want to create two pivot tables, one showing sales grouped by *Month* and the second showing sales grouped by *Year.* Unfortunately, this won't be possible unless each pivot table has its own *pivot table data cache.* There is a work-around to overcome this problem:

1. Create both pivot tables in your workbook (I'll call this *workbook No. 1*).

2. Leave the workbook open and open a new blank workbook (I'll call this *workbook No 2*).

3. Cut and paste one of the pivot tables in *workbook No.1* into *workbook No. 2.*

4. Copy and paste the pivot table from *workbook No. 2* back again into a new worksheet in *workbook No.1.*

This works because a copy of the PivotTable data cache is copied and pasted along with the pivot table. When the pivot table is pasted back again, the second cache is also pasted.

If you expand each year you can also see totals for each quarter.

	A	B	C	D	E
4	Sum of Total	Years ▾	Quarters ▾	Order Date ▾	
5		⊟2014	⊟2015		
6		⊞Qtr4	⊞Qtr1	⊞Qtr2	⊞Qtr3
7	Employee ▾				
8	Anderson,Jane	1551.33	2649.27	691.74	1169.35
9	Armstrong,Dan	2526.81	1714.41	435.63	875.8

You can see that the data only has sales for the fourth quarter of 2014 but has sales for all four quarters in 2015.

Expanding the quarters will display the total for each *Month.*

5 **Remove the *Years* and *Quarters* fields from the Columns pane.**

You can now see sales rolled up into monthly totals.

	A	B	C	D
5	Employee ▾	Jan	Feb	Mar
6	Anderson,Jane	1018.66	632.57	2424.44
7	Armstrong,Dan	244.03	790.71	1521.56

This seems quite useful at first until you realize that the monthly totals include all years. For example, the *March* totals are the combined sales figures for *March 2015* and *March 2016.*

When you group by *Months* it is really important that you also group by *Years.*

6 **Show monthly sales for each employee by *Months* and *Years.***

1. Right-click on any of the months shown in row 5.

2. Click *Group* from the shortcut menu.

   The *Grouping* dialog appears.

3. Select *Months* and *Years.*

Seconds
Minutes
Hours
Days
Months
Quarters
Years

4. Click the *OK* button.

   The pivot table is now grouped by *Year* and by *Month.*

	A	B	C	D	E
4	Sum of Total	Years ▾	Order Date ▾		
5		⊟2014			⊟2015
6	Employee ▾	Oct	Nov	Dec	Jan
7	Anderson,Jane		1525.91	25.42	495.1
8	Armstrong,Dan		1453.87	1072.94	244.03
9	Ashe,Lucille	675.38	281.54	624.23	643.08

7 **Save your work as *Transactions-17.***

Lesson 9-20: Group by numeric value ranges

1　Open *Employee Age Profile-1* from your sample files folder.

2　Convert the range A3:C27 into a table named **Data**.

In Excel 365, it is best practice to base pivot tables upon tables (you would have used a named range in pre 2007 Excel versions).

1. Click anywhere in the range A3:C27.

2. Click: Insert→Tables→Table.

3. Click the *OK* button.

4. Type the name **Data** into:

Table Design→Properties→Table Name

3　Rename the worksheet tab from *Sheet1* to: **Data**

4　Create a pivot table from the *Data* table.

1. Click anywhere inside the table.

2. Click: Insert→Tables→PivotTable.

3. Click the *OK* button.

5　Rename the pivot table worksheet tab to: **Age Profile**

6　Add the following fields to the pivot table:

▼ Filters	�III Columns
▦ Rows	Σ Values
Age ▼	
Name ▼	

(The order is important. *Age* must come before *Name*).

The pivot table now groups employees by age.

	A
8	⊟ 33
9	Jane Anderson
10	Julie Spears
11	Meryl Simpson
12	⊟ 34
13	Howard Simpson

Note that some of the employees may have got a little older by the time you read this book.

Where two or more employees are of the same age, they are grouped together.

The challenge for this lesson will be to group employees into different age bands.

Employee Age Profile-1

7 Group the pivot table into the age bands: *Under 40, 40-49, 50-60* and *Over 60*.

1. Right-click any of the ages in column A (for example: cell A6).

2. Click *Group* from the shortcut menu.

    The *Grouping* dialog is displayed.

3. Type the following values into the dialog:

3	Row Labels	▾
4	⊟ <40	
5	Alfred Hawking	
6	Elizabeth Diamond	
7	Howard Simpson	
8	Jane Anderson	
9	Julia Putin	
10	Julie Spears	
11	Meryl Simpson	
12	Stephen Bell	
13	⊟ 40-49	
14	Dan Armstrong	

Grouping	?	✕
Auto		
☐ Starting at:	40	
☐ Ending at:	60	
By:	10	
OK	Cancel	

This tells Excel to group into the ages:

- Less than 40

- Over 60

- Between 40 and 60 in bands of 10 years

4. Click the *OK* button.

    Ages are now grouped as defined.

    When data is grouped in this way it is sometimes referred to as a *frequency distribution*.

8 Change the *Row Labels* label in cell A3 to: **Age Group**

1. Click once on cell A3.

2. Type **Age Group** into the cell.

	A
3	Age Group
4	⊟ <40
5	Alfred Hawking

3. Press the **<Enter>** key.

9 Save your work as *Employee Age Profile-2*.

	A
3	Age Group ▾
4	⊟ <40
5	Alfred Hawking
6	Elizabeth Diamond
7	Howard Simpson
8	Jane Anderson
9	Julia Putin
10	Julie Spears
11	Meryl Simpson
12	Stephen Bell
13	⊟ 40-49
14	Dan Armstrong
15	Jessica Sagan
16	Margaret Streep
17	Paul Goodman
18	⊟ 50-60
19	Andy Richards
20	Anna Newhart
21	Charles Davis
22	Chuck West
23	Frank Lee
24	John Bradshaw
25	Julia Carrey
26	Lucille Ashe
27	Marilyn Manning
28	Michael Hicks
29	⊟ >60
30	Gloria Silverstone
31	John Jennings
32	Grand Total

Lesson 9-21: Show row data by percentage of total rather than value

In this lesson, you will discover which genres each employee is best at selling. This will enable the company to allocate sales leads for each genre to the most competent salesperson in that genre.

This time you're not interested in total sales but the percentage sales by genre for each employee.

As a bonus, you'll see the percentage market share of each genre.

1   Open *Transactions-17* from your sample files folder (if it isn't already open).

2   Remove all of the existing fields and filters from the pivot table.

You'll often want to remove all fields and filters from your pivot table to start again. To do this, click:

PivotTable Analyze→Actions→Clear→Clear All

3   Add the following fields to the pivot table.

▼ Filters	⫿ Columns
	Genre ▾
⫿ Rows	Σ Values
Employee ▾	Sum of Total ▾

4   Format the *Sum of Total* field to show two decimal places and thousand separators.

This was covered in: *Lesson 9-1: Create a one-dimensional pivot table report* from *a table.*

Sales are now shown for every employee and for every genre.

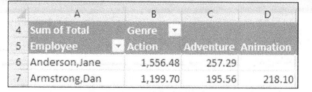

	A	B	C	D
4	Sum of Total	Genre ▾		
5	Employee ▾	Action	Adventure	Animation
6	Anderson,Jane	1,556.48	257.29	
7	Armstrong,Dan	1,199.70	195.56	218.10

5   Show sales values as a percentage of each row total.

1. Right-click on any of the numerical values in the pivot table.

2. Click *Value Field Settings* from the shortcut menu.

The *Value Field Settings* dialog is displayed.

Transactions-17

3. Click the *Show Values As* tab.

Summarize Values By	Show Values As
Show values as	
No Calculation ▼	
Base field:	Base item:
Order No	
Order Date	
Customer	
Title	
Genre	

4. Select *% of Row Total* from the *Show values as* drop down list.

Summarize Values By	Show Values As
Show values as	
No Calculation ▼	
No Calculation	
% of Grand Total	
% of Column Total	
% of Row Total	
% Of	
% of Parent Row Total	
Genre	

5. Click the *OK* button.

    Values are now shown as a percentage of each employee's sales:

	A	B	C	D	E	F	G	H	I	J
5	Employee ▼	Action	Adventure	Animation	Biography	Comedy	Crime	Drama	Fantasy	Sci Fi
6	Anderson,Jane	17.62%	2.91%	0.00%	11.84%	20.93%	7.29%	31.54%	2.37%	3.15%
7	Armstrong,Dan	15.22%	2.48%	2.77%	8.45%	17.37%	11.47%	37.42%	4.09%	0.09%
8	Ashe,Lucille	15.71%	3.84%	2.08%	4.38%	16.87%	12.97%	25.47%	9.70%	1.06%
9	Bell,Stephen	18.34%	7.63%	0.74%	4.52%	18.70%	11.55%	25.14%	7.44%	5.15%
10	Bradshaw,John	16.29%	3.08%	2.20%	10.19%	16.04%	16.16%	29.57%	0.55%	3.69%
11	Carrey,Julia	17.39%	6.06%	0.64%	12.38%	21.05%	12.70%	24.52%	2.81%	1.65%
12	Davis,Charles	23.79%	0.61%	3.50%	5.18%	13.56%	6.44%	31.48%	4.57%	9.17%
13	Diamond,Elizabeth	18.59%	3.62%	5.25%	12.66%	17.38%	5.16%	26.32%	4.21%	4.29%
14	Goodman,Paul	14.57%	3.94%	0.98%	7.17%	15.31%	7.75%	40.02%	4.26%	1.55%
15	Hawking,Alfred	25.86%	4.03%	2.38%	4.57%	16.36%	9.44%	29.77%	2.66%	4.71%
16	Hicks,Michael	12.18%	8.07%	0.00%	9.71%	16.53%	14.92%	31.40%	5.83%	0.00%
17	Jennings,John	16.77%	2.55%	1.76%	4.93%	14.76%	16.04%	31.26%	6.15%	3.35%
18	Lee,Frank	14.50%	2.83%	0.00%	9.12%	19.30%	9.45%	31.79%	9.46%	1.98%
19	Manning,Marilyn	13.37%	7.09%	1.02%	12.65%	15.28%	12.47%	30.31%	3.18%	4.64%
20	Newhart,Anna	16.43%	6.29%	2.81%	3.76%	16.41%	11.90%	23.36%	6.70%	8.56%
21	Putin,Julia	11.78%	3.39%	0.00%	3.48%	25.05%	9.91%	38.17%	4.34%	2.19%
22	Richards,Andy	11.76%	5.50%	0.90%	9.88%	19.06%	17.14%	22.99%	5.47%	3.67%
23	Sagan,Jessica	24.79%	2.32%	7.58%	3.31%	23.17%	4.24%	28.64%	1.90%	3.77%
24	Silverstone,Gloria	21.40%	3.56%	1.02%	9.23%	8.15%	7.86%	23.46%	11.18%	2.98%
25	Simpson,Howard	19.86%	4.61%	1.96%	4.16%	10.04%	10.65%	32.38%	8.44%	4.25%
26	Simpson,Meryl	15.52%	4.01%	3.50%	6.30%	13.78%	6.88%	37.61%	3.41%	5.72%
27	Spears,Julie	9.66%	2.66%	1.02%	11.43%	17.98%	17.54%	32.40%	5.23%	0.00%

You can see at a glance that *Alfred Hawking* does very well with sales in the *Action* genre, and that *Paul Goodman* is our star performer in the *Drama* genre.

You should keep *Michael Hicks* and *Julie Spears* away from *Science Fiction* sales.

6   Save your work as *Transactions-18*.

note

Produce a well formatted report from a pivot table using paste values

Many users work around the formatting limitations of pivot tables like this:

1. Select and copy the cells that you need from the pivot table.

2. Select the destination cell.

3. Click: Home→Clipboard→ Paste Special→ Values and number formats.

4. Format the pasted values in any way you wish.

This works but makes it impossible to refresh the well formatted version.

Lesson 9-22: Use pivot table values in simple formulas

1   Open *Central Park Temperature-1* from your sample files folder (if it isn't already open).

This file contains the average monthly temperatures recorded in New York's Central Park between 2010 and 2015 along with a pivot table that shows the temperatures for April, May and June side by side for the years 2014 and 2015:

	A	B	C
3	Sum of Avg Temp F	Column Labels ▾	
4	Row Labels ▾	2014	2015
5	Apr		52.3 54.3
6	May		64 68.5
7	Jun		72.5 71.2

With the skills you have learned in this session so far, you should have no difficulty understanding how this pivot table was created.

It took me less than 30 seconds to create this pivot table, demonstrating the amazing ability of pivot tables to quickly summarize data. It will not, however, win any design competitions.

2   Type: **Increase/Decrease** into cell D4.

3   Add a formula to cell D5 to show the increase/decrease in temperature for each month.

The automatic insertion of GETPIVOTDATA functions confuses and irritates many Excel users because most Excel users would do this:

1.   Click in cell D5.

2.   Press the equals sign: <=>

3.   Click on cell C5.

4.   Press the minus key <->

5.   Click on cell B5.

6.   Press the <Enter> key.

7.   AutoFill cell D5 down to cell D7.

Here's the result of the above actions:

	A	B	C	D
3	Sum of Avg Temp F	Column Labels ▾		
4	Row Labels ▾	2014	2015	Increase/Decrease
5	Apr		52.3 54.3	2
6	May		64 68.5	2
7	Jun		72.5 71.2	2

If you examine the formula in cell D5 you'll understand why the calculations return incorrect values. You thought you were asking Excel to create the very simple formula:

=C5-B5

Central Park Temperature-1

Instead, Excel has created a complex formula in all three cells:

`=GETPIVOTDATA("Avg Temp F",$A$3,"Month",4,"Years",2015)-GETPIVOTDATA("Avg Temp F",$A$3,"Month",4,"Years",2014)`

note

I really don't like GETPIVOTDATA, how can I switch it off?

Many users do not like the way that Excel automatically inserts GETPIVOTDATA functions when they reference cells within a pivot table.

Students in my classes often ask how they can switch this feature off.

Don't switch it off just yet as you'll be using this feature in the next lesson: *Lesson 9-23: Use the GETPIVOTDATA function.*

If, after completing this lesson, you decide that you would rather Excel didn't automatically insert GETPIVOTDATA functions here's how to switch the feature off:

Uncheck the checkbox:

File→Options→Formulas→ Working with formulas→ Use GetPivotData functions for PivotTable references

There's also a way of doing exactly the same thing from the ribbon:

1. Click inside the pivot table to activate it.

2. Click: PivotTable Analyze→ Pivot Table→Options (drop-down arrow)→ Generate GetPivotData.

This is an odd thing for Excel to do, as it is inconsistent with the way that Excel normally behaves when creating a formula.

If you really wanted to switch off this behaviour you can do so in the Excel options (see sidebar). But I'd encourage you to leave it switched on.

In: *Lesson 9-22: Use pivot table values in simple formulas,* you'll discover that you can make good use of the GETPIVOTDATA function to make your formulas more resilient to changes in the pivot table layout.

Here's how you can use simple formulas in the above scenario:

1. Delete any formulas in cells D5:D7.

2. Type **=C5-B5** (using the keyboard and not the mouse) into cell D5 (or the formula bar).

3. AutoFill cell D5 down to cell D7.

	A	B	C	D
3	Sum of Avg Temp F	Column Labels		
4	Row Labels	2014	2015	Increase/Decrease
5	Apr		52.3	54.3	2
6	May		64	68.5	4.5
7	Jun		72.5	71.2	-1.3

4 Use simple formulas to populate the *Simple Formula Method* range on the *Formatted Report* worksheet.

1. Delete column D from the *TemperaturePivotTable* worksheet.

2. Select the *Formatted Report* worksheet.

3. Enter this formula into cell C7:

`=TemperaturePivotTable!B5`

This formula retrieves the value of cell B5 from the *TemperaturePivotTable* worksheet.

4. AutoFill this formula across to cell D7 and down to cells C8:D9.

The values from the pivot table are displayed:

	A	B	C	D	E	F	G	H
1		Average Monthly & Annual Temperature						
2		Central Park, New York City						
5								
6		Month	2014	2015	Increase/Decrease			
7		Apr	52.3	54.3	2			
8		May	64	68.5	4.5			
9		Jun	72.5	71.2	-1.3			

The table's cells now reference the cell address of the relevant pivot table's cells. It you refresh the pivot table, the values in the formatted report will also update.

5 Save your work as *Central Park Temperature-2.*

note

A value must be visible on the screen for GETPIVOTDATA to work

If you filter a pivot table, or change it in some other way so that a value is no longer visible, the GETPIVOTDATA function will return an error.

Lesson 9-23: Use the GETPIVOTDATA function

In: *Lesson 9-22: Use pivot table values in simple formulas,* you worked with this pivot table:

	A	B	C
3	Sum of Avg Temp F	Column Labels ⏷	
4	Row Labels ⏷	2014	2015
5	Apr	52.3	54.3

In the previous lesson you used simple formulas to reference the correct cell addresses in the pivot table (for example =B5 was used to return the temperature in April 2014).

Unfortunately, there's a problem with this approach. When a pivot table is filtered, cell addresses move. For example, if I were change the filter to also show 2013 temperatures in the pivot table the pivot table would look like this:

	A	B	C	D
3	Sum of Avg Temp F	Column Labels ⏷		
4	Row Labels ⏷	2013	2014	2015
5	Apr		53	52.3 54.3

Cell B5 now points to the temperature in April 2013 instead of April 2014, making my formatted report invalid.

To avoid this type of error you can use the GETPIVOTDATA function to make the formulas resilient to pivot table layout changes.

1 Open *Central Park Temperature-2* from your sample files folder.

2 Automatically create a GETPIVOTDATA function that will return the correct pivot table value to cell C14 in the *Formatted Report* worksheet.

   1. Click in cell C14 on the *Formatted Report* worksheet and press the equals key: **<=>**

   2. Select the *TemperaturePivotTable* worksheet.

   3. Click in cell B5 and press the **<Enter>** key.

     A GETPIVOTDATA function is created in cell C14 on the *FormattedReport* worksheet.

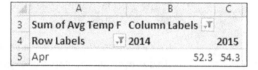

=GETPIVOTDATA("Avg Temp F",TemperaturePivotTable!$A$3,"Month",4,"Years",2014)

3 Adjust the GETPIVOTDATA arguments so that they will AutoFill correctly.

The GETPIVOTDATA function created by Excel is quite difficult to understand. As with all complex functions, things become a lot easier if you launch the function arguments dialog.

   1. Click in cell C14 on the *FormattedReport* worksheet to make it the active cell.

   2. Click the *Insert Function* button on the left of the formula bar. f_x

Central Park Temperature-2

note

The GETPIVOTDATA function works in a different way in regular and OLAP pivot tables

Later, in: *Lesson 12-7: Understand OLAP pivot tables,* you'll learn about a new type of pivot table (introduced in Excel 2013) called an *OLAP pivot table.*

In order to maintain as much similarity as possible between regular pivot tables and OLAP pivot tables, the GETPIVOTDATA function is available in both, but the arguments work in a slightly different way.

An OLAP pivot table also supports a new function that really makes the GETPIVOTDATA function obsolete.

In: *Lesson 12-20: Use the CUBEVALUE function to query a data model,* you'll learn about the new CUBEVALUE function that allows you to bypass an OLAP pivot table entirely and access data directly from the OLAP pivot table's cache.

When you understand how OLAP pivot tables work, you'll realize that the CUBEVALUE function offers a better solution to the problem (solved in this lesson) if you use an OLAP (rather than regular) pivot table.

	A	B	C	D	E	F
4		Simple Formula Method				
5						
6		Month	2014	2015	Increase/Decrease	
7		Apr	53	52.3	-0.7 ▼	
8		May	62.8	64	1.2 ▲	
9		Jun	72.7	72.5	-0.2 ▼	
10						
11		GETPIVOTDATA method				
12						
13		Month	2014	2015	Increase/Decrease	
14		Apr	52.3	54.3	2 ▲	
15		May	64	68.5	4.5 ▲	
16		Jun	72.5	71.2	-1.3 ▼	

3. The *Function Arguments* dialog appears:

Data_field	`Avg Temp F`	↑ =	`Avg Temp F`
Pivot_table	TemperaturePivotTable!$A$3	↑ =	"Sum of Avg Temp F"
Field1	`Month`	↑ =	`Month`
Item1	4	↑ =	4
Field2	`Years`	↑ =	`Years`
Item2	2014	↑ =	2014

Things are now very easy to understand. The function is returning the *Avg Temp F* value displayed at the intersection of month 4 (April) in the *Month* column and 2014 in the *Years* row displayed in the pivot table.

The pivot table as a whole is identified by any cell within the pivot table (in this case cell A3 is used, but any cell within the pivot table would work).

It should be clear that, no matter how the pivot table layout is changed, the correct result will always be returned. It is vital, however, that the values are always displayed somewhere on the pivot table, otherwise the function will return an error.

4. Fix the formula so that it will AutoFill correctly.

There's a small problem with the *Item1* and *Item2* values. They will not autofill correctly. Make the following small changes:

Field1	`Month`	↑ =	`Month`
Item1	MONTH($B14)	↑ =	4
Field2	`Years`	↑ =	`Years`
Item2	C$13	↑ =	2014

$B14 and C$13 are mixed cell references (mixed cell references are covered in depth in the *Essential Skills* book in this series). They mean "always look in column B but adjust the row" and "always look in row 13 but adjust the column".

The month value (the *Item1* argument) is returned using the MONTH function (using the month shown in column B as the function's argument).

The MONTH function works because the months shown in column B are actually date serial numbers formatted as months (you learned about date serial numbers in: *Lesson 3-7: Understand date serial numbers*). The year value (the *Item2* argument) is simply obtained from the year value in row 13.

5. Click the *OK* button.

4 AutoFill the GETPIVOTDATA function across to cell D14 and down to cells C15:D16.

5 Test the formatted reports for resilience when the *Year* filter is changed.

Click the *Column Labels* filter button on the pivot table and change the filter to also display 2013 temperatures. Notice that the *GETPIVOTDATA method* formatted report still shows the correct values while the *Simple Formula Method* formatted report now shows incorrect values.

6 Save your work as *Central Park Temperature-3.*

note

Regular charts vs pivot charts

There are two reasons why you might prefer a regular chart to a pivot chart:

1. A worksheet containing a pivot chart also contains the source data, pivot table data cache and a pivot table. This can result in a very large file size.

2. When you distribute a pivot chart you also give the recipient all of the source data that may contain confidential information.

If you prefer a regular chart instead, follow the instructions in: *Lesson 9-13: Understand pivot table report layouts (sidebar)* to export the required values from the pivot table and then create a regular chart from this data.

You may also consider pasting a picture of the pivot chart into a different workbook. To do this, *Copy* the pivot chart and then *Paste Special* as a picture.

Lesson 9-24: Create a pivot chart from a pivot table

Excel is one of the world's most powerful charting tools. Every aspect of charting is covered in the *Essential Skills* book in this series, where a whole session (28 lessons) covers everything there is to know about Excel charts.

This *Expert Skills* book assumes that you already understand normal Excel charts.

When you create a pivot chart from a pivot table, it is important to realize that the chart always matches the data shown in the pivot table.

1   Open *Transactions-18* from your sample files folder (if it isn't already open).

2   Remove all of the existing fields and filters from the pivot table.

Click: PivotTable Analyze→Actions→Clear→Clear All.

3   Add the following three fields to the pivot table.

Rows		Σ Values	
Genre	▾	Sum of Total	▾
Title	▾		

4   Filter the pivot table so that sales are only shown for the *Adventure*, *Animation* and *Sci-Fi* genres.

You learned how to do this in: *Lesson 9-5: Apply a simple filter and sort to a pivot table.*

	A	B	C
4	**Genre**	**Title**	**Sum of Total**
5	⊟Adventure	Aguirre, the Wrath of God	4666.22
6		Interview With The Vampire	3921.81
7	**Adventure Total**		**8588.03**
8	⊟Animation	Finding Nemo	5098.87
9	**Animation Total**		**5098.87**
10	⊟Sci Fi	Blade Runner	3160.31
11		E.T. the Extra-Terrestrial	4128.87
12	**Sci Fi Total**		**7289.18**
13	**Grand Total**		**20976.08**

5   Collapse the outline so that only the totals are shown.

You learned how to do this in: *Lesson 9-2: Create a grouped pivot table report.*

	A	B	C
4	**Genre**	**Title**	**Sum of Total**
5	⊞Adventure		8588.03
6	⊞Animation		5098.87
7	⊞Sci Fi		7289.18
8	**Grand Total**		20976.08

Transactions-18

note

Advantages of placing charts on chart sheets

In this lesson you embed a chart within an existing worksheet.

While this is sometimes what you want, most of the time you'll want to place your chart into a dedicated *Chart Sheet*. This provides the following advantages:

- They are easier to find, as you can give each sheet a meaningful name.

- They are easier to view, as the chart normally takes up the entire screen. You can re-size a chart on a chart sheet but this isn't often done.

- They are easier to print, as you can simply click the sheet tab and print. You can also print an embedded chart in isolation, but to do so you must first find and activate the chart.

Advantages of embedding charts within worksheets

- You are able to print a chart and worksheet data on the same page.

If you have no need to print worksheet data alongside your chart, it is better to place your charts on chart sheets.

Here's how to move the chart to its own sheet:

1. Click on the chart to activate it.

2. Click: Design→Location→Move Chart.

The *Move Chart* dialog appears.

3. Click the *New sheet* option button.

4. Click the *OK* button.

The chart now resides in its own chart sheet.

6 Create a *Clustered Column* pivot chart from the pivot table.

1. Click anywhere in the pivot table to activate it.

2. Click: PivotTable Analyze→Tools→PivotChart.

The *Insert Chart* dialog appears.

3. Click the *Clustered Column* chart type.

This is usually the default chart type.

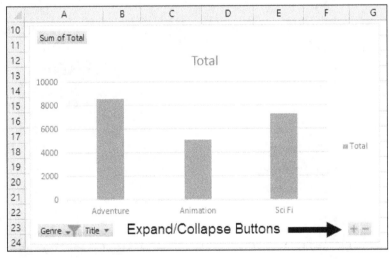

4. Click the *OK* button.

A clustered column chart is shown embedded in the worksheet.

7 Use the *Expand* and *Collapse* buttons on the chart to show the titles of individual films sold within each genre.

Expand/collapse buttons are shown on any pivot chart that includes grouped fields:

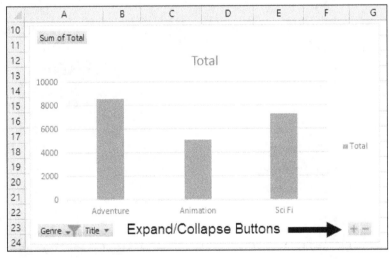

Click the Expand button to show *Titles* in each *Genre*.

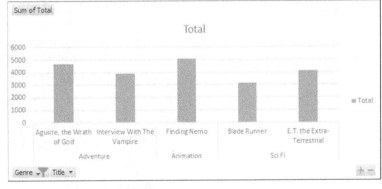

8 Save your work as *Transactions-19*.

Lesson 9-25: Embed multiple pivot tables onto a worksheet

In this lesson, you'll create the following *Sales Summary* worksheet containing three embedded pivot tables:

	A	B	C	D	E	F
1		Sales Summary				
3		Customer ▼	Sales		Employee ▼	Sales
4		Addison-Freelander Screen Agency	17,135.23		Anderson,Jane	8,833.40
5		AV Supplies	15,199.30		Armstrong,Dan	7,880.51
6		Box Office Supplies	22,923.09		Ashe,Lucille	8,755.66
7		Cheapo Cheap DVD's Ltd	20,145.10		Bell,Stephen	11,649.76
8		Cinefocus DVD	22,277.45		Bradshaw,John	9,329.37
9		Classic Films	17,549.80		Carrey,Julia	6,091.91
10		Creative Films	14,637.39		Davis,Charles	6,800.56
11		Lights-Camera-Action Ltd	18,106.20		Diamond,Elizabeth	8,965.29
12		Magic Lantern Classic Film Rental	20,055.78		Goodman,Paul	9,578.01
13		Silver Screen Video	20,757.07		Hawking,Alfred	10,946.28
14		Soft Focus Video Rental	17,870.60		Hicks,Michael	7,091.10
15		Video Flicks International	16,129.79		Jennings,John	11,190.73
16		**Grand Total**	**222,786.80**		Lee,Frank	13,488.16
17					Manning,Marilyn	9,064.16
18		Genre ▼	Sales		Newhart,Anna	8,937.66
19		Action	37,411.40		Putin,Julia	8,590.69
20		Adventure	8,588.03		Richards,Andy	8,302.17
21		Animation	5,098.87		Sagan,Jessica	11,004.66
22		Biography	17,174.78		Silverstone,Gloria	8,349.05
23		Comedy	37,614.16		Simpson,Howard	9,370.30
24		Crime	25,212.68		Simpson,Meryl	6,522.80
25		Drama	67,097.47		Spears,Julie	10,683.14
26		Fantasy	11,785.28		Streep,Margaret	14,513.69
27		Sci Fi	7,289.18		West,Chuck	6,847.74
28		Thriller	5,514.95		**Grand Total**	**222,786.80**
29		**Grand Total**	**222,786.80**			

When several key performance indicators are combined to produce an overview of a business process (in this case Sales) the worksheet is sometimes called a *Dashboard* or *Executive Information System*.

This lesson will also confirm your understanding of many of the skills learned in this session.

1   Open *Transactions-19* from your sample files folder (if it isn't already open).

2   Add a new worksheet and name it: **Summary**

Transactions-19

3   Type **Sales Summary** into cell B1.

4   Apply the *Title* style to cell B1.

Click: Home→Styles→Cell Styles→Titles and Headings→Title.

5   Embed a pivot table starting at cell B3 to show sales value by *Customer.*

1.   Click in cell B3.

2.   Click: Insert→Tables→PivotTable.

3.   Type **Data** into the *Table/Range* box.

4.   Click the *OK* button.

5.   Check the *Customer* and *Total* fields in the *PivotTable Fields* list.

6   Embed a pivot table starting at cell B18 to show sales value by *Genre*.

7   Embed a pivot table starting at cell E3 to show sales value by *Employee.*

8   Format all values to show two decimal places and thousand separators.

This was first covered in: *Lesson 9-16: Add a calculated field to a pivot table.*

9   Change the *Row Labels* text in cells B3, B18 and E3 to read: **Customer, Genre** and **Employee**

This was first covered in: *Lesson 9-16: Add a calculated field to a pivot table.*

10   Change the *Sum of Total* labels in cells C3, C18 and F3 to read: **Sales**

11   Add a *3 Traffic Lights (Unrimmed)* conditional format to cells C4:C15.

Conditional formatting is covered in depth in the *Essential Skills* book in this series.

1.   Select cells C4:C15.

2.   Click: Home→Styles→Conditional Formatting→ Icon Sets→3 Traffic Lights (Unrimmed).

12   Add a *Light Blue Data Bar* conditional format to cells C19:C28.

13   Add a *5 Ratings (Icon Set)* conditional format to cells F4:F27.

14   Re-size the column widths to enhance visual appearance.

15   Save your work as *Transactions-20.*

Lesson 9-26: Use slicers to filter multiple pivot tables

Earlier in this session you learned how to use slicers to provide an elegant user interface when filtering pivot tables.

Slicers become even more powerful when used to filter multiple pivot tables (such as the worksheet created in: *Lesson 9-25: Embed multiple pivot tables onto a worksheet*).

In this lesson you'll refine this worksheet to create an overview of sales using slicers to enable the user to filter all of the pivot tables at the same time.

This is a feat that can only be accomplished using slicers. The filter fields that you learned about in: *Lesson 9-6: Use report filter fields* are only capable of filtering a single pivot table.

1   Open *Transactions-20* from your sample files folder (if it isn't already open).

2   Name the pivot tables: **Customer, Employee** and **Genre**

When working with multiple pivot tables it is useful to give each an intuitive name.

1.   Click on the *Customer* pivot table to activate it.

2.   Click: PivotTable Analyze→PivotTable→ PivotTable Name.

3.   Type **Customer** in the *PivotTable Name* box and press the **<Enter>** key.

4.   Repeat the process to name the *Employee* and *Genre* pivot tables.

3   Add three slicers that will filter the *Customer* pivot table by *Employee, Customer* and *Genre.*

You learned how to do this in: *Lesson 9-7: Filter a pivot table visually using slicers.*

4   Size and format the slicers so that they provide a compact and attractive user interface.

You learned how to do this in: *Lesson 9-7: Filter a pivot table visually using slicers.*

When you have finished, your user interface should be similar to the screen grab on the facing page.

5   Test your slicers.

Notice that the slicers only affect the *Customer* pivot table. No matter what filter condition you set in the slicers, the values in the *Genre* and *Employee* pivot tables remain unaffected.

6   Connect the slicers to all three pivot tables.

1.   Click the *Genre* slicer to select it.

2.   Click: Slicer→Slicer→Report Connections.

Transactions-20

See sidebar for a solution to this problem.

note

How can I stop Excel changing pivot table column widths?

This is caused by a glitch in Excel's *AutoFit* feature.

The easy solution is to switch off AutoFit and size the column widths manually.

To switch off AutoFit:

1. Right-click on each pivot table in turn.

2. Select *PivotTable Options* from the shortcut menu.

3. Click the *Layout & Format* tab.

4. Clear the *Autofit column widths on update* check box.

5. Manually resize each column so that they are wide enough to display their contents correctly.

The *Report Connections* dialog appears.

3. Check the *Employee* and *Genre* check boxes to connect this slicer to all three pivot tables on the *Summary* worksheet.

4. Click the *OK* button.

5. Repeat this process for the *Customer* and *Employee* slicers.

7 Test your slicers.

Notice that the slicers now work the way you want them to. All three pivot tables are filtered in accordance with the slicer filters that you select.

You may find that the columns are not wide enough to display their values when a filter is applied. See sidebar for a solution to this problem.

8 Save your work as *Transactions-21*.

Session 9: Exercise

1   Open *Film Sales-1* from your sample files folder.

2   Convert the range into a table named *Data*.

3   Create a pivot table from the *Data* table.

4   Add *Row Labels* and *Values* so that your pivot table looks like this:

	A	B	C
3	Row Labels ▾	Sum of Qty	Sum of Total
4	Fedex	6929	55793.38
5	Royal Mail	6606	52965.68
6	TNT	7366	58884.38
7	UPS	6902	55143.36
8	**Grand Total**	**27803**	**222786.8**

5   Re-format the values in the pivot table and change the text in the headers, so that your pivot table looks like this:

	A	B	C
3	Carrier ▾	Units	Cost
4	Fedex	6,929	55,793.38
5	Royal Mail	6,606	52,965.68
6	TNT	7,366	58,884.38
7	UPS	6,902	55,143.36
8	**Grand Total**	**27,803**	**222,786.80**

6   Add a calculated field to calculate the average cost per unit for each carrier formatted to two decimal places with a 1000 comma separator.

	A	B	C	D
3	Carrier ▾	Units	Cost	Cost per Unit
4	Fedex	6,929	55,793.38	8.05
5	Royal Mail	6,606	52,965.68	8.02
6	TNT	7,366	58,884.38	7.99
7	UPS	6,902	55,143.36	7.99
8	**Grand Total**	**27,803**	**222,786.80**	**8.01**

7   Embed a second pivot table starting in cell A10 of the same worksheet that will display sales by studio in an attractive format.

	A	B
10	Studio	▾ Sales
11	20th Century Fox	12,819.76
12	BBC TV	2,891.99
13	Columbia Pictures	11,007.66

8   Save your work as *Film Sales-2.*

Film Sales-1

If you need help
slide the page to
the left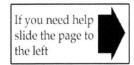

Session 9: Exercise Answers

These are the four questions that students find the most difficult to answer:

Q 7	Q 6	Q 4	Q 2
1. Click in cell A10. 2. Click: Insert→Tables→PivotTable. 3. Type **Data** into the *Table/Range* box. 4. Click the *OK* button. 5. Drag the following fields from the *PivotTable Fields* list to the *Rows* and *Values* lists: Rows: Studio Σ Values: Sum of Total 6. Format the values to show two decimal places and a thousand comma separator (as detailed in the question 6 answer). 7. Click in cell A10 and type: **Studio** 8. Click in cell B10 and type: **Sales** 9. Press the **<Enter>** key. This was covered in: *Lesson 9-3: Understand pivot table rows and columns.*	1. Click: PivotTable Analyze→Calculations→Fields, Items & Sets→Calculated Field… 2. Complete the Calculated field dialog as follows: Name: Cost/Units Formula: = Total/ Qty 3. Click the *OK* button. 4. Right-click one of the values in column D. 5. Click *Number Format…* from the shortcut menu. 6. Select the *Number* category. 7. Check the *Use 1000 Separator (,)* check box. 8. Click the *OK* button. 9. Click cell D3 once and type: **Cost per Unit** This was covered in: *Lesson 9-16: Add a calculated field to a pivot table.*	Drag the following fields from the *PivotTable Fields* list to the *Rows* and *Values* lists: Rows: Carrier Σ Values: Sum of Qty, Sum of Total This was covered in: *Lesson 9-3: Understand pivot table rows and columns.*	1. Click anywhere inside the range. 2. Click: Insert→Tables→Table 3. Click the *OK* button. 4. Click: Table Design→Properties→Table Name 5. Type **Data** into the *Table Name* box. 6. Press the **<Enter>** key. This was covered in: *Lesson 1-13: Convert a range into a table and add a total row.*

If you have difficulty with the other questions, here are the lessons that cover the relevant skills:

3   Refer to: *Lesson 9-1: Create a one-dimensional pivot table report from a table.*

5   Refer to: *Lesson 9-1: Create a one-dimensional pivot table report from a table* and *Lesson 9-7: Filter a pivot table visually using slicers.*

10

Session Ten: 3D Maps

> Regular maps have few surprises: their contour lines reveal where the Andes are, and are reasonably clear. More precious, though, are the unpublished maps we make ourselves, of our city, our place, our daily world, our life; those maps of our private world we use every day.
>
> *Alexander McCall Smith, British writer and professor*
> *(from his book: Love Over Scotland).*

You can use 3D Maps to create stunning video presentations that will amaze, inform, engage and impress your audiences.

The core idea behind 3D Maps is to show visualizations of data upon the surface of a map when data contains geographical locations, but this doesn't begin to describe the huge feature set of this tool.

You can create temporal animations showing how data changes with the passage of time and then position yourself in a "virtual helicopter" above the map to fly your audience around your data in a virtual tour. You are even able to add a narration or musical sound track.

Tours can then be saved in video format, perhaps to publish on YouTube or include inside a PowerPoint presentation. All of this can be done in seconds, with a few clicks of the mouse, and without using any other video editing software.

I can foresee great future demand for 3D Maps skills in the film and TV industries as producers realize the potential of this incredible tool to quickly communicate complex data to audiences in a simple way that anybody can understand.

Session Objectives

By the end of this session you will be able to:

- Understand how 3D Maps use the data model
- Create a simple 3D Map
- Confirm the accuracy of geocoding
- Map using different location fields
- Apply filters to a 3D Map
- Set layer options and customize data cards
- Add a height field to a layer
- Apply different visualization types
- Visualize multiple categories
- Create a visualization with multiple layers
- Add annotations
- Create a video from temporal data
- Set scene options
- Create a tour with multiple scenes

Lesson 10-1: Understand how 3D Maps use the data model

The self-service BI Suite

Since 2010, some versions of Excel (those aimed at enterprise users) were able to install Microsoft's "Power" suite of Business Intelligence (BI) tools. Collectively they are often referred to as the *Self-Service BI suite*.

The suite comprised of four components:

- Power Pivot
- Power Query
- Power Maps
- Power View

Two of these products (*Power Pivot* and *Power Query*) were tools that could only be used by specialized IT staff (with extensive data modeling skills) to create *data models*.

The other two (*Power View* and *Power Maps*) were simple easy-to-learn tools that created visualizations of data within a data model. Excel users could also use a data model as the source data for a pivot table.

The vision behind *self-service BI* was that Excel users with no specialized data modeling skills could make use of the data models created by their IT department to create sophisticated visualizations and reports faster and more easily than was possible with Excel alone.

Data Model

Specialist IT staff with data modeling skills use Power Pivot and Power Query to create a Data Model

Regular users use Pivot Tables, Power Maps and Power View to create visualizations using the data model

In 2013 the *Power Query* tool was added to Excel and re-named Get & Transform. You'll learn how to use Get & Transform later, in: *Session Eleven: Create Get & Transform queries.*

In 2016 *Power Maps* was added to Excel and re-named *3D Maps*. This is the tool that you will learn in this session.

In 2019 *Power Pivot* was added to Excel. You'll learn how to use Power Pivot later, in: *Session Twelve: Power Pivot, Data Modeling, OLAP and Business Intelligence* and *Session Thirteen: An introduction to DAX.*

Power View no longer exists as a self-contained product (or add-in) and cannot be added to current versions of Excel. Instead, Power View has evolved into one component of a new desktop and cloud application called *Power BI.*

You can learn and use 3D Maps without learning data modeling

The data modeling skills that are taught in: *Session Twelve: Power Pivot, Data Modeling, OLAP and Business Intelligence* are very challenging to master.

In recognition of this the 3D Maps feature has been designed so that users with no data modeling skills can use 3D Maps by using a single Excel table (or range) as a data source.

Behind the scenes, 3D Maps automatically converts the table (or range) into a one-table data model. The 3D Maps tool then uses this data model as source data.

If you later create advanced data models everything in this session is equally relevant

Data modeling is a very challenging subject that many Excel users may decide not to invest time learning.

If you decide to progress to: *Session Twelve: Power Pivot, Data Modeling, OLAP and Business Intelligence* and *Session Thirteen: An introduction to DAX*, you will learn some very advanced data modeling skills.

While well-designed data models are very difficult to create, they are amazingly easy to use. All of the skills you will learn in this session will work in exactly the same way when powered by a hand-crafted multi-dimensional data model.

3D Maps can cause "out of memory" errors

3D Maps needs to hold a data model (that is a duplication of the source data) in your computer's memory.

Data models can require a lot of memory (depending upon the size of the source data).

If you encounter crashes or out-of-memory error warnings while working through this session you will need to consult: *Lesson 12-1: Understand data model memory requirements*. This lesson explains the memory issue (and how to solve this problem) in depth.

Lesson 10-2: Create a simple 3D Map

In this lesson you'll create a 3D Map that will show blue squares upon the face of a map. The squares will identify the location of every customer that has made a purchase during 2015.

1   Open *Sales Summary-1* from your sample files folder and examine the data.

This workbook contains a large data set showing details of over 16,000 sales made in the year 2015 to customers located all over the USA.

	A	B	C	D	E	F	G
1	Date	Order Number	Customer	Country	State	City	Postal Code
2	01-Jan-15	SO48740	Modular Cycle Systems	US	TX	Austin	78701
3	01-Jan-15	SO48740	Modular Cycle Systems	US	TX	Austin	78701

The data in column A tells you that several items were sold on *1st January 2015*. The inclusion of the date field tells you that this is *temporal data*. *Temporal data* means any data that changes with the passage of time. As you'll see later, in: *Lesson 10-12: Create a video from temporal data*, 3D Maps have some amazing features that visually depict temporal data at different points in time.

Columns B and C identify the Order Number: *S048740* and the Customer: *Modular Cycle Systems*.

Columns D, E, F and G contain geographical location data. Because *Country, State, City* and *Postal Code* are commonly used names for geographical data, 3D Maps will have no difficulty finding the correct geographical location to display on the map for each row. The remaining columns have details for the *Quantity, Price* and *Category* of the products purchased:

	H	I	J	K
1	Qty	Unit Price	Line Total	Category
2	2	$ 469.79	$ 939.59	Bikes
3	3	$ 469.79	$ 1,409.38	Bikes

You can see that the first item ordered was for 2 items at a unit cost of $469.79, making a total price of $939.59. The items ordered were in the category: *Bikes*.

2   Convert the range into a table named *Sales*.

You learned how to convert a range into a table in: *Lesson 1-13: Convert a range into a table and add a total row*. You learned how to name a table in: *Lesson 1-19: Name a table and create an automatic structured table reference*.

It would also be possible to create a 3D Map from a range but it is best practice to use a table as source data. By using a table any new rows added to the table in the the future will also used by the 3D Map (when it is refreshed).

3   Create a 3D Map from the *Sales* table.

1.   Click inside the table.

Sales Summary-1

2. Click: Insert→Tours→3D Map.

3. If you see a dialog asking to enable the *Data Analysis add-ins* click the *Enable* button.

There will be a short delay as Bing converts the location information contained in your data into longitude and latitude map coordinates.

An impressive visual of the world (expressed as a globe) then appears.

Notice that there's a ribbon at the top of the screen and three panes.

One pane is headed *Tour 1*. This is the *Tour Editor* pane. You'll work with this pane later in: *Lesson 10-14: Create a tour with multiple scenes*.

The center pane shows a map with a blue square for every city that made a purchase during 2015.

The right pane shows details about the current *Layer*. This is the *Layer* task pane. A layer can be thought of as a transparent layer that sits on top of the map. All of the blue squares are located on this layer. You'll discover more about layers in: *Lesson 10-10: Create a visualization with multiple layers*.

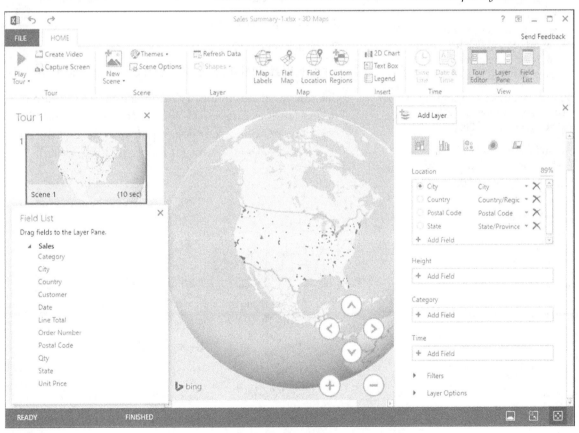

4   Save your work as *Sales Summary-2*

There's no *Save* button in 3D Maps. When you save a workbook that contains one or more *Tours,* they are saved with the workbook. You can close the 3D Maps window while working with Excel without losing any changes that you may have made (provided that you save before closing Excel).

Sales Summary-2

Lesson 10-3: Confirm the accuracy of geocoding

When you first open 3D Maps, place names are converted to points on the map (latitude and longitude). This process is called *geocoding*. The conversion is done (via the Internet) by the *Bing Maps* service.

The geocoding process can fail if your source data contains ambiguous values. For example, there are 235 towns named *San Francisco* in the world. If your data set includes *San Francisco*, then 3D Maps makes a guess and converts the name to the map reference for *San Francisco, California, USA* while your data could really relate to *San Francisco, Mexico*.

For this reason, it is important to confirm that 3D Maps has not incorrectly geocoded any of the locations defined in your source data.

Fortunately, 3D Maps can report any locations that it isn't completely sure of so that you can confirm that all of the guesses are correct.

1   Open *Sales Summary-2* from your sample files folder (if it isn't already open).

2   Open the *Tour 1* tour in the *3D Maps* application.

   1.   Click: Insert→Tours→3D Map.

   2.   Click on the *Open... Tour 1* icon.

3   Check that all fields have been correctly identified.

3D Maps will automatically recognize common column field names (such as *City* and *Country*). To make sure that 3D Maps has correctly identified your geographic data, look at the *Location* pane within the *Layer* task pane (at the right of the screen).

Location		94%
○ Country	Country/Regio ▾	✕
○ Postal Code	Postal Code ▾	✕
○ State	State/Province ▾	✕
● City	City ▾	✕
＋ Add Field		

You can see that, in this case, 3D Maps has done a fine job of identifying the data type of each geographic field.

- City   Recognized as *City*.
- Country: Recognized as *Country/Region*.
- Postal Code: Recognized as *Postal Code*.
- State: Recognized as *State/Province*.

Click one of the drop-down arrows to the right of a data type. A list of all valid 3D Maps geographic data types is shown (see sidebar).

Most 3D Maps use *Latitude* and *Longitude* to identify locations. The alternative X and Y coordinates method can be used with a custom

trivia

Before 1884 there were many different prime meridians

If you visit London, there's a wonderful day-trip I'd recommend. You can take a boat trip along the Thames to Greenwich and visit the *Royal Observatory*. There you can see the *Greenwich Meridian* etched into the ground and see John Harrison's H4 Sea Watch (see facing page sidebar). Tourists love to pose for photographs standing astride the meridian.

The Greenwich Meridian is also known as the *Prime Meridian* and defines zero longitude.

The Greenwich Meridian was defined in 1851 and by 1884 over two thirds of all charts and maps were based upon it.

Not everybody agreed that the Greenwich Meridian should be the world standard. Other meridians were used in different countries (often a nation's capital city).

Competing prime meridians included Jerusalem, Rome, Copenhagen, Pisa, Paris, Philadelphia and Washington. This caused widespread confusion.

In 1884 the US government hosted the *International Meridian Conference*. 25 countries sent delegates to finally settle upon a world standard prime meridian.

The Greenwich Meridian was adopted by 22 votes to one. Only San Domingo (now the Dominican Republic) voted against, while France and Brazil abstained.

France continued to use the Paris Meridian for almost three decades after the standard was agreed and only adopted the Greenwich Meridian in 1911.

---

image. This method will be discussed later, in: *Lesson 10-10: Create a visualization with multiple layers (sidebar).*

4   Show the *Mapping Confidence* dialog to check that all fields have been correctly geocoded.

Geocoding is the process of converting the geographical data in the fields supplied into latitude and longitude coordinates.

3D Maps provides a confidence rating, letting you know how sure 3D Maps is that the locations have been correctly geocoded. You can see a hyperlink on the top right of the pane advising that 3D Maps is 94% sure that all is well:

Click the 94% hyperlink for more information.

The *Mapping Confidence* dialog is displayed.

A quick review of the locations 3D Maps wasn't sure of shows that all have been correctly geocoded.

If any of these guesses were incorrect, you would have to return to the source data and make corrections. Unfortunately, there is no way to correct badly geocoded locations within 3D Maps itself.

You'll notice that the sample file for this lesson included a *Country* field even though all of the locations are in the US. This wasn't really needed but was done to give 3D Maps as many clues as possible when identifying each location.

5   Close the *Mapping Confidence* dialog.

6   You don't need to save your work as nothing has been changed.

Lesson 10-4: Map using different location fields

The geographic fields provided in the source data for this lesson have four levels of detail: *Country, State, City* and *Postal Code.*

1   Open *Sales Summary-2* from your sample files folder (if it isn't already open).

2   Open the *Tour 1* tour in the *3D Maps* application.

   1.   Click: Insert→Tours→3D Map.

   2.   Click on the *Open… Tour 1* icon.

3   Show a map identifying every state that has been sold to.

At the moment the map is showing every *City* that has at least one sale recorded. You can see that the *City* location field has a selected option button next to it.

Location				94%
○ Country	Country/Regic	▾	✕	
○ Postal Code	Postal Code	▾	✕	
○ State	State/Province	▾	✕	
● City	City	▾	✕	
＋ Add Field				

Click the *State* option button. A blue spot is now shown on every state that a sale has been made to.

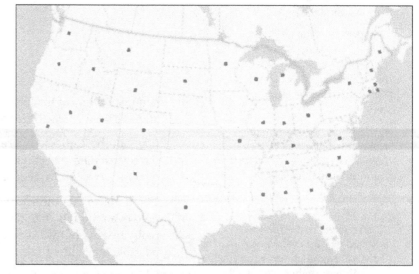

4   Show a flat map (rather than a map shown upon a globe).

Click: Home→Map→Flat Map.

The flat map model used by 3D Maps is a *Mercator Projection* (see sidebar).

5   Display the name upon each state.

Click: Home→Map→Map Labels.

---

note

3D flat maps are created with a Mercator Projection

The flat map displayed by 3D Maps is a *Mercator Projection* (invented by the 16th century Flemish cartographer Gerardus Mercator).

If you wrapped a cylinder of paper around a globe and then projected onto the paper from a light source inside the globe, the result would be a Mercator Projection.

Because the earth is a sphere, distances are not correctly represented on a flat map.

The distortion is most severe at the poles and least severe at the equator. For example, Greenland and Africa seem to be the same size on a Mercator Projection while, in reality, Africa is about fourteen times larger.

Sales Summary-2

---

important

Can I control the level of detail shown on the map?

Unfortunately, the only way you can control the level of detail shown on the map is by zooming in and out.

It would be nice to be able to control which artefacts were displayed upon the map (no matter what level of zoom you used).

Perhaps this feature will be added in a future version of 3D Maps.

6 Zoom the map so that only state names are shown.

Notice a set of five buttons at the bottom-right of the map.

Click the plus and minus buttons repeatedly and observe how the map changes.

As you zoom in to the map, the level of detail changes. At first you will only see country names but as you zoom in state names are added, followed by cities. If you zoom in far enough, you'll even see street names.

Zoom so that only state names are shown.

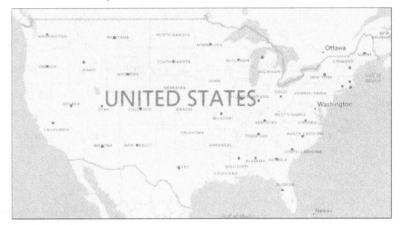

You can now see at a glance the states that have not yet purchased any products (for example, Nebraska and Kansas).

7 Show a map identifying every individual location that has been sold to.

Click: Layer 1→Location→Postal Code.

As each post code has a unique location, you can now see every individual location that a sale has been made to. There are a lot more of them:

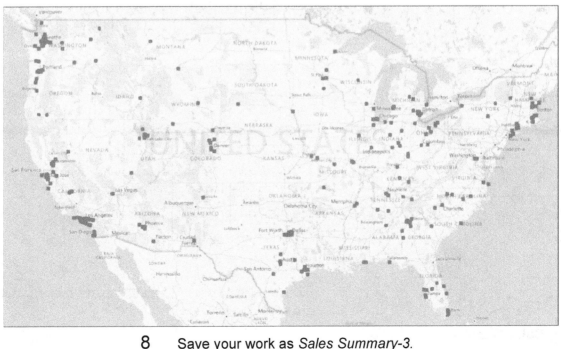

8 Save your work as *Sales Summary-3.*

Lesson 10-5: Apply filters to a 3D Map

In this lesson you'll filter the data points shown on the map so that only data points in Florida are shown.

1 Open *Sales Summary-3* from your sample files folder (if it isn't already open).

2 Open the *Tour 1* tour in the *3D Maps* application.

   1. Click: Insert→Tours→3D Map.

   2. Click on the *Open… Tour 1* icon.

3 Apply a filter so that only data points in Florida are shown.

   1. Click the fly-out menu button shown in front of *Filters* at the bottom of the *Layer* task pane (see sidebar).

   An *Add Filter* button appears.

   2. Click the +*Add Filter* button.

   A field list appears, showing all of the fields in the source data.

   3. Click on the *State* field.

   The *State* field is added as the active filter field. A list showing all states in the data set now appears.

   At present, all states are being shown.

   4. Click the check box next to Florida *(FL)*.

   Note that with larger data sets you will not see all filter values in the list (see sidebar facing page).

   The blue squares on the map change so that only locations in Florida (that have purchased any products in 2015) are shown.

4 Hide the *Tour* and *Layer* task panes.

   1. Click: Home →View→Tour Editor.

   2. Click: Home →View→Layer Pane.

   You could also do this by clicking the close button ☒ at the top right corner of each pane.

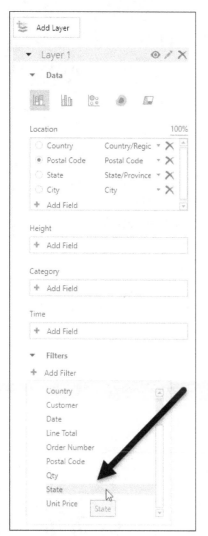

important

If there are a large number of unique values in your filter field, you won't see all of them in the list

In this lesson you filtered by *State*.

Because there are only 50 states in the USA, 3D Maps has no difficulty showing all of them in the filter list.

Sometimes you will use a filter value that has hundreds, or even thousands of unique values. In this case it isn't possible for 3D Maps to display all potential filter values in a list.

When 3D Maps is unable to list all values, a subset will be shown in list form with a *Search* box that can be used to find values that do not exist in the list.

For example, if you tried to filter by *City*, the list would be too long and you would see this:

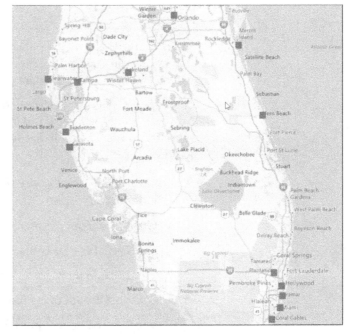

Cities are only listed that begin with A-C. To set a filter for *Orlando,* you'd have to type **Orlando** into the search box.

5   Zoom the map display so that each Florida location is clearly separated.

You can zoom in and out of the display in several ways:

1. Click the plus and minus buttons on the bottom right of the map.

2. Roll the mouse wheel (provided that your mouse has a wheel).

3. Use the plus and minus keys on the keyboard.

4. Double-click on the map to zoom into the map and position the map with the location clicked at the center.

   Unfortunately, it is not possible to zoom out using the double-click method.

6   Position the map so that all of the branches in Florida are visible.

There are two ways to do this:

1. Click and drag the map to re-position it in the map window.

2. Use the arrow keys on the keyboard.

7   Zoom out so that every state is visible on screen.

8   Display the *Tour* and *Layer* task panes.

1. Click: Home →View→Tour Editor.

2. Click: Home →View→Layer Pane.

9   Remove the filter so that data points in all states are shown.

Check the check box next to *All* in the list of states shown in the filter list (see sidebar).

10   Save your work as *Sales Summary-4.*

Lesson 10-6: Set layer options and customize data cards

You can think of a *Layer* as being a sheet of glass laid over the top of the map. Up until now you've only worked with a single layer. Later, in: *Lesson 10-10: Create a visualization with multiple layers,* you'll work with multiple layers stacked on top of each other.

The single layer that you created earlier in this session contains a number of blue squares. Each square marks a single sales location.

If you hover the mouse cursor over any of the location markers, you will see a *data card*:

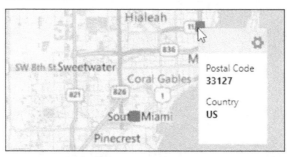

In the example above, the data card simply shows the *Postal Code* and *Country* for the selected location. In this lesson you'll discover how to extensively customize the data card to show other information.

3D Maps also allows you to customize the appearance of each marker. You may want them to be red instead of blue or to be smaller, larger or more transparent. You'll discover how to do all of these things in this lesson.

1 Open *Sales Summary-4* from your sample files folder (if it isn't already open).

2 Open the *Tour 1* tour in the *3D Maps* application.

  1. Click: Insert→Tours→3D Map.

  2. Click on the *Open... Tour 1* icon.

3 Change the location field to: *City*

  You learned how to do this in: *Lesson 10-4: Map using different location fields.*

4 Zoom in to only show *Florida* locations.

5 Change the color of each location marker to red.

  1. Click the fly-out button labeled *Layer Options*. This is located at the bottom of the *Layer* task pane.

  2. Click the *Color* palette and select a red color:

  All of the markers on the map are now colored red.

Sales Summary-4

6 Make all of the markers a little smaller so that they are clearly separated on the map.

Because some locations are close together, they tend to run into each other on the map (unless you are using a very large screen).

Adjust the *Size* slider so that no two markers touch each other.

On my own monitor and zoom level, this worked at a size of 70% but it will be different for you depending upon the size and resolution of your screen.

7 Reduce the opacity of the markers so that you can still read the place names on the map.

If you zoom in to Miami, you'll see that you cannot read the name as it is obstructed by the marker:

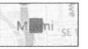

Use the Opacity slider to reduce the opacity of the marker so that it is reasonably easy to read the text:

In the above example I've reduced the opacity to 37%.

8 Customize the data card to show the *Postal Code*, *City* and *State* names.

1. Click: Layer Options→Data Card→Customize at the bottom of the *Layer* task pane.

   The *Customize Data Card dialog* is displayed.

2. Use the *+Add Field* ⎡ + Add Field ⎦ and *Remove* ⎡ × ⎦ buttons to add and remove fields so that the dialog looks like the grab below. You can also click and drag fields to change their position in the list.

3. Click the *OK* button to dismiss the dialog.

4. Hover the mouse cursor over any data point to see the new data card.

9 Save your work as *Sales Summary-5*.

Lesson 10-7: Add a height field to a layer

The data source for this lesson includes sales values:

	A	C	H	I	J	K
1	Date	Customer	Qty	Unit Price	Line Total	Category
2	01-Jan-15	Modular Cycle Systems	2	$ 469.79	$ 939.59	Bikes
3	01-Jan-15	Modular Cycle Systems	3	$ 469.79	$ 1,409.38	Bikes

The first row of the data above tells me that *Modular Cycle Systems* purchased two items in the *Bikes* category for a unit price of *$469.79* and a total price of *$939.59*.

3D Maps can summarize these values by geographical location and then display the total sales value (or quantity of units sold) visually as a bar on the layer.

When you use a value field to visually indicate a value, 3D Maps calls the field a *Height* field.

1   Open *Sales Summary-5* from your sample files folder (if it isn't already open).

2   Open the *Tour 1* tour in the *3D Maps* application.

3   Add a *Height* field to visually indicate the total value of sales (SUM of *Line Total*) to each *City* in the *USA*.

1.   Click: Layer pane→Height→Add Field.

A scrolling field list box appears.

2.   Click on the *Line Total* field.

Note that the field added also shows the aggregation method:

> Height
>
> Line Total (Sum)   ▾ ✕
>
> ✚ Add Field

The SUM aggregation method is used by default, but you can use the drop-down button to the right of the field name to show the other aggregation methods that are available:

> Height
>
> Line Total (Sum)   ▾ ⟩
>
> Sum
> Average
> Count (Not Blank)
> Count (Distinct)
> Maximum
> Minimum
> No Aggregation
> ✚ Add Field

4   Set the layer opacity to 100%.

You learned how to do this in: *Lesson 10-6: Set layer options and customize data cards.*

Sales Summary-5

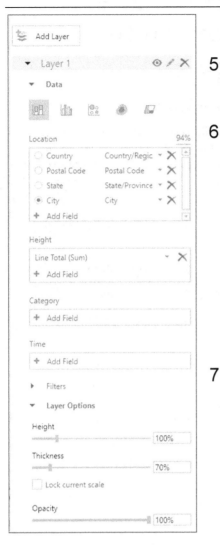

Your *Layer* task pane should now look the same as the one shown in the sidebar.

5   Zoom out from the map so that only Florida locations are visible.

You learned how to do this in: *Lesson 10-5: Apply filters to a 3D Map.*

6   Tilt the map for a more effective visualization.

Bars are shown that visually represent the total sales for each city. Because you are viewing the map from directly overhead this isn't very effective.

Use the *Tilt and Rotate* buttons at the bottom-right of the map to provide a more effective visualization.

A more intuitive way to tilt and rotate the map is to hold down the **<Alt>** key and then click and drag on the map's surface.

7   Customize the layer's data card so that it displays the *State, City* and *Line Total (Sum)* field values.

You learned how to do this in: *Lesson 10-6: Set layer options and customize data cards.*

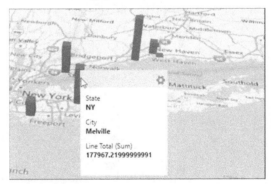

Note the strangely formatted currency value shown in the *Data Card*. This is caused by 3D Maps using a floating point numeric data type internally.

Unfortunately 3D Maps has no option to format the values displayed upon a data card (even rounding in the source data will not work).

In: *Lesson 10-1: Understand how 3D Maps use the data model* you learned that a 3D map uses a data model as the data source. Later, in: *Lesson 12-18: Format values in a data model*, you will learn how to format values within the data model to solve this problem.

8   Adjust the color, height and opacity of the bars to suit your taste.

You learned how to do this in: *Lesson 10-6: Set layer options and customize data cards.*

9   Save your work as *Sales Summary-6*.

tip

Three useful buttons

There are three useful buttons on the bottom-right of the 3D Maps window:

The buttons allow you to return to default settings, zoom to selection and to toggle the navigation buttons on and off.

Lesson 10-8: Apply different visualization types

3D Maps supports five different types of visualization.

One layer may only have one visualization type. The maps you have worked with so far have only had one layer. Later, in: *Lesson 10-10: Create a visualization with multiple layers*, you'll work with 3D Maps that have more than one layer. This will allow you show more than one visualization on the same map.

1 Open *Sales Summary-6* from your sample files folder (if it isn't already open).

2 Open the *Tour 1* tour in the *3D Maps* application.

3 Make sure that the *Location* field is set to: *City*.

You learned how to do this in: *Lesson 10 6: Set layer options and customize data cards*.

4 Set the visualization type to: *Clustered Column*.

The visualization type can be selected by clicking on one of the icons at the top of the *Layer* task pane.

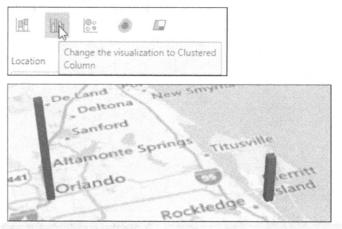

Even though there are two column visualizations (*Clustered Column* and *Stacked Column*), both will produce an identical display with the currently selected options.

Later, in: *Lesson 10-9: Visualize multiple categories*, you'll add a *Category* field to the layer and then you'll better understand the difference between the two different column visualization types.

In the above visualization it is easy to see that *Orlando* is generating more sales volume than *Merritt Island*.

5 Set the visualization type to: *Heat Map*

6 Tilt the map so that it is viewed from directly above.

Sales Summary-6

The easiest way to do this is by clicking the *Return the view to its default zoom and pitch levels* button at the bottom-right of the 3D maps window.

The *Heat Map* visualization shows differently colored circles. Blue is the coldest level (lowest sales) and the colors cycle through green, yellow and red as sales increase.

7   Set the visualization type to: *Bubble*

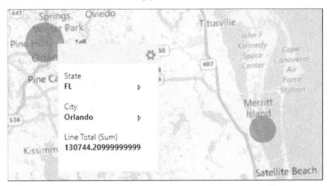

A *Bubble* visualization is similar to a *Heat Map* except that the size of each circle (bubble) indicates the relative sales value of each location.

8   Set the location field to: *State* and the visualization type to: *Region*

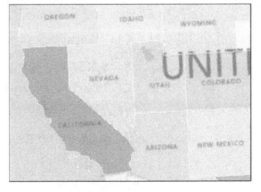

A *Region* visualization indicates sales values by shading in areas. The darkest shaded states indicate the highest sales values. In the above example it is easy to see that *California* is producing a higher sales value than *Arizona*.

9   Save your work as *Sales Summary-7*.

Lesson 10-9: Visualize multiple categories

Up until now, you've only visualized a single data value for each geographical data point.

In this lesson you will visualize multiple data values by displaying *Stacked Column, Clustered Column* and *Pie* charts upon the layer.

1   Open *Sales Summary-7* from your sample files folder (if it isn't already open).

2   Open the *Tour 1* tour in the *3D Maps* application.

3   Replace the layer's *Value* field with the SUM of the *Qty* field.

1.   Cick: Layer task pane→Value→Line Total(Sum)→Delete Button, to remove the existing *Value* field.

If you do not see a window labelled: *Value* on the *Layer* task pane you may have set a different visualization type (see facing page sidebar).

2.   Click: Layer task pane→Value→+ Add Field.

3.   Click on the *Qty* field in the drop-down list.

The Qty(Sum) field is now displayed in the the *Value* window.

4   Customize the data card to show the *State, Qty (Sum)* and *Category* fields.

You learned how to do this in: *Lesson 10-6: Set layer options and customize data cards.*

5   Add the *Category* field from the source data as a *Category*.

The sample data for this lesson has a field called *Category*. This records the product category for each item sold.

There are only four categories of product: *Accessories, Bikes, Clothing* and *Components*.

1.   Click: Layer task pane→Category→+ Add Field.

A list appears showing all of the fields in the source data.

2.   Click on the *Category* field.

The *Category* field is added as the *Category* field for this layer.

6   Select a *Clustered Column* visualization.

You learned how to do this in: *Lesson 10-8: Apply different visualization types.*

7   Zoom and tilt the map so that it most effectively visualizes sales by *Category*.

You learned how to do this in: *Lesson 10-7: Add a height field to a layer.*

Sales Summary-7

note

The value window is labeled: Value, Size or Height depending upon the current visualization type

3D Maps will show a different label for the Layer task pane's value window depending upon the currently selected visualization type.

Region and *Heatmap* visualization types name the label as: *Value*.

The *Bubble* visualization type names the label as: *Size*.

Size
Qty (Sum)
✚ Add Field

The *Stacked Column* and *Clustered Column* visualization types name the label as: *Height*.

Height
Qty (Sum)
✚ Add Field

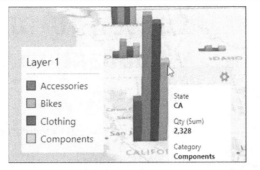

You are now able to visualize the quantities ordered in different states for each product category.

In this example you can see at a glance that *2328* units in the *Components* category were sold in *California* during 2015.

8 Select the *Stacked Column* visualization.

A stacked column visualization shows the same data in a more compact form. Bars are less likely to overlap each other when there is only a single bar.

9 Change the visualization's tilt so that it is viewed from directly overhead.

The easiest way to do this is by clicking the *Return the view to its default zoom and pitch levels* button 🔲 at the bottom-right of the 3D Maps window.

Column visualizations are not very effective when viewed from directly overhead.

10 Show a Pie chart visualization to display categorized values for each State.

Change the visualization type to *Bubble*. When you use the *Bubble* visualization with categorized data, pie charts are shown instead of plain bubbles.

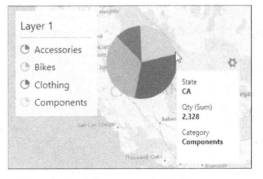

11 Save your work as *Sales Summary-8*.

note

Formatting longitude and latitude values for 3D Maps

There are many ways to format longitude and latitude values but only one is understood by 3D Maps.

The globe is split into 360 equal degrees of longitude. Starting at the *Greenwich Meridian,* longitude is measured in degrees east or west. 3D maps require you to specify *longitude degrees East* as positive values and *longitude degrees West* as negative values.

The globe is also split into 180 equal degrees of *latitude* (each forming a circle called a *parallel*). The central parallel (the equator) represents zero degrees, making the *North Pole* 90 degrees North and the *South Pole* 90 degrees South.

In a similar way to longitude, 3D Maps requires you to specify *latitude degrees North* as positive values and *latitude degrees South* as negative values.

	A	B
1	Longitude	Latitude
2	-96.8892	32.94914

The above example shows correctly formatted coordinates for 3D Maps. You'll often see this formatted as:

32.94914 N 96.8892 W

note

Show/Hide layers

An eyeball icon 👁 is shown next to each layer name.

You can click this toggle to hide or show the layer.

US Population-1

Lesson 10-10: Create a visualization with multiple layers

Up until now you've only created visualizations that have a single layer.

If you create several layers (stacked on top of each other) it is possible to create some interesting presentation effects that are not possible with a single-layer visualization.

1 Open *US Population-1* from your sample files folder.

This workbook contains a single worksheet containing a table called: *USPopulation.* This table contains the *Population, Area in Square Miles* and *Population Density* for each major US city.

Notice that nothing has been left to chance for the location of each city, as latitude and longitude coordinates have been defined.

See sidebar for a discussion of how latitude and longitude values need to be defined for 3D Maps to recognize them.

2 Create a 3D Map to show a heat map visualization of population density by city.

1. Click anywhere in the *USPopulation* table.

2. Click: Insert→Tours→3D Map.

   Notice that Latitude and Longitude have been correctly recognized in the *Location* pane.

3. Set the *Visualization Type* to: *Heat Map.*

4. Set the *Location* field to: *City*

5. Set the *Value* field to: *Population/Square Mile (Sum)*

6. Click: Home→Map→Flat Map to change the map view from a globe to a flat map.

7. Click: Home→Map→Map Labels to show names upon the map.

   What you have just done demonstrates the incredible power of 3D Maps. In just eight clicks you can clearly visualize which USA cities have the highest population density:

note

Help – one of my layers has disappeared

When you first start to work with multiple layers, you can gain the impression that a layer has disappeared.

This is because layers are shown one beneath the other in the *Layers task pane*. You will often have to scroll down the *Layers task pane* in order to find the other layers.

Layers can also be expanded and collapsed using the triangle shown before the layer name. This is usually easier than scrolling down the task pane.

Expand/Collapse Button

note

It is possible to use the 3D Maps tool without using Bing Maps

Bing Maps converts all location data to longitude and latitude in order to show visualizations on the correct part of a Bing map.

Sometimes you may wish to visualize location-specific data on a custom image instead of a map.

For example, you might want to visually indicate sales values in different shops within a shopping mall.

In this case you would use x and y co-ordinates to refer to pixels in a custom background graphic.

3   Rename the *Layer 1* layer to: **City Population Heat Map**

When working with multiple layers, things are a lot easier if you give each layer a descriptive name.

1.   Click the *Rename this layer* icon to the right of the words *Layer 1* at the top of the *Layer* task pane.

2.   Type: **City Population Heat Map** into the text box and then press the **<Enter>** key.

4   Create a new layer and name it: **City Population Column**

1.   Click the *Add Layer* button at the top of the *Layer* task pane.

2.   Click the *Rename this layer* icon to the right of the words *Layer 2* at the top of the *Layer* task pane.

3.   Type: **City Population Column** into the text box and then press the **<Enter>** key.

5   Set up the *City Population Column* layer to show *a Clustered Column* visualization of each city's population.

1.   Set the *Visualization Type* to: *Clustered Column*.

2.   Set the *Location* field to: *City*.

3.   Set the *Height* field to: *Population/Square Mile (Sum)*

4.   Zoom and tilt the map to most effectively visualize population densities in the *New York* and *Boston* area.

6   Adjust the *Height* and *Thickness* values of the columns and the *Color Scale* and *Radius of Influence* values of the heat map to best visually illustrate population density.

You learned how to do this in: *Lesson 10-6: Set layer options and customize data cards.*

You now have a two-layer visualization that provides more visual information than would be possible with a single layer visualization.

7   Save your work as: *US Population-2.*

Lesson 10-11: Add annotations

In: *Lesson 10-6: Set layer options and customize data cards,* you learned how to control the information that appears on *data cards*.

Data cards appear when you hover the mouse cursor over any of the objects on a 3D Maps layer (see example in sidebar).

Sometimes you may want to add information to a 3D Map that goes beyond what is possible with a data card. In this lesson you'll add *Annotations* to a 3D Map visualization.

Annotations contain information about a specific object on a layer.

1 Open *Popular Names-1* from your sample files folder.

The sample file contains a table called *PopularNames* that lists the most popular male and female names, by state, given to children born in 2014.

	A	B	C
3	State	Male	Female
4	Alabama	William	Ava
5	Alaska	Liam	Emma

You can see that the most popular *Male* name given to children born in 2014 in *Alabama* was *William*.

2 Create a flat map with a *Region* visualization, showing which states had the same most popular *Male* name in 2014.

1. Click anywhere inside the table.

2. Click: Insert→Tours→3D Map.

3. Click: Home→Map→Flat Map.

4. Click the *State* option button in the *Location* pane.

5. Set the *Visualization type* to: *Region*.

6. Set the *Category* field to: *Male*.

7. Zoom into the map to see all of the states except Alaska and Hawaii.

You can see that states are now colored to show those that shared the same most popular name in 2014.

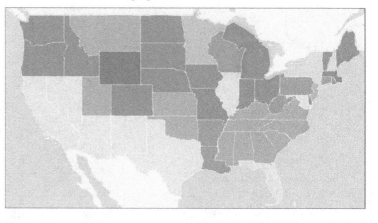

note

You can add an image to an annotation

When you add an annotation to an object, it is possible to add an image instead of custom text or fields.

This opens up a huge range of possibilities as you can create an image that also includes text.

Here's an example:

Popular Names-1

Add Annotation

Choose data fields you would like to add, or type

| Segoe UI | v | 12 | v | **B** | *I* |

TITLE ○ Custom ● State

State: Arizona

DESCRIPTION

○ Custom ● Fields ○ Image

☐ State

☐ Male (Count - Not Blank)

☑ Male

PLACEMENT

○ Left ● Right

note

You can also add text boxes to a map

A text box is similar to an annotation but is not connected to any object. They can be used for titles or freehand notes.

To add a text box to a layer:

1. Right-click on the map.

2. Click: *Add Text Box* from the shortcut menu.

3 Add an annotation to *Arizona* to show the most popular name in this (and similarly colored) states.

1. Right-click on the location of *Arizona* on the map.

2. Click: *Add Annotation* from the shortcut menu.

3. Click the option button to the left of *State* to set the annotation's *TITLE* field to show the state.

4. Set the font size for the *TITLE* field to *12* points.

5. Click on the *Fields* options button underneath *DESCRIPTION* to select a description field to be shown in the annotation.

6. Click the *Male* check box to show the most popular male name in the annotation.

Note that the *CONTENT PREVIEW* pane now shows how the annotation will look when it is added to the map.

7. Click the *OK* button.

The annotation is now shown on the map:

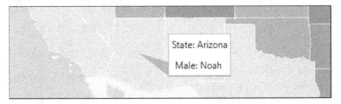

4 Add more annotations, one for each of the nine colors shown on the map.

You may have to select one of the *Left* or *Right* PLACEMENT option buttons at the bottom of the *Add Annotation* dialog to prevent some annotations from overlapping.

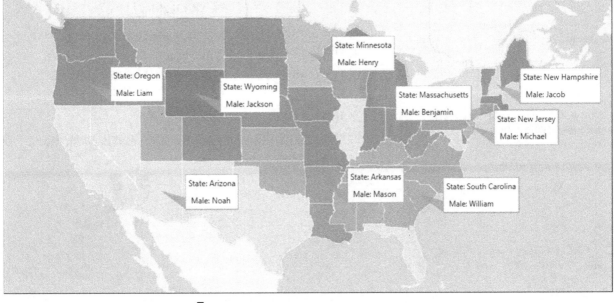

5 Save your work as: *Popular Names-2.*

note

Save a temporal visualization as a movie file

You can use your temporal visualization to create a video in 1080p (full HD), 720p (slightly better than DVD) or 360p (low quality, low file size).

Creating a video uses a lot of processor and memory resources. This means that it can take an older computer a considerable amount of time to render your video.

On a fast, modern i7 computer with solid state hard drive and plenty of memory, it will take less than 30 seconds to create this video in full HD.

If you are using a 32-bit version of Excel with limited memory, it is possible that Excel will be unable to render your video and will report an *Out of Memory* error. If this happens you may find that you are still able to create a video at a lower resolution (the lowest is 360p).

In order to do make a movie of your visualization:

1. Click: Home→Tour→ Create Video.

2. Select the quality you want (1080p, 720p or 360p).

3. Click *Soundtrack Options* if you would like to add a sound file. This will enable you to add music or a voice narration.

4. Click the *Create* button.

5. Select a location to save the video to.

6. Click the *Save* button.

7. Click the *Open* button to view the MP4 video that Excel has created.

Lesson 10-12: Create a video from temporal data

In: *Lesson 10-9: Visualize multiple categories*, you visualized the total sales volume by category during 2015. The total sales volume values were aggregated from over 16,000 individual transactions occurring on different days during the year.

When a data set includes a time dimension, it becomes possible to do some very interesting things with 3D maps. A video presentation can be automatically generated that shows an animation of accumulated sales with the passage of time.

In this lesson you will create a video by adding a *Time* dimension to a 3D Maps layer.

1 Open *Sales Summary-8* from your sample files folder (if it isn't already open).

2 Open the *Tour 1* tour in the *3D Maps* application.

3 Change the values of the fields in the *Layer 1* task pane.

   1. Set the *Location* field to: *City*.

   2. Set the *Visualization Type* to: *Stacked Column*.

   3. Make sure that the *Height* field is set to: *Qty (Sum)*.

   4. Set the *Category* field to: *Category*.

4 Tilt and zoom the map so that the bars are clearly visible.

5 Add the *Date* field from the source data to the layer's *Time* dimension.

   1. Click: Layer 1→Time→+ Add Field.

   A drop-down list of all fields in the source data that contain valid time information appears.

   In this case there is only one field (*Date*) that contains Date/Time information.

   2. Click the *Date* field.

   Notice that a video play bar has appeared beneath the visualization.

6 Play a video showing sales as they occurred in 2015.

Click the *Play* button.

note

You can use the time scrubber to move to any point in the video

Click and drag the *time scrubber* to move to a specific point in time.

Go to a specific time in the current scene.

note

Selecting how data should be animated

When you add a *Time* field, a clock icon appears above the selected field:

Data shows for an instant
Data accumulates over time
Data stays until it is replaced

You can see that there are three options.

1. Data accumulates over time.

This is clearly the correct option for this lesson. As each sale is made, you want the total sales to date (a running total) to be visualized.

2. Data stays until it is replaced.

Imagine you are showing how the population of a city has changed over the years. You'd want to replace the previous population figure with the new updated population figure at each census.

3. Data shows for an instant.

In this case, the data disappears as the timeline moves forwards. You might use this to document a road trip when you are only present in one location at one time.

A video plays for ten seconds. Each stacked column gradually grows in height as sales occur during the year. When the video stops playing, a visualization of the total sales for 2015 remains visible.

7   Display only calendar months at the top left of the visualization.

By default, the visualization displays the day, hour and second as it travels through the year.

Perhaps you'd like to keep the display simpler by only displaying the calendar month.

1. Right click on the date and time display at the top left of the visualization.

2. Click *Edit* from the shortcut menu.

    The *Edit Time* dialog is displayed.

    Edit Time

    Segoe UI   26   B   I   A

    Time Format

    18/06/2010 08:30

3. Click inside the *Time Format* box.

    A drop-down menu appears listing a huge variety of built-in format types.

4. Select a format that shows only the month and year.

    Notice that you can also customize the font type, font size, font color and background color from this dialog.

5. Click the *Accept* button.

    The time display now only shows the month and year:

    December 2015

    CANADA

8   Play the video again.

This time the visualization displays each calendar month of 2015 as it animates.

It is possible to save the video you are seeing as an industry-standard MP4 video file (see facing page sidebar). You could then distribute the video or incorporate it into a PowerPoint presentation.

9   Save your work as *Sales Summary-9*.

Lesson 10-13: Set scene options

In: *Lesson 10-12: Create a video from temporal data*, you learned how to animate your data. The video that you created was a little uninteresting as it was viewed from a single viewpoint. You could imagine that you were looking down upon the map from a hovering helicopter.

The next time you watch a Hollywood movie, notice that the camera rarely stays still. The viewpoint constantly moves as the camera zooms in and out of the scene and moves around the subject. This adds interest and engages the viewer.

When you create a 3D Maps movie, you can use the same production techniques. You'll find that this creates a more interesting and engaging display.

1 **Open *New Jersey Sales-1* from your sample files folder.**

   This sample file contains a table called *NewJerseySales* containing details of 11,500 sales made by a consumer electronics retailer in the state of *New Jersey* during 2015.

2 **Create a flat map with a *City* visualization showing total *Sales Amount* by *City*.**

   1. Click anywhere inside the table.

   2. Click: Insert→Tours→3D Map.

   3. Click: Home→Map→Flat Map.

   4. Click: Home→Map→Map Labels to show place names on the map.

   5. Set the *Location* field to: *City*.

   6. Set the *Height* field to: *Sales Amount(Sum)*.

   7. Zoom and tilt the map to best visualize sales.

3 **Add a *Time* and *Category* field to create a video presentation of 2015 sales by *Category*.**

   Add the following fields:

New Jersey Sales-1

Category

Category   ✕

Time   ⏱ ▾

Date (None)   ▾ ✕

4   Name the layer: **New Jersey Sales**

1.   Click the *Rename this layer* 🖊 icon at the top right of the *Layer* task pane and type: **New Jersey Sales** into the text box.

2.   Press the **<Enter>** key.

5   Name the scene: **Sales by Category**

As you'll discover later in: *Lesson 10-14: Create a tour with multiple scenes,* a *Tour* can have many *Scenes.* The visualization you have created in this lesson only has a single scene. It will still be useful to name it now, so that things don't become confusing if you add another scene in the future.

1.   Click: Home→Scene→Scene Options.

The *Scene Options* dialog appears.

2.   Type: **Sales by Category** into the *Scene Name* text box.

3.   Close the *Scene Options* dialog.

Scene Options   ✕

Scene duration (sec)   10.00 ↕

Scene Name

Sales by Category

Effects

Transition duration (sec)   3.00 ↕

Effect   Circle ▾

Effect Speed   ━━━━●━

Time

Start date   01/01/2015 00:00:00 ▾

End date   31/12/2015 00:00:00 ▾

Speed   ━━━━━●━

Map Type

Change

6   Play the video.

Note that the viewpoint stays still during the video.

7   Add a *Circle* effect to fly around the visualization in a circle.

1.   Click: Home→Scene→Scene Options.

2.   Click the *Effect* drop-down arrow and set the *Effect* to: *Circle.*

3.   Close the *Scene Options* dialog.

8   Play the tour.

Click: Home→Tour→Play Tour.

You won't see the effect if you click the *Play* button at the bottom of the screen.

When you play a *Tour* the display changes to full screen. Notice how much more effective the visualization is as you fly in a partial circle around the visualization.

You will not fly in a full circle. You could achieve this (if required) by changing the *Effect Speed* or *Scene Duration* settings in the *Scene Options dialog.*

Later, in: *Lesson 10-14: Create a tour with multiple scenes,* you'll discover how you can combine scenes and effects to create a stunning presentation. For now, try experimenting with the different effects available in order to become familiar with them.

9   Close full screen view by pressing the **<Escape>** key.

10   Save your work as: *New Jersey Sales-2.*

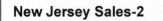

Lesson 10-14: Create a tour with multiple scenes

In this lesson you'll create a tour that begins with a scene that shows total sales by category for each branch (the scene that you created in: *Lesson 10-13: Set scene options*).

This retailer makes most of its income from computer sales. For this reason, you'll then create a second scene showing sales in the *Computers* category for each city.

1   Open *New Jersey Sales-2* from your sample files folder.

2   Open the *Tour 1* tour in the *3D Maps* application.

There is only one scene in the current tour. This scene has only one layer. It would be correct to call this: "The *New Jersey Sales* layer in the *Sales by Category* scene".

3   Change the Visualization type to *Clustered Column*.

Change the visualization from *Stacked Column* to *Clustered Column*.

This will work better for the multi-scene tour.

4   Add a new scene to the Tour called *Computer Sales*.

1.   Click: Home→Scene→New Scene (drop-down list)→ Copy Sales by Category.

Notice that a second scene has now appeared beneath the first. There is a green line around this scene to show that it is the active scene.

2.   Click: Home→Scene→Scene Options.

The *Scene Options* dialog appears, showing options for the currently active scene.

3.   Click in the *Scene Name* box and type the new name: **Computer Sales**

5   Make sure that the *Computer Sales* scene is the active scene.

One scene is always the active scene.

You can see which scene this is in the *Tour Editor* task pane (the task pane shown on the left of the screen). The active scene has a green outline.

If the *Computer Sales* scene is not the active scene, click on it once to select it.

6   Change the layer settings for the *Computer Sales* scene so that only sales in the *Computers* category are displayed.

1.   Click: Layer task pane→Filters→+Add Filter.

2.   Click the *Category* field from the field list.

3.   Check the *Computers* check box in the filter field list.

New Jersey Sales-2

The visualization changes to only show sales in the *Computers* category.

7   Change the visualization for the *Computer Sales* scene so that the bars are shown at full height for the entire duration of the second scene.

1.   Make sure that the *Computer Sales* scene is active (selected).

2.   Remove the *Date (None)* field from the *Time* pane in the *Layer* task pane.

Without a *Time* field, the scene will show total sales for the entire duration of the scene.

8   Remove the transition effect from the *Sales by Category* scene and the *Circle* effect from the *Computer Sales* scene.

It may be overkill to have effects for both scenes.

1.   Make sure that the *Sales by Category* scene is active (selected).

2.   Click Home→Scene→Scene Options.

3.   Set the *Transition Duration (sec)* to: **0.00**

Transition effects are used to smoothly move to the starting view point of any follow-on scene.

In the next step, you'll synchronize the starting view point of the *Computer Sales* scene with the ending view point of the Sales by *Category* scene. If you do this well, you won't need a transition effect.

4.   Click on the *Computer Sales* scene to activate (select) it.

5.   Click Home→Scene→Scene Options.

6.   Set the *Effect* to: *No Effect.*

9   Move the starting view point of the *Computer Sales* scene to the approximate finishing location of the *Sales by Category* scene.

Because the view point of the first scene is travelling around the visualization in a circle, the ending view point of the first scene will be in a different position to the starting view point of the second scene.

1.   Make sure that the *Computer Sales* scene is active (selected).

2.   Use the *Rotate* arrows at the bottom right of the visualization to move around the visualization.

Avoid clicking the *Tilt Up* and *Tilt Down* arrows to maintain the view point at the same altitude as the previous scene.

3.   Play the tour to see how well you did. You may have to do this a few times before you are happy with the effect.

10   Refine and improve your tour.

You may find it useful to compare the New *Jersey Sales-3* sample file (in your sample files folder) to your own work.

11   Save your work as *New Jersey Sales-3.*

Session 10: Exercise

1   Open *European Climate-1* from your sample files folder.

This workbook contains a single range, showing average monthly temperatures in twelve European cities.

2   Convert the range into a table named: **EuropeanClimate**

3   Create a 3D Maps tour from the table.

4   Review the geocoding to confirm that all locations have been correctly identified.

5   Change the map display so that it shows a *Flat Map* displaying place names (*Map Labels*).

6   Set the *Location, Height* and *Category* fields to display a *Clustered Column* visualization upon each *City* showing the average temperature for each month.

7   Rename the layer to: **Average Temperature** and change the tilt and zoom settings, column *Height* and column *Thickness* to make the visualization as effective and informative as possible.

8   Add a *Fly Over* motion effect to the scene and play the tour.

9   Save your work as *European Climate-2*.

European Climate-1

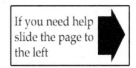

If you need help slide the page to the left

Session 10: Exercise Answers

These are the three questions that students find the most difficult to answer:

Q 8	Q 7	Q 6
1. Click: Home→Scene→ Scene Options. The *Scene Options* dialog appears. 2. Change the *Effect* to: *Fly Over.* 3. Click: Home→Tour→Play Tour This was covered in: *Lesson 10-13: Set scene options.*	1. Click the *Rename this Layer* icon at the top of the *Layer* task pane and then type: **Average Temperature** into the text box. This was covered in: *Lesson 10-10: Create a visualization with multiple layers.* 2. Use the *Tilt* and *Zoom* buttons to zoom and tilt the map. This was covered in: *Lesson 10-7: Add a height field to a layer.* 3. At the bottom of the *Layer* task pane, click: Layer Options→ Height/Thickness … to change the height and thickness of the bars. This was covered in: *Lesson 10-6: Set layer options and customize data cards*	Set the fields in the *Layer 1* task pane so that they look like this: This was covered in: *Lesson 10-9: Visualize multiple categories.*

If you have difficulty with the other questions, here are the lessons that cover the relevant skills:

2   Refer to: *Lesson 1-13: Convert a range into a table and add a total row.*

3   Refer to: *Lesson 10-2: Create a simple 3D Map.*

4   Refer to: *Lesson 10-3: Confirm the accuracy of geocoding.*

5   Refer to: *Lesson 10-4: Map using different location fields.*

Session Eleven: Create Get & Transform queries

> The goal is to transform data into information, and information into insight.
>
> *Carly Fiorina (1954-),*
> *American former technology business executive and former*
> *Presidential candidate in the 2016 Republican primaries.*

Get & Transform integrates well with both Excel and Power Pivot (an advanced data modeling add-in that is included with Excel). You'll learn more about data modeling with Power Pivot in: *Session Twelve: Power Pivot, Data Modeling, OLAP and Business Intelligence.*

Get & Transform is a powerful and complex professional tool. Entire books have been written to explain how to use Get & Transform. This short session will teach you everything you need to know to use this tool effectively in most business scenarios. By the end of this session you'll have skills that could potentially save an enormous amount of time in your day-to-day work with Excel.

Session Objectives

- Understand Get & Transform and ETL
- Create a simple extract and load web query
- Understand queries and connections
- Move, remove, rename, filter and sort columns
- Split delimited data
- Understand data types
- Create and use a linked data type
- Add a linked data type field using a data card
- Resolve geocoding errors in the Geography linked data type
- Understand Get & Transform data types
- Specify data types
- Understand steps and PQFL
- Remove empty, error and top and bottom rows
- Understand and work with null values
- Transform date and time columns
- Transform number columns
- Add a custom calculated column

- Create an aggregated data query
- Unpivot aggregated data
- Work with multiple queries
- Create an append query
- Understand Column From Examples
- Use Column From Examples with selected source columns
- Use Column From Examples to extract characters from strings
- Understand primary and foreign keys
- Link primary and foreign keys using VLOOKUP
- Efficiently import data using a view
- Understand linked table and Pivot Table refresh
- Load a query directly into the Pivot Table cache
- Understand normal and de-normalized data
- Create a simple two-table merged query
- Create a five-table merged query
- Create a merged query using fuzzy logic

Lesson 11-1: Understand Get & Transform and ETL

Get & Transform is an advanced ETL tool. ETL is an acronym for *Extract, Transform and Load*.

Before Get & Transform was added to Excel, users had to import data into a worksheet and then transform the data inside Excel. The new *Get & Transform* tool enables you to import data (from one or more external sources) and then transform it *before* it is loaded into Excel (or a data model). This provides many advantages.

The diagram below should make it clear what is meant by the terms *Extract, Transform* and *Load*.

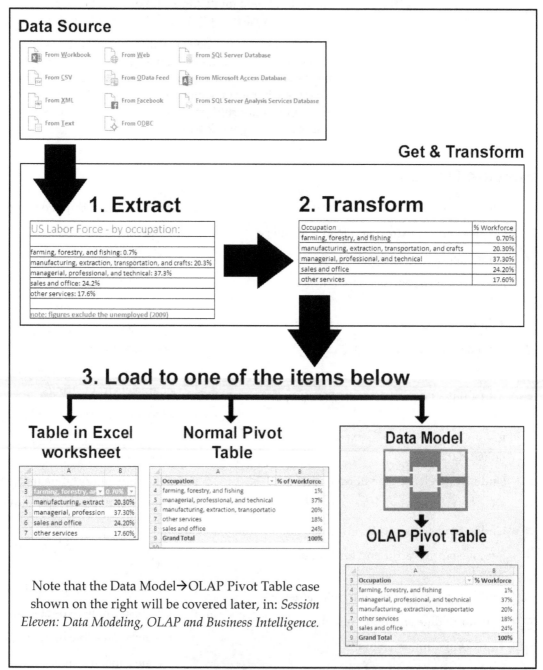

Note that the Data Model→OLAP Pivot Table case shown on the right will be covered later, in: *Session Eleven: Data Modeling, OLAP and Business Intelligence.*

note

Confusing terminology

In the world of IT, we are very fond of terminology.

The process that I describe as *Data Transformation* is often referred to using the following alternative terminology:

- Data Wrangling
- Data Cleansing
- Data Scrubbing
- Data Shaping
- Data Pre-Processing
- Data Munging

In this session I will exclusively use the term *Data Transformation*.

You can, of course, use the above terminology liberally in meetings. This will make you sound very important and help to confuse your co-workers.

Personally, I'd rather be referred to as a transformer than a munger, scrubber or wrangler.

The ETL methodology

Extract: Most data that is analyzed with Excel doesn't start its life in an Excel workbook but is imported from an external data source (often from a database or CSV file). *Extract* simply means moving this data from the external data source into the Get & Transform tool.

Transform: Extracted data often isn't in a form that can be easily analyzed by Excel. There may be unwanted columns, badly named fields, badly formatted fields or corrupted data. The Get & Transform tool includes a vast array of features that enable you to clean your data before loading it into an Excel table or Pivot Table. This cleaning process is called *Data Transformation* (see sidebar).

Load: This simply means exporting the transformed data from the Get & Transform tool to its destination. A Get & Transform query can export (load) transformed data into an Excel table or into an Excel Pivot Table.

Get & Transform can also load data into a special construct called a *Data Model*. Data Modeling will be covered later, in: *Session Twelve: Power Pivot, Data Modeling, OLAP and Business Intelligence.*

Why is ETL better than ELT?

When you add and delete columns, change column headers, re-format columns and add calculated columns to Excel tables you are *transforming* your data. Excel users that do not understand how to use the *Get & Transform* tool use an ELT methodology (*Extract* from data source, *Load* into Excel and *Transform* within Excel). Here are some of the advantages in using Get & Transform to implement an ETL methodology:

1. **Re-usable and sharable queries:** The Get & Transform tool generates a re-usable *Query*. This means that all of the Get & Transform actions that you define can be repeated to refresh the data in a table on your worksheet with a single click. You'll learn more about queries later, in: *Lesson 11-3: Understand queries and connections.*

2. **Automatically refreshed data:** You can configure a query to automatically refresh an Excel table at a timed interval. You'll learn how to automatically refresh data later, in: *Lesson 11-3: Understand queries and connections.*

3. **The ability to transform big data:** Get & Transform does not share Excel's limits (of approximately a million rows of data) so it can be used to transform big data (sending the result directly to the data model, 3D Map, or to an Excel worksheet after aggregation). You'll learn more about pre-aggregating data later, in: *Lesson 11-18: Create an aggregated data query.*

4. **Better tools:** Get & Transform has some advanced transformation tools that are not found in the standard Excel product (for example, the *Unpivot Columns* tool that you'll learn about in: *Lesson 11-19: Unpivot aggregated data*).

5. **The ability to combine data:** Get & Transform enables you to merge queries. This enables you to combine relational data from disparate data sources to create a de-normalized data extract. You'll learn about this later, in: *Lesson 11-31: Understand normal and de-normalized data.*

Lesson 11-2: Create a simple extract and load web query

There are many sites on the Internet containing useful data that is constantly changing. Obvious examples are currency exchange rates and stock prices. This type of information is often presented on a web page.

Get & Transform allows you to create a web query that will extract data from a specified table on a specified web page.

When a web query has been created, it is possible to refresh the information in your worksheet (from the source web page) at any time, either manually or automatically (at a specified time interval).

1 Open a new blank workbook.

2 Open your web browser and go to:

https://tinyurl.com/version2002

Type the above URL into your web browser's address bar.

A simple web page appears showing eight current (fictitious) currency exchange rates.

Notice that the exchange rates update every five seconds.

3 Create a web query to extract currency exchange rates from: https://tinyurl.com/version2002

1. Return to Excel and select cell A1.

2. Click:

Data→Get & Transform Data→From Web

The *From Web* dialog appears, requesting a URL.

3. Type: https://tinyurl.com/version2002

…into the *URL* box.

4. Click the *OK* button.

5. If you see a security prompt asking whether to allow access click: *Connect*.

The *Navigator* pane appears, listing a single table and a document.

On a more complicated web page you could see many tables. This is a simple page with only one table.

6. Select the *Table 0* table.

A preview of the table appears in the right-hand pane of the dialog.

Notice that there are three buttons at the bottom of the dialog: *Load*, *Transform Data* and *Cancel*. The *Transform Data* button would take you to the *Power Query Editor* window where you

note

Sometimes refresh takes longer than expected

When tested with build: 13127.20910 I noticed that the refresh feature does not always work correctly. This may have been corrected via a later build by the time you read this book.

note

The Import Data dialog options

1. *Table* in *New Worksheet*.

Sends the output to a linked Excel table in a new worksheet.

2. *Table* in *Existing Worksheet*.

Sends the output to an Excel linked table in a specified location in an existing worksheet (the option you used in this lesson).

3. *Only Create Connection*.

This option allows you to save a query to use later. You'll learn how to use saved queries later, in: *Lesson 11-3: Understand queries and connections*.

4. *Add this data to the Data Model*.

If this check box is checked, the data returned by the query will be sent to a table in a special in-memory construct called the data model.

The data model will be covered later, in: *Session Twelve: Power Pivot, Data Modeling, OLAP and Business Intelligence*.

would be able to transform your data. (You'll use many of Get & Transform's transformation tools later in this session).

For the moment you will use the Get & Transform tool only to *extract* and *load* the data. You've already *extracted* the data and are now ready to *load* it into the worksheet.

4   Load the extracted data into cell A1 on the currently selected worksheet.

1.   Click: Load (drop-down arrow)→Load To…

The *Import Data* dialog appears. Notice that the default load location is a table in a new worksheet.

2.   Click the *Existing worksheet* option button.

Cell A1 is already selected, so the data will be loaded into a table in cell A1 of the currently selected worksheet. See sidebar for a discussion of the other load options.

3.   Click the *OK* button.

The exchange rates are displayed in a table upon the worksheet.

	A	B	C	D	E
1	Place	Currency	Symbol	1 USD	Inverse
2	Atlantis	Orich	ATO	0.8061	1.2406
3	Narnia	Lion	NAL	0.6848	1.4602
4	Middle Earth	Castar	MEC	67.7414	0.0148
5	Hogsmeade Village	Gringott	HOG	1.2182	0.8209
6	Kingdom of Zamunda	Pound	ZAP	0.9407	1.0631
7	El Dorado	Gold Dollar	ELD	1.4877	0.6722
8	Lilliput	Sprug	LIS	125.6879	0.008
9	San Seriffe	Corona	SSC	1.4199	0.7043

Note that this is a rather special table (called a *linked table*). If you click inside the table, you'll see a new *Query* ribbon tab. This tells you that the table is linked to a *Get & Transform* query. The default color of the table (green instead of blue) also provides a visual clue that this is a linked table.

5   Refresh the data shown in the table.

Because the table is linked to a *Get & Transform* query, you can execute the query at any time to update the exchange rates.

1.   Click inside the table to select it.

2.   Click: Query→Load→Refresh.

Every time you click the *Refresh* button you'll see the values change to show up-to-the-second exchange rates. If this doesn't seem to work for you see sidebar.

Later, in: *Lesson 11-3: Understand queries and connections,* you'll learn how to automatically refresh the query at a timed interval (of as little as one minute). The worksheet data will then always be up to date.

6   Save your work as *Exchange Rates-1*.

note

Where are queries and connections saved?

When you save an Excel workbook containing a query, the query (that includes both a connection and transformation instructions) is automatically saved as part of the workbook.

Lesson 11-3: Understand queries and connections

A *Get & Transform* query contains two items:

1. A *Connection* that the query uses to connect to a data source and *Extract* raw data.

2. All of the steps needed for the query to *Transform* the data after it is extracted using the connection. Later, in: *Lesson 11-12: Understand steps and PQFL,* you'll learn that these steps are stored in a special language called: *Power Query Formula Language.*

Crucially, the query does not know what to do with the data after transforming it. In other words, it does not contain any *Load* information.

This provides many advantages. You can share a query with other users who can decide where they want to load the resulting query data.

1   Open a new blank workbook.

2   Create a web query to extract currency exchange rates from: https://tinyurl.com/version2002

     1.   Select cell A1.

     2.   Click: Data→Get & Transform Data→From Web.

     3.   Type: https://tinyurl.com/version2002
        …into the *URL* box.

     4.   Click the *OK* button.

     5.   Select the *Table 0* table.

     6.   Click: Load (drop-down)→Load To…

        The *Import Data* dialog appears. Notice that the default load location is a table in a new worksheet.

     7.   Click the *Only Create Connection* option button.

        Only Create Connection is rather confusing terminology, as you are actually creating a *Query* that includes both a connection and transformation instructions (and not a simple connection).

     8.   Click the *OK* button.

3   View query information using the *Queries & Connections* task pane.

     1.   The *Queries & Connections* task pane should now be visible on the right of your screen. If you have closed it, click:

        Data→Queries & Connections→Queries & Connections

        … to bring it back again.

     2.   Hover the mouse cursor over the *Table 0* query.

        A large amount of information about the query is shown in an information box.

note

Unlinking a linked table

When you import a table using a query, the table is linked to the source data.

You may, however, wish to break the link between the source data and the table.

To do this:

1. Right-click on the table.

2. Click:

Table→
Unlink from Data Source

… from the shortcut menu.

4 Give the query a meaningful name.

1. Right-click on the *Table 0* query in the *Queries & Connections* task pane.

2. Click: *Properties* from the shortcut menu.

3. Type: **Currency Exchange Rates** into the *Query name* box.

4. Click the *OK* button.

5 Use the *Currency Exchange Rates* query to provide data to a table on the current worksheet.

1. Right-click on the *Currency Exchange Rates* query in the *Queries & Connections* task pane.

2. Click: *Load To…* from the shortcut menu.

3. Click the *Table* option button.

4. Click the *Existing worksheet* option button.

5. Click the *OK* button.

The data returned by the query is displayed in a linked table on the current worksheet.

You learned about linked tables in: *Lesson 11-2: Create a simple extract and load web query.*

6. Click inside the table to select it.

7. Look in the: Table Design→Properties→Table Name box.

Notice that Excel has automatically named the table: *Currency_Exchange_Rates.*

You learned about table names in: *Lesson 1-19: Name a table and create an automatic structured table reference.*

6 Change the connection properties so that the query refreshes every minute.

1. Right-click on the *Currency Exchange Rates* query in the *Queries & Connections* task pane.

2. Click: *Properties* from the shortcut menu.

The *Query Properties* dialog appears.

3. On the *Usage* tab, check the *Refresh every* check box and set the time interval to 1 minute (the minimum available).

4. Click the *OK* button to close the dialog.

5. Observe the table. Notice that every 60 seconds the currency exchange rates all refresh to show current values. If this doesn't seem to work for you see sidebar.

7 Save your work as *Exchange Rates-2* and close the workbook.

---

note

The Get & Transform query created in this lesson is re-usable

A CSV (comma separated values) file is typically extracted from a database. In this lesson's example the CSV file would probably have been created from the company's HR system.

In a large company the *Employees* CSV file would change on a regular basis.

If the CSV were to change in the future, you wouldn't have to do any more work to update the *Phone List* generated in this lesson.

Get & Transform has created a linked table. As you discovered in: *Lesson 11-2: Create a simple extract and load web query,* you can manually (or automatically) refresh the linked table at any time without having to recreate the Get & Transform query.

Lesson 11-4: Move, remove, rename, filter and sort columns

1   Open a new blank workbook.

2   Create a *Get & Transform* query to extract the values contained in the *Employees-1* comma separated values (CSV) file.

The CSV file format is often used when exporting data from other applications. If you were to open the *Employees-1* CSV file in *Notepad,* you'd see this:

```
Employees-1 - Notepad
File  Edit  Format  View  Help
Last Name,First Name,Job Description,Title Of Courtesy,Birth Date,
Davolio,Nancy,Sales Representative,Ms.,08-Dec-1968,"507 - 20th Ave
Fuller,Andrew,"Vice President, Sales",Dr.,19-Feb-1952,908 W. Capit
```

You can see that the first line of the file has column names (sometimes called field names) separated by commas. The second (and subsequent) lines have column values, also separated by commas.

Get & Transform can use a CSV file as a data source.

1.   Click:

Data→Get & Transform Data→From Text/CSV

2.   Navigate to the *Employees-1* CSV file in your sample files folder.

Name	Date modified	Type
Employees-1	18/02/2016 14:23	Microsoft Excel Comma Separated Values File

3.   Either double-click the file name or click once on the file name to select and then click the *Import* button.

The contents of the *Employees-1* csv file is displayed.

Notice that, this time, *Get & Transform* didn't ask you to select a table, as a CSV file can only contain a single table.

You can see that the sample file contains thirteen different fields (columns) with an assortment of information about each employee. In this lesson you will transform this into a compact telephone number listing by removing many of the existing columns.

3   Remove unwanted columns so that only the *Last Name, First Name, Job Description, Title of Courtesy, Country* and *Home Phone* fields remain.

1.   Click the *Transform Data* button.

The *Power Query Editor* appears.

2.   Click: Home→Manage Columns→Choose Columns.

Employees-1 (CSV)

Choose Columns

Choose the columns to keep

Search Columns

- ■ (Select All Columns)
- ☑ Last Name
- ☑ First Name
- ☑ Job Description
- ☑ Title Of Courtesy
- ☐ Birth Date
- ☐ Address
- ☐ City
- ☐ Region
- ☐ Postal Code
- ☑ Country
- ☑ Home Phone
- ☐ Extension
- ☐ Reports To

3. Clear the *(Select All Columns)* check box to uncheck all check boxes.

4. Check the boxes for the fields you want to keep.

5. Click the *OK* button.

The query editor grid now shows only six columns.

4   Rename the *Title Of Courtesy* field to: **Title**

1. Double-click on the text: *Title Of Courtesy* in the column header.

2. Type: **Title** followed by the **<Enter>** key.

5   Change the order of the columns so that they match the screen grab below.

Click and drag each column header to the required position.

	A^B_C Country	A^B_C Title	A^B_C First Name	A^B_C Last Name	A^B_C Job Description	A^B_C Home Phone
1	USA	Ms.	Nancy	Davolio	Sales Representative	(206) 555-9857
2	USA	Dr.	Andrew	Fuller	Vice President, Sales	(206) 555-9482
3	USA	Ms.	Janet	Leverling	Sales Representative	(206) 555-3412

6   Sort Alphabetically, first by *Country* and then by *Last Name*.

1. Click on the drop-down arrow to the right of the *Country* column header.

2. Select *Sort Ascending* from the drop-down list.

3. Click on the drop-down arrow to the right of the *Last Name* column header.

4. Select *Sort Ascending* from the drop-down list.

Notice that this has resulted in a two-level sort. All countries are grouped together, and within each country last names are sorted from A-Z.

7   Filter the list so that only USA telephone numbers are shown.

1. Click the drop-down arrow to the right of the *Country* column header.

2. Remove the check from the *UK* check box and click the *OK* button.

8   Close the query editor and load the query result to a table in cell A1 of the worksheet (there is only one worksheet in this workbook).

1. Click: Home→Close→Close & Load (drop-down arrow)→ Close and Load To...

The *Import Data* dialog appears.

2. Select the *Table* and *Existing Worksheet* options.

3. Make sure that cell **A1** is selected in the *Existing worksheet* cell box.

4. Click: *OK*.

9   Save your work as *Phone List-1*.

---

note

Other ways to remove unwanted columns in the Query Editor

1. Select one or more columns by clicking on the column headers. (You can use **<Ctrl>+Click** to select individual columns or **<Shift>+Click** to select an adjacent set of columns).

2. Right-click on any of the selected column headers and (from the shortcut menu) either click *Remove Columns* (to remove the selected columns) or *Remove Other Columns* (to remove the unselected columns).

These shortcut menu options are also available on the ribbon at:

Home→Manage Columns→ Remove Columns (drop-down list)

Lesson 11-5: Split delimited data

1   Open *Top 20 Films-1* from your sample files folder.

The sample file has a single table named: *Top20Films.*

	A	B	C	D
3	Title	Studio	Gross*	Director
4	Avatar (2009)	20th Century Fox	2,187	James Cameron

The table is very easy to read for a human but is badly designed from a data perspective. In: *Lesson 2-1: Split fixed width data using Text to Columns*, you learned why you should not have more than one data element in each table column.

In this sample file the *Title* column contains two data elements (*Title* and *Year*). They should be in separate columns.

2   Create a *Get & Transform* query to extract the values contained in the *Top20Films* table.

Up until now you've used *Get & Transform* to connect to external data sources. In this lesson you'll extract data from an Excel table, transform the data, and then load the query result back into the same workbook.

1. Click inside the *Top20Films* table.

2. Click: Data→Get & Transform Data→From Table/Range.

    The *Power Query Editor* appears, showing the contents of the *Top20Films* table.

3   Extract the date from the *Title* column and place it into a new column.

In: *Lesson 2-2: Split delimited data using Text to Columns,* you learned how you could achieve this using Excel's *Text to Columns* tool.

Get & Transform's *Split Column* feature works in a similar way.

1. Click anywhere in the *Title* column.

2. Click: Transform→Text Column→
    Split Column (drop-down list)→By Delimiter.

    Note that there's also a *By Number of Characters* option. You could use this option to split fixed width data (you learned about fixed width data in: *Lesson 2-1: Split fixed width data using Text to Columns*).

    The *Split Column by Delimiter* dialog appears.

3. Select -- *Custom* -- from the *Select or enter delimiter* drop-down list.

4. Type an opening bracket into the text box (if one isn't already there).

5. Click the: *Right-most delimiter* option button.

Top 20 Films-1

Split Column by Delimiter

Specify the delimiter used to split the text

Select or enter delimiter

--Custom--

(

Split at

○ Left-most delimiter

● Right-most delimiter

○ Each occurrence of the delimiter

In this data it doesn't really matter which option you select as there is only one opening bracket in each title. The option you have just selected specifies that the split should take place at the right-most occurrence of a bracket character.

6. Click the *OK* button.

The *Title* field now only contains the film title and a new column has been inserted showing the year along with a closing bracket.

	Title.1	Title.2	Studio
1	Avatar	2009)	20th Century Fox
2	Titanic	1997)	20th Century Fox/Paramount

4 Rename the *Title.1* column header to: **Title** and the *Title.2* column header to: **Year**.

You learned how to do this in: *Lesson 11-4: Move, remove, rename, filter and sort columns.*

5 Remove the closing bracket from the *Year* column.

1. Click anywhere in the *Year* column.

2. Click: Transform→Any Column→Replace Values.

   The *Replace Values* dialog appears.

Replace Values

Replace one value with

Value To Find

)

Replace With

3. Type a closing bracket into the *Value To Find* box.

4. Leave the *Replace With* box empty.

   This will replace any closing brackets found in the column with nothing.

5. Click the *OK* button.

   All of the closing brackets are removed from the *Year* column.

6 Close the query editor and load the query result to a table in cell A1 of a new worksheet.

You learned how to do this in: *Lesson 11-2: Create a simple extract and load web query.*

	A	B	C
1	Title	Year	Studio
2	Avatar	2009	20th Century Fox

7 Save your work as *Top 20 Films-2.*

note

Solutions to the "penny rounding" problem

Consider the simple addition of two values:

	A	B
1	1.4	1
2	1.4	1
3	2.8	3

In the examples above, cell A3 and B3 contain the formula: =A1+A2 and =B1+B2

In the right-hand example, the values have been formatted to only show one decimal place.

Best practice

Excel has a ROUND function that can be used to round the result to two decimal places at the point of calculation.

The new formula for cell B3 would be:

=ROUND(B1,1) + ROUND(B2,1)

… producing a result of 2.

Changing precision

Click: File→Options→ Advanced.

In the *When calculating this workbook* group, click the *Set precision as displayed* check box.

This alters the default behavior of Excel so that each value in the worksheet is regarded as being precisely the same as its display value when performing calculations.

Using this option can cause data to become inaccurate as it is a global setting, affecting the entire worksheet (and any other worksheets you may open before turning it off).

Use this feature with extreme caution, or better still, don't use it at all!

Lesson 11-6: Understand data types

What are scalar data types?

Excel only supports four native scalar data types: *Number, Text, Logical* and *Error*.

Data Type	Example
Number	22.4567
Text	John Smith
Logical	TRUE or FALSE
Error	#DIV/0, #N/A, #NULL! etc

These are called scalar data types because they can only hold a single data item.

Relational database products such as Access and SQL Server have far more scalar data types. For example, Access supports six different numeric data types (such as *Integer* and *Currency*) and SQL server supports eleven.

Excel simulates data types by formatting

In: *Lesson 3-7: Understand date serial numbers*, you learned that Excel uses the *Number* data type to store date and time values. The ingenious use of date serial numbers enables Excel to mimic a *date/time* data type.

You're familiar with using Excel's formatting features to display numbers on a worksheet with a fixed number of decimal places (simulating the *Decimal* data type) or as whole numbers with no decimal places (simulating the *Integer* data type).

Common Excel data type problems

Excel's lack of a *Currency* or *Decimal* data type often causes rounding errors (sometimes referred to as the "penny rounding problem"). The sidebar discusses this problem and some solutions. Because RDBMS (Relational Data Management Systems) such as SQL Server and Access support these data types they do not experience this problem.

Excel's lack of a *Date* data type means that Excel is unable to work with dates that are before 1900. The SQL Server *Date* data type can work with any dates between 1st Jan 0001 and 31st Dec 9999.

You can see that there will often be problems converting values from other data sources into a form that is usable by Excel.

What are non-scalar data types?

Excel's *Linked Data Types* and *Dynamic Arrays* are more complex non-scalar data types. Non-scalar data types contain a collection of many values (in the case of a *Dynamic Array* each value is an *Element*, and in the case of *Linked Data Types* each value is called a *Field*).

The Linked Data Type

A *Linked Data Type* is non-scalar and can contain many different fields each of which has its own data type and contains a value.

For example, the *Geography* object contains fields for *Population, Longitude* and *Latitude*. You'd obtain the values of these fields using syntax such as:

- City.Population
- City.Longitude
- City.Latitude

It is not possible to create your own linked data types within Excel, they must be downloaded from Microsoft's servers via the Internet. Once downloaded they are saved within the workbook (along with the information contained in all of the fields) and can then be used (but not refreshed) within Excel even if you are no longer connected to the Internet.

Linked data types will be discussed in depth later, in*: Lesson 11-7: Create and use a linked data type* and *Lesson 11-8: Add a linked data type field using a data card.*

Here is an example of a linked data type:

In the above example cells A2:A6 each contain a *Geography Linked Data Type* containing information about a single *City*. The linked data type feature is being used to retrieve the value of the population of *London*.

When the user clicks on the *Population* field, the formula *=A1.Population* is added to cell B2 and a value representing the population of London is returned to the cell.

The Dynamic Array Data Type

Dynamic arrays (introduced in the July 2020 semi-annual version 2002) are a non-scalar data type. You learned about this data type in: *Session Four: Working with Dynamic Arrays.*

---

important

Dynamic Arrays

Dynamic arrays (introduced in the July 2020 semi-annual version 2002) are a non-scalar data type.

Consider this dynamic array:

=E7#
Returns a *non-scalar* two-dimensional six-cell dynamic array.

=E7

Returns the scalar value: *Aniseed Syrup*. This is one of the elements contained within the dynamic array.

The formula:

=INDEX(E7#,2,2)

Returns the scalar value: *Beverages*. This is the element at row 2 and column 2 in the two dimensional dynamic array.

Lesson 11-7: Create and use a linked data type

1   Open a new blank workbook.

2   Type the following text into the new workbook:

	A	B
1	City	
2	London	
3	Paris	
4	New York	
5	Munich	
6		

3   Convert the range A1:A5 into a table and name it: **City**

You learned how to do this in: *Lesson 1-13: Convert a range into a table and add a total row* and *Lesson 1-19: Name a table and create an automatic structured table reference.*

It isn't necessary to convert a range into a table to use the *linked data types* feature but is recommended best practice.

4   Convert cells A2:A5 into the *Geography* linked data type.

1.   Select cells A2:A5.

2.   Click: Data→Data Types→Geography.

3.   After a short delay, two things happen:

	A	B
1	City ▼	
2	📖 London	
3	📖 Paris	
4	📖 New York	
5	📖 Munich	

Icons appear to the left of each *City* name: The icons confirm that the names in cells A2:A5 are able to identify a single *Geography* object on Microsoft's servers (via the Internet).

Be aware that Microsoft is guessing that you mean London, England (there are many more towns and cities in the world named London). You'll learn how to resolve ambiguous names later, in: *Lesson 11-9: Resolve geocoding errors in the geography linked data type.*

An *Add Column* button appears at the top-right of the table.

5   Add a non-existent City to cell A6.

note

There are many ways to identify a Geography or Stocks object

A *Geography* object can be identified using a *Country, Province, Territory* or *City* name.

A *Stocks* object can be identified using a *Ticker Symbol, Company Name* or *Fund Name.*

note

The Stocks data type

The *Stocks* linked data type can be used in exactly the same way as the *Geography* linked data type.

	A	B
1	Company	Price
2	🏛 Microsoft Corp (XNAS:MSFT)	$ 133.97
3	🏛 Apple Inc (XNAS:AAPL)	$ 199.13
4	🏛 Netflix Inc (XNAS:NFLX)	$ 367.56
5	🏛 Facebook Inc (XNAS:FB)	$ 192.19

Note that the *Stocks* linked data type icon is different to the *Geography* linked data type icon.

note

Alternative ways to add a field

1. If you begin to type a field name in the header row of the table, this will happen:

	A	B
1	City	Population
2	🏛 London	City
3	🏛 Paris	
4	🏛 New York	Population

... then when you press the **<Enter>** key the new column is added to the table.

2. If you add a formula to a table column that references a linked data type cell an AutoComplete list will appear enabling you to add a field.

	A	B
1	City	
2	🏛 London	=A2
3	🏛 Paris	◯ Admin D
4	🏛 New York	◯ Admin D
5	🏛 Munich	◯ Area

	A	B
1	City	Population
2	🏛 London	8,908,081
3	🏛 Paris	2,148,271
4	🏛 New York	8,537,673
5	🏛 Munich	1,456,039
6	🏛 Madrid	3,223,334

	A	B	C
1	City		
2	🏛 London		
3	🏛 Paris		
4	🏛 New York		
5	🏛 Munich		
6	⍰ abc123		
7			

Notice the question mark icon. This informs you that Microsoft is unable to identify a single *Geography* object from the text that you have entered in cell A6.

6 Change the text in cell A6 to: **Madrid**

The icon returns to normal as Microsoft is able to identify a single *Geography* object from the text: *Madrid*.

	A	B
6	🏛 Madrid	

7 Use the *add column* button to retrieve the population of each city.

1. Click anywhere in the table.

An *Add Column* button appears at the top right of the table. 🗒

2. Click on the *Add Column* button.

Something interesting happens. You can see that Excel now presents a list of fields:

	A	B	C	D
1	City	🗒		
2	🏛 London	City		
3	🏛 Paris			
4	🏛 New York	Admin Division 1 (State/provi...		
5	🏛 Munich	Admin Division 2 (County/dist...		

The field list you are seeing is actually provided by a *Geography* object located on a remote Microsoft server. You can select any of them to add a new column that contains the value of the selected field.

3. Click on the *Population* field.

Name
Population ▷
Time zone(s)

A new *Population* column is added to the table containing up-to-date values for the population of each city.

8 Save your work as *Linked City Data-1*.

important

You need an Internet connection to use this feature

Linked data types allow you to retrieve information via the Internet from objects stored on Microsoft's servers.

This is not possible unless your computer is connected to the Internet.

Once the fields associated with a linked data type have been downloaded they are saved within the workbook. This means that you can still access all properties when offline, but you cannot refresh the data to current values unless you are online again.

note

How to refresh the data obtained from a linked data type

Linked data types do not automatically refresh. For this reason it is important to manually refresh the data they retrieve from time to time.

To refresh the data, right-click a cell that contains a linked data type and select:

Data Type→Refresh

…from the shortcut menu.

You can also select:

Data→
Queries & Connections→
Refresh All

… from the Ribbon to refresh all data types, data connections and Pivot Tables in the entire workbook.

Lesson 11-8: Add a linked data type field using a data card

Open a new blank workbook.

1   Type the following text into the new workbook:

	A	B
1	Country	
2	USA	
3	China	
4	Japan	
5	Germany	
6	UK	
7	Tuvalu	

These are the world's five largest economies (by GDP) along with Tuvalu, the nation with the world's smallest economy.

2   Convert the range A1:A7 into a table and name it: **Country**

You learned how to do this in: *Lesson 1-13: Convert a range into a table and add a total row* and *Lesson 1-19: Name a table and create an automatic structured table reference.*

It isn't necessary to convert a range into a table to use the *linked data types* feature but is recommended best practice.

3   Convert cells A2:A7 into the *Geography* linked data type.

You learned how to do this in: *Lesson 11-7: Create and use a linked data type.*

4   View the card for the USA.

Click on the icon to the left of cell A2.

	A	B
1	Country ▾	
2	🗺 United States	
3	🗺 China	
	Show card (Ctrl+Shift+F5)	
4	🗺 Japan	

A card is displayed showing information about the United States.

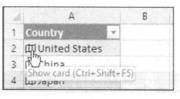

⊿	A	B
1	**Country** ▾	**Capital** ▾
2	⊞ United States	Washington, D.C.
3	⊞ China	Beijing
4	⊞ Japan	Tokyo
5	⊞ Germany	Berlin
6	⊞ United Kingdom	London
7	⊞ Tuvalu	Funafuti

note

Converting a linked data type back into text

1. Right click on a cell containing a linked data type.

2. Click: Data Type→Convert To Text from the shortcut menu.

5   Extract the value of the *Capital* field shown on the card to the table.

1. Hover over the *Capital* field on the data card.

Notice that an icon has appeared on the card.

United States

Capital
Washington, D.C.

Extract Capital to grid

Leader(s)

2. Click on the icon to extract the contents of the *Capital* field to the table for all countries.

6   Extract the value of the *Gasoline Price* field shown on the card to the table.

1. Click on the icon to the left of cell A2.

The card for the United States appears.

2. Hover the mouse over the *Gasoline Price* field and click the *Extract to Grid* button.

This time one of the field values displays an error.

⊿	A	B	C
1	**Country** ▾	**Capital** ▾	**Gasolin** ▾
2	⊞ United States	Washington, D.C.	$ 0.71
3	⊞ China	Beijing	$ 0.96
4	⊞ Japan	Tokyo	$ 1.06
5	⊞ Germany	Berlin	$ 1.39
6	⊞ United Kingdom	London	$ 1.46
7	⊞ Tuvalu	Funafuti	#FIELD!

As you might expect, the data contained in the *Geography* object for Tuvalu is not as comprehensive as that for the world's five largest economies. You'd need to do further research if you needed to know the *Gasoline Price* in Tuvalu.

7   View the card for Tuvalu.

Notice that this card is much shorter than the USA card and does not contain a *Gasoline* field.

8   Replace the error message in cell C7 with the text: **Not Available**

Edit the formula in cell C2 to the following:

```
=IFERROR([@Country].[Gasoline price], "Not Available")
```

You learned how to use the IFERROR function in: *Lesson 3-24: Use an IFERROR function to suppress error messages.*

9   Save your work as *Linked Country Data-1.*

Wikipedia · CC0

Tuvalu

Capital
Funafuti

Leader(s)
Elizabeth II (Monarch), Enele Sopoaga (Prime Minister), Iakoba Italeli (Governor-general)

Population · 2017
11,192

⊿	A	C
1	**Country** ▾	**Gasoline price** ▾
2	⊞ United States	$ 0.71
3	⊞ China	$ 0.96
4	⊞ Japan	$ 1.06
5	⊞ Germany	$ 1.39
6	⊞ United Kingdom	$ 1.46
7	⊞ Tuvalu	Not Available

Lesson 11-9: Resolve geocoding errors in the geography linked data type

When you create a *Stocks* data type it is possible to uniquely identify a stock by specifying a *Ticker Symbol* along with a *Market Identifier Code*. In this example there is no scope for ambiguity:

	A	B
1	Company	Price
2	🏛 Microsoft Corp (XNAS:MSFT)	$ 133.97
3	🏛 Apple Inc (XNAS:AAPL)	$ 199.13
4	🏛 Netflix Inc (XNAS:NFLX)	$ 367.56
5	🏛 Facebook Inc (XNAS:FB)	$ 192.19

You can see that the *Microsoft Corp* ticker symbol: *MSFT* has been used in conjunction with the *US NASDAQ* Market Identifier Code: *XNAS*.

Geographical data has far more potential for error.

In: *Lesson 11-7: Create and use a linked data type,* you created a geographic linked data type for several cities.

	A	B
1	City	Population
2	🏙 London	8,825,000
3	🏙 Paris	2,140,526
4	🏙 New York	8,537,673
5	🏙 Munich	1,456,039
6	🏙 Madrid	3,223,334

Excel has used the *Bing Maps Service* to guess that the London you are referring to is London UK. There are, however, many different cities in the world also named London. In this lesson you'll create a linked data type to report the population of three different Londons:

- London, England, United Kingdom
- London, Ohio, USA
- London, Kentucky, USA

1   Open a new blank workbook.

2   Type the following text into the new workbook:

	A	B	C
1	City	Country	State/Country
2	London	United Kingdom	England
3	London	USA	Ohio
4	London	USA	Kentucky

3   Convert the range A1:C4 into a table and name it: **London**

You learned how to do this in: *Lesson 1-13: Convert a range into a table and add a total row* and *Lesson 1-19: Name a table and create an automatic structured table reference.*

note

The field values within a linked data type do not automatically refresh

Note that it is not possible to automatically refresh data from a linked data type at a timed interval.

While this would be really useful for the Stocks linked data type, Microsoft have probably not implemented this feature to avoid overloading their servers.

You are, however, able to manually refresh the data obtained from a linked data type.

To refresh the data:

1. Right-click a cell that contains a linked data type.

2. Select: Data Type→Refresh from the shortcut menu.

You can also refresh data using the ribbon by clicking:

Data→
Queries & Connections→
Refresh All

This will refresh all data types, data connections and Pivot Tables in the entire workbook.

It isn't necessary to convert a range into a table to use the *linked data types* feature but is recommended best practice.

4   Convert cells A2:A4 into the *Geography* data type.

You learned how to do this in: *Lesson 11-7: Create and use a linked data type.*

5   Add a column to report the population of each city.

You learned how to do this in: *Lesson 11-7: Create and use a linked data type.*

◢	A	B	C	D
1	City	Country	State/Country	Population
2	London	United Kingdom	England	8,825,000
3	London	USA	Ohio	8,825,000
4	London	USA	Kentucky	8,825,000
5				

6   Inspect the data card for each row.

You learned how to do this in: *Lesson 11-8: Add a linked data type field using a data card.*

Notice that, in every row, Excel has reported the population of *London, England, United Kingdom.*

7   Correct each row to retrieve the correct population figure.

The Excel terminology for this procedure is *switching out* data.

1.   Right-Click on the icon in cell A3.

2.   Select: Data Type→Change… from the shortcut menu.

The *Data Selector* task pane appears.

3.   Click on the *Select* button beneath *London, Madison County, Ohio.*

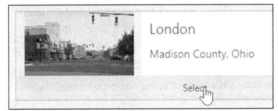

London
Madison County, Ohio

Select

(Be careful to click on the *Select* button rather than upper part of the menu item).

The figure shown in the *Population* column updates.

4.   Use the same method to update row 4 to point to *London, Laurel County, Kentucky.*

The population figures now display correctly:

◢	A	B	C	D
1	City	Country	State/Country	Popula
2	London	United Kingdom	England	8,825,000
3	London	USA	Ohio	10,158
4	London	USA	Kentucky	8,157

8   Save your work as *Three Londons-1.*

Lesson 11-10: Understand Get & Transform data types

The Excel suite includes several different applications

The Excel suite consists of three major applications:

Excel: This is the core Excel product that you've been using in sessions 1-9 of this book. As you discovered in: *Lesson 11-6: Understand data types,* Excel only supports four native data types.

Get & Transform: This is Microsoft's ETL (Extract, Transform and Load) tool that you are learning to use in this session. Get & Transform was originally a separate application called *Power Query.* Because Get & Transform needs to work with data from many different sources it supports twelve different data types.

Power Pivot: This is Microsoft's OLAP (Online Analytical Processing) and data modeling tool. You'll learn how to use Power Pivot later, in: *Session Twelve: Power Pivot, Data Modeling, OLAP and Business Intelligence.* Power Pivot supports five different data types.

Data type conversion (from source)

In order to be able to import (get) data from sources such as SQL Server, Access and Excel, *Get & Transform* must convert source data into one of the data types it supports.

It is often possible for *Get & Transform* to guess the most appropriate data type to convert the source data into. For example, if a source data column contained numeric values with no decimal places, *Get & Transform* might guess that the *Whole Number* data type was most appropriate.

Get & Transform will often play it safe and convert most data into the *Text* data type. You then need to manually set the correct data type using *Get & Transform*. You'll learn how to do this in: *Lesson 11-11: Specify data types.*

Data type conversion (to target)

As well as performing data type conversion during the *Get* and *Transform* operations, data sometimes needs to go through another data type conversion when it is loaded to its final destination.

Later, in: *Session Twelve: Power Pivot, Data Modeling, OLAP and Business Intelligence,* you'll discover that Get & Transform is also the correct tool to use when loading data into a Power Pivot data model.

The *Power Pivot* tool supports more data types than Excel, meaning that fewer data type conversions are needed when loading data into Power Pivot.

Get & Transform supported data types

Data Type	Description
Decimal Number	This corresponds exactly to the Excel Number data type. The Decimal Number data type is a floating-point number that can have decimal places. The largest value that can be represented by a Decimal Number data type is 15 digits long (the decimal separator can occur anywhere in the number).
Currency	The Currency data type allows a maximum of four decimal places.
Whole Number	Numbers that have no decimal places. These are often also called Integers. Whole Numbers can be positive or negative. The largest value that can be represented by a Whole Number data type is 19 digits long.
Percentage	In a similar way to Excel, a percentage value (for example 5%) will be automatically recognized as a percentage value and then converted into a two-digit precision decimal number (in this example 0.05) that can be used for arithmetical operations in the Query Editor, Data Model or a worksheet.
Date/Time	This is stored in the same way as an Excel date/time serial number using a Decimal number type. Valid dates are from 1 Jan 1900 to 31 Dec 9999. Date serial numbers were explained in depth in: *Lesson 3-7: Understand date serial numbers.*
Date	This is stored in the same way as an Excel date/time serial number using a Decimal number type with no decimal places.
Time	This is stored in the same way as an Excel date/time serial number using a Decimal number type with no digits to the left of the decimal place.
Date/Time/Timezone	This represents a UTC Date/Time.
Duration	The Duration data type represents a length of time. This is stored in the same way as an Excel date/time serial number, using a Decimal number type. The Duration data type can be added or subtracted from a Date/Time field with correct results.
Text	A set of Unicode characters. These are often also called Strings. Strings can also represent numbers or dates stored in a text format. The maximum length of a string is 268,435,456 Unicode characters.
True/False	Either a True or False value.
Binary	Binary data is the type of data that is typically stored in a file (such as a picture or video).

Lesson 11-11: Specify data types

In: *Lesson 11-10: Understand Get & Transform data types* you discovered that the *Get & Transform* tool supports twelve different data types. When you import data, *Get & Transform* must convert the source data into one of the data types that it supports.

While *Get & Transform* tries to guess the most appropriate data type to convert the source data into it will often play it safe and convert most data into the *Text* data type.

In this lesson you'll learn how to manually set the correct data type for each column.

1   Open a new blank workbook.

2   Create a *Get & Transform* query to extract the values from the *Invoice* table in the *Invoices-1* Access database.

    1.   Click: Data→Get & Transform Data→Get Data→ From Database→From Microsoft Access Database.

    2.   Navigate to the *Invoices-1* Access file in your sample files folder and then click the *Import* button.

    3.   Select the *Invoice* table and then Click the *Transform Data* button.

          ◢ ▦   Invoices-1.accdb [1]

              ▦ Invoice

The *Power Query Editor* opens.

3   Remove the *InvoiceID* column.

You learned how to do this in: *Lesson 11-4: Move, remove, rename, filter and sort columns.*

4   Correct the *InvoiceDate* and *InvoiceTime* data types.

You can immediately see that the *InvoiceDate* and *InvoiceTime* columns have the wrong data type as they are both displaying both date and time values.

    1.   Right-click on the *InvoiceDate* column header.

    2.   Hover the mouse cursor over: *Change Type* from the shortcut menu.

        A list of data types appears with the *Date/Time* data type checked.

    3.   Click: *Date* to change the data type to *Date.*

    4.   Repeat this process for the *InvoiceTime* field, changing the data type to *Time.*

        Notice the descriptive icons at the top of each column that visually indicate the column's data type.

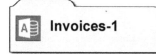
Invoices-1

note

You can also change the data type by clicking on the data type icon

There are icons in each column header that indicate the data type. For example:

You can see that in the column header above that Genre has the *Text* data type and *Qty* has the *Number* data type.

The data type icon is also a split button and if you click on it you can change the data type.

5 Confirm that the other columns have the most appropriate data type.

You can see that Get & Transform has done a great job on the other columns by identifying the correct data types.

Get & Transform has decided that the safest option is to use the *Text* data type for the *InvoiceNumber* column. You might think that the *Whole Number* data type would be more appropriate as all of the values in this column are whole numbers.

In this case, Get & Transform may have a good argument. Consider an invoice number with leading zeroes (such as 000001). Converting this number to a *Whole Number* data type would remove the leading zeroes and this might make the value more confusing.

6 Close the query editor and load the query result to a table that begins in cell A1 of a new worksheet.

You learned how to do this in: *Lesson 11-4: Move, remove, rename, filter and sort columns.*

7 Save your work as *Invoices-2.*

Lesson 11-12: Understand steps and PQFL

Every transformation that you apply in *Get & Transform* generates a formula that is written in the *Power Query Formula Language* (PQFL). A PQFL formula looks very much like an Excel formula. Unlike Excel formulas, PQFL language formulas are case sensitive.

Get & Transform creates a PQFL formula every time you apply a transformation action.

1   Open *Phone List-1* from your sample files folder.

This is the workbook that you created in: *Lesson 11-4: Move, remove, rename, filter and sort columns.*

2   Click the *Enable Content* button if shown.

3   Display the *Queries & Connections* task pane.

Click: Data→Queries & Connections→Queries & Connections.

The *Queries & Connections* task pane appears.

4   Open the query in the Power Query Editor.

Double-click on the *Employees-1* query (visible in the *Queries & Connections* task pane).

The *Power Query Editor* opens, showing the rows returned by the query.

Notice that there is a *Query Settings* task pane on the right-hand side of the query editor. This should look the same as (or similar to) the one shown in the sidebar.

In the *Applied Steps* list you can see all of the transformations that you applied to this query in: *Lesson 11-4: Move, remove, rename, filter and sort columns.*

Each of the *Applied Steps* contains a PQFL formula.

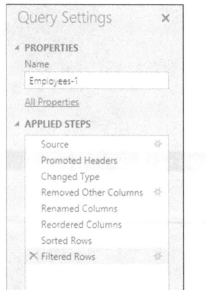

5   Inspect the PQFL formula for the *Filtered Rows* step.

You may remember that in: *Lesson 11-4: Move, remove, rename, filter and sort columns,* the last transformation you specified was to filter the list to only show USA employees.

This created the *Filtered Rows* step.

1.   If the formula bar is not visible check: View→Layout→ Formula Bar.

2.   Click on the *Filtered Rows* step in the *Query Settings* task pane.

Observe the PQFL formula in the formula bar.

```
= Table.SelectRows(#"Sorted Rows", each ([Country] = "USA"))
```

Even without knowing PQFL, you can probably guess broadly how this formula works.

6   Manually edit the PQFL formula for the *Filtered Rows* step so that UK employees are shown instead of USA employees.

Phone List-1

trivia

What's in a name?

The Power Query Formula Language (PQFL)

As you are aware, *Get & Transform* is a re-branding of a product that was originally known as *Power Query*.

The old name lives on in the name of the query language.

The M Language

When PQFL was being developed, Microsoft's original internal code name for the language was "M Language".

The letter *M* comes from the common Business Intelligence term: *Mashup*.

A *Data Mashup* simply means combining data from different data sources.

Much of the PQFL help refers to the language in a rather long-winded way as:

The Power Query Formula Language (informally known as "M").

note

Some steps have arguments

Notice that some steps have a small gear wheel icon next to them, such as the *Source* step shown below:

When you see this icon, you know that the step has arguments that you can edit.

If you click on the icon for the *Source* step, you'll find that you are able to edit the file location of the original CSV file.

Where you see "USA" in the formula bar, change the text to read "UK" and press the **<Enter>** key.

```
= Table.SelectRows(#"Sorted Rows", each ([Country] = "UK"))
```

The grid changes to show UK employees.

Of course, it would be easier to simply change the filter using the filter button next to *Country*.

This does, however, illustrate the link between the things that you are doing using the ribbon and grid, and the PQFL formula that is generated to implement each of your actions.

7 Step through the *Applied Steps* one by one.

1. Click on the *Source* action in the *Query Settings* task pane.

    This was one of two actions that *Get & Transform* automatically created when you first opened the CSV file. You can see the original CSV file just after import. Notice that the column headers have not yet been named.

2. Click on the *Promoted Headers* action.

    This action was also automatically created when you first opened the CSV file.

    Get & Transform intelligently guessed that the first row of the CSV file contained column headers. The term *Promoted* means that the first row is used to define the column names.

3. Click on each of the other actions in turn and watch your data transform as each transformation is applied.

8 Delete the *Sorted Rows* step.

You may remember that one of the transformations you applied was to sort the data in A-Z order, first by *Country* and then by *Last Name*.

If you delete the *Sorted Rows* step, the data will be listed in the order that it originally appeared in the CSV file.

1. Click on the *Sorted Rows* step to select it.

    Notice that there is a delete icon on the left-hand side of the step.

2. Click the *Delete* icon.

3. Click the *Delete* button when prompted to confirm the deletion.

    The step is removed.

4. Click on the last *Filtered Rows* step.

    Notice that the *Last Name* column is no longer sorted in alphabetical order.

9 Close the Power Query Editor (click *Keep* if prompted).

10 Save your work as *Phone List-2*.

Lesson 11-13: Remove empty, error and top and bottom rows

While you can freely remove columns from a query, you need to use different techniques when removing rows.

When you simply need a subset of the rows in the source data, this is normally done by applying a filter.

Sometimes data contains error rows, or top and bottom rows, that need to be removed.

1   Open a new blank workbook.

2   Create a *Get & Transform* query to extract the values from the *Gold-1* CSV file in your sample files folder.

   You learned how to do this in: *Lesson 11-4: Move, remove, rename, filter and sort columns.*

   This file contains average monthly spot price of gold (in US dollars) for the period January 2006 to December 2015.

3   Click the *Transform Data* button to enter the Power Query Editor.

4   Use the values in the first row as column headers.

   In: *Lesson 11-4: Move, remove, rename, filter and sort columns,* you worked with a well-structured CSV file and *Get & Transform* was able to automatically detect that the first row should be used as column headers.

   The first rows in this CSV file are a little harder to understand:

Column1	Column2
1 Date	Average Price
2 Month/Year	in US Dollars
3 Jan 2006	548.1404
4 Feb 2006	554.2743478

   You can see that the column header information is contained in both rows 1 and 2.

   Click: Transform→Table→Use First Row as Headers.

   This solves part of the problem, as the values in row 1 are now used as column headers.

Date	Average Price
1 Month/Year	in US Dollars
2 Jan 2006	548.1404
3 Feb 2006	554.2743478

5   Remove row 1.

   You'll often find one or more rows of unwanted header or footer data at the top or bottom of an imported data table.

   Get & Transform provides a fast way to remove the unwanted rows.

   1.   Click: Home→Reduce Rows→Remove Rows→ Remove Top Rows.

Gold-1 (CSV)

The *Remove Top Rows* dialog appears.

2. Type: **1** into the *Number of rows* box.

3. Click the *OK* button.

6 **Change the data types to appropriate values.**

You learned about data types in: *Lesson 11-6: Understand data types.*

1. Right-click on the *Average Price* column header.

2. Click: Change Type→Currency.

3. Right-click on the *Date* column header.

4. Click: *Change Type* from the shortcut menu.

Notice that the data type is currently set to *Text*.

5. Click: *Date* to change the data type.

Notice that two interesting things have happened.

	Date	$ Average Price
1	1/1/2006	548.1404
2	2/1/2006	554.2743
3	3/1/2006	555.3573
4	4/1/2006	609.2191

Because there is no information to suggest the correct day of the month, *Get & Transform* has guessed that an appropriate date might be the first day of each month. Later, in: *Lesson 11-15: Transform date and time columns*, you'll find out how you could choose a different day of the month.

There are some values in this column (for example the words: *Average 2007*) that could not be converted to dates. In these cases, Get & Transform is showing the word *Error* in place of a date.

Note that in the above grab the dates are shown in *m/dd/yyyy* format because my Windows *Region format* was set to *English (United States)*. Depending upon your operating system's region format settings, you will see an appropriate format for your geographical location.

7 **Remove error rows.**

Click: Home→Reduce Rows→Remove Rows→Remove Errors.

The error rows are removed from the grid.

8 **Close the Power Query Editor and load the query result to a linked table in cell A1 of the worksheet (there is only one worksheet in this workbook).**

You learned how to do this in: *Lesson 11-4: Move, remove, rename, filter and sort columns.*

9 **Save your work as** *Gold-2*.

Import Data dialog:

Import Data   ? ✕

Select how you want to view this data in your workbook.
- ◉ Table
- ○ PivotTable Report
- ○ PivotChart
- ○ Only Create Connection

Where do you want to put the data?
- ◉ Existing worksheet:
  =Sheet1!$A$1
- ○ New worksheet

☐ Add this data to the Data Model

Properties...   OK   Cancel

	A	B
1	Date	Average Price
2	1/1/2006	548.1404
3	2/1/2006	554.2743
4	3/1/2006	555.3573
5	4/1/2006	609.2191

Lesson 11-14: Understand and work with null values

When you see a blank cell in a worksheet, you might interpret this as a value of zero. Computers (and databases) are more sophisticated and support a concept called null. Null is not a value but is the *absence* of a value.

Empty cells often do not contain null values but are left blank because most readers will assume a value that is not stated.

Here's an example:

With nulls

	A	B	C
1	First Name	Last Name	Occupation
2	John	Smith	Electrician
3	Bill	Jones	
4	Arthur	Williams	Bricklayer

Without nulls

	A	B	C
1	First Name	Last Name	Occupation
2	John	Smith	Electrician
3	Bill	Jones	Unemployed
4	Arthur	Williams	Bricklayer

What is the status of Bill Jones in the *With nulls* example above? Is he unemployed, or do you simply not know? Excel would consider the blank cell as having a null value (in other words, you don't know whether Bill has an occupation or not).

Ideally the nulls should be replaced with words similar to: *Not Stated, Withheld, Unemployed, Retired* or *Unknown*.

The issue is far more common (and can cause more errors) with numeric fields. Consider this example:

With nulls

	A	B
1	Item	Quantity
2	Apples	25
3	Oranges	
4	Pears	35
5		

Without nulls

	A	B
1	Item	Quantity
2	Apples	25
3	Oranges	0
4	Pears	35
5		

In the *With nulls* example above, a human might assume that we have zero oranges. Excel would just note the absence of any meaningful data (in other words, a null value) and assume that you have no idea how many oranges you have.

Null values will also affect many of Excel's functions.

In the *With nulls* example above, the formula **=AVERAGE(B2:B4)** returns a value of 30.

In the *Without nulls* example above, the same formula returns a value of 20. A **COUNT** function would also return different results (2 and 3).

The above two examples both illustrate the concept of false null values.

Sometimes (though rarely) you may have real null values (see sidebar for examples). In these special cases it may be better to leave the cells empty.

1   Open a new blank workbook.

Olympics-1 (CSV)

2   Create a *Get & Transform* query to extract the values from the *Olympics-1* CSV file in your sample files folder.

You learned how to do this in: *Lesson 11-4: Move, remove, rename, filter and sort columns.*

3   Click the *Transform Data* button to enter the Power Query Editor.

1²₃ Rank		A⁸C Country	A⁸C Continent	1²₃ Summer Olympics		A⁸C Years (Summer Olympics)	1²₃ Winter Olympics	A⁸C Years (Winter Olympics)
10	8	Soviet Union/Russia	Europe		1	1980	1	2014
11	8	Greece	Europe		2	1896, 2004	null	
12	8	Australia	Oceania		2	1956, 2000	null	
13	8	Norway	Europe		null		2	1952, 1994
14	8	Austria	Europe		null		2	1964, 1976

This data contains a list of countries that have hosted one or more Olympic Games.

Notice that there are several null values.

In the above grab you can see that Norway and Austria have a null value in the *Summer Olympics* column.

These are false null values. You actually know that Norway and Austria have never hosted a Summer Olympics. The value should more properly be stated as zero.

Notice also that there are empty values in the *Years* columns when a country has never hosted the Olympics. This is because *Get & Transform* has assigned the *Text* data type to these columns (see sidebar).

4   Correct the null values.

It is generally good practice to remove false null values from data (unless you really intend the value to signify the absence of data).

In this case, the nulls clearly signify zero values

1. Click on the *Summer Olympics* column header to select the entire column.

2. Hold down the **<Ctrl>** key and then click on the *Winter Olympics* column header.

   Both columns are now selected.

3. Click: Home→Transform→Replace Values.

   The *Replace Values* dialog appears.

4. Type **null** into the *Value To Find* box.

5. Type **0** into the *Replace With* box.

6. Click the *OK* button.

   The null values are replaced with zeroes.

5   Close the Power Query Editor and load the query result to a table in cell A1 of the existing worksheet (there is only one worksheet in this workbook).

You learned how to do this in: *Lesson 11-4: Move, remove, rename, filter and sort columns.*

6   Save your work as *Olympics-2*.

note

Why do the Year columns not contain null values?

Get & Transform will represent a null textual value as an *Empty String*.

An empty string can be thought of as a textual value that does not contain any actual text.

For example, the Excel formula:

="Extra" & "" & "terrestrial"

… concatenates an empty string in between the words *Extra* and *terrestrial*.

If you typed the above formula into an Excel cell, the result would be the single word:

Extraterrestrial

Database designers can argue all day about whether a blank textual value should be represented as an empty string or a null value.

In the context of data that will be used by Excel there isn't any real difference, as Excel will regard a cell containing an empty string to be the same as any other empty cell.

In this lesson's data you could, of course, replace the empty text values with meaningful text such as: *Not Applicable*. The resulting data would then produce different results with Excel functions such as COUNTA and COUNTBLANK.

note

How can I return day and month names instead of numbers?

When you return day and month numbers instead of names you are able to sort by week or month number and have the days or months appear in the correct order.

This is why the Get & Transform *Day of Week* and *Month* transformations return numbers instead of text.

For example:

1=January, 2=February
and
0=Monday, 1=Tuesday

Sometimes, for display purposes, you'd rather have textual month and day values such as:

Jan, Feb, Mar
and
Mon, Tue, Wed

You can do this by adding a duplicate column and then applying one of the following transformations to it:

Transform→
Date & Time Column→
Date→Month→
Name of Month

Transform→
Date & Time Column→
Date→Day→
Name of Day

Lesson 11-15: Transform date and time columns

When source data contains transactional information (such as a listing of individual sales), you will often want to analyze total sales by *Quarter*, *Month* or *Year*.

As you learned in: *Lesson 9-19: Group by date*, regular pivot tables have always had the ability to group by *Seconds, Minutes, Hours, Days, Months, Quarters* and *Years*.

This means that you probably won't have to create *Second, Minute, Hour, Day, Month, Quarter* and *Year* fields within your *Get & Transform* queries if you intend to load the query into a pivot table.

While pivot tables can group by these seven different date and time fields, *Get & Transform* supports sixteen additional date and time grouping types. For example:

- You might want to group by the *Week of Year*, to compare this week's sales with the same week's sales last year.

- You might want to group by *Day of Week*, to discover the average sales figure for *Monday*.

In this lesson you'll learn how to add a new *Week of Year* grouping field to a *Get & Transform* query and then use it to analyze sales by week in a pivot table.

1   Open a new blank workbook.

2   Create a *Get & Transform* query to extract the values from the *DVDSales* table in the *DVD Sales-1* Excel workbook in your sample files folder.

The *DVD Sales-1* workbook contains two Excel tables called *DVDSales* and *Data*.

1. Click: Data→Get & Transform Data→Get Data→ From File→From Workbook.

2. Navigate to and select the *DVD Sales-1* Excel workbook file in your sample files folder.

3. Select the *DVDSales* table.

4. Click the *Transform Data* button to open the query in the *Power Query Editor*.

	1²₃ No	▾	Date	▾	A⁸C Customer	▾	A⁸C Employee
1	136438		10/2/2014		Silver Screen Video		Lee,Frank
2	136438		10/2/2014		Silver Screen Video		Lee,Frank
3	136438		10/2/2014		Silver Screen Video		Lee,Frank

5. Click the *Refresh* button if prompted.

3   Create a duplicate *Date* column named *Week*.

1. Click anywhere in the *Date* column.

2. Click: Add Column→General→Duplicate Column.

A duplicate column is added, named: *Date - Copy*.

DVD Sales-1

3. Double-click in the column header and type: **Week**

4. Press the **<Enter>** key.

1.2 Total	1²₃ Week
106.13	40
54.56	41
140.31	41
202.36	41
50.01	41
178.51	41
155.88	41
124.87	41

4 **Transform the value in the *Week* column so that it displays the week number of each transaction.**

1. Click anywhere in the *Week* column to make it the active column.

2. Click: Transform→Date & Time Column→Date→ Week→Week of Year.

   The values in the *Week* column change to show the week number for each transaction.

5 **Load the query results directly into a pivot table.**

This time you will output the query result directly to a pivot table without loading to a linked table first.

This results in a more compact workbook, both in file size (when you save it) and in memory usage (when it is open).

1. Click: File→Close & Load To…

   The *Import Data* dialog appears.

2. Click the *PivotTable Report* option button.

3. Click the *OK* button.

   You are returned to a new worksheet containing a pivot table.

6 **Use the pivot table to show sales by *Customer* for each *Year* and *Week*.**

Do this using the same technique you learned in: *Lesson 9-19: Group by date*.

The field settings are:

Filters	Columns
	Years
	Week
Rows	Σ Values
Customer	Sum of Total

	A	B	C	D	E
3	Sum of Total	Column Labels			
4		2014			
5	Row Labels	40	41	42	43
6	Addison-Freelander Screen Agency				289.69
7	AV Supplies	308.11	331.23		169.58
8	Box Office Supplies	667.27		784.73	400.89

7 Save your work as *DVD Sales-2*.

Lesson 11-16: Transform number columns

You will often find a need to transform the scale and rounding of number columns.

For example, in this table, column C shows numbers using the *Thousand* number scale and percentages as floating-point numbers:

	A	B	C	D
3	From ▼	To ▼	Individuals (thousands) ▼	% In Group ▼
4	0	2,500.00	12,686	5.996350951
5	2,500.00	4,999.00	7,202	3.404203023
6	5,000.00	7,499.00	9,645	4.558947259

You might prefer the *Individuals (thousands)* column to show values without scaling and the *% In Group* column to show values rounded to four decimal places, like this:

	A	B	C	D
1	From ▼	To ▼	Individuals ▼	% In Group ▼
2	0	2500	12686000	5.9964
3	2500	4999	7202000	3.4042
4	5000	7499	9645000	4.5589

You could, of course, do this inside Excel but it is best practice to transform values within Get & Transform.

By transforming the values within *Get & Transform* the linked table will display the correct values as soon as it is created. You are then able to right-click→refresh the table to update and display any future changes that may occur in the data source without having to manually reformat the table after refreshing.

1   Open a new blank workbook.

2   Create a *Get & Transform* query to extract the values from the *IncomeDistribution* table in the *USA Income-1* Excel workbook in your sample files folder and display them in the Power Query Editor.

You learned how to do this in: *Lesson 11-15: Transform date and time columns.*

This workbook contains details of individual incomes in the United States in 2010:

⊞▼	From ▼	To ▼	Individuals (thousands) ▼	% In Group ▼
21	50000	52499	6320	2.987303958
22	52500	54999	2186	1.033266844
23	55000	57499	3455	1.633091009
24	57500	59999	1876	0.886737694

You can see that *6,320,000* Americans had an income between *$50,000* and *$52,499*, which constituted *2.987303958%* of all individuals.

3   Change the scale of the *Individuals (thousands)* column to show the number without thousand scaling.

USA Income-1

1. Click anywhere in the *Individuals (thousands)* column.

2. Click: Transform→Number Column→Standard→Multiply.

   The *Multiply* dialog appears.

3. Type: **1000** into the *Value* box.

4. Click the *OK* button.

   All values in the *Individuals (thousands)* column are transformed:

Multiply

Enter a number by which to multiply

Value

| 1000 |

⊞▾ From	▾ To	▾	Individuals (thousands)	▾	% In Group	▾
1	0	2500		12686000	5.996350951	
2	2500	4999		7202000	3.404203023	
3	5000	7499		9645000	4.558947259	

4 Change the column header of the *Individuals (thousands)* column to: **Individuals**

1. Double-click on the *Individuals (thousands)* column header.

2. Replace the existing text with: **Individuals**

3. Press the **<Enter>** key.

5 Round the values in the *% In Group* column so that values are rounded to four decimal places.

1. Click anywhere in the *% In Group* column.

2. Click: Transform→Number column→Rounding→Round…

   The *Round* dialog appears.

3. Type **4** into the *Decimal Places* box.

4. Click the *OK* button.

   All values in the *% In Group* column are rounded to four decimal places:

⊞▾ From	▾ To	▾	Individuals	▾	% In Group	▾
1	0	2500		12686000	5.9964	
2	2500	4999		7202000	3.4042	
3	5000	7499		9645000	4.5589	

Import Data ? ✕

Select how you want to view this data in your workbook.

⊙ ⦿ **T**able

▦ ○ **P**ivotTable Report

▯ ○ Pivot**C**hart

▯ ○ **O**nly Create Connection

Where do you want to put the data?

⦿ **E**xisting worksheet:

| SA$1 | ⬆ |

○ **N**ew worksheet

☐ Add this data to the Data **M**odel

| Properties... ▾ | OK | Cancel |

6 Close the Power Query Editor and load the query result to a table beginning in cell A1 of the existing worksheet (there is only one worksheet in this workbook).

You learned how to do this in: *Lesson 11-4: Move, remove, rename, filter and sort columns.*

◢	A	B	C	D
1	From ▾	To ▾	Individuals ▾	% In Group ▾
2	0	2500	12686000	5.9964
3	2500	4999	7202000	3.4042
4	5000	7499	9645000	4.5589

7 Save your work as *USA Income-2*.

Lesson 11-17: Add a custom calculated column

In a few clicks you can add a calculated column to a *Get & Transform* query.

1 Open a new blank workbook.

2 Create a *Get & Transform* query to extract the values from the *Sales* table in the *Bonus-1* Excel workbook in your sample files folder and display them in the Power Query Editor.

You learned how to do this in: *Lesson 11-15: Transform date and time columns.*

This workbook contains details of individual sales generated by a DVD wholesaler:

	1²₃ Order No	Order Date	A^BC Customer	A^BC Employee	A^BC Title	A^BC Genre	1²₃ Qty	1.2 Total
1	136438	10/2/2014	Silver Screen Video	Lee,Frank	Lawrence of Arabia	Biography	15	122.76
2	136438	10/2/2014	Silver Screen Video	Lee,Frank	The Discreet Charm of the Bourgeoisie	Comedy	9	67.46
3	136438	10/2/2014	Silver Screen Video	Lee,Frank	Berlin Alexanderplatz	Drama	25	250.6
4	136438	10/2/2014	Silver Screen Video	Lee,Frank	Gone With The Wind	Drama	14	107.72
5	136439	10/3/2014	Cinefocus DVD	Diamond,Elizabeth	Mouchette	Drama	5	31.77

You can see that *Frank Lee* sold order *136438* to *Silver Screen Video.* The order was for four different DVD titles.

By adding the *Qty* and *Total* field values in rows 1-4 you can see that Frank sold 63 DVDs on this order, for a total price of $548.54.

In this lesson you will calculate a monthly bonus for each employee. The bonus will be calculated as 3% of the total sale value.

3 Add a custom column to the Get & Transform query named: **Bonus** that will calculate 3% of the value shown in the *Total* column.

  1. Click: Add Column→General→Custom Column.

  2. The *Custom Column* dialog appears.

  3. Type: **Bonus** into the *New column name* box.

  4. Click inside the *Custom column formula* box.

  5. Click the *Total* field in the right-hand list.

  6. Click the << *Insert* button to add the *Total* field to the *Custom column formula* box.

     Notice that the field name is shown inside square brackets. This is PQFL syntax for a field name.

  7. Click to the right of the *[Total]* field and type: ***0.03** to complete the formula.

     Multiplying the *Total* field by 0.03 will calculate 3% of the field's value.

Bonus-1

New column name

Bonus

Custom column formula:

`= [Total]*0.03`

1²₃ Qty	▾	1.2 Total	▾	$ Bonus	▾
15		122.76		3.6828	
9		67.46		2.0238	
25		250.6		7.518	
14		107.72		3.2316	
5		31.77		0.9531	
19		136.71		4.1013	

8. Click the *OK* button.

A new custom (calculated) column called *Bonus* is added to the query and shows values that are 3% of the value in the *Total* column:

You can see that *Frank Lee* made $3.68 bonus on his sale of 15 copies of *Lawrence of Arabia*.

4 Set the data type of the *Bonus* field to *Currency*.

You learned how to do this in: *Lesson 11-11: Specify data types*.

5 Load the query results directly into a pivot table.

You learned how to do this in: *Lesson 11-15: Transform date and time columns*.

6 Select fields in the pivot table that will show the monthly *Bonus* earned for each *Employee*.

Do this using the same technique you learned in: *Lesson 9-19: Group by date*.

The field settings are:

▼ Filters	▥ Columns
	Years ▾
	Order Date ▾

▥ Rows	Σ Values
Employee ▾	Sum of Bonus ▾

7 Set the *Number Format* for the values shown in the pivot table to *Currency*.

1. Right-click on any value in the pivot table.

2. Select *Number Format…* from the shortcut menu.

3. Set the number format to *Currency*.

4. Click the *OK* button.

You can now see the monthly bonus earned by each *Employee* for each year and month in the period Oct 2014 to Mar 2016.

	A	B	C	D	E
3	Sum of Bonus	Column Labels ▾			
4		⊟2014			2014 Total
5	Row Labels ▾	Oct	Nov	Dec	
6	Anderson,Jane		$45.78	$0.76	$46.54
7	Armstrong,Dan		$43.62	$32.19	$75.80
8	Ashe,Lucille	$20.26	$8.45	$18.73	$47.43

Note that the currency symbol shown in your own pivot table may differ depending upon your Windows region format settings.

8 Save your work as *Bonus-2*.

Import Data

Select how you want to view this data in your workbook.

- ☐ ○ Table
- ☑ ◉ PivotTable Report
- ☐ ○ PivotChart
- ☐ ○ Only Create Connection

Where do you want to put the data?

- ○ Existing worksheet:
  - =$A$1 ⬆
- ◉ New worksheet

☐ Add this data to the Data Model

Properties ▾ | OK | Cancel

Lesson 11-18: Create an aggregated data query

Normally you will use *Get & Transform* to transform data and then use a pivot table to aggregate (summarize) the query result.

There may be some special circumstances where you would like the query to aggregate values *before* sending the query results to Excel.

This lesson will bring together many of the skills you have learned so far in this session.

1   Open a new blank workbook.

2   Create a *Get & Transform* query to extract the values from the *Products and Categories View* in the Inventory-1 Access database in your sample files folder and display them in the *Power Query Editor*.

> You will learn more about views later, in: *Lesson 11-28: Efficiently import data using a view.*
>
> You learned how to connect a *Get & Transform* query to an Access database in: *Lesson 11-11: Specify data types.*
>
> This view returns inventory details. Each product has been allocated a *Category*.

▥	ProductName ▾	CategoryName ▾	QuantityPerUnit ▾	UnitPrice ▾	UnitsInStock ▾	UnitsOnOrder ▾	ReorderLevel ▾	Discontinued ▾
1	Chai	Beverages	10 boxes x 20 bags	18	39	0	10	FALSE
2	Chang	Beverages	24 - 12 oz bottles	19	17	40	25	FALSE
3	Guaraná Fantástica	Beverages	12 - 355 ml cans	4.5	20	0	0	TRUE

> Your challenge in this lesson will be to create a *Get & Transform* query that will return aggregated (summarized) values for each *Category*. This is very similar to the results you could obtain using a pivot table (see facing page sidebar for the advantages an aggregated data query).
>
> For each *Category*, the query needs to report the total *Units in Stock, Units on Order, Inventory Value* and *Projected Inventory Value* (the value that would result if all goods on order had already arrived).

3   Set the data type of the *UnitPrice* column to *Currency* (if it isn't already set to *Currency*) and the data type of the *UnitsInStock* and *UnitsOnOrder* columns to *Whole Number*.

> You learned how to do this in: *Lesson 11-11: Specify data types.*

4   Add a custom column named *InventoryValue* that contains a value equal to the *UnitPrice* field multiplied by the *UnitsInStock* field.

> You learned how to do this in: *Lesson 11-17: Add a custom calculated column.*

5   Add a custom column named *ProjectedInventoryValue* that contains a value equal to the *UnitsOnOrder* field multiplied by the *UnitPrice field* added to the (already calculated) *InventoryValue* field.

Custom Column

New column name

InventoryValue

Custom column formula:

= [UnitPrice]*[UnitsInStock]

Custom Column

New column name

ProjectedInventoryValue

Custom column formula:

= [UnitsOnOrder]*[UnitPrice]+ [InventoryValue]

Inventory-1

note

Advantages of a linked table containing an aggregated query over a pivot table

Automatic refresh capability

You can schedule automatic refreshes with an aggregated query.

In: *Lesson 11-3: Understand queries and connections*, you learned how to automatically refresh a table linked to a *Get & Transform* query every minute.

It isn't possible to automatically refresh data in a pivot table.

Small file and memory size

A worksheet table does not have any associated PivotTable data cache. This can result in a much smaller file size and memory requirement.

You learned how to do this in: *Lesson 11-17: Add a custom calculated column.*

6   Set the data type of both custom columns to *Currency.*

You learned how to do this in: *Lesson 11-11: Specify data types.*

7   Group the query by *CategoryName* to show aggregated values for the total of the four numeric columns.

1.   Click any cell in the *CategoryName* column.

2.   Click: Transform→Table→Group By.

The *Group By* dialog appears.

3.   Click the *Advanced* option button.

4.   Select *CategoryName* from the *Group by* drop-down list (if it isn't already selected).

5.   Type **UnitsInStock** into the *New column name* box.

6.   Select: *Sum* from the *Operation* drop-down list.

7.   Select *UnitsInStock* from the *Column* drop-down list.

8.   Click the *Add aggregation* button to add a second group field for *UnitsOnOrder.*

9.   Add three more fields so that your dialog looks like this:

Group by		
CategoryName		
Add grouping		
New column name	**Operation**	**Column**
UnitsInStock	Sum	UnitsInStock
UnitsOnOrder	Sum	UnitsOnOrder
InventoryValue	Sum	InventoryValue
ProjectedInventoryValue	Sum	ProjectedInventoryValue

10.   Click the *OK* button.

8   Close the Power Query Editor and load the query result to a table in cell A1 of the existing worksheet.

You learned how to do this in: *Lesson 11-4: Move, remove, rename, filter and sort columns.*

	A	B	C	D	E
1	CategoryName	UnitsInStock	UnitsOnOrder	InventoryValue	ProjectedInventoryValue
2	Beverages	559	60	12480.25	13850.25
3	Condiments	507	170	12023.55	14423.55
4	Confections	386	180	10392.2	13009.7

9   Save your work as *Inventory-2.*

Lesson 11-19: Unpivot aggregated data

Recognizing pivoted data

You'll often find data showing rolled-up totals in columns. For example, consider this data:

	A	B	C	D
2	Customer	Jan	Feb	Mar
3	Addison-Freelander Screen Agency	2,195.49	1,673.32	488.52
4	AV Supplies	1,298.66	1,862.95	1,792.25
5	Box Office Supplies	795.39	3,029.79	1,793.12

The data shows aggregated monthly sales.

Data in this format is nicely presented for human readers but is not useful when you need to analyze it using an Excel worksheet or pivot table.

Here is the correct format for easy analysis of the above data:

	A	B	C
2	Customer	Month	Sales
3	Addison-Freelander Screen Agency	Jan	2195.49
4	Addison-Freelander Screen Agency	Feb	1673.32
5	Addison-Freelander Screen Agency	Mar	488.52
6	AV Supplies	Jan	1298.66
7	AV Supplies	Feb	1862.95
8	AV Supplies	Mar	1792.25
9	Box Office Supplies	Jan	795.39
10	Box Office Supplies	Feb	3029.79
11	Box Office Supplies	Mar	1793.12

This transformation would take a substantial amount of time using traditional Excel tools but takes just three clicks in the *Get & Transform* query editor. Many more things can be done when the data is transformed into the correct format for analysis.

- You can create a pivot table from it.

- You can filter by month.

- You can use many of Excel's aggregation functions and features (for example the automatic subtotal feature that you learned to use in: *Lesson 2-3: Automatically subtotal a range*).

1 Open a new blank worksheet.

2 Create a *Get & Transform* query to extract the values from the *MonthlySales* table in the *Sales by Employee-1* Excel workbook in your sample files folder and display them in the Power Query Editor.

You learned how to do this in: *Lesson 11-15: Transform date and time columns*.

Sales by Employee-1

This workbook contains monthly total sales figures for each employee.

	ABC 123 Employee		ABC 123 Genre		ABC 123 Jan-15		ABC 123 Feb-15		ABC 123 Mar-15	
4	Anderson,Jane		Comedy			116		0		777.2
5	Anderson,Jane		Crime			217.12		152.22		0
6	Anderson,Jane		Drama			161.98		0		397.63

note

Why are there two Month fields shown in the PivotTable Field List

When you add the *Month* pivot table field to the *Columns* box, two different values are shown:

Columns
Months (Month) ▾
Month ▾

In: *Lesson 11-6: Understand data types*, it was noted that Excel does not support any true *Date* or *Time* data types.

Instead, Excel relies upon formatting numerical values that are regarded as being *date serial numbers*.

Date serial numbers were covered in depth in: *Lesson 3-7: Understand date serial numbers*.

Get & Transform originally assigned the *Text* data type to the *Month* column.

When you changed the data type of the *Month* column to *Date*, Get & Transform assigned the first day of each month to the date values in the column.

The pivot table was not sure whether you wanted date values (such as 01/01/18) or month values (such as *Jan, Feb, Mar*) in the column headers.

For this reason, it helpfully added both *Months (Month)* to show the month name and *Month* (the field name on its own) to show the full date.

▼ Filters	▦ Columns
	Months (Month) ▾
☰ Rows	Σ Values
Genre ▾	Sum of Sales ▾

You can see that this is a classic example of pivoted data. The *Employee* and *Genre* columns don't have a problem but all of the other columns (*Jan-15* to *Dec-15*) need to be unpivoted.

3 Unpivot all of the monthly total columns.

1. Click on the *Jan-15* column header to select it.
2. Hold down the **<Shift>** key.
3. Click on the *Dec-15* column header.

   All monthly columns are now selected.
4. Click: Transform→Any Column→Unpivot Columns.

   The columns are unpivoted:

	A_C B Employee		A_C B Genre		A_C B Attribute		1.2 Value	
1	Anderson,Jane		Action		Jan-15			0
2	Anderson,Jane		Action		Feb-15			173.29
3	Anderson,Jane		Action		Mar-15			409.48

4 Rename the *Attribute* column to: **Month** and the *Value* column to: **Sales**

You learned how to do this in: *Lesson 11-4: Move, remove, rename, filter and sort columns.*

5 Change the data type of the *Month* column to *Date* and the data type of the *Sales* column to *Currency.*

You learned how to do this in: *Lesson 11-11: Specify data types.*

6 Load the query results directly into a pivot table.

You did this in: *Lesson 11-15: Transform date and time columns.*

7 Select fields in the pivot table that will show monthly *Sales* for each *Genre.*

Do this using the same technique you learned in: *Lesson 9-19: Group by date.*

The field settings are shown in the sidebar.

8 Set the *Number Format* for the values shown in the pivot table to *Currency.*

1. Right-click on any value in the pivot table.
2. Select *Number Format…* from the shortcut menu.
3. Set the number format to *Currency.*
4. Click the *OK* button.

	A	B	C	D	E	F
1	Sum of Sales	Column Labels ▾				
2	Row Labels ▾	Jan	Feb	Mar	Apr	May
3	Action	$1,112.11	$1,249.08	$2,630.88	$769.55	$1,001.89
4	Adventure	$246.59	$167.83	$285.65	$379.22	$581.30

9 Save your work as: *Sales by Employee-2.*

Lesson 11-20: Work with multiple queries

Up until now you've worked with a single query.

Get & Transform can also combine data from multiple queries. You'll learn how to do this in: *Lesson 11-21: Create an append query*.

Get & Transform also has some features that work well with queries containing related data (you'll learn about relational data later, in: *Lesson 11-26: Understand primary and foreign keys*).

As each query can potentially draw data from a different data source, it is possible to combine data from one or more web queries, CSV files, Excel workbooks and database tables or views.

You could create queries individually (as you have up to now in this session). This lesson will teach you how to work more efficiently by creating multiple queries in a single *Get & Transform* session.

1   Open a new blank workbook.

2   Open the Power Query Editor.

Up until now you've always selected the data source type before entering the query editor. You could do that in this lesson but, for variety, you'll do things a little differently.

Click: Data→Get & Transform Data→Get Data→
Launch Power Query Editor...

The empty query editor opens.

3   Create four queries named *Confections, DairyProduce, Beverages* and *Condiments* from the four sample files of the same name in the *Session 10/Append* folder in your sample files folder.

The *Session 10/Append* folder contains three Excel sample files and one CSV sample file. Each of the files contains data with the same structure (the same number of columns and the same column header names in each column).

Name	Type	Size
Beverages	Microsoft Excel Comma Separated Values File	1 KB
Condiments	Microsoft Excel Worksheet	10 KB
Confections	Microsoft Excel Worksheet	11 KB
DairyProduce	Microsoft Excel Worksheet	10 KB

1.   Click: Home→New Query→New Source→File→Excel.

2.   Navigate to the *Session 10/Append* folder and double-click the *Condiments* workbook.

3.   Select the *Condiments* table within the workbook.

4.   Click the *OK* button.

The Power Query Editor now shows the contents of the *Condiments* table.

Set of four files in:
Session 10/Append

Notice that the query editor has automatically named the query *Condiments* and that it has appeared in the query list on the left of the screen.

Queries [1] <
Condiments

5. Click: Home→New Query→New Source→File→Text/CSV.

6. Navigate to the *Session 10/Append* folder and double-click the *Beverages* CSV file.

The *Get & Transform* query editor now shows the contents of the *Beverages* CSV file.

7. Click the OK button.

Notice that the query editor has automatically named the query *Beverages* and that it has appeared underneath the *Condiments* query in the query list on the left of the screen.

Queries [2] <
Condiments
Beverages

8. Repeat the same process for the *Confections* and *DairyProduce* Excel workbooks.

4 Save the four queries as connection only queries.

The four queries will be used in the next lesson. For the moment you do not want to load the data returned by the queries anywhere.

Queries [4] <
Condiments
Beverages
Confections
DairyProduce

1. Click: Home→Close→Close & Load (Drop-down list)→ Close & Load To…

2. Click the *Only Create Connection* option button.

Import Data   ?   ×

Select how you want to view this data in your workbook.
○ Table
○ PivotTable Report
○ PivotChart
● Only Create Connection
Where do you want to put the data?
Existing worksheet:
=$A$1
New worksheet
☐ Add this data to the Data Model

Properties...   OK   Cancel

Make sure that the *Add this data to the Data Model* check box is **not** checked.

A *data model* is an in-memory construct that can be analyzed using a new type of pivot table (called an OLAP pivot table). You'll learn about data models later, in: *Session Twelve: Power Pivot, Data Modeling, OLAP and Business Intelligence*.

3. Click the *OK* button.

You are returned to the empty workbook with four *Connection only* queries shown in the *Queries & Connections* task pane.

5 Save your work as *Multiple Queries-1*.

Queries & Connections

Queries | Connections

4 queries

Condiments
Connection only.

Beverages
Connection only.

Confections
Connection only.

DairyProduce
Connection only.

Lesson 11-21: Create an append query

You will often find a need to append rows of data from different data sources.

In: *Lesson 11-20: Work with multiple queries,* you created four queries that returned data from three similar workbooks and a CSV file.

This is the data that was returned from the *Condiments* table in the *Condiments* Excel workbook:

Product Name	Supplier	Category
Aniseed Syrup	Exotic Liquids	Condiments
Chef Anton's Cajun Seasoning	New Orleans Cajun Delights	Condiments
Genen Shouyu	Mayumi's	Condiments

… and here is the data returned from the *Beverages* CSV file:

Product Name	Supplier	Category
Chai	Exotic Liquids	Beverages
Chang	Exotic Liquids	Beverages
Chartreuse verte	Aux joyeux eccl,siastiques	Beverages

Notice that the column headers (field names) are identical and that each column has the same data type.

You'll often find that you have rows of data residing in different data sources that you need to combine into one table that contains all rows of data. You can do this with a *Get & Transform append query.*

If the above two queries were appended, the resulting table would look like this:

Product Name	Supplier	Category
Aniseed Syrup	Exotic Liquids	Condiments
Chef Anton's Cajun Seasoning	New Orleans Cajun Delights	Condiments
Genen Shouyu	Mayumi's	Condiments
Chai	Exotic Liquids	Beverages
Chang	Exotic Liquids	Beverages
Chartreuse verte	Aux joyeux eccl,siastiques	Beverages

1   Open *Multiple Queries-1* from your sample files folder (if it isn't already open).

This is the workbook that you created in: *Lesson 11-20: Work with multiple queries.*

The workbook is empty apart from four *Connection only* queries that point to four different data sources.

2   Create an append query that will return appended data from the *Condiments*, *Beverages*, *Confections* and *DairyProduce* queries.

1.   Click: Data→Get & Transform Data→Get Data→ Combine Queries→Append.

The *Append* dialog appears.

2. Click the *Three or more tables* option button.

3. Select all four tables in the left-hand *Available table(s) list.*

4. Click the *Add* >> button.

The four tables are displayed in the right-hand *Tables to append* list.

Append

○ Two tables   ● Three or more tables

Available table(s)   Tables to append

Condiments   Condiments
Beverages   Beverages
Confections   Confections
DairyProduce   DairyProduce

                                      Add >>

5. Click the *OK* button.

The Power Query Editor appears, showing the rows from all four queries appended into a single table.

6. Look at the PQFL formula in the formula bar.

fx   = Table.Combine({Condiments,Beverages, Confections, DairyProduce})

note

PQFL formulas and blank spaces

In this lesson I was careful to name one of the queries: *DairyProduce* (without a space) rather than *Dairy Produce* (with a space).

If you include spaces in query names you will have to refer to them in a special way within PQFL formulas.

To refer to a query called *Dairy Produce* (with a space) you'd need to type:

#"Dairy Produce"

The complete formula would be:

=
Table.Combine({Condiments, Beverages, Confections, #"Dairy Produce"})

Unless you think it likely that you will want to create PQFL code by hand this is unlikely to be of any importance.

3 Rename your query to: **Full Stock List**

Notice that in the *Query Settings* task pane the query has been named *Append1*.

Click in the *Name* box and type the new query name: **Full Stock List**

▲ PROPERTIES
Name
Full Stock List

4 Close the Power Query Editor and load the query result to a table in cell A1 of the existing worksheet (there is only one worksheet in this workbook).

You learned how to do this in: *Lesson 11-4: Move, remove, rename, filter and sort columns.*

Import Data   ?   ×

Select how you want to view this data in your workbook.
☐ ● Table
☐ ○ PivotTable Report
☐ ○ PivotChart
☐ ○ Only Create Connection
Where do you want to put the data?
● Existing worksheet:
=$A$1   ⬆
○ New worksheet
☐ Add this data to the Data Model

Properties...   OK   Cancel

5 Save your work as *Multiple Queries-2*.

Lesson 11-22: Understand Column From Examples

Column from Examples can save you an enormous amount of time when implementing many common transformations.

In: *Lesson 11-5: Split delimited data,* you learned how to transform delimited text using Get & Transform's *Extract* feature. In this lesson you'll split some simple delimited text in a different and far faster way using the *Column from Examples* feature.

1 Open *Column From Examples-1* from your sample files folder.

2 Create a query that will extract the contents of the *Employee* table and open it in the Power Query Editor.

   1. Select the *Employees* worksheet.

   2. Click anywhere inside the *Employee* table.

   3. Click: Data→Get & Transform Data→From Table/Range.

      The query opens in the Power Query Editor.

3 Use the *Column from Examples* feature to extract each Employee's first name into a new column called *First Name*.

   1. Click: Add Column→General→Column From Examples.

      An empty example column appears.

   2. Type: **Jessica**

   3. Press the **<Enter>** key.

      All of the Employees' first names have appeared grayed out in the column (see sidebar).

      The header text at the top of the column has also changed to *Text Before Delimiter*.

Text Before Delimiter
Jessica

This lets you know that Get & Transform has intelligently guessed that there is a delimiter (in this case a space) between the first and second names.

   4. Click the *OK* button to apply the transformation and add the column.

   5. Rename the new column: **First Name**

	A^B_C Full Name		A^B_C First Name	
1	Jessica Sagan		Jessica	
2	Stephen Bell		Stephen	

4 Examine the PQFL code that Get & Transform has generated.

   1. If the *Query Settings* task pane is not displayed click:

**Sidebar:**

Text Before Delimiter
Jessica
Stephen
John
Meryl
Alfred
Lucille
Julia
Marilyn
Charles
Elizabeth
Margaret
Howard
Paul
Frank
Anna
Andy
Jane
Michael
Dan
John
Chuck
Julie
Julia
Gloria

Column From Examples-1

APPLIED STEPS

Source
Changed Type
✕ Inserted Text Before Delimiter
Renamed Columns

View→Layout→Query Settings.

2. Click on the *Inserted Text Before Delimiter* step in the *Query Settings* task pane.

3. Look at the PQFL code in the formula bar.

```
= Table.AddColumn(#"Changed Type", "Text Before Delimiter", each Text.BeforeDelimiter([Full Name], " "), type text)
```

Even without an in-depth knowledge of PQFL you can see what Get & Transform has done. The code:

Transform: Text.BeforeDelimiter([Full Name], " ")

… is taking each value in the *[Full Name]* column and extracting the text before the space delimiter (" "). This is exactly what you wanted Get & Transform to do.

5   Load the result of the query to a table that begins in cell C1 in the *Employees* worksheet.

1. Click: Home→Close & Load→Close & Load To…

2. Set the *Import Data* settings as follows:

3. Click OK.

6   Set the new linked table to automatically refresh every minute.

You learned how to do this in: *Lesson 11-3: Understand queries and connections.*

7   Add a new name to the *Employees* table and wait one minute.

The new name also appears in the linked table.

	A	B	C	D
1	Full Name ▼		Full Name ▼	First Name ▼
24	Julia Carrey		Julia Carrey	Julia
25	Gloria Silverstone		Gloria Silverstone	Gloria
26	Arthur Daly		Arthur Daly	Arthur

8   Save your work as *Column From Examples-2*.

Lesson 11-23: Use Column From Examples with selected source columns

The *Jan 2020 Semi-Annual Version 1908* release added the ability to define multiple source columns when working with *Column from Examples*. This enables far more complex transformations to be automatically created.

1 Open *Column From Examples-2* from your sample files folder.

2 Use *Column From Examples* to add a new *Last Name* column to the *Employee* query.

1. Open the *Employee* query in the *Power Query* editor.

2. Click the column header of the *Full Name* column.

   Every employee's full name is now selected.

3. Click: Add Column→General→Column From Examples→ From Selection.

   This instructs *Column From Examples* to only consider the contents of the *Full Name* column when deciding the most appropriate PQFL code to generate.

4. Type: **Sagan**

5. Press the **<Enter>** key.

   All of the employee last names are shown (grayed out) in the example column (see sidebar).

6. Click the OK button

   A new column is added that contains each employee's last name.

7. Change the name of the column to: **Last Name**

	ABC Full Name	ABC First Name	ABC Last Name
1	Jessica Sagan	Jessica	Sagan
2	Stephen Bell	Stephen	Bell
3	John Jennings	John	Jennings

3 Use *Column From Examples* to add a new *Initials* column to the *Employee* query.

1. Select the *First Name* and *Last Name* columns.

   You need to make *Column From Example's* job as easy as possible by trying to make the method of arriving at your example text clearer.

2. Click: Add Column→General→Column From Examples→ From Selection.

   This informs *Column From Examples* to only consider the contents of the *First Name* and *Last Name* columns when figuring out the appropriate PQFL code to generate.

**Sidebar:**

Text After Delimiter

Sagan
Bell
Jennings
Simpson
Hawking
Ashe
Putin
Manning
Davis
Diamond
Streep
Simpson
Goodman
Lee
Newhart
Richards
Anderson
Hicks
Armstrong
Bradshaw
West
Spears
Carrey
Silverstone
Daly

Column From Examples-2

---

3. Click in the first cell in the *Column1* table.

4. Type: **JS**

5. Press the **<Enter>** key.

Nothing happens. *Column From Examples* needs another example to understand your requirement.

6. Type: **SB**

7. Press the **<Enter>** key.

This time *Column From Examples* understands what is needed and all of the employee initials are shown (grayed out) in the example column (see sidebar).

8. Click the *OK* button.

A new column is added containing all of the Employee initials

9. Change the name of the new column to: **Initials**

	AᴮC Full Name	AᴮC First Name	AᴮC Last Name	AᴮC Initials
1	Jessica Sagan	Jessica	Sagan	JS
2	Stephen Bell	Stephen	Bell	SB
3	John Jennings	John	Jennings	JJ

4 Use *Column From Examples* to add a new *Reverse Full Name* column to the *Employee* query to show [Last Name], [First Name].

It is common to list names in the form:

Sagan, Jessica

This makes a column of names easy to sort.

1. Select the *First Name* and *Last Name* columns.

2. Use the same technique you used to add the *Initials* column.

Your first example will look like this:

Column1
Sagan, Jessica

When you have finished, the *Power Query Editor* window should look like this:

	AᴮC Full Name	AᴮC First Name	AᴮC Last Name	AᴮC Initials	AᴮC Reverse Full Name
1	Jessica Sagan	Jessica	Sagan	JS	Sagan, Jessica
2	Stephen Bell	Stephen	Bell	SB	Bell, Stephen
3	John Jennings	John	Jennings	JJ	Jennings, John

5 Close the Power Query editor window keeping changes made.

When the window closes you may be asked to click the *Keep* button. Notice that the linked table has been updated (and will continue to update as you set a timed refresh for it to automatically execute the query in: *Lesson 11-22: Understand Column From Examples*).

6 Save your work as *Column From Examples-3*.

note

You can add an example in any row of the example column

In this lesson you typed the example text in the first row of the example column:

A^B_C Telephone	☑	
+44 (0)113-4960227		+44
+356 (0)2138-3393		▢ +44
+44 (0)115-4960498		

Sometimes you will need to place your example in a different row of the example column.

For example, imagine that you want to capitalize the first letter of the following names:

▦▾	A^B_C Mixed Case	▾
1	Jessica Sagan	
2	stephen Bell	
3	john Paul Jennings	

You can see that the first entry is already correct. Get & Transform will not know what you need to do if you simply repeat it in the first row.

Instead you would place your example into the second or third row, as they are incorrect.

A^B_C Mixed Case	☑	Capitaliz
Jessica Sagan		Jessica Sagan
stephen Bell		Stephen Bell
john Paul Jennings		John Paul Jennings

In the above grab, the text: **Stephen Bell** has been typed into the second row of the example column.

This was all Get & Tansform needed understand that you wanted to capitalize each word.

Lesson 11-24: Use Column From Examples to extract characters from strings

In: *Lesson 3-21: Extract text from delimited strings using the FIND and LEN functions* you used Excel formulas to extract the Country Code, NDD and Area Code from some international telephone numbers.

▲	A	B	G	H	I
			Country		Phone
3	Company	Telephone	Code	Area Code	Number
4	Books A Million	+44 (0)113-4960227	+44	113	4960227
5	Maltese Books	+356 (0)2138-3393	+356	2138	3393
6	Bargain Bookstore	+44 (0)115-4960498	+44	115	4960498
7	Books for Less	+44 (0)116-4960593	+44	116	4960593

This was quite a complex task.

In this lesson you'll use *Column From Examples* to complete the same operation in a fraction of the time.

1   Open *Column From Examples-3* from your sample files folder.

2   Select the *Phone Book (Formatted)* worksheet.

3   Create a query that will extract the contents of the *FormattedPhoneNumbers* table and open it in the Power Query Editor.

   1.   Select the *Phone Book (Formatted)* worksheet.

   2.   Click anywhere inside the *FormattedPhoneNumbers* table.

   3.   Click: Data→Get & Transform Data→From Table/Range.

      The query opens in the Power Query Editor.

4   Use the *Column from Examples* feature to create a new column containing the Country Code.

   You learned how to do this in: *Lesson 11-23: Use Column From Examples with selected source columns.*

   Begin by selecting the *Telephone* column as the source.

   Your first example will be:

Column1
+44

▦▾	A^B_C Company	▾	A^B_C Telephone	▾	A^B_C Country Code	▾
1	Books A Million		+44 (0)113-4960227		+44	
2	Maltese Books		+356 (0)2138-3393		+356	

5   Use the *Column from Examples* feature to create a new column containing the Area Code.

   Begin by selecting the *Telephone* column as the source.

   Your first example will be:

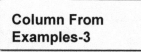

Column From Examples-3

Column1
113

A^B_C Telephone	A^B_C Country Code	A^B_C Area Code
+44 (0)113-4960227	+44	113
+356 (0)2138-3393	+356	2138

6   Use the *Column from Examples* feature to create a new column containing the Phone Number.

Begin by selecting the *Telephone* column as the source.

Your first example will be:

Column1
4960227

A^B_C Telephone	A^B_C Country Code	A^B_C Area Code	A^B_C Phone Number
+44 (0)113-4960227	+44	113	4960227
+356 (0)2138-3393	+356	2138	3393

7   Load the result of the query to a table that begins in cell D1 in the *Phone Book (Formatted)* worksheet.

   1.   Click: Home→Close & Load→Close & Load To…

   2.   Set the *Import Data* settings as follows:

   Import Data   ?   ×

   Select how you want to view this data in your workbook.
       ⊙ Table
       ○ PivotTable Report
       ○ PivotChart
       ○ Only Create Connection
   Where do you want to put the data?
       ⊙ Existing worksheet:
       Book (Formatted)'!$D$1   ↑
       ○ New worksheet
   □ Add this data to the Data Model

   Properties...   OK   Cancel

8   Set the new linked table to automatically refresh every minute.

You learned how to do this in: *Lesson 11-3: Understand queries and connections.*

9   Add a new company and telephone number to the *FormattedPhoneBook* table and wait one minute.

You may have to begin the number with an apostrophe to indicate that it is a string and prevent Excel from regarding it as a formula.

The new phone number also appears in the linked table.

	A	B	C	D	E	F	G	H
13	The Book Depository	+44 (0)20-79460345		The Book Depository	+44 (0)20-79460345	+44	20	79460345
14	Blackwells	+44 (0)191-4980562		Blackwells	+44 (0)191-4980562	+44	191	4980562
15	Brilliant Books	+44 (0)28-90180295		Brilliant Books	+44 (0)28-90180295	+44	28	90180295
16	Laxey Bookshop	+44 (0)29-20180948		Laxey Bookshop	+44 (0)29-20180948	+44	29	20180948
17	La Manoeuvre, Paris	+33 (0)745-558081		La Manoeuvre, Paris	+33 (0)745-558081	+33	745	558081

10   Save your work as *Column From Examples-4*.

Lesson 11-25: Appreciate the potential of Column From Examples

Column From Examples is one of Get & Transform's most useful features.

This lesson gives examples of many common transformations that can be quickly and simply completed using *Column From Examples.* I've also included all of the examples in the sample file: *Column From Examples Samples.*

Column From Examples is able to apply many more transformations than those shown below but the examples may help you to appreciate the potential of this feature.

In each example, *Column From Examples* created the shaded columns.

Split text and extract initials

Full Name	First Name	Last Name	Initials
Jessica Sagan	Jessica	Sagan	JS
Stephen Bell	Stephen	Bell	SB
John Jennings	John	Jennings	JJ

This is similar to the example you created in: *Lesson 11-22: Understand Column From Examples* and *Lesson 11-23: Use Column From Examples with selected source columns.*

Concatenate text

First Name	Last Name	Full Name
Jessica	Sagan	Jessica Sagan
Stephen	Bell	Stephen Bell
John	Jennings	John Jennings

Remove title from names

Full Name	Short Name
Miss Jessica Sagan	Jessica Sagan
Mr Stephen Bell	Stephen Bell
Mr John Jennings	John Jennings

Add commas
(a useful name format for alphabetical sorting)

First Name	Last Name	Sort Name
Jessica	Sagan	Sagan, Jessica
Stephen	Bell	Bell, Stephen
John	Jennings	Jennings, John

Column From
Examples Samples

This is similar to the example that you created in: *Lesson 11-23: Use Column From Examples with selected source columns.*

Concatenate text and insert extra text

First Name	Last Name	Full Name
Jessica	Sagan	First Name: Jessica, Last Name: Sagan
Stephen	Bell	First Name: Stephen, Last Name: Bell
John	Jennings	First Name: John, Last Name: Jennings

Change capitalization

Mixed Case	Capitalize Each Word	UPPERCASE	lowercase
jessica elizabeth sagan	Jessica Elizabeth Sagan	JESSICA ELIZABETH SAGAN	jessica elizabeth sagan
stephen Bell	Stephen Bell	STEPHEN BELL	stephen bell
john Paul jennings	John Paul Jennings	JOHN PAUL JENNINGS	john paul jennings

Extract the day, month or year from a date

When using a date as the source column for *Column From Examples* it is important that the data type (within Get & Transform) is set to *Date, Time* or *DateTime*.

Date	Day Name	Day	Month Name	Year	Quarter
1/19/2013	Saturday	19	January	2013	1
8/5/1967	Saturday	5	August	1967	3
9/20/1999	Monday	20	September	1999	3

Extract the domain name and addressee from an e-mail address

E-mail address	Domain	Addressee
Mary@QuiteContrary.com	QuiteContrary.com	Mary
Humpty@Dumpty.com	Dumpty.com	Humpty
Jack@Nimble.com	Nimble.com	Jack

Extract and Format telephone numbers

Company Name	Phone	Area	Exchange	Number	Formatted Number
Great Lakes Food Market	5035557555	503	555	7555	(503)-555-7555
Hungry Coyote Import Store	5035556874	503	555	6874	(503)-555-6874
Lazy K Kountry Store	5095557969	509	555	7969	(509)-555-7969

This is similar to the example you created in: *Lesson 11-24: Use Column From Examples to extract characters from strings.*

In this example it would not be possible to create the *Formatted Number* directly from the *Phone* column.

Column From Examples is first used to extract the *Area, Exchange* and *Number* columns using the *Phone* column as the source.

The *Formatted Number* column is then created using the *Area, Exchange* and *Number* columns as the source.

note

Virtually all of the world's databases work like this

Dr Edgar F Codd (1923-2003) invented the relational database when working for IBM in the 1970's.

The first relational database products came to market in the late 1970's and were quickly adopted by big business.

So good and great was Codd's design that nothing better has been developed in over thirty years.

The entire world of commerce is now powered by relational databases.

You'll usually find a requirement to analyze data from a relational database in all but the very smallest enterprises.

Lesson 11-26: Understand primary and foreign keys

A set of tables that are *related* to each other are referred to as a relational database. Some of Get & Transform's most useful features require an understanding of basic relational database theory.

What is a primary key?

A relational database consists of several tables, each containing data. A database table is conceptually no different to an Excel table except that each row must have a unique *primary key*.

Here's an example of a table from a relational database:

CategoryID	CategoryName	Description
1	Beverages	Soft drinks, coffees, teas, beers, and ales
2	Condiments	Sweet and savory sauces, relishes, spreads, and seasonings
3	Confections	Desserts, candies, and sweet breads

The above example comes from a database table called *Category*. It is good relational database design practice to name a primary key as the table name plus the letters *ID*. This designer has followed best practice and called the primary key *CategoryID*.

The only important quality of a primary key is that all primary key values must be different (unique) within the primary key column. That's because the primary key is used (by a relationship) to identify a single, row in a table. If there were two table rows with the same primary key, a relationship wouldn't be able to correctly identify which single row was being referenced.

In the above example the primary key is a number but primary keys can consist of numbers, letters or both.

What is a foreign key?

note

Primary and foreign keys should have the same name

Any database designer worthy of the name will use the same name for the primary key column and the related foreign key column.

I've found that, in the real world of business, I often need to work with a badly designed database where this is not the case. This makes the data a lot more difficult to work with.

Here is an example of two related tables from a relational database:

CategoryID	CategoryName	Description
1	Beverages	Soft drinks, coffees, teas, beers, and ales
2	Condiments	Sweet and savory sauces, relishes, spreads, and seasonings
3	Confections	Desserts, candies, and sweet breads

ProductID	ProductName	CategoryID	QuantityPerUnit	UnitPrice
1	Chai	1	10 boxes x 20 bags	18.00
3	Aniseed Syrup	2	12 - 550 ml bottles	10.00
16	Pavlova	3	32 - 500 g boxes	17.45
24	Guaraná Fantástica	1	12 - 355 ml cans	4.50
25	NuNuCa Nuß-Nougat-Creme	3	20 - 450 g glasses	14.00
34	Sasquatch Ale	1	24 - 12 oz bottles	14.00

You can see how it is possible to determine that *Aniseed Syrup* is in the *Condiments* category:

- In the *Product* table, *Aniseed Syrup* has a *CategoryID* of 2.

- The item in the *Category* table with a primary key (*CategoryID*) of 2 is *Condiments.*

While *CategoryID* is the primary key column in the *Category* table, it is a *foreign key* column within the *Product* table.

You can think of the *CategoryID* values in the *Product* table as belonging to the *Category* table, making them foreign keys in the *Product* table.

You can probably now see the wisdom of the naming convention for primary keys. It makes it possible to spot which are the primary and foreign keys in a table at a glance.

- The column named with the table name plus *ID* is the primary key.

- Any other column name that is suffixed with *ID* (has *ID* at the end of the name) is a foreign key.

- Any column not suffixed with *ID* is a regular data field containing information.

Meaningful and meaningless primary keys

In the above example, the primary key is a *meaningless* number. The number 2 tells you nothing about any attribute of the *Condiments* category. It simply provides a way to find where the correct *Condiments* row is located within the table.

It is also possible to use a *meaningful* primary key (though a professional database designer would never do this). For example, you could argue that because category names are unique, it is fine to use the *CategoryName* column in the above table as the primary key.

If you decided to use the category name as the primary key the tables would look like this:

CategoryID	Description
Condiments	Sweet and savory sauces, relishes, spreads, and seasonings
Beverages	Soft drinks, coffees, teas, beers, and ales
Confections	Desserts, candies, and sweet breads

ProductID	ProductName	CategoryID	QuantityPerUnit	UnitPrice
50	Valkoinen suklaa	Confections	12 - 100 g bars	16.25
1	Chai	Beverages	10 boxes x 20 bags	18.00
77	Original Frankfurter grüne Soße	Condiments	12 boxes	13.00
8	Northwoods Cranberry Sauce	Condiments	12 - 12 oz jars	40.00
68	Scottish Longbreads	Confections	10 boxes x 8 pieces	12.50
70	Outback Lager	Beverages	24 - 355 ml bottles	15.00

From a database design perspective, this is generally a bad idea

You'll often find, however, that you need to create this type of relationship when creating relationships between tables that originate from different databases. In this case, no formal primary key/foreign key relationship will exist.

For example, you may need to join a table from your corporate database containing customer addresses with a table detailing sales tax rates by state that you've downloaded from the Internet. In this case you would need to create a primary key/foreign key relationship between the state columns in each table.

note

XLOOKUP is the modern replacement for the old VLOOKUP function

XLOOKUP is one of the new dynamic array function included in the *Excel July 2020 Semi-Annual Version 2002* release.

Unless you have a need to share your workbooks with users of legacy Excel versions (Excel 2019 and earlier) you should always use XLOOKUP and not VLOOKUP for new work.

Lesson 11-27: Link primary and foreign keys using XLOOKUP

In: *Lesson 11-26: Understand primary and foreign keys,* you learned how relational databases use primary key/foreign key relationships to relate tables to each other.

In this lesson you'll leverage upon your understanding of primary and foreign keys by using a simple XLOOKUP to retrieve information from a related table.

1 Open *Primary and Foreign Keys-1* from your sample files folder.

Notice the following:

- This workbook contains two worksheets: *Category* and *Product.*

- The *Product* worksheet contains a single table called *Product.*

- The *Category* worksheet contains a single table called *Category.*

- The *Product* table has two fields with the suffix: *ID.* (*ProductID* and *CategoryID*).

- The *Category* table has one field with the suffix: *ID.* (*CategoryID*).

- In: *Lesson 11-26: Understand primary and foreign keys,* you learned that these fields are, in fact, Primary Keys and Foreign Keys.

- In the *Product* table, the *ProductID* field is the primary key and the *CategoryID* field is a foreign key.

- In the *Category* table, the *CategoryID* field is the primary key.

In this lesson you'll use a simple XLOOKUP to add the correct *Category Name* to each row in the *Product* table.

2 Insert a column to the left of the *QuantityPerUnit* column (column D) in the *Product* table.

3 Name the new column: **Category Name**

	B	C	D	E	
1	ProductName ▾	CategoryID ▾	Category Name ▾	QuantityPerUnit ▾	
2	Chai		1		10 boxes x 20 bags
3	Chang		1		24 - 12 oz bottles

4 Add an XLOOKUP function to cell D2 that will return the *CategoryName* field that matches the *CategoryID* value in cell C2.

You learned how to use the XLOOKUP function in: *Lesson 4-18: Understand XLOOKUP (part one).* The correct function arguments in this case are:

Lookup_value	[@CategoryID]
Table_array	Category
Col_index_num	2
Range_lookup	False

```
=XLOOKUP([@CategoryID],Category[CategoryID],Category[CategoryName])
```

Primary and Foreign Keys-1

Because this is a table, the function should be automatically replicated to all table cells in column D.

If this does not happen for you, somebody has disabled automatic calculated column creation on your machine. Refer to: *Lesson 1-22: Understand unqualified structured table references (sidebar)*, for instructions showing how to switch calculated columns back on.

	B	C	D	E
1	ProductName	CategoryID	Category Name	QuantityPerUnit
2	Chai		1 Beverages	10 boxes x 20 bags
3	Chang		1 Beverages	24 - 12 oz bottles
4	Aniseed Syrup		2 Condiments	12 - 550 ml bottles

5 **Hide the primary and foreign key columns A and C.**

The primary key columns are crucial when linking tables in a relational database but the data within them is of no interest.

To hide the columns, right click on the column header of each column and click: *Hide* from the shortcut menu.

	B	D	E	F
1	Produc	Category Name	QuantityPerUnit	UnitPrice
2	Chai	Beverages	10 boxes x 20 bags	18
3	Chang	Beverages	24 - 12 oz bottles	19

6 **Create a pivot table from the Product table.**

Later, in: *Lesson 12-6: Use an OLAP pivot table to analyze data residing in a data model,* you'll learn about a different type of pivot table that can work with multiple tables.

Regular pivot tables can only work with one table. Now that you have added a *Category Name* to the *Product* table, you can use a pivot table to analyze products by category name.

1. Click inside the table.

2. Click: Insert→Tables→PivotTable.

3. Click the *OK* button.

7 **Use the pivot table to show the total units in stock by category.**

Click the check boxes next to the *Category Name* and *UnitsInStock* fields in the *PivotTable Fields* task pane.

Take a moment to consider what you have just achieved.

You've just joined two related tables together via their primary and foreign keys using an XLOOKUP function to show the related categories in the *Product* table.

You then used the *Product* table to create a pivot table that reports the total units in stock analyzed by category.

	A	B
3	Row Labels	Sum of UnitsInStock
4	Beverages	559
5	Condiments	507
6	Confections	386
7	Dairy Products	393
8	Grains/Cereals	308
9	Meat/Poultry	165
10	Produce	100
11	Seafood	701
12	Grand Total	3119

8 **Save your work as *Primary and Foreign Keys-2.***

note

Views can contain calculated fields

A *View* is defined within a database using a powerful relational query language called SQL (Structured Query Language).

SQL isn't an Excel skill. Books of over 600 pages have been written that teach the SQL language.

Every professional DBA (database administrator) will have excellent SQL skills and will be able to create any view that you need in a few minutes.

You need to be aware that you can also ask your DBA to include calculated fields in a view.

The example view used in this lesson contains a simple primary key/foreign key lookup from the *Product* table to the *Category* table.

It is effectively doing what you did with an XLOOKUP in: *Lesson 11-27: Link primary and foreign keys using XLOOKUP.*

It only took me about 30 seconds to create this view using SQL.

Here's an example of a view that contains a calculated field:

Chai	$18.00	39	702.00
Chang	$19.00	17	323.00

In this example the *Product Name, Unit Price* and *Units In Stock* fields exist in the source table.

The right-hand field is a calculated field that shows the total inventory value (*Units in Stock* multiplied by *Unit Price*).

Lesson 11-28: Efficiently import data using a view

In: *Lesson 11-27: Link primary and foreign keys using XLOOKUP*, you had to add a related column to a table in order to make it suitable for a pivot table to analyze (as regular pivot tables can only work with one table of source data).

In a corporate setting the database is normally maintained by a data professional called a DBA (database administrator). Because relational table data is awkward for Excel (and other reporting tools) to analyze, database software (such as SQL Server, Oracle and Access) supports a concept called a *View*.

If you ask the DBA to create a *View* containing all of the information you need, you won't need to do any more work when you import the data.

A few minutes' work by the DBA might save you many hours of work if you have to work with raw tables.

Sometimes you'll have no choice other than to work with raw tables of course. This might be the case if you use an off-the-shelf package, if your company do not allow any changes to the database, or if it takes too long to get your IT department to respond to change requests.

1   Open a new blank workbook.

2   Import the *Products and Categories View* from the *With View* Access database in your sample files folder into a new worksheet in the workbook.

1.   Click: Data→Get & Transform Data→Get Data→ From Database→From Microsoft Access Database.

2.   Select the Access database file *With View* from your sample files folder.

With View	Microsoft Access Database

3.   Click the *Import* button.

   The *Navigator* dialog appears:

   ⁂ With View.accdb [3]
   - 📑 Products and Categories View
   - 📊 Category
   - 📊 Product

   Notice that this there's a different icon for a view.

4.   Click on the *Products and Categories View* to select it.

5.   Click: Load (drop-down arrow)→Load To…

   The *Import Data* dialog appears:

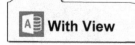
With View

6. Click the *Table* option button (if it isn't already selected).

7. Click the *OK* button.

A new table is added to a new worksheet. It already contains everything you need for the pivot table:

	A	B	C	D	E	F	G	H
1	ProductName	CategoryName	QuantityPerUnit	UnitPrice	UnitsInStock	UnitsOnOrder	ReorderLevel	Discontinued
2	Chai	Beverages	10 boxes x 20 bags	18	39	0	10	FALSE
3	Chang	Beverages	24 - 12 oz bottles	19	17	40	25	FALSE
4	Guaraná Fantástica	Beverages	12 - 355 ml cans	4.5	20	0	0	TRUE

note

You can also create the equivalent of a view outside the database

Later, in: *Lesson 11-31: Understand normal and de-normalized data,* you'll learn that a view is also referred to as *de-normalized data.*

Later, in: *Lesson 11-32: Create a simple two-table merged query,* you'll create a de-normalized data extract that is similar to the view used in this lesson.

In this way you can create something that is functionally equivalent to a view without having to bother your IT department.

You can now appreciate what a huge time saver views are when importing data from a relational database.

3 Rename the new worksheet: **Products and Categories**

4 Rename the table: **ProductsAndCategories**

This time Excel has given the table the name:

Products and Categories View

1. Click inside the table.

2. Click: Table Design→Properties→Table Name.

3. Change the table name to: **ProductsAndCategories**

5 Create a pivot table from the *ProductsAndCategories* table.

1. Click inside the table.

2. Click: Insert→Tables→PivotTable.

3. Click the *OK* button.

6 Change the pivot table worksheet's name to: **Pivot Table**

7 Use the pivot table to show the total units in stock by category.

Click the check boxes next to the *CategoryName* and *UnitsInStock* fields in the *PivotTable Fields* task pane.

8 Save your work as *With View-1.*

	A	B
3	Row Labels	Sum of UnitsInStock
4	Beverages	559
5	Condiments	507
6	Confections	386
7	Dairy Products	393
8	Grains/Cereals	308
9	Meat/Poultry	165
10	Produce	100
11	Seafood	701
12	**Grand Total**	**3119**

Lesson 11-29: Understand linked table and pivot table refresh

A linked table is an Excel table that was created by a Get & Transform query. The linked table is shaded green (instead of the normal default blue) to provide a visual clue that it is a linked table.

Linked tables can be refreshed at any time by re-running the Get & Transform query that they are linked to. In: *Lesson 11-28: Efficiently import data using a view* you also created a pivot table, using a linked Excel table as the pivot table's data source.

In: *Lesson 9-4: Understand the pivot table data cache*, you learned that a pivot table does not access its data source directly. Instead it creates a *pivot table data cache* from its own data source. It is also possible for the user to refresh the pivot table. In this case the pivot table cache will refresh from the linked table.

This diagram makes things clearer:

You can see that two refresh options are possible.

A linked table refresh can be done by right-clicking the table and then selecting *Refresh* from the shortcut menu. This refresh goes to the database and fetches the latest data from it.

A linked pivot table refresh can be done by right-clicking the pivot table and then selecting *Refresh* from the shortcut menu. A pivot table refresh goes to its own data source (in this case the linked table) and updates its *pivot table data cache* from the values found there.

You can see that in order to make sure that the pivot table is showing the very latest data you would have to first refresh the linked table and then refresh the pivot table.

With View-1

1 Open *With View-1* from your sample files folder (if it isn't already open).

2 Click on the *Pivot Table* worksheet and note that the total units in stock for the *Beverages* category is 559 units.

3 Change the value in cell E2 on the *Products and Categories* worksheet from 39 to 1,039.

Cell E2 contains the number of *Chai* units in stock. Note that *Chai* is in the *Beverages* category.

4 Select the *Pivot Table* worksheet. Notice that the total *Beverages* units in stock remains unchanged at 559 units.

The *Beverages* units have not updated because the pivot table gets its data from the *pivot table data cache*.

Because the *pivot table data cache* has not been refreshed, it does not yet know that its source data (the *ProductsAndCategories* table) has changed.

5 Refresh the pivot table. Notice that the total *Beverages* units in stock has increased to 1,559 units.

Right-click inside the pivot table and click: *Refresh* from the shortcut menu. The pivot table cache has now been refreshed to reflect the values displayed in its source data (the source data for the pivot table is the *ProductsAndCategories* table).

6 Refresh the *ProductsAndCategories* table. Notice that the Chai *UnitsInStock* (in cell E2) has decreased to 39 units.

Right-click inside the *ProductsAndCategories* table and click: *Refresh* from the shortcut menu.

The linked table has now been refreshed to show the values from its source data (the source data for the table is the *With View* Access database).

Because the values in the database have not changed, the linked table is updated to match the current values in the database.

In a real-world database, the values can be expected to constantly change as goods are sold or received and as prices and other data are changed.

7 Select the *Pivot Table* worksheet. Notice that the total *Beverages* units in stock remains unchanged at 1559 units.

The *Beverages* units have not updated because the pivot table gets its data from the *pivot table data cache*.

Because the *pivot table data cache* has not been refreshed, it does not yet know that its source data (the *ProductsAndCategories* table) has changed.

8 Refresh the pivot table. Notice that the total *Beverages* units in stock has decreased to 559 units.

Right-click inside the pivot table and click: *Refresh* from the shortcut menu. The pivot table cache has now been refreshed to reflect the values displayed in its source data (the source data for the pivot table is the *ProductsAndCategories* table).

important

Out of memory errors

To complete this lesson, the *PivotTable Data Cache* has to be loaded into memory.

If you only have a small amount of free memory on your computer, you may encounter out of memory errors.

note

What is big data?

In 2010 it was estimated that the world was generating 2.5 Exabytes of new data every day. An Exabyte is approximately one million Terabytes.

The amount of data generated today is far greater. In 2019 it was estimated that the Internet alone was generating 44,000 Exabytes of new data every day. This is expected to grow to 175,000 Exabytes a day by 2025.

Worrying though it sounds, every click you make, every e-mail you send and every telephone call you make is being stored somewhere.

This explosion of data is often referred to as *big data*. Big data doesn't mean any particular number but refers to data of such a size that analysis (with tools such as Excel) can be a problem.

Perhaps Excel would regard *big data* as being data with more than a million rows (an Excel worksheet cannot have more than 1,048,576 rows).

You may find that memory and speed constraints sometimes impose a far lower limit on the size of worksheet-based data you can usefully work with.

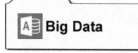

Big Data

Lesson 11-30: Load a query directly into the PivotTable cache

In *Lesson 11-28: Efficiently import data using a view,* you loaded data into a single Excel table and then created a pivot table from this table. There is absolutely nothing wrong with this approach and it is appropriate for many data analysis tasks. There are, however, three potential problems:

- You cannot analyze a data source that has more than approximately a million rows (1,048,576 to be precise) as that is the largest number of rows that a worksheet can contain. Very large data sets are often referred to as: *Big Data* (see sidebar).

- It can take a long time to create the *pivot table data cache* when working with large data sets stored in worksheets.

- Storing data in worksheets means that data is loaded into the computer's memory twice when you open the workbook. Once from the table in the workbook (the entire Excel workbook is held in the computer's memory) and again from the *pivot table data cache* (also held in the computer's memory). This means that you could start to see "out of memory" errors when working with very large data sets.

In this diagram you can see how Excel can be used to analyze big data:

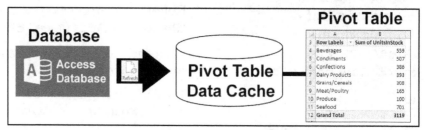

If the pivot table cache is created directly from the external data source, you can avoid all of the above three problems. There is a physical limit to the amount of data you can store in a *pivot table data cache,* but it is very large (theoretically 2.1 billion data items or individual values).

Later, in: *Session Twelve: Power Pivot, Data Modeling, OLAP and Business Intelligence,* you'll learn how to work with even bigger data (that can contain up to two thousand million rows – each of which can contain many data items).

1   Open a new blank workbook.

2   Import the *BigData* table from the *Big Data* Access database directly into a Pivot Table Data Cache.

   1. Click: Data→Get & Transform Data→Get Data→ From Database→From Microsoft Access Database.

   2. Navigate to the *Big Data* Access database in your sample files folder.

   3. Double-click on the *Big Data* Access database file.

      The *Navigator* dialog appears:

note

An Access database can't really handle big data

You're simulating big data techniques in this lesson using an Access database.

An Access database can only contain 2 Terabytes of data. That is still enough to store several million rows in one table.

SQL Server and Oracle databases can handle really big data with billions of rows.

note

The 64-bit version of Excel is best when working with big data

Both Windows and Excel are available in 32-bit and 64-bit editions.

If you work a lot with big data and are finding that you encounter *out of memory* errors, you should consider switching to the 64-bit version of Excel (to run this you must also have the 64-bit version of Windows).

The normal 32-bit version of Excel can only make use of 2 gigabytes of memory, but the 64-bit version can effectively use all of the memory installed on your computer.

You'll learn more about memory issues and how they can be overcome later, in: *Lesson 12-1: Understand data model memory requirements.*

4. Select the *BigData* table and click:

   Load (drop-down arrow)→Load To…

   The *Import Data* dialog is displayed.

5. Click the *PivotTable Report* option button and then click the *OK* button. A pivot table is created showing the fields in the *BigData* table.

   The *BigData* table in the sample file contains 1,301,840 rows of data. Because an Excel table can only contain 1,048,576 rows of data you clearly cannot load this data into an Excel table.

   If you had selected *Table* in the above dialog (and then clicked the *OK* button) the import would have failed, and you would (eventually) have seen an error message.

3 Use the pivot table to show the total *InvoiceAmount* for each *ProductCode* for each *year*, *quarter* and *month*.

This is a very similar pivot table to the one you created in: *Lesson 9-19: Group by date.*

In order to keep the *Big Data* sample Access database as small as possible, I have only included three fields:

InvoiceDate:	The date the product was invoiced.
ProductCode:	A number that identifies the product.
InvoiceAmount:	The amount that was charged.

Drag the *ProductCode* to the *Rows* pane, the *InvoiceAmount* to the *Values* pane and the *InvoiceDate* to the *Columns* pane.

	A	B	C	D	E
4	Sum of InvoiceAmount	Column Labels			
5		⊟2008			
6		⊟Qtr1			⊞Qtr2
7	Row Labels	Jan	Feb	Mar	
8	101001	7609.542	5157.03	4123.5456	20027.4624
9	101002	5210.9385	5638.8291	6063.2124	21036.006
10	101003	6926.04	8865.7668	6142.3956	21984.732
11	101004	12569.9175	7330.3488	11230.6362	29042.2794

4 Save your work as *Big Data-1.*

trivia

Third normal form

This sidebar was also included in: Lesson 2-1: Split fixed width data using Text to Columns. I've also included it here as an overview of Third Normal Form is needed to understand the concept of normal and de-normalized data.

Dr E.F. Codd (1923-2003) is a cult figure to every database designer worthy of the name.

He was not only the inventor of the relational database (while working for IBM) but he also wrote the rulebook for excellence in database design.

Codd's books are essential (and even exciting) reading for anybody who designs relational databases for a living. I have read all of them and hung on every word!

Codd defined a set of rules that are collectively called third normal form (or 3NF for short).

Codd's rules are broken into three parts: First Normal Form, Second Normal Form and Third Normal Form.

Each set of rules builds upon the earlier set so that a database design cannot conform to 2NF unless it first conforms to 1NF (and a 3NF design must first conform to 2NF).

In theory, all of the corporate databases that you work with should be third normal form compliant. In practice you'll often find database design errors that may make some databases difficult to work with.

Lesson 11-31: Understand normal and de-normalized data

What is normal data?

Most relational databases conform to design rules that are collectively called *Third Normal Form* (often abbreviated to 3NF).

A data source that complies with these rules is said to contain normal (or normalized) data. Compliance with 3NF is a pre-requisite for an efficient relational database that can reliably allow rows to be added, edited or deleted.

What is de-normalized data?

Regular Excel pivot tables can only use a single table of source data.

When data is extracted from multiple tables (usually residing in a relational database such as SQL Server, Oracle or Access) and combined into a single table, the data in the single table is referred to as *de-normalized data*.

In: *Session Twelve: Power Pivot, Data Modeling, OLAP and Business Intelligence* you'll learn to build a relational (multi-table) in-memory construct called a *data model* that can be analyzed using a new type of pivot table (called an OLAP pivot table).

To create efficient OLAP data models you'll often need to de-normalize data (combine two or more related tables into a single de-normalized table).

De-normalizing by adding derived values

One of the most important normal form rules prohibits *derived* values in a relational database table. There are very good reasons for this (see facing page sidebar).

A *derived value* is a value that can be calculated from other columns in the same row. In: *Lesson 11-18: Create an aggregated data query*, you worked with this view:

	A	B	C	D
1	**ProductName**	**CategoryNa**	**UnitsInStock**	**UnitPrice**
2	Chai	Beverages	39	18.00
3	Chang	Beverages	17	19.00
4	Guaraná Fantástica	Beverages	20	4.50

One of the challenges in: *Lesson 11-18: Create an aggregated data query*, was to calculate the total *Inventory Value*. A correctly designed database cannot contain a column showing *Inventory Value* because it can be calculated by multiplying the *UnitsInStock* column by the *UnitPrice* column (in other words it would be a *derived value*).

You de-normalized the data by adding a custom column containing a calculated (derived) field to show the *Inventory Value*. Here is the de-normalized data that you created:

Add Custom Column

New column name

Inventory Value

Custom column formula:

= [UnitPrice]*[UnitsInStock]

	A	B	C	D	E
1	ProductName	CategoryNa	UnitsInStock	UnitPrice	Inventory Value
2	Chai	Beverages	39	18.00	702.00
3	Chang	Beverages	17	19.00	323.00
4	Guaraná Fantástica	Beverages	20	4.50	90.00

Learning more about third normal form

Third normal form is a subject that sometimes even confuses specialized IT personnel. Apart from professional specialist database designers it is unusual to find IT workers who can create a correctly normalized database from a business requirement specification.

This lesson has only presented a simplified overview of third normal form, but it will be enough for your work with *Get & Transform*.

If you want to learn more about third normal form, an Internet search will uncover a huge amount of information upon this widely misunderstood subject.

De-normalizing by combining tables

In: *Lesson 11-26: Understand primary and foreign keys,* you learned about related tables. Here's the data that you worked with:

CategoryID	CategoryName	Description
1	Beverages	Soft drinks, coffees, teas, beers, and ales
2	Condiments	Sweet and savory sauces, relishes, spreads, and seasonings
3	Confections	Desserts, candies, and sweet breads

ProductID	ProductName	CategoryID	QuantityPerUnit	UnitPrice
1	Chai	1	10 boxes x 20 bags	18.00
3	Aniseed Syrup	2	12 - 550 ml bottles	10.00
16	Pavlova	3	32 - 500 g boxes	17.45
24	Guaraná Fantástica	1	12 - 355 ml cans	4.50
25	NuNuCa Nuß-Nougat-Creme	3	20 - 450 g glasses	14.00
34	Sasquatch Ale	1	24 - 12 oz bottles	14.00

An important normal form rule is that you cannot have information about more than one entity in the same table. Think of an entity as a noun (or thing). A *Category* is a noun and a *Product* is a noun.

Now consider the de-normalized version of the above tables that you worked with in: *Lesson 11-28: Efficiently import data using a view*:

	A	B	C	D
1	ProductName	CategoryName	QuantityPerUnit	UnitPrice
2	Alice Mutton	Meat/Poultry	20 - 1 kg tins	39.00
3	Aniseed Syrup	Condiments	12 - 550 ml bottles	10.00
4	Boston Crab Meat	Seafood	24 - 4 oz tins	18.40

You can see that this de-normalized view breaks normal form rules because the *Category Name* field rightly belongs in the *Category* table.

It is quite correct for a database administrator to create this type of de-normalized read-only view within a correctly designed relational database, as the view is only used for reporting purposes.

Later, in: *Lesson 11-32: Create a simple two-table merged query,* you'll learn how to create this type of de-normalized table using the *Get & Transform* tool.

note

What is a join?

When a relationship is defined within a query it is called a *join*.

There are different types of join that define the data that is returned when there is a missing foreign key in a foreign key column.

There is a drop-down list at the bottom of the *Merge* dialog used in this lesson, that allows you to specify a *Join Kind*.

> Left Outer (all from first, matching from second)
> Right Outer (all from second, matching from first)
> Full Outer (all rows from both)
> Inner (only matching rows)
> Left Anti (rows only in first)
> Right Anti (rows only in second)

The *Left Outer* join is the default join kind and it is the join type that you'll use nearly all of the time. In this lesson, imagine that there are some *Product* rows that have a missing (or invalid) *CategoryID*.

The *Left Outer* join will return all of the rows in the *Product* table. No category data is returned if there is a missing *CategoryID* (in other words the *Category* field will be left blank).

Sometimes you might want to only return *Product* records if the *Category ID* field is not blank and there is a matching *CategoryID* field in the *Category* table. This type of join is called an *Inner* join.

With this knowledge, you should be able to figure out (from the description provided in brackets) what the other four (lesser used) join types would return in different situations.

> Queries [2]   <
> ▦ Product
> ▦ Category

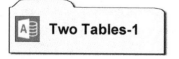
Two Tables-1

Lesson 11-32: Create a simple two-table merged query

In: *Lesson 11-27: Link primary and foreign keys using XLOOKUP,* you opened a worksheet that contained two related Excel tables. One table contained *Product* information and the other contained *Category* information.

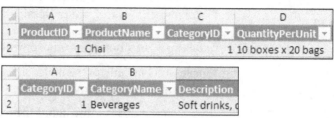

In: *Lesson 11-26: Understand primary and foreign keys,* you learned that the two tables had a relationship linking the *CategoryID* primary key (in the *Category* table) to the *CategoryID* foreign key (in the *Product* table).

1 Open *Merge-1* from your sample files folder.

2 Create two connection-only *Get & Transform* queries to extract all values from the *Product* and *Category* tables.

   You learned how to do this in: *Lesson 11-20: Work with multiple queries.*

   1. Click anywhere in the *Product* table.

   2. Click: Data→Get & Transform Data→From Table/Range.

      The Get & Transform query editor opens.

   3. Click the Expand button ⟩ in the left-hand *Navigator* Pane.

      The *Product* query is now visible in the *Navigator* pane.

      > Queries [1]   <
      > ▦ Product

   4. Click: Home→Close→Close & Load→Close & Load To…

   5. Click the *Only Create Connection* option button and click OK.

   6. Click anywhere in the *Category* table.

   7. Click: Data→Get & Transform Data→From Table/Range.

      The Get & Transform query editor opens.

   8. Click the Expand button ⟩ in the left-hand *Navigator* Pane.

   9. Both the *Product* query and the *Category* query are now shown in the Navigator pane (see sidebar).

3 Create a merged query to show the *Category* name in the *Product* query.

   1. Select the *Product* query in the left-hand *Navigator* pane.

   2. Click: Home→Combine→Merge Queries.

      The *Merge* dialog appears.

note

XLOOKUP, View or de-normalized Get & Transform query?

You have now discovered three different ways to work with relational data.

You may wonder when to use each. Here are the advantages of each approach:

1. XLOOKUP

XLOOKUP is the modern replacement for the old VLOOKUP function. This is the most primitive way to create a de-normalized data extract from related tables. It may also be the one you see most often as it is the only method that most Excel users understand.

The XLOOKUP method is slow and cumbersome to implement and maintain. It is the least preferred way to work with relational data.

2. View

A *View* is the best way to obtain a de-normalized data extract from a relational database.

While *Views* are wonderful, they can only be used with a relational database data source and can only be created by specialized IT staff.

3. Get & Transform Query

A de-normalized extract created by a *Get & Transform* query can be used as the data source of a linked table as well as a normal pivot table.

Get & Transform queries can be automatically refreshed at a timed interval (when used to populate a linked table).

Later, in: *Session Twelve: Power Pivot, Data Modeling, OLAP and Business Intelligence,* you'll learn yet another way (and the most powerful way of all) to work with relational data by creating an in-memory relational data model.

3. Click in the *CategoryID* (foreign key) column in the *Product* table shown at the top of the *Merge* dialog.

4. Select the *Category* table from the drop-down list in the middle of the dialog.

5. Click in the *CategoryID* (primary key) column in the *Category* table.

6. Click *OK* to merge the queries.

Notice that a new *Category* column has appeared on the right of the preview window.

4 Expand the new column to see the contents of the *Category* table.

1. Click the expand button ⊞ on the right of the *Category* column header.

2. Click the *OK* button.

The *Category* names are now shown in the preview window.

5 Remove the *ProductID, CategoryID, Category.CategoryID and Category.Description* columns from the query.

You learned how to do this in: *Lesson 11-4: Move, remove, rename, filter and sort columns.*

6 Move the *Category.CategoryName* field so that it is next to the *ProductName* field.

You learned how to do this in: *Lesson 11-4: Move, remove, rename, filter and sort columns.*

	ABC ProductName	ABC Category.CategoryName	ABC QuantityPerUnit
1	Chai	Beverages	10 boxes x 20 bags
2	Chang	Beverages	24 - 12 oz bottles

7 Close the Power Query Editor, creating *Connection only* queries in the workbook.

You learned how to do this in: *Lesson 11-20: Work with multiple queries.*

8 Save your work as *Merge-2*.

Lesson 11-33: Create a five-table merged query

In this lesson you'll create a *Merge* query to extract data from five related tables and then combine them all into a single de-normalized table.

1   **Open a new blank workbook.**

Here is a diagram showing the tables and primary key/foreign key relationships used in this lesson. This type of diagram is often referred to as a *schema*:

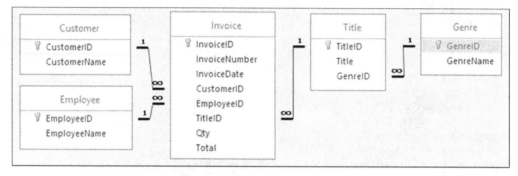

The challenge for this lesson will be to extract a single de-normalized table from the five related tables using *Get & Transform Merge Queries*. The single-table extract will merge the values of every field in the database (seventeen fields) into one table.

2   **Create five queries containing all of the data from all five tables in the *Film Sales-1* Excel workbook.**

Because all of these tables are contained in the same workbook, there's a really quick way to do this.

1.   Click: Data→Get & Transform Data→Get Data→ From File→From Workbook.

2.   Navigate to the *Film Sales-1* workbook and open it.

3.   Check the *Select multiple items* check box.

4.   Check the check boxes next to each of the five tables (see sidebar).

5.   Click the *Transform Data* button.

The Power Query Editor opens, and five queries are shown in the left-hand query list. There is one query for each table (see sidebar).

3   **Merge the five queries together so that the Invoice query returns all of the data contained in the four related tables.**

You learned how to do this in: *Lesson 11-32: Create a simple two-table merged query.*

1.   Select the *Title* query and then merge the *Genre* query into the *Title* query using the *GenreID* key to link the tables.

2.   Select the *Invoice* query and then merge the *Customer* query into the *Invoice* query using the *CustomerID* key to link the tables.

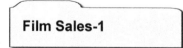

Film Sales-1

note

Merge queries are easier to create when using a relational database source

Later, in: *Lesson 12-9: Create a data model directly from a relational database,* you will use Get & Transform to import an entire relational database.

When Get & Transform imports data from a relational data source it also imports the relationships.

When Get & Transform is already aware of the relationships between tables a

Merge button [ ] is automatically displayed in related tables. This makes merging tables a lot easier.

The *Invoice* query should now return all fields from both the *Invoice* and *Customer* tables.

3. Select the *Invoice* query and then merge the *Employee* query into the *Invoice* query using the *EmployeeID* key to link the tables.

   The *Invoice* query should now return all fields from the *Invoice, Customer* and *Employee* tables.

4. Select the *Invoice* query and then merge the *Title* query into the *Invoice* query using the *TitleID* key to link the tables.

   Remember that the *Title* query is itself a merged query (that includes fields from the *Genre* table). By merging the *Title* query with the *Invoice* query, you have made both the *Title* and *Genre* table's data available within the *Invoice* query.

4 Select the Invoice query and expand all of the new columns.

You learned how to do this in: *Lesson 11-32: Create a simple two-table merged query.*

The new columns are those where every cell contains the word: *Table.*

The *Invoice* query should now return all seventeen fields from the *Invoice, Customer, Employee, Title* and *Genre* tables

5 Remove all of the primary and foreign key columns from the query (all of the fields that are suffixed with *ID*).

You learned how to do this in: *Lesson 11-4: Move, remove, rename, filter and sort columns.*

6 Close the Power Query Editor, creating *Connection only* queries.

You learned how to do this in: *Lesson 11-20: Work with multiple queries.*

7 Create a new linked table using the *Invoice* query.

1. Right-click on the *Invoice* query in the *Queries & Connections* task pane.

2. Select *Load to…* from the shortcut menu.

   The *Import Data* dialog appears.

3. Click the *Table* option button and the *Existing worksheet* option button.

4. Select cell A1 as the location for the linked table and click the *OK* button.

	A	B	C	D	E	F	G	H
1	InvoiceNumber	InvoiceDate	Qty	Total	CustomerName	EmployeeName	Title	GenreName
2	136438	10/1/2012	15	122.76	Silver Screen Video	Lee,Frank	Lawrence of Arabia	Biography
3	136438	10/1/2012	9	67.46	Silver Screen Video	Lee,Frank	The Discreet Charm of the Bourgeoisie	Comedy

You could also have loaded the output of this query directly into the Pivot Table Data Cache (using the *PivotTable Report* option button) to further analyze the data.

8 Save your work as *Five Table Query-1*.

note

Fuzzy logic uses Jaccard similarity

Paul Jaccard (1868-1944) was a professor of botany at the *Swiss Federal Institute of Technology* in Zurich.

Jaccard published his paper on the Jaccard index of similarity (*coefficient de communauté*) in 1901.

Jaccard developed this technique to combine regional floras.

When comparing two sample sets Jaccard realized that similarity could be measured by considering the *intersection* and *union* of two sets. For example, consider these two sets:

- John Peter Travolta
- John Simon Travolta

Each word in each set is called a *token*.

Jaccard's *intersection* value would be 2 because two of the tokens (John and Travolta) are the same in each set.

Jaccard's *union* value would be 4 because there are four unique tokens (John Peter Simon and Travolta) in both sets.

This allows the *Jaccard Similarity* to be calculated using the formula: intersection/union, in this case 2/4=0.5.

As you will discover in: *Lesson 11-35: Improve fuzzy logic results using a custom transformation table*, Excel's fuzzy logic implementation is more sophisticated than the simple *Jaccard Similarity* method described above.

Sales Performance-1

Lesson 11-34: Create a merged query using fuzzy logic

Computers like things to be very precise. While a human will instanty realize that *John Smith* and *Johnny Smith* are the same person, it is difficult for a computer to do this. Fuzzy logic is a type of artificial intelligence that allows you to work with data that imperfectly matches.

Artificial intelligence isn't perfect (as anybody who has had a conversation with Amazon's Alexa, Apple's Siri or Microsoft's Cortana will know) so use this feature with caution.

1 Open *Sales Performance-1* from your sample files folder.

You can see that this workbook contains two tables.

The *Salesman* table contains the correct spelling of each salesman's full name.

The *Sales* table contains details of each sale made. Unfortunately the staff who log the sales are not very consistent in how they name each salesman.

Salesman	Region		Salesman	Invoice Value	
Tom Cruise	North		john travolta	$	84.76
Johnny Depp	Midlands		Mr John Travolta	$	106.73
John Travolta	South		John Travvolta	$	118.93
			mr jonny depp	$	121.56

In this lesson you'll use Excel's fuzzy logic feature to automatically match the different variations of each salesman's name.

2 Create two connection-only *Get & Transform* queries to extract all values from the *Salesman* and *Sales* tables.

You learned how to do this in: *Lesson 11-20: Work with multiple queries*.

3 Merge the *Sales* query into the *Salesman* query using fuzzy logic to match the *Salesman* field in each table.

1. Click: Data→Get & Transform Data→Get Data→Combine Queries→Merge.

   The *Merge* dialog appears.

2. Select *Salesman* for the first (top) table. Select *Sales* for the second table.

3. Click inside the *Salesman* field in both of the tables displayed in the dialog to indicate which fields to join.

4. Change the *Join Kind* to *Full Outer (all rows from both)*. You learned about join types in: *Lesson 11-32: Create a simple two-table merged query* (sidebar).

5. Click the *Use fuzzy matching to perform the merge* check box.

   Your dialog should now look like this:

trivia

How John Travolta and Johnny Depp got their nicknames

Johnny Depp is a member of the *Honorable Order of Kentucky Colonels*. His close friend Hunter S. Thompson nominated him for the honor and always refers to Johnny as "The Colonel".

John Travolta was nicknamed "Bone" when he was young because he was long and lean.

Tom Cruise	Tom Cruise
Tom Cruise	tom cruise
Tom Cruise	Tom cruize
Tom Cruise	Mr tom cruise
Tom Cruise	tom cruise jr
Tom Cruise	Cruise
Johnny Depp	Johnny Depp
Johnny Depp	john depp
Johnny Depp	Johnny dep
Johnny Depp	jonny deppp
Johnny Depp	johnny Depp jr
Johnny Depp	Depp
Johnny Depp	mr jonny depp
John Travolta	john travolta
John Travolta	john Travolta
John Travolta	John Travolta
John Travolta	John Travvolta
John Travolta	Jon Travolta
John Travolta	Mr John Travolta
John Travolta	John Travolta Jr
John Travolta	Travolta
John Travolta	John Travolta-jr
null	Bone
null	The Colonel

Merge

Select tables and matching columns to create a merged table.

Salesman

Salesman	Region
Tom Cruise	North
Johnny Depp	Midlands
John Travolta	South

Sales

Salesman	Invoice Value
john travolta	84.76
Mr John Travolta	106.73
John Travvolta	118.93
mr jonny depp	121.56
John Travolta Jr	121.02

Join Kind

Full Outer (all rows from both)

☑ Use fuzzy matching to perform the merge

▷ Fuzzy matching options

✓ The selection matches 3 of 3 rows from the first table, and 17 of 24 rows f...

Notice that Excel is only able to match 17 of the 24 salesman names.

6. Click on *Fuzzy matching options*.

   Notice the *Similarity threshold (optional)* box. This allows you to set the *Jaccard similarity* (see facing page sidebar). By default this is set to 0.8.

7. Set the *Similarity threshold* to 0.6. Note that Excel is now able to match 18 salesman names.

8. Set the similarity threshold to 0.5. Excel is now able to match 22 of the 24 salesman names.

9. Click the *OK* button.

10. Click the expand button �लᵖ on the right of the *Sales* column header.

11. Click the *OK* button to merge all fields from both tables.

    You can see that Excel has done an almost perfect job in identifying all of the similar names (see sidebar).

    There are two names that cannot be matched. It is not possible to determine that *The Colonel* is a nickname for *Johnny Depp* and *Bone* is a nickname for *John Travolta* using *Jaccard similarity*. In the next lesson: *Lesson 11-35: Improve fuzzy logic results using a custom transformation table*, you'll learn how to solve this problem.

4   Close the Get & Transform window saving the merge query as a connection only query.

5   Save your work as *Sales Peformance-2*.

note

Fuzzy logic uses token weighting, edit distance and transformations

Token weighting

Excel will look for tokens that appear frequently and those that are more novel.

For example, in a list of company names, *Corporation* might appear many times but a company name such as: *Amazon* might appear less frequently. A direct match on the word *Amazon* would then have more importance than a match on *Corporation*.

Edit distance

Edit distance counts the number of changes that need to be made to convert one word to another.

For example, when comparing *Jonny* with *Johnny* the edit distance is only 1. This would be considered a higher value match than comparing *Johnny* with *Jon* (edit distance 3).

Transformations

A transformation table allows tokens to be converted from one string to another before considering a match.

When a transformation table is defined, the original value will still be considered (along with the values defined in the transformation table).

For example, you may wish that Excel considers the token *Robert* to also have the values *Bob* and *Bobby*.

From	To
Robert	Bob
Robert	Bobby

Sales Performance-2

Lesson 11-35: Improve fuzzy logic results using a custom transformation table

In: *Lesson 11-34: Create a merged query using fuzzy logic* (sidebar), you learned that fuzzy logic uses Jaccard similarity to find similar (but not exact) matches between sets of data.

Excel's fuzzy logic feature uses more sophisticated techniques than simplistic Jaccard similarity. *Token weighting, transformations* and *edit distance* are also used to improve fuzzy matches (see sidebar if you are interested in how these work).

While you have no control over *token weighting* and *edit distance* you can improve Excel's fuzzy logic accuracy by defining a custom transformation table.

In: *Lesson 11-34: Create a merged query using fuzzy logic,* you matched some names using fuzzy logic. Excel was able to correctly match:

- *Tom Cruise* with *tom cruize*
- *Johnny Depp* with *Mr Jonny Depp*

There were two names that Excel was unable to pair. They were:

- *Johnny Depp* with *The Colonel*
- *John Travolta* with *Bone*

You can see that it is impossible to match the above names with their nicknames simply by applying logical rules to the text.

In order for Excel to regognize similarity, in these cases, a custom transformation table is needed.

The transformation table is a table with two fields named *From* and *To*. When performing a fuzzy match Excel will convert the tokens using this table and also consider the converted values before establishing a match.

1   Open *Sales Performance-2* from your sample files folder.

    This is the workbook you created in: *Lesson 11-34: Create a merged query using fuzzy logic.*

2   Add a custom transformation table to transform *John Travolta* to *Bone* and *Johnny Depp* to *The Colonel*.

    Here is the table you need to create:

From	To
John Travolta	Bone
Johnny Depp	The Colonel

3   Name the new table: **Transform**

4   Create a connection-only *Get & Transform* query to extract all values from the *Transform* table

5   Open the *Merge1* query.

    1.   If the *Queries & Connections* task pane is not visible click:

Queries & Connections

Queries | Connections

5 queries

☐ Salesman
   Connection only.

☐ Sales
   Connection only.

☐ Merge1
   Connection only.

Tom Cruise	Tom Cruise
Tom Cruise	tom cruise
Tom Cruise	Tom cruize
Tom Cruise	Mr tom cruise
Tom Cruise	tom cruise jr
Tom Cruise	Cruise
Johnny Depp	Johnny Depp
Johnny Depp	john depp
Johnny Depp	The Colonel
Johnny Depp	Johnny dep
Johnny Depp	jonny deppp
Johnny Depp	johnny Depp jr
Johnny Depp	Depp
Johnny Depp	mr jonny depp
John Travolta	john travolta
John Travolta	john Travolta
John Travolta	John Travolta
John Travolta	John Travvolta
John Travolta	Bone
John Travolta	Jon Travolta
John Travolta	Mr John Travolta
John Travolta	John Travolta Jr
John Travolta	Travolta
John Travolta	John Travolta-jr

Data➔Queries & Connection➔Queries and Connections

Note the *Merge1* connection. This is the connection you saved in: *Lesson 11-34: Create a merged query using fuzzy logic.*

2. Double click on the *Merge1* connection to open the query.

Notice that there are two applied steps in this query.

▴ APPLIED STEPS

   Source

  ✕ Expanded Sales

3. Double click on the *Source* applied step.

The *Merge* dialog opens.

4. Click *Fuzzy matching options* to add merge options to the bottom of the dialog.

5. Select the *Transform* table in the *Transformation table (optional)* drop-down list.

Transformation table (optional)

Transform   ▾ ⓘ

Sales

Salesman

Transform

6. The *Merge* dialog should now look like this:

Join Kind

Full Outer (all rows from both)   ▾

☑ Use fuzzy matching to perform the merge

▴ Fuzzy matching options

Similarity threshold (optional)

0.5   ⓘ

☑ Ignore case

☑ Match by combining text parts ⓘ

Maximum number of matches (optional)

     ⓘ

Transformation table (optional)

Transform   ▾ ⓘ

✓ The selection matches 3 of 3 rows from the first table, and 24 of 24 rows f...

You can see that all 24 rows now match.

7. Click the *OK* button.

8. Click the *Expanded Sales* step in the *Query Settings* pane on the right of the *Power Query Editor.*

▴ APPLIED STEPS

   Source

  ✕ Expanded Sales

Notice that Excel has now matched every name (see sidebar).

9. Close the *Power Query Editor* keeping changes when prompted.

6   Save your work as *Sales Peformance-3.*

Session 11: Exercise

For this exercise there is an *Exercise* folder in your session ten sample files folder that contains three workbooks: *Customer-1, Order-1* and *Product-1*.

1   Open a new blank workbook.

2   The *Customer-1* workbook contains three tables called: *FranceTable, UKTable* and *USATable*. Create three *Connection only* queries that return the data from each table.

3   Create a new *Append* query called *AllCustomers* that will combine all of the rows contained in the other three queries into one query.

4   The *Order-1* and *Product-1* workbooks each contain a single table (*OrderTable* and *ProductTable*). Create two new *Connection only* queries that return the data from each table.

5   Add a *Custom Column* to the *OrderTable* query named *Total Price* that will calculate the total price of each row using the formula: **[Quantity]*[Unit Price]**

6   Set the data type of the new *Total Price* column to: *Currency*.

7   Load the *OrderTable* query results directly into a pivot table.

8   Use the pivot table to show total sales by year and month for each *Country*.

	A	B	C	D	E	F
3	Sum of Total Price	Column Labels				
4		⊞2014	⊟2015			
5	Row Labels		Jan	Feb	Mar	Apr
6	France	$17,189.90	$4,225.60	$6,682.40	$3,072.80	$4,226.80
7	UK	$9,654.00	$3,063.00	$1,084.60	$3,151.80	$352.00
8	USA	$43,654.00	$3,971.00	$10,129.10	$12,472.10	$6,123.94
9	Grand Total	$70,497.90	$11,259.60	$17,896.10	$18,696.70	$10,702.74

In the screen grab above the *Currency* number format has been applied to the values.

9   Save your work as: *Exercise 10-End*.

Customer-1, Order-1, Product-1

If you need help slide the page to the left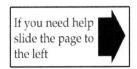

Session 11: Exercise Answers

These are the three questions that students find the most difficult to answer:

Q 5	Q 3	Q 2
1. Click: Add Column→ General→ Custom Column (from inside the Get & Transform editor). The *Custom Column* dialog appears. 2. Type: **Total Price** into the *New column name* box. 3. Click *Quantity* in the *Available columns* list and then click the << *Insert* button. 4. Type the multiplication operator <*>. 5. Click *Unit Price* in the *Available columns* list and then click the << *Insert* button. 6. Click the OK button. This was covered in: *Lesson 11-17: Add a custom calculated column.*	1. Click: Data→ Get & Transform Data→ Get Data→ Combine Queries→Append. The *Append* dialog appears. 2. Click the *Three or more tables* option button. 3. Select the three tables from the left-hand window and use the *Add >>* button to copy them to the right-hand window. 4. Click the *OK* button. A new query appears in the left-hand navigator pane called: *Append1*. 5. Double-click on the *Append1* query and type: **AllCustomers** 6. Press the <**Enter**> key. This was covered in: *Lesson 11-21: Create an append query.*	1. Click: Data→ Get & Transform Data→ Get Data→ Launch Power Query Editor… 2. Click: Home→ New Query→ New Source→File→Excel. 3. Select the *Customer-1* workbook from the *Exercise* folder beneath your *Session 10* sample files folder. 4. Check the *Select multiple items* checkbox. 5. Select the *FranceTable, UKTable* and *USATable* tables. 6. Click the *OK* button. The three queries appear in the left-hand navigaor bar. 7. Click: Home→Close→ Close & Load→ Close and Load To… 8. Click the *Only Create Connection* option button. 9. Click the *OK* button. This was covered in: *Lesson 11-20: Work with multiple queries.*

If you have difficulty with the other questions, here are the lessons that cover the relevant skills:

4   Refer to: *Lesson 11-20: Work with multiple queries.*

6   Refer to: *Lesson 11-11: Specify data types.*

7   Refer to: *Lesson 11-15: Transform date and time columns.*

8   Use these fields in your pivot table:

▼ Filters	▥ Columns	
	Years	▾
	Order Date	▾
▤ Rows	Σ Values	
Country ▾	Sum of Total Price	▾

Introduction to the Data Modeling and Power Pivot sessions

The contents of the next two sessions will be challenging to most readers

Your Excel skills are now very advanced and would already be regarded as Expert level by any employer. The concepts presented in the next two sessions are not commonly understood by Excel users (even IT professionals often struggle with relational database and OLAP concepts).

Excel 365 (and Excel 2019) added Microsoft's powerful *Power Pivot* data modeling add-in to all versions of Excel. This new tool enables you to create sophisticated relational data models.

Power Pivot is only used to create OLAP data models

Excel users are often confused about exactly what Power Pivot does (especially if they have been browsing the Internet). Power Pivot is a very sophisticated data modeling tool that enables you to construct tabular data models (called *Relational OLAP tabular databases*) from multiple related data sources (whose data has ideally been imported and prepared using *Get & Transform*).

When an OLAP data model has been constructed it is very easy (even for unsophisticated Excel users) to use a special new type of pivot table (called an OLAP pivot table) to quickly and efficiently create a huge variety of reports using the data contained in the model.

If you cannot understand the above two paragraphs don't worry. The following sessions will enable you to acquire all of the theory you need to make use of Power Pivot.

It has been estimated that only 10% of Excel users are able to use the regular pivot tables that you mastered in: *Session Nine: Pivot Tables*. It is likely that far less than 1% of Excel users (even those with expert skills) will venture into the bold new world of OLAP multidimensional analysis using Power Pivot.

The material that follows is of necessity more complex than in the previous sessions

To create efficient Power Pivot data models, you must first master relational database theory along with many DAX (Data Analysis eXpression) concepts.

By the end of the next two sessions, you will have mastered the core concepts needed to effectively create efficient OLAP data models using Get & Transform and Power Pivot. You'll also be able to include DAX expressions (referred to as *calculated measures*) in the data models you build.

Do not be discouraged if the material in the next two sessions proves difficult to understand upon first reading. It is unlikely that any reader will find the material easy to digest (unless you have existing relational database modeling skills).

Things will become a lot clearer upon a second or third read, as you put the entire subject of multidimensional analysis into a broader context.

12

Session Twelve: Power Pivot, Data Modeling, OLAP and Business Intelligence

> Any sufficiently advanced technology is indistinguishable from magic.
>
> *Sir Arthur C. Clarke, British Science Fiction Writer (1917 - 2008)*

This session will give you the data modeling skills that you need to build OLAP-friendly relational data models and to create OLAP pivot tables from them.

Later, in: *Session Thirteen: An introduction to DAX*, you'll learn how to use DAX expressions to further refine your data model.

Session Objectives

By the end of this session you will be able to:

- Understand data model memory requirements
- Install the Power Pivot add-in
- Add tables to a data model
- Understand the Power Pivot window
- Add a relationship to a data model using Power Pivot
- Use an OLAP pivot table to analyze data residing in a data model
- Understand OLAP pivot tables
- Understand modern data analysis
- Understand many-to-many relationships
- Create a data model directly from a relational database
- Understand OLTP database design
- Understand OLAP database design
- Create a snowflake data model from a relational database
- Convert a snowflake data model into a star data model
- Hide, remove and rename data model columns
- Add a calendar table to a data model
- Format values in a data model
- Understand MDX queries and OLAP pivot table limitations
- Use the CUBEVALUE function to query a data model
- Convert CUBEVALUE functions to include MDX expressions
- Create an asymmetric OLAP pivot table using Named Sets

note

How to check how much memory you have available

Click in the Windows search box (at the bottom left of your screen) and type: **System Information** and then press the **<Enter>** key.

A screen appears showing how much memory is installed, and how much is currently available, for your computer.

Installed Physical Memory (RAM)	32.0 GB
Total Physical Memory	31.9 GB
Available Physical Memory	23.1 GB

The above grab was from my own computer, running the 64-bit version of Windows. On my computer I have 32 GB of memory installed.

If I ran the 32-bit version of Windows on the same computer I would only have 2GB of memory available.

You should also make sure that you are running the 64-bit version of Windows 10. Look for this item:

System Type	x64-based PC

x64 indicates that a 64-bit version of Windows 10 is installed.

note

SSAS version history

Microsoft's first OLAP product was released in 1998 as part of SQL Server 7. It was called *OLAP services*.

OLAP services could host an OLAP data model that could be accessed via the MDX query language.

In the year 2000, *OLAP services* was renamed *Analysis Services*. The current version is *Microsoft SQL Server 2019 Analysis Services* (usually referred to using the acronym: *SSAS*).

Lesson 12-1: Understand data model memory requirements

In this book's remaining sessions, you will create and use data models. The data models created in this book reside within the Excel workbook in which they are created. When you save the workbook you also save the data model and the data it contains.

For some of the lessons in this session you will need to open sample files. Though it is very unlikely, you may have a computer that has insufficient free memory to load the sample files into memory.

When you create your own real-world data models you may need to work with very large data sets. This may cause you to experience memory-related problems.

Why memory issues can occur

When a data model is hosted inside Excel, the Power Pivot engine must reside in your computer's memory, along with the data model you create. This can cause out-of-memory errors on computers running the 32-bit version of Windows or on computers with very little memory (RAM) installed.

Make sure you are using the 64-bit version of Windows

Microsoft still produce a 32-bit version of Windows 10, but this is only provided to support very old computer hardware (that cannot run a 64-bit operating system) or for companies that run very old software (that cannot run in a 64-bit environment).

The 32-bit version of Windows 10 can only use up to 4GB of RAM (no matter how much memory you install in your computer).

If you are using the 32-bit version of Windows 10 you will be unable to install the 64-bit version of Microsoft Office.

See sidebar to find out how to check whether you are using the 32-bit or 64-bit version of Windows 10.

Solving memory issues with the 64-bit version of Excel

There are two versions of Office available and you have access to both with your 365 subscription.

- The 32-bit version (the default for installations before 2019)

- The 64-bit version (the default for installations after 2019).

To discover the version of Office you are using:

1. Start Excel.

2. Click: File→Account→About Excel.

(?) About Excel	**About Excel**
	Learn more about Excel, Support, Product ID, and Copyright information.
	Version 2002 (Build 12527.20880 Click-to-Run)
	Semi-Annual Enterprise Channel (Preview)

You'll now see which version you are using.

About Microsoft® Excel® for Office 365

Microsoft® Excel® for Office 365 MSO (16.0.11929.20536) 64-bit ⬅

note

Out of memory errors may crash or hang your computer

If your computer hangs or crashes when using an Excel workbook that contains a data model the cause could be a memory-related issue. You may have to do the following to close Excel:

1. Open the *Windows Task Manager* application (the easiest way to do this is to press the **<Ctrl>+<Alt>+<Delete>** keys) and then select *Task Manager* from the shortcut menu.

2. Click the *Processes* tab.

3. In the *Apps* list, right-click on *Microsoft Excel* and select *End Task* from the shortcut menu.

4. Restart Excel.

note

Some modern computers support an enormous amount of RAM

For example, the Hewlett Packard Integrity MC990X supports up to 48 Terabytes of RAM (though it does cost over $70,000).

Until January 2019 the 32-bit version of Office was automatically installed by default. This was to avoid potential problems with older 32-bit items such as add-ins or embedded media. Since January 2019 the 64 bit version has been installed by default (a welcome change). If your copy of Office 365 was installed before February 2019 you may find that you are still using the 32-bit version.

The Excel 32-bit version can only utilize 2GB of memory while the Office 64-bit version can address up to 8 Terabytes. It is difficult to imagine any data analysis task that would need more memory than this.

Users of the 64-bit version of Excel can thus always overcome out-of-memory problems by installing more memory.

Solving memory issues by pre-compression

When a data model is loaded into memory it is compressed (by the Power Pivot engine) into a much more compact form. Compression can reduce the data model's size by as much as 90%.

In: *Appendix A: Power Pivot Rules*, you can find out how to make your data model compression-friendly so that Power Pivot can achieve optimal compression.

If you have access to a 64-bit version of Excel running on a machine with a lot of memory, you may be able to create a data model that can be used by 32-bit users with limited memory. When you create the data model and then save the workbook (that contains the data model) you may find that it opens without issues on computers that would have been unable to create the model themselves.

If you adopt this strategy be aware that users will be unable to refresh data models (from the original source data) on their machines.

Solving memory issues by hosting your data model on SSAS

Microsoft have a product called SSAS (SQL Server Analysis Services). A Power Pivot data model can be exported (including any DAX expressions it may contain), without modification, into a tabular model that can be hosted on an SSAS server (rather than in your computer's memory).

Out of memory problems can then be avoided (even by 32-bit users with modest hardware) as the data model is stored in the SSAS server's memory (and not in the user's own computer memory).

There are other advantages to hosting a data model on an SSAS server:

- **The ability to work with bigger data:** The size of the model is no longer limited by the size of your computer's memory.

- **Better security:** It is easier to restrict the data that the user of the data model is permitted to see.

- **Refresh scheduling:** SSAS allows the data model to be refreshed on a scheduled basis.

- **Centralized data:** The data model is held at one central location.

Lesson 12-2: Install the Power Pivot add-in

Until the January 2020 Version 1908 release the Power Pivot add-in was not installed by default. If the Power Pivot add-in is missing from your Ribbon you may need to install it to complete this session.

1 Open Excel and create a new blank workbook.

2 Install Power Pivot.

1. Click Data→Data Tools→Manage Data Model.

If Power Pivot is already installed then the Power Pivot window will open. If this is the case you can close the Power Pivot window and move to the next lesson.

If Power Pivot is not already installed, a dialog may appear asking you to *Enable the Data Analysis add-ins.*

This is Excel's way of asking for permission to install the Power Pivot add-in.

2. Click the *Enable* button.

Power Pivot could take 30 seconds or more to install on a slower computer.

When the installation process is complete the Power Pivot application is opened:

trivia

PowerPivot or Power Pivot (with a space)?

Between 2010 and 2013 Microsoft used the product name PowerPivot (without a space).

On July 8, 2013 Microsoft announced that PowerPivot would now form part of a new *Power BI* suite of self-service tools.

The suite comprised of:

- Power Pivot
- Power Query
- Power Maps
- Power View

PowerPivot had been renamed *Power Pivot* to maintain consistency with the naming convention of the other applications in the suite.

As you know from the earlier OLAP sessions, *Power Query* has now been renamed *Get & Transform* and *Power Maps* has now been renamed *3D Maps*.

Power View (now obsolete) was an early incarnation of the product Microsoft now call: *Power BI*.

Power BI is a fast-evolving stand-alone tool that aims to allow unsophisticated users to create visual representations of data from data models created by more sophisticated users (such as yourself when you have finished this book).

Power BI includes *Get & Transform* (that you learned about in: *Session Eleven: Create Get & Transform queries*) and *Power Pivot* (the subject of this session).

Your Excel OLAP skills will be equally relevant if you later use the Power BI tool to create your data models.

3. Close the *Power Pivot* window.

Notice that a new *Power Pivot* tab has now appeared on the ribbon:

3   **Open the Power Pivot window.**

Now that the Power Pivot add-in has been installed you can open the Power Pivot window in two ways:

Either

Click: Power Pivot→Data Model→Manage.

Or

Click: Data→Data Tools→Manage Data Model.

Lesson 12-3: Add tables to a data model

In this lesson you'll create your first data model using Get & Transform and Power Pivot.

A data model contains one or more tables and defines the (primary key/foreign key) relationships between them. You learned about primary keys and foreign keys in: *Lesson 11-26: Understand primary and foreign keys.*

It is possible to import data directly into a data model from many different data sources. In this lesson you will import data from two Excel tables.

1   Open *Stock List-1* from your sample files folder.

2   Select the *Product* worksheet.

3   Add the *Product* table to the data model.

1.   Click on any cell inside the *Product* table.

2.   Click: Data→Get & Transform Data→From Table/Range.

The Get & Transform editor opens. Note that the left-hand bar contains a new query called *Product*.

(You may have to click the *Expand* button to expand the *Navigator Pane*).

3.   Click: Home→Close→Close & Load→Close & Load To...

The *Import Data* dialog appears.

4.   Click the *Only Create Connection* option button.

5.   Check the *Add this data to the Data Model* check box.

note

Data models that source data from Excel tables in the same workbook are inefficient

In this lesson's example, data is sourced from Excel tables that are in the same workbook that the data model resides in. This means that Excel must maintain two copies of the same data (one in the data model and one in the Excel tables). This is not best-practice when creating data models.

Both Excel and the data model must fit in the computer's available memory. When dealing with large data sets there is an increased risk of encountering out-of-memory errors when the data is duplicated in the way described above.

For this reason, importing data into a data model from a linked Excel table (in the same workbook) is not considered to be best-practice when creating data models.

The best-practice rule:

Do not use linked Excel tables.

… is included in: *Appendix A: Power Pivot Rules.*

6. Click: *OK.*

You are returned to Excel with the *Queries & Connections* task pane visible. You cannot see the *Data Model* yet (the Data Model is an in-memory construct that is invisible within the Excel application).

4 Add the *Category* table to the data model.

Do this in the same way you added the *Product* table.

Don't forget to check the *add this data to the Data Model* check box (as you did with the *Product* query).

You should now be inside Excel with two queries shown in the *Queries & Connections* task pane.

5 Save your work as *Stock List-2.*

Lesson 12-4: Understand the Power Pivot window

1   Open *Stock List-2* from your sample files folder.

2   Open the Power Pivot window.

Click: Power Pivot→Data Model→Manage.

The Power Pivot window opens.

This is your first view of the Power Pivot application.

note

You can paste data directly into a new data model table

To do this:

1. Select and copy the range of data that you want to import into a new Power Pivot table.

2. Open the Power Pivot window.

3. Click: Home→Clipboard→ Paste (from within the Power Pivot window).

4. Provide a name for the new table when prompted.

The differences between the Power Pivot window and Excel

The Power Pivot window seems very similar to Excel but you are really looking at a completely different application that has been engineered to "look and feel" like Excel. This is intended to make you feel instantly at home with Power Pivot.

You can see that there is a data grid that is similar to Excel with rows and columns. You can also see tabs showing that there are two tables in the above data model (very similar to two worksheets in a workbook).

Just like Excel, you can:

- Rename and delete columns.

- Change column widths.

- Insert new columns.

- Click and drag columns to new locations.

- Rename and delete sheet tabs.

- Click and drag sheet tabs to re-arrange them.

- Use AutoSum to aggregate all of the values in a column.

note

If data in the workbook changes the data model will not automatically update

The data you are looking at is an independent copy of the data residing in the Excel *Product* and *Category* tables.

If the data in the *Product* and *Category* tables changes, you will not see any change in the data model (unless you refresh the model from the original source data).

important

Do not import or transform data using Power Pivot

The Power Pivot application is a tool to construct and refine data models.

Power Pivot is not a good tool for importing data into the data model.

You should always import data into the data model using Get & Transform (in the way you did for this model in: *Lesson 12-3: Add tables to a data model*).

Using Get & Transform provides powerful data transformation features that enable you to edit and refine your data in the future.

The best-practice rule:

Do not use Power Pivot to import or transform data.

… is included in: *Appendix A: Power Pivot Rules.*

This creates a *calculated measure*. You'll learn how to use calculated measures later in: *Lesson 13-3: Create a DAX calculated measure.*

- Format cells.

- Sort columns.

Unlike Excel, you can't:

- Type a value into a cell or change any of the information you see displayed (although you can refresh the data from the original data source).

- Have more than one table in a sheet. A Power Pivot sheet contains a single table rather than a worksheet.

- Refer to a cell using A1 notation (A1 notation means cell references such as B12 or A1:C14). Power Pivot does not recognize letters to identify columns. Columns must be referred to by name.

- Assign different data types within a column. You cannot, for example, have text in some cells and numbers in other cells in the same column. You learned about data types in: *Lesson 11-6: Understand data types.*

- Have more than one formula in a column. When a formula is added to a Power Pivot column it always applies to every cell in that column. You'll learn more about calculated columns later, in: *Lesson 13-2: Add a DAX calculated column.*

Some things Power Pivot can do that Excel cannot

- Create relationships between tables.

- Assign a larger range of data types to columns.

- Use DAX functions (you'll learn about DAX later, in: *Session Thirteen: An introduction to DAX*).

- Create calculated measures. You'll learn more about measures later, in: *Lesson 13-3: Create a DAX calculated measure.*

- Work with *Big Data*. An Excel worksheet can contain a maximum of just over a million rows. A Power Pivot table can contain a maximum of just over a thousand million rows.

- Produce extremely fast (often perceived as instant) results even when analyzing data sets containing many millions of rows. Power Pivot uses Microsoft's *xVelocity in-memory analysis engine*. This engine can scan billions of data rows per second and can produce reports in a tiny fraction of the time needed by Excel.

3   Close the Power Pivot window.

4   Close Excel without saving the workbook.

note

Classic Data Analysis and Modern Data Analysis

In: *Lesson 11-27: Link primary and foreign keys using XLOOKUP,* you effectively created a primary key/foreign key relationship using a simple XLOOKUP function.

This methodology is often described as belonging to *Classic Data Analysis.*

In this lesson you use Power Pivot to define a primary key/foreign key relationship within a data model without the use of any function.

This methodology is often described as belonging to *Modern Data Analysis.*

You'll discover more about the differences between Classic Data Analysis and Modern Data Analysis later, in: *Lesson 12-8: Understand modern data analysis.*

Lesson 12-5: Add a relationship to a data model using Power Pivot

In: *Lesson 12-3: Add tables to a data model,* you added two tables to a data model.

If you completely understood: *Lesson 11-26: Understand primary and foreign keys,* you will see at a glance that:

- *ProductID* is the primary key of the *Product* table.

- *CategoryID* is the primary key of the *Category* table.

- The *Product* table contains a single foreign key called *CategoryID.*

The data model is not yet aware that there is a relationship between the tables. In this lesson you'll add the relationship to the data model.

1   Open *Stock List-2* from your sample files folder.

2   Open Power Pivot.

Click: Power Pivot→Data Model→Manage.

3   Change the Power Pivot window view to *Diagram View*

In the Power Pivot window click:

Home→View→Diagram View

The window contents change to show a graphical representation of both tables. This type of graphical representation of tables (and their relationships) within a database is often referred to as a *Schema.*

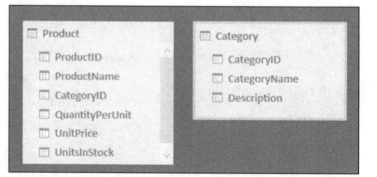

You can drag the tables around the window or click and drag the edge of a table to re-size it.

Stock List-2

4 **Add a Primary Key/Foreign Key relationship between the tables.**

Click on the *Category ID* primary key (in the *Category* table) and drag it on top of the *Category ID* foreign key (in the *Product* table).

It doesn't really matter which table you drag the key field from, and which you drag it to. Power Pivot is clever enough to figure out which table contains the primary key column and which table contains the foreign key (whichever direction you drag a field in).

A relationship appears in the diagram window:

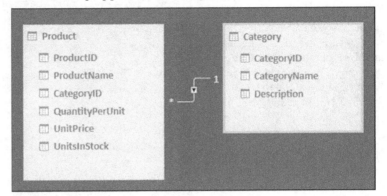

Notice the number **1** next to the *Category* table and the asterisk next to the *Product* table.

You can read this relationship as follows:

***One** Category can be associated with **Many** products, but each product can be associated with one (**and only one**) category.*

This type of relationship is called a one-to-many relationship and is the only relationship used in Power Pivot data models (often called OLAP databases).

Relational databases often contain a different (but rarer) relationship called a many-to-many relationship. You'll learn about this type of relationship in: *Lesson 12-10: Understand many-to-many relationships.*

5 **Close the Power Pivot window.**

6 **Save your work as** *Stock List-3.*

You've now created your very first data model.

In this very simple data model you imported data from two small Excel tables and then defined a relationship between them.

You can probably appreciate how you can use Power Pivot to create large data models that import table data from multiple sources with defined relationships between them.

The data model is invisible (unless you open Power Pivot). In the next lesson: *Lesson 12-6: Use an OLAP pivot table to analyze data residing in a data model,* you will make use of the data model by using it as the source data for a new type of Pivot Table (called an OLAP Pivot Table).

Microsoft's *Modern Data Analysis* vision will then become a little clearer.

Lesson 12-6: Use an OLAP pivot table to analyze data residing in a data model

In: *Lesson 12-3: Add tables to a data model* and *Lesson 12-5: Add a relationship to a data model using Power Pivot,* you created a very simple data model that contained two tables and one relationship.

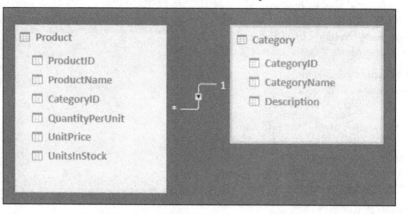

In this lesson you'll analyze the data contained in this model using an OLAP pivot table.

1   Open *Stock List-3* from your sample files folder.

2   Open Power Pivot.

Click: Power Pivot→Data Model→Manage.

3   Create an OLAP pivot table that uses the data model as source data.

1.   Click: Home→PivotTable→Pivot Table (in the Power Pivot window).

The *Create PivotTable* dialog appears.

2.   Click: OK.

A special type of pivot table is created that references the data model. While the pivot table looks almost the same as the pivot tables you worked with in: *Session Nine: Pivot Tables*, it is actually a completely new type of pivot table called an *OLAP pivot table.* OLAP is an acronym for *OnLine Analytical Processing.*

Later in this session you'll learn a lot more about OLAP pivot tables. OLAP pivot tables can do many things that regular pivot tables cannot do. Conversely, there are some features available in a regular pivot table that are not supported (or needed) in OLAP pivot tables.

Notice that the *PivotTable Fields* pane is headed with two tabs: *Active* and *All* (although there are no active fields at present). This is one way to immediately identify OLAP pivot tables (as they look very similar to regular pivot tables).

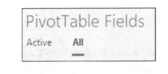

4   Rename the pivot table worksheet tab: **Pivot Table**

5   Use the OLAP pivot table to show total units in stock for each category.

1. Click on the pivot table to activate it.

    In the *PivotTable Fields* pane, tables in the data model are shown with a orange icon on the bottom-right corner. Tables in the regular Excel workbook do not have this icon (see sidebar).

Data Model Tables
Excel Tables

2. Click the fly out menu button next to the Data Model *Category* table and check the *CategoryName* check box.

3. Click the fly out menu button next to the Data Model *Product* table and check the *UnitsInStock* check box.

Row Labels	Sum of UnitsInStock
Beverages	559
Condiments	507
Confections	386
Dairy Products	393
Grains/Cereals	308
Meat/Poultry	165
Produce	100
Seafood	701
Grand Total	3119

PivotTable Fields
Active   **All**
Choose fields to add to report:
Search

▲ Category
☐ CategoryID
☑ CategoryName
☐ Description

▲ Product
☐ ProductID
☐ ProductName
☐ CategoryID
☐ QuantityPerUnit
☐ UnitPrice
☑ UnitsInStock

▷ Category

You have now created a single OLAP pivot table based upon a data model. The data model:

- Contains two tables (that were imported using *Get & Transform* queries).

- Contains a relationship (that was created using *Power Pivot*).

- Is being used by an OLAP Pivot Table (within *Excel.*)

In the lessons and sessions that follow you'll appreciate the huge advantages of assembling data into a data model prior to analysis with an OLAP pivot table.

6   Save your work as *Stock List-4*.

© 2021 The Smart Method® Ltd

note

Another way to automatically detect and add relationships

On the facing page sidebar you learned that Excel can add relationships to a data model automatically – and that you should use this feature with caution.

You can also launch the Auto-Detect feature from the Power Pivot ribbon tab (within Excel).

1. Select a pivot table that uses the data model as its source:

2. Click: Power Pivot→ Relationships→Detect

Detect
Relationships

The relationships will then be automatically detected and created.

Lesson 12-7: Understand OLAP pivot tables

In: *Lesson 9-4: Understand the pivot table data cache* you learned that a normal pivot table does not access the source data directly. Instead, a *pivot table data cache* is created from the data source. The pivot table then takes its data from the cache.

In: *Lesson 11-30: Load a query directly into the PivotTable cache*, you learned that a pivot table data cache doesn't need to use an Excel worksheet as its data source. It is possible to construct the cache directly from an external data source.

In: *Lesson 12-3: Add tables to a data model, Lesson 12-5: Add a relationship to a data model using Power Pivot* and *Lesson 12-6: Use an OLAP pivot table to analyze data residing in a data model*, you created a data model and then used it as the data source for a new type of pivot table called an OLAP pivot table.

You may wonder why a different type of pivot table is needed when you create a pivot table from a data model rather than a single Excel table.

Normal and OLAP Pivot Tables

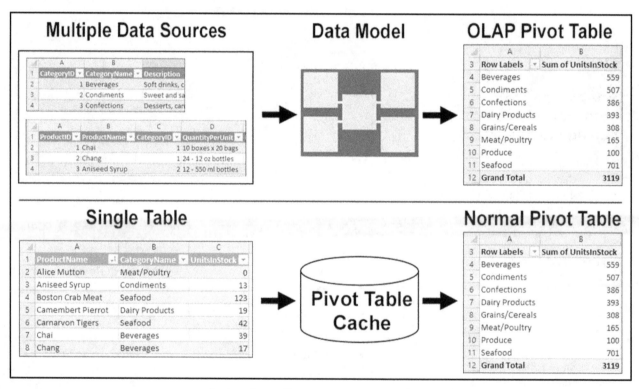

In the above diagram you can see that both the regular pivot table and the OLAP pivot table look identical.

The difference between them is that the *OLAP pivot table* obtains its data from a *Data Model* created from one or more related tables. The ability to select fields from more than one related table is one of the biggest advantages of working with OLAP pivot tables.

The *regular pivot table* obtains its data from a *pivot table data cache* created from a single table residing in an Excel worksheet or external data source.

OLAP pivot tables are standards-based

The *PivotTable data cache* can be thought of as a non-standard OLAP implementation that is restricted to a single table data source.

In contrast, when data resides in a data model it can be retrieved directly from the data model using an industry-standard query language called MDX (Multi-Dimensional eXpressions). You'll learn more about MDX queries later, in: *Lesson 12-19: Understand MDX queries and OLAP pivot table limitations*.

MDX is also used by many non-Microsoft products such as *Crystal Reports*.

An OLAP pivot table automatically generates the MDX queries it needs to return values to display in the OLAP pivot table.

OLAP pivot tables can work with big data

Excel worksheets are limited to approximately one million rows. OLAP pivot tables obtain their data from a Data Model. Data Models can contain about two thousand million data rows.

In: *Lesson 11-30: Load a query directly into the PivotTable cache*, you learned how a regular pivot table can work with big data by using Get & Transform to load data (from an external non-Excel data source) directly into the *PivotTable Data Cache*.

While it is true that a regular pivot table can also overcome the million-row limitation in this way, the *PivotTable Data Cache* is still restricted to 2.1 thousand million data items (rather than rows) and is unable to work with more than one table.

What is Business Intelligence?

Business Intelligence is a very broad term that was first used in 1865 to describe how the banker Sir Henry Furnese prospered by receiving and acting upon information before his contemporaries.

When IT professionals talk about Business Intelligence (BI) today, they usually mean the analysis and presentation of data sourced from an OLAP database (data model).

Dr E.F. Codd (the inventor of OLAP) wrote a paper in 1985 that proposed 12 rules for defining OLAP. Two of his rules were:

- *The tool (and not the user) should be concerned with where the physical data comes from.*

- *Reporting facilities should present information in any way the user wants to view it.*

You can see how Microsoft's BI solution complies with Codd's rules by separating the data modeling (difficult) and reporting (easy) tasks and by enabling complete reporting flexibility via the OLAP pivot table.

note

Power Pivot has been available for selected versions of Excel for a long time

Power Pivot was first released in May 2010 as part of the *SQL Server 2008 R2* product line. It was also possible to install Power Pivot onto any version of Excel 2010 as a free add-in.

For Excel 2013 and Excel 2016 the full Power Pivot add-in was only available for Pro Plus versions of Excel.

In the standard version of Excel 2013 it became possible to create a relational data model and analyze the model using an OLAP pivot table or chart. Without access to Power Pivot it wasn't possible to create DAX calculated fields or calculated measures or to display a schema. You'll learn more about DAX later, in: *Session Thirteen: An introduction to DAX*.

Excel 2016 also added the *Get & Transform* tool (previously named Power Query) as an integral part of all Excel versions.

Excel 2019 (and the Jan 2019 semi-annual Excel 365 release) finally added Power Pivot to all Excel versions. It then became possible to realize the full *modern data analysis* vision using any Excel version.

Lesson 12-8: Understand modern data analysis

You now have an in-depth understanding of *Get & Transform*. You also have a limited understanding of relational database theory and Power Pivot. With this foundation knowledge you should now be able to understand how these tools and technologies work together to provide a new paradigm for data analysis using Excel that is often described as: *Modern Data Analysis*.

What does modern data analysis mean?

When the *Get & Transform* and *Power Pivot* tools were added to Excel (in the Excel 2019 perpetual licence version and the January 2019 Excel 365 semi-annual update) they enabled a new paradigm for data analysis.

The term: *Modern Data Analysis* is often used to describe the use of these new tools in their intended fashion. The term: *Classic Data Analysis* has been used to describe the "old way" of doing things.

The five steps in the modern data analysis workflow

Most data analysis tasks require five clearly defined steps: Get, Transform, Relate, Aggregate (summarize) and Visualize.

1. **Get** the data. This means importing data (that may be located in a database, Excel worksheet, CSV file or other source).

2. **Transform** the data. This might include removing unwanted columns, converting text fields to dates, rounding numeric values, filtering, sorting, renaming columns, adding calculated columns and other similar tasks.

3. **Relate** the data. If data resides in several different tables, there needs to be a method to either define the relationships between them or to consolidate the data into a single table.

4. **Aggregate** (summarize) the data. Values usually need to be aggregated (for example by creating grouped totals or averages) into a digestible form.

5. **Visualize** the data. This may involve adding charts, pivot charts, conditional formatting, sparklines and other visualizations.

How data analysis was done in the past (classic data analysis)

1. **Get** the data. This was traditionally done by importing data into a collection of Excel tables or ranges.

2. **Transform** the data. This might include removing unwanted columns from the worksheet, adding new calculated columns containing Excel functions and formulas, converting text fields to dates, rounding numeric values, renaming columns, formatting cells and other similar tasks.

3. **Relate** the data. Traditional (non OLAP) pivot tables can only summarize data from a single table so data from several different tables would often have to be consolidated into a single table. This was traditionally done with VLOOKUP, SWITCH, INDEX, MATCH, IF and IFS functions.

4. **Aggregate** the data. Excel contains many methods to summarize data. Popular methods include Automatic Subtotals, Data Tables, traditional (as opposed to OLAP) Pivot Tables and aggregation functions such as SUM, SUMIFS, AVERAGE, MAX, MIN, COUNT and COUNTIF.

5. **Visualize** the data. This might involve summarizing data in a traditional pivot table or pivot chart, adding charts, conditional formatting, sparklines and other visualizations.

How modern data analysis achieves faster and better results

1. **Get** the data. This is done using the *Get and Transform* tool. Data can be imported from a huge range of data sources using this tool (including relational databases, Excel worksheets, CSV files and web pages). Get & Transform can work with very large data sets (often called *Big Data*) as it is not restricted to Excel's million row limitation (see sidebar).

2. **Transform** the data. This is also done using the *Get and Transform* tool. Unlike Excel, the transform actions are stored in PQFL (Power Query Formula Language) expressions. Both the connection details and the PQFL steps are stored in a query. This means that the query can be re-run, avoiding repetitive work in the future if the source data changes.

3. **Relate** the data. Power Pivot enables tables to be related in a *data model* using primary key/foreign key relationships. This provides huge flexibility and avoids the use of any Excel functions (such as VLOOKUP) to relate data.

4. **Summarize** the data. While a traditional pivot table can only access data residing in a single table, data models can be analyzed with a new type of pivot table (called an OLAP pivot table). The OLAP pivot table can do just about anything that a regular pivot table can do but can access data residing in multiple related tables.

   Power Pivot also enables DAX (Data Analysis Expressions) to be added to the data model. DAX enables calculated columns and calculated measures (aggregations) to be simply defined. You'll learn about DAX later, in: *Session Thirteen: An introduction to DAX.*

5. **Visualize** the data. OLAP Pivot Tables and OLAP Pivot Charts provide the primary method of visualizing data residing in data models. It is also possible to use any of Excel's classic analysis and visualization features by using CUBEVALUE functions to extract data directly from a data model into Excel cells. You'll learn more about the CUBEVALUE function later, in: *Lesson 12-20: Use the CUBEVALUE function to query a data model.*

note

Relationships imported from a relational database are reliable

When you import data from a relational database (via Get & Transform) both tables and relationships are imported.

Get & Transform can then load both the tables and the relationships into a data model.

Note that this is very different to the auto-detect feature discussed in: *Lesson 12-6: Use an OLAP pivot table to analyze data residing in a data model*(sidebar).

When you import data from a relational database there is no scope for error as the relationships defined by the database designer are also imported.

Lesson 12-9: Create a data model directly from a relational database

In: *Lesson 11-26: Understand primary and foreign keys,* you learned how a relational database consists of several tables linked by relationships.

In: *Lesson 11-30: Load a query directly into the PivotTable cache,* you created a *PivotTable data cache* directly from a single database table (without importing any data into a worksheet).

Of course, the *PivotTable data cache* doesn't understand the concept of multiple related tables. You can only create a *PivotTable data cache* from a single worksheet or single external table (or view). Data models don't have this limitation.

A relational database (such as Access, Oracle or SQL Server) already contains defined relationships between tables. When the data source has defined relationships, Get & Transform imports both the tables and the relationships. Get & Transform can then load both the tables and the relationships into a data model.

In this lesson you'll import a complete relational database (along with its relationships) into a data model. You won't need to define the relationships yourself. You'll then use the data model as the source for an OLAP pivot table.

1   Open a new blank workbook.

2   Import the *Categories* and *Products* tables from the *Two Related Tables* Access database in your sample files folder directly into a data model.

    1.   Click: Data→Get & Transform Data→Get Data→ From Database→From Microsoft Access Database.

       The *Import Data* dialog appears.

    2.   Select the Access database file *Two Related Tables* from your sample files folder and click the *Import* button.

> 🅰️ Two Related Tables   Microsoft Access Database

       The *Navigator* dialog appears.

    3.   Check the *Select multiple items* check box.

       Check boxes appear next to each table.

    4.   Check the check boxes next to the *Category* and *Product* tables.

> ☑ Select multiple items
>
> Display Options ▾   ▯
>
> ▲ ▦ Two Related Tables.accdb [2]
>
>   ☑ ▦ Category
>
>   ☑ ▦ Product

🅰️ **Two Related Tables**

    5.   Click: Load (drop-down arrow)→Load To…

Import Data dialog:

Select how you want to view this data in your workbook.

- ☐ _T_able
- ☑ _P_ivotTable Report
- ☐ Pivot_C_hart
- ☐ _O_nly Create Connection

Where do you want to put the data?

- ☐ _E_xisting worksheet:
  - =SAS1
- ☑ _N_ew worksheet

☑ Add this data to the Data Model

Properties... ▾   OK   Cancel

The _Import Data_ dialog appears (sometimes this takes a few moments to appear).

6. Click the _PivotTable Report_ option button. Notice that when you select this option the _Add this data to the Data Model_ checkbox is automatically checked and cannot be changed. This happens because Get & Transform knows that the data source contains two or more tables along with their relationships.

7. Click the _OK_ button.

   When you click the OK button Excel uses Get & Transform queries that access the _Category_ and _Product_ tables from the Access database to create a new data model with primary key/foreign key relationships that match those defined in the database.

   An empty OLAP pivot table is then created. _The PivotTable Fields_ list references this data model. You can see that all of the fields from both the _Category_ and _Product_ tables are available.

   Notice the small orange database symbols shown on each table. This indicates that the data source resides in the data model and not in an Excel worksheet.

3   View the relationships in the data model.

1. Click: Power Pivot→Data Model→Manage.

   The Power Pivot window opens.

2. In the Power Pivot window, click: Home→View→ Diagram View.

   The Schema is displayed.

3. Click the relationship line between the tables.

   The _CategoryID_ field is highlighted in both tables, proving that the relationship between the _Category_ and _Product_ tables has been correctly applied:

4   Close the Power Pivot window.

5   Use the OLAP pivot table to show the total _UnitsInStock_ for each _CategoryName_.

Row Labels ▾	Sum of UnitsInStock
Beverages	559
Condiments	507

6   Save your work as _Two Related Tables-1._

note

Even IT professionals often find many-to-many relationships difficult to understand

Unfortunately, database design is one of the least understood skills in the world of IT.

I have spent a great deal of my professional life implementing clumsy work-arounds to overcome badly designed databases (even when working on multi-million-dollar projects).

One of the most common errors I have encountered in corporate databases all over the world is the incorrect modeling of many-to-many relationships. Often a programmer that doesn't really understand database design will try to "muddle through".

The normal error is when the programmer didn't "get" many-to-many relationships and tried to model a series of one-to-many relationships instead.

If you see this type of table:

Invoice
🔑 invoiceID
CustomerID
InvoiceDate
Product1
Quantity1
Product2
Quantity2
Product3
Quantity3

… you will know at once that the designer didn't understand many-to-many relationships.

The designer of the above table has tried to work-around their inability to model many-to-many relationships by defining three one-to-many relationships.

You are almost certain to encounter design errors like this if you work with corporate data.

Lesson 12-10: Understand many-to-many relationships

Power Pivot data models cannot contain many-to-many relationships

As you will learn in this lesson, many-to-many relationships are found in most commercial databases.

Later in this session you'll discover that Power Pivot data models need to be designed in a different way to commercial databases as they cannot contain many-to-many relationships. You'll learn how to convert any many-to-many relationships in the source data into the one-to-many relationships needed in a correctly designed Power Pivot data model.

One-to-many relationships

Up until now you have only modeled a one-to-many relationship.

In: *Lesson 12-5: Add a relationship to a data model using Power Pivot,* you created a relationship between a *Product* table and a *Category* table. This defined the following relationship:

- Each Product can be associated with one, and only one, Category.

- *One* Category can potentially be associated with *Many* Products.

This type of relationship is called a *one-to-many* relationship, with the Category on the *One* side of the relationship and the Product on the *Many* side.

One-to-many relationships are by far the most common type of relationship.

A one-to-many relationship is displayed in the Power Pivot window's *diagram view* like this:

You can see how the *One* and *Many* sides of the relationship are marked.

Many-to-many relationships

This type of relationship is more difficult to model than a simple one-to-many relationship.

In the world of commerce, a many-to-many relationship that is often encountered is that between *Products* and *Invoices.*

- One *Invoice* can bill many *Products*.

- One *Product* can appear on many *Invoices.*

note

Many Power Pivot users never overcome the many-to-many issue

You can design a data model that can effectively analyse data that originated in a database containing many-to-many relationships.

To do this you'll need to convert those relationships into the one-to-many relationships needed by a correctly designed data model.

With the skills you've already acquired you can already do a lot of useful data analysis using Get & Transform and Power Pivot.

In the lessons that follow you'll learn why commercial (transactional) databases need to be designed differently to Power Pivot data models.

With this understanding you'll learn how to overcome the many-to-many issue and will be able to design data models that work perfectly with Power Pivot.

How many-to-many relationships are modeled

In: *Lesson 11-26: Understand primary and foreign keys,* you learned that a one-to-many relationship uses a primary key on the "one" side of the relationship and a foreign key on the "many" side.

For a many-to-many relationship, a link table is required. This sits between the tables on either side of the many-to-many relationship like this:

In the example above, the primary key of the link table (*InvoiceProduct*) is a concatenation of the primary keys found in the two related tables. Remember that you cannot use this type of relationship in a Power Pivot data model (though you will usually find them in commercial databases).

The Invoice table

This table contains information about the invoice as a whole.

Think of it as the invoice before any items have been added. In this simple example it only contains the *InvoiceDate* and the *InvoiceID.* You could also use this table to store information such as the ship-to address or due date. Notice that there is also a *CustomerID* foreign key. This identifies the customer to invoice in a separate *Customer* table (not shown in the schema above).

The Product table

This table contains information about each product. In this simple example it only contains *ProductName, QuantityPerUnit* and *UnitPrice* fields. Notice that there is also a *CategoryID* foreign key pointing to the category that the product belongs to (not shown in the above schema).

You could also use this table to store other information about the product such as the cost price or wholesale discount.

The InvoiceProduct table

This is the many-to-many link table. It is a good relational database naming convention to name link tables as a concatenation of the two tables on either side of the many-to-many relationship (in this case the *InvoiceProduct* table joins the *Invoice* and *Product* tables in a many-to-many relationship). The *InvoiceProduct* table has a row for each line item in the invoice.

Each row has a column that stores the number of units sold on each invoice line. The *ProductID* is a foreign key that identifies the row in the *Product* table that contains details of the product sold.

Lesson 12-11: Understand OLTP database design

OLTP databases

A database that is used to support day-to-day business transactions is called an OLTP (OnLine Transactional Processing) database.

OLTP relational databases are designed around the need to quickly perform four actions: *Create, Retrieve, Update* and *Delete*. The anagram CRUD is often used for these four requirements.

Imagine that your computer application manages employee records (stored in a database). If an employee's details change you would need to first *Retrieve* (find) the employee's record. You'd then have to *Update* the record with the new information.

If an employee left the company, you might want to *Delete* their record. If a new employee was then recruited, you'd need to *Create* a new employee record.

OLTP database schema example

The above schema example comes from an OLTP database. You can see a many-to-many relationship between the *Orders* and *Product* tables (you learned about many-to-many relationships in: *Lesson 12-10: Understand many-to-many relationships*).

You don't need to understand the difference between ROLAP, MOLAP and HOLAP to use Power Pivot. You may find this terminology used in articles about Power Pivot however, so I thought I'd give you an overview of what they mean.

Power Pivot uses a *tabular data model*. An SSAS (SQL Server Analysis Services) server supports three models: *tabular*, *multidimensional* and *hybrid*. The newer tabular model was introduced by Microsoft in 2012 (the multidimensional model is an older technology). Excel uses the newer tabular model (that can be simply exported to an SSAS server if required).

OLAP (*OnLine Analytical Processing*) is an acronym that is used to describe a database (data model) that is used to interactively analyze data from multiple perspectives. In the Excel implementation a tabular data model is analyzed using an OLAP pivot table.

To differentiate between the tabular and multidimensional models, the term ROLAP (Relational OLAP) and MOLAP (Multi-dimensional OLAP) can be used.

Another type of OLAP database is sometimes referred to as HOLAP (Hybrid OLAP). This refers to an OLAP database that combines ROLAP and MOLAP features.

So which OLAP model is best? IT professionals could spend hours arguing the answer, but Microsoft have stated:

"For new projects, we generally recommend tabular models".

In this book I use the more generic term: OLAP though it would also be correct to use the term ROLAP as Power Pivot uses the tabular model.

The *Orders* table contains values that relate to items you'd typically find in the header area of a paper order (such as *OrderDate*).

The *OrderDetails* table contains one row for each item ordered. These would be the values defined in the body area of a paper order (first order item, second order item, etc).

This schema describes a perfectly designed OLTP database, but it is not useful for an OLAP database (a Power Pivot data model is a type of OLAP database).

A Power Pivot data model is an OLAP database

The data model that you create in Power Pivot is a copy of data (from one or more data sources) at a given point in time. This is sometimes called a *Snapshot* of the data (as a photograph does not change after it has been taken).

The data model is a special type of database that has to be designed around the need to quickly analyze data. This type of database is called an *OLAP database* (OnLine Analytical Processing).

Terminology confusion

Current Excel documentation refers to an OLAP database hosted by Excel as a *Data Model*.

If the same model is created using Power Pivot, it is sometimes called a *Power Pivot Model*.

OLAP databases are also often referred to as an *OLAP data source*.

SSAS data models that use the Multidimensional Model (see sidebar) are often referred to as *OLAP Cubes*.

You'll also find the term *OLAP Cube* referred to extensively in OLAP-related discussions as multi-dimensional analysis concepts are often explained using the analogy of a three-dimensional cube (a little like a Rubik's cube) with aggregated values in each cell.

Lesson 12-12: Understand OLAP database design

OLAP databases and OLTP databases are designed differently

OLTP design criteria

In: *Lesson 12-11: Understand OLTP database design* you learned that an OLTP (On Line Transaction Processing) database is designed around the need to quickly perform four actions: *Create, Retrieve, Update* and *Delete.*

Well-designed OLTP databases must also conform to Third Normal Form (3NF) and are said to contain *Normalized Data.* A normalized database reduces the risk of data corruption during transactional processing. You learned a little about 3NF in: *Lesson 11-31: Understand normal and de-normalized data.* OLTP databases can contain one-to-many and many-to-many relationships. You learned about relationship types in: *Lesson 12-10: Understand many-to-many relationships.*

OLAP design criteria

The data model that you create in Power Pivot is an OLAP (On Line Analytical Processing) database. An OLAP database is read-only and has no need to *Create, Retrieve, Update* and *Delete* records. Instead it is designed around the need to quickly analyze data.

Data analysis is most easily performed using a special table and relationship arrangement called a *Star* or *Snowflake* schema that has a central *Fact* table surrounded by several *Dimension* tables.

OLAP databases used with Power Pivot cannot contain many-to-many relationships.

Because OLAP databases do not process transactions they have no need to conform to third normal form. For this reason several dimension tables are often de-normalized into a single dimension table.

Snowflake schema

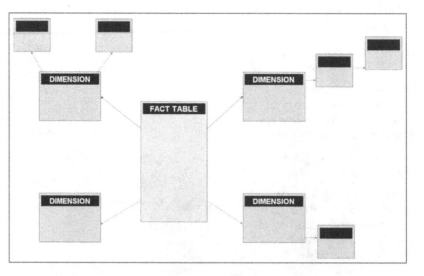

A Snowflake schema has a central *Fact* table surrounded by several *Dimension* tables.

Notice that some of the dimension tables have sub-dimensions giving the schema the appearance of a snowflake.

You can think of the dimension tables as filters that enable aggregations of the values in the fact table.

Star schema (the best choice for OLAP)

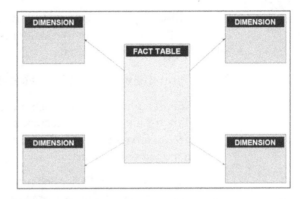

In the above diagram, you can see that a star schema has only one level of dimension tables, giving the schema the appearance of a star.

While Power Pivot will work with either a snowflake or star schema, Power Pivot works faster and better with a star schema. Star schemas are also easier for users to work with.

For these reasons the star schema is the recommended choice when working with Power Pivot.

The best-practice rule:

Use a star schema (rather than a snowflake schema) when constructing data models.

… is included in: *Appendix A: Power Pivot Rules.*

Creating a star schema from an OLTP database

To create an OLAP star schema database from an OLTP database it is first necessary to create a snowflake schema database by converting any many-to-many relationships into one-to-many relationships. You'll do this later, in: *Lesson 12-14: Create a snowflake data model from a relational database.*

The snowflake schema can then be converted into a star schema by de-normalizing any chains of dimension tables into single dimension tables. You'll do this later in: *Lesson 12-15: Convert a snowflake data model into a star data model.*

Lesson 12-13: Understand how to resolve many-to-many relationships

In: *Lesson 12-11: Understand OLTP database design,* you discovered that relational databases use a different type of schema to Power Pivot data models (also called OLAP databases).

When importing data from an OLTP database into a data model (OLAP database) the first problem to consider is the existence of many-to-many relationships in the source data.

1 Open the source OLTP database using Microsoft Access.

Not all editions of Office 365 include Microsoft Access (a tool that allows databases to be designed and used). Microsoft Access is often referred to as a desktop RDBMS (relational database management system).

If your edition of Office 365 includes Microsoft Access, open the *Orders* Access database from your sample files folder using Microsoft Access and then click:

Database Tools→Relationships→Relationships

The following schema will then be displayed:

2 Identify any many-to-many relationships.

Microsoft Access makes it very easy for you to identify many-to-many relationships because it graphically represents primary keys with a small key symbol. 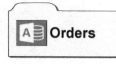 .

You can see that all of the tables (except one) have a single primary key. The *OrderDetails* many-to-many link table has a compound primary key made from a concatenation of the OrderID and ProductID.

You can read this as:

- One *Product* may be related to many *Orders*

- One *Order* can be related to many *Products*.

3 Understand how the many-to-many issue can be solved.

In: *Lesson 12-12: Understand OLAP database design*, you learned that an OLAP database cannot contain a many-to-many relationship.

In: *Lesson 11-31: Understand normal and de-normalized data,* you learned that two tables can be merged together. The resulting table contains de-normalized data.

De-normalized data cannot be used in an OLTP database as it would break third normal form rules. (You learned a little about third normal form in: *Lesson 11-31: Understand normal and de-normalized data - sidebar*). It is, however, perfectly correct to include de-normalized data within an OLAP database.

In*: Lesson 11-32: Create a simple two-table merged query,* you learned how to use Get & Transform to merge two tables together.

If the *Orders* table and *OrderDetails* table are merged the database will consist only of one-to-many relationships. The model would then look like this:

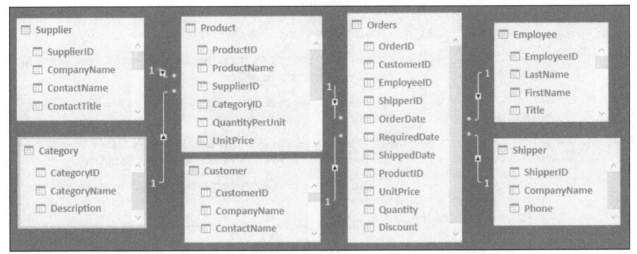

In: *Lesson 12-12: Understand OLAP database design*, you learned that correctly designed OLAP databases need to have a *Snowflake* or *Star* schema arrangement.

You may recognize that the above is a snowflake schema. The *Orders* table is the *Fact* table and all other tables are *Dimension* tables.

Note that in the above snowflake schema, the *Orders* table (that previously contained a single row for each order) will now contain multiple rows for each order – each row containing a single product order item.

This means that the *OrderID* field (previously the primary key) will no longer be unique. This does not present a problem because the *Orders* table is the central *Fact* table in this snowflake schema and a Fact table does not require a primary key (though see sidebar for further discussion).

In the next lesson: *Lesson 12-14: Create a snowflake data model from a relational database*, you'll create the OLAP database shown above.

4 Close Microsoft Access (if it is open).

important

In this lesson you never leave the "Power" environment

The Power tools (Power Pivot and Get & Transform) can work with Big Data containing billions of rows.

Excel can only deal with data that contains approximately a million rows. In this lesson you have never entered the Excel environment so do not have this restriction.

Data was imported and transformed using Get & Transform and then loaded directly into the data model without involving Excel.

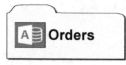

Lesson 12-14: Create a snowflake data model from a relational database

In: *Lesson 12-13: Understand how to resolve many-to-many relationships,* you developed a strategy to convert a many-to-many relationship into a one-to-many relationship by merging two tables together.

In this lesson you'll create a snowflake schema OLAP database (Power Pivot data model) from an OLTP database.

To do this you'll need to perform three operations:

- Create Get & Transform queries for each of the tables in the (Access) Orders database.

- Merge the *OrderDetails* query into the *Orders* query.

- Load all of the queries into a Power Pivot data model.

1   Open a new blank Excel workbook.

2   Import all of the tables from the *Orders* Access database into the Get & Transform editor.

You learned how to do this in: *Lesson 12-9: Create a data model directly from a relational database.*

1. Click: Data→Get & Transform Data→Get Data→ From Database→From Microsoft Access Database.

2. Navigate to the *Orders* Access database in your sample files folder.

3. Click the *Select multiple items* checkbox.

4. Select all eight tables.

5. Click the *Transform Data* button   Transform Data

The *Power Query Editor* window opens.

You can see eight queries listed in the left-hand *Navigator Pane,* one for each table in the Orders database.

3   Merge the *ProductID, UnitPrice, Quantity* and *Discount* fields from the *OrderDetails* query into the *Order* query.

You learned how to do this in: *Lesson 11-32: Create a simple two-table merged query.*

1. Select the *Orders* query in the left-hand *Navigator Pane.*

2. Click the expand button on the right of the *OrderDetails* column header.

    OrderDetails
    Table

A dialog appears.

3. Make sure that the *Expand* option button is selected.

4. Select the *ProductID, UnitPrice, Quantity* and *Discount* fields.

5. De-select the *Use original column name as prefix* check box.

Your dialog should now look like the one shown in the sidebar.

6. Click the OK button.

You have now created a single de-normalized *Orders* table that includes data that was previously in the *Orders* and *OrderDetails* tables.

4 Delete the *OrderDetails* query from the query list.

1. Right-click on the *OrderDetails* query in the left-hand *Navigator Pane.*

2. Click *Delete* from the short cut menu.

5 Create Connection Only queries that will Load the output of all queries to the data model.

You learned how to do this in: *Lesson 12-3: Add tables to a data model.*

1. Click Close & Load→Close & Load To…

2. Select the *Only Create Connection* option button.

3. Check the *Add this data to the Data Model checkbox.*

4. Click the OK button.

You will see the queries executing in the right-hand *Queries & Connections* task pane. It may take some time to import and transform all of the data in the database.

6 Open the Power Pivot window in *Diagram* view.

The diagram shows that you have created a snowflake schema from the OLTP relational database.

Notice how Get & Transform has automatically created the relationships for you to match those defined withing the source database.

You may wish to move the tables around in diagram view to match the arrangement shown below.

7 Close the Power Pivot window.

8 Save your work as *Orders-1*

Lesson 12-15: Convert a snowflake data model into a star data model

1   Open *Orders-1* from your sample files folder.

2   Open the Power Pivot window in *Diagram View.*

You can see that the schema only deviates from being a star schema because of the *Product* table that has two sub-dimensions (the *Supplier* and *Category* tables).

3   Merge the *Category* table and *Supplier* table into the *Product* table using Get & Transform.

1. Close the Power Pivot window.

2. Click: Data→Get & Transform Data→Get Data→ Launch Power Query Editor.

3. Select the *Product* query from the left-hand *Queries* bar.

4. Scroll to the right until you see the *Category* and *Supplier* tables.

▦ Category	↭↮	▦ OrderDetails	↭↮	▦ Supplier	↭↮
Value		Table		Value	
Value		Table		Value	
Value		Table		Value	

5. Click the expand button on the right of the *Category* column header.

▦ Category	↭↮	▦ Or
Value		Table

A dialog appears.

6. Select the *CategoryName* and *Description* fields.

7. Make sure that the *Use original column name as prefix* check box is checked. This will make the data model easier to use as each field will be prefixed with the original (pre-merge) table name for example: *Category.Description*

Your dialog should now look like this:

▣ (Select All Columns)
☐ CategoryID
☑ CategoryName
☑ Description
☐ Product
☑ Use original column name as prefix

8. Click the OK button.

9. Click the expand button on the right of the *Supplier* column header.

Orders-1

A dialog appears.

10. Select all fields except the *SupplierID* and *Product*.

11. Make sure that the *Use original column name as prefix* check box is checked.

   Your dialog should now look like the one shown in the sidebar.

12. Click the OK button.

4 Delete the *Category* and *Supplier* queries from the left-hand *Queries* bar.

   1. Right-click on the *Category* query.

   2. Select *Delete* from the shortcut menu.

   3. Delete the *Supplier* query in the same way.

5 Close the Power Query editor and load the query results back into the data model.

Click: Home→Close→Close & Load→Close & Load.

6 Open the Power Pivot window in *Diagram View*

7 Refresh the data model.

Click: Home→Refresh→Refresh All.

You should now see a perfect star schema:

If you re-size the *Product* table, you will find that it now contains all of the information that was previously contained in the *Category* and *Supplier* tables (see sidebar).

While the data model could be used in its present form there are many fields that are of no interest to users (for example, most of the primary and foreign key fields).

You can also see that some of the field names do not conform to the naming conventions defined in: *Appendix A: Power Pivot Rules.*

Both of these issues will be dealt with in the next lesson.

8 Close the Power Pivot window.

9 Save your work as *Orders-2.*

Lesson 12-16: Hide, remove and rename data model columns

You have now created a good basic star schema from a relational database. In this lesson you'll refine the data model to make it more compact and easier to use.

1   Open *Orders-2* from your sample files folder.

2   Remove any columns from the data model that are not needed by your users.

Don't be tempted to bloat your data model by including columns just in case you might need them later. You know how easy it is to add and delete columns using Get & Transform should future requirements change.

When removing redundant columns, the most important table to consider is the fact table (the *Orders* table in this case). You need to particularly focus upon columns that contain unique values (such as dates) as power pivot will be unable to compress them (see: *Appendix A: Power Pivot Rules* for more information about making your tables file-compression friendly).

The sidebar shows the results of user feedback for this data model. Remove the columns that users have indicated are not required.

1.   Close the power pivot window if it is open.

2.   Click: Data→Get & Transform Data→Get Data→ Launch Power Query Editor…

3.   Select the *Orders* query from the left-hand *Queries* sidebar.

4.   Right-click on the *Required Date* column header.

5.   Select *Remove* from the shortcut menu.

6.   Do the same for the other fields in the *Orders* and *Product* tables that are listed in the sidebar.

3   Hide all primary and foreign key columns from your users.

Some columns are needed in the data model but are of no interest to users. For example, primary and foreign key columns are required to maintain relationships but of no interest for reporting purposes. These columns need to be hidden from end users.

1.   Click: Home→Close→Close & Load, to close the Get & Transform query editor and save your changes to the data model.

It may take some time for your updates to be applied.

2.   Open the Power Pivot window in data view.

3.   Click the *Customer* tab at the bottom of the Power Pivot window to view the contents of the Customer table.

4.   Right-click on the *CustomerID* column header.

---

important

Users have identified that the following columns are not required for reporting purposes

Orders Table

Required Date
Shipped Date

Product Table

Category.Description
QuantityPerUnit
Supplier.HomePage

Orders-2

important

Why not delete the OrdersID column?

It is normally best practice to remove the primary key from the fact table (in this model the Orders table is the fact table).

Normally the primary key is meaningless and is only used to create relationships between tables.

In this exceptional case the designer of the source database has broken normal design rules and used the *Order Number* as the primary key of the *Orders* table.

For this reason, the primary key column needs to be retained but renamed to a more descriptive name (*Order Number*).

5. Select *Hide from Client Tools* from the shortcut menu.

Notice that the column is grayed out when hidden.

6. Do the same for all primary and foreign key columns in the model except the *OrderID* in the *Orders* table (see sidebar). The primary and foreign keys can be identified as they all have a suffix of *ID*.

4 **Correct all column names so that they adhere to the naming convention defined in: *Appendix A: Power Pivot Rules.***

1. Close the power pivot window if it is open.

2. Click: Data→Get & Transform Data→Get Data→ Launch Power Query Editor…

3. For each query, where required, rename field names, or add spaces to existing field names to conform with the naming conventions defined in: *Appendix A: Power Pivot Rules.*

5 **View the schema in Power Pivot.**

1. Close Get & Transform and save your changes.

Click: Home→Close→Close & Load.

It may take some time for your changes to update.

2. Open the Power Pivot window in diagram view.

Your schema should now look like this:

6 **Close the Power Pivot window and save your work as *Orders-3*.**

note

It is possible to update the range of dates in a Calendar table manually

In this lesson Power Pivot added a self-updating calendar table. Power Pivot established a date range for the calendar by looking at every table in the data model that contained dates.

The *Employee* table contained an employee with a date of birth in 1952 so Power Pivot used this as a starting date.

You could make the Calendar table more compact in two ways:

1. Remove the *BirthDate* column from the *Employee* table (by editing the Get & Transform query) and refresh the data model.

The query would then update the data model, causing Power Pivot to scan the tables once again (but this time the earliest date found would be in 2017).

2. Manually adjust the start date of the calendar table. This can be done by selecting the date table tab and then clicking:

Design→Calendars→Date Table→Update Range.

Lesson 12-17: Add a calendar table to a data model

Most fact tables (in this model the fact table can be identified by its plural name: *Orders*) will contain transactional data that includes a date field.

Many reporting requirements will include the need to aggregate values by time dimensions (such as week, month, quarter and year).

While it would be possible to add calculated columns to the fact table, or to create these aggregations inside a pivot table, best OLAP practice is to add a *Calendar* dimension table to the data model.

The best-practice rule: *Use a calendar table for date dimensions* is included in: *Appendix A: Power Pivot Rules*.

You'll only fully appreciate the advantages of using a calendar table later, in: *Lesson 13-4: Understand Implicit and Explicit measures*.

Power Pivot automates the process of creating a calendar table

In earlier versions of Power Pivot you had to do a lot of work to add a calendar table to a data model. Fortunately, Power Pivot has recently added a feature that enables you to add a self-updating calendar table with a single click.

1 Open *Orders-3* from your sample files folder.

2 Open the Power Pivot window.

3 Create a calendar table.

Click: Design→Calendars→Date Table→New

A new table is created named *Calendar*.

4 Inspect the contents of the new Calendar table.

1. Click: Home→View→Data View.

2. Select the *Calendar* tab.

Date	Year	Month Number	Month	MMM-YYYY	Day Of Week Number	Day Of Week
1	1/1/1952 12:00:00 AM	1952	1	January	Jan-1952	3 Tuesday
2	1/2/1952 12:00:00 AM	1952	1	January	Jan-1952	4 Wednesday
3	1/3/1952 12:00:00 AM	1952	1	January	Jan-1952	5 Thursday
4	1/4/1952 12:00:00 AM	1952	1	January	Jan-1952	6 Friday

Notice that the calendar contains several columns. Each column except the primary key column (the primary key is the *Date* column) contains a formula rather than a value. This keeps the table very compact as Power Pivot is easily able to compress the table.

Notice that the table contains sequential rows of dates that include a date for every date value found in any column, and in any table of your data model. This is an outstanding feature as it means that you don't have to update the calendar table

Orders-3

What is a hierarchy?

When you create a calendar table (as you do in this lesson), Power Pivot creates a hierarchy for you.

This appears in an OLAP pivot table like this:

When you add the hierarchy field to a pivot table you can add the above three fields to a row or column with one click (instead of three).

Row Labels	▾
⊟1952	
⊟January	
1/1/1952	
1/2/1952	

You may think that the hierarchy is more confusing for users of the pivot table than it is worth. If you feel this way it is easily removed like this:

1. Open the data model in Diagram View.

2. Right-click on the *Date Hierarchy* column.

3. Click: *Delete* from the shortcut menu.

Creating a hierarchy is also very easy:

1. Open the data model in Diagram View.

2. Select the *Date, Year* and *Month* columns.

3. Right-click one of the selected fields and select: *Create Hierarchy* from the shortcut menu.

4. Right-click the hierarchy and select: *Rename* from the shortcut menu to give the hierarchy a meaningful name.

5. Click and drag the fields within the hierarchy to put them in the right order (*Year, Month, Date*).

when the model is refreshed (and new date rows may be needed).

The calendar begins in 1952 as this is the date of birth of the Vice President of Sales: Dr. Andres Fuller. It would be possible to adjust the date range manually to make the table more compact (see facing page sidebar).

You can add, delete or change any of the columns in the new Calendar table. There's also a *Set Default* option (Design→Calendars→Date Table→Set Default), to restore the table to its original form (if you have altered the columns and want to start again).

5 **Define a relationship between the *Calendar* table and the *Orders* table.**

1. The Calendar table's *Date* column is the Calendar table's primary key. You will need to relate this to the *Order Date* column in the fact (Orders) table.

2. Change the view to *Diagram* view.

Click: Home→View→Diagram View.

3. Drag the *Order Date* field from the *Orders* table and place it on top of the *Date* field in the *Calendar table*.

6 **Hide the Order Date field from users.**

Having two different date fields visible in pivot tables may be confusing for users.

1. Right-click on the *Order Date* field in the *Orders* table.

2. Select: *Hide from Client Tools* from the shortcut menu.

7 **View the schema.**

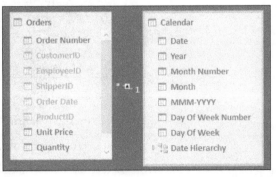

The calendar table's fields will now appear in the PivotTable fields list enabling values to be aggregated by many different time periods. Notice that Power Pivot has also created a *Date Hierarchy* for you (see sidebar).

The fields that are grayed out will not appear in the PivotTable

If a new time aggregation (such as quarter) was required, it would be a simple matter to add a new calculated column to the calendar table. You'll learn how to add calculated columns later, in: *Lesson 13-2: Add a DAX calculated column*.

8 **Close the Power Pivot window and save your work as *Orders-4*.**

Lesson 12-18: Format values in a data model

If you format values inside the data model, you'll never have to re-format when you use a column within a pivot table. This makes the data model easier to use by untrained users (who may not even know how to format a value in a pivot table).

Remember that the data model may be used by many pivot tables. By formatting once in the data model, you avoid formatting many times each time you add the value to a pivot table.

1   Open *Orders-4* from your sample files folder.

2   Open the Power Pivot window.

3   View the data model in Data View.

Click: Home→View→Data View.

4   Review the formatting of all values in the fact table.

The fact table in this model is the *Orders* table. You learned about fact and dimension tables in: *Lesson 12-12: Understand OLAP database design.*

If you have followed our naming convention detailed in: *Appendix A: Power Pivot Rules,* it is obvious that this must be the fact table as it is the only table named in the plural.

The fact table usually contains all of the numeric fields in a data model.

You can see that there are four value columns visible to users and that none of them have yet been correctly formatted:

Quantity	Discount	Order...	Unit Price	Order Number
30	0.05000000...	9/25/2017 12:..	10.4	10483
60	0.05000000...	10/3/2017 12:..	11.2	10492
20	0.05000000...	10/3/2017 12:..	11.2	10492

Format them as follows:

1.   Click on the *Quantity* column header.

2.   Click: Home→Formatting→Format.

3.   Select: *Whole Number* from the drop-down list.

4.   Format the other fields as follows:

Discount:	Percentage.
Unit Price:	Currency.
Order Number:	Whole number.

The columns now display correctly in Power Pivot and, more importantly, will display correctly when used within a pivot table:

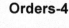

Orders-4

Quantity	Discount	Order ...	Unit Price	Order Number
30	5.00%	9/25/2017 12:...	$10.40	10483
60	5.00%	10/3/2017 12:...	$11.20	10492
20	5.00%	10/3/2017 12:...	$11.20	10492

5   Review the formatting of all values in the *Product* table.

The Product table is the only other table in this model that contains values.

You can see that there are four value columns and that none of them have yet been correctly formatted:

Unit Price	Units In Stock	Units On Order	Reorder Level
6	24	0	5
23.25	35	0	0
15.5	39	0	5
17.45	29	0	10

Format them as follows:

- **Unit Price:**   Currency.

- **Units In Stock:**   Whole Number.

- **Units On Order:**   Whole Number.

- **Reorder Level:**   Whole number.

The columns now display correctly:

Unit Price	Units In Stock	Units On Order	Reorder Level
$6.00	24	0	5
$23.25	35	0	0
$15.50	39	0	5
$17.45	29	0	10

6   Close the Power Pivot window.

7   Save your work as *Orders-5*.

Lesson 12-19: Understand MDX queries and OLAP pivot table limitations

How an OLAP pivot table obtains its data using MDX

The above diagram shows a data model that has been created from a relational database using Get & Transform and Power Pivot.

When the OLAP pivot table needs to get information from the data model, it requests the information using an MDX query.

The OLAP pivot table creates the MDX query and submits it to the data model. This is done individually with a new MDX query for every value displayed in the pivot table. Each requested value is then returned to the pivot table.

In: *Lesson 12-21: Convert CUBEVALUE functions to include MDX expressions*, you'll get a glimpse of some MDX code that has been created by an OLAP pivot table.

What is MDX?

MDX (Multi-Dimensional eXpressions) is the standard query language used to request data that resides in an OLAP database (a data model is an OLAP database).

History of MDX

MDX was invented by Microsoft and was used as the query language for Microsoft's first OLAP product in 1998.

Even though MDX is owned by Microsoft, it has become the standard OLAP query language and has been adopted by a wide range of OLAP

info

Increasing the default drill-down items in an OLAP pivot table

By default, data models only include 1,000 rows from the source data that was used to aggregate totals.

This is a sensible restriction as it reduces the size of the data model.

If there is a special need to drill-down to more than the default 1,000 rows of source data, you can increase this limit in the connection properties.

1. Click:

Data→
Queries & Connections→
Queries & Connections

The *Queries & Connections* task pane appears.

2. Select *Connections* at the top of the *Queries and Connections* task pane.

Queries & Connections

Queries | Connections

3. Right-click on the *ThisWorkbookDataModel* connection.

4. Select *Properties* from the shortcut menu.

5. Click on the *Usage* tab.

You are now able to select a maximum number of rows to store (for drill-through purposes) within the data model:

OLAP Drill Through

Maximum number of records to retrieve: 4500

Note that (because drill-through items are shown on an Excel worksheet) this is restricted to a maximum of 1,048,576 items.

vendors including Oracle Corporation, SAP, Cognos and Business Objects.

You don't need to learn MDX to use OLAP pivot tables

Hand-crafting an MDX query is not an Excel skill. You don't have to know anything about the MDX query language to work with Excel's data model and OLAP pivot tables.

Some dedicated MDX books stretch to over 700 pages so, of course, this book will not attempt to teach you how to hand-craft an MDX query.

OLAP pivot table limitations

Because OLAP pivot tables can only retrieve data from an OLAP database (the data model is an OLAP database) using MDX, there are some features found in regular pivot tables that are not used in OLAP pivot tables

Here are some regular pivot table features that are not supported in OLAP pivot tables:

Show Report Filter Pages is not supported: The *Show Report Filter Pages* feature discussed in: *Lesson 9-10: Use report filter fields to automatically create multiple pages* cannot be used with OLAP pivot tables.

Drill-down is restricted (by default) to 1,000 items: In regular pivot tables you can double-click any pivot table aggregated value to "drill down" to the data source items that were used to calculate the value. When you drill down, Excel creates a new worksheet that contains every row of source data used for the aggregation (without restricting the number of rows available).

OLAP pivot tables (that are often used to analyze big data containing millions, or even billions of rows) could potentially be enormous if unlimited drill-down data was included. For this reason, drill down is limited (by default) to 1,000 rows. It is possible to manually increase this limit (see sidebar).

Calculated Fields and Calculated Items are not needed: You learned how to use these features in regular pivot tables in: *Lesson 9-16: Add a calculated field to a pivot table* and *Lesson 9-17: Add a calculated item to a pivot table*.

These features are not needed in OLAP pivot tables because any calculated fields that may be required should already exist in the data model (removing the need for the Pivot Table to calculate them).

You already know how to add calculated columns using Get & Transform so that calculated columns are added before data is exported to the data model. This is best practice.

Later, after you have completed: *Session Thirteen: An introduction to DAX,* you'll discover that DAX also enables the addition of *calculated columns* to the data model. While you can do this, it is better practice to add calculated columns using Get & Transform (for the reasons explained in: *Appendix A: Power Pivot Rules*).

note

Why does the CUBEVALUE function have the prefix CUBE?

It is common to teach and visualize OLAP concepts in the context of an imaginary three-dimensional *OLAP Cube.*

The imaginary cube is a little like a Rubik's cube but contains a set of aggregated values in each cell.

OLAP concepts are taught in the context of *Slicing, Dicing* and *Rotating* (Pivoting) the cube of data.

MDX queries (created by the CUBE functions) retrieve aggregated totals from specified cells (intersections of three values) from a cube of data.

Lesson 12-20: Use the CUBEVALUE function to query a data model

In: *Lesson 9-23: Use the GETPIVOTDATA function,* you discovered a way to reference data that is visible on the screen within a pivot table.

If you've completely understood this session so far, you'll now realize that an OLAP pivot table is simply a visual and user-friendly way to display, format and present the values stored in a data model.

The CUBEVALUE function enables you to obtain values directly from the data model without a pivot table. This opens up many new possibilities when presenting and formatting data.

1   Open *Stock List-4* from your sample files folder (if it isn't already open).

This workbook contains the pivot table that you created from a data model in: *Lesson 12-6: Use an OLAP pivot table to analyze data residing in a data model.*

	B	C
3	Row Labels	Sum of UnitsInStock
4	Beverages	559
5	Condiments	507
6	Confections	386
7	Dairy Products	393
8	Grains/Cereals	308
9	Meat/Poultry	165
10	Produce	100
11	Seafood	701
12	Grand Total	3119

2   Attempt to insert a column or row within the pivot table.

Notice that (as with all pivot tables) this isn't possible.

When you attempt to insert a row or column, a warning dialog is shown:

Microsoft Excel   ×

⚠ We can't make this change for the selected cells because it will affect a PivotTable. Use the field list to change the report. If you are trying to insert or delete cells, move the PivotTable and try again.

OK

3   Convert the pivot table into a set of CUBEVALUE functions.

1.   Click inside the pivot table to activate it.

2.   Click:

PivotTable Analyze→Calculations→
OLAP Tools→Convert to Formulas

(This option is grayed out when working with regular pivot tables).

Notice that the OLAP pivot table no longer exists but the data previously displayed remains:

note

The GETPIVOTDATA function is also supported by OLAP pivot tables

In: *Lesson 9-23: Use the GETPIVOTDATA function,* you learned how to use the GETPIVOTDATA function to access values in a regular pivot table from outside the pivot table.

The GETPIVOTDATA function can only be used to reference values *that are visible in a pivot table*.

This can be a huge problem, as a user may change the fields displayed in a pivot table, causing functions that use the GETPIVOTDATA function to fail.

If there were a function that directly accessed data from the *pivot table data cache* (that regular pivot tables use instead of the data model) this problem would be overcome.

Unfortunately, there is no way to do this in a regular pivot table.

The CUBEVALUE function has none of these problems as data is accessed directly from the data model without any interaction with a pivot table.

OLAP pivot tables still support the GETPIVOTDATA function but you'll probably prefer to use CUBEVALUE functions in their place when working with data that originates in a data model.

	B	C
3	Row Labels	Sum of UnitsInStock
4	Beverages	559
5	Condiments	507
6	Confections	386
7	Dairy Products	393
8	Grains/Cereals	308
9	Meat/Poultry	165
10	Produce	100
11	Seafood	701
12	Grand Total	3119

Each value is now directly accessed from the data model using CUBEVALUE functions.

4 **Examine the CUBEVALUE function for the *Sum of UnitsInStock* column in the *Beverages* category.**

1. Click once in cell C4.

2. Look at the function displayed in the formula bar:

```
=CUBEVALUE("ThisWorkbookDataModel",$B4,C$3)
```

The first argument identifies the name of the connection to the data model. In this case it is the data model that you defined in: *Lesson 12-3: Add tables to a data model* and *Lesson 12-5: Add a relationship to a data model using Power Pivot.*

The last two arguments are MDX expressions. You learned about the MDX query language in: *Lesson 12-19: Understand MDX queries and OLAP pivot table limitations.*

3. Click on cell B4 and C3 to see how the MDX expressions have been created. With your understanding of data models, you should be able to broadly understand how the references work.

You have used an OLAP pivot table to automatically create the MDX code for you. This technique allows you to create CUBEVALUE functions without any understanding of the MDX language.

5 **Insert a column before column C and a row before row 5.**

	B	C	D
1			
2			
3	Row Labels		Sum of UnitsInStock
4	Beverages		559
5			
6	Condiments		507
7	Confections		386

There is now no barrier to inserting rows and columns, as each cell contains a normal function.

You can also format the values in any way you wish.

6 **Save your work as *Stock List-5.***

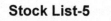

Stock List-5

Lesson 12-21: Convert CUBEVALUE functions to include MDX expressions

At the moment the CUBEVALUE functions (created in: *Lesson 12-20: Use the CUBEVALUE function to query a data model*) are not very transportable.

The CUBEVALUE functions reference MDX code contained in other cells. This creates two potential problems:

1. If you copy and paste a function to a different worksheet, the references to the MDX expressions may be adjusted to point to incorrect cells.

2. If the cells containing the MDX functions are deleted, the functions will fail.

The functions will be far more robust if they contain the actual MDX expressions rather than references to cells containing the MDX expressions.

1 Open *Stock List-5* from your sample files folder (if it isn't already open).

This workbook contains the CUBEVALUE functions that you created automatically from an OLAP pivot table in: *Lesson 12-20: Use the CUBEVALUE function to query a data model.*

	B	C	D
3	Row Labels		Sum of UnitsInStock
4	Beverages		559
5			
6	Condiments		507
7	Confections		386
8	Dairy Products		393
9	Grains/Cereals		308
10	Meat/Poultry		165
11	Produce		100
12	Seafood		701
13	Grand Total		3119
14			

2 Convert the formula in cell D4 so that it contains no cell references.

1. Click in cell D4.

2. Look at the formula in the formula bar:

```
=CUBEVALUE("ThisWorkbookDataModel",$B4,D$3)
```

You can see that MDX expressions in cells B4 and D3 are being referenced.

3. Click in cell B4.

Look at the formula in the formula bar.

You can see that this cell is using the CUBEMEMBER function to access the data model:

fx | =CUBEMEMBER("ThisWorkbookDataModel","[Category].[CategoryName].&[Beverages]")

4. Select and copy all of the contents of the formula bar after the = sign.

5. Press the **<Escape>** key.

6. Click in cell D4.

7. Click the *Insert Function* button on the left of the formula bar.

   [fx]

   The *Function Arguments* dialog is displayed.

Connection	'ThisWorkbookDataModel'	⬆
Member_expression1	$B4	⬆
Member_expression2	D$3	⬆

8. Click in the *Member_expression1* text box and delete the current contents.

9. Paste the CUBEMEMBER function into the text box.

Connection	'ThisWorkbookDataModel'	⬆
Member_expression1	CUBEMEMBER('ThisWorkbookD	⬆
Member_expression2	D$3	⬆

10. Press the **<Enter>** key.

11. Use a similar technique to copy the formula behind cell D3 into the *Member_expression2* box.

Connection	'ThisWorkbookDataModel'	⬆
Member_expression1	CUBEMEMBER('ThisWorkbookD	⬆
Member_expression2	CUBEMEMBER('ThisWorkbookD	⬆

12. Click the *OK* button.

    The formula in cell D4 now directly references the data model without any references to other cells in the workbook.

3   Copy the formula in cell D4 to any other cell on any other worksheet in the workbook.

    You can see that you can now show the *Sum of UnitsInStock* for the *Beverages* category absolutely anywhere in the workbook.

    The value will update if any referenced value in a table within the data model changes.

4   On the *Product* worksheet, change the *UnitsInStock* value for any product in the *Beverages* category.

5   Refresh the data model.

    Click: Data→Queries & Connections→Refresh All.

    Notice that both cells showing *Sum of UnitsInStock* for the *Beverages* category have now updated.

6   Save your work as *Stock List-6*.

note

You could achieve a similar result by using CUBEVALUE functions

In: *Lesson 12-20: Use the CUBEVALUE function to query a data model*, you discovered how to obtain values directly from a data model. It would be easy to reproduce the solution described in this lesson using this technique. To do this you would proceed as follows:

1. Open *Americas and Europe-1* from your sample files folder.

2. Enable external data connections if necessary.

3. Click inside the pivot table to activate it.

4. Click:

PivotTable Analyze→
Calculations→
OLAP Tools→
Convert to Formulas

5. Delete rows 6, 9, 11, 13, 15, 16 and 17.

6. Delete the values in cells B4 and B9.

The worksheet would then look like this:

	A	B
3	Row Labels	Sum of InvoicePrice
4	2011	
5	Austria	70600.68
6	France	35654.88
7	Germany	109595.61
8	USA	130834.27
9	2012	
10	Brazil	41941
11	USA	114845.12
12	Venezuela	26404.77

To refresh the values displayed by the CUBEVALUE functions, click:

Data→Queries & Connections→
Refresh All

Americas and Europe-1

Lesson 12-22: Create an asymmetric OLAP pivot table using Named Sets

OLAP pivot tables have an interesting feature that is not available in regular pivot tables: the ability to create *Named Sets*. Named Sets are a little like filters in that they allow you to hide specific rows or columns from your pivot table. You can also implement named sets using CUBEVALUE functions (see sidebar) and many users may find this easier than using the Named Sets feature demonstrated in this lesson.

The sample file for this lesson contains a data model consisting of an *Invoice* table with over 1,400 rows and a related *Category* table.

The invoice table lists sales to all customers in 2011 and 2012. It is easy to generate a pivot table showing annual sales for each year by country like this:

	A	B
3	Row Labels ▾	Sum of InvoicePrice
4	2011	475,836.30
5	Austria	70,600.68
6	Brazil	66,848.42
7	France	35,654.88
8	Germany	109,595.61
9	UK	31,897.11
10	USA	130,834.27
11	Venezuela	30,405.33
12	2012	430,332.72
13	Austria	57,402.38
14	Brazil	41,941.00
15	France	45,263.40
16	Germany	117,402.02
17	UK	27,074.03
18	USA	114,845.12
19	Venezuela	26,404.77

But imagine that management have requested a different report. They want to see sales to Europe (Austria, France, Germany and the UK) for 2011 followed by sales to the Americas (Brazil, USA and Venezuela) for 2012.

Here's the report they want:

	A	B
3	Row Labels	Sum of InvoicePrice
4	2011	
5	Austria	70,600.68
6	France	35,654.88
7	Germany	109,595.61
8	UK	31,897.11
9	2012	
10	Brazil	41,941.00
11	USA	114,845.12
12	Venezuela	26,404.77

You couldn't do this with a regular pivot table as regular pivot tables are always *symmetric*.

note

Named sets and MDX

As you know from: *Lesson 12-19: Understand MDX queries and OLAP pivot table limitations,* OLAP pivot tables use MDX to retrieve data from the data model.

Microsoft have designed their *named sets* feature to enable users to create and use named sets without needing to know anything about the MDX language.

Users who understand the MDX query language are able to create hand-crafted custom MDX code.

Click the *Edit MDX...* button on the *New Set* dialog to view (and even edit) the MDX code that the dialog has automatically generated.

With an in-depth understanding of MDX it is possible to implement more advanced requirements (such as adding subtotals by named set).

See also facing page sidebar for a more versatile solution using CUBEVALUE functions.

	A	B
3	Row Labels	Sum of InvoicePrice
4	2011	
5	Austria	70,600.68
6	France	35,654.88
7	Germany	109,595.61
8	UK	31,897.11
9	2012	
10	Brazil	41,941.00
11	USA	114,845.12
12	Venezuela	26,404.77

If you showed European sales for 2011 you'd also have to display European sales for 2012. The OLAP pivot table in the above screen grab is *asymmetric.* It displays just what you specify using *Named Sets.*

1 **Open *Americas and Europe-1* from your sample files folder.**

2 **Enable external data connections if necessary.**

You may see a security warning advising that external data connections have been disabled:

> ⚠ SECURITY WARNING External Data Connections have been disabled   Enable Content

Excel regards all OLAP data sources as external databases.

Click the *Enable Content* button to allow the OLAP pivot table in this worksheet to access the data.

This workbook contains two tables: An *Invoice* table and a related *Category* table. A data model has been created from these related tables and then used to create an OLAP pivot table summarizing sales by year and by country.

3 **Create a named set to show sales for Europe in 2011 and for the Americas in 2012.**

1. Click anywhere within the pivot table (in the *Pivot Table* worksheet).

2. Click: PivotTable Analyze→Calculations→
   Fields, Items & Sets→Create Set Based on Row Items...

   The *New Set* dialog appears.

   You can see all countries that have sales in 2011 and 2012. It is possible to delete rows by selecting them and then clicking the *Delete Row* button.

3. Type the set name: **Americas and Europe** into the *Set Name* box.

4. Remove the 2011 *Americas* country rows (*Brazil, USA* and *Venezuela*).

5. Remove the 2012 *European* country rows (*Austria, France, Germany* and *UK*).

6. Remove the two rows that have *All* shown for the *Country.*

   These are the rows that listed total sales for each year. As you have removed some countries from each year, the totals will no longer show the correct value.

   In order to add subtotals for each named set you would need an advanced understanding of the MDX query language (see sidebar). You could also do this more easily using the CUBEVALUE method (see sidebar facing page).

7. Click the *OK* button.

   The OLAP pivot table now lists European sales for 2011 and Americas sales for 2012.

4 **Save your work as *Americas and Europe-2.***

Session 12: Exercise

1 Open *Film Sales-1* from your sample files folder.

This contains five tables detailing sales from a DVD film wholesaler.

2 Use Get & Transform and Power Pivot to create a snowflake data model containing all of the tables and relationships defined in the schema shown below.

3 Add a *Calendar* table to the data model and create a relationship between the *Calendar* table and *Invoice* table.

4 Within the data model, format the *Invoice* Table's *Total* field as *Currency.*

5 Create an OLAP pivot table (in a new worksheet) from the data model.

6 Use the OLAP pivot table to report each customer's *Total* purchase value by *Genre.*

	B	C	D
2	Sum of Total	Column Labels ▾	
3	Row Labels ▾	Action	Adventure
4	Addison-Freelander Screen Agency	$2,961.43	$1,051.02
5	AV Supplies	$3,044.27	$438.40

7 Use the OLAP pivot table to report the total cash value of goods (*Sum of Total*) sold by each *Employee* during each *Month* and *Year.*

	B	C	D	E	F	G	H
2	Sum of Total	Column Labels ▾					
3		⊟2012			⊟2013		
4	Row Labels ▾	October	November	December	January	February	March
5	Anderson,Jane		$1,525.91	$25.42	$495.10	$395.53	$1,758.64
6	Armstrong,Dan	$590.41	$1,246.73	$689.67	$244.03	$182.02	$1,288.36
7	Ashe,Lucille	$675.38	$281.54	$624.23	$643.08	$385.10	$298.94

8 Save your work as *Film Sales-2.*

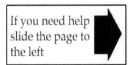

If you need help slide the page to the left

Film Sales-1

Session 12: Exercise Answers

These are the three questions that students find the most difficult to answer:

Q 7	Q 6	Q 2
1. Add the following fields to the pivot table:	Make sure that you drag down fields from the data model tables (and not from the tables that are also shown in the PivotTable Fields list).	1. Click inside the *Invoice* table (located on the *Invoice* worksheet):
		2. Click: Data→ Get & Transform Data→ From Table/Range.
Rows EmployeeNa... ▼	Data model tables have a small orange icon in their bottom-right corner.	This was covered in: *Lesson 12-3: Add tables to a data model.* The Power Query editor opens.
Columns Year ▼ Month ▼	▷ ⊞ Customer	3. Click: Home→ Close→ Close & Load→ Close & Load To…
Σ *Values* Sum of Total ▼	Set up the pivot table like this:	The *Import Data* dialog appears.
	Filters *Columns* GenreName ▼	4. Select the following options:
Note that the *Year* and *Month* fields are added from the *Calendar* table.	*Rows* Σ *Values* CustomerNa... ▼ Sum of Total ▼	◉ Only Create Connection Where do you want to put the data? ○ Existing worksheet =$B$2 ● New worksheet ☑ Add this data to the Data Model
This was covered in: *Lesson 12-6: Use an OLAP pivot table to analyze data residing in a data model.*	This was covered in: *Lesson 12-6: Use an OLAP pivot table to analyze data residing in a data model.*	5. Do the same for the other four tables.
		6. Click: Power Pivot→ Data Model→Manage.
		7. Inside the Power Pivot window click: Home→View→Diagram View
		8. Define the relationships by dragging each primary key across to the corresponding foreign key.
		This was covered in:
		Lesson 12-5: Add a relationship to a data model using Power Pivot.

If you have difficulty with the other questions, here are the lessons that cover the relevant skills:

3   Refer to: *Lesson 12-17: Add a calendar table to a data model.*

4   Refer to: *Lesson 12-18: Format values in a data model.*

5   Refer to: *Lesson 12-6: Use an OLAP pivot table to analyze data residing in a data model.*

13

Session Thirteen: An introduction to DAX

> You can't build a great building on a weak foundation. You must have a solid foundation if you're going to have a strong superstructure.
>
> *Gordon B. Hinckley (1910-2008)*
> *American religious leader and author*

In: *Lesson 11-1: Understand Get & Transform and ETL* and *Session Twelve: Power Pivot, Data Modeling, OLAP and Business Intelligence* you learned how to create an efficient star schema data model.

The data model that you created can already support most reporting requirements (when used as the data source for an OLAP pivot table or chart), but you may encounter some reporting requirements that cannot be satisfied. In these cases, the DAX language will enable you to further refine the data model by adding *DAX calculated measures*.

The DAX language has over 200 functions and there are 500-page books published that are entirely devoted to the subject of DAX. The purpose of this session is to provide you with a solid grounding in key DAX concepts and to cover a few of the most widely used DAX functions.

In this session you'll create DAX measures that conform to the best-practice rules defined in: *Appendix A: Power Pivot Rules.* This will provide you with a solid foundation for future learning, enabling you to explore DAX in greater depth, when you apply your data modeling and DAX skills to solve real-world reporting problems.

Session Objectives

By the end of this session you will be able to:

- Understand the Power Pivot window
- Add a DAX calculated column
- Create a DAX calculated measure
- Understand Implicit and Explicit measures
- Understand row and filter context
- Create a calculated measure using the measure dialog
- Use a DAX DISTINCTCOUNT function
- Create a Key Performance Indicator
- Use a DAX CALCULATE function
- Use a DAX measure to calculate year-on-year growth
- Use a DAX ALL function

Lesson 13-1: Understand the Power Pivot window

1   Open *Orders-5* from your sample files folder.

This workbook contains a copy of the data model that you created in: *Session Twelve: Power Pivot, Data Modeling, OLAP and Business Intelligence.*

2   Click the Enable Content button if prompted to do so.

ⓘ SECURITY WARNING External Data Connections have been disabled	Enable Content

Excel regards all OLAP data sources as external databases. Click the *Enable Content* button to allow the queries in this worksheet to access the data.

3   Open Power Pivot in data view.

You learned how to do this in: *Lesson 12-2: Install the Power Pivot add-in.*

4   Make sure that the Calculation Area is enabled.

If the calculation area is not visible (the area at the bottom of the window), click:

Home→View→Calculation Area

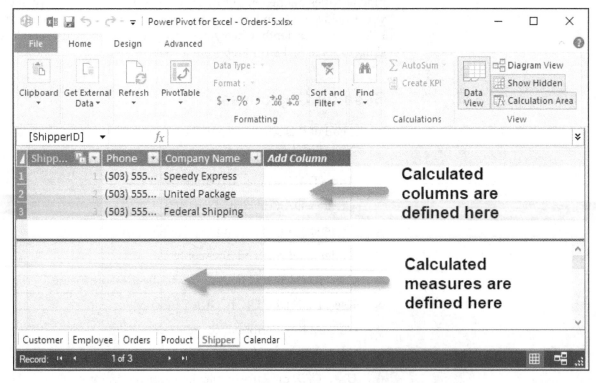

Power Pivot supports two very different types of calculated fields

Power Pivot enables you to create two different types of calculated fields: *Calculated Columns* and *Calculated Measures.*

Orders-5

Calculated Columns

In the screen grab on the previous page you can see can see that Calculated Columns are defined in the column headed *Add Column* within the Power Pivot data view window.

Calculated Columns are very easy to understand as they are very similar to the calculated fields that you created in: *Lesson 9-16: Add a calculated field to a pivot table.* You'll create a calculated column later, in: *Lesson 13-2: Add a DAX calculated column.*

Calculated Measures

In the facing page screen grab you can see can see that calculated measures are defined in the area beneath the table called the *Calculation Area.*

Calculated measures contain aggregations of data contained in one or more table columns.

Calculated measures are one of Power Pivot's most important features. Very complex business analysis scenarios can be delivered using a well-designed data model containing DAX calculated measures.

You'll create your first calculated measure later, in *Lesson 13-3: Create a DAX calculated measure.*

5   Keep the workbook open for the next lesson.

Lesson 13-2: Add a DAX calculated column

DAX enables you to create two different types of calculated fields: *Calculated Columns* and *Calculated Measures.*

In this lesson you'll create a *Calculated Column.* This is the simpler of the two types of DAX formula.

1   Open *Orders-5* from your sample files folder.

This workbook contains a copy of the data model that you created in: *Session Twelve: Power Pivot, Data Modeling, OLAP and Business Intelligence.*

2   Open the data model using Power Pivot.

Click: Power Pivot→Data Model→Manage.

3   Make sure that you are viewing the model in Data View.

Click: Home→View→Data View.

4   Add a calculated column to the *Orders* table that will show the *Order Value.*

Third normal form (3NF) is a set of rules that must be followed when designing OLTP databases. You learned about the difference between OLTP and OLAP databases in: *Lesson 12-11: Understand OLTP database design.*

One important 3NF rule is that a table cannot contain a value that can be calculated from other columns in the table. In the case of the *Orders* table, the order value can be calculated from other columns using this formula:

Order Value = Quantity * Unit Price * (1-Discount)

The final multiplication of (1-Discount) is needed because the discount values in the table are percentages. A 10% discount would have a value of 0.1.

If a 10% discount value is subtracted from 1 the result is 0.9. Multiplying by 0.9 will return 90% of the value (a discount of 10%).

Because this is an OLAP database it is perfectly correct (and desirable) to have calculated columns.

1.   Select the *Orders* table tab.

2.   Click anywhere in the rightmost column with the header *Add Column.*

3.   Press the <=> key to begin the formula (your keypresses will appear in the formula bar and not the column) .

4.   Click once anywhere in the *Quantity* column.

5.   Press the multiplication <*> key.

6.   Click once anywhere in the *Unit Price* column.

7.   The formula bar now contains this DAX formula:

Orders-5

f_x =Orders[Quantity]*Orders[Unit Price]

8. Add the following to the DAX formula:

f_x =Orders[Quantity]*Orders[Unit Price]*(1-

9. Click anywhere in the *Discount* column.

10. Finish the formula with a closing bracket.

The DAX formula should now look like this:

f_x =Orders[Quantity]*Orders[Unit Price]*(1-Orders[Discount])

11. Press the **<Enter>** key.

After a short time, all of the calculated values are displayed.

Unit Price	Order Number	Calculated Column 1
$36.80	10294	552
$27.20	10294	571.2
$6.20	10294	37.2

Notice that Power Pivot calculated columns are shaded differently to regular columns.

5 Change the name of the new calculated column to: **Order Value**

Double-click in the column header and type the new name: **Order Value**

6 Format the new calculated column as *Currency.*

1. Click anywhere in the *Order Value* column.

2. Click: Home→Formatting→Format→Currency.

The calculated column should now look like this:

Quantity	Discount	Order ...	Unit Price	Order Number	Order Value
10	0.00%	1/9/2017 12:0...	$7.70	10250	$77.00
40	0.00%	1/10/2017 12:...	$27.20	10252	$1,088.00
20	0.00%	1/20/2017 12:...	$8.00	10261	$160.00

There is some debate amongst Power Pivot professionals regarding whether it is better to create a calculated column using *Get & Transform* or as a Power Pivot calculated column.

My own preference would be to create calculated columns as close to the source data as possible. For this reason, I would tend to do this using Get & Transform (though you could argue that it doesn't really matter).

The *Order Value* calculated column will now be available to your users in any OLAP pivot table that uses this data model.

7 Close the Power Pivot window.

8 Save your work as *Orders-6.*

Lesson 13-3: Create a DAX calculated measure

In: *Lesson 13-2: Add a DAX calculated column* you added a calculated column to a data model.

Calculated columns are very easy to understand as each cell only references values that are in the same row. Calculated measures are more difficult to understand as they contain aggregations of data contained in one or more table columns.

In this lesson you'll create your first calculated measure.

1 Open *Orders-6* from your sample files folder.

2 Open the Power Pivot window.

3 Make sure you have *Data View* enabled.

Click: Home→View→Data View.

4 Select the *Orders* table (if it isn't already selected).

5 Use AutoSum to create a *Sum of Order Value* calculated measure.

Notice that the Power Pivot window is split into two panes. The lower pane is called the *Calculation Area.*

Calculated measures are created in the calculation area.

1. Click in the calculation area in the first cell underneath the *OrderValue* column (see facing page sidebar if this area is not visible).

2. Click: Home→Calculations→AutoSum. Σ AutoSum ▾

A calculated measure called *Sum of Order Value* is created.

[Order Value] ▾	f_x	Sum of Order Value:=SUM([Order Value])					⊻
Quantity	Discount	Order Number	Order ...	Unit Pri...	Order Value	Add Column	
10	0.00%	10250	1/9/2017 12:0...	$7.70	$77.00		
40	0.00%	10252	1/10/2017 12:...	$27.20	$1,088.00		
20	0.00%	10261	1/20/2017 12:...	$8.00	$160.00	DAX formula	
20	0.00%	10261	1/20/2017 12:...	$14.40	$288.00		
18	0.00%	10294	3/3/2017 12:0...	$14.40	$259.20		
15	0.00%	10294	3/3/2017 12:0...	$31.20	$468.00		

Calculation Area   **Calculated Measure** → Sum of Order Value: $1,467,199.39

Customer | Employee | Orders | Product | Shipper | Calendar

Notice the syntax of the DAX formula shown in the formula bar:

Sum of Order Value:=SUM([Order Value])

When you define a calculated measure, you begin with the measure name (in this case: **Sum of Order Value**), you then add a colon followed by an equals sign (:=) before creating the DAX formula: **SUM([Order Value])**.

Orders-6

note

If you don't see the calculation area

The calculation area is visible by default but can be toggled on and off.

If the calculation area is not visible on your computer click:

Home→View→
Calculation Area

… to bring it back.

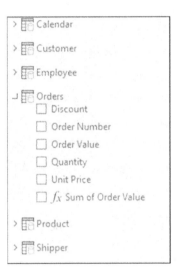

> ⊞ Calendar

> ⊞ Customer

> ⊞ Employee

⌐ ⊞ Orders
   ☐ Discount
   ☐ Order Number
   ☐ Order Value
   ☐ Quantity
   ☐ Unit Price
   ☐ *fx* Sum of Order Value

> ⊞ Product

> ⊞ Shipper

6 **Correct the calculated measure formula to conform with naming convention rules.**

AutoSum has done a good job in creating the DAX calculated measure. Unfortunately, AutoSum hasn't read this book so it doesn't know our naming convention rules.

One of the naming convention rules in: *Appendix A: Power Pivot Rules* is:

Include the table name when you reference a column.

There are two reasons for this rule:

- It is perfectly correct (in database design) to have the same field name in two different tables. By prefixing column names with table names, you will ensure that Power Pivot is always referencing the correct field.

- Because DAX formulas can include references to other measures, it can be difficult to identify which parts of a formula are column references and which are measure references. If you include the table name when you reference a column and do not include the table name when referencing a measure, it is always clear (when auditing a formula) where the values are coming from.

Edit the formula (in the formula bar) so that it reads as follows:

Sum of Order Value:=SUM(Orders[Order Value])

If a pivot table is created that references this data model, the calculated measure will appear in the PivotTable fields list in exactly the same way as the other fields (see sidebar).

Notice that the *Sum of Order Value* field (in the sidebar) is prefixed with *fx* to identify it as a calculated measure.

☐ *fx* Sum of Order Value

You may wonder why you would bother creating this calculated measure. You can, after all, sum the *Order Value* field in a pivot table simply by dragging it into the *Values* window.

The reason that calculated measures are better practice than simple pivot table aggregations will only be become clear later, in: *Lesson 13-4: Understand Implicit* and *Explicit measures.*

7 **Rename the calculated measure from *Sum of Order Value* to: CM – Sum of Order Value**

Edit the formula (in the formula bar) so that it reads as follows:

CM - Sum of Order Value:=SUM(Orders[Order Value])

You wouldn't normally rename the measure in this way. *Sum of Order Value* is a really great name for this field as users will instantly understand the value that the field is returning. The new name is being used only for the purpose of clarity in the next lesson: *Lesson 13-4: Understand Implicit and Explicit measures.*

8 **Close the Power Pivot window.**

9 **Save your work as *Orders-7*.**

Lesson 13-4: Understand Implicit and Explicit measures

1 Open *Orders-7* from your sample files folder.

2 Open the Power Pivot window.

3 Create a new OLAP pivot table in a new worksheet using the data model.

    1. Click: Home→Pivot Table.

    2. Click the OK button.

4 Name the new OLAP pivot table's worksheet tab: **Implicit and Explicit Measures**

5 Delete the *Sheet1* worksheet.

6 Use the OLAP pivot table to show *Sum of Order Value* by *Category Name* using the *CM - Sum of Order Value* calculated measure in the *Orders* table.

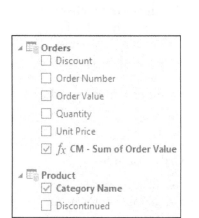

Rows	Σ Values
Category Name ▼	CM - Sum of Order Value ▼

Row Labels ▼	CM - Sum of Order Value
Beverages	$317,055.20
Condiments	$122,372.68
Confections	$186,880.13
Dairy Products	$273,542.81
Grains/Cereals	$105,933.41
Meat/Poultry	$191,412.40
Produce	$123,686.33
Seafood	$146,316.42
Grand Total	**$1,467,199.39**

7 Drag the *Order Value* field from the *Orders* table to the pivot table's *Values* pane.

Rows	Σ Values
Category Name ▼	CM - Sum of Order Value ▼
	Sum of Order Value ▼

Both the *CM - Sum of Order Value calculated measure* and the *Sum of Order Value measure* are returning exactly the same values.

Row Labels ▼	CM - Sum of Order Value	Sum of Order Value
Beverages	$317,055.20	$317,055.20
Condiments	$122,372.68	$122,372.68
Confections	$186,880.13	$186,880.13
Dairy Products	$273,542.81	$273,542.81
Grains/Cereals	$105,933.41	$105,933.41
Meat/Poultry	$191,412.40	$191,412.40
Produce	$123,686.33	$123,686.33
Seafood	$146,316.42	$146,316.42
Grand Total	**$1,467,199.39**	**$1,467,199.39**

It is important to appreciate the difference between them.

Orders-7

note

You cannot apply further aggregations to explicit measures

1. Click on *the CM – Sum of Order Value calculated measure* (in the Pivot Table's *Values* box).

2. Click *Value Field Settings…* on the pop-up menu.

3. Click the *Summarize Values By* tab.

Notice that the summation methods (for this explicit measure) are all disabled:

4. Now do the same thing for the *Sum of Order Value* measure.

Notice that the summation methods (for this implicit measure) are all enabled:

Summarize value field by
Choose the type of calcula
data from the selected fiel

Sum
Count
Average
Max
Min
StdDev

This is exactly what you would expect. Because the explicit measure only returned eight values to the pivot table it is not possible for the pivot table to apply any other summation method to the measure.

If your users needed several summation methods, you would need to provide several calculated measures in the data model.

The values returned by the *CM - Sum of Order Value calculated measure* column were explicitly calculated by Power Pivot before they were sent to the pivot table. This type of measure is called an *Explicit Measure.* This meant that only eight values had to be sent from the Power Pivot engine to Excel.

The regular *Order Value* PivotTable field returned 2,448 values from the Power Pivot engine to Excel. Excel's Pivot Table then calculated the *Sum of Order Value measure* by adding these values together. This type of measure is called an *Implicit Measure.*

8 Understand the advantages of using explicit measures.

- **Explicit measures calculate much faster than implicit measures:**

    Implicit measure values are calculated by the pivot table's own formula engine. Power Pivot explicit measures use Microsoft's *xVelocity in-memory analysis engine*. This engine can scan billions of data rows per second and can produce reports in a tiny fraction of the time needed by the Excel pivot table.

    Power Pivot's xVelocity engine produces extremely fast (often perceived as instant) results even when dealing with data sets containing many millions of rows.

- **Explicit measures are more sophisticated than implicit measures:**

    Implicit measures in the *Values* pane are aggregated using one of the pivot table's ten aggregation methods such as *Sum, Count* and *Average*. Sometimes your aggregation needs may go beyond what is possible using the pivot table's ten simple aggregation methods.

    Explicit measures are far more sophisticated than implicit measures as they can implement complex business logic using DAX functions.

- **Explicit measures are re-usable:**

    Explicit measures are defined within the data model. A single data model can be used by many pivot tables. Implicit measures are defined within (and can only be used by) one pivot table.

    For these reasons, it is best practice to always use explicit measures in your work.

    The best-practice rule:

    Always use explicit measures rather than implicit measures.

    … is included in: *Appendix A: Power Pivot Rules.*

9 Save your work as *Orders-8*.

note

You wouldn't normally use a DAX aggregation function in a calculated column

In this lesson you discovered a key difference between DAX aggregation functions and their Excel namesakes. You used a DAX SUM aggregation function and found that it behaved differently to an Excel SUM function.

DAX aggregation functions always apply to an entire table column (they do not recognize the concept of a traditional Excel range).

For this reason, you would not normally use a DAX aggregation function (one whose Excel equivalent uses a range of cells as an argument) in a calculated column.

Non-aggregation functions (functions that require single cell arguments) work well in calculated columns.

For example, you'll find the LEFT, RIGHT and MID string manipulation functions and IF logical function useful in calculated columns. You'll find that these functions have the same syntax (and work in the same way) as their Excel equivalents.

Some DAX functions (such as CALCULATE and ALL) have no Excel equivalent. You'll learn how to use some of these functions later in this session.

Lesson 13-5: Understand row and filter context

When working with classic Excel data analysis you don't have to consider the issue of context.

When working with a data model and an associated OLAP pivot table an understanding of context (sometimes called *Evaluation Context*) is essential.

1 **Open *Orders-8* from your sample files folder.**

2 **Open the Power Pivot window.**

3 **Make sure you have *Data View* enabled.**

   Click: Home→View→Data View.

4 **Select the *Orders* table.**

   This table contains a calculated measure called: *CM – Sum of Order Value* that aggregates the sum of the total order value for all 2,448 rows in the table.

Order Value	CC - Sum of Order Value
$77.00	$1,467,199.39
$1,088.00	$1,467,199.39
$160.00	$1,467,199.39
CM - Sum of Order Value: $1,467,199.39	

   You created this calculated measure in: *Lesson 13-3: Create a DAX calculated measure.* (All fields defined in the calculation area below the table are calculated measures).

   Calculated measures always have *Filter Context.* (You'll discover how this differs from *Row Context* in a moment).

5 **Add a new calculated column to show the total Order value.**

   To do this you'll use a DAX aggregation function. The DAX aggregation functions have familiar names (such as SUM and AVERAGE) but can sometimes behave differently to their Excel namesakes.

   1. Click anywhere in the column that has the header: *Add Column.*

   2. Add the following formula in the formula bar:

       =SUM(Orders[Order Value])

   Aggregation functions (such as the SUM function) shouldn't normally be used in a calculated column (see sidebar). You are only doing this to illustrate the difference between row and filter context.

6 **Rename the new calculated column to: CC – Sum of Order Value**

   You learned how to do this in: *Lesson 13-2: Add a DAX calculated column.*

Orders-8

7 Format the new calculated column as *Currency*.

You learned how to do this in: *Lesson 13-2: Add a DAX calculated column.*

	$199.50	$1,467,199.39
	$1,064.00	$1,467,199.39
	$310.00	$1.467.199.39
CM - Sum of Order Value: $1,467,199.39		

Notice that, exactly as you would expect, the same value is shown in every row in the *CC – Sum of Order Value calculated column* and is exactly the same as the value returned by the *CM – Sum of Order Value calculated measure.*

The difference between the two is that calculated columns always have *Row Context* and calculated measures always have *Filter Context.* (You'll discover the difference between the two contexts in a moment).

8 Create a new OLAP pivot table from the data model on a new worksheet.

9 Rename the new worksheet: **Context**

10 Use the new pivot table to show *Sum of Order Value by Category* using both the *CM – Sum of Order Value calculated measure* and the *CC – Sum of Order Value calculated column.*

Rows	Σ Values
Category Name ▼	Sum of CC - Sum of Order Value ▼
	CM - Sum of Order Value ▼

Row Labels ▼	Sum of CC - Sum of Order Value	CM - Sum of Order Value
Beverages	$689,583,714.79	$317,055.20
Condiments	$360,931,050.72	$122,372.68
Confections	$542,863,775.47	$186,880.13

⌐ ▦ Orders
  ☑ CC - Sum of Order Value
  ☐ Discount
  ☐ Order Number
  ☐ Order Value
  ☐ Quantity
  ☐ Unit Price
  ☑ *fx* CM - Sum of Order Value

⌐ ▦ Product
  ☑ Category Name

The calculated measure has *filter context*. This means that the aggregated values respect the *context* of any row and column headers, slicers and report filters in the pivot table.

This means that the calculated measure is correctly returning the *Sum of Order Value by Category.*

The calculated column has row context. Row context does not respect the row and column headers so is showing incorrect results.

You may be curious about how these incorrect results have been calculated. The values have been calculated by multiplying the *Sum of Order Value* calculated column value ($1,467,199.39) by the number of orders in each category.

11 Save your work as *Orders-9.*

Lesson 13-6: Create a calculated measure using the measure dialog

In: *Lesson 13-3: Create a DAX calculated measure*, you created a calculated measure using the Power Pivot window's calculation area.

When working with OLAP pivot tables it is useful to be able to quickly create calculated measures without opening the Power Pivot window. This method creates the measure using the *Measure* dialog box rather than the calculation area.

1   Open *Orders-9* from your sample files folder.

2   Open the Power Pivot window.

3   Create a new pivot table on a new sheet in the workbook.

    1.   Click: Home→PivotTable (from inside the Power Pivot window).

    2.   Click OK.

4   Rename the new worksheet: **Measure Dialog**

5   Use the new pivot table to show the total *Quantity* (from the *Orders* table) sold by *Company Name* (from the *Customer* table).

    1.   Check the box next to *CompanyName* in the *Customer* table.

    2.   Check the box next to *Quantity* in the *Orders* table.

Row Labels	Sum of Quantity
Alfreds Futterkiste	264
Ana Trujillo Emparedados y helados	74
Antonio Moreno Taquería	359
Around the Horn	871
Berglunds snabbköp	1036

6   Change the *Sum of Quantity* field into an Explicit Measure using the *Measure* dialog.

The pivot table works perfectly but you have used an *Implicit Measure* (the *Sum of Quantity* field). *In: Lesson 13-4: Understand Implicit and Explicit measures,* you learned that it is better to use an *Explicit Measure.*

Explicit measures are created by defining a calculated measure in the data model.

In: *Lesson 13-3: Create a DAX calculated measure,* you did this using Power Pivot's calculation area. This time you will create the calculated measure directly from the pivot table.

    1.   Right-click on the *Orders* table in the *PivotTable Fields* list.

Orders-9

note

You can also open the Measure dialog from the Power Pivot ribbon tab

If you click:

Power Pivot→Calculations→
Measures→New Measure

… you will open exactly the same *Measure* dialog.

 This formula has no errors

2. Select *Add Measure…* from the shortcut menu.

Orders
CC · ✚ Add Measure…
Disc   Remove from Active Tab

The *Measure* dialog appears.

3. Type: **Total Quantity** into the *Measure Name* box. (The *Value Description* is optional so leave this box blank).

4. Type this formula into the *Formula* box:

   =SUM(Orders[Quantity])

   You'll notice Excel offering to help you with drop-down lists as you type.

5. Click the *Check DAX Formula* button [Check DAX Formula] to make sure that your formula has no errors.

6. In the *Category* box click *Number* to apply a number format.

7. Use the values to the right of the *Category* box to set the number format to *Whole Number* with a thousand separator.

   The dialog should now look like this:

Measure	? ✕
Table Name:	Orders
Measure Name:	Total Quantity
Value Description:	

   Formula: *fx*   Check DAX Formula

   =SUM(Orders[Quantity])

   ✓ This formula has no errors

Category:	Format:	Whole Number
General		
Date		
Number		
Currency	☑ Use 1000 separator (,)	
TRUE\FALSE		

   OK   Cancel

8. Click the *OK* button to create the calculated measure.

9. Remove the existing *Sum of Quantity* implicit measure from the *Values* box and replace it with the new *Total Quantity* explicit measure.

   The pivot table displays the same values but now uses an *Explicit* measure rather than an *Implicit* measure. The measure is pre-formatted (note the comma thousands separator) and will calculate large data sets much faster.

☑ *fx* Total Quantity

> Product

Drag fields between areas below:

▼ Filters   ▥ Columns

≡ Rows   Σ Values
Company Na… ▼   Total Quantity ▼

Row Labels	▼ Total Quantity
Alfreds Futterkiste	264
Ana Trujillo Emparedados y helados	74
Antonio Moreno Taquería	359
Around the Horn	871
Berglunds snabbköp	1,036

7   Save your work as *Orders-10*.

Lesson 13-7: Use a DAX DISTINCTCOUNT function

1 Open *Orders-10* from your sample files folder.

Inspect the workbook's schema using Power Pivot diagram view.

In this lesson you will work with the *Orders* and *Customer* tables. (You can see these two tables in the sidebar).

2 Understand the report specification.

Imagine that a manager has asked you for this report:

"I need to know average order value per working day. I'll need these figures summarized into years, months and days".

To produce this report, you will need to create three calculated measures:

1. The *Sum of Order Value* for all sales recorded in the *Orders* table (you have already created this calculated measure).

2. The *Count of Working Days* from the *Orders* table.

3. The *Average Order Value Per Working Day*. This will use the other two calculated measures to divide the *Sum of Order Value* by the *Count of Working Days*.

Because calculated measures will have *Filter Context*, the three new calculated measures will always calculate correctly within the *context* of any row and column headers, slicers and report filters in the pivot table.

3 Add a calculated measure that will calculate the *Count of Working Days*.

For the purposes of this calculation it is assumed that the business was never open for an entire day without taking at least one order. If this assumption is correct, the number of days upon which the business was open will be the total unique instances of the *Order Date* field.

This can be easily calculated using the DAX DISTINCTCOUNT function. DISTINCTCOUNT is an example of a DAX function that has no counterpart in Excel.

1. Change the Power Pivot view to: *Data View*.

2. Select the *Orders* table.

3. Click in any empty cell in the calculation area beneath the table.

4. Type this formula into any empty cell in the calculation area:

f_x | Count of Working Days:=DISTINCTCOUNT(Orders[Order Date])

5. Press the **<Enter>** key.

Count of Working Days: 516

note

You can also create a *Distinct Count* implicit measure

Unlike a traditional pivot table, an OLAP pivot table has a built-in implicit *Distinct Count* aggregation method but I don't recommend that you use it.

In: *Appendix A: Power Pivot Rules*, you'll find that I discourage the use of implicit measures, advising you to use explicit measures in every case.

Orders-10

4 Add a calculated measure that will calculate the *Average Order Value per Working Day* from the *CM – Sum of Order Value* and *Count of Working Days* calculated measures.

A wonderful feature of calculated measures is the ability to use them within other calculated measures.

1. Type this formula into any empty cell in the Calculation Area:

f_x Average Order Value per Working Day:= [CM - Sum of Order Value]/[Count of Working Days]

This formula demonstrates one of the advantages of the naming convention defined in: *Appendix A: Power Pivot Rules*.

Because you have adhered to the rules:

Include the table name when you reference a column.

Do not include the table name when you reference a measure.

…it is obvious that two calculated measures are being used in the above formula (rather than columns). This makes formulas (especially very complex ones) far simpler to work with.

2. Press the **<Enter>** key.

5 Format the new calculated measure as *Currency*.

Click: Home→Formatting→Format and select *Currency* from the drop-down list.

Average Order Value per Working Day: $2,843.41

6 Create a pivot table from the data model in a new worksheet and use it to report the *Average Order Value per Working Day* summarized by *Month and Year*.

Now that the data model is complete it is quite a trivial matter to create the report requested:

⊞ Rows		Σ Values	
Year	▼	Count of Working Days	▼
Month	▼	Average Order Value per Working Day	▼
Date	▼		

Row Labels ▼	Count of Working Days	Average Order Value per Working Day
⊞ 2017	257	$1,893.85
⊞ 2018	259	$3,785.64
Grand Total	**516**	**$2,843.41**

The manager is also able to collapse and expand the left-most column from *Years* to *Months* and to *Days*.

7 Name the pivot table's worksheet: **DISTINCTCOUNT**

8 Save your work as *Orders-11*.

Calendar
> ☐ Date Hierarchy
More Fields
  ☑ Date
  ☐ Day Of Week
  ☐ Day Of Week Number
  ☐ MMM-YYYY
  ☑ Month
  ☐ Month Number
  ☑ Year
> Customer
> Employee
Orders
  ☐ CC - Sum of Order Value
  ☐ Discount
  ☐ Order Number
  ☐ Order Value
  ☐ Quantity
  ☐ Unit Price
  ☐ f_x CM - Sum of Order Value
  ☐ f_x Total Quantity
  ☑ f_x **Count of Working Days**
  ☑ f_x **Average Order Value per Working Day**

Lesson 13-8: Create a Key Performance Indicator

The scenario used in this lesson is as follows:

The business has communicated their sales expectations to their employees:

- Your Sales Target is $2,000 per working day.

- If you exceed your sales target by 20% you will receive a bonus.

- If you consistently under-perform your sales target by 30% you may be re-assigned to a non-sales position.

Here is a pivot table with a KPI (Key Performance Indicator):

The KPI status field provides the colored indicator shown next to each employee. You can see at a glance that, in September, *Davolio* and *Callahan* had excellent performance, *Dodsworth* and *Fuller* had acceptable performance, but *Buchanan* had unacceptable performance.

To create a KPI in Power Pivot three values are needed:

Base Value: In the above example the base value is the calculated measure: *Average Order Value per Working Day*.

Target Value: In the above example the target value is $2,000. In some scenarios this could reference a calculated measure rather than the absolute value ($2,000) used in this example.

Status Threshold: This consists of two values (a high and a low) that will define the color of the KPI indicator. In the above example this would be $2,400 (20% above target) and $1,400 (30% below target).

1 Open *Orders-11* from your sample files folder.

2 Create a KPI to the specifications shown above.

1. Open the Power Pivot window.

2. Make sure you are displaying *Data View*.

3. Select the *Orders* table.

4. Right-click on the *Average Order Value per Working Day* calculated measure.

5. Select *Create KPI…* from the shortcut menu.

   The *Key Performance Indicator (KPI)* dialog appears. Note that the KPI base field: *Average Order Value per Working Day* is pre-selected.

6. Click the *Absolute value* option button.

7. Type: **2000** into the *Absolute value* text box.

note

Other ways to open the KPI dialog

In this lesson I right-clicked on a calculated measure and then clicked: *Create KPI…* from the shortcut menu.

This is the method I prefer as the correct calculated measure is pre-selected, reducing the scope for error.

Excel provides several other ways to invoke the KPI dialog.

From the Power Pivot ribbon

1. Open the Power Pivot window.

2. Click on a calculated measure to select it.

3. Click: Home→Calculations→ Create KPI.

Prom the Power Pivot tab in Excel

Click: Power Pivot→ Calculations→ KPIs→New KPI…

Note that you can also click:

Power Pivot→ Calculations→ KPIs→Manage KPIs…

… to edit the settings of an existing KPI.

Orders-11

This is the *Target Value.*

8. Click and drag the sliders to define a *lower status threshold* of **1400** and an *upper status threshold* of **2400.**

The dialog should now look like this:

The icon style gallery at the bottom of the dialog can be used to choose from a range of visualizations.

9. Click the OK button.

3   Create a new OLAP pivot table on a new worksheet.

4   Rename the new worksheet: **KPI**

5   Use the new pivot table to show the *Average Sales per Working Day* (along with the KPI *Status*) achieved by each employee summarized by month and by year.

1. Notice that a special new KPI item has appeared in the *PivotTable Field List* within the *Orders* table (see sidebar).

2. Drag fields down to define the pivot table as follows:

☰ Rows		Σ Values	
Year	▾	Average Order Value per Working Day	▾
Month	▾	Average Order Value per Working Day Status	▾
Last Name	▾		

3. The pivot table now shows the sales performance for each employee:

Row Labels	▾	Average Order Value per Working Day	Ave
⊞ 2017		$1,893.85 ◯	
⊟ 2018			
⊞ January		$2,071.42 ◯	
⊟ February			
Callahan		$1,123.43 ●	
Davolio		$2,477.92 ●	
Dodsworth		$1,446.00 ◯	

⊿ ⛟ Average Sales per Working Day
  ☑ *fx* Value (Average Sales per Working Day)
  ☐ Goal
  ☑ Status

6   Save your work as *Orders-12.*

Lesson 13-9: Use a DAX CALCULATE function

The *CALCULATE* function is regarded by many Power Pivot experts as being the most important function in the vast DAX function library.

The CALCULATE function enables you to pre-filter a table (by adding one or more filters) prior to aggregating the values within it.

1   Open *Orders-12* from your sample files folder.

2   Add a new worksheet and name it: **CALCULATE**

3   Add a pivot table to the worksheet beginning in cell B3 using the workbook's data model as the data source.

    1.   Click in cell B3.

    2.   Click: Insert→Tables→Pivot Table.

    3.   Click OK.

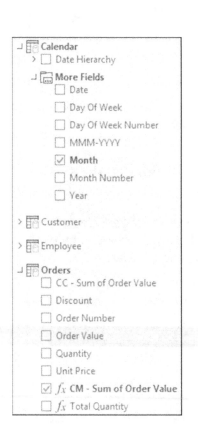

4   Create a pivot table to show the *Sum of Sales Value* by *Month*.

Rows	Σ Values
Month ▼	CM - Sum of Order Value ▼

Row Labels ▼	CM - Sum of Order Value
January	$74,862.30
February	$72,049.97
March	$82,174.07

This isn't a very useful pivot table. The January figure of $74,862.30 is actually the addition of the January 2017 and January 2018 sales.

5   Add a *Year* field (from the Calendar table) to the *Rows* window.

Rows	Σ Values
Year ▼	CM - Sum of Order Value ▼
Month ▼	

Row Labels ▼	CM - Sum of Order Value
⊟ 2017	
January	$27,219.69
February	$22,095.17
March	$30,125.70

The pivot table is now more useful as it shows sales by year and month.

6   Create a calculated measure to show the Sum of Sales Value in the year 2017 and format it as *Currency*.

You can address this requirement by pre-filtering the *Orders* table **before** any Pivot Table row and column headers, slicers and report filters are applied.

    1.   Create the following calculated measure in the *Orders* table:

Orders-12

**Sum of 2017 Order Value:=CALCULATE(
[CM - Sum of Order Value],
YEAR(Orders[Order Date])=2017)**

The second argument in the CALCULATE function pre-filters the value returned by the *CM - Sum of Order Value* calculated measure so that only sales occurring in 2017 are aggregated.

2. Format the calculated measure as *Currency* with two decimal places.

Sum of 2017 Order Value: $486,718.69

7 Add the new calculated measure to the pivot table.

Rows	Σ Values
Year ▾	CM - Sum of Order Value ▾
Month ▾	Sum of 2017 Order Value ▾

Row Labels ▾	CM - Sum of Order Value	Sum of 2017 Order Value
⊞ 2017	$486,718.69	$486,718.69
⊞ 2018	$980,480.70	
Grand Total	$1,467,199.39	$486,718.69

You can see that the pre-filtered calculated measure results in the pivot table displaying no sales for 2018.

8 Create a Pivot table that shows monthly sales for 2017 and 2018 alongside each other.

1. Use the same technique as you used to create the **Sum of 2017 Order Value** calculated measure to create a new calculated measure: **Sum of 2018 Order Value**

2. Set up the pivot table using these settings:

Rows	Σ Values
Month ▾	Sum of 2017 Order Value ▾
	Sum of 2018 Order Value ▾
	CM - Sum of Order Value ▾

Row Labels ▾	Sum of 2017 Order Value	Sum of 2018 Order Value	CM - Sum of Order Value
January	$27,219.69	$47,642.61	$74,862.30
February	$22,095.17	$49,954.79	$72,049.97
March	$30,125.70	$52,048.37	$82,174.07

You may wonder what the point is of doing this.

You could have achieved exactly the same result by adding the *Year* PivotTable field to the *Columns* window and the *Month* PivotTable field to the *Rows* window.

You would not normally use a CALCULATE function that simply filtered a field that is already in the PivotTable field list. You've done it in this case merely as a simple example.

Later, in: *Lesson 13-10: Use a DAX measure to calculate year-on-year growth*, you'll use the two calculated measures that you created in this lesson to create a *Percentage Growth* calculated measure. This will enable you to create a useful OLAP pivot table that could not be easily created without the use of calculated measures.

9 Save your work as *Orders 13*.

Lesson 13-10: Use a DAX measure to calculate year-on-year growth

It is a very common business requirement to measure business growth by comparing a business metric (such as sales) with the same metric during a previous period.

In this example you will calculate the percentage growth of orders received in 2018 compared to orders received in 2017.

1 Open *Orders-13* from your sample files folder.

2 Add a new calculated field named: **Percentage Growth 2017/2018** to calculate the percentage sales growth in 2018 compared to 2017.

   This is quite easy using the formula:

   (2018 Sales – 2017 Sales)/2017 Sales

   You already have the calculated measures for both values.

   1. Open the Power Pivot window.

   2. Click inside any blank cell in the calculation area.

   3. Type this formula into the formula bar:

f_x Percentage Growth 2017/2018:=([Sum of 2018 Order Value]-[Sum of 2017 Order Value])/[Sum of 2017 Order Value]

3 Format the new calculated field as a percentage.

   Click: Home→Formatting→Format→Percentage.

   You can already see that sales in 2018 had grown by 49.64% when compared to 2017.

   Percentage Growth 2017/2018: 101.45%

4 Create a new pivot table on a new sheet in the workbook.

   1. Click: Home→PivotTable.

   2. Click OK.

5 Rename the new worksheet: **Year on Year**

6 Set up the pivot table to show three columns showing 2017 orders, 2018 orders and the percentage growth in 2018 (compared to 2017).

   Add the following fields to the pivot table:

☰ Rows		Σ Values	
Month	▼	Sum of 2017 Order Value	▼
		Sum of 2018 Order Value	▼
		Percentage Growth 2017/2018	▼

Orders-13

Calendar
> ☐ Date Hierarchy
  More Fields
    ☐ Date
    ☐ Day Of Week
    ☐ Day Of Week Number
    ☐ MMM-YYYY
    ☑ Month
    ☐ Month Number
    ☐ Year
> Customer

> Employee

Orders
    ☐ CC - Sum of Order Value
    ☐ Discount
    ☐ Order Number
    ☐ Order Value
    ☐ Quantity
    ☐ Unit Price
    ☐ *fx* CM - Sum of Order Value
    ☐ *fx* Total Quantity
    ☐ *fx* Count of Working Days
    ☑ *fx* Sum of 2017 Order Value
    ☑ *fx* Sum of 2018 Order Value
    ☑ *fx* Percentage Growth 2017/2018
> Average Order Value per Working Day

Row Labels ⌄	Sum of 2017 Order Value	Sum of 2018 Order Value	Percentage Growth 2017/2018
January	$27,219.69	$47,642.61	75.03%
February	$22,095.17	$49,954.79	126.09%
March	$30,125.70	$52,048.37	72.77%
April	$28,236.30	$69,477.05	146.06%
May	$52,507.48	$46,007.83	-12.38%
June	$43,628.41	$60,688.96	39.10%
July	$56,619.44	$97,836.88	72.80%
August	$45,678.66	$108,474.59	137.47%
September	$36,839.31	$91,100.62	147.29%
October	$54,137.42	$135,026.86	149.42%
November	$52,824.70	$110,794.43	109.74%
December	$36,806.38	$111,427.71	202.74%
Grand Total	$486,718.69	$980,480.70	101.45%

In: *Lesson 13-4: Understand Implicit and Explicit measures* you learned the importance of explicit measures.

Because the pivot table only contains explicit measures, all calculation and aggregation has been done by the Power Pivot xVelocity engine. This means that results will be almost instantaneous (even when working with tables that contain millions of rows).

In: *Lesson 13-5: Understand row and filter context* you learned the importance of filter context.

Because the pivot table only contains calculated measures (that always have filter context) the pivot table can be used for many other year-on-year comparisons.

For example, here's how each employee performed:

Row Labels ⌄	Sum of 2017 Order Value	Sum of 2018 Order Value	Percentage Growth 2017/2018
Buchanan	$28,441.99	$42,821.79	50.56%
Callahan	$48,390.25	$114,223.05	136.05%
Davolio	$64,990.90	$144,682.65	122.62%
Dodsworth	$16,553.59	$70,384.27	325.19%
Fuller	$51,382.51	$155,599.24	202.83%
King	$46,778.42	$98,895.69	111.41%
Leverling	$80,918.95	$150,740.38	86.29%
Peacock	$114,914.01	$151,345.09	31.70%
Suyama	$34,348.05	$51,788.53	50.78%
Grand Total	$486,718.69	$980,480.70	101.45%

… and here are some sales changes for the best customers:

Row Labels	Sum of 2017 Order Value	Sum of 2018 Order Value	Percentage Growth 2017/2018
Save-a-lot Markets	$24,932.84	$98,181.85	293.79%
Ernst Handel	$35,001.82	$89,803.37	156.57%
QUICK-Stop	$42,784.81	$81,414.40	90.29%
Hungry Owl All-Night Grocers	$17,513.30	$33,160.10	89.34%
Hanari Carnes	$4,943.92	$30,130.15	509.44%
Folk och fä HB	$8,172.74	$26,678.07	226.43%
Rattlesnake Canyon Grocery	$26,964.03	$26,673.86	-1.08%

You can see that OLAP's other name: *Business Intelligence* is well deserved. Executives with very little training can make strategic decisions in moments based upon up-to-date data.

Of course, executives will need a data modeling expert with advanced Excel and Power Pivot skills to create easy-to-use and efficient data models.

7   Save your work as *Orders 14*.

Lesson 13-11: Use a DAX ALL function

The DAX *ALL* function cannot be used on its own (as it returns a table rather than an aggregation). It is very useful inside another function that requires a table as an argument.

In this lesson you will use the ALL function in conjunction with the CALCULATE function that you learned to use in: *Lesson 13-9: Use a DAX CALCULATE function.*

The ALL function is used to return a table containing all of the values from a table, single column or multiple columns, ignoring any filters that may have been applied.

In this lesson you'll use an ALL function to create a very useful report.

Consider this common business requirement:

Show me the total order value for each month in 2017 and, for each month, what percentage this is of the total order value for the entire year 2017.

You need these calculated measures to satisfy this requirement.

- Sum of order value for each month of 2017.

  You already have this calculated field (*Sum of 2017 Order Value*). Because the field has filter context it can easily be used to show order value by month.

- Sum of order value for the entire 2017 year. This value should remain constant even when filters are applied to the pivot table. This is the calculated field you'll create in this lesson that will require the DAX ALL function.

1 Open *Orders-14* from your sample files folder.

2 Add a new worksheet, name it: **ALL** and add a pivot table to cell B3 that references the data model.

3 Create a calculated measure named: **Sum of All 2017 Orders** that will calculate the total annual orders for 2017 (irrespective of any filters that may be applied).

   Create this calculated measure:

   fx | Sum of All 2017 Orders:=CALCULATE([Sum of 2017 Order Value], ALL(Orders))

4 Format the new calculated measure as currency.

   The calculated measure seems to return exactly the same value as the *Sum of 2017 Order Value* calculated measure:

   Sum of 2017 Order Value: $486,718.69

   Sum of All 2017 Orders: $486,718.69

   There is, however, an important difference between the values. The *Sum of All 2017 Orders* calculated measure will not be affected by any pivot table filter applied by a user.

   To see this in action, return to the *ALL* worksheet and create this pivot table:

Orders-14

	Rows		Σ Values
	Month	▼	Sum of 2017 Order Value ▼
			Sum of All 2017 Orders ▼

Row Labels ▼	Sum of 2017 Order Value	Sum of All 2017 Orders
January	$27,219.69	$486,718.69
February	$22,095.17	$486,718.69
March	$30,125.70	$486,718.69

In: *Lesson 13-5: Understand row and filter context,* you learned that all calculated measures have *filter context.*

You might expect that even the *Sum of All 2017 Orders* column would show monthly sales because it has filter context (as do all measures). The reason that the *Sum of All 2017 Orders* column is unaffected by the monthly filter is a little difficult for some users to grasp.

The *ALL(Orders)* part of the DAX expression created a new (invisible) table in memory that was a duplicate of the *Orders* table. The CALCULATE function then used the existing *Sum of 2017 Order Value* calculated measure to calculate the total order value while referencing this duplicate (in memory) table.

Any filters applied to the *Orders* table will thus not affect the value returned because the filters are (correctly) not applied to this (invisible) duplicate table.

5 **Create a pivot table to show sales for each month in 2017 along with the percentage of annual sales this represents.**

You now have a calculated measure that returns the total annual orders for 2017 (*Sum of All 2017 Orders*). This calculated measure works as if it does not have filter context.

You also have a calculated measure for 2017 orders that does have filter context (*Sum of 2017 Order Value*).

You have a pivot table that shows these two calculated measures alongside each other. A simple division of *Sum of 2017 Order Value /All 2017 Orders* will return a percentage of the annual order value.

1. Create a new calculated measure as follows:

fx 2017 Sales as % of Annual Total:=[Sum of 2017 Order Value]/[Sum of All 2017 Orders]

2. Format the new calculated measure using the *Percentage* format.

3. Add the new calculated measure to the pivot table.

   Create this pivot table:

	Rows		Σ Values
	Month	▼	Sum of 2017 Order Value ▼
			2017 Sales as % of Annual Total ▼

Row Labels ▼	Sum of 2017 Order Value	2017 Sales as % of Annual Total
January	$27,219.69	5.59%
February	$22,095.17	4.54%
March	$30,125.70	6.19%

6 Save your work as *Orders 15.*

Session 13: Exercise

1 Open a new blank workbook.

2 Use Get & Transform to import all seven tables from the *2018 Film Sales* Access database.

3 Close Get & Transform, loading the data from all tables into the Data Model.

4 Open the Power Pivot window and view the schema in *Diagram View*. Familiarize yourself with the data model's relationships (imported automatically from the Access database).

5 Switch from *Diagram View* to *Data View*. The *Orders* table has a *Qty* and *UnitPrice* column. Add an *Extended Price* calculated column to the *Orders* table by multiplying these two values together.

[Extended Price] ▾		*fx* =Orders[Qty]*Orders[UnitPrice]		
▲ploy... 📇 ▾ Fil... 📇 ▾	Qty ▾	UnitPrice ▾	Extended Price	▾
1	23	26	14	$29.98	$419.72
2	3	37	20	$29.98	$599.60

6 Use AutoSum to add two calculated measures to the *Orders* table that calculate the *Sum of Qty* and *Sum of ExtendedPrice*.

> Sum of Qty: 18409   Sum of Extended Price: $478,557.22

7 Rename the two calculated measures: **Qty Sold** and **Sum of Order Value**

> Qty Sold: 18409   Sum of Order Value: $478,557.22

8 Add a calculated measure to the *Orders* table that uses the calculated measures already defined to calculate the *Average Price Per Unit*.

> *fx* Average Price Per Unit:=[Sum of Order Value]/[Qty Sold]

> Average Price Per Unit: 25.9958

9 Format the *Average Price Per Unit* calculated measure as *Currency*.

> Average Price Per Unit: $26.00

10 Add a KPI (Key Performance Indicator) to the *Average Price Per Unit* calculated measure that uses a *Target Value* of $26.00, a *Status Threshold (High)* of $27.00 and a *Status Threshold (Low)* of $25.00.

11 Create a pivot table that will show, for each *Employee*, the *Qty Sold, Sum of Order Value, Average Price Per Unit* and the KPI visual *Status* indicator.

Row Labels ▾	Qty Sold	Sum of Order Value	Average Price Per Unit	Average Price Per Unit Status
Anderson,Jane	993	$25,580.13	$25.76 ◯	
Armstrong,Dan	687	$17,174.05	$25.00 ⬤	
Ashe,Lucille	895	$23,556.94	$26.32 ◯	
Bell,Stephen	861	$23,588.72	$27.40 ⬤	
Bradshaw,John	608	$16,497.20	$27.13 ⬤	

12 Save your work as: *2018 Film Sales*.

2018 Film Sales

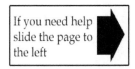
If you need help slide the page to the left

Session 13: Exercise Answers

These are the three questions that students find the most difficult to answer:

Q 11	Q 5 & 6	Q 2 & 3
1. Click: Home→PivotTable (from the Power Pivot window). The *Create Pivot Table* dialog appears. 2. Click the OK button. You are taken back to an Excel worksheet containing an OLAP pivot table that references the data model. 3. Drag the following fields from the *PivotTable Fields* list to the lower panes: ▤ Rows EmployeeName ▾ Σ Values Qty Sold ▾ Sum of Order Value ▾ Average Price Per Unit ▾ Average Price Per Unit Status ▾ This was covered in: *Lesson 13-8: Create a Key Performance Indicator.*	1. Click: View→Data View (in the Power Pivot window). 2. Click the *Orders* tab. 3. Click anywhere inside the column headed: *Add Column.* 4. Type this formula into the formula bar: `=Orders[Qty]*Orders[UnitPrice]` 5. Press the **<Enter>** key. 6. Double-click the *Calculated Column 1* column header and type: **Extended Price** 7. Click in the first cell in the calculation area that is below the *Qty* column. 8. Click: Home→Calculations→Autosum. 9. Do the same thing for the *Extended Price* column. This was covered in: *Lesson 13-2: Add a DAX calculated column and Lesson 13-3: Create a DAX calculated measure.*	1. Click: Data→ Get & Transform Data→ Get Data→From Database→ From Microsoft Access Database. 2. Navigate to the *2018 Film Sales* Access database and open it. 3. Click the *Select multiple items* checkbox. 4. Select every table. 5. Click the *Load* button. This was covered in: *Lesson 12-9: Create a data model directly from a relational database.*

If you have difficulty with the other questions, here are the lessons that cover the relevant skills:

4   Refer to: *Lesson 12-5: Add a relationship to a data model using Power Pivot.*

7   Click on the *Sum of Extended Price* calculated measure and edit the text before the := operator.

8   Refer to: *Lesson 13-2: Add a DAX calculated column* and *Lesson 13-7: Use a DAX DISTINCTCOUNT function.*

9   Click on the *Average Price Per Unit* calculated measure (to select it) and then click: Home→Formatting→Format→Currency (from the Power Pivot window).

10   Refer to: *Lesson 13-8: Create a Key Performance Indicator.*

Appendix A: Power Pivot Rules

> Rules are for the obedience of fools and the guidance of wise men.
>
> *Douglas Bader (British World War II fighter pilot) 1910-1982*

When working with Power Pivot the very best practitioners are fanatical about rules.

Some rules are so self-evidently good and great that it's almost impossible to find anybody that could disagree with them.

Proposing some rules can cause debate, and even sometimes anger, amongst others who do not want to change the way they work. For this reason, whenever a team project is undertaken it is a good idea to publish the rules and spend the first morning in a meeting to ensure that everybody agrees with the rules and "buys into" them. During this meeting it must be made clear that all rules are entirely negotiable, providing that a case for changes can be logically argued. Some of our best rules have come from these brainstorming sessions.

The rules presented in this appendix include generally accepted best-practice as well as some of The Smart Method's own unique standards. Rules that apply to concepts not covered in this book are not included in order to avoid confusion.

You can use the "rule book" to QA your work prior to releasing the first version of your data model. All lessons in this book should conform to the rules (please let us know if you discover any that do not).

You don't need to adopt The Smart Method's rules, but they are a good starting point to derive your own rules.

Never be afraid to break the rules when you have good reason to. As Douglas Bader observed, they are only for guidance. When you do break the rules, however, make sure you can justify (to yourself at least) why you did it.

Never break the rules in a misguided attempt to save time by producing a "quick and dirty" data model. You'll waste far more time unravelling the mess than you'll ever save.

Adhere to the standard defined in this appendix (or your own derivative of it) and create beautiful, robust, extendable data models.

1: Get & Transform

1-1 When importing data from a database, transform data (as much as possible) with a View.

In an ideal world (when data resides in a database) your DBA would create a *View* for you that will remove a lot of transforming work (from Get & Transform).

A View can:

- Remove columns you don't need.

- Rename columns to the names you need (which are often different to the source data field names).

- De-normalize several source tables into a single View.

- Add calculated columns.

Because this is all done in the source database you have a flying start for your Get & Transform session and can re-use the View in any future Get & Transform queries.

You learned about Views in: *Lesson 11-28: Efficiently import data using a view.*

Because we do not live in an ideal world you may find resistance from your DBA when requesting views, or unacceptably long lead times to have them implemented. In this case you will need to use Get & Transform instead.

1-2 Do not use Power Pivot to import or transform data.

Get & Transform should be used to import and transform data before it is modeled using Power Pivot. You may have noticed that Power Pivot still retains limited direct import features. You should regard these as legacy features that date back to the days before Get & Transform was available.

1-3 Create compression-friendly columns with as few unique values as possible.

A Power Pivot data model contains compressed data.

How data compression works

You may be familiar with products such as WinZip that can compress a file so that it is many times smaller than the original file.

Compression is achieved using a lookup table.

For example, consider all the words in a novel stored as a text file. The word "and" takes up three characters (or three bytes) in the file. If you replaced all occurrences of the word: "and" with the number: 1 along with a lookup table defining that "1 = and" you would significantly reduce the size of the text file.

When you compressed the file, you'd substitute the number 1 (one byte) for every occurrence of "and" (3 bytes) and then do the reverse when you uncompressed the file.

This may be a slight over-simplification but it is essentially how Power Pivot compresses data.

How to make columns compression friendly

Here are some examples of how to reduce the unique values in a column.

If you had a column that contained date and time values, but you were only really interested in summarizing by date, you'd greatly reduce the number of unique values in the column by only storing the *date* part of the data in the model (removing the time component using Get & Transform). To take this further, if you were only interested in creating aggregations of monthly data, you'd make the column even more compression-friendly by converting the dates into month names.

If you had an address table with a column called *Location* (containing names such as *Orlando, FL)* you could reduce the size of the data model by splitting the column into two (*City* and *State*). This would work because there would be fewer unique values in each column. This is, of course, also better practice as it gives users more scope when filtering by dimension.

1-4 Only store numerical data and foreign keys in the fact table.

The central *fact* table in your star schema should not contain dimension columns. If any dimension columns exist, they should be split out into their own tables. Any correctly normalized relational database will already follow this rule.

Degenerate dimensions may break this rule

There are exceptions to this rule in respect of *degenerate dimensions*. These are dimensions that are so insignificant that there's no need to normalize the fact table column into its own dimension table. If a fact table column *could* be a foreign key (but there is no extra information about it that could appear in a separate dimension table) it would be correct to describe it as a *degenerate dimension.*

Here's a degenerate dimension example:

If an *Invoices* fact table had a field named *Discount Coupon Number*, it would be possible to regard it as a degenerate dimension but only if nothing else was known about the discount coupon in the data source. If there was extra data about each *Discount Coupon* within the data source (such as the *Issued Date* and *Expiry Date*) then *Discount Coupon Number* should be modeled as a foreign key (within the *Invoices* fact table) that relates to a *Discount Coupon* dimension table. The *Discount Coupon* dimension table would then contain the *Issued Date* and *Expiry Date* (and the primary key would contain the *Discount Coupon Number*).

1-5 When creating a fact table do not import the primary key.

It is necessary to have a primary key for each dimension table, but the primary key has no value in the fact table. Because the fact table's primary key consumes a substantial amount of space it should not be imported into the data model.

1-6 Remove redundant columns and tables.

There is often a huge amount of redundant data within a data source that is of little interest for reporting purposes. Don't be tempted to include all the source data tables and columns "just in case" they are needed in the future. It is easy to add tables and columns using Get & Transform if they are needed in the future.

You should pay particular attention to unnecessary columns in the fact table. Fact tables can contain millions of rows (while dimension tables are usually quite small). For this reason, an unnecessary column in a fact table can hugely impact upon the data model size.

There are many advantages in keeping your data models compact:

- The data model will use less memory.

- Reports (visualizations) will usually load faster.

- The Excel file size will be smaller.

- Users will find the model easier to use.

2: Data Modeling

2-1   Use a calendar table for date dimensions.

Whenever there is a date column in a fact table you should add a calendar dimension table.

Power Pivot makes it easy to add a self-updating calendar table with a single click. A calendar table opens many more possibilities when creating aggregations that use time dimensions.

2-2   Use a Star schema (rather than a Snowflake schema) when constructing data models.

A Snowflake schema is said to resemble a snowflake:

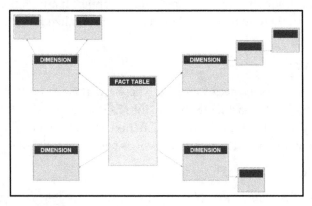

A Star schema de-normalizes the dimension tables into a single dimension:

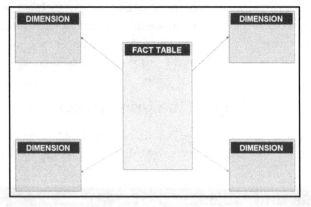

While Power Pivot will work well with either a Snowflake or Star schema, Power Pivot works faster and better with a Star schema. Star schemas are also easier for users to work with.

For these reasons the Star schema is the preferred choice when working with Power Pivot.

2-3   Do not model many-to-many relationships.

Many-to-many relationships (using a link table) are not supported in Power Pivot data models. In order to create accurate aggregations, Power Pivot needs a single path between tables.

Many-to-many relationships that exist in source data should be de-normalized to create a one-to-many relationship.

2-4   Do not use linked Excel tables.

If you import data into Get & Transform using a linked Excel table (in the same workbook) and then load it into Power Pivot you will create two copies of your data.

Data in Power Pivot is compressed in memory (and can shrink to as little as 10% of the source data size). For this reason, you may bloat the workbook's size by as much as 90% by duplicating data in both the data model and an Excel workbook linked table.

2-5 Always format columns inside the data model (and not in the Pivot Table).

If you format columns and calculated measures inside the data model, you'll never have to re-format when you use a column within a pivot table. This makes the data model easier to use by untrained users (who may not even know how to format a value in a pivot table).

Remember that the data model may be used by many pivot tables. By formatting once in the data model, you avoid formatting each time you add the measure to a pivot table.

3: Table, Column and Measure naming

3-1 Never use prefixes for table names.

You will often see star schemas with a fact table prefixed with *fact* (or sometimes *Fact* or *fct*) and dimension tables prefixed with *Dim* (or sometimes *dim*). This results in names such as: *FactOrders, fctOrders, Fact_Orders, DimProduct, dimProduct and Dim_Product.*

This convention originates in Ralph Kimball's *Business Dimensional Lifecycle* methodology.

While the Kimball naming convention works really well for data warehouses it is not a great fit for a Power Pivot data model. Data models are often used by ordinary, unsophisticated users to visualize their data (either using an OLAP pivot table or Microsoft's Power BI product).

Users reasonably expect a Product dimension table to have a plain English name such as *Product* rather than *DimProduct*.

Another advantage of using plain English nouns for tables is that the data model will work well with the Q&A tool in Microsoft's Power BI product. The Q&A tool enables users to type *natural language queries* such as: "List all Orders by Product and Month". A user would be unlikely to type "List all DimOrders by FactProduct and DimMonth".

Because many badly designed data models use cryptic names, Power Pivot allows you to define synonyms for table names (you can do this in Power Pivot by clicking: Advanced→Language→Synonyms). By avoiding prefixes, you will not have to define a synonym for each table.

3-2 Apart from acronyms, never use abbreviations for Table, Column, Measure (or any other) names.

A good yardstick for choosing a name is to try to imagine that there is an extraordinary reward for two programmers if they can independently come up with the same program text for the same problem. Both programmers know the reward but cannot otherwise communicate. Such an experiment would be futile, of course, for any sizable problem, but it is a neat goal. The reward of real life is that a program written by someone else, which is identical to what one's own program would have been, is extremely readable and modifiable.

Dr. Charles Simonyi (formerly Microsoft's Chief Architect)

Example: A dimension table contains Customer information. One of the fields in the table contains the Customer's first name. It was badly named in the source data as a table named *Cust* and a field named *CusFN*. How would you rename the field in Get & Transform?

If you were playing Charles Simonyi's game and you needed to guess which name another developer had come up with you'd probably win with:

Table Name: Customer
Field Name: First Name

A long time ago, when memory was a precious commodity, there was a small performance gain to be had by abbreviating names. There isn't any more (and hasn't been for many years). So why do 21st century developers still create cryptic, bug prone, and difficult-to-maintain data models by abbreviating names? It is one of the great mysteries of life!

Some data modelers might argue that you don't have to type as much if you use abbreviations. You may save a few keystrokes when you design the model, but you'll waste many hours later on when you have to consult documentation in order to establish what your cryptically named columns actually contain.

This rule can, of course, be sometimes waived in the case of commonly used acronyms. For example, if everybody in an organization refers to the *Gross Domestic Product* as the *GDP* it may be clearer to users if the abbreviation is used (though you'd probably define *Gross Domestic Product* as a synonym in this case by clicking: Advanced→Language→Synonyms).

3-3 Name dimension tables, fields, and everything else except the fact table, in the singular.

As previously noted, one of the goals of our naming convention is that you should be able to intuitively guess the correct name of any dimension table, column name or measure.

The use of plurals makes this goal more difficult. Consider a dimension table containing customer records. It would be difficult to guess whether the name of the table should be *Customer* or *Customers*.

This problem can be avoided by always using singular names for table names (except the fact table), column names and measure names.

You should be aware that some designers turn this convention upside down and make all dimension table names plural. It is (vastly) preferable to enforce an "everything in the singular" convention as column names are prefixed with the table name and may look confusing in the plural.

3-4 Name the fact table in the plural.

The fact table is the central table in a star schema. This table should be named in the plural because the table contains one-to-many relationships with the dimension tables. For example, an *Invoices* fact table contains many invoices, but each field only connects to one row in the *Customer* dimension table.

Using the "dimension table names singular/fact table name plural" convention provides several advantages:

- It is always apparent (at a glance) which table is the fact table in a star schema.

- Queries sound just like the spoken word:

    "Show me the Sales by Customer"

    … instead of:

"Show me the Sale by Customers" or "show me the Sale by Customer" or "Show me the Sales by Customers".

3-5 Use a single noun for table names whenever possible.

Most tables (such as Customer and Product) lend themselves to the use of a single noun. Where this is the case you should not use two words to describe the table.

3-6 Do not use spaces in table names.

There may be a very unusual case where you need to use two words to describe a table. When this is the case, use Upper Camel Case (also known as Pascal Case) with names such as *InternetSales* and *ProductSubcategory*, rather than spaces.

If you use spaces in table names you will need to enclose the table name in single quotation marks whenever you reference the table name in a formula.

3-7 Always use spaces in column names and measures.

Unlike table names, it is very common to need more than one word to clearly describe the data in a column. For example: *Company Name* and *Contact Name* (that might both appear in a *Supplier* table).

Unlike table names, you don't have to use quotation marks when referring to column names as they are always enclosed by square brackets such as: [Company Name] and [Contact Name].

Data models are often used by ordinary, unsophisticated users to visualize their data (either using an OLAP pivot table or Microsoft's Power BI product). They will find plain English column names (with spaces) easier to work with than underscores or camel case.

4: Creating DAX calculated measures

4-1 Place measures in the same table that they reference.

This is the most logical place for measures. The table in which the measure resides also determines where it will appear in the *Pivot Table Fields* list. It will be less confusing for users if the field appears in the correct table.

Power Pivot will allow you to place measures in any table but if you place measures in a different table than the one they reference, Power Pivot may become confused and trigger a relationship warning.

4-2 Always use explicit measures rather than implicit measures.

You learned about explicit and implicit measures in: *Lesson 13-4: Understand Implicit and Explicit measures*. Explicit measures have so many advantages over implicit measures that it is best practice to use them exclusively.

Make sure that you provide enough explicit measures for all likely reporting scenarios.

4-3 Use many simple measures rather than one complex measure.

Because measures can reference other measures it is better to create several interim measures and then to create a more complex measure by referencing the simpler measures that you have already defined.

4-4 Always format measures inside the data model (and not in the pivot table).

Just like columns, you should always format measures inside the data model and not in any pivot tables that are created from it.

4-5 Include the table name when you reference a column.

It is perfectly correct (in database design) to have the same field name in two different tables. By prefixing column names with table names, you will ensure that Power Pivot is referencing the correct field.

Good: =Product[FirstName] & " " & Product[LastName]
Bad: = [FirstName] & " " & [LastName]

4-6 Do not include the table name when you reference a measure.

Because DAX formulas can include references to other measures, it can be difficult to identify which parts of a formula are column references and which are measure references.

If you include the table name when you reference a column and do not include the table name when referencing a measure, it is always clear (when auditing a formula) where the values are coming from.

Appendix B: Skills Covered in the Essential Skills Course

> You have to learn to crawl before you can walk.
> You have to learn to walk before you can run.
>
> *Proverbs, unknown authors*

In order to get the most out of this book you should already be very comfortable with Excel's main features. We also have an *Essential Skills* course for absolute beginners.

978-1-909253-45-2
385 pages

978-1-909253-48-3
(This book)

This (Expert Skills) book assumes that you have already mastered the skills taught in the *Essential Skills* book.

So how do you know if your skills are already advanced enough to tackle this book?

This appendix lists the objectives for each of the eight sessions in the *Essential Skills* course.

If you already have all (or at least most) of the skills taught in the *Essential Skills* course, you are ready to upgrade your skills to Expert level with this course.

Essential skills course outline

Session 1: Basic Skills

- Start Excel and open a new blank workbook
- Understand update channels
- Check that your Excel version is up to date
- Change between Touch Mode and Mouse Mode
- Change the Office Theme
- Maximize, minimize, re-size, move and close the Excel window
- Download the sample files and open/navigate a workbook
- Save a workbook to a local file
- Understand common file formats
- Pin a workbook and understand file organization
- View, move, add, rename, delete and navigate worksheet tabs
- Use the Versions feature to recover an unsaved Draft file
- Use the Versions feature to recover an earlier version of a workbook
- Use the Ribbon
- Understand Ribbon components
- Customize the Quick Access Toolbar and preview the printout
- Use the Mini Toolbar, Key Tips and keyboard shortcuts
- Understand views
- Hide and Show the Formula Bar and Ribbon
- Use the Tell Me help system
- Use other help features

Session 2: Doing Useful Work with Excel

- Enter text and numbers into a worksheet
- Create a new workbook and view two workbooks at the same time
- Use AutoSum to quickly calculate totals
- Select a range of cells and understand Smart Tags
- Enter data into a range and copy data across a range
- Select adjacent and non-adjacent rows and columns
- Select non-contiguous cell ranges and view summary information
- AutoSelect a range of cells
- Re-size rows and columns
- Use AutoSum to sum a non-contiguous range

- Use AutoSum to calculate average and maximum values
- Create your own formulas
- Create functions using Formula AutoComplete
- Use AutoFill for text and numeric series
- Use AutoFill to adjust formulas and use AutoFill options
- Speed up your AutoFills and create a custom fill series
- Understand linear and exponential series
- Use Flash Fill to split and concatenate text
- Analyze Data with the Ideas feature
- Use the zoom control
- Print out a worksheet

Session 3: Taking Your Skills to the Next Level

- Insert and delete rows and columns
- Use AutoComplete and fill data from adjacent cells
- Cut, copy and paste
- Cut, copy and paste using drag and drop
- Use Paste Values
- Increase/decrease decimal places displayed
- Transpose a range
- Use the Multiple Item Clipboard
- Use Undo and Redo
- Insert, View and Print cell notes and cell comments
- Understand absolute, relative and mixed cell references
- Understand templates and set the default custom template folder
- Create a template
- Use a template
- Add an Office Add-In to a workbook
- Freeze columns and rows
- Split the window into multiple panes
- Check spelling

Session 4: Making Your Worksheets Look Professional

- Format dates
- Understand date serial numbers
- Format numbers using built-in number formats

- Create custom number formats
- Horizontally and Vertically align the contents of cells
- Merge cells, wrap text and expand/collapse the formula bar
- Unmerge cells and Center Across Selection
- Understand themes
- Use cell styles and change themes
- Add color and gradient effects to cells
- Add borders and lines
- Create your own custom theme
- Create your own custom cell styles
- Use a master style book to merge styles
- Use simple conditional formatting
- Manage multiple conditional formats using the Rules Manager
- Bring data alive with visualizations
- Create a formula driven conditional format
- Insert a Sparkline into a range of cells
- Apply a common vertical axis and formatting to a Sparkline group
- Apply a date axis to a Sparkline group and format a single Sparkline
- Use the Format Painter
- Rotate text

Session 5: Charts and Graphics

- Understand chart types, layouts and styles
- Create a simple chart with two clicks
- Move, re-size, copy and delete a chart
- Create a chart using the Recommended Charts feature
- Add and remove chart elements using Quick Layout
- Apply a pre-defined chart style and color set
- Manually format a chart element
- Format 3-D elements and add drop shadows
- Move, re-size, add, position and delete chart elements
- Apply a chart filter
- Change a chart's source data
- Assign non-contiguous source data to a chart
- Understand data series and categories
- Add data series using the Select Data Source dialog tools
- Chart non-contiguous source data by hiding rows and columns

- Create a chart with numerical axes
- Deal with empty data points and add data labels to a chart
- Highlight specific data points with color and annotations
- Add gridlines and scale axes
- Emphasize data by manipulating pie charts
- Create a chart with two vertical axes
- Create a combination chart containing different chart types
- Work with trend lines and forecast sheets
- Add a gradient fill to a chart background
- Create your own chart templates
- Create a filled map chart

Session 6: Working with Multiple Worksheets and Workbooks

- View the same workbook in different windows
- View two windows side by side and perform synchronous scrolling
- Duplicate worksheets within a workbook
- Move and copy worksheets from one workbook to another
- Hide and unhide a worksheet
- Create cross worksheet formulas
- Understand worksheet groups
- Use find and replace

Session 7: Printing Your Work

- Print Preview and change paper orientation
- Use Page Layout view to adjust margins
- Use Page Setup to set margins more precisely and center the worksheet
- Set paper size and scale
- Insert, delete and preview page breaks
- Adjust page breaks using Page Break Preview
- Add auto-headers and auto-footers and set the starting page number
- Add custom headers and footers
- Specify different headers and footers for the first, odd and even pages
- Print only part of a worksheet
- Add row and column data labels and gridlines to printed output

- Print several selected worksheets and change the page order
- Suppress error messages in printouts

Session 8: Cloud Computing

- Understand cloud computing
- Save a workbook to a OneDrive
- Open a workbook from a OneDrive
- Understand operating systems and devices
- Understand Office versions
- Understand Excel for the web
- Open a workbook using Excel for the web
- Share a link to a workbook
- Understand OneDrive AutoSave and Version History
- Edit a workbook simultaneously with other users using Excel for the web

Index

E

G

H

Q

Further Reading

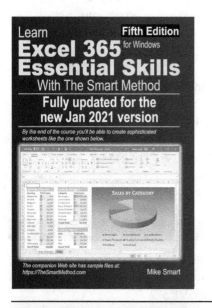

The Essential Skills book isn't only for beginners! Experts find it useful too.

Many purchasers of *Expert Skills* also decide to purchase the *Essential Skills* book (the first book in this series). *Essential Skills* isn't only for Excel beginners. I often teach this course (as a classroom course) to professionals that have used Excel for over ten years and they *always* gain some fantastically useful skills from the course.

Essential Skills assumes no previous exposure to Excel and teaches all of the core skills. Charts and Graphics are extensively covered in a 30-lesson session and there's comprehensive coverage of Excel's cloud computing features (including collaborative working with Excel Online).

Available as both a printed paper book and e-book.

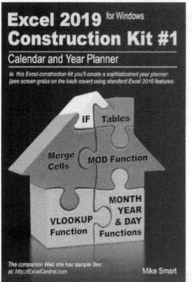

Learn how to apply your new Excel skills with a Smart Method construction kit.

For over 900 years craftsmen have traditionally taught their skills to an apprentice. In this model the apprentice learned his trade by observing how the master craftsman used his skills. This construction kit will teach you advanced Excel skills in the same way. Even if you only have basic Excel skills, the construction kit is designed in such a way that you'll be able to construct a complex, polished professional Excel application that would be well beyond the powers of most advanced Excel users. Available as both a printed paper book and e-book.

Preview the first chapter free at:

https://thesmartmethod.com

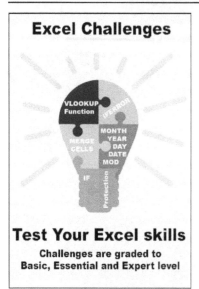

Excel Challenges.

Our Excel online challenges are a little like the exercises at the end of each session in this book. Unlike the exercises, the online challenges will test the application of many skills (covered in different sessions in the book).

We began trialling challenges in July 2018 and (at time of writing in Jan 2021) we'd published three challenges. By the time you read this book we may have produced more.

Access the challenges online at:

https://thesmartmethod.com/excel-challenges/

Use your new Excel skills to teach your own classroom courses

If you've worked through this book carefully you are now a true Excel expert. There is a huge demand, everywhere in the world, for Excel training at all levels. The skills you have learned in this book (and the preceding *Essential Skills* book) will enable you to teach Excel at all levels – from beginner to expert.

This book is available for all Excel versions in common use (Excel 2007, 2010, 2013, 2016, 2019 and 365 for Windows along with Excel 2016 & 2019 for Apple Mac). You can use the books as courseware during your classes and then give each student a copy of the book to take home as reference material when the course is over.

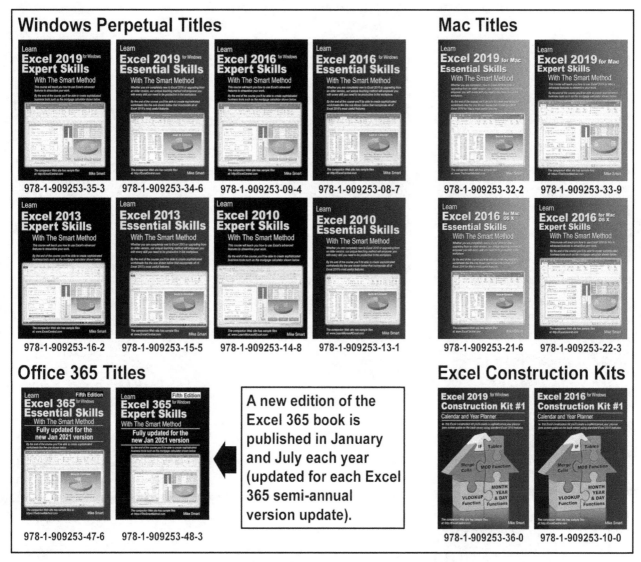

Windows Perpetual Titles

Learn **Excel 2019** for Windows **Expert Skills** — 978-1-909253-35-3
Learn **Excel 2019** for Windows **Essential Skills** — 978-1-909253-34-6
Learn **Excel 2016** for Windows **Expert Skills** — 978-1-909253-09-4
Learn **Excel 2016** for Windows **Essential Skills** — 978-1-909253-08-7

Learn **Excel 2013 Expert Skills** — 978-1-909253-16-2
Learn **Excel 2013 Essential Skills** — 978-1-909253-15-5
Learn **Excel 2010 Expert Skills** — 978-1-909253-14-8
Learn **Excel 2010 Essential Skills** — 978-1-909253-13-1

Mac Titles

Learn **Excel 2019** for Mac **Essential Skills** — 978-1-909253-32-2
Learn **Excel 2019** for Mac **Expert Skills** — 978-1-909253-33-9

Learn **Excel 2016** for Mac OS X **Essential Skills** — 978-1-909253-21-6
Learn **Excel 2016** for Mac OS X **Expert Skills** — 978-1-909253-22-3

Office 365 Titles

Learn **Excel 365** Fifth Edition **Essential Skills** — 978-1-909253-47-6
Learn **Excel 365** Fifth Edition **Expert Skills** — 978-1-909253-48-3

A new edition of the Excel 365 book is published in January and July each year (updated for each Excel 365 semi-annual version update).

Excel Construction Kits

Excel 2019 for Windows **Construction Kit #1** Calendar and Year Planner — 978-1-909253-36-0
Excel 2016 for Windows **Construction Kit #1** Calendar and Year Planner — 978-1-909253-10-0

You can quote the ISBN numbers shown above to any book retailer or wholesaler. All major distributors (in every country of the world) have our books in stock for immediate delivery.

Place a direct order for 5+ books for wholesale prices and free delivery worldwide

To place a publisher-direct order you only need to order five books or more (of the same title). To view wholesale prices, go to this web page:

https://thesmartmethod.com/wholesale-printed-books

CPSIA information can be obtained
at www.ICGtesting.com
Printed in the USA
LVHW062356290621
691473LV00007B/687